P9-BJB-873

Geography in Early Judaism and Christianity focuses on a particular Old Testament pseudepigraphon – the *Book of Jubilees*, which is presented as a revelation that Moses received at Mount Sinai, although it actually consists of a rewriting and interpretation of the biblical narrative from Genesis 1 to Exodus 16. The study traces the appropriation of the *Book of Jubilees* in early Christian sources from the New Testament to Hippolytus and beyond, and more specifically focuses on the reception of *Jubilees* 8–9, an expansion of the so-called Table of Nations in Genesis 10 (1 Chronicles 1).

The book takes an interdisciplinary approach based on detailed analysis of primary sources, much of which is seldom considered by New Testament scholars, and explores the neglected topic of ancient geographical conceptions. By studying geographical aspects of the work, James M. Scott is able to relate *Jubilees* to both Old and New Testament traditions, bringing important new insights into several Christian texts.

JAMES M. SCOTT is Professor of Religious Studies at Trinity Western University, British Columbia. He is author of *Adoption as Sons of God* (1992), *Paul and the Nations* (1995), and *2 Corinthians* (1998), and is editor of *Exile: Old Testament, Jewish, and Christian Conceptions* (1997), and *Restoration: Old Testament, Jewish, and Christian Conceptions* (2001).

SOCIETY FOR NEW TESTAMENT STUDIES

MONOGRAPH SERIES

General editor: Richard Bauckham

113

GEOGRAPHY IN EARLY JUDAISM AND CHRISTIANITY

229.911
Sco 84

Geography in Early Judaism and Christianity

The Book of Jubilees

JAMES M. SCOTT

CAMBRIDGE
UNIVERSITY PRESS

LIBRARY ST. MARY'S COLLEGE

PUBLISHED BY THE PRESS SYNDICATE OF THE UNIVERSITY OF CAMBRIDGE
The Pitt Building, Trumpington Street, Cambridge, United Kingdom

CAMBRIDGE UNIVERSITY PRESS
The Edinburgh Building, Cambridge CB2 2RU, UK
40 West 20th Street, New York, NY 10011-4211, USA
477 Williamstown Road, Port Melbourne, VIC 3207, Australia
Ruiz de Alarcón 13, 28014 Madrid, Spain
Dock House, The Waterfront, Cape Town 8001, South Africa

http://www.cambridge.org

© James M. Scott 2002

This book is in copyright. Subject to statutory exception
and to the provisions of relevant collective licensing agreements,
no reproduction of any part may take place without
the written permission of Cambridge University Press.

First published 2002

Printed in the United Kingdom at the University Press, Cambridge

Typeface Times 10/12 pt.   *System* LᴬTEX 2ε   [TB]

A catalogue record for this book is available from the British Library.

Library of Congress Cataloguing in Publication data
Scott, James M.
Geography in early Judaism and Christianity : the book of Jubilees / by James M. Scott.
    p.   cm. – (Society of New Testament Studies monograph series ; 113)
Includes bibliographical references and index.
ISBN 0 521 80812 X   hardback
1. Book of Jubilees VIII–IX – Geography.   2. Bible. O. T. Genesis X – Geography.
3. Geography, Ancient.   4. Geography, Ancient – Maps.   5. Book of Jubilees
VIII–IX – Criticism, interpretation, etc. – History – To 1500.   6. Christian literature,
Early – History and criticism. I. Title.   II. Monograph series (Society for New
Testament Studies) ; 113.

BS1830.J8 S45   2001
229′.911 – dc21   2001035282

ISBN 0 521 80812 X hardback

CONTENTS

PREFACE

The present study represents the fruit of my Sabbatical research in 1996–97, during which I had the very pleasant opportunity of working both in the Oxford Centre for Hebrew and Jewish Studies and in the Evangelisch-theologisches Seminar of the University of Tübingen. This research would have been impossible without fellowships from the OCHJS and the Alexander von Humboldt-Stiftung and a research grant from the Social Sciences and Humanities Research Council of Canada. My sincere thanks go to these institutions for their generous support.

I also owe a tremendous debt of gratitude to many individuals for their help and encouragement along the way. The following scholars deserve special mention in this regard: William Adler, Peter Barber, Richard Bauckham, Dean Béchard, Peder Borgen, Benjamin Braude, Katherine Clarke, Catherine Delano Smith, Evelyn Edson, Jörg Frey, Martin Hengel, Chris Howgego, F. Stanley Jones, Nikos Kokkinos, Fergus Millar, Matthew Morgenstern, Stanley Porter, Ferdinand Rohrhirsch, Peter Stuhlmacher, James C. VanderKam, John Williams, and David A. Woodward.

I would like to express my thanks to the staff at Cambridge University Press for facilitating the publication of this book, and to Susanne Staryk and Nathan Van Seters for checking the manuscript and preparing the indexes.

Finally, I would like to express my love and appreciation for my wife Gail and our two children, Kathryn and Elizabeth, whose flexibility and spirit of adventure made this Sabbatical year not only possible but also thoroughly enjoyable. As in the past, Gail has labored with me during every phase of the research, writing, and publication of this volume. I could not have done it without her, nor would I have wanted to.

INTRODUCTION

This book seeks to trace the appropriation of a particular "Old Testament pseudepigraphon"[1] – the *Book of Jubilees*[2] – in early Christian sources from the New Testament (NT) to Hippolytus (and beyond). More specifically, our study focuses on the reception of *Jubilees* 8–9, an expansion on the so-called Table of Nations in Genesis 10 (1 Chronicles 1). There are three primary motivations for undertaking such a study at this particular time. First, my previous work on the Table of Nations tradition has led me to the conclusion that *Jubilees* 8–9 had a powerful influence on geographical conceptions found not only in Second-Temple Jewish sources but also in early Christian writings.[3] In order further to articulate and substantiate this thesis, the present study delves more thoroughly than before into some of the important primary source material. For instance, our study gives greater scope to a Hellenistic epigram that opens up the possibility of Jewish cartographic activity in the Second-Temple period (Chapter 1). The study also augments my previous work by reconsidering the relationship of *Jubilees* 8–9 both to the lost "Book of Noah" and to other writings of the Second-Temple period (Chapter 2). The study greatly expands our earlier discussion on the geography of Luke-Acts (Chapter 3) and penetrates more deeply into early Christian literature outside the NT (Chapters 4–6). Finally, the study ventures a foray into the medieval *mappaemundi* as possibly our earliest extant cartographic remains of the *Jubilees* 8–9 tradition (Chapter 7). First and foremost, therefore, the present study is motivated by the desire to offer further evidence of the influence of the *Jubilees* 8–9 tradition.

Second, our study is motivated by the need to base the investigation of the NT on a firmer historical foundation. NT scholars have often been negligent in investigating historical geography, let alone ancient geographical conceptions. William Ramsay decries "the general lack of interest taken by scholars in mere geographical matters – which are commonly regarded as beneath the dignity of true scholarship..."[4] Moreover, as Philip S. Alexander observes, "It has long been understood that our images of the world can be extraordinarily revealing about our mentality, yet this insight has taken some time to make any real impact on the study of the ancient world. Ancient historians have been quite happy to investigate man's relationship to time (e.g. through a study of his concept of history), but reluctant to investigate his orientation towards and organisation of space, as revealed, for example, in his ideas about the geographical world."[5]

Clearly, the historical investigation of the NT must have its proper boundaries in time and space, its beginning, its aim, and its localities. It presupposes some sort of basic *chronology* and *geography*.[6] To this end, our study contributes particularly to the geographical framework of the NT. Unfortunately, NT scholars often simply assume geographical knowledge of the past, thus regarding a thoroughgoing geographical investigation as practically superfluous.[7] Indeed, most attempts to write the history of early Christianity use the benefit of modern hindsight and global perspective to trace the larger patterns and developments. They describe the developments, as it were, from the "outside." The danger of such an approach is that it reads back later perspectives into the earlier material, and thereby fails to respect the inevitably more limited horizons of the ancient writers themselves.[8] A classic example of this can be seen in the standard maps of "The Journeys of Paul the Apostle," included in most Bible atlases or appended to many modern Bibles. Such maps have become so familiar that we hardly stop to consider that the image of the world portrayed on them looks strangely modern in orientation, outline, and scale.[9] Thus, we unwittingly read back into the biblical text our image of the world, an image that itself is the product of a centuries-long development.[10] The present book attempts the more difficult task of describing the process from the "inside." How did the Jerusalem apostles, for example, imagine the world of their day? What conception(s) of world geography informed early Christians as they carried their message from place to place throughout the oikoumene? Such questions have scarcely been asked and yet require answers. As P. M. Fraser aptly observes, "full understanding of the outlook of any individual in antiquity – or indeed any period before the modern era – depends to a considerable extent on our ability to assess his geographical horizon."[11]

To answer such questions is no easy matter, given the paucity of the extant evidence. There is no ancient map to which we may facilely appeal, and other relevant sources are few and far between. We must carefully sift through a great quantity of exotic materials to extract even a few clues that may help us, and some of these are subtle. To complicate matters even further, our investigation must be interdisciplinary by its very nature, incorporating the insights and methods of such disparate disciplines as Jewish Studies, classical philology, ancient and medieval cartography, ancient history, and patristics. At the risk of becoming mere dilettantes, we must have the courage to pass over the boundaries of our too narrowly specialized field and so become much more familiar with allied disciplines. Only in this way can we avoid what Martin Hengel has rightly called a science of surmises and a merry-go-round of hypotheses which has so long characterized NT Studies.[12] Admittedly, more thorough acquaintance with the ancient sources will not solve all of the problems that currently bedevil our discipline and even threaten its demise,[13] but it will hopefully provide a firmer historical basis on which to build in various directions.

Third, the present study is motivated by the desire to provide a case study of the reception of the so-called "OT pseudepigrapha" in the early Christian literature.[14] The pseudepigrapha are a rather amorphous collection of writings that have been preserved to the modern period primarily by Christian efforts but are attributed to or closely identified with various heroes of the pre-Christian Jewish tradition. For instance, before their discovery as part of the Qumran scrolls, important Jewish works like *1 Enoch* and *Jubilees* were known only in the versions transmitted in Christian communities. Hence, Robert A. Kraft may well be right when he insists that the pseudepigrapha should first be studied as witnesses to Christian interest and activities before they are mined for information about pre-rabbinic Judaism.[15] By the same token, Christian material cannot always be illuminated by Second-Temple sources without first placing those sources in a trajectory of Jewish development. The point is, however, that the NT's exegesis of the OT may be seen within a continuum of Jewish biblical interpretation that begins already in the OT itself, continues through the Greco-Roman period, and extends all the way to Jewish and Christian literatures of the Middle Ages.

The pseudepigrapha are no strangers to Christian tradition, and the pervasiveness of their influence on the NT and early Christian literature should be reckoned as highly probable, even if direct citations are comparatively rare. The most famous example, of course, is the citation of *1 Enoch* 1:9 in Jude 14–15 as a prophecy coming from the seventh patriarch from Adam; however, several other Christian writers called a book of Enoch "scripture" (e.g., ἡ γραφή in Barn. 16:5).[16] There was a remarkable continuity of exegetical tradition from the Second-Temple period through the first few centuries of the early Christian period, and the line between "Jewish" and "Christian" is frequently either blurred or non-existent.[17] Thus, a tradition that is found in *Jubilees* (e.g., the testing of Abraham through the offering of Isaac [*Jub.* 17:16–18]) is recycled in Augustine, *De civ. D.* 16.32. Similarly, a Qumran pseude-pigraphon (4QPs.-Ezekiel) is apparently cited in 1 Clem. 50:4.[18] The *Book of Jubilees* itself is called "divine scripture" (θεία γραφή) in the 'Εκλογὴ 'Ιστοριῶν, which is preserved in a thirteenth-century copy.[19] On the other hand, in the recently discovered papyri at Tura near Cairo, a commentary on Job by Didymus the Blind (ca. 310–98 CE) was found that refers to a story in *Jubilees* (17:16) with the proviso, "if one wants to recognize the Book of the Covenant (εἰ τῷ φίλον παραδέξασθαι τὴν βίβλον τῆς διαθήκης)."[20] Hermann Rönsch adduces numerous examples of the use of *Jubilees* in ancient and medieval Christian literature.[21]

Along with *1 Enoch*, the *Book of Jubilees* is among the very earliest and most extensive of the Jewish pseudepigrapha from the Second-Temple period. Since the discovery of the Ethiopic version by Western scholars in the nineteenth century, *Jubilees* has sustained intense scholarly interest as a document of central relevance for the understanding of ancient Judaism, not least as a prime example of the so-called "Rewritten Bible."[22] This interest has only increased since the official publication in 1994 of the entirety of the *Jubilees* manuscripts from Qumran cave 4.[23] With this improved textual basis for studying the book, a research symposium on *Jubilees* was organized in Leipzig in 1996, and its proceedings have recently been published.[24] Curiously, however, the scripture index to the volume contains only five references to the NT, none of which relates to the possible influence of *Jubilees* on the NT. Likewise, the 27th edition of the Nestle-Aland edition of the Greek NT records only three allusions to *Jubilees* in the whole NT, all of them in Romans.[25] Since *Jubilees* obviously had a strong influence on Second-Temple Jewish sources and on later Christian literature,[26] being on par with scripture in some quarters,[27] we may suspect that this pseudepigraphon – "the Little Genesis,"[28] as it was sometimes called – also influenced the NT. As we shall see, the traces of the *Jubilees* 8–9 geographical tradition found in early Christian literature may be useful in detecting its influence on the NT as well. The influence of *Jubilees* need not have been constant over time,[29] but it sustained a remarkable legacy over a considerable period.

1

THE *MAPPAMUNDI* OF QUEEN KYPROS

Introduction

A most interesting and enigmatic cartographic text has apparently escaped the notice of historians of cartography – an epigram of Philip of Thessalonica, who wrote in Rome during the reigns of Tiberius (14–37 CE) and Gaius (37–41 CE).[1] This epideictic epigram (*Anth. Pal.* 9.778) praises an artistically woven tapestry that was sent as a gift from a queen to an unnamed, reigning Caesar, presumably one of the aforementioned Roman emperors. The tapestry itself is said to display the inhabited world and the surrounding Ocean. We are evidently dealing here with a world "map" done in either wool or linen,[2] making it perhaps one of the earliest recorded *mappaemundi* in the literal sense of the term (i.e., "cloth of the world").[3] It should be noted here that the image of weaving is used extensively in connection with weaving narratives, so literary and visual productions, in which the world may be described, are neatly linked.[4]

Philip's tantalizingly brief poem prompts several questions. Who was the queen who made the tapestry and sent it as a gift? What picture of the world are we to imagine on the tapestry? What is the cartographic source(s) for the "map"?[5] In seeking to answer these questions, however provisionally, the present chapter opens our discussion of Jewish geographical conceptions with a cameo of the subject at hand. This will provide us not only with a fitting example of the kind of evidence that is available for our work, but also with a salient reminder of the difficulties inherent in the task.

Philip's Epigram (*Anth. Pal.* 9.778)

We begin our investigation with the text of Philip's epigram:[6]

> Γαῖαν τὴν φερέκαρπον ὅσην ἔζωκε περίχθων
> ὠκεανὸς μεγάλωι Καίσαρι πειθομένην
> καὶ γλαυκήν με θάλασσαν ἀπηκριβώσατο [Κύπρος]

κερκίσιν ἱστοπόνοις πάντ᾽ ἀπομαξαμένη·
Καίσαρι δ᾽ εὐξείνωι χάρις ἤλθομεν, ἦν γὰρ ἀνάσσης
δῶρα φέρειν τὰ θεοῖς καὶ πρὶν ὀφειλόμενα.

Modelling all with shuttle labouring on the loom, [Kypros] made me, a perfect copy of the harvest-bearing earth, all that the land-encircling ocean girdles, obedient to great Caesar, and the gray sea too. We have come as a grateful return for Caesar's hospitality; it was a queen's duty, to bring gifts so long due to the gods.

Here, we read of a woman's skillful handiwork at the loom. Philip's description suggests that the resulting tapestry was a genuine work of art, for the participle ἀπομαξαμένη comes from a verb (ἀπομάσσω) which in the middle voice is used in the sense of "model" as a sculptor (cf. LSJ, s.v., 209). Moreover, the participle is construed with a main verb (ἀπακριβόομαι) which is likewise used of sculpturing, this time in the sense of "make exact."[7] Hence, the tapestry is described not only as a work of art but also as an exact replica of the world that it sought to portray.[8] Allowing for some exaggeration and poetic license, we may nevertheless conclude that the tapestry must have been quite impressive to behold.[9] We will return to Philip's description of the tapestry after attempting to identify the "queen" who made it and the "Caesar" for whom she made it.

The identification of the queen and the reigning Caesar

It is difficult to ascertain who the maker and giver of this artistic tapestry may have been. We know that the artist must have been a woman, for in line 5 she is called an ἄνασσα ("queen, lady"). Furthermore, the name of the queen is undoubtedly to be found in Κάρπος, which is the reading preserved in line 3 of the manuscript. While the masculine Κάρπος is not usually a name for a woman, the text clearly presupposes that the name belongs to a woman, as seen by the feminine participle ἀπομαξαμένη, which takes its gender from the assumed subject of the main clause. Very likely, therefore, Κάρπος is a corruption for another name. The identification of this person is indeed the linchpin for the interpretation of the entire epigram.

As a solution to this problem, Conrad Cichorius made the ingenious suggestion that Κάρπος should be emended to the orthographically similar name Κύπρος, and that this Kypros should be identified as the grand-daughter of Herod the Great and the wife of Agrippa I, another grandchild of Herod.[10] Kypros, too, seems to be a relatively uncommon name for a woman, which may perhaps explain why the textual corruption happened in the first place.[11] Indeed, we may note that apparently the only women of royal lineage who are known to have had this name belonged to the Herodian dynasty.[12]

Interpreting the emended name as a reference to Kypros, the wife of Agrippa I, is consistent with the description of the woman in Philip's epigram. First, the term ἄνασσα applies to a "queen" or a "lady" of a royal household.[13] Used mostly in poetry rather than in prose (cf. LSJ, s.v., 121), ἄνασσα is not one of the most common terms for the queen of a Roman client kingdom.[14] Nevertheless, it is used apparently of Cleopatra Selene (*Anth. Pal.* 9.752.3), the daughter of Antony and Cleopatra VII whom Augustus married to King Juba II of Mauretania (ca. 20 BCE).[15] Hence, the reference to Kypros as an ἄνασσα may signal that she belongs to one of the client kingdoms that stand in a vassal relationship with Rome.[16] Upon his accession to the throne in 37 CE, Emperor Gaius declared Agrippa "king" (βασιλεύς) of the former tetrarchies of Philip and Lysanias (*JW* 2.181; *Ant.* 18.237),[17] thus making Kypros a "queen" of a Roman client kingdom.[18]

Second, the poem seems to suggest that the queen in question has some kind of rapport with the reigning "Caesar."[19] Again, this fits Kypros, whose husband enjoyed a close, personal relationship with Emperor Gaius.[20] Like other sons of client kings, Agrippa had lived in Rome from childhood under patronage of the imperial family (Josephus, *Ant.* 18.143). He had, in fact, been brought up with Gaius (§191). When Emperor Tiberius later accepted Agrippa into his own inner circle, Agrippa deepened his relationship with Gaius and tried to impress him with extravagant spending (Josephus, *JW* 2.178; *Ant.* 18.166–7). Agrippa went so far in currying favor with Gaius that he expressed the hope that Gaius would soon replace Tiberius as emperor, a remark which provoked Tiberius and landed Agrippa in prison (*JW* 2.179–80; *Ant.* 18.168–9, 186–92). After Tiberius' death, Gaius released Agrippa from prison and appointed him king as a reward for his loyalty. If Agrippa's wife is the one described in Philip's epigram, then her gift pays tribute to the Roman emperor as an expression of the long-standing, personal relationship between Agrippa and Caesar.[21]

Third, Philip's epigram implies that the queen in question was politically involved for the sake of her husband. Again, this fits Kypros.[22] As Josephus tells us, Agrippa had a particularly intelligent wife, who often intervened on behalf of her husband.[23] For example, when Agrippa was destitute and at the point of suicide, Kypros' intercession won for Agrippa the help of his sister's husband, Antipas (*Ant.* 18.147–9). On another occasion, when he was again in dire financial straits, Agrippa begged Alexander the alabarch to loan him a large sum of money, but Alexander refused. Only when Kypros intervened did Alexander relent, "because he marveled at her love for her husband and all her other good qualities" (*Ant.* 18.159). If Agrippa's wife is the one described in Philip's epigram, then her gift to Caesar provides yet another example of how she intervened with a political benefactor on behalf of her husband. It could be argued that weaving was the ideal for Jewish women of high repute who enhanced their husbands' political standing.[24] The epigram does not state the occasion for the gift to Caesar. If the queen is Kypros, then Josephus records an episode during the reign of Agrippa, probably in the summer of 39 CE,[25] which may have been the occasion for Kypros' gift. Herod Antipas was urged by his wife Herodias, Agrippa's sister, to go to Italy to petition Gaius for the status of king, to equal his brother-in-law (Josephus, *Ant.* 18.240–54). But Agrippa, when he learned of their plan and of the lavish gifts that they were bringing to Gaius, made his own preparations. "And when he heard that they had set sail," Josephus writes, "he himself also dispatched Fortunatus, one of his freedmen, to Rome, charged with presents for the emperor and letters against Herod..." (§ 247).[26] Perhaps Kypros' artistic tapestry was among the presents that were delivered to Gaius on this occasion. Certainty is, of course, impossible.

Nikos Kokkinos suggests another possible occasion for the queen's gift.[27] If, as he believes, Agrippa I and Kypros accompanied Gaius to the western extremes of the Empire in 39/40 CE,[28] then Kypros may have wanted to commemorate this grand expedition with the production of a *mappamundi*. Kokkinos surmises that the tapestry must have been prepared in Rome, for Agrippa's return to Palestine occurred only in the autumn of 41. Therefore, Roman influences, such as the famous "map" of M. Vipsanius Agrippa, may be relevant here (see further below). We may wonder, however, whether the emperor's invitation to accompany the expedition was prompted by the gift, or rather the gift by the expedition. Moreover, the commonly accepted date for publication of the *Garland* of Philip (40 CE) seems to point toward the earlier date for the gift and the epigram, although the date of publication is disputed and may have been during the reign of Nero (see above).

The *imago mundi* of the tapestry

As befitting an epigram, Philip's description is quite laconic, mentioning only the two most basic components of the world map depicted on the tapestry – land and sea. Nevertheless, by carefully examining the poem line by line, we may be able to make some reasonable deductions about the nature of the image.

In line 1, Philip refers to the "harvest-bearing earth" (γαῖαν φερέκαρπον). Although an Orphic hymn addresses the "goddess Gaia" (Γαῖα θεά) as, among other things, "harvest-bearing" (φερέκαρπε), [29] we need not conclude from this that Philip also uses γαῖα as a proper noun. For the very next clause in line 1 – "as much as the land-encircling Ocean girdles" (ὅσην ἔζωκε περίχθων ὠκεανός) – modifies γαῖα, thus showing that γαῖα is meant primarily in the geographical sense of "earth." On the other hand, the whole concept may reflect Homeric mythology, for in the *Iliad* (14.200; cf. 301) Hera is made to say: "For I shall see the bounds of the fertile Earth, and Ocean, progenitor of the gods" (εἶμι γὰρ ὀψομένη πολυφόρβου πείρατα γαίης Ὠκεανόν τε θεῶν γένεσιν).[30] Strabo, who defends the Homeric picture of the known world as substantially true, also refers to this passage in the *Iliad* (*Geog.* 1.1.7), showing that this conception persisted even to the first century BCE.

Philip describes Kypros' *mappamundi* in terms that would have been readily understandable in both Greco-Roman and Jewish cultures.[31] The Homeric notion of Earth as an island landmass encircled by Ocean retained an astonishingly persistent hold.[32] Homer conceived of Ocean as a great river that compasses the earth's disk, returning into itself (*Il.* 18.399; *Od.* 20.65).[33] Ocean is represented as wrought on the circular rim of Achilles' shield (*Il.* 18.607–8),[34] which provides a fitting parallel to Kypros' artistic production.[35] Anaximander (610–540 BCE) is reportedly the first to have mapped such a conception.[36] Already in the fifth century BCE, Herodotus (4.36; cf. 2:23) scoffed at this conception: "I laugh to see how many have now drawn maps of the world, not one of them showing the matter reasonably; for they draw the world as round as if fashioned by compasses, encircled by the river of Ocean . . ."[37] Nevertheless, this image of the world never really died out. In fact, it experienced a renaissance in the first century BCE precisely because it so well suited Roman imperial ideology and aspiration. Thus, Cicero (*Somn.* 20) describes the inhabited world which the Romans dominate as a "small island," oblong in shape and surrounded by Ocean.[38] Strabo (*Geog.* 2.5.17) states that the "inhabited world" (οἰκουμένη) is "surrounded by water" (περίρρυτος), a view that he explicitly attributes to Homer as the first geographer correctly to describe the earth as surrounded by Ocean (1.1.3–10).[39] Ovid (43 BCE –17 CE) regards Delphi as the center of the earth (*Met.* 10.167–8), and holds the Homeric concept of the earth as a disk surrounded by Ocean (*Met.* 2.5–7). An epigram of Antipater of

Thessalonica (*Anth. Pal.* 9.297), which was probably addressed to Gaius Caesar when sent by Augustus to the East in 1 BCE, describes the Roman Empire as "bounded on all sides by Ocean" (ὠκεανῷ περιτέρμονα πάντοθεν). Writing in 43/44 CE, Pomponius Mela (*De chorographia* 1.3–8) likewise describes the earth in his pioneering Latin geography as encircled by Ocean.[40] Obviously, the Ocean as a definer of the Roman Empire was a crucial feature of the Roman mental map.[41] In light of all the other strong Homeric echoes in our epigram, it seems clear that Philip describes Kypros' tapestry map in terms of the Homeric geographic tradition that had recently been reinstated for use in Roman imperial ideology.

The Old Testament (OT) contains a similar conception of the world, whose closest Near Eastern parallel is the famous Babylonian world map from Sippar, dating to the late eighth or seventh century BCE.[42] This celebrated, little map (ca. 90 mm in diameter), which is unique among ancient Mesopotamian maps, shows the world as a circular disk surrounded by Ocean (*marratu*). A hole at the center of the map is evidently the result of the compass used to carve the concentric circles; it does not seem to represent a city or other landmark conceived of as the center or navel of the world. Circles are used to indicate cities or countries, but none of them is at the center of the disk. Eight outlying regions, triangular in shape and radiating out from the outer edge of the world, are the home of strange or legendary beings. At the top the scribe has written, "Where the sun is not seen," to indicate the north. The accompanying text, apparently describing these regions, mentions Utnapishtim (the well-known hero of the flood story in the *Gilgamesh Epic*), Sargon of Akkad (the famous third-millennium king who was remembered as the conqueror of the entire world), and the "four quandrants" of the earth's surface. Evidently, we are dealing here with a map that is concerned to show the worldwide extent of the Babylonian Empire.[43]

According to Job 26:10, God "has described a circle on the face of the waters, at the boundary between light and darkness." This could be interpreted as meaning that the disk-shaped world is bounded by water all around. According to Gen. 1:9–10, describing the third day of creation, "God said, 'Let the waters under the sky be gathered together into one place, and let the dry land appear.' And it was so. God called the dry land Earth, and the waters that were gathered together he called Seas." *4 Ezra*, a late first-century pseudepigraphon, goes beyond Gen. 1:9–10 by adding that the ratio of earth-to-sea was six-to-one: "On the third day you commanded the waters to be gathered together in the seventh part of the earth; six parts you dried up and kept so that some of them might be planted and cultivated and be of service for you" (*4 Ezra* 6:42).[44]

This suggests perhaps that the earth is composed predominantly of a landmass surrounded by a relatively thin strip of water.[45] According to the *Exagoge* of Ezekiel the Tragedian, who wrote probably during the second century BCE in Alexandria, Moses dreamed of ascending a throne on Mt. Sinai, from which he beheld "the entire circular earth" (γῆν ἅπασαν ἔγκυκλον, line 77), i.e., "the whole earth or inhabited world" (γῆν ὅλην τ᾽ οἰκουμένην, line 87).[46] Rabbinic literature makes similar statements about Alexander the Great.[47]

In line 2, Philip further describes the whole earth as "obedient to great Caesar" (μεγάλωι Καίσαρι πειθομένην). To underscore the emperor's claim to universal sovereignty, the text adds, as we have seen, that the whole earth, "as much as the land-encircling Ocean girdles," is subject to Caesar. At this point, Philip is simply reflecting the grandiose Roman imperial ideology of his day, which held that the Roman Empire was coextensive with the inhabited world.[48] According to Plutarch (*Caes.* 58.6–7), Julius Caesar "planned and prepared to make an expedition against the Parthians; and after subduing these and marching around the Euxine by way of Hyrcania, the Caspian Sea, and the Caucasus, to invade Scythia; and after overrunning the countries bordering on Germany and Germany itself, to come back by way of Gaul to Italy, and so to complete the circuit of his empire, which would then be bounded on all sides by Ocean" (καὶ συνάψαι τὸν κύκλον τοῦτον τῆς ἡγεμονίας τῷ πανταχόθεν 'Ωκεανῷ περιορισθείσης).[49] This plan failed to materialize. In the Preamble of his *Res Gestae*, however, Augustus, the first emperor of the Roman Empire, announces that he has attained dominion over the whole *orbis terrarum* ("*circle* of the world").[50] During the early Empire, the fiction of the emperor's ruling the whole world was perpetuated in the imperial ruler cult. Thus, an altar inscription from Narbo dated to 11 CE honors Augustus, referring to the "day on which he received imperium over the *orbis terrarum* ..."[51] Likewise, Gaius Caligula was expected to become "ruler of the inhabited world" (ἡγεμὼν τῆς οἰκουμένης) when he acceded to the throne (Josephus, *Ant.* 18.187).[52] Philo (*Legat.* 8) reports that after the death of Tiberius, Gaius succeeded to "the sovereignty of the whole earth and the sea" (τὴν ἡγεμονίαν πάσης γῆς καὶ θαλάσσης).

In line 3, Philip refers to the "gray sea" (γλαυκὴ θάλασσα). Since he has already mentioned Ocean that encircles the earth (lines 1–2), a reference to the "gray sea" might suggest a different body of water. On the other hand, the idea that the earth is surrounded by the *Mare Oceanum*, as graphically portrayed in the maps of Macrobius and of Isidore of Seville, allows us perhaps to equate the "gray sea" with the surrounding Ocean.

Like other terms in Philip's epigram, γλαυκὴ θάλασσα has Homeric roots (*Il.* 16.34), although it is also found in the Jewish *Sibylline Oracles* (1.11; 2.198; 7.5). In Hesiod (*Theog.* 440), "gray stormy" (γλαυκὴ δυσπέμφελος) is used as a general epithet of the sea. The adjective γλαυκός ("gray"), the color of the sea, is often applied to water deities. For example, Glaucus Pontius or Thalassius is a sea-god with prophetic powers (e.g., Euripides, *Or.* 362–5; Aristotle frg. 490), located, at least since Aeschylus' *Glaucus Pontius*, in the vicinity of the Euboean strait. Like many sea-gods, he is regarded as an old man (Virgil, *Aen.* 5.823). Job 41:24 (32) uses "gray hair" (שֵׂיבָה) in a figurative reference to the sea. We have not found evidence that "gray sea" refers to a specific body of water like the Mediterranean, which, in any case, was often conceived of as an arm of the surrounding Ocean.

In sum, the terms that Philip uses to describe the map apply from Homeric times to a conception of the earth as a large disk-shaped landmass surrounded by a relatively thin strip of Ocean. The size of the image cannot be ascertained from Philip's description. Perhaps investigation into the nature and size of artistic tapestries in the ancient world would provide a basis for comparison.[53] The fact that Kypros' tapestry was singled out for special praise in an epigram may imply that it was of monumental size.[54]

The source(s) of the *imago mundi*

Our investigation of the possible source(s) of the image of the world on the tapestry is hampered by the fact that the only description of it is extremely brief and comes from a Hellenistic court poet in Rome who is clearly writing from a Roman imperial perspective. Nevertheless, in view of the paucity of material evidence that survived from the ancient world, we cannot afford to overlook any shred of literary evidence. From what we have seen so far, the source(s) of Kypros' *mappamundi* could be either Roman or Jewish. We shall consider each of these possibilities in turn, without forgetting that both of these potential sources had undergone strong Hellenistic influence.

A possible Roman source

A Roman source for Kypros' map is particularly attractive, for it might explain why Caesar (Gaius) was so flattered by the tapestry. As we have seen, Philip writes that the tapestry displayed the whole earth "obedient to great Caesar,"[55] which conveys the universal sovereignty of the Roman emperor. Thus, there may be a direct connection between Kypros' map and the famous world "map" of M. Vipsanius Agrippa (64/3–12 BCE), which was erected in the Porticus Vipsania in Rome after his death and was meant, like the aforementioned Preamble of the *Res Gestae*, to proclaim that Augustus ruled the whole inhabited world. The great and successful wars of conquest initiated by Augustus and M. Vipsanius Agrippa became one of the key sources of legitimacy and prestige of the newly founded Roman Empire.[56] In the years up to his death, Agrippa acted as almost coregent of the Empire. Therefore, a public memorial to Augustus' right-hand man was most appropriate, and Augustus himself saw to the completion of the project (Pliny, *HN* 3.17).

If, as seems likely, Kypros had lived in Rome,[57] then she may have seen the Agrippa "map," which became her inspiration at the loom.[58] Perhaps she would have taken special note of this "map" not only because her husband had been named after the famous M. Vipsanius Agrippa,[59] but also because the latter had been a close personal friend of Herod the Great and benevolent toward the Jews.[60] A Jewish community in Rome was even named after him (*CIJ* 365, 425, 503), although the reason is not clear. More importantly, however, M. Agrippa was Gaius' grandfather through his mother, Agrippina the elder. In honor of his grandfather, Gaius issued a vast coinage of asses with Agrippa obverse, which performed a major role of circulation outside Italy.[61] According to Philo (*Legat.* 294–7), Agrippa I appealed specifically to the example of M. Agrippa as Gaius' maternal grandfather, in order to dissuade the emperor from violating the sanctity of the Jerusalem Temple.[62] Hence, if Kypros was looking for a way to impress Gaius, she could not have done better than to model her tapestry after the memorial of M. Agrippa.[63] Indeed, when Philip extols the tapestry as an exact copy of the earth and sea, he may well be referring to the fact that Kypros imitated the Agrippa "map," which would have been regarded as the ultimate standard of world cartography in that day.[64] Just as M. Agrippa had been Herod the Great's model for the architectural and cultural responsibilities of a dynast,[65] so now Herod Agrippa's wife may have followed that model in order to ingratiate her husband with the emperor. If, as Kokkinos suggests, the tapestry commemorated Gaius' grand expedition to the western limits of the known world, which Kypros and her husband may have accompanied (see above), then the gift of a world map would have been all the more appropriate.[66]

There is great doubt, however, whether the work set up in Agrippa's memory was really a "map" at all. Certainly, the map, if there ever was one, did not survive from antiquity. Based on the literary evidence, scholars have generally assumed that a map is being described.[67] However,

Kai Brodersen has recently called this whole assumption into question, arguing instead that the monument set up in the Porticus Vipsania was nothing more than a list of landmarks and the distances between them.[68] Brodersen begins by discussing the many vastly different reconstructions of the alleged map.[69]

> It was a mosaic, a mural, a bronze engraving, or a marble carving.
> It was round, oval, or rectangular.
> It was 9 × 18 m, 24 × 12 m, or 75 × 4.5 m.
> It was oriented on the east, the south, or the north.

Brodersen's critique makes it abundantly clear that, whether or not there was a map, we have very little concrete idea what Agrippa's monument actually looked like.[70]

Brodersen goes on to argue that the three pieces of literary evidence that are usually adduced to show that Agrippa's monument was a map fail to substantiate the case.[71] According to Brodersen, neither of the passages in Pliny's *Natural History* stands up to closer scrutiny. In *HN* 3.17, the elder Pliny (23/24–79 CE) expresses astonishment at Agrippa's measurements for the southern Spanish province of Baetica: "Who would believe that Agrippa, who was very careful and took great pains over this work, should, when he was going to set up the world to be looked at by the citizens of Rome (*cum orbem terrarum urbi spectandum propositurus esset*), have made this mistake, and together with him the deified Augustus? For it was Augustus, who, when Agrippa's sister had begun building the portico, carried it out from the intention and notes (*commentarii*) of M. Agrippa."[72] Brodersen contends that the expression *orbem terrarum urbi spectandum* refers not to a map but to a text, as Pliny's usage of *spectare* elsewhere shows.[73] The second text is *HN* 6.139, where Pliny writes that the Porticus Vipsania has Charax by the sea (*et maritimum etiam Vipsania porticus habet*). This passage has been thought to reveal a direct reference to the map on the portico wall in Rome rather than to the commentary, because on a relatively small-scale world map Charax – an unimportant town of Arabia – may have looked closer to the Persian Gulf than it really was. Brodersen points out, however, that Pliny's geographical commentary sometimes uses coastal cities as endpoints for measurements (e.g., Chalcedon, Byzantium, Panticapeum, Pelusium, and Arsinoe).[74] The third piece of literary evidence for the Agrippa map is found in Strabo, who repeatedly refers to "the chorographer" (ὁ χωρόγραφος), and once to a "choreographic tablet" (χωρογραφικὸς πίναξ). While these are sometimes taken as references to Agrippa and his map, Brodersen points out that Strabo could not have seen a map in the Porticus Vipsania, for the portico had not been completed by 7 BCE (cf. Dio Cassius 55.8.3–4), which is the year when Strabo's *Geography* was supposedly completed.[75] Thus, Brodersen completely dismisses the literary evidence for Agrippa's map.

Brodersen's case against the existence of an Agrippa world map must be seen in light of broader trends in the current discussion of the history of cartography. A debate is presently taking place among historians, geographers and cartographers over ancient conceptions of geography and the use of maps in antiquity. Two schools of thought have shaped discussion of this subject. Some scholars assume that ancient map use must be similar to our own, although limited by technology, and that any investigation of ancient geography should concentrate on ancient cartography.[76] On the other hand, a growing number of scholars contend that map consciousness and map use are almost totally absent in the ancient world.[77] "As pointed out by Fergus Millar, what we know about ancient map-making indicates that the Romans did not have a sufficiently clear or accurate notion of topographical realities to allow them to conceive of the overall military situation in global strategic terms."[78] Even more poignantly, R. J. A. Talbert remarks: "Up till then [i.e., the seventeenth century!], what we would consider accurate planning of long-term conquest could hardly have been feasible, while any army (or navy) operating away from 'home' (however you need to define that) must have been, to our way of thinking, 'lost.'"[79]

So far neither side of the debate appears even to have seen Philip's epigram, let alone consider its possible significance for the discussion.[80] If, as we have discussed, the queen of a Roman client kingdom could have produced a work of art in the form of a world map, that would seem to indicate more "map consciousness" than is often admitted.[81] Moreover, as we have seen, there is a possibility that Kypros' map may have been a reproduction of the famous Agrippa map, which she had seen in Rome. The symbolic significance of such a gift is readily apparent: the queen would be saying in essence that Gaius had achieved the domination of the inhabited world and thereby succeeded to the Empire of Divus Augustus.[82] Indeed, this corresponds to the meaning that Philip's epigram attaches to the tapestry. Just as Agrippa's map of the tributary world had been made to honor Augustus and his universal reign,[83] so also Kypros' map was produced to honor Gaius and given to him in tribute. The very fact that the map was woven would have further underscored imperial values, for, according to Suetonius (*Aug.* 64.2), Caesar Augustus had his daughter Julia (the wife of M. Agrippa) and his granddaughters (including Agrippina, the mother of Gaius Caligula) taught the art of spinning and weaving.[84] Suetonius (*Aug.* 73) also claims that Augustus wore only clothing woven by the women of his family.[85] Furthermore, Plato's *Politicus* (279b–311c) had long since made weaving a fitting analogy for the role of the consummate ruler. Seen in this light, Kypros' tapestry becomes a metaphor for Caesar's statecraft in weaving together every disparate aspect of Rome's world empire into a united and orderly whole under his imperium.[86]

We may perhaps suppose that the Agrippa map was disk-shaped. Several lines of evidence can confirm this. First, we may consider numismatic evidence from the early Principate. A simple form of world "map" occurs regularly on Roman imperial coinage, in which the globe is portrayed as dominated by either Victory or the emperor. Many specimens of this coin type were minted during the reigns of Augustus[87] and Gaius.[88] Admittedly, however, the authenticity of a unique gold medallion, whose inscription dates it to the reign of Augustus, remains disputed: the obverse reportedly contains the image of Augustus with the inscription AUGUSTO DIVI FILIO COS XI TR P II IMP VIII; the reverse contains three circles representing the tripartite world with the entry EUR ASI AFR.[89] David Woodward regards the medallion as the beginning of the Roman tradition of representing the earth as a sphere on coins,[90] whereas Brodersen rejects it as a modern forgery, because the date of Augustus' TR P II (i.e., his second *tribunicia potestas* = 26 June 22 to 25 June 21 BCE) conflicts with the imprint by the III VIR (i.e., *tresviri monetales*), which began after 20 BCE.[91] However, the chronology of the monetary *collegia* is not as certain as Brodersen seems to suggest. According to the numismatist, C. H. V. Sutherland, only one of the monetary *collegia* active under Augustus is specifically dated (i.e., that of L. Mescinius Rufus, L. Vinicius, and C. Antistius Vetus in 16 BCE), the rest of the chronology being largely a matter of conjecture.[92] Nevertheless, the medallion in question is almost certainly a relatively modern confection, for it is quite out of place in Francesco Gnecchi's catalogue of gold medallions.[93]

In any case, the numismatic evidence demonstrates that an image of the world in the shape of a circle (or sphere) was used during the reign of Augustus and the rest of the early Principate to portray Roman domination of the world. In particular, the reverse of a coin of Faustus Cornelius Sulla (ca. 56 BCE) contains a globus surrounded by four wreaths: the large, jeweled wreath at the top represents Pompey's golden crown, whereas the plainer wreaths represent the three continents over which Pompey triumphed.[94]

Second, the medieval *mappaemundi* may confirm that the Agrippa map was a disk-shaped landmass encircled by a relatively thin strip of Ocean. For on the basis of statements by a number of ancient and medieval writers, the Agrippa map is generally believed to be the prototype for a succession of later world maps such as the thirteenth-century Hereford *mappamundi*.[95] These medieval world maps are also disk-shaped and encircled by Ocean. The main difference is that they depict Christ, rather than Caesar, as the one who dominates the world.[96] Like many medieval *mappaemundi*, the Agrippa map may have had a center. Although the medieval *mappaemundi* never put Rome in the center, we would expect the Agrippa map to have done so. Similarly, Strabo (*Geog.* 17.3.24) conceptualized the Roman Empire and the entire world as spreading in concentric circles around Rome: Italy, the regions around Italy in a circle (κύκλῳ), and the three continents (Europe, Libya, Asia).[97] Arrian's *Anabasis* begins with a description of the lands under control of the Romans, proceeding in a counterclockwise direction: beginning at the Pillars of Hercules, the account circumnavigates the Mediterranean eastward across North Africa, northward up the coast of Syria-Palestine, and across Asia Minor and Europe, and back to the Pillars of Hercules (Prooem. 1–3).

A possible Jewish source

A Jewish source for Kypros' world map is also possible, especially since Kypros is a Jewess who had intimate contact with Judea.[98] By the first century CE, Jews throughout the eastern Mediterranean had undergone Hellenization to one degree or another;[99] hence, it is not always possible to distinguish sharply a Jewish source from other contemporary influences.[100] Some Jews in Palestine read Homer,[101] and, as *Jubilees* 8–9 (second-century BCE) demonstrates, even the most rigorous of Jewish groups in Palestine were influenced by Hellenistic conceptions of world geography.[102] It is not surprising, then, to find that the mosaic floor in the third- or fourth-century CE synagogue of Hammath-Tiberias portrays Helios in the center of a zodiac circle, riding a quadriga and holding a globus containing a crossband.[103] The quadriga, the zodiac circle, and the globus are Greco-Roman motifs commonly associated with Helios.[104] Obviously, the synagogue appropriated these elements from the culture at large and adapted them to its own uniquely Jewish cult.[105] Therefore, acknowledging that Kypros was Jewish hardly settles the issue of cartographic sources for her tapestry.

Nevertheless, at least three pieces of evidence allow us to consider a possible Jewish source for Kypros' world map. First, Kypros' weaving activity itself may provide an important clue to the source of the image on her tapestry. Spinning and weaving was an art practiced already in ancient Israel. According to Exodus, the construction of the tabernacle involved considerable spinning and weaving, including many textiles with images of cherubim worked into them (e.g., Exod. 26:1, 31). Women did some of the spinning for the tabernacle and the priestly vestment. Exod. 35:25 states that "All the skillful women spun with their hands, and brought what they had spun in blue and purple and crimson yarns and fine linen..." Josephus (*Ant.* 3.107; cf. *JW* 5.213) rephrases this text to read that "Women themselves vied with one another in providing priestly vestments..." implying that the women not only did the spinning, but the weaving as well. Of particular interest for our purposes is Josephus' description in *Ant.* 3.183–4 of the cosmological symbolism woven into the fabrics used in the tabernacle and the high priest's vestment:[106]

> The tapestries woven of four materials denote the natural elements: thus the fine linen appears to typify the earth, because from it springs up the flax, and the purple the sea, since it is incarnadined with the blood of fish; the air must be indicated by the blue, and the crimson will be the symbol of fire. (184) The high-priest's tunic likewise signifies the earth, being of linen, and its blue the arch of heaven, while it recalls the lightnings by its pomegranates, the thunder by the sound of its bells.

Since this description of the tabernacle and the high priestly vestment goes beyond Scripture, Josephus, himself a native of Jerusalem and a priest (*JW* 1.3), presumably reflects here an actual knowledge of the Temple cult in his own day which he has interjected into the biblical account.[107] In any case, it is significant that Josephus shows familiarity with tapestries and other woven goods bearing cosmological symbolism.[108]

The *Wisdom of Solomon* contains similar comments about the high priest's vestment, which may corroborate Josephus' description. According to Wisd. 18:24 (alluding to Exodus 28), Aaron's high-priestly vesture was endowed with symbolic and cosmic significance: "For on his long robe the whole world was depicted..." (ἐπὶ γὰρ ποδήρους ἐνδύματος ἦν ὅλος ὁ κόσμος).[109] Again, this may reflect actual knowledge of the Temple cult in the writer's own day (in this case, probably the first century BCE). If so, we can only speculate what the image of the world may have looked like, although the collection of the Temple tax from the worldwide Diaspora would suggest that priestly circles in Jerusalem possessed an actual map of the world. This possibility is strengthened by several observations. (1) A priestly source forms the basic framework of the Table of Nations in Genesis 10.[110] As we shall see in the next chapter, Genesis 10 is more than a genealogical list; it reflects an *imago mundi* that comes to expression in subsequent centuries. (2) *M. Sheq.* 3:1, 4 describes how the Temple tax was disbursed for Temple expenditures in three separate drawings, according to the geographical area from which the tax had been collected, proceeding in concentric circles around Jerusalem: the first drawing was made before Passover, on the shekels from the Land of Israel; the second was made before Pentecost, on the offering from the neighboring countries; and the third was made before the Feast of Tabernacles, on the money from Babylonia, Media, and the distant lands. Hence, there is enough evidence from Judea during the Second-Temple period of hand-woven textiles containing cosmological symbols and perhaps actual images of the world worked into them that Kypros could have gained the inspiration for her tapestry directly from the Jerusalem Temple.[111] Given the fact that foreign envoys often brought the Roman emperor gifts displaying the exotic nature of their country (e.g., Strabo, *Geog.* 15.1.73), we might expect Kypros' gift to display distinctively Jewish characteristics, at least in part.

Second, archaeological evidence may provide a clue to the source of the image on the Kypros map. For example, in light of the Babylonian world map, it is tempting to compare a somewhat similar artifact found at Qumran:[112] a shallow bowl measuring 145 mm in diameter, with a hole in the center, four concentric furrows progressively further away from it, and three pairs of concentric circles in the flat spaces between the furrows. Each pair of circles is joined by a series of short lines that fill the interstitial space and radiate toward the center of the disk. It is estimated that there were approximately 60 of these lines between the inner pair of rings, 72 between the middle ones,[113] and 90 between the outer ones. In addition, the artifact contains several striking orientation marks: a circle around one of the short lines in the first pair of concentric circles and a notch on the outer rim of the disk. The artifact has been tentatively identified as a kind of sundial or "astronomical measuring instrument," for which there is no known parallel.[114] This hypothesis requires several assumptions, including (1) the original existence of a vertical post (gnomon) in the center hole that served the function of casting a shadow so that the user could determine the season and the hour of the day,[115] and (2) the purpose of the shallow bowl was to hold water as a means of controlling the vertical position of the gnomon.[116]

If, on the other hand, the artifact is seen as a sort of schematic world map, then the center may represent the Jerusalem Temple, which the Qumran community undoubtedly considered the "navel of the world" (cf. *Jub.* 8:12, 19);[117] the first furrow may separate the walled city of Jerusalem from the rest of Israel; the second furrow may separate Israel from the nations round about, symbolized by the series of 72 lines;[118] and the outermost band or furrow may represent Ocean.[119] The notion of concentric circles around Jerusalem and the Temple is well documented in Jewish literature of the period (cf. 1 Chronicles 1–9;[120] the Temple Scroll;[121] *m. Kelim* 1:6–9;[122] and *m. Sheq.* 3:1, 4;[123] Midr. Tanḥuma, *Qedoshim* 10 [124]). For the overall conception, it is interesting to compare qiblah world maps, and especially the qiblah chart prepared in 570/1562 by Mahmud al-Khatib al-Rumi, showing 72 sectors about the Kaʻba in the center.[125] Another qibla diagram dating to 958/1551 depicts the Kaʻba in the center of a thirty-two-division windrose, the outside perimeter of which is lined with the names of the lands of the world in groups of three.[126] Perhaps most important for comparison with our bowl from Qumran is a shallow, ceramic qiblah-bowl from Damascus dating to ca. 1516–20, which could have been filled with water and would have had a floating magnetic needle to establish the cardinal directions.[127] The outside perimeter of this bowl with concentric circles also contains 72 marks, corresponding to the 72-sector scheme of sacred geography in early Islamic tradition.[128]

The Temple and Jerusalem contain many elements that point to a strong geographical orientation. For instance, the huge and highly ornamented "molten sea" or "bronze sea" that reportedly stood in the courtyard of Solomon's temple. According to 1 Kgs. 7:23–6 (cf. 2 Chr. 4:2–5) this "sea" was supported on four sets of bronze oxen, with three oxen in each set. Each set of oxen faced a direction of the compass, with their hindquarters facing inward and supporting the basin. Similarly, according to both the OT (Ezek. 48:30–5) and a Qumran manuscript (4Q554 1 i:12–ii:9), the gates in outer walls of eschatological Jerusalem will be arranged in four sets of three, corresponding to the cardinal points, and named after the twelve tribes of Israel.[129] The same Qumran scroll (4Q554 1 i:3–6) describes the new Jerusalem as containing a broad main street running east–west and a somewhat narrower main street running north–south.[130] As to the molten sea's symbolic function, Carol Meyers suggests:[131]

> One of the features of ANE temples was their utilization of artistic and architectural elements relating to the idea of the temple as the cosmic center of the world. The great deep, or cosmic waters, is one aspect of the array of cosmic attributes of such a holy spot. The temple of Marduk at Babylon, for example, had an artificial sea (*ta-am-tu*) in its precincts; and some Babylonian temples had an *apsû*-sea, a large basin. Such features symbolize the idea of the ordering of the universe by the conquest of chaos; or they represent the presence of the 'waters of life' at the holy center. Ancient Israel shared in this notion of watery chaos being

subdued by Yahweh and of the temple being built on the cosmic waters. The great 'molten sea' near the temple's entrance would have signified Yahweh's power and presence.

Subsequent Jewish interpretation underscores the universal significance of the molten sea.[132] As Josephus (*Ant.* 3.180–7) explains, every object in the Temple is intended to imitate and represent the universe in some way. We see, then, that the Kypros map would have had numerous possible sources in the material culture of Jerusalem and the Second Temple.

Third, a letter from Agrippa I to Emperor Gaius may provide a clue to the source of the image on the Kypros map. According to Philo's vindictive treatise, *Embassy to Gaius* (§§276–329), Agrippa wrote the letter to Gaius when the latter ordered a colossal statue of himself to be introduced into the Jerusalem Temple. If, as many scholars suspect, Philo himself composed the letter,[133] then its value for the present discussion is negligible. If, on the other hand, Philo's version reflects the substance of an actual letter to Gaius, then it may be relevant, for in his response to the enormity of Gaius' order, Agrippa includes a geographic survey of the worldwide Jewish Diaspora, which had gone out from Jerusalem to form colonies in the mainlands, the islands, and the countries beyond the Euphrates (*Legat.* 281–3). The conception of the world presupposed here is distinctively Jewish, as seen particularly by the centrality of Jerusalem in it. By stating that colonies went out from Jerusalem ("the metropolis") to form colonies in the rest of the inhabited world, Jerusalem is thereby indirectly compared to Delphi, which, in Greco-Roman thought, was often considered the omphalos of the world.[134] Agrippa's wife Kypros may have been imbued with such an *imago mundi* when she set to work on the tapestry.

Conclusion

Enough has been said to give some impression of the diversity and richness of the evidence that is potentially available for any attempt to understand ancient Jewish geographical conceptions. By its very nature, the evidence is tantalizingly sketchy and highly evocative. As so often, if we try to generalize too confidently when confronted with the intermingling of languages, cultures, and forms of religious belief and practice that influence Jewish conceptions, the evidence will not quite fall into the patterns we would like. This is indeed partly because, when and if literary or documentary evidence from the period is particularly explicit, it in itself may constitute an observer's interpretation, not a report which can be taken at face value.

It is precisely for these reasons that the epigram of Philip of Thessalonica is of such significance for our quest. Although our only glimpse of Kypros' tapestry is through the eyes of a Hellenistic court poet, whose description is too terse and enigmatic to support unequivocal conclusions, we are nevertheless ineluctably drawn to consider the scant evidence left to us by the ravages of time and to attempt an interpretation. The context is one where Jews and Romans interface on the basis of their respective cultural heritages, part of which is Hellenistic and shared and part of which is not. The result is not merely the coexistence of multivalent perspectives but the possible amalgamation of geographical conceptions. Unequivocal conclusions are hardly possible when the conceptions we are trying to describe are themselves equivocal. What seems virtually certain is that we have evidence for cartographic activity and geographical speculation among Jews during the first century. This is not at all surprising when we consider how fundamentally geography informs and shapes the historical imagination of Judaism, with its persistent contrast between the Land of Israel and other lands.[135]

The Kypros map provides a convenient point of departure for further consideration of Jewish geographical conceptions. In Chapters 2–6, we shall examine the Jewish geographical tradition that probably most influenced Jewish and Christian geographical conceptions. In Chapter 7, we shall return to the Kypros map to explore the possible relevance of our investigation for understanding the medieval *mappaemundi*. With the discussion of Chapters 2–6 in view, it is almost inevitable that speculation should lead one to consider a possible connection between the Kypros map and the *mappaemundi*.

2

JUBILEES 8–9

Introduction

Any description of Jewish geographical conceptions must deal with the Table of Nations in Genesis 10 and the influential tradition to which it gave rise.[1] For Genesis 10, along with a few other biblical data,[2] provided the main source of information for latter Jewish and Christian attempts to describe world geography and ethnography. As we shall see in Chapter 7, the Genesis 10 tradition arguably had a major influence on the medieval *mappaemundi*.

There is a certain irony in this Table of Nations tradition. For, although Genesis 10 presents the reader with a static view of the world and its inhabitants after the flood, the Genesis 10 tradition itself underwent numerous changes in the course of its centuries-long transmission. As Elias Bikerman observes in his justly famous article, "Origines Gentium" (1952):[3]

> The Bible taught the unity of mankind. We are all sons of Adam, and the chosen people is only a secondary branch on the common stem. This meek idea made pre-history static for the Hebrews. . . . The Jews could mechanically transfer an old name to some new people. First the Macedonians, then the Romans received the name of Kittim, which originally referred to the inhabitants of Citium (Cyprus). Such identification is purely nominal.

Hence, although the Table of Nations long remained the undisputed standard of world geography and ethnography, it nevertheless underwent a process of shaping, translation, and development to meet changing historical circumstances.[4] This can be seen already in the OT itself, where Genesis 10 is re-edited in 1 Chronicles 1. There were many subsequent versions and revisions of the table, including *Jubilees 8–9*, *Genesis Apocryphon* 12–17, Josephus' *Antiquities* 1.122–47, and Pseudo-Philo's

Biblical Antiquities 4(–5). For purposes of the present study, we shall focus on the use of Genesis 10 in *Jubilees* 8–9. For, as we shall argue, it is primarily through this text that the Genesis 10 tradition is later received in Christian circles and from there is passed on to the Middle Ages. We begin by examining Genesis 10 itself.

The Table of Nations in Genesis 10

Form and structure of the Hebrew version

Situated between the genealogical notice of Noah's death (Gen. 9:28–9) and the Tower of Babel story (Gen. 11:1–9), the Table of Nations in Genesis 10 is presented as a genealogy (תּוֹלְדֹת, "generations") of the sons of Noah to whom children were born after the flood. The use of the term תּוֹלְדֹת links Genesis 10 with the larger genealogical structure of the Priestly work (Gen. 2:4b; 5:1; 6:9; 11:10, 27; 25:12, 19; 36:1, 4, 9; 37:2; Num. 3:1).[5] Together with the story of the Tower of Babel, Genesis 10 marks the end of the primeval history (Genesis 1–11) and the transition to the patriarchal history (Genesis 12–50), which is set against the background of a world filled with nations. Thus, when God promises Abram that "in you all the families of the earth will be blessed" (Gen. 12:3), this refers back to the Table of Nations, where the descendants of Noah are separated "by their families" (see below).

Structurally, the table proceeds from Japheth (10:2–5), to Ham (vv. 6–20), and then to Shem (vv. 21–31), although the sons' names appear in the reverse order (Shem–Ham–Japheth) in the opening verse (v. 1). Thus, being the most important son of Noah, Shem both begins and ends the list.[6] Each of the three sections concludes with a formulaic, summary statement:

> <u>Japheth</u> (v. 5): "From these the coastland peoples spread. These are the descendants of Japheth in their lands, with their own language, by their families, in their nations."
>
> מֵאֵלֶּה נִפְרְדוּ אִיֵּי הַגּוֹיִם בְּאַרְצֹתָם אִישׁ לִלְשֹׁנוֹ לְמִשְׁפְּחֹתָם בְּגוֹיֵהֶם
>
> <u>Ham</u> (v. 20): "These are the descendants of Ham, by their families, their languages, their lands, and their nations."
>
> אֵלֶּה בְנֵי־חָם לְמִשְׁפְּחֹתָם לִלְשֹׁנֹתָם בְּאַרְצֹתָם בְּגוֹיֵהֶם
>
> <u>Shem</u> (v. 31): "These are the descendants of Shem, by their families, their languages, their lands, and their nations."
>
> אֵלֶּה בְנֵי־שֵׁם לְמִשְׁפְּחֹתָם לִלְשֹׁנֹתָם בְּאַרְצֹתָם לְגוֹיֵהֶם

Finally, the whole genealogy in Genesis 10 concludes with an all-encompassing summary statement (v. 32) which employs some of the same vocabulary found in the preceding summary statements for each section: "These are the families of Noah's sons, according to their genealogies, in their nations; and from these the nations spread abroad on the earth after the flood" (אֵלֶּה מִשְׁפְּחֹת בְּנֵי־נֹחַ לְתוֹלְדֹתָם בְּגוֹיֵהֶם וּמֵאֵלֶּה נִפְרְדוּ הַגּוֹיִם בָּאָרֶץ אַחַר הַמַּבּוּל).

Table 1 provides an overview of the list as a whole, according to the sequence of the 70 names in Genesis 10.[7] The number 70 emerges, of course, only if we omit from the count the three sons of Noah themselves and Nimrod, whose inclusion in the list seems non-genealogical (cf. Gen. 10:8–12).[8] In any case, the idea of the 70 (or 72) nations is traditional.[9]

The Septuagint version

The list is substantially the same in the Septuagint, except for a few changes, some of them quite significant.[10] First, the Septuagint lists Ελισα as Japheth's fifth son, thus giving him a total of eight sons, instead of seven as in the Hebrew text. Nevertheless, the Septuagint also lists Ελισα as the first son of Javan, just as in the MT. Second, whereas the MT has Shelah as the son of Arpachshad in the genealogy of Shem, the Septuagint has Καιναν as the son of Arpachshad and the father Shelah. The *Book of Jubilees* gives considerable scope to Kainan son of Arpachshad (cf. *Jub.* 8:1–4), and this will be a matter of some importance to us in the next chapter. Third, the name Καιναν appears again at the end of the list of Shem's sons. Fourth, Obal, Joktan's eighth son in the MT, is not present in the list of Shem's sons.

Geography

Genesis 10 includes within the genealogy several pieces of geographical information. The first geographical detail is found, as we have seen, in the summaries at the end of each of the three sections and also at the end of the whole chapter. These summaries reflect a consciousness of "their lands" that will be highly influential in the subsequent tradition. Because the exact boundaries of these ethnic territories are not specified, they invited geographical speculation and allowed revision in the course of time.

The second geographical detail occurs in Gen. 10:18–19, where the actual borders of one specific ethnic territory are mentioned: "Afterward the families of the Canaanites spread abroad. And the territory of the Canaanites extended from Sidon, in the direction of Gerar, as far as Gaza,

Table 1. *The Table of Nations according to the sequence of the "70" names in Genesis 10*

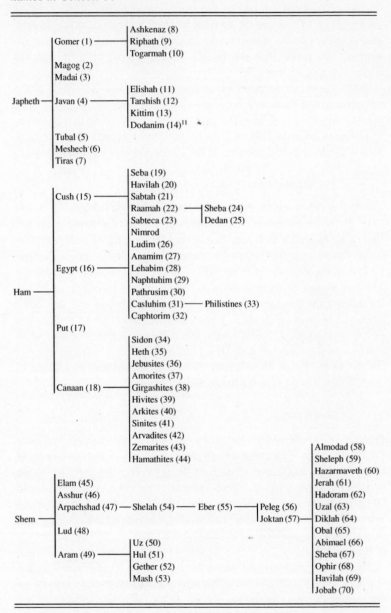

and in the direction of Sodom, Gomorrah, Admah, and Seboiim, as far as Lasha."[12] As we shall see, the legitimacy of the Cannanites' territory was a contentious issue in later Jewish thinking.

The third geographical detail is found in Gen. 10:25, which states that Peleg (פֶּלֶג) was so called "because in his days the earth was divided (נִפְלְגָה)...." The passive voice of the verb (niphal) leaves open how the earth was divided and by whom (God or Noah?). Subsequent tradition will seek to clarify these points, whether by adducing a parallel passage of scripture (cf. Deut. 32:8) or by expanding the Genesis story.

Finally, Gen. 10:30 gives the borders for Joktan and his sons: "The territory in which they lived extended from Mesha in the direction of Sephar, the hill country of the east." As mentioned above, the Table of Nations describes more degrees of Shem's descendants than for any of the other sons of Noah. It is, in fact, Joktan and his sons who make the list of Shem's descendants so exceptional in this regard, and as if that were not enough, their territory is also described. However, this is not the line through which the Israelites will eventually come; that distinction is reserved for Joktan's brother Peleg.

Jubilees' revision of Genesis 10

Introduction to the *Book of Jubilees*

The *Book of Jubilees* is a thorough rewriting[13] of Genesis 1 to approximately Exodus 20 that dates to the mid-second century BCE (ca. 170–150 BCE).[14] As the fifteen or sixteen manuscripts of *Jubilees* found at Qumran (caves 1, 2, 3, 4, and 11) now verify, the *Book of Jubilees* was originally written in Hebrew[15] and was closely connected with the Qumran community.[16] In the course of time, the book was translated from Hebrew into Greek, and from Greek into Latin, Ethiopic, and perhaps also Syriac.[17] Some textual evidence survives from each of these languages, although the only complete text of *Jubilees* now extant is the Ethiopic version, which appeared relatively late in the book's textual transmission. Insofar as a comparison can be made on the basis of the *Jubilees* manuscripts at Qumran, the Ethiopic text has been judged a remarkably reliable translation.[18]

Taken as a whole, *Jubilees* purports to be the account of a divine revelation that was revealed to Moses on Mt. Sinai. According to *Jub.* 1:26–9, an angel of the divine presence read the revelations from heavenly tablets to Moses who in turn wrote them down by dictation.[19] In the process, Moses is told about everything "from the beginning of creation till my sanctuary has been built among them for all eternity" (*Jub.* 1:27). The revelation, which, as we have mentioned, is essentially a rewriting of the first one and a half books of the Torah, is structured by a chronology which divides time into units of forty-nine years (= jubilees), each of which consists of seven "weeks of years."

None of the manuscripts of *Jubilees* found at Qumran contains material from *Jub.* 8:11–9:15;[20] therefore, we are reliant on the Ethiopic version for our investigation, which in turn is a translation of the lost Greek version.[21] We may wonder, of course, whether *Jubilees* 8–9 represents a later insertion into the Greek or Ethiopic texts,[22] but the Genesis Apocryphon (1QapGen. 16–17) contains a very similar description of the distribution of the earth among the sons of Noah.[23] Hence, although it is still debated whether *Jubilees* is dependent on the Genesis Apocryphon or vice versa,[24] or whether both are dependent on a common source,[25] there can be little doubt that the original Hebrew version of *Jubilees* contained chapters 8–9. Moreover, these chapters form an integral part of the argument within its present context in *Jubilees*.[26]

Translation of *Jubilees* 8:11–9:15[27]

1   *The Book of Noah*

(8:11) When he [sc. Noah] summoned his children, they came to him – they and their children. He divided the earth into the lots that his three sons would occupy. They reached out their hand and took the book from the bosom of their father.

2   *The contents of the Book of Noah*

Shem's lot. (12) In the book there emerged as Shem's lot the center of the earth which he would occupy as an inheritance for him and for his children throughout the history of eternity: from the middle of the mountain range of Rafa, from the source of the water from the Tina River. His share goes toward the west through the middle of this river. One then goes until one reaches the water of the deeps from which this river emerges. This river emerges and pours its waters into the Me'at Sea. This river goes as far as the Great Sea. Everything to the north belongs to Japheth, while everything to the south belongs to Shem. (13) It goes until it reaches Karas. This is in the bosom of the branch that faces southward. (14) His share goes toward the Great Sea and goes straight until it reaches to the west of the branch that faces southward, for this is the sea whose name is the Branch of the Egyptian Sea. (15) It turns from there southward toward the mouth of the Great Sea on the shore of the waters. It goes toward the west of Afra and goes until it reaches the water of the Gihon River and to the south of the Gihon's waters along the banks of this river. (16) It goes eastward until it reaches the Garden of Eden, toward the south side of it – on the south side and from the east of the entire land of Eden and of all the east. It turns to the east and comes until it reaches to the east of the mountain range named Rafa. Then it goes down toward the bank of the Tina River's mouth.

(17) This share emerged by lot for Shem and his children to occupy it forever, throughout his generation until eternity. (18) Noah was very happy that this share had emerged for Shem and his children. He recalled everything that he had said in prophecy with his mouth, for he had said: 'May the Lord, the God of Shem, be blessed, and may the Lord live in the places where Shem resides' [Gen. 9:27]. He knew that the Garden of Eden is the holy of holies and is the residence of the Lord; (that) Mt. Sinai is in the middle of the desert; and (that) Mt. Zion is in the middle of the navel of the earth. The three of them – the one facing the other – were created as holy (places). (20) He blessed the God of gods, who had placed the word of the Lord in his mouth, and (he blessed) the Lord forever. (21) He knew that a blessed and excellent share had come about for Shem and his children throughout the history of eternity: all the land of Eden, all the land of the Erythrean Sea, all the land of the east, India, (that which is) in Erythrea and its mountains, all the land of Bashan, all the land of Lebanon, the islands of Caphtor, the entire mountain range of Sanir and Amana, the mountain range of Asshur which is in the north, all the land of Elam, Asshur, Babylon, Susan, and Madai; all the mountains of Ararat, all the area on the other side of the sea which is on the other side of the mountain range of Asshur toward the north – a blessed and spacious land. Everything in it is very beautiful.

Ham's lot. (22) For Ham there emerged a second share toward the other side of the Gihon – toward the south – on the right side of the garden. It goes southward and goes to all the fiery mountains. It goes westward toward the Atel Sea; it goes westward until it reaches the Mauk Sea, everything that descends into which *is* destroyed. (23) It comes to the north to the boundary of Gadir and comes to the shore of the sea waters, to the waters of the Great Sea, until it reaches the Gihon River. The Gihon River goes until it reaches the right side of the Garden of Eden.

(24) This is the land that emerged for Ham as a share that he should occupy for himself and his children forever throughout their generations until eternity.

Japheth's lot. (25) For Japheth there emerged a third share on the other side of the Tina River toward the north of the mouth of its waters. It goes toward the northeast, (toward) the whole area of Gog and all that is east of them. (26) It goes due north and goes toward the mountains of Qelt, to the north and toward the Mauq Sea. It comes to the east of Gadir as far as the edge of the sea waters. (27) It goes until it reaches the west of Fara. Then it goes back toward Aferag and goes eastward toward the water of the Me'at Sea. (28) It goes to the edge of the Tina River toward the northeast until it reaches the bank of its waters toward the mountain range of Rafa. It goes around the north. (29) This is the land that emerged for Japheth and his children as his hereditary share that he would occupy for himself and his children throughout their generations forever; five large islands and a large land in the north. (30) However, it is cold while the land of Ham is hot. Now Shem's land is neither hot nor cold but it is a mixture of cold and heat.

3   *The subdivision of the lots among Noah's grandsons*

Ham's lot. (9:1) Ham divided (his share) among his sons. There emerged a first share for Cush to the east; to the west of him (one) for Egypt; to the west of him (one) for Put; to the west of him (one) for Canaan; and to the west of him was the sea.

Shem's lot. (2) Shem, too, divided (his share) among his sons. There emerged a first share for Elam and his children to the east of the Tigris River until it reaches the east of the entire land of India, in Erythrea on its borders, the waters of the Dedan,

all the mountains of Mebri and Ela, all the land of Susan, and
everything on the border of Farnak as far as the Erythrean Sea
and the Tina River. (3) For Asshur there emerged as the second share the whole land of Asshur, Nineveh, Shinar, and Sak
as far as the vicinity of India, (where) the Wadafa River rises.
(4) For Arpachshad there emerged as a third share all the land
of the Chaldean region to the east of the Euphrates which is
close to the Erythrean Sea; all the waters of the desert as far
as the vicinity of the branch of the Sea which faces Egypt; the
entire land of Lebanon, Sanir, and Amana as far as the vicinity of the Euphrates. (5) There emerged for Aram as the fourth
share the entire land of Mesopotamia between the Tigris and
Euphrates to the north of the Chaldeans as far as the vicinity of
the mountain range of Asshur and the land of Arara. (6) For Lud
there emerged as the fifth share the mountain range of Asshur
and all that belongs to it until it reaches the Great Sea and reaches
to the east of his brother Asshur.

Japheth's lot. (7) Japheth, too, divided the land among his sons
as an inheritance. (8) There emerged for Gomer a first share
eastward from the north side as far as the Tina River. North
of him there emerged (as a share) for Magog all the central
parts of the north until it reaches the Me'at Sea. (9) For Madai
there emerged a share for him to occupy on the west of his two
brothers as far as the islands and the shores of the islands. (10)
For Javan there emerged as the fourth share every island and the
islands that are in the direction of Lud's border. (11) For Tubal
there emerged as the fifth share the middle of the branch which
reaches the border of Lud's share as far as the second branch,
and the other side of the second branch into the third branch.
(12) For Meshech there emerged a sixth share, namely all the
(region on the) other side of the third branch until it reaches to
the east of Gadir. (13) For Tiras there emerged as the seventh
share the four large islands within the sea which reach Ham's
share. The islands of Kamaturi emerged by lot for Arpachshad's
children as his inheritance.

4   *The oath against trespassing*

(14) In this way Noah's sons divided (the earth) for their sons
in front of their father Noah. He made (them) swear by oath to

curse each and every one who wanted to occupy the share that
did not emerge by his lot. (15) All of them said: "So be it!"
So be it for them and their children until eternity during their
generations until the day of judgment on which the Lord God
will punish them with the sword and fire because of all the evil
impurity of their errors by which they have filled the earth with
wickedness, impurity, fornication, and sin.

Overview of *Jubilees* 8–9

Jub. 8:11–9:15 consists of two interrelated parts that are based on Genesis
10 but go well beyond the biblical text.[28] In the first part (*Jub.* 8:11–30),
Noah divides the earth by lot among his three sons – Shem, Ham, and
Japheth. This is the same order as they are at first listed in Gen. 10:1,
that is, the order of their priority (and primogeniture).[29] In the second
part (*Jub.* 9:1–15), Noah's sons, still in the presence of their father, sub-
divide their portions among their own sons, according to the order Ham,
Shem, and Japheth, that is, from south to north. As a result the whole
world is covered twice, first by the three major lines of demarcation and
then by the smaller subdivisions. Whereas the original Table of Nations
in Genesis 10 contains merely a list of Noah's descendants in which
his grandsons appear directly after listing of each son (see Table 1),
Jubilees 8–9 contains separate sections for the sons and the grandsons
and provides explicit geographical boundaries between them. The procedure in *Jubilees* is thus more akin to the famous geographic work of
Dionysius Periegetes of Alexandria, Περιήγησις τῆς οἰκουμένης
("Geographical Description of the Inhabited World"), written during the
reign of Hadrian (117–38 CE), which first outlines the world by continents (Africa/Libya, Europe, Asia [line 9]) and then subdivides the continents by tracing lines according to major geographical landmarks and
noting the nations along the way (lines 170–1165).[30] *Jubilees* 8–9 and
Dionysius' work also have many other points in common.[31] It may be that
Jubilees is adapting the *periegesis* tradition of geographical description,
in which, for example, Hecataeus of Miletus and Strabo of Amaseia are
also located.[32]

The first section of the *Jubilees* account begins in 8:11 by setting the
scene: "When he [sc. Noah] summoned his children, they came to him –
they and their children. He divided the earth into the lots that his three
sons would occupy. They reached out their hands and took the book from
the bosom of their father Noah." This mention of a "book" of Noah is
important, for the whole rest of chapters 8–9 goes on to describe the lots

contained in that book.[33] Thus, beginning with Shem, we read: "In the book there emerged as Shem's lot the center of the earth ..." (*Jub.* 8:12). Unlike the "book" of Noah to which 1QapGen. 5.29 refers,[34] the "book" in *Jub.* 8:11, 12 does not record Noah's autobiography, but rather a title deed drawn up by Noah for distributing land among his sons which is analogous to the distribution of the promised land among the twelve tribes.[35] As often in *Jubilees*, Noah is portrayed here as a Moses-like figure.[36]

From this "book" of Noah, it becomes clear that Shem receives the most favorable portion in the temperate "center of the earth" (8:12–21), with Mt. Zion "in the middle of the navel of the earth" (v. 19); Ham receives the hot southern portion (vv. 22–4); and Japheth receives the cold northern portion (vv. 25–30). This division follows the Greek geographical model of κλίματα or "zones of the world," ranging from torrid to arctic, with the temperate climate in between.[37] According to Strabo (*Geog.* 2.3.1), Posidonius (ca. 135–51 BCE) also represented zones by "ethnic distinctions" (ταῖς ἐθνικαῖς διαφοραῖς): "the Ethiopic zone," "the Scythian-Celtic zone," and "the intermediate zone" (τὴν ἀνὰ μέσον).[38]

Shem's strategic allotment in the temperate center of the earth may have been understood in geopolitical terms. For within a few lines, Vitruvius (early Augustan period) relocates the center of the world from Greece (*De arch.* 6.1.6), where it was earlier set by the Greeks, to Rome (6.1.10), where it serves once again as a justification for rule: "And so by its policy, it curbs the courage of the Northern barbarians, by its strength the imaginative South. Thus the Divine Mind has allotted to the Roman State an excellent and temperate region to rule the world."[39] Strabo (*Geog.* 6.4.1) has a similar conception of Rome: "... being in the middle (ἐν μέσῳ) ... and through its superiority in courage and size ... it is naturally suited to hegemony (πρὸς ἡγεμονίαν εὐφυῶς ἔχει)."[40] Likewise, the *Book of Jubilees* clearly expects the descendants of Shem to rule the world from their privileged position in the center of the earth.[41] Thus, in *Jub.* 22:11–14, Abraham (sic!) blesses Jacob with the words:

> May my son Jacob and all his sons be blessed to the most high Lord throughout all ages. May the Lord give you righteous descendants, and may he sanctify some of your sons *in the midst of all the earth. May the nations serve you, and may all the nations bow down before your descendants.* (12) *Be strong before people and continue to exercise power among all of Seth's descendants.* Then your ways and the ways of your sons will be

> proper so that they may be a holy people. (13) May the most
> high God give you all the blessings with which he blessed me
> and with which he blessed Noah and Adam. May they come to
> rest on the sacred head of your descendants throughout each and
> every generation forever. (14) May he purify you from all filthy
> pollution so that you may be pardoned for all the guilt of your
> sins of ignorance. May he strengthen you and bless you; may
> you *possess the entire earth.*

We find similar expectations of universal sovereignty for Jacob's descendants in *Jub.* 19:21–2 and 32:18–19.[42] The fact that all four holy places in the *Book of Jubilees* (i.e., the Garden of Eden, Mt. Sinai, Mt. Zion, and the Mountain of the East) are located in Shem's territory further underscores the privileged position of Shem's territory.[43] Since the first three of these were created as holy places "facing each other" (*Jub.* 8:19), this creates two medians that intersect at Zion: an east–west median running through the Garden of Eden and the Straits of Gibraltar and a north–south median running through Mt. Zion and Mt. Sinai.[44]

In *Jub.* 8:19, the notion of Jerusalem as the omphalos (navel) of the earth goes back to Ezek. 38:12 (cf. 5:5).[45] Although Philip S. Alexander has recently argued that the earliest clear reference to Jerusalem as omphalos occurs in *Jubilees* 8,[46] it is nevertheless probable that the author of *Jubilees* (or his source) interpreted Ezek. 38:12 in this way.[47] For the Ezekiel text is set within a passage that looks forward to the defeat of hostile, intruding nations and their judgment by fire (Ezek. 38: 1–39:29). As we shall see, this is precisely the emphasis of *Jubilees* 8–10 (cf. *Jub.* 9:15). Alexander argues further that *Jubilees* is a Hasmonean document that is politically motivated: it contrasts Jerusalem to Delphi, makes Greek influence in the East illegitimate, and justifies Hasmonean expansion.[48] Just how grandiose those expansionistic dreams could be during this period becomes apparent when we examine the Qumran War Rule presently. For the moment, it is important to recognize that *Jubilees* regards Jerusalem and the Land as the sacrosanct place of divine favor and the position from which the world will ultimately be brought under subjection.

Jubilees describes the geographical extent of the allotted portions and the natural physical boundaries between them in great detail, following a circular path in each case: the descriptions of the territories of Shem and Japheth make a counterclockwise circuit beginning at the source of the Tina River; and the description of Ham's territory makes a clockwise circuit beginning at a place beyond the Gihon River, to the right (south) of the Garden of Eden.[49] Each description ends with a formula indicating that the portion allotted to that son became a possession to him and his descendants "forever" (vv. 17, 24, 29).

The second section of the *Jubilees* account describes the further sub-division of the earth among the sons of Ham (9:1), Shem (vv. 2–6), and Japheth (vv. 7–13). Again, the natural boundaries of the portions are set out. At the conclusion of the process, Noah compels his sons and grand-sons in vv. 14–15 to "swear by oath to curse each and every one who wanted to occupy the share that did not emerge by his lot. All of them said: 'So be it!' So be it for them and their children until eternity during their generations until the day of judgment on which the Lord God will punish them with the sword and fire because of all the evil of their errors by which they have filled the earth with wickedness, impurity, fornica-tion, and sin."[50] *Jubilees* 8–10 seeks to establish Israel's ancestral right to the promised land,[51] a conception that is probably derived from the Song of Moses. For Deut. 32:8–9 strongly implies that during the original divi-sion of the world among the nations, God established Israel's right to the Land.[52] This oath gives *Jubilees* 8–9 an apocalyptic orientation.[53] Here there seems to be a connection between violation of territorial boundaries and the future divine judgment by sword and fire.[54] In that case, imperia-listic world conquerors such as the Greco-Macedonians (Seleucids)[55] and later the Romans would be particularly subject to the coming judgment.[56] Indeed, *Jub.* 23:30 claims that the time of peace will arrive when foreign enemies are finally expelled.

Nachwirkung of the "Book of Noah" in Jewish texts of the Second-Temple period

It is beyond the scope of the present study to delve too far into the ongoing debate over the possible existence of a "Book of Noah" in antiquity. The difficulty is that although we have several references to a "Book of Noah" in antiquity, most recently in a fragment of the *Genesis Apocryphon*,[57] the book itself has not survived as an independent writing. This has prompted some scholars, including Florentino García Martínez, to attempt to re-construct the supposed book from various pieces, drawn from different sources.[58] Suffice it to say that there are several problems with such an attempt. First, the pseudepigraphic "Book of Noah" may never have exi-sted at all, except as a literary fiction within certain works.[59] Second, it is practically impossible to show that the various pieces from different sources, divergent as they are in language, form, and content, actually fit together coherently based on a common "Book of Noah."[60] Third, the attempt to reconstruct a single "Book of Noah" may be misguided, for there may have been several different writings attributed to Noah in the ancient world that focused on various aspects of the Noah story.[61] For example, in an addition to the *Testament of Levi*, Isaac instructs Levi about the prohibition against eating blood, "for so my father Abraham commanded me; for so he found [it] in the writing of the book of Noah concerning the blood (οὕτως γάρ μοι ἐνετείλατο ὁ πατήρ μου Ἀβραάμ, ὅτι οὕτως εὗρεν ἐν τῇ γραφῇ τῆς βίβλου τοῦ Νῶε περὶ τοῦ αἵματος)."[62] Similarly, there may have been "books of Noah" on other topics.

This possibility deserves further consideration in light of our passage. For when *Jub.* 8:11–12 characterizes the contents of chapters 8–9 as stemming from a "book," this may indicate that the *Vorlage* of *Jubilees* 8–9 circulated independently during the Second Temple.[63] There is evidence that another "book" of Noah mentioned in *Jubilees* (10:1–14) circulated independently of *Jubilees* and eventually found its way into the Jewish magical book, *Sefer ha-Razim*,[64] and the medieval *Book of Asaph the Physician*.[65] Moreover, the recently published material from the *Genesis Apocryphon* (1QapGen. 16–17), which, as we have mentioned, is very similar to *Jubilees* 8–9, shows that this material on the division of the earth among the sons of Noah was being transmitted, modified and adapted.[66] We get the same impression from other Jewish texts from the Second-Temple period.[67] Both the Third Sibyl (§§110–61) and the War Rule (1QM 1–2) retain the aforementioned apocalyptic thrust of the *Jubilees* tradition. The War Rule presupposes an apocalyptically oriented Table of Nations tradition when it describes the plan for the final, eschatological war against all nations in terms of the sons and grandsons of Noah. Josephus (*Ant.* 1.122–47) clearly uses the *Jubilees* tradition for antiquarian purposes,[68] but he modifies the tradition, depriving it of any apocalyptic significance.[69] Looking beyond the Second-Temple period, the medieval text, *Midrash Aggadah*, continues to reflect the *Jubilees* 8–9 tradition. We conclude our survey with the *Asatir*, a Samaritan text of uncertain date.

The Third Sibyl

We begin by comparing *Jubilees* 8–9 and the Third Sibyl, both of which stem from the second century BCE.[70] The Third Sibyl recounts the biblical story of Noah and his three sons in much the same way as *Jubilees* does, albeit with a thick overlay of Greek mythology. The Sibyl, herself a daughter (or daughter-in-law) of Noah (cf. *Sib. Or.*, Prol. 33; 1.288–90;

3.827), explains that after the Flood, the earth was divided by lot (κατὰ κλῆρον), into three territories according to the three sons of Gaia and Ouranos: Kronos, Titan, and Iapetos (*Sib. Or.* 3.110–14).[71] The Iapetos of Hesiod (*Theog.* 18, 134, 507, 746), who is equivalent to the biblical Japheth,[72] facilitates the connection between the Greek myth and the Table of Nations tradition in Genesis 10.[73] Each son reigned over his own territory and was bound by oath not to violate the others' portions (lines 115–16). But after Ouranos died, the sons began to transgress their oaths by stirring up strife against each other "as to who should have royal honor and reign over all men" (110–20). At first, diplomacy was able to bring about an uneasy truce that allowed the eldest son, Kronos, to rule over all on a provisional and temporary basis (121–31). However, when Titan discovered that Kronos had deceived him, a war broke out between the families (147–53), a war which is described as "the beginning of war for mortals" (154–5). The subsequent list of nations shows that the struggle for world empire continued even after all the descendants of Titan and Kronos had died (156–8). As the text states, "But then as time pursued its cyclic course, the kingdom of Egypt arose, then that of the Persians, Medes, and Ethiopians, and Assyrian Babylon, then that of the Macedonians, of Egypt again, then of Rome" (158–61). The point of the Third Sibyl is that the oath imposed by the father was broken, that a struggle for world domination began among the three sons, and that before setting up his own kingdom (implicitly with Israel[74]), God will judge all nations by sword and fire (cf. 2, 492–519, 689–90), including Magog (cf. 319, 512–13, both passages with Gog [Ezek. 38:1]) and Rome. The parallel to *Jubilees* 8–9 is obvious, for there too three sons after the Flood are assigned portions by lot (cf. *Jub.* 8:11), and the territories are held inviolable by an oath imposed by their father, which, if broken, would bring a curse upon the offender and ultimately divine judgment by sword and fire (cf. *Jub.* 9:14–15), alluding to Ezek. 38:22.[75] Apparently, therefore, the "Book of Noah" preserved in *Jubilees* 8–9 also circulated in Alexandria, Egypt, where the Third Sibyl originated and later the Alexandrian World-Chronicles as well.[76]

The War Rule

Another text to which we can compare *Jubilees* 8–9 is the War Rule (1QM). The first two columns detail the sequence of events during the forty-year war of the Sons of Light against all the nations of the world,[77] led by the Kittim, that is, the Hellenistic kingdoms in the early Qumran compositions and later the Romans.[78] This war is proleptically summarized in 1QM 1.1–7, culminating in lines 6–7: "... and the supremacy of the Kittim shall cease, that wickedness be overcome without a remnant. There shall be no survivors of [all Sons of] Darkness." Clearly alluding to Dan. 12:1, the passage goes on to describe this war as the last and greatest tribulation: "It is a time of distress fo[r al]l the people who are redeemed by God. In all their afflictions none exists that is like it, hastening to its completion as an eternal redemption. On the day of their battle against the Kittim, they shall g[o forth for]carnage in battle" (1.11–13). According to Dan. 12:1 (NRSV), "There shall be a time of anguish, such as has never occurred since nations first came into existence. But at that time your people shall be delivered, everyone who is found written in the book."[79] This reference to the beginning of the nations can be compared to 1QM 10.14–15, which, alluding to Genesis 10–11, refers to the "confusion of language (בלה לשון)[80] and the separation of peoples (ומפרד עמים),[81] the dwelling-place of clans (מושב משפחות)[82] (15) and the inheritance of lands (ונחלת ארצות)."[83] After thus alluding to the Table of Nations and the Tower of Babel, cols. 11–12 proceed to list the nations by name that will be defeated in battle.[84] Hence, like Dan. 12:1, the War Rule juxtaposes the *Urzeit* and the *Endzeit*, the beginning of the nations and their cataclysmic end.

The forty-year war against the nations listed in Genesis 10 is to be conducted in two phases interrupted by the requisite sabbatical years.[85] In the first phase, the entire holy congregation is to participate in a six-year war against Israel's neighbors and traditional enemies (Edom, Moab, Ammon, etc.), the Kittim, and the offenders against the covenant. After the conclusion of the first phase and a sabbatical year, selected units from the tribes of Israel are to continue the fight for twenty-nine years, with four intervening sabbatical years (totaling thirty-three years), against the remaining nations. 1QM 2.10–14 outlines the plan of attack during this twenty-nine-year period, listing the nations to be fought according to the order given in Genesis 10:1. Thus, the first nine years of this last major offensive is to be fought against the sons of Shem (1QM 2.10–13);[86] the next ten years of the war is to be fought against "all the sons of Ham according to their clans in their dwelling-places" (2.13–14), where the phrase "according to their clans"(למשפחתם) comes from Gen. 10:20; and the final ten years of the war is to be fought against "all the sons of Japheth in their dwelling-places" (2.14).[87] The War Rule expects that all nations will fall under divine judgment, and that universal sovereignty will pass from the Kittim to Israel. Indeed, 1QM 17.7–8 refers to "the dominion of Israel over all flesh" (cf. also 19.8). Hence, like *Jubilees* 8–9 and the Third Sibyl, the War Rule uses the division of the earth among Noah's sons to express the expectation not only of eschatological divine judgment of the nations by fire and sword but also of universal sovereignty for Israel.

Midrash Aggadah

A final Jewish text that should be considered here goes well beyond the Second-Temple period. Martha Himmelfarb discusses the use of *Jubilees* 8–9 (or perhaps rather the work of an excerptor who incorporates the *Jubilees* material) in *Midrash Aggadah*, a writing drawn from the commentary on the Torah of R. Moses the Preacher of Narbonne, who lived in the eleventh century.[88] On Gen. 12:6 ("The Canaanite was then in the land"), *Midrash Aggadah* Lek-Leka 13.7 comments:[89]

> For the land of Israel had fallen to the portion of Shem, as it says, "Melchizedek, king of Salem" (Gen. 14:18). When the Holy One, blessed be he, divided the world among them, Noah made his three sons swear that none of them would enter the territory of another [cf. *Jub.* 9:14]. But the seven nations passed through the land of Israel and transgressed the oath [cf. *Jub.* 10:32]. Therefore the Holy One, blessed be he, commanded, "You shall utterly destroy them [cf. *Jub.* 9:15]." At the time that Abraham passed through they had not yet entered there except for the Canaanites. Thus the land of the seven nations fell to Israel, for all the lands of the seven nations had fallen to the portion of Shem [cf. *Jub.* 8:12–21; 9:2–6]. Thus it says, "He set up boundaries for the nations according to the number of the children of Israel" (Deut. 32:8).

This commentary cites neither *Jubilees* 8–9 nor the putative "Book of Noah," but it does show influence from this tradition. What makes it different from the later Christian *Diamerismos* tradition (see Chap. 6) is the emphasis here on Melchizedek as evidence that the Land had been allotted to Shem.[90]

Asatir

Written in Aramaic, this Samaritan book of the "Secrets of Moses" is a midrash that contains legendary material on biblical themes, ranging from the time of Adam to the death of Moses, to whom it is ascribed.[91] The formal parallel to *Jubilees* is obvious, although, unlike *Jubilees*, the *Asatir* covers the whole Pentateuch rather than only Genesis and part of Exodus. Moreover, unlike *Jubilees*, the Samaritan text includes an account of how

Adam divided the world among his sons Cain and Abel, which seems to anticipate the later division of the earth by Noah.[92] Most importantly for our purposes, the *Asatir*, like *Jubilees*, contains the story of Noah's division of the world among his three sons after the flood. Although the Samaritan account does not purport to have been recorded in a "Book of Noah,"[93] there are nonetheless many similarities between it and *Jubilees* 8–9:[94]

(13) And after sixty-two years, he [sc. Noah] divided the earth among his sons Shem, Ham and Japheth. (14) And to **Shem** he gave three portions and Japheth four and Ham four; [Shem divided his portion, giving to] Elam, Lud, Aram and Asshur four portions and Arpachshad one portion. (15) And he gave the Book of Signs to Arpachshad, and the Book of Astronomy to Elam and the Book of the Wars to Asshur. And he made them the foremost of all his sons. (17) And **Japhet** divided the four portions, among Gomer, Magog, Maddai, Javan, Tubal, Meshech and Tiras each one portion. (18) And **Ham** divided his land into four portions, Kush one portion and Misraim one portion, Put one portion and Canaan one portion.

(19) And when Noah had finished the division of the land by the astronomical calculation of the day, he found that there were still four thousand three hundred years less seven years to come after the flood, of the six thousand from the beginning of the creation and three hundred and seven since the flood. (20) For from the beginning of the days of creation there shall be 6,000 years. (21) From the day of creation until the day of the visitation of the generations (through the flood) were one thousand three hundred and seven years. (22) And from the day when Noah made the division among his children, until the day of the visitation of the generations were four hundred and ninety-three years. (23) And he divided his kingdom to his three sons in the year three hundred and twenty. (24) And Noah was on the day when he divided [the land] among his sons nine hundred and thirty years old. (25) And he divided the land among his three sons on the tenth day of the month of Elul.

(26) And then he sent proclamations to his sons that each should go to his country. (27) And they took leave of him, and Elam and Asshur went to the north of Ur Kasdim, which is called by them the place of Bab el Abwab (Gate of Gates), (28) and which is

on the border of Elam and Asshur. (29) And Gomer and Magog were from Bab el Abwab and onwards. (30) And Lud and Aram settled in Great Kutah whose name is Charassan the Black, which is called Algezirah in Afrikia (Phrygia). (31) And Arpachshad settled in Ur Kasdim in Brktrs (Bactria?), whose name is Romi. And Nimrod began to rule over all the children of Ham. (32) And he built great Babel and they gathered themselves all together and they went to build it, and Nimrod started to walk as a giant in the land. (33) And Noah was nine hundred and forty-five years old when the report of it reached Noah. (34) But Shem his son was the one whom he had placed on the throne of the kingdom because he was the firstborn. (35) And Shem sent also to Elam, Asshur, Lud, Aram, and Arpachshad, and they came and built Nineveh and Calah, Rehoboth Ir, and Resen, which is the big town.

(36) And the day drew near for Noah to die, so he sent and called Shem, Ham and Japheth, and they came to him to Shalem the Great and built an altar and they brought upon it thank offerings. (37) And he completed his division and gave to Shem six and to Japhet six, and he made Shem greater than Japhet [cf. Gen. 9:27?]. (38) And Noah commanded them the keeping of peace and died.

Several comparisons can be made between this account and *Jubilees* 8–9.[95] First, *Asatir* describes a similar twofold division of the earth: Noah first divides the earth among his three sons (4.13; cf. *Jub.* 8:11–30), and they, in turn, divide it among their own sons (*Asatir* 4.14, 17, 18; cf. *Jub.* 9:1–13). The allotted territories are described in different terms from those in *Jubilees*, but the principle is similar. Second, *Asatir* emphasizes that Noah made the Shemites of "the foremost of all his sons" (4.15), that he placed Shem on the throne of his kingdom because he was the firstborn (34), and that he made Shem greater than Japheth (37). This corresponds, in general, to the primacy that is given to Shem in *Jubilees* 8 (i.e., his privileged position in the temperate middle of the earth, the holy sites located within his territory). Third, *Asatir* records that Noah commanded his descendants to keep the peace (4.38). This recalls the oath that Noah required his sons to take so that they would not violate each other's territories (*Jub.* 9:14). Fourth, *Asatir* contains a strongly eschatological perspective. Like *Jubilees*, which encompasses everything "from the beginning of creation till my sanctuary has been built among them for all eternity" (*Jub.* 1:27), *Asatir* (4.19–20) reckons with 6,000 years of world history from the beginning of the days of creation to the end of time. From this, Noah calculates that there are still "four thousand three hundred years less seven years to come after the flood . . . " (19). As we shall see in Chap. 6, the *Jubilees* tradition of the division of the earth among the sons of Noah apparently fueled an imminent apocalyptic expectation in some early Christian circles. When a date for the end of time is set, apocalyptic speculation increases as the date seems to be approaching.

Interestingly enough, this discovery of the time remaining before the end was made "when Noah had finished the division of the land by the astronomical calculation of the day . . . " (*Asatir* 4.19). Although the precise nature of this astronomical calculation is not spelled out, it should be noted that descriptions of the heavens and the earth have long been associated, for a correspondence between them is widely held in antiquity. *Asatir* may provide evidence for the concept of large-scale mapping of earth based on astronomical observation. Unfortunately, the uncertain date of the text makes it difficult further to locate this conception.

Conclusion

In sum, we have seen that *Jub.* 8:11 refers to *Jubilees* 8–9 as giving the contents of an apocalyptically-oriented "book" purportedly written by Noah. Certain Jewish texts from the Second-Temple period (the Third Sibyl and the War Rule) provide evidence that this "book" was in circulation before the Maccabean crisis, and that it was reused in apocalyptic oracles against the nations, and particularly against the Kittim. If this hypothesis is correct, then we must ask what circumstances would have prompted the writing of such a book, perhaps as early as the third century BCE. We may suppose that the period of imperialistic expansion under Antiochus III (ca. 223–187), when Palestine became a political football between two rival powers in the East, was the occasion of writing.[96] The perceived infringement of the Ptolemies and then Seleucids on the inherited land of Israel may have sparked a strong reaction from a nationalistic author with an apocalyptic bent.[97] We shall see more on this hypothesis in Chap. 6.

Before delving into the further history of this material, a word of caution must be sounded. At this stage in the research, we are unable to trace precisely the highly ramified tradition to which the "Book of Noah" and the *Book of Jubilees* gave rise in Jewish and Christian circles during the following millennium. There are at least two complicating factors.

First, the ancient Near East contains other traditions about the descendants of Noah. Josephus writes, for instance, in *Ap.* 1.130–1: "This Berossus [fl. 290 BCE], following the most ancient records, has, like

Moses, described the flood and the destruction of humanity thereby, and told of the ark in which Noah, the founder of our race, was saved when it landed on the heights of the mountains of Armenia. *Then he enumerates Noah's descendants*, appending dates, and so comes down to Nabopalassar, king of Babylon and Chaldea."[98] Such extrabiblical traditions may influence various strands of the Jewish tradition based on Genesis 10.

Second, the very fact that the "Book of Noah" may have circulated independently, as well as part of the *Book of Jubilees* (8–9), significantly complicates the tradition history. How shall we ever be certain that we are looking at traces of one or the other in the subsequent literary tradition? Perhaps the best that we can do at present is to assume the influence of *Jubilees* unless there is an explicit reference to the "Book of Noah" or other factors that point toward an independent tradition. Of course, when we speak of the "influence" of the "Book of Noah" or of *Jubilees* on subsequent literary works, this leaves open the question as to the exact literary relationship between them. By it one could mean at least two forms of connection – direct and indirect. In the former, the overlap in content between the two works is the result of one author deriving material directly from the other composition. In the latter case, the overlap between the works is due to the younger work standing more loosely in the *Jubilees*/"Book of Noah" tradition. It is often difficult or impossible to decide between these alternatives, especially if an author takes liberties with his received text or tradition. Moreover, we should note that both the "Book of Noah" and the *Book of Jubilees* probably underwent significant changes as they were repeatedly appropriated, translated, and epitomized in the long history of their transmission in several different languages and literatures. We should perhaps think of various forms of the *Jubilees* 8–9 tradition circulating among different Jewish and Christian communities. Given the many uncertainties of the situation, we must settle in the following chapters for limited objectives and interim results, hoping that in the future, more thoroughgoing philological work along the lines suggested by Robert A. Kraft will help further to clarify the picture.[99]

3

LUKE-ACTS

Introduction

Having investigated the Jewish tradition steming from the Table of Nations in Genesis 10, especially that reflected in *Jubilees* 8–9, we are now in a position to consider the Christian reception of that tradition. There is, of course, no firm dividing line between "Jewish" and "Christian" in the first century, and what eventually came to be known as "Christianity" developed originally within a Jewish matrix. Hence, we turn now to the NT with the expectation of an essential continuity of tradition, without assuming complete correspondence at every point. Since the *Jubilees* 8–9 tradition was obviously in circulation during the Second-Temple period, we shall not be surprised if it influenced the NT as well. This is at least a possibility that can be tested. The two-volume work of Luke-Acts[1] provides an excellent test case because of its strongly geographic and ethnic orientation – the two foci of the *Jubilees* tradition.[2] In the following, we shall examine in turn both Luke's Gospel and the Book of Acts, being careful in the process also to note some of their overarching themes.

The Gospel of Luke

Jesus' Genealogy and the Table of Nations (Luke 3:23–38)

Our investigation of the possible reception of Genesis 10 tradition in Luke begins with the genealogy of Jesus (Lk. 3:23–38). There has been much discussion about the possible source(s) of the Lukan genealogy. Some scholars have traced it back to the Septuagint version of either Genesis 5 and 11, or 1 Chronicles 1ff. On the one hand, Gert J. Steyn, for example, has made a case that the last part of the Lukan genealogy (3:34–8) is dependent on Greek Gen. 11:10–32 and Gen. 5:1–32.[3] His clinching argument is the occurrence of the name Καινάμ son of Arpachshad in ways, the probability amplitude, this 'a' number, is the sum of the 'a's for each of the various alternatives. If an experiment is performed which is capable of determining which alternative is taken, the probability of the event is changed; it is then the sum of the probabilities for each alternative. That is, you lose the interference.

The question now is, how does it really work? What machinery is actually producing this thing? Nobody knows any machinery. Nobody can give you a deeper explanation of this phenomenon than I have given; that is, a description of it. They can give you a wider explanation, in the sense that they can do more examples to show how it is impossible to tell which hole the electron goes through and not at the same time destroy the interference pattern. They can give a wider class of experiments than just the two slit interference experiment. But that is just repeating the same thing to drive it in. It is not any deeper; it is only wider. The mathematics can be made more precise; you can mention that they are complex numbers instead of real numbers, and a couple of other minor points which have nothing to do with the main idea. But the deep mystery is what I have described, and no one can go any deeper today.

What we have calculated so far is the probability of arrival of an electron. The question is whether there is any way to determine where an individual electron really arrives? Of course we are not averse to using the theory of probability, that is calculating odds, when a situation is very complicated. We throw up a dice into the air, and with the various resistances, and atoms, and all the complicated business, we are perfectly willing to allow that we do not know enough details to make a definite prediction; so we calculate the odds that the thing will come this way or that way. But here what we are proposing, is it not, is that there is probability all the way back: that in the fundamental laws of physics there are odds.

Suppose that I have an experiment so set up that with the light out I get the interference situation. Then I say that even with the light on I cannot predict through which hole

145

an electron will go. I only know that each time I look it will be one hole or the other; there is no way to predict ahead of time which hole it will be. The future, in other words, is unpredictable. It is impossible to predict in any way, from any information ahead of time, through which hole the thing will go, or which hole it will be seen behind. That means that physics has, in a way, given up, if the original purpose was – and everybody thought it was – to know enough so that given the circumstances we can predict what will happen next. Here are the circumstances: electron source, strong light source, tungsten plate with two holes: tell me, behind which hole shall I see the electron? One theory is that the reason you cannot tell through which hole you are going to see the electron is that it is determined by some very complicated things back at the source: it has internal wheels, internal gears, and so forth, to determine which hole it goes through; it is fifty-fifty probability, be-cause, like a die, it is set at random; physics is incomplete, and if we get a complete enough physics then we shall be able to predict through which hole it goes. That is called the hidden variable theory. That theory cannot be true; it is not due to lack of detailed knowledge that we cannot make a prediction.

I said that if I did not turn on the light I should get the interference pattern. If I have a circumstance in which I get that interference pattern, then it is impossible to analyse it in terms of saying it goes through hole 1 or hole 2, because that interference curve is so simple, mathematically a com-pletely different thing from the contribution of the two other curves as probabilities. If it had been possible for us to determine through which hole the electron was going to go if we had the light on, then whether we have the light on or off is nothing to do with it. Whatever gears there are at the source, which we observed, and which permitted us to tell whether the thing was going to go through 1 or 2, we could have observed with the light off, and therefore we could have told with the light off through which hole each electron was going to go. But if we could do this, the resulting curve would have to be represented as the sum of those that go through hole 1 and those that go through hole 2, and it is not. It must then be impossible to have any information ahead of time about which hole the electron is going to go through, whether the light is on or off, in any circumstance when the experiment is set up so that it can produce the interference with the light off. It is not our ignorance of the internal gears, of the internal complications, that makes nature appear to have probability in it. It seems to be somehow intrinsic. Someone has said it this way – 'Nature herself does not even know which way the electron is going to go'.

A philosopher once said 'It is necessary for the very existence of science that the same conditions always produce the same results'. Well, they do not. You set up the circumstances, with the same conditions every time, and you cannot predict behind which hole you will see the electron. Yet science goes on in spite of it – although the same conditions do not always produce the same results. That makes us unhappy, that we cannot predict exactly what will happen. Incidentally, you could think up a circumstance in which it is very dangerous and serious, and man *must* know, and still you cannot predict. For instance we could cook up – we'd better not, but we could – a scheme by which we set up a photo cell, and one electron to go through, and if we see it behind hole No. 1 we set off the atomic bomb and start World War III, whereas if we see it behind hole No. 2 we make peace feelers and delay the war a little longer. Then the future of man would be dependent on something which no amount of science can predict. The future is unpredictable.

What is necessary 'for the very existence of science', and what the characteristics of nature are, are not to be determined by pompous preconditions, they are determined always by the material with which we work, by nature herself. We look, and we see what we find, and we cannot say ahead of time successfully what it is going to look like. The most reasonable possibilities often turn out not to be

147

the situation. If science is to progress, what we need is the ability to experiment, honesty in reporting results – the results must be reported without somebody saying what they would like the results to have been – and finally – an important thing – the intelligence to interpret the results. An important point about this intelligence is that it should not be sure ahead of time what must be. It can be prejudiced, and say 'That is very unlikely; I don't like that'. Prejudice is different from absolute certainty. I do not mean absolute prejudice – just bias. As long as you are only biased it does not make any difference, because if your bias is wrong a perpetual accumulation of experiments will perpetually annoy you until they cannot be disregarded any longer. They can only be disregarded if you are absolutely sure ahead of time of some precondition that science has to have. In fact it is necessary for the very existence of science that minds exist which do not allow that nature must satisfy some preconceived conditions, like those of our philosopher.

7

Seeking New Laws

What I want to talk about in this lecture is not, strictly speaking, the character of physical law. One might imagine at least that one is talking about nature when one is talking about the character of physical law; but I do not want to talk about nature, but rather about how we stand relative to nature now. I want to tell you what we think we know, what there is to guess, and how one goes about guessing. Someone suggested that it would be ideal if, as I went along, I would slowly explain how to guess a law, and then end by creating a new law for you. I do not know whether I shall be able to do that.

First I want to tell you what the present situation is, what it is that we know about physics. You may think that I have told you everything already, because in the lectures I have told you all the great principles that are known. But the principles must be principles about *something*; the principle of the conservation of energy relates to the energy of *something*, and the quantum mechanical laws are quantum mechanical laws about *something* – and all these principles added together still do not tell us what the content is of the nature that we are talking about. I will tell you a little, then, about the stuff on which all of these principles are supposed to have been working.

First of all there is matter – and, remarkably enough, all matter is the same. The matter of which the stars are made is known to be the same as the matter on the earth. The character of the light that is emitted by those stars gives a kind of fingerprint by which we can tell that there are the same kinds of atoms there as on the earth. The same kinds of atoms appear to be in living creatures as in non-living creatures; frogs are made of the same 'goup' as rocks, only in different arrangements. So that makes our problem simpler; we have nothing but atoms, all the same, everywhere.

The atoms all seem to be made from the same general constitution. They have a nucleus, and around the nucleus there are electrons. We can make a list of the parts of the world that we think we know about (fig. 32).

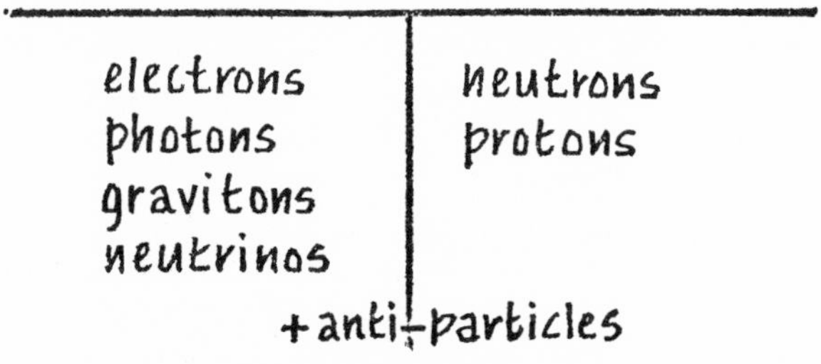

electrons	neutrons
photons	protons
gravitons	
neutrinos	

+ anti-particles

Figure 32

First there are the electrons, which are the particles on the outside of the atom. Then there are the nuclei; but those are understood today as being themselves made up of two other things which are called neutrons and protons – two particles. We have to see the stars, and see the atoms, and they emit light, and the light itself is described by particles which are called photons. In the beginning we spoke about gravitation; and if the quantum theory is right, then the gravitation should have some kind of waves which behave like particles too, and these are called gravitons. If you do not believe in that, just call it gravity. Finally, I did mention what is called beta-decay, in which a neutron can disintegrate into a proton, an electron and a neutrino – or really an anti-neutrino; there is another particle, a neutrino. In addition to all the particles I have listed there are of course all the anti-particles; that is just a quick statement that takes care of doubling the number of particles, but there is no complication.

150

Seeking New Laws

With these particles that I have listed, all of the low energy phenomena, in fact all ordinary phenomena that happen everywhere in the Universe, so far as we know, can be explained. There are exceptions, when here and there some very high energy particle does something, and in the laboratory we have been able to do some peculiar things. But if we leave out these special cases, all ordinary phenomena can be explained by the actions and the motions of particles. For example, life itself is supposedly understandable in principle from the movements of atoms, and those atoms are made out of neutrons, protons and electrons. I must immediately say that when we state that we understand it in principle, we only mean that we think that, if we could figure everything out, we would find that there is nothing new in physics which needs to be discovered in order to understand the phenomena of life. Another instance, the fact that the stars emit energy, solar energy or stellar energy, is presumably also understood in terms of nuclear reactions among these particles. All kinds of details of the way atoms behave are accurately described with this kind of model, at least as far as we know at present. In fact, I can say that in the range of phenomena today, so far as I know there are no phenomena that we are sure cannot be explained this way, or even that there is deep mystery about.

This was not always possible. There is, for instance, a phenomenon called super-conductivity, which means that metals conduct electricity without resistance at low temperatures. It was not at first obvious that this was a consequence of the known laws. Now that it has been thought through carefully enough, it is seen in fact to be fully explainable in terms of our present knowledge. There are other phenomena, such as extra-sensory perception, which cannot be explained by our knowledge of physics. However, that phenomenon has not been well established, and we cannot guarantee that it is there. If it could be demonstrated, of course, that would prove that physics is incomplete, and it is therefore extremely interesting to physicists whether it is right or wrong. Many experiments exist

151

which show that it does not work. The same goes for astrological influences. If it were true that the stars could affect the day that it was good to go to the dentist – in America we have that kind of astrology – then physics theory would be proved wrong, because there is no mechanism understandable in principle from the behaviour of particles which would make this work. That is the reason that there is some scepticism among scientists with regard to those ideas.

On the other hand, in the case of hypnotism, at first it looked as though that also would be impossible, when it was described incompletely. Now that it is known better it is realized that it is not absolutely impossible that hypnosis could occur through normal physiological, though as yet unknown, processes; it does not obviously require some special new kind of force.

Today, although our theory of what goes on outside the nucleus of the atom seems precise and complete enough, in the sense that given enough time we can calculate anything as accurately as it can be measured, it turns out that the forces between neutrons and protons, which constitute the nucleus, are not so completely known, and are not understood at all well. What I mean is that we do not today understand the forces between neutrons and protons to the extent that if you wanted me to, and gave me enough time and computers, I could calculate exactly the energy levels of carbons, or something like that. We do not know enough. Although we can do the corresponding thing for the energy levels of the outside electrons of the atom, we cannot for the nucleus, since the nuclear forces are still not understood very well.

In order to find out more about this, experimenters have gone on to study phenomena at very high energy. They hit neutrons and protons together at very high energy to produce peculiar things, and by studying these peculiar things we hope to understand better the forces between neutrons and protons. Pandora's box has been opened by these experiments! Although all we really wanted was to get a better idea of the forces between neutrons and protons, when we hit these things together hard we discovered that there are more particles in the world. In fact more than four dozen other particles have been dredged up in an attempt to understand these forces; we will put these four dozen others into the neutron/proton column (fig. 33), because they inter-

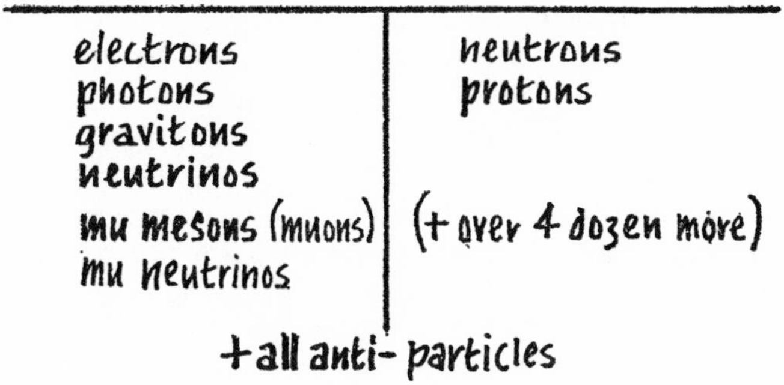

electrons   neutrons
photons   protons
gravitons
neutrinos
mu mesons (muons)   (+ over 4 dozen more)
mu neutrinos

+ all anti-particles

Figure 33

act with neutrons and protons, and have something to do with the forces between them. In addition to that, while the dredge was digging up all this mud it picked up a couple of pieces that are irrelevant to the problem of nuclear forces. One of them is called a mu meson, or muon, and the other is a neutrino which goes with it. There are two kinds of neutrino, one which goes with the electron and one which goes with the mu meson. Incidentally, most amazingly, all the laws of the muon and its neutrino are now known, as far as we can tell experimentally, and the law is that they behave in precisely the same way as the electron and its neutrino, except that the mass of the mu meson is 207 times heavier than the electron; but that is the only difference known between those objects, which is rather curious. Four dozen other particles is a frightening array – plus the anti-particles. They have various names, mesons, pions, kaons, lambda, sigma . . . it does not make any difference . . . with four dozen particles there are going to be a lot of names!

153

But it turns out that these particles come in families, which helps us a little. Actually some of these so-called particles last such a short time that there are debates about whether it is in fact possible to define their very existence, but I will not enter into that debate.

In order to illustrate the family idea, I will take the cases of a neutron and a proton. The neutron and the proton have the same mass, within a tenth of a per cent or so. One is 1,836, the other 1,839 times as heavy as an electron. More remarkable is the fact that for the nuclear forces, the strong forces inside the nucleus, the force between two protons is the same as between a proton and a neutron, and is the same again between a neutron and a neutron. In other words, from the strong nuclear forces you cannot tell a proton from a neutron. So it is a symmetry law; neutrons may be substituted for protons without changing anything – provided you are only talking about the strong forces. But if you change a neutron for a proton you have a terrific difference, because the proton carries an electrical charge and the neutron does not. By electrical measurement you can immediately see the difference between a proton and a neutron, so this symmetry, that you can replace one by the other, is what we call an approximate symmetry. It is right for the strong interactions of nuclear forces, but it is not right in any deep sense of nature, because it does not work for electricity. This is called a partial symmetry, and we have to struggle with these partial symmetries.

Now that the families have been extended, it turns out that substitutions of the type of neutron for proton can be extended over a wider range of particles. But the accuracy is still lower. The statement that neutrons can always be substituted for protons is only approximate – it is not true for electricity – but the wider substitutions which have been found possible give a still poorer symmetry. However, these partial symmetries have helped to gather the particles into families and thus to locate places where particles are missing and to help to discover new ones.

This kind of game, of roughly guessing at family relationships and so on, is illustrative of the kind of preliminary sparring which one does with nature before really discovering some deep and fundamental law. Examples are very important in the previous history of science. For instance, Mendeleev's* discovery of the periodic table of the elements is analogous to this game. It is the first step; but the complete description of the reason for the atomic table came much later, with atomic theory. In the same way, organization of the knowledge of nuclear levels was made by Maria Mayer and Jensen† in what they called the shell model of nuclei some years ago. Physics is in an analogous game, in which a reduction of the complexity is made by some approximate guesses.

In addition to these particles we have all the principles that we were talking about before, the principles of symmetry, of relativity, and that things must behave quantum mechanically; and, combining that with relativity, that all conservation laws must be local.

If we put all these principles together, we discover that there are too many. They are inconsistent with each other. It seems that if we take quantum mechanics, plus relativity, plus the proposition that everything has to be local, plus a number of tacit assumptions, we get inconsistency, because we get infinity for various things when we calculate them, and if we get infinity how can we ever say that this agrees with nature? An example of these tacit assumptions which I mentioned, about which we are too prejudiced to understand the real significance, is such a proposition as the following. If you calculate the chance for every possibility – say it is 50% probability this will happen, 25% that will happen, etc., it should add up to 1. We think that if you

*Dimitri Ivanovitch Mendeleev, 1834–1907, Russian chemist.

†Maria Mayer, American physicist, Nobel Prize 1963, Professor of Physics at University of California since 1960. Hans Daniel Jensen, German physicist, Nobel Prize, 1963. Director of Institute for Theoretical Physics at Heidelberg since 1949.

add all the alternatives you should get 100% probability. That seems reasonable, but reasonable things are where the trouble always is. Another such proposition is that the energy of something must always be positive – it cannot be negative. Another proposition which is probably added in before we get inconsistency is what is called causality, which is something like the idea that effects cannot precede their causes. Actually no one has made a model in which you disregard the proposition about the probability, or you disregard the causality, which is also consistent with quantum mechanics, relativity, locality and so on. So we really do not know exactly what it is that we are assuming that gives us the difficulty producing infinities. A nice problem! However, it turns out that it is possible to sweep the infinities under the rug, by a certain crude skill, and temporarily we are able to keep on calculating.

O.K., that is the present situation. Now I am going to discuss how we would look for a new law.

In general we look for a new law by the following process. First we guess it. Then we compute the consequences of the guess to see what would be implied if this law that we guessed is right. Then we compare the result of the computation to nature, with experiment or experience, compare it directly with observation, to see if it works. If it disagrees with experiment it is wrong. In that simple statement is the key to science. It does not make any difference how beautiful your guess is. It does not make any difference how smart you are, who made the guess, or what his name is – if it disagrees with experiment it is wrong. That is all there is to it. It is true that one has to check a little to make sure that it is wrong, because whoever did the experiment may have reported incorrectly, or there may have been some feature in the experiment that was not noticed, some dirt or something; or the man who computed the consequences, even though it may have been the one who made the guesses, could have made some mistake in the analysis. These are obvious remarks, so when I say if it disagrees with experiment it is wrong, I mean after the experiment has been checked, the calculations have been checked, and the thing has been rubbed back and forth a few times to make sure that the consequences are logical consequences from the guess, and that in fact it disagrees with a very carefully checked experiment.

This will give you a somewhat wrong impression of science. It suggests that we keep on guessing possibilities and comparing them with experiment, and this is to put experiment into a rather weak position. In fact experimenters have a certain individual character. They like to do experiments even if nobody has guessed yet, and they very often do their experiments in a region in which people know the theorist has not made any guesses. For instance, we may know a great many laws, but do not know whether they really work at high energy, because it is just a good guess that they work at high energy. Experimenters have tried experiments at higher energy, and in fact every once in a while experiment produces trouble; that is, it produces a discovery that one of the things we thought right is wrong. In this way experiment can produce unexpected results, and that starts us guessing again. One instance of an unexpected result is the mu meson and its neutrino, which was not guessed by anybody at all before it was discovered, and even today nobody yet has any method of guessing by which this would be a natural result.

You can see, of course, that with this method we can attempt to disprove any definite theory. If we have a definite theory, a real guess, from which we can conveniently compute consequences which can be compared with experiment, then in principle we can get rid of any theory. There is always the possibility of proving any definite theory wrong; but notice that we can never prove it right. Suppose that you invent a good guess, calculate the consequences, and discover every time that the consequences you have calculated agree with experiment. The theory is then right? No, it is simply not proved wrong. In the future you could compute a wider range of consequences, there could be a wider range of experiments, and you might then discover that the thing is wrong. That is why laws like Newton's laws for the motion of planets last such a long time. He guessed the law of gravitation, calculated all kinds of consequences for the system and so on, compared them with experiment – and it took several hundred years before the slight error of the motion of Mercury was observed. During all that time the theory had not been proved wrong, and could be taken temporarily to be right. But it could never be proved right, because tomorrow's experiment might succeed in proving wrong what you thought was right. We never are definitely right, we can only be sure we are wrong. However, it is rather remarkable how we can have some ideas which will last so long.

One of the ways of stopping science would be only to do experiments in the region where you know the law. But experimenters search most diligently, and with the greatest effort, in exactly those places where it seems most likely that we can prove our theories wrong. In other words we are trying to prove ourselves wrong as quickly as possible, be-cause only in that way can we find progress. For example, today among ordinary low energy phenomena we do not know where to look for trouble, we think everything is all right, and so there is no particular big programme looking for trouble in nuclear reactions, or in super-conductivity. In these lectures I am concentrating on discovering funda-mental laws. The whole range of physics, which is interest-ing, includes also an understanding at another level of these phenomena like super-conductivity and nuclear reactions, in terms of the fundamental laws. But I am talking now about discovering trouble, something wrong with the fundamental laws, and since among low energy phenomena nobody knows where to look, all the experiments today in this field of finding out a new law, are of high energy.

Another thing I must point out is that you cannot prove a vague theory wrong. If the guess that you make is poorly expressed and rather vague, and the method that you use for figuring out the consequences is a little vague – you are not sure, and you say, 'I think everything's right because it's

all due to so and so, and such and such do this and that more
or less, and I can sort of explain how this works . . .', then
you see that this theory is good, because it cannot be
proved wrong! Also if the process of computing the consequences is indefinite, then with a little skill any experimental results can be made to look like the expected
consequences. You are probably familiar with that in other
fields. 'A' hates his mother. The reason is, of course, because
she did not caress him or love him enough when he was a
child. But if you investigate you find out that as a matter of
fact she did love him very much, and everything was all
right. Well then, it was because she was over-indulgent when
he was a child! By having a vague theory it is possible to
get either result. The cure for this one is the following. If it
were possible to state exactly, ahead of time, how much love
is not enough, and how much love is over-indulgent, then
there would be a perfectly legitimate theory against which
you could make tests. It is usually said when this is pointed
out, 'When you are dealing with psychological matters
things can't be defined so precisely'. Yes, but then you
cannot claim to know anything about it.

You will be horrified to hear that we have examples in
physics of exactly the same kind. We have these approximate
symmetries, which work something like this. You have an
approximate symmetry, so you calculate a set of consequences supposing it to be perfect. When compared with
experiment, it does not agree. Of course – the symmetry
you are supposed to expect is approximate, so if the agreement is pretty good you say, 'Nice!', while if the agreement
is very poor you say, 'Well, this particular thing must be
especially sensitive to the failure of the symmetry'. Now you
may laugh, but we have to make progress in that way. When
a subject is first new, and these particles are new to us, this
jockeying around, this 'feeling' way of guessing at the
results, is the beginning of any science. The same thing is
true of the symmetry proposition in physics as is true of
psychology, so do not laugh too hard. It is necessary in the
beginning to be very careful. It is easy to fall into the deep

end by this kind of vague theory. It is hard to prove it wrong, and it takes a certain skill and experience not to walk off the plank in the game.

In this process of guessing, computing consequences, and comparing with experiment, we can get stuck at various stages. We may get stuck in the guessing stage, when we have no ideas. Or we may get stuck in the computing stage. For example, Yukawa* guessed an idea for the nuclear forces in 1934, but nobody could compute the consequences because the mathematics was too difficult, and so they could not compare his idea with experiment. The theories remained for a long time, until we discovered all these extra particles which were not contemplated by Yukawa, and therefore it is undoubtedly not as simple as the way Yukawa did it. Another place where you can get stuck is at the experimental end. For example, the quantum theory of gravitation is going very slowly, if at all, because all the experiments that you can do never involve quantum mechanics and gravitation at the same time. The gravity force is too weak compared with the electrical force.

Because I am a theoretical physicist, and more delighted with this end of the problem, I want now to concentrate on how you make the guesses.

As I said before, it is not of any importance where the guess comes from; it is only important that it should agree with experiment, and that it should be as definite as possible. 'Then', you say, 'that is very simple. You set up a machine, a great computing machine, which has a random wheel in it that makes a succession of guesses, and each time it guesses a hypothesis about how nature should work it computes immediately the consequences, and makes a comparison with a list of experimental results it has at the other end'. In other words, guessing is a dumb man's job. Actually it is quite the opposite, and I will try to explain why.

The first problem is how to start. You say, 'Well I'd start off with all the known principles'. But all the principles

*Hideki Yukawa, Japanese physicist. Director of Research Institute for Fundamental Physics at Kyoto. Nobel Prize 1949.

that are known are inconsistent with each other, so something has to be removed. We get a lot of letters from people insisting that we ought to makes holes in our guesses. You see, you make a hole, to make room for a new guess. Somebody says, 'You know, you people always say that space is continuous. How do you know when you get to a small enough dimension that there really are enough points in between, that it isn't just a lot of dots separated by little distances?' Or they say, 'You know those quantum mechanical amplitudes you told me about, they're so complicated and absurd, what makes you think those are right? Maybe they aren't right'. Such remarks are obvious and are perfectly clear to anybody who is working on this problem. It does not do any good to point this out. The problem is not only what might be wrong but what, precisely, might be substituted in place of it. In the case of the continuous space, suppose the precise proposition is that space really consists of a series of dots, and that the space between them does not mean anything, and that the dots are in a cubic array. Then we can prove immediately that this is wrong. It does not work. The problem is not just to say something might be wrong, but to replace it by something – and that is not so easy. As soon as any really definite idea is substituted it becomes almost immediately apparent that it does not work.

The second difficulty is that there is an infinite number of possibilities of these simple types. It is something like this. You are sitting working very hard, you have worked for a long time trying to open a safe. Then some Joe comes along who knows nothing about what you are doing, except that you are trying to open the safe. He says 'Why don't you try the combination 10:20:30?' Because you are busy, you have tried a lot of things, maybe you have already tried 10:20:30. Maybe you know already that the middle number is 32 not 20. Maybe you know as a matter of fact that it is a five digit combination. . . . So please do not send me any letters trying to tell me how the thing is going to work. I read them – I always read them to make sure that I have not already thought of what is suggested – but it takes too long to answer them, because they are usually in the class 'try 10:20:30'. As usual, nature's imagination far surpasses our own, as we have seen from the other theories which are subtle and deep. To get such a subtle and deep guess is not so easy. One must be really clever to guess, and it is not possible to do it blindly by machine.

I want to discuss now the art of guessing nature's laws. It is an art. How is it done? One way you might suggest is to look at history to see how the other guys did it. So we look at history.

We must start with Newton. He had a situation where he had incomplete knowledge, and he was able to guess the laws by putting together ideas which were all relatively close to experiment; there was not a great distance between the observations and the tests. That was the first way, but today it does not work so well.

The next guy who did something great was Maxwell, who obtained the laws of electricity and magnetism. What he did was this. He put together all the laws of electricity, due to Faraday and other people who came before him, and he looked at them and realized that they were mathematically inconsistent. In order to straighten it out he had to add one term to an equation. He did this by inventing for himself a model of idler wheels and gears and so on in space. He found what the new law was – but nobody paid much attention because they did not believe in the idler wheels. We do not believe in the idler wheels today, but the equations that he obtained were correct. So the logic may be wrong but the answer right.

In the case of relativity the discovery was completely different. There was an accumulation of paradoxes; the known laws gave inconsistent results. This was a new kind of thinking, a thinking in terms of discussing the possible symmetries of laws. It was especially difficult, because for the first time it was realized how long something like Newton's laws could seem right, and still ultimately be wrong. Also it was difficult to accept that ordinary ideas of time and space, which seemed so instinctive, could be wrong.

Seeking New Laws

Quantum mechanics was discovered in two independent ways – which is a lesson. There again, and even more so, an enormous number of paradoxes were discovered experimentally, things that absolutely could not be explained in any way by what was known. It was not that the knowledge was incomplete, but that the knowledge was too complete. Your prediction was that this should happen – it did not. The two different routes were one by Schrödinger,* who guessed the equation, the other by Heisenberg, who argued that you must analyse what is measurable. These two different philosophical methods led to the same discovery in the end.

More recently, the discovery of the laws of the weak decay I spoke of, when a neutron disintegrates into a proton, an electron and an anti-neutrino – which are still only partly known – add up to a somewhat different situation. This time it was a case of incomplete knowledge, and only the equation was guessed. The special difficulty this time was that the experiments were all wrong. How can you guess the right answer if, when you calculate the result, it disagrees with experiment? You need courage to say the experiments must be wrong. I will explain where that courage comes from later.

Today we have no paradoxes – maybe. We have this infinity that comes in when we put all the laws together, but the people sweeping the dirt under the rug are so clever that one sometimes thinks this is not a serious paradox. Again, the fact that we have found all these particles does not tell us anything except that our knowledge is incomplete. I am sure that history does not repeat itself in physics, as you can tell from looking at the examples I have given. The reason is this. Any schemes – such as 'think of symmetry laws', or 'put the information in mathematical form', or 'guess equations' – are known to everybody now, and they are all tried all the time. When you are stuck, the answer cannot be one of these, because you will have tried these right away.

*Erwin Schrödinger, Austrian theoretical physicist. Won Nobel Prize for Physics 1933 with Paul Dirac.

163

There must be another way next time. Each time we get into this log-jam of too much trouble, too many problems, it is because the methods that we are using are just like the ones we have used before. The next scheme, the new discovery, is going to be made in a completely different way. So history does not help us much.

I should like to say a little about Heisenberg's idea that you should not talk about what you cannot measure, because many people talk about this idea without really understanding it. You can interpret this in the sense that the constructs or inventions that you make must be of such a kind that the consequences that you compute are comparable with experiment – that is, that you do not compute a consequence like 'a moo must be three goos', when nobody knows what a moo or a goo is. Obviously that is no good. But if the consequences can be compared to experiment, then that is all that is necessary. It does not matter that moos and goos cannot appear in the guess. You can have as much junk in the guess as you like, provided that the consequences can be compared with experiment. This is not always fully appreciated. People often complain of the unwarranted extension of the ideas of particles and paths, etc., into the atomic realm. Not so at all; there is nothing unwarranted about the extension. We must, and we should, and we always do, extend as far as we can beyond what we already know, beyond those ideas that we have already obtained. Dangerous? Yes. Uncertain? Yes. But it is the only way to make progress. Although it is uncertain, it is necessary to make science useful. Science is only useful if it tells you about some experiment that has not been done; it is no good if it only tells you what just went on. It is necessary to extend the ideas beyond where they have been tested. For example, in the law of gravitation, which was developed to understand the motion of planets, it would have been no use if Newton had simply said, 'I now understand the planets', and had not felt able to try to compare it with the earth's pull on the moon, and for later men to say 'Maybe what holds the galaxies together is gravitation'. We must try that. You could say, 'When you get to the size of the galaxies, since you know nothing about it, anything can happen'. I know, but there is no science in accepting this type of limitation. There is no ultimate understanding of the galaxies. On the other hand, if you assume that the entire behaviour is due only to known laws, this assumption is very limited and definite and easily broken by experiment. What we are looking for is just such hypotheses, very definite and easy to compare with experiment. The fact is that the way the galaxies behave so far does not seem to be against the proposition.

I can give you another example, even more interesting and important. Probably the most powerful single assumption that contributes most to the progress of biology is the assumption that everything animals do the atoms can do, that the things that are seen in the biological world are the results of the behaviour of physical and chemical phenomena, with no 'extra something'. You could always say, 'When you come to living things, anything can happen'. If you accept that you will never understand living things. It is very hard to believe that the wiggling of the tentacle of the octopus is nothing but some fooling around of atoms according to the known physical laws. But when it is investigated with this hypothesis one is able to make guesses quite accurately about how it works. In this way one makes great progress in understanding. So far the tentacle has not been cut off – it has not been found that this idea is wrong.

It is not unscientific to make a guess, although many people who are not in science think it is. Some years ago I had a conversation with a layman about flying saucers – because I am scientific I know all about flying saucers! I said 'I don't think there are flying saucers'. So my antagonist said, 'Is it impossible that there are flying saucers? Can you prove that it's impossible?' 'No', I said, 'I can't prove it's impossible. It's just very unlikely'. At that he said, 'You are very unscientific. If you can't prove it impossible then how can you say that it's unlikely?' But that is the way that *is* scientific. It is scientific only to say what is more likely and what less likely, and not to be proving all the time the possible and impossible. To define what I mean, I might have said to him, 'Listen, I mean that from my knowledge of the world that I see around me, I think that it is much more likely that the reports of flying saucers are the results of the known irrational characteristics of terrestrial intelligence than of the unknown rational efforts of extra-terrestrial intelligence'. It is just more likely, that is all. It is a good guess. And we always try to guess the most likely explanation, keeping in the back of the mind the fact that if it does not work we must discuss the other possibilities.

How can we guess what to keep and what to throw away? We have all these nice principles and known facts, but we are in some kind of trouble: either we get the infinities, or we do not get enough of a description – we are missing some parts. Sometimes that means that we have to throw away some idea; at least in the past it has always turned out that some deeply held idea had to be thrown away. The question is, what to throw away and what to keep. If you throw it all away that is going a little far, and then you have not much to work with. After all, the conservation of energy looks good, and it is nice, and I do not want to throw it away. To guess what to keep and what to throw away takes considerable skill. Actually it is probably merely a matter of luck, but it looks as if it takes considerable skill.

Probability amplitudes are very strange, and the first thing you think is that the strange new ideas are clearly cock-eyed. Yet everything that can be deduced from the ideas of the existence of quantum mechanical probability amplitudes, strange though they are, do work, throughout the long list of strange particles, one hundred per cent. Therefore I do not believe that when we find out the inner guts of the composition of the world we shall find these ideas are wrong. I think this part is right, but I am only guessing: I am telling you how I guess.

On the other hand, I believe that the theory that space is continuous is wrong, because we get these infinities and other difficulties, and we are left with questions on what determines the size of all the particles. I rather suspect that the simple ideas of geometry, extended down into infinitely small space, are wrong. Here, of course, I am only making a hole, and not telling you what to substitute. If I did, I should finish this lecture with a new law.

Some people have used the inconsistency of all the principles to say that there is only one possible consistent world, that if we put all the principles together, and calculate very exactly, we shall not only be able to deduce the principles, but we shall also discover that these are the only principles that could possibly exist if the thing is still to remain consistent. That seems to me a big order. I believe that sounds like wagging the dog by the tail. I believe that it has to be given that certain things exist – not all the 50-odd particles, but a few little things like electrons, etc. – and then with all the principles the great complexities that come out are probably a definite consequence. I do not think that you can get the whole thing from arguments about consistencies.

Another problem we have is the meaning of the partial symmetries. These symmetries, like the statement that neutrons and protons are nearly the same but are not the same for electricity, or the fact that the law of reflection symmetry is perfect except for one kind of reaction, are very annoying. The thing is almost symmetrical but not completely. Now two schools of thought exist. One will say that it is really simple, that they are really symmetrical but that there is a little complication which knocks it a bit cock-eyed. Then there is another school of thought, which has only one representative, myself, which says no, the thing may be complicated and become simple only through the complications. The Greeks believed that the orbits of the planets were circles. Actually they are ellipses. They are not quite symmetrical, but they are very close to circles. The question is, why are they very close to circles? Why are they nearly symmetrical? Because of a long complicated effect of tidal friction – a very complicated idea. It is possible that nature in her heart is completely unsymmetrical in these things, but in the complexities of reality it gets to look approximately as if it is symmetrical, and the ellipses look almost like circles. That is another possibility; but nobody knows, it is just guesswork.

Suppose you have two theories, A and B, which look completely different psychologically, with different ideas in them and so on, but that all the consequences that are computed from each are exactly the same, and both agree with experiment. The two theories, although they sound different at the beginning, have all consequences the same, which is usually easy to prove mathematically by showing that the logic from A and B will always give corresponding consequences. Suppose we have two such theories, how are we going to decide which one is right? There is no way by science, because they both agree with experiment to the same extent. So two theories, although they may have deeply different ideas behind them, may be mathematically identical, and then there is no scientific way to distinguish them.

However, for psychological reasons, in order to guess new theories, these two things may be very far from equivalent, because one gives a man different ideas from the other. By putting the theory in a certain kind of framework you get an idea of what to change. There will be something, for instance, in theory A that talks about something, and you will say, 'I'll change that idea in here'. But to find out what the corresponding thing is that you are going to change in B may be very complicated – it may not be a simple idea at all. In other words, although they are identical before they are changed, there are certain ways of changing one which looks natural which will not look natural in the other. Therefore psychologically we must keep all the theories in our heads, and every theoretical physicist who is any good knows six or seven different theoretical representations for exactly the same physics. He knows that they are all equivalent, and that nobody is ever going to be able to decide which one is right at that level, but he keeps them in his head, hoping that they will give him different ideas for guessing.

That reminds me of another point, that the philosophy or

168

ideas around a theory may change enormously when there
are very tiny changes in the theory. For instance, Newton's
ideas about space and time agreed with experiment very well,
but in order to get the correct motion of the orbit of Mercury, which was a tiny, tiny difference, the difference in the
character of the theory needed was enormous. The reason
is that Newton's laws were so simple and so perfect, and
they produced definite results. In order to get something
that would produce a slightly different result it had to be
completely different. In stating a new law you cannot make
imperfections on a perfect thing; you have to have another
perfect thing. So the differences in philosophical ideas between Newton's and Einstein's theories of gravitation are
enormous.

What are these philosophies? They are really tricky ways
to compute consequences quickly. A philosophy, which is
sometimes called an understanding of the law, is simply a
way that a person holds the laws in his mind in order to
guess quickly at consequences. Some people have said, and
it is true in cases like Maxwell's equations, 'Never mind the
philosophy, never mind anything of this kind, just guess the
equations. The problem is only to compute the answers so
that they agree with experiment, and it is not necessary to
have a philosophy, or argument, or words, about the equation'. That is good in the sense that if you only guess the
equation you are not prejudicing yourself, and you will
guess better. On the other hand, maybe the philosophy helps
you to guess. It is very hard to say.

For those people who insist that the only thing that is
important is that the theory agrees with experiment, I would
like to imagine a discussion between a Mayan astronomer
and his student. The Mayans were able to calculate with
great precision predictions, for example, for eclipses and for
the position of the moon in the sky, the position of Venus,
etc. It was all done by arithmetic. They counted a certain
number and subtracted some numbers, and so on. There
was no discussion of what the moon was. There was no
discussion even of the idea that it went around. They just

calculated the time when there would be an eclipse, or when the moon would rise at the full, and so on. Suppose that a young man went to the astronomer and said, 'I have an idea. Maybe those things are going around, and there are balls of something like rocks out there, and we could calculate how they move in a completely different way from just calculating what time they appear in the sky'. 'Yes', says the astronomer, 'and how accurately can you predict eclipses?' He says, 'I haven't developed the thing very far yet'. Then says the astronomer, 'Well, we can calculate eclipses more accurately than you can with your model, so you must not pay any attention to your idea because obviously the mathematical scheme is better'. There is a very strong tendency, when someone comes up with an idea and says, 'Let's suppose that the world is this way', for people to say to him, 'What would you get for the answer to such and such a problem?' And he says, 'I haven't developed it far enough'. And they say, 'Well, we have already developed it much further, and we can get the answers very accurately'. So it is a problem whether or not to worry about philosophies behind ideas.

Another way of working, of course, is to guess new principles. In Einstein's theory of gravitation he guessed, on top of all the other principles, the principle that corresponded to the idea that the forces are always proportional to the masses. He guessed the principle that if you are in an accelerating car you cannot distinguish that from being in a gravitational field, and by adding that principle to all the other principles, he was able to deduce the correct laws of gravitation.

That outlines a number of possible ways of guessing. I would now like to come to some other points about the final result. First of all, when we are all finished, and we have a mathematical theory by which we can compute consequences, what can we do? It really is an amazing thing. In order to figure out what an atom is going to do in a given situation we make up rules with marks on paper, carry them into a machine which has switches that open and close in some complicated way, and the result will tell us what the atom is going to do! If the way that these switches open and close were some kind of model of the atom, if we thought that the atom had switches in it, then I would say that I understood more or less what is going on. I find it quite amazing that it is possible to predict what will happen by mathematics, which is simply following rules which really have nothing to do with what is going on in the original thing. The closing and opening of switches in a computer is quite different from what is happening in nature.

One of the most important things in this 'guess – compute consequences – compare with experiment' business is to know when you are right. It is possible to know when you are right way ahead of checking all the consequences. You can recognize truth by its beauty and simplicity. It is always easy when you have made a guess, and done two or three little calculations to make sure that it is not obviously wrong, to know that it is right. When you get it right, it is obvious that it is right – at least if you have any experience – because usually what happens is that more comes out than goes in. Your guess is, in fact, that something is very simple. If you cannot see immediately that it is wrong, and it is simpler than it was before, then it is right. The inexperienced, and crackpots, and people like that, make guesses that are simple, but you can immediately see that they are wrong, so that does not count. Others, the inexperienced students, make guesses that are very complicated, and it sort of looks as if it is all right, but I know it is not true because the truth always turns out to be simpler than you thought. What we need is imagination, but imagination in a terrible strait-jacket. We have to find a new view of the world that has to agree with everything that is known, but disagree in its predictions somewhere, otherwise it is not interesting. And in that disagreement it must agree with nature. If you can find any other view of the world which agrees over the entire range where things have already been observed, but disagrees somewhere else, you have made a great discovery. It is very nearly impossible, but not quite, to find any theory which agrees with experiments over the entire range in which all theories have been checked, and yet gives different consequences in some other range, even a theory whose different consequences do not turn out to agree with nature. A new idea is extremely difficult to think of. It takes a fantastic imagination.

What of the future of this adventure? What will happen ultimately? We are going along guessing the laws; how many laws are we going to have to guess? I do not know. Some of my colleagues say that this fundamental aspect of our science will go on; but I think there will certainly not be perpetual novelty, say for a thousand years. This thing cannot keep on going so that we are always going to discover more and more new laws. If we do, it will become boring that there are so many levels one underneath the other. It seems to me that what can happen in the future is either that all the laws become known – that is, if you had enough laws you could compute consequences and they would always agree with experiment, which would be the end of the line – or it may happen that the experiments get harder and harder to make, more and more expensive, so you get 99·9 per cent of the phenomena, but there is always some phenomenon which has just been discovered, which is very hard to measure, and which disagrees; and as soon as you have the explanation of that one there is always another one, and it gets slower and slower and more and more uninteresting. That is another way it may end. But I think it has to end in one way or another.

We are very lucky to live in an age in which we are still making discoveries. It is like the discovery of America – you only discover it once. The age in which we live is the age in which we are discovering the fundamental laws of nature, and that day will never come again. It is very exciting, it is marvellous, but this excitement will have to go. Of course in the future there will be other interests. There will be the interest of the connection of one level of phenomena to another – phenomena in biology and so on, or, if you are talking about exploration, exploring other planets, but there will not still be the same things that we are doing now.

Another thing that will happen is that ultimately, if it turns out that all is known, or it gets very dull, the vigorous philosophy and the careful attention to all these things that I have been talking about will gradually disappear. The philosophers who are always on the outside making stupid remarks will be able to close in, because we cannot push them away by saying, 'If you were right we would be able to guess all the rest of the laws', because when the laws are all there they will have an explanation for them. For instance, there are always explanations about why the world is three-dimensional. Well, there is only one world, and it is hard to tell if that explanation is right or not, so that if everything were known there would be some explanation about why those were the right laws. But that explanation would be in a frame that we cannot criticize by arguing that that type of reasoning will not permit us to go further. There will be a degeneration of ideas, just like the degeneration that great explorers feel is occurring when tourists begin moving in on a territory.

In this age people are experiencing a delight, the tremendous delight that you get when you guess how nature will work in a new situation never seen before. From experiments and information in a certain range you can guess what is going to happen in a region where no one has ever explored before. It is a little different from regular exploration in that there are enough clues on the land discovered to guess what the land that has not been discovered is going to look like. These guesses, incidentally, are often very different from what you have already seen – they take a lot of thought.

What is it about nature that lets this happen, that it is possible to guess from one part what the rest is going to do? That is an unscientific question: I do not know how to answer it, and therefore I am going to give an unscientific answer. I think it is because nature has a simplicity and therefore a great beauty.

Lk. 3:36, where Luke agrees with the LXX (Gen. 5:9–14: Καινάν; cf. also 10:24, where Codex A has Καινάμ) against the MT and the Samaritan Pentateuch, which do not have this generation at all. On the other hand, William S. Kurz has argued that Lk. 3:23–38 is more probably based on Greek 1 Chronicles 1–9.[4] For him, the following considerations are decisive: (1) Lk. 3:34 has Ἀβραάμ with Chronicles rather than Ἀβραμ with Genesis; (2) the list form of the genealogies in Chronicles would have been much easier to use than culling the names from Genesis 5 and 11, which have much extraneous material interspersed; and (3) the likelihood that the Lukan genealogy used Chronicles for later names suggests its use for earlier ones as well; and (4) like the Chronicler, Luke extends his genealogy back to Adam.[5]

It seems unlikely, however, that the Lukan genealogy of Jesus stems directly from any of these OT passages.[6] More probably, it represents an independent tradition. Several reasons can be adduced to support this contention. First, despite Kurz's assertion, the genealogy actually shows striking independence of the Septuagint in the generations after Perez; therefore, it is probably not dependent on the Septuagint for the generations between Adam and Perez.[7] For example, the Lukan genealogy ignores Chronicles and makes Shealtiel and Zerubbabel descendants of David through Nathan.[8]

Second, the inclusion of Kainam as son of Arpachshad is found not only in LXX Gen. 10:24 and 11:12,[9] but also in *Jub.* 8:1. In his work on the chronology of the patriarchs from Adam to Joseph, John T. Rook has shown that the Septuagint and *Jubilees* represent independent traditions.[10] Moreover, there is no reason why the Lukan genealogy of Jesus from Adam to Perez could not have been culled from the *Book of Jubilees*, as Table 2 shows. Hence, *Jubilees* provides evidence that another source is possible for at least the latter part of Lk. 3:23–38. Perhaps we must reckon with a source that incorporated the *Jubilees* tradition into a more comprehensive genealogy that is partially or wholly independent of the relevant biblical genealogies.

Third, if the Lukan genealogy originally had 77 generations from Adam to Jesus,[11] then it displays a possibly heptadic structure ($77 = 7 \times 11$) which is found neither in LXX Genesis 5 and 11 nor in LXX 1 Chronicles. It must be stressed, however, that, unlike the Matthean genealogy of Jesus, with its explicit structure of 3×14 generations (Matt. 1:17), the Lukan genealogy does not expressly make anything of the 77 generations as a multiple of seven.[12] Are there, nevertheless, any extrabiblical parallels for such a scheme? It is interesting to note that *Jubilees* has a heptadic structure by the very nature of the chronology of jubilees

Table 2. *Luke 3:33–8 and* Jubilees

Lk. 3:33–8	Jubilees	Birth	Jubilee	Week	Year	Annus mundi
Ἀδάμ	2:14, 23	Adam	[1]	1		1–7
Σήθ	4:7	Seth	3	5	4	130
Ἐνώς	4:11	Enosh	5	5	4	228
Καϊνάμ	4:13	Kenan	7	5	3	325
Μαλελεήλ	4:14	Malalael	9	1	3	395
Ἰάρετ	4:15	Jared	10	3	6	461
Ἐνώχ	4:16	Enoch	11	5	4	522
Μαθουσαλά	4:20	Methuselah	12	7	6	587
Λάμεχ	4:27	Lamech				
Νῶε	4:28	Noah	15	3		701–7
Σήμ	4:33	Shem	25	5	3	1207
Ἀρφαξάδ	7:18	Arpachshad				
Καϊνάμ	8:1	Kainan	29	1	3	1375
Σαλά	8:5	Shelah	30	2	4	1432
Ἔβερ	8:7	Eber	31	5	5	1503
Φάλεκ	8:8	Peleg	32	7	6	1567
Ῥαγαύ	10:18	Ragew	33	2	4	1579
Σερούχ	11:1	Serug	35	3	7	1687
Ναχώρ	11:7	Nahor	36	5	1	1744
Θάρα	11:10	Terah	37	6	7	1806
Ἀβραάμ	11:15	Abram	39	2	7	1876
Ἰσαάκ	16:13	Isaac				
Ἰακώβ	19:13	Jacob	42	6	2	2046
Ἰούδα	28:15	Judah	44	4	1	2129
Φάρες	44:15	Perez				

(7 × 7 years) which runs throughout the text.[13] As Table 2 shows, for example, the birth of the patriarchs from Adam to Judah is painstakingly dated as to the jubilee in which it occurred. Within the heptadic chronology of *Jubilees*, however, the birthdates of the patriarchs themselves do not form a neat, heptadic scheme of 7 × 11 generations like that possibly found in the Lukan genealogy. Yet, as Richard Bauckham has argued, the closely related Enochic *Apocalypse of Weeks* (*1 Enoch* 93:3–10; 91:11–17) can be so construed that a scheme of ten weeks of seven generations each emerges which encompasses the whole history of the world from Adam to last judgment.[14] This argument necessitates several assumptions: (1) the scheme in the *Apocalypse of Weeks* is generational rather than chronological;[15] (2) the *Apocalypse* implicitly includes Kainam as one of the seven generations in the second week, based

on knowledge of the closely related *Jubilees* tradition;[16] and (3) the *Apocalypse* follows a shorter, priestly genealogy for the sixth week, which incorporates the whole period of the divided monarchy down to the destruction of the Temple.[17] For all of this to have any relevance for the Lukan genealogy, two more assumptions must be made: (1) the Lukan genealogy adapted a supposedly *priestly* generational scheme of world history to the *royal* genealogy of Jesus;[18] and (2) the Lukan genealogy expanded the ten-week scheme in the *Apocalypse of Weeks* to an eleven-week system based on *1 Enoch* 10:12 (= 4Q202 [4QEnoch^b ar] 4.10–11).[19] This requires that the 70 generations for which the Watchers are to be bound (*1 Enoch* 10:12) commence with the lifetime of Enoch's son Methuselah in the eighth generation and conclude with the final judgment in the seventy-seventh generation.[20]

Bauckham's suggestion is a valiant attempt to account for the scope and structure of the Lukan genealogy. However, the endeavor to fit the Lukan genealogy into a scheme of 77 generations, which is crucial for Bauckham's comparison to the *Apocalypse of Weeks*, presents several major difficulties. First, it is possible that 77 may not be the original number of generations in Luke's genealogy. Although the Nestle-Aland text (27th edn.) includes the full 77 names, it should be noted that there are other manuscript traditions.[21] Some manuscripts contain, for example, only 76 names (B), 74 names (A) or 73 names (N).[22] As Fitzmyer has correctly seen, the Lukan list has been more open to scribal tampering than the Matthean because of the many unknown persons mentioned in it (thirty-six are otherwise completely unknown!) and because nothing is explicitly said about the number of names or structure of the genealogy, such as is found in Matt. 1:17.[23] Furthermore, some of the doublets in the list (e.g., Joseph and Jesus) may have arisen by scribal accident. Hence, faced as we are with a bewildering variety of readings and name counts, we should be open to reexamining the issue.

Second, there could be a *theological* reason why a scribe would have wanted to ascribe 77 generations to Jesus' genealogy, for if "seven indicates fullness, seventy-seven implies ultimacy, a fullness beyond measure..."[24] According to Gen. 4:24, "If Cain is avenged sevenfold, truly Lamech seventy-sevenfold." Likewise in Matt. 18:22: "Not seven times, but, I tell you, seventy-seven times." In that case, the reason for the 77 names in the Lukan genealogy may have nothing at all to do with an apocalyptic scheme of 11 × 7 generations, but may instead express ultimacy. For the author or redactor of the Lukan genealogy, Jesus may have been viewed as the ultimate generation of the human race in terms of significance but not necessarily in number.[25]

Third, there is the strong possibility that, as in manuscript N (sixth century CE) and in Irenaeus (ca. 130–202 CE), the original Lukan genealogy contained inclusively only 72 names from Jesus to Adam.[26] Since Joseph M. Heer provides a detailed argument for the originality of 72 names,[27] we may restrict our comments here to a few salient points.

(1) The general principle of textual criticism is that, with some exceptions, the shorter reading (*lectio brevior*) is more likely to represent the original text.[28] In the case of Lk. 3:23–38, however, scholars have frequently assumed that it is easier for names to drop out of a list of this kind than for names to be added, so that here "shorter" is not necessarily "better."[29] This assumption does not seem to stand up under scrutiny. Several manuscripts (D, N^c, Θ) clearly add τοῦ 'Ιακώβ between 'Ιωσήφ and τοῦ 'Ηλί at 3:23; another manuscript (1071) adds τοῦ 'Ιαννά in the same place. Moreover, an example like the *Chronicon* of Hippolytus – a handbook of history from Adam to 234/5, replete with extensive genealogies drawn from scripture and tradition – shows that lists such as Luke's could also undergo significant expansion in the course of textual transmission.[30] The same is true in similar texts of the Syriac tradition.[31]

(2) Irenaeus' explanation of the Lukan genealogy is of signal importance for understanding the significance of the number 72:[32]

> *Propter hoc Lucas genealogiam quae est a generatione Domini nostri usque ad Adam LXXII generationes habere ostendit, finem coniungens initio et significans quoniam ipse est qui omnes gentes exinde ab Adam dispersas et uniuersas linguas et generationes hominum cum ipso Adam in semetipse recapitulatus est.*
>
> Therefore, Luke shows that the genealogy which is from the generation of our Lord all the way to Adam contains 72 generations, connecting the end with the beginning, and indicating that it is he who recapitulated in himself all nations spread abroad thereafter from Adam, and all languages and generations of men, together with Adam himself.

Thus, according to Irenaeus, the 72 generations from Adam to Jesus symbolize a relationship between Jesus and the 72 nations of the world.[33] As we shall see below, the tradition of the 72 nations of the world was quite widespread in the ancient world, both in Jewish and in Greco-Roman tradition. Moreover, Luke himself may allude to this relationship between Jesus and the 72 nations of the world when he sends out his 70/72 disciples for mission (see below on Lk. 10:1–24). In that case, Luke would be using the Table of Nations to emphasize the universalistic aspect of Jesus and his ministry. The genealogy of Jesus in Lk. 3:23–38 traces Jesus' lineage back to Noah, Adam, and ultimately to God. This not only predicates divine sonship of all humanity (cf. Acts 17:28), but also – and more importantly – describes Jesus in relationship both to the nations of the world and to his own people Israel. It is possible that in the early period of the transmission of Luke's text, 72 was a more obviously symbolic number than 77, and that this could have led to the deliberate reduction of the number of names in some manuscripts.[34] This seems unlikely, however, for as a comment in Clement of Alexandria shows, even the number 75 could be pressed into service as the number of nations in the world (perhaps under the influence of Jewish tradition or even an alternative manuscript tradition of the Lukan genealogy of Jesus).[35] On the other hand, it is possible that the number 72, which is consistent with Luke's own universalistic theology, may well be original, and that it was a later interpolator who added names to the list in order to express the ultimate significance of Jesus in world history.

If we are correct, the Lukan genealogy of Jesus is composed of two extrabiblical sources that articulate at a natural seam. First, Luke excerpted the genealogical material of *Jubilees* from Adam to Perez, including Kainam son of Arpachshad.[36] Indeed, the very last of the generations that Luke could have appropriated from *Jubilees* (i.e., Judah and Perez) are found in the list of the 70 sons and grandsons of Jacob who went down into Egypt with Jacob (*Jub.* 44:11–34; cf. Gen. 46:8–27; Ps.-Philo, *LAB* 8:11). Second, picking up where the *Jubilees* tradition left off, Luke added a separate Davidic genealogy of Jesus, which began with Hezron son of Perez, another of the 70 persons enumerated in the list of the family of Jacob who, according to Gen. 46:12, migrated to Egypt. Significantly, the family of David came from Hezron through his son Ram, and David's lineage is therefore subsumed under the genealogy of Hezron in 1 Chr. 2:9–24 (esp. 10–15). However, Luke's source did not simply appropriate the genealogy of Hezron from 1 Chr. 2:9–24 LXX.[37] For it is no coincidence that the Lukan genealogy begins to diverge most radically from the Septuagint precisely where Luke's two extrabiblical sources articulate. Whereas Luke has Ἐσρώμ, the Septuagint has Ἐσερών (1 Chr. 2:5, 9; A: Ἐσρώμ) and Ἐσρών (Ruth 4:18–19; A: Ἐσρών, Ἐσρών). Even more significantly, the descendants of Hezron that follow in the Lukan genealogy – τοῦ Ἀμιναδάβ τοῦ Ἀδμὶν τοῦ Ἀρνί (Lk. 3:33) – present a bewildering variety of readings having little or nothing to do with the Septuagint, which knows nothing of Admin, and which, instead of Arni, has either Ἀράμ (1 Chr. 2:9–10; B: Ἀρράν) or Ἀρράν (Ruth 4:19; *v.l.* Ἀράμ).[38]

Luke's emphasis on the Nations

If, as we have argued, the Lukan genealogy of Jesus incorporates genealogical material from the *Book of Jubilees*, including the Genesis 10 tradition of *Jubilees* 8–9, and if the number of generations listed in the Lukan genealogy reflects the traditional number of the nations, then Luke's ethnic and geographic emphasis in the rest of Luke-Acts is potentially very significant for our study. In a special way, Luke-Acts focuses on the "nations" (ἔθνη)[39] and the whole "inhabited world" (οἰκουμένη).[40] In fact, Marilyn Salmon argues that "Luke perceives himself to be a Jew," because, among other reasons, his use of ἔθνος (in the sense of "not Jewish") "reflects a Jewish perspective of the world."[41] In support of this argument, David Ravens points out that ἔθνος in Luke's Gospel is found either on the lips of Jews (usually Jesus) or in quotations of the OT; however, in Acts, it occurs not only in its use by Jews, but also in editorial descriptions (Acts 11:1, 14; 2:5, 27; 15:3, 12).[42]

In several cases, Luke uses scripture about the nations in a way that overarches both volumes of Luke-Acts. In Luke's Gospel, for example, Simon, upon seeing Jesus, praises God for granting him the privilege of witnessing "your salvation, which you have prepared in the presence of all peoples, a light for revelation to the nations . . ." (Lk. 2:30–2). This alludes to Isa. 49:6 ("I will set you as a light to the nations that my salvation may reach to the end of the earth"), which is explicitly cited in Acts 13:47 with reference to the preaching of Paul and Barnabas to non-Jews. Thus, the mission to the nations in Acts is the extension and fulfillment of Jesus' own divinely appointed destiny. In Luke's Gospel, this theme is continued in the citation of Isa. 40:3, in which Luke goes beyond his Markan source by including v. 5: " . . . and all flesh shall see the salvation of God" (Lk. 3:6). Acts closes with a statement by Paul that recalls the same passage in Isaiah: "Let it be known to you, then, that this salvation of God has been sent to the nations . . . " (Acts 28:28). Further examples of such overarching themes will be seen below.

Luke's universalistic message is found elsewhere in his Gospel. In his programmatic address to the synagogue in Nazareth, for instance, Jesus casts himself in the role of Elijah and Elisha, sent to outcasts beyond the borders of Israel (Lk. 4:16–30). Later, Jesus speaks of places at the messianic banquet in the kingdom: "There will be weeping and gnashing of teeth when you see Abraham and Isaac and Jacob and all the prophets in the kingdom of God, and you yourselves thrown out. Then, people will come from east and west, from north and south, and will eat in the kingdom of God" (13:28–9). This presumably means that the Gentile nations from the four points of the compass will participate in the messianic banquet, although it could also imply the ingathering of the exiles (cf. Ps. 107:2–3).[43] Perhaps the equivocation is intentional, for, as we shall argue, Luke sees a relationship between the restoration of Israel and the participation of the nations.

The mission of the seventy(-two) (Luke 10:1–24)

Having considered Luke's special emphasis on the nations, we turn now to examine a text that is particularly relevant to our investigation of the possible reception of Genesis 10 tradition in Luke's Gospel – the mission of the seventy(-two) in Lk. 10:1–24. In Luke 9, Jesus sends out the Twelve, representing the number of the tribes of Israel (cf. Lk. 22:30) and thus the nucleus of a restored and reconstituted nation,[44] in order "to proclaim the kingdom of God and to heal" (Lk. 9:1–6).[45] Later, at the beginning of his journey to Jerusalem (Lk. 9:51–18:14), Jesus sends out the seventy (-two),[46] in order to accomplish a similar mission (10:1–24). Thus, the type of mission that the twelve had already been doing is now to be carried out more extensively by an expanded group of disciples. Is the number 70/72 symbolic as well?

Two main lines of interpretation have been suggested. On the one hand, the number has been interpreted as a reference to the seventy elders who were appointed to share the burden of Moses' work (Num. 11:16–17, 24–5; cf. Exod. 24:1).[47] Thus, for example, William Horbury argues that "The 'seventy' or 'seventy-two' of Luke 10. 1, 17–20 reflect, it may be suggested, a pre-Lukan attempt to include the elders in the apostolic commission."[48] On the other hand, the 70/72 has been interpreted in light of the traditional number of nations in the world based on the Table of Nations.[49] For example, Ephrem the Syrian (306–73 CE) connects the 72 languages of the descendants of Noah with the "seventy" chosen by Jesus, as reported in Lk. 10:1, 17.[50] On this interpretation, the sending of the 70/72 in Luke's Gospel foreshadows the later evangelization of the nations by the early church in Acts. In order to evaluate this second possibility, it is necessary to consider in more detail the number 70/72 as it applies to the nations of the world.

Excursus

The 70 or 72 nations of the world

The Jewish notion of 70 or 72 nations of the world is based not only on counting the number of nations listed in Genesis 10 (and 1 Chronicles 1),[51] but also in part on Deut. 32:8, where we read of the method that God used in originally dividing the nations: "When the Most High was separating the nations, when he was scattering the sons of Adam, he set the boundaries of the nations according to the number of the sons of God" (ὅτε διεμέριζεν ὁ ὕψιστος ἔθνη ὡς διέσπειρεν υἰοὺς Ἀδὰμ ἔστησεν ὅρια ἐθνῶν κατὰ ἀριθμὸν υἰῶν θεοῦ). The LXX translator of this passage may well have had in mind the story of the Tower of Babel, according to which the Lord scattered (διέσπειρεν) the peoples over the face of the whole earth (Gen. 11:8). From this developed the concept of the guardian angels of the nations, sometimes but not always specified as 70 (or 72) in number.[52] Instead of "according to the number of the sons [= angels] of God,"[53] the MT has "according to the number of the sons of Israel" (למספר בני ישראל).[54] Later Jewish tradition regarded this number as 70,[55] for according to Gen. 46:27 MT[56] (cf. also Exod. 1:5; Deut. 10:27), "all the persons of the house of Jacob who came into Egypt were seventy" (cf. *Tg. Ps-J* Deut. 32:8–9; *Num. Rab.* 9:14).[57] In the *Animal Apocalypse* (*1 Enoch* 85–90), the seventy shepherds to which the flock (Israel) is transferred (chaps. 89–90) are commonly thought to be the patron angels of the seventy gentile nations (cf. Dan. 10:13, 20) and thus symbolize the dominance of the nations over the Judeans.[58] *Jub.* 44: 33–4 may have already presupposed the correspondence between the two numbers, for the text mentions the "seventy nations" immediately after referring to the "seventy persons" of Jacob who entered Egypt.[59] In subsequent Jewish interpretation, any occurrence of the number 70, whether expressed or implied in the biblical text, can be taken as a reference to the 70 nations.[60]

All of these interpretations of Deut. 32:8 resurface in Christian sources. On the one hand, Ps.-Clementine *Homilies* (18.4.3) regards "the number of the sons of Israel" in Deut. 32:8 as 70, corresponding to the 70 languages of the nations.[61] Epiphanius, *Panarion* 2.8–13 regards the original number of nations as 72.[62] Hippolytus (*Chronicon* 53) tries to harmonize the two numbers: "Therefore, the confused languages were 72 (γλῶσσαι οβ'), but those who built the tower were 70 nations (ἔθνη ο'), who were also separated by their languages upon the face of the earth."[63] On the other hand, Ps.-Clementine *Recognitions* 2.42.3–4 interprets Deut. 32:8 as a division of the earth according to the angels.[64]

Both 70 and 72 are important numbers also in Greco-Roman sources.[65] In Greek literature 70 is frequently used as a rhetorical number to signify "eine homogene geschlossene Gruppe," as well as "all cities" of a country or kingdom and "eine in sich geschlossene historische Epoche."[66] Writing in the third century CE, Horapollon (*Hieroglyphica* 1.14) refers to a tradition (φασί) that there are "seventy-two ancient countries of the inhabited earth" (ἑβδομήκοντα δύο χώρας τὰς ἀρχαίας ... τῆς οἰκουμένης).[67] Furthermore, the number 72 is found in Greco-Roman astrological tradition.[68] For example, in some manuscripts of Claudius Ptolemy's *Tetrabiblos* 2.3, "Total, 72 countries" (γίνονται χῶραι οβ′) occurs at the end of the list of countries that come under the influence of the twelve signs of the zodiac (although the actual total is slightly off from that figure).[69] In speaking of the influence of the heavens on animals, Pliny (*HN* 2.110) mentions that the heavens are divided "into seventy-two signs (*in duo atque septuaginta signa*), that is, shapes of things or of animals into which the learned have mapped out the sky."[70] Already in MUL.APIN, a Babylonian astronomical compendium composed ca. 700 BCE, the number of the stars and constellations is 71.[71] Similarly, Iamblichus (*Myst.* 8.3) reports that the Egyptians divided the heavens into 72 parts. Several writings refer to 72 stars that influence the world. The *Liber Hermetis Trismegisti* (chaps. 3, 25) contains a list of 68 individual stars which is thought to have been 72 originally.[72] *P. Oxy.* 465 (late second century CE) is a fragmentary astrological calendar that includes the names of deities called κραταιοί ("presiding deities"), each of which governs five days (= one week) or five degrees of a 360-day year; hence, there are a total of 72 deities, each corresponding to the sixth part of one of the signs or constellations of the zodiac.[73]

Is the use of the number 72 in early Jewish and Christian sources influenced by the Greco-Roman astrological usage of the same number? Certainly there is precedence for seeing the sons of Israel as stars. In Gen. 37:9, Joseph dreams that the sun, the moon, and eleven stars bow down before him. Based on this passage, Philo makes an explicit connection between the twelve tribes of Jacob and the twelve signs of the zodiac.[74] MUL.APIN is thought to have influenced a Qumran text (4Q318) and the astronomical section of the *Books of Enoch*.[75] Furthermore, a unique "astronomical measuring instrument" found at Qumran

contains three concentric rings of graduated scales, the middle
one of which consists of about 72 marks.[76] A mosaic pavement in
the floor of the western aisle of the En-Gedi synagogue (4th–5th
century CE) contains four sections, the first of which, written
in Hebrew, cites 1 Chr. 1:1–4, listing the first thirteen fathers
of humanity from Adam to Japheth (which is followed in the
biblical text by the Table of Nations!).[77] The second section,
written in Aramaic, contains a verbal list of the twelve signs
of the zodiac, the Hebrew months of the year, the three patriarchs (Abraham, Isaac and Jacob), and the three companions
of Daniel (Hananiah, Mishael and 'Azariah).[78] The juxtaposition of these elements may represent astrological speculation
on the twelve tribes of Israel (//the twelve signs of the zodiac)
and the 70/72 nations.[79] This possibility is strengthened by the
mosaic pavement in the nave of the fourth-century synagogue at
Hammath-Tiberias, where the middle panel consists of two concentric circles framed within a square: the outer circle is divided
into twelve segments, in each of which a sign of the zodaic is
depicted and its name is written in Hebrew; the inner circle contains a picture of Helios riding a quadriga and holding a globe
in his left hand.[80] This globe contains a crossband representing
the zodiac and the equator.[81] Presumably, the twelve signs of
the zodiac represent the twelve tribes of Israel[82] and the globe
represents the 70/72 nations that come under the influence of
the zodiac. Burrows goes so far as to argue that the pattern of
the sums in the Table of Nations (Genesis 10; 1 Chronicles 1)
and the genealogy of Jacob's descendants (Gen. 46:8–27) stems
from the same uranographical tradition as MUL.APIN.[83]

Our survey shows that 72 as the number of the nations of the world is not
so uncommon as is sometimes assumed. Hence, in dealing with the textual
problem in Luke 10, 72 can no longer be regarded as the *lectio difficilior*,
which was subsequently changed by scribes to the more familiar 70. There
is ample motivation for either reading based on Jewish, Christian, and
Greco-Roman tradition. Since the external evidence for the two readings
seems to be about equal,[84] and the internal evidence is also equivocal,
we must be content with presenting both options as strong possibilities.[85]
In light of our discussion of the Lukan genealogy of Jesus, however, 72
seems more probable.

The fact that the sending of the 72 occurs in pairs cannot be used
against this interpretation.[86] For the whole account of the sending speaks

of mission in ways that foreshadow the universal mission in Acts. For instance, the mission of healing and proclaiming the kingdom of God in Lk. 10:9 continues in Acts. Jesus' instructions to the 70/72 disciples in Lk. 10:10–11 (cf. 9:5) to shake off the dust from their feet if a town rejects their message continues in Acts, when Paul and Barnabas "shook off the dust of their feet in protest" against the city of Pisidian Antioch (Acts 13:51); Paul did the same thing in Corinth (Acts 18:6). Hence, although the 72 do not themselves go to the ends of the earth, they were sent ahead to every town and place where Jesus himself intended to go (Lk. 10:1), which after the resurrection extended to the whole world.

Before his ascension, Jesus explains to his disciples what scripture says about him: "Thus it is written, that the Messiah is to suffer and to rise from the dead on the third day, and that repentance and forgiveness of sins is to be proclaimed in his name to all nations (εἰς πάντα τὰ ἔθνη), beginning from Jerusalem" (Lk. 24:46–47). This mission "to all nations" is viewed as the continuation of the mission of the seventy-two, for the same sequence of numbers is at least implied at the beginning of Acts: twelve apostles (1:26; 2:14)[87] and seventy-two nations (cf. 2:5: "every nation under heaven"). This dual emphasis on Israel and on the nations is quite extensive in Luke-Acts, as we have seen. It begins already in Lk. 2:25–38, where the hopes of Simeon and Anna are juxtaposed. Simeon expresses a messianic hope for the nations (v. 32), while Anna, the daughter of Phanuel, of the northern tribe of Asher,[88] proclaims the messianic hope of the exiles for the redemption of Jerusalem (v. 38), which traditionally includes regathering of all the tribes of Israel to the center.[89]

Summary

In sum, Luke's Gospel focuses considerable attention on the nations and the whole inhabited world, although it does so without losing sight of Israel and her national restoration. The seminal impulse for this emphasis on the nations is the Genesis 10 tradition, particularly as reflected in *Jubilees* 8–9. Set at the beginning of the Gospel, Jesus' genealogy provides the biblical framework through which the rest of Luke's universalism is refracted, for, like the rest of humanity, Jesus is identified there as a descendant of Adam and Noah, based on the Table of Nations tradition. To underscore this point, the number of generations from Jesus to Adam is evidently set at 72, one of the traditional numbers of the nations in the world. If this is correct, the identity of the messianic Son of God becomes the foundation for universal mission in the rest of the two-volume work.

In Luke's Gospel, Jesus' identity and his identification with humankind are appropriated and extended by the disciples. Jesus' ministry of teaching and healing, which is directed first and foremost to Israel, carries over to a commission of the Twelve and then of the 72. Although both groups minister exclusively to Israel, the very number of the seventy-two seems to adumbrate and anticipate the universalistic aspect of Jesus' mission. Thus, based again on the Table of Nations tradition, the seventy-two almost certainly represent proleptically the nations of the world, which will become the focus of the Book of Acts. Although the twin foci of Luke-Acts (i.e., Israel and the nations) are inextricably intertwined in both volumes, Luke's Gospel stresses the particularistic aspect, while Acts emphasizes the universalistic aspect. It is becoming increasingly obvious that these two aspects are really two sides of the same coin – the restoration of Israel, which Jesus sought to bring about.

The Book of Acts

Having examined the Genesis 10 tradition in Luke's Gospel, we now proceed to the Book of Acts. Here again, the emphasis on the nations and the whole inhabited world, as well as the influence of the Genesis 10 tradition from *Jubilees* 8–9, are unmistakable throughout. We begin by examining Jesus' final words before his ascension (Acts 1:1–11), before going on to the Pentecost event (2:1–13), Peter's speech in the Temple (3:11–26), the Apostolic Council (15:1–29), and Paul's speech on the Areopagus (17:22–31).

Jesus' final words (Acts 1:1–11)

Acts takes up where Luke's Gospel leaves off with Jesus' final words to his disciples before his ascension (Acts 1:1–11). The idea that the disciples would preach "to all nations ($\pi\acute{\alpha}\nu\tau\alpha$ $\tau\grave{\alpha}$ $\check{\epsilon}\theta\nu\eta$) beginning at Jerusalem" (Lk. 24:46–7) is reiterated in Acts 1:8, where Jesus promises, "and you will be my witnesses in Jerusalem, and in all Judea and Samaria, and to the end of the earth." This Spirit-impelled mission begins in Jerusalem, traditionally the center of the world, and radiates out in concentric circles "to the end of the earth" ($\check{\epsilon}\omega\varsigma$ $\grave{\epsilon}\sigma\chi\acute{\alpha}\tau\sigma\upsilon$ $\tau\tilde{\eta}\varsigma$ $\gamma\tilde{\eta}\varsigma$).[90] Thus, the programmatic statement of the Book of Acts puts the whole concept of mission in a geographical perspective relative to Jerusalem (cf. Acts 13:47). In Luke-Acts, as in the exposition of the Table of Nations in *Jubilees* 8–9 (cf. *Jub.* 8:19), Jerusalem functions as "the navel of the earth" (Ezek. 38:12; cf. 5:5).[91] That the ascension takes place just outside

Jerusalem underscores that Jerusalem is the omphalos connecting heaven and earth, a veritable *axis mundi* of intersecting horizontal and vertical planes.[92]

As R. Bauckham rightly stresses, the centrality of Jerusalem was, above all, eschatologically important.[93] Not only was the Jewish Diaspora to be regathered to Jerusalem from all four cardinal points (e.g., Isa. 11:12; 43:5–6), but also the Gentile nations were to come from all directions to Jerusalem to worship God in order to participate in the messianic salvation (Isa. 2:2–3; cf. Matt. 8:11; Lk. 13:29, interpreting Isa. 49:12 in this sense). In some texts, the returning exiles and the Gentile pilgrims form a single movement converging on Jerusalem (Isa. 60:3–16; Zech. 8:20–3; Tob. 13:11–13).

The geographical movement in Acts is centrifugal – away from Jerusalem. The announcement of Jesus in Acts 1:8, "You will be my witnesses in Jerusalem and in all Judea and Samaria and to the end of the earth," is carried out by the narrative: the ministry in Jerusalem (chaps. 1–7) is followed by the evangelization of Judea and Samaria (chaps. 8–12), then by Asia Minor and Europe (chaps. 13–28).[94] Each movement outward, however, also circles back to Jerusalem (cf. Acts 12:25; 15:2; 18:22; 19:21; 20:16; 21:13; 25:1).[95] Thus, Jerusalem remains the center and focal point of Acts from first to last.[96] Only when Paul finally comes to Rome does Jerusalem recede from view.

Acts 1:8 is often understood as broadly programmatic for the structure of Acts.[97] Yet as an explication of what it means that the disciples would preach "to all nations beginning at Jerusalem" (Lk. 24:46–7), the concentric circles radiating out from Jerusalem in a northwesterly direction to the ends of the earth suggest influence from the Table of Nations tradition. For, as M. Kartveit has shown, 1 Chronicles 1 lists the nations of the world "in a circle" which proceeds counterclockwise – from north, to west, to south, and to east – with Jerusalem in the center.[98] Likewise in Ezek. 5:5, Jerusalem is described as lying in the center of a "circle" of nations. In Jewish literature of the Second-Temple period, this Table of Nations tradition is appropriated by *Jubilees* 8–9. In its exposition of the Table of Nations, *Jubilees* 8–9 does not merely list the nations around Israel but actually describes the geography of the world and Israel's central position in it. The *Jubilees* world extends from the Garden of Eden in the East (*Jub.* 8:16) to Gadir in Spain (8:23, 26; 9:12). As we have seen, Noah divides the earth by lot among his three sons: Shem receives the temperate "middle of the earth" (*Jub.* 8:12–21), with Mt. Zion "in the middle of the navel of the earth" (v. 19); Ham receives the hot southern portion (vv. 22–4); and Japheth, the cold northern portion (vv. 25–30).

If we apply this traditional, tripartite division of the earth to Acts, the following structure emerges for the book. The Spirit-impelled witness which goes out from Jerusalem (the center) to "all the nations of the world" can be broadly divided into three missions in accordance with the Table of Nations tradition: (1) Acts 2:1 – 8:25 records the mission to *Shem* concentrating on Judea and Samaria; (2) Acts 8:26–40 provides a glimpse at the burgeoning mission to *Ham* in Africa (8:26–40); and (3) the rest of Acts is devoted primarily to the rapidly expanding mission to *Japheth* in Asia Minor and Europe.[99] Admittedly, the names of Noah and his sons do not occur in the Book of Acts. Nevertheless, Luke-Acts focuses on the "nations" (ἔθνη) and the whole "inhabited world" (οἰκουμένη) in such a manifestly scriptural way that the influence of a prominent tradition like the Table of Nations should be considered probable, especially since this same tradition is found in other early Christian literature. As we shall see, *Jubilees* 8–9 influenced such writings as Theophilus of Antioch, Hippolytus of Rome, and the Jewish–Christian source of the Pseudo-Clementine *Recognitions*. The latter is particularly important because it is also dependent on Acts.

Excursus

The meaning of "To the end of the Earth"

The meaning of "to the end of the earth" (ἕως ἐσχάτου τῆς γῆς) in Acts 1:8 remains disputed.[100] The simplest solution is to identify "the end" (singular!) of the earth with Rome, to which Paul finally comes at the conclusion of Acts. Indeed, *Ps. Sol.* 8:15 is often used to support this interpretation, since Pompey is seen there as someone whom God brought "from the end of earth" (ἀπ᾽ ἐσχάτου τῆς γῆς) in order to conquer Jerusalem in 63 BCE. It is not certain, however, whether the end of the earth in that passage actually refers to Rome, for Pompey came to Syria from Spain, where he had commanded troops in the 70s.[101] Thus, Sallust reports in *Cat.* 16.5 that *Pompeius in extremis terris bellum gerebat.* By the first century CE, it is doubtful that Rome itself could be seen as one of the ends of the earth, although there was a Greek-derived myth of Rome's founding which put the city on the fringes of the world,[102] and there were rumors of Julius Caesar's supposed intention of moving the seat of the Roman Empire to Alexandria or Ilium (cf. Nicolaus of Damascus, *Vita Caes.* 20; Suetonius, *Iul.* 79.3), presumably so that it would be closer to the supposed geographical center of the inhabited world.[103] By the first century, however, Rome had become the new center of the world, as we have seen in Strabo. Thus, the phrase περὶ τὰς ἐσχατιὰς τόπων τῆς καθ' ἡμᾶς οἰκουμένης (Polybius 3.58.2) most naturally means the most distant parts from the center of the world.[104]

E. E. Ellis suggests a solution that again depends on seeing "the end" as referring to one specific place.[105] For him, "the end of the earth" refers to Spain, which reveals Luke's knowledge of Paul's travel plans (Rom. 15:24, 28). Indeed, 1 Clem. 5:7 regards Paul's mission as having reached "the extremity of the West" (τὸ τέρμα τῆς δύσεως), which is similar to Luke's formulation and may even be dependent on it.[106] Ellis argues that the plural expression τὰ ἔσχατα τῆς γῆς is used when all the ends of the earth are meant. In response to Ellis' suggestion, it is important to observe that even the singular ἔσχατος is sometimes used in contexts where it clearly denotes all the ends of the earth (e.g., Isa. 8:9; 45:22; Jer. 38[31]:8; 1 Macc. 3:9).[107] Rome might be *terra incognita* to many peoples in the East,[108] but it hardly qualifies as one of the traditional ends of the earth – India, Scythia, Spain, and Ethiopia.[109]

Indeed, we may surmise that Ethiopia, to which the gospel was brought even before Paul's Damascus road experience (Acts 8:25–41), is almost certainly one of the ends of the earth that Acts 1:8 has particularly in view. As David Goldenberg notes, "The association of racial extremes with geographical extremes apparently lies behind the choice of an Ethiopian as the first Gentile convert to Christianity (Acts 8:26–40). Nothing could more visibly indicate the universalist posture of the early church than the conversion of those from the remotest parts of the world. Indeed, Philip's conversion of the Ethiopian became a symbol of Christianity's conversion of the world, and in Christian metaphor the 'Ethiopian' later became (beginning primarily with Origen, emphasized by Augustine) the symbol for the church of the Gentiles. As Augustine said, explaining 'Ethiopians' in Ps. 72(71):9, 'By the Ethiopians, as by a part the whole, he signified all nations, selecting that nation he named especially, which is at the ends of the earth (Per Aethiopes, a parte totium, omnes gentes significavit, eam ligens gentem, quam potissimum nominaret, quae in finibus terrae est)', and 'Is he God only of the Jews? Is he not also of the nations . . . ? But Ethiopia, which appears to be the extreme of the nations, is justified through faith without the works of the law...' Similarly, explaining Ps. 68:32 (67:31), 'Ethiopia, which seems to be the farthest limit of the Gentiles', *Enarrationes in Psalmos* 71.12 (*CCL* 39:980f) and 67.40 (*CCL* 39:897). For the same reason, used to make the opposite point, Amos 9:7 compares Israel to the Ethiopians..."[110]

Luke's phrase is best interpreted in light of Isa. 49:6, which, as we have seen, is used twice in Luke-Acts (Lk. 2:36; Acts 13:47) and provides an important clue to Luke's view of the mission to the nations from Jesus to Paul (cf. Acts 22:21, where the resurrected Christ speaks to Paul in the Temple: "Go, for I will send you far away to the nations [εἰς ἔθνη μακράν]"). This Servant Song expresses an eschatological expectation in which the kingdom of God is universalized to include all nations. In Isa. 49:6, the phrase "to the end [singular!] of the earth" (ἕως ἐσχάτου τῆς γῆς; MT: עַד־קְצֵה הָאָרֶץ) receives its meaning from v. 1, where God directly addresses the "islands" (νῆσοι; MT: אִיִּים) and the "nations" (ἔθνη; MT: אֻמִּים מֵרָחוֹק). A similar parallelism between "to the end(s) of the earth" and the "nations" is found in 1 Macc. 1:1–4 (esp. v. 3), which refers to Alexander's universal empire: "After Alexander son of Philip, the Macedonian, who came from the land of Kittim, had defeated King Darius of the Persians and the Medes, he succeeded him as king. (He had previously become king of Greece.) (2) He fought many battles, conquered strongholds, and put to death the kings of the earth. (3) He advanced to the ends of the earth (ἕως ἄκρων τῆς γῆς), and plundered many nations (πλήθους ἐθνῶν). When the earth became quiet before him, he was exalted, and his heart was lifted up. (4) He gathered a very strong army and ruled over countries, nations, and princes, and they became tributary to him." Pompey's conquests in Asia are said to have extended the frontiers of the Empire "to the limits of the earth" (τοῖς ὅροις τῆς γῆς), and a list of fourteen conquered nations is provided to substantiate this (Diod. Sic. 40.4).[111] Cicero (*Pis.* 16) goes so far as to praise Pompey as *victor omnium gentium*.[112] Thus, the phrase in Isa. 49:6, "to the end of the earth," means all the nations of the earth to the outer edges of the inhabited world.[113] Seen in this light, "from Jerusalem... to the ends of the earth" in Acts 1:8 has the same meaning as "to all nations, beginning from Jerusalem" in Lk. 24:47.[114] This explains the aforementioned emphasis in Luke-Acts on the οἰκουμένη.

In the process of evangelizing to the ends of the earth, the missionaries turn the inhabited world (οἰκουμένη) upside down and are accused of "acting contrary to the decrees (δόγματα) of the emperor, saying that there is another king named Jesus" (Acts 17:6–7). This alludes to the statement found earlier in Luke's Gospel that the Roman emperor issues a "decree" (δόγμα) to "the whole inhabited world" (Lk. 2:1–2), which in turn is based on Augustus' claim in the Preamble of the *Res Gestae Divi Augusti* that he has gained dominion over the whole *orbis terrarum*.[115] By the end of Acts, however, even Rome, the imperial capital, is being effectively reached with the proclamation of the kingdom of God (Acts 28:31), the gospel of the real Lord of All (cf. Acts 10:36) and Judge of the οἰκουμένη (Acts 17:31; cf. Lk. 4:5–8), whose post-resurrection decree has sent Spirit-impelled witnesses to the ends of the earth (Acts 1:8). Rome itself is not the end of the world, but the Roman Empire is, from its own grandiose imperial ideology and aspiration, coextensive with the inhabited world.[116] Hence, reaching the center of the Empire for the kingdom of God is tantamount to reaching the ends of the earth,[117] even if the actual work of evangelization was expected to continue after reaching Rome. There can be little doubt that Luke-Acts presents us with a dynamic picture of how the static Romanocentric Empire is in the process of being supplanted by a new kingdom and a new center through the conquest of the gospel.

Historically, the worldwide mission to "the ends of the earth" progressed in stages, much as the schematic summary statement in Acts 1:8 describes it. The expulsion of the Hellenists and the conversion of Paul led to the first Jewish–Christian mission in Arabia (by Paul), Syria and Cilicia, countries in the immediate neighborhood. About the year 40 CE the new messianic movement had already reached Antioch, Tarsus, Cyprus, and probably, Rome, and at the beginning of the fifties, Western Asia Minor and Greece. By then Paul was already looking westward toward Spain, to the end of the *oikoumene*. In the year 70, Mark (13:10) could write that the gospel must be preached to all peoples before the imminent parousia of the Lord, but another one hundred years pass before we hear the rather optimistic progress report from Irenaeus that the church had "dispersed throughout the whole world, even to the ends of the earth" (*Ecclesia enim per universum orbem usque ad fines terrae seminata*).[118]

The concentric circles radiating out from Jerusalem to the ends of the earth can also be compared to the subsidiary circles of missionary activity portrayed in the Book of Acts. The best example is Paul, who on each of his three missionary journeys makes a circuitous route out from and eventually back to Antioch, except on the last one which he concludes in Jerusalem (Acts 13:4–14:28; 15:36–18:22; 18:23–21:17). In discussing this cyclical pattern, Doron Mendels argues that Luke was apparently familiar with literary topoi concerning the Hellenistic culture-hero and thus cast Paul's mission in the mold of wandering missionaries, such as Heracles, Myrina, Semiramis, Osiris, Sesostris, and Dionysus, who traveled a complete circle in carrying out their missions to civilize the world.[119] Mendels finds only one "Jewish wanderer," Abraham, who according to the *Genesis Apocryphon* (1QapGen. 21.13–20), makes a similar circuit around the eastern *oikoumene*, although Abraham was not a civilizatory figure at all; he simply moves from place to place: "In this context it strengthens the argument that Jewish literature of the hellenistic period was not the source for Luke in his description of Paul's mission."[120] Mendels is convinced that Luke's conception has nothing to do with the OT and Jewish tradition: "Here it should be mentioned that scholars have associated the universalistic concept in Judaism (especially from the Hebrew Bible) with Paul's mission . . . However, ideas that we find in Isaiah 2 and elsewhere never speak of Jews who will *go* to the nations, thus being active in spreading their religion. In Paul's case as in the hellenistic culture-heroes, the apostle is *active* in walking from one place to another, spreading his mission."[121] This ignores a passage like Isa. 66:18–21, which contains the divine promise that Jews who survive the exile will go out (from Jerusalem?) to the nations and bring them back to the Lord in the Holy City, together with gifts and Diaspora Jews.[122] Indeed, Rainer Riesner argues that Isa. 66:18–21 was important for understanding the geographical expansion of earliest Christianity as described by the Book of Acts.[123] In view of Luke's emphasis on the restoration of Israel (cf. Acts 1:6 and further below), he was probably more familiar with Isa. 66:18–21 than with literary topoi concerning the Hellenistic culture-hero.

The Pentecost event (Acts 2:1–13)

Having examined the programmatic verse of Acts, we turn now to the Pentecost event itself, which describes the beginning of the early Christian mission in Jerusalem. The scene is set in Acts 2:1–4:

> (1) When the day of Pentecost had come, they were all together in one place. (2) And suddenly from heaven there came a sound

like the rush of a violent wind, and it filled the entire house where they were sitting. (3) Divided tongues, as of fire, appeared among them, and a tongue rested on each of them. All of them were filled with the Holy Spirit and began to speak in other languages, as the Spirit gave them ability.

This description of the Pentecost event gives us another important glimpse into Luke's perspective on the nations, including foreshadowing of the worldwide mission and the role of Israel in it.

1   *Festival of Pentecost (v. 1)*

According to Acts 2:1, the crucial event occurred "when the day of Pentecost had come." As a designation for a particular religious observance, the Greek word appears only twice in the LXX (Tob. 2:1; 2 Macc. 12:32). In the Hebrew Bible, the customary name for the observance is the Feast of Weeks (*Shavuot*). It is regarded as the second of three obligatory observances, coming between Passover and Tabernacles (cf. Exod. 23:14–17; 34:18–24; Deut. 16:16; 2 Chr. 8:13).[124] In Exod. 23:16, it is called "the festival of harvest, of the first fruits of your labor, of what you sow in the field." In Exod. 34:22, the Feast of Weeks is further described as "the first fruits of wheat harvest."

It is often pointed out that Jewish tradition held that the Law was given on this day, seven weeks after Passover. Perhaps more importantly for the message of Acts, the *Book of Jubilees* makes Pentecost the most important of the annual festivals on the Jewish liturgical calendar (cf. *Jub.* 22:1). As we have seen above, *Jubilees* is a source for Luke-Acts; hence, *Jubilees'* view of Pentecost may well have special relevance for our discussion.[125] According to *Jub.* 6:15–19, the Feast of Pentecost was instituted in connection with the covenant with Noah and was to be renewed annually in perpetuity:

> He [sc. God] gave Noah and his sons a sign that there would not again be a flood on the earth. (16) He put his bow in the clouds as a sign of the eternal covenant that there would not henceforth be flood waters on the earth for the purpose of destroying it throughout all the days of the earth. (17) For this reason it has been ordained and written on the heavenly tablets that they should celebrate the festival of weeks during this month – once a year – to renew the covenant each and every year. (18) ... Then Noah and his sons kept it for seven jubilees and one week of years until Noah's death. From the day of Noah's death his sons corrupted (it) until Abraham's lifetime and were eating blood.

> (19) Abraham alone kept (it), and his sons Isaac and Jacob kept
> it until your lifetime. During your lifetime the Israelites had for-
> gotten (it) until I renewed (it) for them at this mountain [= Sinai].

According to this intepretation, the covenant with Noah (cf. Gen. 8:20–2;
9:8–17) was the covenant that was being renewed at each stage of history
during the time of Pentecost. Even the revelation at Sinai was a renewal of
the Noachic covenant.[126] Hence, Pentecost was originally an observance
that was incumbent upon all humanity, just as the Noachic decree itself
was. According to Zech. 14:16–19, all nations would come to worship
the Lord in Zion and keep the Feast of Tabernacles.[127] Perhaps in a
similar way the Book of Acts sees Pentecost in light of the eschatological
pilgrimage of the nations to Zion.[128] As Peter's sermon goes on to make
clear, the Spirit was poured out at Pentecost "upon all flesh" (ἐπὶ πᾶσαν
σάρκα) in fulfillment of Joel 2:28–32 (Acts 2:17).[129]

We may note that Luke, unlike Matthew, traces Jesus' lineage through
Noah (Lk. 3:36) to Adam (v. 38). The reverse sequence is found in 1
Chronicles 1, whose condensed version of Genesis 1–10 moves from
Adam to a reformulation of the Table of Nations in Genesis 10. Both
Matthew (24:37–8) and Luke (17:26–7) incorporate the same Q saying,
in which the coming of the Son of Man is compared to the judgment
and destruction experienced during the days of Noah. Moreover, as we
shall see, Luke's description of the Apostolic Decree (Acts 15:20, 29;
21:25) probably echoes the Noachic Decree, which, according to Jewish
tradition, was incumbent upon all human beings after the flood. Given
Luke's emphasis on Noah and Noachic traditions, he may well have
known about the origins of Pentecost according to the *Book of Jubilees*.

2   *Miracle of Tongues (vv. 1–4)*

When the day of Pentecost arrived, the twelve apostles were all together
in one place (v. 1). It was at this time that the gift of the Spirit came
upon them, thus giving the initial fulfillment of Jesus' words in Acts
1:8, that they would receive power when the Holy Spirit had come upon
them, enabling them to be his witnesses beginning in Jerusalem. This
divine enablement manifests itself in the apostles' spontaneous ability to
speak in foreign languages (v. 4).[130] Luke wants to show that "The church
from the beginning, though at the beginning located only in Jerusalem,
is in principle a universal society in which universal communication is
possible."[131] The old language-based division of humanity (cf. Gen. 10:5,
20, 31; 11:1–9), which resulted from the episode at the Tower of Babel

(Gen. 11:1–9), had now been overcome. Already in the OT, Zeph. 3:9 expects the reversal of Babel at the time of the restoration of Israel, when the nations will be converted, and their speech is changed to a pure speech. There is now significant evidence that this expectation was maintained (or at least preserved) in Qumran.[132]

Although the Pentecost event did not cause the nations to revert to one language,[133] the account in Acts 2 nevertheless contains clear allusions to the story of the Tower of Babel and the restoration of Israel. First, our passage alludes to the Tower of Babel. For example, just as the Tower episode is said to have been accompanied by a violent wind,[134] Acts 2:2 reports that the Pentecost event was attended by "a sound like the rush of a violent wind." Furthermore, Acts 2:6 indicates that the great mass of the people in Jerusalem were "confounded" (συνεχύθη) by the Pentecost event, which can be compared to the confounding (συγχεῖν) of the people in Gen. 11:7, 9. Also, the "divided tongues" (διαμεριζόμεναι γλῶσσαι) in Acts 2:3 may well symbolize the divided language groups that were created as a result of the confusion of languages at Babel.[135]

Second, Acts 2 alludes to the restoration of Israel. In particular, the coming of the Spirit at Pentecost fulfills a key element of the traditional expectation of Israel's restoration.[136] In Isa. 11:1–9, a messianic king who is endowed with the Spirit restores the fortunes of Israel and establishes the righteous reign of God on earth (cf. Isa. 42:1). Isaiah 40–66 has much to say about the restoration of Israel, including the coming of the Spirit to the nation. According to Isa. 44:3, the Spirit will bring the nation new life and cause it to flourish. In Ezekiel's prophecy of hope, the Spirit is integral to the future restoration of Israel and Judah. According to Ezek. 36:26–7, the Lord promises to put his Spirit within the people and to remove their heart of stone (cf. Ezek. 11:19). The prophet's vision of the valley of dry bones in Ezekiel 37 pictures the exiled nation, which was as good as dead, as reanimated by the life-giving Spirit of God when it is reestablished in the Land under a Davidic king. Ezekiel 39:25–9 goes on to state that when God regathers the people from the lands of their exile, he will restore the fortunes of Jacob and have mercy on the whole house of Israel; and he will never again hide his face from them, when he pours out his Spirit upon them. In Joel, the outpouring of the Spirit on all flesh (2:28) is a precursor to the great and terrible day of the Lord, after which God will restore the fortunes of Judah and Jerusalem (3:1). It can be no accident that Peter's speech at Pentecost cites Joel 2:28–32 (3:1–5 LXX). By using this text, Peter was announcing that the restoration of Israel was in the process of coming to pass right before their very eyes. Before his death, Jesus had conferred the kingdom on the Twelve

(Lk. 22:29–30). With the death of Jesus, however, the disciples' hopes were dashed (cf. Lk. 24:21: "But we had hoped that he was the one to redeem Israel"). When the resurrected Lord started speaking about the kingdom (Acts 1:3), the disciples immediately asked him whether this was the time when he would restore the kingdom to Israel (v. 6). And now, at Pentecost, one of the great pilgrimage festivals of the nation, the long-expected time of national restoration had finally begun to dawn. It is no coincidence that the prophesied outpouring of the Spirit takes place precisely at the time of the eschatological ingathering of the exiles to the Land.[137] By the same token, it is perhaps significant that the number of people who respond positively to Peter's speech ("about three thousand" [Acts 2:41]) is approximately the same as the number of Judeans who were taken away into exile during the first deportation to Babylon ("three thousand twenty-three" [Jer. 52:28 MT]).

3   *"Jews from every nation under heaven" (v. 5)*

In v. 5, the objects of the apostles' witness on this occasion are described as "Jews from every nation under heaven" ('Ιουδαῖοι... ἀπὸ παντὸς ἔθνους τῶν ὑπὸ τὸν οὐρανόν)" who were staying in Jerusalem. This statement raises several questions. (1) How can these Jews be *both* "dwelling in Jerusalem" (2:5, εἰς 'Ιερουσαλὴμ κατοικοῦντες; cf. v. 14, ἄνδρες 'Ιουδαῖοι καὶ οἱ κατοικοῦντες 'Ιερουσαλὴμ πάντες) *and* "dwelling in Mesopotamia, etc." (2:9, οἱ κατοικοῦντες τὴν Μεσοποταμίαν, κτλ.)? (2) Why does Luke consider it worth mentioning that there were Jews living in Jerusalem? (3) How can he say that Jews are "from every nation under heaven"?[138]

All of these questions can be answered if we assume that Diaspora Jews had come to Jerusalem for the pilgrimage festival.[139] First, there are evidently two senses of "dwelling" here. Although the Jews listed in vv. 9–10 normally live in the Diaspora,[140] they temporarily dwell in Jerusalem for the special occasion. It has been pointed out that κατοικεῖν is not used of temporary residence. Perhaps, then, v. 5 has a different provenance from that of the list of nations, and the two senses of κατοικεῖν (to reside permanently and to dwell temporarily) come from the juxtaposition of originally separate traditions.[141]

Second, Luke considers it supremely worthwhile to mention that Jews were dwelling in Jerusalem because the *Diaspora* Jews had returned to the city at an auspicious moment in history. This was more than just an annual pilgrimage festival. From Luke's perspective, Pentecost is the beginning of the restoration of Israel.

Third, the idea that Jews were "from every nation under heaven" is crucial to Luke's point. This is the language of the Diaspora, as Haman's information to the king in Esth. 3:8 shows: "There is a nation scattered among the nations in your kingdom (ὑπάρχει ἔθνος διεσπαρμένον ἐν τοῖς ἔθνεσιν ἐν πάσῃ τῇ βασιλείᾳ σου)." Those who gather in Jerusalem for Pentecost represent not only Diaspora Judaism but also the nations whose languages they speak. The scene is programmatic for the worldwide mission to follow. If the account has any basis in historical reality, the Pentecost event itself may have given direct impetus to the worldwide mission, insofar as these first believers returned to the Diaspora after their sojourn in Jerusalem and established churches there, including perhaps the church in Rome.[142]

Yet there is more to the expression "every nation under heaven." It is no coincidence that the expression is found several times in Deuteronomy.[143] For example, Deut. 2:25 refers to the fear that Israel will put "upon all nations under heaven" (ἐπὶ πρόσωπον πάντων τῶν ἐθνῶν τῶν ὑποκάτω τοῦ οὐρανοῦ).[144] Similarly, Deut. 4:19 reads: "And do not look up into heaven and look at the sun, the moon, the stars and all the world of heaven, lest being led astray, you might worship them and serve them, which the Lord your God has shown to all the nations under heaven" (πᾶσιν τοῖς ἔθνεσιν τοῖς ὑποκάτω τοῦ οὐρανοῦ).[145] Here again, we see a relationship between Israel and the nations of the world, albeit a negative one in this case. More importantly, Deuteronomy speaks of Israel's exile and return as taking place "under heaven." Thus we read in Deut. 30:4–5 LXX: "If your dispersion be from one end of heaven to the other, the Lord your God will gather you from there, and the Lord your God will receive you from there, and the Lord your God will lead you into the Land ..." In Neh. 1:8–9 (2 Esdras 11:8–9), precisely this promise is brought to God's attention: "Now remember the word that you commanded to Moses your servant, saying, 'If you break the covenant, I will scatter you among the peoples, and if you return to me and keep my commandments and do them, [even] if your dispersion is from the end of heaven, I will gather them from there and bring them into the place where I have chosen to cause my name to dwell'" (cf. also Deut. 12:5; 28:64).[146] 2 Macc. 2:18 alludes to the same Deuteronomic promise, specifying that the ingathering would come from everywhere under heaven: "We have hope in God that he will soon have mercy on us and will gather us from everywhere under heaven (ἐκ τῆς ὑπὸ τὸν οὐρανόν) into his holy place ..." (cf. 1:27; Deut. 30:3). Moreover, God had promised that he would gather his people from the ends of the earth particularly at the time of one of the great pilgrimage festivals: "Look, I am bringing them from the north, and I will gather them from the end of the earth during the feast of Passover" (ἰδοὺ ἐγὼ ἄγω αὐτοὺς ἀπὸ βορρᾶ καὶ συνάξω αὐτοὺς ἀπ' ἐσχάτου τῆς γῆς ἐν ἑορτῇ φασεκ, Jer. 38[31]:8).[147] Hence, when Acts 2:5 describes the Pentecost event as occuring when Diaspora Jews had gathered from every nation under heaven, this language strongly implies the restoration of Israel.[148] For Luke, Jerusalem was more than merely the center from which the centrifugal movement of the gospel went out to the ends of the earth;[149] rather, Jerusalem was the center to which, in corresponding centripetal movement, the eschatological people of God must return. Even if he was writing after 70 CE,[150] when maintaining the centrality of Jerusalem would no longer seem viable, Luke faithfully places the focus on Jerusalem for the nascent church and does not repress the eschatological function of the Holy City.[151]

As we have seen, Isa. 49:6 influences both Luke (2:31–2) and Acts (1:8; 13:47). This Isaianic text encompasses both aspects – the restoration of Israel and the mission to the nations: "to restore the survivors of Israel" and to "give you as a light to the nations, that my salvation may reach to the end of the earth." The logic of Acts thus proceeds as follows:[152]

> Jesus' response to the disciples' question [Acts 1:6] is not formulated in order to correct the readers' ... 'eschatology', but to introduce the whole narrative of Acts as a testimony to the deployment of the reign of God's Messiah through his twelve apostles who declare repentance and forgiveness to Israel. First the twelve are restored (Acts 1:12–26). Then the Spirit is poured out upon devout Jews 'from every nation under heaven' (Acts 2).
>
> The logic stems directly from Second Isaiah: the promise of God's reign is not simply the restoration of the preserved of Israel, but the renewal of the vocation of Israel to be a light to the nations to the end of the earth. Have God's promises failed? No, the restoration which the exalted Jesus is now about to inaugurate through the Holy Spirit (the promise of the Father: Lk. 24:49) is the renewal of Isaiah's prophetic calling in the world.

4   *List of nations (vv. 9–11)*

Acts 2:9–11 goes on to list the Diaspora Jews who had gathered in Jerusalem from every nation in terms of their countries of origin. This list raises another set of questions.[153] (1) Did Luke himself construct the list, or did he appropriate it from a source? (2) If the latter, what is the background of the list? (3) What explains the structure and contents of the list? Let us begin with the last question first.

Despite the widely recognized importance of the list, little attention has been given to a basic structural analysis of the text, resulting in the proliferation of interpretations based on incomplete or faulty observations. The following diagram illustrates the structure of the passage:

(8) καὶ πῶς ἡμεῖς ἀκούομεν ἕκαστος τῇ ἰδίᾳ διαλέκτῳ ἡμῶν ἐν ᾗ ἐγεννήθημεν;

(9) Πάρθοι
καὶ Μῆδοι
καὶ Ἐλαμῖται

καὶ οἱ κατοικοῦντες τὴν Μεσοποταμίαν,
Ἰουδαίαν
τε καὶ Καππαδοκίαν,
Πόντον
καὶ τὴν Ἀσίαν,
(10) Φρυγίαν
τε καὶ Παμφυλίαν,
Αἴγυπτον
καὶ τὰ μέρη τῆς Λιβύης τῆς κατὰ
Κυρήνην,

καὶ οἱ ἐπιδημοῦντες Ῥωμαῖοι, (11) Ἰουδαῖοί τε
καὶ προσήλυτοι,
Κρῆτες
καὶ Ἄραβες

ἀκούομεν λαλούντων αὐτῶν ταῖς ἡμετέραις γλώσσαις τὰ μεγαλεῖα τοῦ θεοῦ.

Structurally, the list is framed by the first-person reaction of the Diaspora Jews in attendance: "And how is it that we hear, each of us, in our own native language?" (v. 8) and ". . . in our own languages we hear them speaking about God's deeds of power" (v. 11). This repetition may indicate that what comes in between is an insertion of possibly traditional material, especially since it is difficult to imagine that those dwelling in Judea would be astonished that they could understand the

Galileans who were speaking to them. We shall come back to this issue in a moment.

The list itself consists of three clearly identifiable parts joined by καί: three *nations* at the beginning (Parthians, Medes, Elamites) and three at the end (Romans, Cretans, Arabs) sandwich an articular substantival participle in the middle that has nine *lands/countries* as objects ("those who inhabit Mesopotamia, Judea and Cappadocia, Pontus and Asia, Phrygia and Pamphylia, Egypt and the parts of Libya adjacent to Cyrene"). Obviously this is a carefully constructed, tripartite list consisting of multiples of three (3–9–3).[154] As we shall see, this is probably not a coincidence, and we should therefore resist the temptation to identify individual members of the list as secondary insertions, even if one of the names may have been corrupted in the process of transmission (see further below).

Further structural observations can be made within each of the three parts of the list. The first part consists of three adjacent Near Eastern nations, which establish a generally southwesterly line from Parthia to Elam. The third part consists of three nations that establish an almost perfect southeasterly line from Rome to Arabia. Indeed, the trajectories of both the first and third parts of Luke's list seem to converge on Arabia, depending of course how we understand this toponym.[155] In the third part, the Romans are given special emphasis by the extra modifiers (an adjectival participle and a compound appositive) that are used to describe them: they are "sojourning" Romans who include "both Jews and proselytes."[156] Moreover, the Romans are the only occidental nation/land included in the list. In the middle part of the list the first accusative object of the participle κατοικοῦντες (i.e., Mesopotamia) stands alone, whereas the other eight form dyads connected alternately by τε καί and καί (i.e., Judea–Cappadocia, Pontus–Asia, Phrygia–Pamphylia, Egypt–Libya).[157] This puts special emphasis on Mesopotamia, just as the aforementioned piling up of modifiers puts emphasis on the Romans. Compared with the other three dyads in the series, each of which applies to adjacent geographical areas, the first dyad is clearly anomalous, since Judea and Cappadocia do not belong together geographically.[158] Although the external evidence for Ἰουδαίαν is unassailable, various suggestions, both ancient and modern, have been made to emend the text on internal grounds.[159] For example, Martin Dibelius suggests Γαλατίαν, which at least coheres better with Cappadocia.[160] It is extremely doubtful, however, that "Judea" is a relic of an older list, made from a different geographical standpoint and perhaps for a different purpose.[161]

A completely different structural analysis is suggested by Richard Bauckham, who argues that "the names in Acts 2:9–11 are listed in four groups corresponding to the four cardinal points, beginning in the east and moving counterclockwise," with Jerusalem in the center.[162] Whereas other scholars have considered the inclusion of Judea in the list to be anomalous, for Bauckham, "Recognizing that Judaea is in the list because it is the centre of the pattern described by the names is the key to understanding the list."[163] His suggestion is elucidated on the chart.

	Cappadocia Pontus Asia Phrygia Pamphylia	
Egypt Libya Romans Cretans	**JUDEA**	Parthians Medes Elamites Mesopotamia
	Arabs	

According to Bauckham, the first group of names in the list (Parthians, Medes, Elamites, Mesopotamia) begins in the far east and moves in toward Judea. The second group of names (Cappadocia, Pontus, Asia, Phrygia, Pamphylia) contains places to the north of Judea, and follows an order which moves out from and back to Judea, ending at the point from which one might sail to Judea. The third group of names moves west from Judea through Egypt and Libya to Rome, and then back to Judea by a sea route calling at Crete. The last name (Arabs) represents the movement south from Judea.

Superficially, Bauckham's suggestion is attractive, for it seems to solve a number of interpretative difficulties, while supplying additional evidence that Jerusalem and the Land are central to Luke's thinking. At first sight, it would seem compelling geographically to group the first five names in the list (i.e., Parthians, Medes, Elamites, Mesopotamia, Judea), the next five names (i.e., Cappadocia, Pontus, Asia, Phrygia, Pamphylia), and the next two as well (i.e., Egypt, Libya). However, Bauckham's suggestion imposes a pattern on the list that largely ignores the actual grammatical structure of the text and thus misses how Luke designed the list to be read. The list contains no indication that it was constructed with the four cardinal points in mind.[164] Moreover, the asymmetry between the supposed cardinal points (north is represented by five names, whereas the south is represented by only one) and the convoluted pattern within several of them (away from Judea and back again) make this suggestion unlikely. Most importantly, it is impossible to isolate Judea as the centerpiece of the list (assuming, of course, that Ἰουδαίαν is original). Judea is merely one of the objects of the participle, and indeed one that is inextricably paired with Cappadocia ("both Judea and Cappadocia," Ἰουδαίαν τε καὶ Καππαδοκίαν).[165] In contrast, Mesopotamia or the Romans have much more claim to being emphasized in the text.[166]

Having examined the structure of the list, we turn next to its contents and background. As mentioned above, the repetition that we observed in the reaction of the astonished crowd (vv. 8, 11) may indicate that the intervening list is an insertion of possibly traditional material, especially since it is difficult to imagine that those dwelling in Judea would be astonished that they could understand the Galileans who were speaking to them. The difference in regional dialect could hardly be the cause of astonishment. If the Jews came "from every nation under heaven," then this must be a *pars pro toto*[167] list for all 70 or 72 nations of the world to which the Jewish people had been scattered.[168] Certainly, Luke knew that Jews were living in other parts of the world, as Acts itself shows (e.g., Syria, Cilicia, Macedonia, Greece).[169] This might indicate that the list was not of Luke's own making,[170] or it might mean that Luke has some reason for selecting these particular names (see below).[171] It has sometimes been alleged that the names "Medes" and "Elamites" are out of place in a list of contemporary nations, since these peoples had long since passed from the stage of history.[172] We may also point out that by the first century, the Parthian Empire would have subsumed all of them, listing them separately may be evidence either of archaicism or of an earlier source.[173]

A glance at the *Tübinger Atlas des Vorderen Orients* might be used to reinforce this point. Before the sixth century BCE, the Elamite Empires controlled much of the land east of the Tigris and Euphrates.[174] During the Achaemenid Age from the sixth to fourth centuries BCE, the Parthians, the Medes, and the Elamites appear on the map as separate peoples within their own distinguishable borders.[175] From the time of Alexander and onward, however, the distinctions begin to blur and fade. The map of Alexander's empire (336–323 BCE) includes Parthyene (without borders), but Elam and Media drop out of sight.[176]

When Alexander's empire was divided among his successors (ca. 303 BCE), the Seleucid territory was subdivided, in part, into the neighboring satrapies of Parthyaia and Media; Elam is once again absent from the map.[177] This situation continues through the third century BCE in the Seleucid Empire.[178] In the second century BCE, the Parthians begin to encroach on the Seleucid Empire and advance up to the Euphrates, swallowing up the territory that used to belong to Media and Elam; Media appears on the map as part of the Seleucid Empire, but Elam does not.[179] From 67 BCE to 14 CE, the Parthian Empire extends even further westward to engulf both the Tigris and Euphrates all the way to Zeugma.[180] Finally, in 14–138 CE, the Parthian Empire includes greatly reduced satrapies of Elymaïs and Media, which is actually divided into three smaller satrapies.[181] From this brief survey we could surmise that the first three nations in the list of Acts 2:9 refers back to a time when the Parthians, Medes and Elamites were still seen as separate peoples, that is, to the Achaemenid Age.

Here we must be cautious, however. Nomenclature is a constant impediment in such a study. The same regions occur under various appellations, and the same name may carry a meaning ethnical, political, or geographical.[182] Thus, "Medes" and "Elamites" continued to be called by their ancient names for a very long time after they had been conquered, even into the first century CE and beyond.[183] For example, in describing the northern border of Media, Polybius (5.44.9) mentions the Elamites. Strabo frequently refers to the Elamites and the Medes (e.g., *Geog.* 11.13.6 and 16.1.8, where both occur in the same context).[184] Appian (*Syr.* 32) lists "Elamites and Arabs" among those amassed in Antiochus' army. According to Pliny (*HN* 6.31.136–7), Marcus Agrippa gave measurements for Elymais, Media, Parthia, and Persis. According to Plutarch (*Pompey* 36.2), "the kings of the Elamites and the Medes" sent ambassadors to Pompey when he was in Lesser Armenia. Epiphanius (*Pan.* 9.4.5) shows that it is still possible to speak of a "king of Medes and Elamites." For the Rabbis, Elam was nothing other than another name for Persia and Media, which were themselves generally considered to be one entity.[185] It is difficult, therefore, to deduce very much from the first three names about the source of Luke's list.

Many suggestions have been made about the background of Luke's list,[186] and only a few can be discussed here. First of all, Gerd Lüdemann suggests that Luke has made use of an astrological list of nations similar to the one in Paulus Alexandrinus' *Elementa Apotelesmatica* (second

Table 3.

Acts 2:9–11	Zodiac Sign	Paulus Alexandrinus	Manilius	Dorotheus	Hermes Trismegistos	Ptolemy
1. Parthians	Aries	Persia	Hellespont, Propontis, Syria, Persia, Egypt (11)	Babylon, Arabia (15)	Ocean, Vactricani, Lydia	Britain, Gaul, Germany; in the center, Coele Syria, Palestine, Idumea, Judea (5)
2. Medes	Taurus	Babylonia	Scythia, Asia, Arabia	Media (2), Arabia (15), Egypt (11)	Medes (2), Amazonians, Semiramiden (=Babylon?)	Parthia (1), Media (2), Persia; in the center, the Cyclades, Cyprus, the coastal region of AM (8)
3. Elamites	Gemini	Cappadocia (6)	Black Sea	Cappadocia (6), Perrhabia, Phoenicia	Teukrians (Troas), Persis, Parthians (1)	Hyrcania, Armenia, Matiana: in the center, Cyrenaica, Marmarica, Lower Egypt (11)
4. Mesopotamia	Cancer	Armenia	India, Ethiopia	Thrace, Ethiopia	Syria, Assyria, Ethiopia	Numidia, Carthage, Africa; in the center, Bithynia, Phrygia (9), Colchica
5. Judea	Leo	Asia (8)	Phrygia, Bithynia, Cappadocia, Armenia, Macedonia	Greece, Phrygia (9), Pontus (7)	India, (two unknown lands)	Italy, Cisalpine Gaul, Sicily, Apulia; in the center, Phoenicia, Chaldea, Orchenia
6. Cappadocia	Virgo	Greece, Ionia	Rhodes, Caria, Doris, Ionia, Arcadia	Rhodes, Cyclades, Peloponnesus	Arabia (15), Armenia, Elephantine	Mesopotamia (4), Babylonia, Assyria: in the center, Hellas, Achaia, Crete (14)
7. Pontos	Libra	Libya (12), Cyrene	Italy	Cyrene, Italy	Egypt (11), Trachonitrum (Trachonitis?), Lybia (12)	Bactriana, Casperia, Serica: in the center, Thebais, Oasis, Troglodytica

8. Asia	Scorpio	Italy (13)	Carthage, Libya, Cyrenaica, Sardinia, Mediterranean Isles	Carthage, Libya (12), Sicily	Palestine (5). Phoenicia, Cilicia, Cappadocia (6), Galatia, Phrygia (9)	Metagonitis, Mauretania, Gaetulia; in the center, Syria, Commagene, Cappadocia (6)
9. Phrygia	Sagittarius	Cilicia, Crete (14)	Crete, Sicily	Gaul, Crete (14)	Achaia, Pamphylia (10), Sea of Nikere, Africa	Tyrrhenia, Celtica, Spain; in the center, Arabia Felix (15)
10. Pamphylia	Capricorn	Syria	Spain, Gaul, Germany	Cimmeria	Mauretania, Pannonia, Galatia	India, Ariana, Gedrosia; in the center, Thrace, Macedonia, Illyria
11. Egypt	Aquarius	Egypt (11)	Phoenicia, Cilicia, Lower Egypt	—	Syria, Germania, Sarmatia	Sauromatica, Oxiana. Sogdiana; in the center, Arabia (11), Azania, Middle Ethiopia
12. Libya	Pisces	Red Sea, India	Chaldea, Mesopotamia, Parthia, Red Sea	—	Britannia, Dacia, Chaukilikaonia, Etruria, Italia, Campania	Phazania, Nasamonitis, Garamantica; in the center, Lydia, Cilicia, Pamphylia (10)
13. Romans						
14. Cretes						
15. Arabs						

half of the 4th cent. CE),[187] in which each zodiac-god is paired with one or more countries.[188] This suggestion deserves careful consideration, because Luke's list of nations is obviously meant to elucidate the expression "Jews from every nation *under heaven*"[189] in v. 5, and, as we have seen above, the number 70/72 has astrological signficance in some texts.[190] While there are some interesting similarities between the lists, the differences are appreciable.[191] Besides the obvious differences in sequence and content, Paulus' list consists exclusively of *lands* that come under the influence of the zodiac-gods, whereas Luke's list consists exclusively of *peoples*. Even when Luke mentions lands (vv. 9b–10a), they occur as objects of οἱ κατοικοῦντες, thus emphasizing the peoples who inhabit the lands, rather than the lands themselves. If Luke's list were dependent on an astrological chorography such as that of Paulus, then we would expect a list of *lands* (see Table 3).[192] As Manilius puts the matter after giving his own list of correspondences, "Thus is the world forever distributed among the twelve signs, and from the signs themselves must the law prevailing among them be applied to the areas they govern..." (*Astronomica* 4.807–10). While the 3–9–3 structure of Luke's list is comparable to the Greco-Roman astrological lists, insofar as the latter often include for each sign of the zodiac three lands corresponding to three decan deities,[193] only the first and third parts of Acts 2:9–11 are triads. As we have seen, the middle part of Luke's list has instead a dyadic structure. In view of these considerations, an astrological background for Luke's list seems unlikely.

Second, C. K. Barrett argues that the nearest analogy to Luke's list appears to be the accounts of the distribution of Jews throughout the world.[194] Elsewhere, I have drawn particular attention to the alleged letter of King Agrippa I to Emperor Gaius (Philo, *Legat.* 276–329), which describes the Jewish Diaspora by listing many of the countries in which Jews lived and placing them in relationship to the metropolis Jerusalem as the implicit center of the worldwide Diaspora (§§ 281–4).[195] Although Barrett curiously neglects to mention any examples from the OT,[196] he appears correct in seeking a Jewish background for Luke's list. In Jewish usage, for example, Media and Medes remained current terms, designating the place and the members of one of the two main areas of the eastern Diaspora (the other being Babylonia).[197] The Medes may have been mentioned in Luke's list, because according to 2 Kgs. 17:6; 18:11, the ten tribes had been deported to the Medes.[198] As we have seen, Luke's mention of Anna from the tribe of Asher (Lk. 2:36) seems to reveal an interest in the Median Diaspora.[199]

Third, M. D. Goulder suggests that the list should be understood on the basis of the Table of Nations in Genesis 10: the first thirteen names (twelve Gentile peoples + the Jews) in Acts 2:9–11 correspond, with some telescoping, to the sixteen grandsons of Noah, arranged in an order from east to west, culminating in Rome; the last two names were added by "an over-careful scribe" who noticed that Crete and Arabia are "the only two pieces of land which do not send representatives to Pentecost, in the circle around Jerusalem covered by the first twelve peoples . . . "[200] Although Goulder's rather complicated suggestion fails to convince,[201] he may nevertheless be on the right track. I have independently argued that Luke's table of nations does indeed go back to the Table of Nations tradition based on Genesis 10.[202] This is not at all surprising if we think of scriptural emphasis on the nations in Luke-Acts,[203] and especially of Luke's use of the Table of Nations tradition in constructing the genealogy of Jesus (Lk. 3:23–38), which, as we have seen, is another evidence of Luke's universalistic perspective. Where else would one look first for a list of all the nations of the world that would fit the context of Acts than in the Table of Nations tradition?[204] For if the Jewish audience that is assembled in Jerusalem from "every nation under heaven" hears the speakers "in our own tongues" (ταῖς ἡμετέραις γλώσσαις, v. 11), then it is well to remember that the Table of Nations in Genesis 10 (vv. 5, 20, 31) explicitly lists the nations of the world stemming from the three sons of Noah not only "according to their tongues" (κατὰ γλώσσας αὐτῶν), but also "in their countries" (ἐν ταῖς χώραις αὐτῶν) and "in their nations" (ἐν τοῖς ἔθνεσιν αὐτῶν). Indeed, as we have seen, the expression "divided tongues" in Acts 2:3 may allude to the confusion of languages that resulted from the Tower of Babel episode. Moreover, the allusions in Acts 2 to the Tower of Babel in Genesis 11 put us in the same context as the Table of Nations in Genesis 10. When we put this together with the *Jubilees* interpretation of Pentecost as an observance initially given to Noah and hence to all humanity, it is difficult to avoid the conclusion that the list of nations in our text is purposely alluding to the Table of Nations tradition.

The Table of Nations tradition has a long and venerable history. According to Josephus (*Ap.* 1.130–1), the tradition was familiar in the East, even among non-Jews.[205] Not only is the tradition well represented in the Second-Temple period, but, as we shall see in the next two chapters, the Table of Nations tradition as mediated through the *Book of Jubilees* clearly influenced early Christian literature, including Ps.-Clementine *Recognitions* 1.27–71[206] and the *Diamerismos* of Hippolytus (*Chron.* 44–239).[207]

Both of these writings are important to our considerations here, although they cannot be properly introduced until later.

Providing a very full list of *both* the nations *and* the countries which belong to Shem, Ham, and Japheth, Hippolytus' *Diamerismos* contains a parallel for practically every name in Acts 2:9–11, except 'Ιουδαίαν, whose occurrence in Luke's list is often considered to be anomalous on other grounds (see above). Let us examine the parallels between Acts 2:9–11 and the *Diamerismos* according to the order in Luke's list:[208]

(1)   Parthians (Πάρθοι): Hippolytus' *Diamerismos* mentions the Πάρθοι both in the list of the 16 nations of Shem (§190.10) and in the list of colonies of the "unknown" nations (§204).[209] According to the latter, there is a direct relationship between the Medes and Persians and the Parthians: "Colonies of Persians and Medians became Parthians and the surrounding nations of Eirene to Coele Syria" (τῶν Περσῶν καὶ Μήδων ἄποικοι γεγόνασι Πάρθοι καὶ τὰ πέριξ ἔθνη τῆς Εἰρήνης ἕως τῆς Κοίλης Συρίας).

(2)   Medes (Μῆδοι): The *Diamerismos* frequently mentions the Μῆδοι. They appear first in the list of the sons and grandsons of Japheth and the nations that stem from them, where Madai (Gen. 10:2; 1 Chr. 1:5) is given as the forefather of the Medes (§59, Μαδάι, ἀφ' οὗ Μῆδοι).[210] Later, they appear in another list of the nations of Japheth (§0.1), including the list of six Japhethite nations that understand writing (§82.5). The Medes next appear in the list of the nations of *Shem* (§190.3), the very list in which, as we have seen, the Parthians appear (§190.10). Is this a simple mistake or is there another explanation? We may note that according to *Jub.* 10:35, Madai, who was allotted territory in the Far West but who had married into Shem's family, did not like the land near the sea and requested other territory "from Elam, Asshur, and Arpachshad, his wife's brother. He has settled in the land of Medeqin near his wife's brother until the present." With some plausibility, therefore, the Medes can be listed under the Shemites, based on the Table of Nations tradition in *Jubilees*. Evidently, Hippolytus' *Diamerismos* is dependent on *Jubilees* for this point.[211] The Medes also appear in the list of the Shemite nations that know writing (§192.3). Finally, the Medes

are mentioned in the table of 72 nations whose languages were confused (§ 200.4).

(3)   Elamites ('Ελαμῖται): In the list of the sons, grandsons and great-grandsons of Shem, the *Diamerismos* mentions the Elamites as descendants of Elam (§ 160, 'Ελάμ, ὅθεν οἱ 'Ελυμαῖοι).[212] The change in vocalization from alpha to upsilon may seem surprising, but Josephus also has 'Ελυμαῖοι (*Ant.* 1.143). Moreover, Epiphanius, *Ancoratus* 113.2, who is dependent on Hippolytus' *Diamerismos*,[213] has both 'Ελυμαῖοι and 'Ελαμῖται. Hippolytus also includes the Elamites in another list of the nations of Shem (§ 190.12), the same list in which the Parthians (§ 190.10) and the Medes (190.3) appear, as we have seen above. Hence, from the perspective of the *Diamerismos*, the first three names in Acts 2:9–11 can be regarded as nations of Shem.

(4)   Those who inhabit Mesopotamia (οἱ κατοικοῦντες τὴν Μεσοποταμίαν): The *Diamerismos* lists Mesopotamia as one of the countries of the sons of Shem (§ 194.7).

(5)   [Those who inhabit] Judea ('Ιουδαίαν): The *Diamerismos* does not list Judea, not even among the countries of the sons of Shem (§§ 193–4). However, the 'Ιουδαῖοι[214] are listed among the nations of Shem (§ 190.1), together with other nations that Luke's list also includes (i.e., Medes [§ 190.3], Parthians [§ 190.10], and Elamites [§ 190.12]). The *Diamerismos* also lists the Jews among the Shemite nations who understand writing (§ 192.1). Finally, Jews are anachronistically included among the 72 nations whose languages were confused at the Tower of Babel (§ 200.1).

(6)   [Those who inhabit] Cappadocia (Καππαδοκίαν): The *Diamerismos* lists Cappodocia among the countries of Japheth (§ 84.5).[215] Cappadocia is mentioned once again in a list of the twelve most famous mountains, which includes the "Taurus [mountains] in Cilicia and in Cappadocia" (§ 235.3).

(7)   [Those who inhabit] Pontos (Πόντον): The *Diamerismos* includes Pontos among the colonies of the "unknown" nations (§ 214.15; cf. 233).

(8)   [Those who inhabit] Asia (τὴν Ἀσίαν): The *Diamerismos* refers to "a certain part of Asia called 'Ionia'" (μέρος τι τῆς Ἀσίας τὸ καλούμενον 'Ιωνία) as one of "the islands of Japheth" (§ 88.12). Subsequently, "Asians" are listed between "Bosporans" and "Isaurians" among the 72 nations whose languages were confused (§ 200.39). "Asians" are also listed among the colonies of the "unknown" nations, specifically among the colonies of the Greek nations (§ 209.4).

(9)   [Those who inhabit] Phrygia (Φρυγίαν): The *Diamerismos* lists Phrygia among the countries of Ham in Asia Minor (§ 151.18, 26). Likewise, the Phrygians are included in the list of the nations of Ham (§ 132.16), including those that understand writing (§ 135.4). The identification of Phrygia with Ham seems to be idiosyncratic in the Table of Nations tradition.[216] We would expect Phrygia to be regarded as the territory of either Japheth (cf. Josephus, *Ant.* 1.126) or possibly Shem (cf. *Jub.* 9:6).[217] Even the *Diamerismos* otherwise restricts the territory of Ham to Africa (e.g., §§ 48, 130, 136). The Phrygians also appear in the list of the 72 nations whose languages were confused (200.45).

(10)   [Those who inhabit] Pamphylia (Παμφυλίαν): The *Diamerismos* lists Pamphylia as another one of the countries of Ham in Asia Minor (§ 151.14). Again, this seems idiosyncratic in the Table of Nations tradition (see above on Phrygia).

(11)   [Those who inhabit] Egypt (Αἴγυπτον): The *Diamerismos* indicates that the Hamite peoples inhabit from Egypt to the Southern Ocean (§ 133). Egypt is included among the countries of Ham in Africa (§ 138, Αἴγυπτος σὺν τοῖς περὶ αὐτὴν πᾶσιν). Ham is said to have the River Geon, called the Nile, which circles all Egypt and Ethiopia (§ 156). Rinocoroura separates Syria and Egypt (§§ 188, 196).

(12)   [Those who inhabit] the parts of Libya adjacent to Cyrene (τὰ μέρη τῆς Λιβύης τῆς κατὰ Κυρήνην):[218] The *Diamerismos* lists two countries named Libya as countries of Ham in Africa: (a) Λιβύη ἡ παρεκτείνουσα μέχρι Κορκυρίνης (§ 143) and

(b) Λιβύη ἑτέρα ἡ παρεκτείνουσα ⟨ἀπὸ Λέπτεως⟩ μέχρι μικρᾶς Σύρτεως (§146). Furthermore, in the list of the 12 most famous mountains, the Altas mountains are located in Libya to the Great River (§235.4).

(13) Romans (Ῥωμαῖοι): Like Acts 2:9–11, the *Diamerismos* puts special emphasis on the Romans, who are mentioned some five times.[219] In the list of the sons and grandsons of Japheth, Kitioi (= Kittim) is given as one of the sons of Javan (Gen. 10:4; 1 Chr. 1:7) and as the forefather of the Romans (§72, Κίτιοι, ἀφ᾽ οὗ Ῥωμαῖοι ⟨οἱ⟩ καὶ Λατῖνοι).[220] The Romans also appear in a list of the nations of Japheth (§80.33, ⟨Λα⟩τῖνοι οἱ καὶ Ῥωμαῖοι), including those Japhethite nations that, like the Medes (see above), understand writing (§82.2). The Romans are mentioned in the table of the 72 nations whose languages were confused, where they are once again identified with the Kittim (§200.58, Ῥωμαῖοι οἱ καὶ Λατῖνοι καὶ Κιτιαῖοι). Finally, in the list of the colonies of the "unknown" nations, the *Diamerismos* refers to the seven nations and colonies of the Romans/Kittim (§215, Ῥωμαίων δὲ τῶν καὶ Κιτιέων [τῶν καὶ Λατίνων κεκλημένων] ἔθνη καὶ ἀποικίαι εἰσὶν ἑπτά).

(14) Cretans (Κρῆτες): The *Diamerismos* lists the Cretans among the nations of Ham (132.28).[221] Furthermore, Crete is given as one of the islands of Ham (153.11). In the list of colonies of the "unknown" nations, Crete is listed as a Greek colony (212.2).

(15) Arabs (Ἄραβες): In the list of the nations of Shem, the *Diamerismos* distinguishes two Arab peoples: (a) Ἄραβες [οἱ] πρῶτοι οἱ καλούμενοι Κεδρούσιοι (§190.14) and (b) Ἄραβες δεύτεροι [οἱ καλούμενοι] (§190.15).[222] This is the same list in which, as we have seen, the Jews (§190.1), the Medes (§190.3), the Parthians (§190.10), and the Elamites (§190.12) also appear. The *Diamerismos* goes on to distinguish two countries of Shem called Arabia (§§194.8, Ἀραβία ἡ ἀρχαία; 194.11, Ἀραβία ἡ εὐδαίμων). Both Arab nations are listed among the 72 nations whose languages were confused

(§ 200.6). And in the list of colonies of "unknown" nations, there is talk of the colonies of the Arabs (§ 205, Ἀράβων δὲ ἄποικοι γεγόνασιν Ἄραβες οἱ εὐδαίμονες). Finally, the list of the 12 most famous mountains includes Mt. Sinai in Arabia (§ 235.9, Ναυσαῖον τὸ καὶ Σινᾶ ἐν τῇ Ἀραβίᾳ).

If we apply the *Diamerismos'* identifications to Luke's list,[223] an interesting triadic pattern emerges, based on the three sons of Noah. The first three names in Acts 2:9–11 represent nations of Shem, and the last three names represent all three sons of Noah (Japheth, Ham, and Shem – the same order as in Genesis 10 and 1 Chronicles 1), thus producing a ring structure. In between, we have a list of nine countries – one that stands alone (Shem) and four pairs ([Shem]–Japheth, Japheth–Japheth, Ham–Ham, Ham–Ham) – so that, once again, all three sons of Noah are represented.[224] The whole 3–9–3 structure of the list seems to reinforce the perceived emphasis on the three sons of Noah. If Luke's purpose was to construct a representative *pars pro toto* list of "Jews from every nation under heaven" (Acts 2:5), then the list that we find in Acts 2:9–11 provides a good sample.[225] The same procedure can be seen in Isa. 66:18–20,[226] where each of the three sons of Noah is represented in a *pars pro toto* list of "all nations and tongues" that God intends to gather to Jerusalem.[227] Moreover, the same question applies to the Isaianic list that is often asked of Acts 2:9–11: why were these particular nations selected (or why were others, such as Greece and Syria, omitted)? Frequently, it is impossible to ascertain the precise criteria for inclusion in ancient ethnic lists. Some lists have a recognizable order.[228] In the case of Acts 2:9–11 and Isa. 66:18–20, there may be no definitive answer to the question in every detail.[229]

In a few cases, scriptural allusions may provide a rationale for the inclusion of a particular people in Luke's list.[230] Isa. 11:10–12, for example, may explain the inclusion of the Elamites in Acts 2:9, for the former is also a *pars pro toto* list of the Jewish Diaspora. According to this Isaianic text, the dispersed will be gathered from the "four corners of the earth" in the messianic age. This fits well with Luke's Christological thrust in context (cf. Acts 2:14–36) and reinforces the restoration idea that we noticed in v. 5 and elsewhere in Luke-Acts. We should not be surprised, therefore, if one name from Isaiah's list of nations – the Elamites – was included in Acts 2:9–11 precisely because it provides an allusion to Isa. 11:11. Although the variation in the spelling of the name in the two texts (i.e., Ἐλαμῖται,

Αἰλαμιτῶν) may speak against this possibility, we should note that Symmachus and other Greek manuscripts of Isa. 11:11 read ᾽Ελαμιτῶν (Göttingen edition). Interestingly enough, Eusebius interprets Isa. 11:11 in light of Acts 2:5–11 in his *Commentary on Isaiah* (63).[231] Similarly, the mention of the Arabs in Luke's list may find an explanation in Psalm 72, which contains a *pars pro toto* list of the nations of the world that will come to pay tribute to the messiah and specifically mentions the Arabs (cf. Ps. 72[71]:10).

If Isaiah 11 is a source for Luke's list, then it is worth noting that the same passage also refers to the hope of the "nations": "And in that day there will be the root of Jesse and he who will arise to rule the nations. The nations will hope in him, and his rest will be honor. (11) And it will be in that day [that] the Lord will again show his hand to be zealous for the remnant that is left of the people, which is left by the Assyrians, and [the remnant] from Egypt and Babylonia and Ethiopia and from the Elamites and from the rising of the sun and from Arabia. (12) And he will lift up a sign to the nations and gather the lost ones of Israel and gather the dispersed ones of Judah from the four ends of the earth." Hence, Isa. 11:10–12 has both the centrifugal and the centripetal aspects that we have become accustomed to seeing in OT restoration texts. Moreover, Isa. 11:10–12 gives Bauckham's geographical analysis of Acts 2:9–11 a possible traditional basis. For Isaiah 11 does refer to "the four ends of the earth." Even though our structural analysis shows that Luke (or his source) constructed the list to be read in a different way, nevertheless the traditional background of the list may allow it to be read as Bauckham suggests. This must remain speculation, however.

In sum, Hippolytus' *Diamerismos* helps us to see how the table of nations in Acts 2:9–11 could be derived from the Table of Nations tradition. Thus, P. S. Alexander appears to be substantially correct: " . . . if the outpouring of the Spirit at Pentecost is seen in Acts as a reversal of God's confusion of tongues after the Flood (Gen. 11:7), then the catalogue of nations is most obviously related to Genesis 10. The brief list in Acts is only an allusion to the longer Table in Genesis."[232] To this we would merely add that Luke's list does not allude directly to Genesis 10, but to Genesis 10 as mediated through Jewish (and possibly Jewish–Christian) tradition, especially *Jubilees* 8–9. Certainly, there is some concrete evidence in early Christian literature that Pentecost was indeed understood in this light. For example, Ephrem the Syrian (*Nat.* 1.46) relates the division of the earth in the days of Peleg (Gen. 10:25) to Christ's division of earth among the apostles through tongues at Pentecost.[233]

In the context of Luke's two-volume work, the Pentecost event in Acts 2:1–47 presents a crucial turning point in the history of the nascent Christian movement. For Pentecost inaugurates the Spirit-impelled mission that the resurrected Lord had already promised. At the end of Luke's Gospel, the resurrected Lord had promised his disciples: "And see, I am sending upon you the promise of my Father; so stay here in the city until you have been clothed with power from on high" (Lk. 24:49). Acts 1:8 picks up the same promise, expressed in other words: "But you will receive power when the Holy Spirit has come upon you; and you will be my witnesses in Jerusalem, in all Judea and Samaria, and to the end of the earth." Now Pentecost brings outpouring of the Spirit on the disciples (and on "all flesh" [2:17]) and thus the beginning of the mission in Jerusalem, the first stage in the Spirit-impelled mission that would eventually reach the end of the earth. As such, the Pentecost event is an anticipation of the whole mission to the nations which unfolds in the rest of the Book of Acts. Our passage contains both the centripetal and centrifugal movements which are characteristic of the Book of Acts as a whole and of traditional expectations of the restoration of Israel.

Seen in this light, the Diaspora Jews who gathered in Jerusalem represent "every nation under heaven" (Acts 2:5) and point to the universalistic thrust of the Book of Acts. The allusion to the Tower of Babel in the previous context helps us see that the list of nations in vv. 9–11 goes back to the Table of Nations. According to the *Book of Jubilees*, the Feast of Pentecost itself was originally incumbent upon all people, when it was given to Noah after the Flood. Just as the sending out of the 70/72 disciples, based on the Table of Nations tradition, anticipates the mission to the nations in the Book of Acts, so also the *pars pro toto* list of nations in Acts 2:9–11, again based on the Table of Nations tradition, anticipates the later mission to the nations.[234]

Peter's speech in the Temple (Acts 3:11–26)

In Acts 3:11–26, Peter's speech in the Temple continues both the theme of Israel's restoration and the universalistic aspect of Luke-Acts. Indeed, the restoration of Israel is seen here as a means to wider blessing, which includes "all the families of the world."[235] The repentance of Israel will bring "times of refreshment," until God culminates these by sending his Messiah, Jesus, who remains in heaven until the prophesied "times of restoration of all things" (χρόνοι ἀποκαταστάσεως πάντων) reach their fulfillment (v. 21).

The speech concludes with the statement directed to Peter's Jewish audience, but with an eye again on the nations: "You are the descendants of the prophets and of the covenant that God gave to your ancestors, saying to Abraham, 'And in your descendants all the families of the earth shall be blessed (καὶ ἐν τῷ σπέρματί σου [ἐν]ευλογηθήσονται πᾶσαι αἱ πατριαὶ τῆς γῆς)'" (v. 25). This is a citation of Gen. 12:3 (καὶ ἐνευλογηθήσονται ἐν σοὶ πᾶσαι αἱ φυλαὶ τῆς γῆς), which is often repeated in Genesis.[236] We should not treat this citation atomistically and divorced from its OT context, for Luke was obviously acquainted with the cycle of scripture reading in the synagogue (cf. Lk. 4:16–22; Acts 13:13–16). According to the Babylonian Talmud (b. Meg. 29b), the Torah reading was so ordered that the whole of the Pentateuch was read consecutively in a triennial cycle. Both Philo (Op. 128) and Josephus (Ap. 2.175) acknowledge that Jews regularly attended the synagogue, where the scripture was read and expounded. Deut. 31:10 requires the public reading of the law once every seven years, at the Feast of Tabernacles, but by the first century the practice was to read portions of the law weekly in the synagogue. Those having such a thorough grounding in scripture would immediately understand "all the families/nations of the earth" as recalling the Table of Nations in Genesis 10, where these families/nations[237] are listed for the first time. Seen in this light, the citation of Gen. 12:3 in Acts 3:25 resonates with the list in Acts 2:9–11, understood against the background of the Table of Nations. Both Israel and the nations are included in this promise to Abraham.

The apostolic council (Acts 15)

In Luke's portrayal, the Christian mission emanates from the center, Jerusalem, and proceeds to the ends of the earth. However, as we have already mentioned, the mother church is not simply left behind in this centrifugal movement outward. It continues to exercise decisive control even over the developing mission to the nations. The most important example of the Jerusalem church's authority over and influence on this mission is found in the account of the Jerusalem council in Acts 15. Even Paul's own description of this event in Gal. 2:1–10 admits that in coming to Jerusalem, Paul was seeking the recognition and approval of the mother church for his mission to the nations (Gal. 2:1–10).[238] While this may have been partly a pragmatic matter, Paul, who understands himself in context as an apostle with divine authority independent of the Jerusalem church, would hardly admit any dependence on the Jerusalem church unless this was very important to him. Moreover, Paul elsewhere acknowledges that in some fundamental sense, his gospel proceeds from Jerusalem (Rom. 15:19) on its way ultimately to Spain (Rom. 15:24, 28).

According to Acts 15, the main issue at stake at the Jerusalem council was whether Gentile believers must be circumcised (i.e., become Jews) in order to belong to the eschatological people of God. This issue arose in Antioch, when "certain individuals came down from Judea and began teaching the brothers, 'Unless you are circumcised according to the custom of Moses, you cannot be saved'" (v. 1). The question here is not merely one of table fellowship, but rather more fundamentally one of entrance requirements: what Gentiles must do to be *saved*. As Markus Bockmuehl puts the question: "Should Gentiles who believed in Christ be treated as proselytes or as Noachides?"[239] So Paul and Barnabas and a few others were appointed to go up to Jerusalem in order to discuss this problem with the apostles and the elders (v. 2) and to ask for an authoritative ruling. When the delegates arrived in Jerusalem, Jewish Christians from the sect of the Pharisees added the demand of observing the law of Moses: "It is necessary for them to be circumcised and ordered to keep the law of Moses" (v. 5).[240]

During the meeting, Peter and James address these issues with complementary arguments. On the one hand, Peter argues *experientially* that, like Jewish Christians, believing Gentiles have already received the Holy Spirit (vv. 7–9; cf. 10:44–8; 11:17), showing that the latter are acceptable to God without circumcision,[241] and that there is therefore no need for them to proselytize. Peter also argues *historically* (and implicitly *scripturally*) that Israel was never been able to keep the law of Moses, demonstrating that the Gentiles should not be subjected to a failed system (v. 10). On the other hand, James, after voicing his agreement with Peter's position,[242] goes on to argue *scripturally* that the prophets, when they predicted that the nations would participate in the eschatological, messianic Temple, also made it clear that they would do so as Gentile nations and not as proselytes (vv. 15–18, citing Amos 9:11–12; Jer. 12:15; Isa. 45:21). From this James concludes with an authoritative judgment (διὸ ἐγὼ κρίνω) that Gentile Christians are not obligated to the law of Moses, but that four specific prohibitions are nevertheless binding on them (Acts 15:19–20). These are the terms of the so-called Apostolic Decree (vv. 28–29; cf. 21:25).[243]

Let us look more closely at James' crucial argument from scripture, introduced by καθὼς γέγραπται. The citation (or combination of citations) is shown in Table 4.

Table 4.

Acts 15:16–18	Hos. 3:5 LXX	Amos 9:11–12 LXX	Jer. 12:15–16 LXX	Isa. 45:20–22 MT
After this I will return, and I will rebuild the dwelling of David, which has fallen; from its ruins I will rebuild it, and I will set it up, (17) so that all other peoples may seek the Lord – even all nations over whom my name has been called. Thus says the Lord, who has been making these things (18) known from long ago.	And after these things, the children of Israel will return and will seek the Lord their God and David their king.	In that day, I will raise up the tent of David that has fallen, and repair its breaches, and raise up its ruins, and rebuild it as in the days of old, (12) so that the rest of humanity – even all nations, over whom my name is called – may seek earnestly. Thus says the Lord God who does these things.	And it will be that, after I have cast them [sc. the nations] out, I will return and have mercy on them, and will cause them to dwell, each in his inheritance and each in his land. And it shall be that, if they will indeed learn the way of my people, to swear by my name, "The Lord lives," as they taught my people to swear by Baal, then also they shall be built in the midst of my people.	Assemble yourselves and come together, draw near, you survivors of the nations! They have no knowledge – those who carry about their wooden idols, and keep on praying to a god that cannot save. (21) Declare and present your case; let them take counsel together! Who told this long ago? Who declared it of old? Was it not I, the LORD? There is no other god besides me, a righteous God and a Savior; there is no one besides me. (22) Turn to me and be saved, all the ends of the earth! For I am God, and there is no other.

This citation strongly emphasizes the restoration of Israel and the consequent inclusion of the nations. However, it remains disputed exactly what aspect of the restoration is in view. Much depends on what the rebuilding of the "the tent of David" (τὴν σκηνὴν Δαυειδ) means. Several possibilities have been suggested.[244] (1) Bruce Chilton and Jacob Neusner interpret it as a reference to the restoration of the house of David through Jesus and his brother James.[245] (2) Jacob Jervell regards the rebuilding of the tent of David as a metaphor for the restoration of Israel itself.[246] (3) Richard Bauckham interprets "the tent of David" as "the eschatological Temple which God will build, as the place of his eschatological presence, in the messianic age when Davidic rule is restored to Israel."[247] He will build this new Temple so that all the Gentile nations may seek his presence there. Deciding between these alternatives is not easy, and for our purposes, the question can be left open.[248] It should be pointed out, however, that in the pre-70 situation of Luke's account, a literal Temple in Jerusalem cannot be immediately ruled out in favor of a metaphorical interpretation of "the tent of David."[249] Even a later, Jewish–Christian writing, such as Pseudo-Clementine *Recognitions* 1.27–71, to which we shall turn in the next chapter, may well have reckoned with the renewal of the literal Temple in Jerusalem, albeit on a new basis.[250] The OT contains many texts which speak of the participation of the Gentile nations in the eschatological Temple in Jerusalem.[251] For example, Isa. 56:3–8 is directed against the exclusion of God-fearing foreigners from participation in the Temple cult and promises such foreigners full participation in the cult on the basis of the universal character of the Jerusalem Temple as a "house of prayer for all nations" at the time of the restoration of Israel.[252] As we have seen, Isa. 66:18–21, which has many features in common with 56:3–8,[253] expects that YHWH will gather all nations to Jerusalem (v. 18), and that in the process they will bring the Jewish exiles with them (v. 20). Yahweh will send those who have been saved as missionaries to the nations (v. 19). According to Claus Westermann, Isaiah 66 even states that some of these Gentiles who make the eschatological pilgrimage to Zion will be made into priests and Levites for the Lord (v. 21)![254]

> Like the parallel passage in Matt. 21:13, Luke's account of the Cleansing of the Temple (Lk. 19:45–6) omits πᾶσιν τοῖς ἔθνεσιν from the citation of Isa. 56:7, leaving merely "My house will be called a house of all prayer . . ." This omission is perhaps surprising in light of Luke's universalistic perspective. On the one hand, it may indicate that with the destruction of Jerusalem in 70 CE, the Temple ceased to be a place of prayer for all nations,

and that the church gradually came to be seen as the new place of prayer.[255] Hence, the evangelists modified Mark's longer and more original version.[256] On the other hand, it seems possible that Luke deleted πᾶσιν τοῖς ἔθνεσιν because for him the mission to the nations began with Pentecost (see above on Acts 2:5–11). In that case, the omission is not a sign that the Temple has been spiritualized in Acts, but rather that Jesus' criticism may have been viewed as premature.

Luke obviously thinks of the Jerusalem Temple as a house of prayer (cf. Lk. 2:37; 18:10). From the very beginning, the Temple had been a place of prayer, as Solomon's prayer of dedication makes clear (1 Kgs. 8:29–30, 41–3; cf. 3 Macc. 2:10). Jostein Ådna argues that the original meaning of Jesus' Temple action was as a messianic sign of the replacement of the sacrifical cult in the Jerusalem Temple by his own atoning death.[257] Overturning the tables of the money-changers signified that the money which sustained the daily whole burnt offerings had been cut off; hence, the sacrifices that provided atonement and forgiveness of sins had been abrogated.[258] This interpretation of Jesus' Temple action seems to be confirmed by the fact that in the time immediately after Jesus' death and resurrection, the earliest Christians in Jerusalem continue to treat the Temple as a house of prayer.[259] Thus, just as Jesus taught (Mk. 11:17) and practiced (cf. Mk. 14:49 par.; John 7:14, 28; 8:20; Lk. 18:10), the early Christians regarded the Temple as having an ongoing function as a house of prayer, but no longer as a place of atonement for the nation.[260] According to Hegesippus' legendary account in Eusebius (*HE* 2.23.6), James the Lord's brother went alone to the Temple, where he "constantly went down on his knees to pray to God and to ask him for forgiveness for his people."[261]

This contrast between prayer and sacrifice may seem like a false dichotomy, for contemporary Jewish sources describe an integral relationship between the two.[262] Nevertheless, we have evidence of a Palestinian, Jewish–Christian source in the Pseudo-Clementines (*Rec.* 1.27–71) which, written approximately forty-five years after the destruction of the Temple and in obvious dependence on Luke-Acts, maintained a sharp distinction between the proper function of the Temple as a house of prayer and its idolatrous misuse as a place of sacrifice.[263] While we need not assume that all the earliest Jewish Christians in Jerusalem regarded the sacrificial cult as idolatrous, they may

well have held a similar view about the proper function of the
Temple as primarily or exclusively a house of prayer. Luke himself seems to hold this view when he repeatedly emphasizes the
post-Easter function of the Temple for the church.

Having shown from scripture that the nations would participate in the
eschatological Temple as nations (and not as proselytes), James argues
emphatically against those who insist on circumcision and other obliga-
tions of the Mosaic law as an entrance requirement for Gentile believers.
Yet how does James conclude on the basis of this argument (διὸ ἐγὼ
κρίνω) that Gentile believers are nevertheless required to observe four
specific prohibitions (Acts 15:19–20)? It seems at first like a *non se-
quitur*. The text states: "(19) Therefore I have reached the decision that
we should not trouble those Gentiles who are turning to God, (20) but we
should write to them to abstain only from things polluted by idols and
from fornication and from whatever has been strangled and from blood
(τοῦ ἀπέχεσθαι τῶν ἀλισγημάτων τῶν εἰδώλων καὶ τῆς πορνείας
καὶ τοῦ πνικτοῦ καὶ τοῦ αἵματος)." On the basis of this authoritative
decision, a letter is sent from the Jerusalem church to Antioch containing
the following decree: "(28) For it has seemed good to the Holy Spirit and
to us to impose on you no further burden than these essentials: (29) that
you abstain from what has been sacrificed to idols and from blood and
from what is strangled and from fornication (ἀπέχεσθαι εἰδωλοθύτων
καὶ αἵματος καὶ πνικτῶν καὶ πορνείας). If you keep yourselves from
these, you will do well."

Most NT scholars interpret the prohibitions of this decree in light of
prohibitions in the Holiness Code of Leviticus 17–26 that apply to resident aliens who live with the people of Israel (esp. 17–20 or 17–18 or
18–20).[264] This seems to be confirmed by the scriptural reason that James
gives for his decision: "For in every city, for generations past, Moses has
had those who proclaim him, for he has been read aloud every sabbath
in the synagogues" (Acts 15:21).[265] Moreover, the Holiness Code contains prohibitions which approximate the four listed in Acts 15 (cf. also
21:25).[266] The difficulty with the view is that the Apostolic Decree is
directed not to resident aliens in the Land of Israel but to Gentiles outside the Land. It would seem arbitrary to reapply these regulations to a
Diaspora situation.

Another prominent approach is to see the prohibitions of the Apostolic
Decree as a reflection of the Noachic Decree in Genesis 9.[267] These two
interpretations are not necessarily mutually exclusive, for, as Matthias
Millard has argued, there is an intertextual relationship between Genesis 9

and Leviticus 18 and 20.[268] Moreover, as Michael E. Stone has observed, there seems to have been an attempt in several OT pseudepigrapha to trace priestly traditions back to Noah.[269] Furthermore, Bockmuehl argues convincingly that the form in which the prohibitions are given in Acts 15 is reminiscent of the second-century lists of Noachic Commandments.[270] Although these commandments never assume a fixed and final definition in early Judaism, the first explicit mention of the Noachic Commandments in the formal sense occurs in the Tannaitic period. The *locus classicus* is found in *t. AZ* 8.4 (before 230 CE): "Seven commandments were given to the children of Noah: regarding the establishment of courts of justice, idolatry, blasphemy, fornication, bloodshed, theft [and the torn limb]." This list alone covers two of four prohibitions in Acts 15: "idolatry" and "fornication."

Our evidence for the Noachic Commandments is not limited to rabbinic sources.[271] Already in *Jub.* 7:20, we find the commandments given by Noah to his grandsons to "bless the one who had created them" and to "keep themselves from fornication, uncleanness, and from all injustice."[272] Ps.-Clementine *Rec.* 1.27–71, which is probably the earliest extensive commentary on Acts,[273] identifies the first commandment given to Noah after the flood as the prohibition against eating blood, "for the flood had taken place precisely because of this" (1.30.1).[274] While this prohibition against eating blood obviously derives from God's covenant with Noah in Gen. 9:4,[275] the idea of a causal relationship between the flood and violating the commands later given to Noah after the flood most likely stems from *Jub.* 7:21–4 (or possibly a source common to *Rec.* 1.27–71 and *Jub.* 7:21–4).[276] For according to this passage, Noah gave his sons the commandments after the flood with the explanation: "For it was on account of these three things that the flood was on the earth . . . " (*Jub.* 7:21).[277] As we have already mentioned and will examine more thoroughly in Chap. 4, Ps.-Clem. *Rec.* 1.27–71 is dependent on *Jubilees.* Hence, despite the doubts of some modern scholars about the relevance of *Jub.* 7:20 for the situation of Gentiles in the early church, a good argument can be made in favor of it.[278] In reflecting on Gen. 9:4 and the double prohibition against eating blood in Acts 15:20, 29 (πνικτόν/πνικτά and αἷμα),[279] *Rec.* 1.30.1 seems to reinterpret *Jub.* 7:21–4 as a prohibition against eating blood.[280] Outside of our Jewish–Christian source, however, the Pseudo-Clementines interpret the Apostolic Decree with reference to Leviticus 17–18.[281] In the final analysis, this need not mean a fundamental difference in interpretation, if, as we have mentioned, there is an intertextual relationship between these passages already in the OT. Moreover, as James C. VanderKam points out, Leviticus 18 appears to be part of the basis of Noah's actions and words in *Jubilees* 6–7.[282] Or, to put it another way, "The Noachide covenant is transformed [in *Jubilees*] into a paradigm of the covenant with Israel on Sinai."[283]

The importance of the Noachic prohibition against blood cannot be overemphasized.[284] According to *Jub.* 6:18 (cf. 6:38; 11:2), eating blood was among the first great evils committed by Noah's children after his death, even though it had been strictly proscribed in the covenant with Noah (*Jub.* 6:7, 10, 12; 21:18). In *Jub.* 7:27–32, Noah sternly warns his children not to consume blood, predicting dire consequences if they do and linking the act with shedding blood.[285] In *Jub.* 21:1–11, Abraham teaches Isaac the prohibition of eating blood (vv. 6–7) and other laws pertaining to sacrifice which "I found written in the book[s] of my ancestors, in the Words of Enoch and in the Words of Noah" (v. 10).[286] Similarly in an addition to the *Testament of Levi*, Isaac instructs Levi about the prohibition against eating blood, basing his teaching on the following reason: "For so my father Abraham commanded me; for so he found [it] in the writing of the book of Noah concerning the blood (οὕτως γάρ μοι ἐνετείλατο ὁ πατήρ μου Ἀβραάμ, ὅτι οὕτως εὗρεν ἐν τῇ γραφῇ τῆς βίβλου τοῦ Νῶε περὶ τοῦ αἵματος)."[287] Evidently, the prohibition of blood in the *Book of Jubilees* became the basis of an ongoing (written) tradition.[288]

There is evidence that the church in the second century maintained a ban on the consumption of blood based on the Noachic commandment.[289] The first Christian writer after Luke to mention the prohibition of blood is Justin Martyr (*Dial.* 20.1), who refers to it in connection with the Noachic commandments in Gen. 9:3–4: "Moreover, you were commanded to abstain from certain kinds of food, in order that you might keep God before your eyes while you ate and drank, seeing that you were prone and very ready to depart from his knowledge, as Moses also says: 'The people ate and drank, and rose up to play' (Exod. 32:6). And again: 'Jacob ate, and was satisfied, and grew fat; and he who was beloved kicked: he grew fat, became thick, was enlarged, and he forsook God who had made him' (Deut. 32:15). For it was told you by Moses in the book of Genesis, that God granted to Noah, being a just man (Gen. 6:9),[290] to eat of every animal, but not of flesh with the blood (Gen. 9:3–4), which is dead."[291] Tertullian (*Apol.* 9.13) explicitly connects the prohibition of strangulated meat and the consumption of blood: "Blush for your vile ways before the Christians, who have not even the blood of animals at their meals of simple and natural food, who abstain from strangled meat and carrion, so that they may by no means be contaminated by blood or that secreted in the viscera."[292]

If eating blood was *the* cause of the flood (so Ps.-Clem. *Rec.* 1.30.1), this may explain the double prohibition against (eating) blood in the Apostolic Decree.[293] Indeed, one of the only explicit references to Noah in Luke-Acts tends to confirm this hypothesis.[294] For according to Lk. 17:26–7 (par. Matt. 24:37–9), which compares the days of the Son of Man to the days of Noah, indiscriminate eating, among other things, characterized the antediluvians: "Just as it was in the days of Noah, so too it will be in the days of the Son of Man. (27) They were eating and drinking, and marrying and being given in marriage, until the day Noah entered the ark, and the flood came and destroyed all of them." Superficially, these activities seem to represent the normal human activity of daily life; yet they are actually meant to connote the corruption of the earth in God's sight mentioned in Gen. 6:4, 11 (cf. 2 Pet. 2:5).[295]

In order to understand Luke's typological use of the Noah tradition, we must look at a precedent in the prophetic tradition that may have been influential here, specifically Isa. 54:9–10.[296] After referring to the desolations of the exile caused by divine wrath (Isa. 54:7–8), the prophet adds: "this is like the waters of Noah to me; just as I swore that the waters of Noah would never again inundate the earth, so I do forswear future anger and wrath against you. For though the mountains may move and the hills be displaced, my graciousness will not depart from you, nor shall my covenant of peace be disrupted – says YHWH, your consoler" (vv. 9–10). What is expressed here is a typological association between the flood and the late Judean exile.[297] Just as the former was an expression of wrath, but ended with a divine promise of permanence in the natural order (Gen. 8:21–2; 9:15–17), so now the wrath of exile will give way to an era of eternal divine grace.[298] In this way, the ancient covenant with Noah and his descendants will be recapitulated in the post-exilic period. For just as the post-diluvian world involved a divine renewal of the primordial creation, and a divine promise that such destruction would "never again" be repeated (cf. עוד...לא, Gen. 8:21), so now Isaiah repeatedly emphasizes the theme of YHWH as Creator (e.g., 40:12–31; 42:5; 44:24; 45:9–13, 18; 47:13; 51:13, 16) – even of a new heaven and new earth (65:17) – and emphasizes that the wrath of the past will "never again" recur (cf. עוד...לא, 51:22; 52:1; 54:4; 60:18–20; 62:4; 65:19–20). For Isaiah 54, God's covenant promise with Noah, the first covenant by which God restored the creation (Genesis 9), is both a guarantee of creation and a model and prototype for God's dealing with Israel after the catastrophe of the exile.[299]

Against this background, we can see that Luke uses the story of Noah typologically but in a negative way, much as it is in the Qumran literature.[300] The prohibitions in the Apostolic Decree relate to the Noachic Commandments. In Jewish–Christian circles of the early church, obedience to the Noachic Commandments, especially the prohibition against eating blood, were considered absolutely essential[301] for Gentile believers, in order that they might not fall under divine judgment.[302] Once again, the key to the interpretation is the *Book of Jubilees* and the Jewish–Christian tradition dependent on it. At the same time, we should not underestimate the possibility that Gentile adherence to the Noachic decree may have been seen in the early church as a way for all humanity to participate in the restoration both of Israel and of the whole creative order.[303]

As we have seen in our discussion of Pentecost in Acts 2, the revelation at Sinai is connected in *Jubilees* with the renewal of the Noachic covenant at the time of the annual Feast of Pentecost. If Luke (or his tradition) was aware of this connection, then James' answer to the question posed in Antioch was readily available: not the renewal of the Sinaitic covenant was needed, but rather the renewal of the prior Noachic covenant. For the early church, Noah was the supreme example of a person who was saved from divine judgment without observing circumcision and other prescriptions of the Mosaic law.[304] By appealing to a universal decree that was given before the Mosaic Law, the church's message gains universal relevance.[305]

Paul's speech on the Areopagus (Acts 17:22–31)

Paul's speech on the Areopagus contains allusions to Genesis 10 and Deut. 32:8 which reconfirm our thesis that the Table of Nations tradition influences Luke's perspective in Acts. On the Areopagus Paul is reported first to have established common ground with his Athenian audience, which included Epicurean and Stoic philosophers (v. 18), by proclaiming to them the "unknown god" invoked on one of their local altar inscriptions (vv. 22–3). Then, abbreviating the story line in Genesis 1–10, Paul goes on to describe this God as (1) the one "who made the world and everything in it" (Acts 17:24–5; cf. Gen. 1:1–25), and as (2) the one "who made from one man [sc. Adam? Noah?] every nation (ἔθνος) of men to dwell on the face of the earth (e.g. ἐπὶ παντὸς προσώπου τῆς γῆς)", having determined allotted periods and the boundaries of their habitation" (Acts 17:26a; cf. Gen. 1:26–8; 9:1, 7, 19; 10:1–32).[306] This foreshortening of the narrative is consistent with the Genesis account itself, for the mandate to "be fruitful and multiply, and fill the earth (γῆ)" in Gen. 1:28 is reiterated verbatim to Noah and his sons in Gen. 9:1 (cf. v. 7).[307] Indeed, according to Gen. 9:19, it was from these sons of Noah that people spread out "over the whole earth" (e.g. ἐπὶ πᾶσαν τὴν γῆν) after the flood. Therefore, the idea of "every nation" (πᾶν ἔθνος) in Paul's speech clearly alludes to the Table of Nations itself,[308] which concludes with the statement: "These are the tribes of the sons of Noah, according to their generations, according to their nations (ἔθνη); from them were the islands of the nations (ἔθνη) scattered over the earth (γῆ) after the flood" (Gen. 10:32). B. Gärtner quite rightly compares Acts 17:26 with Josephus, *Ant.* 1.120: "From that hour, therefore, they were dispersed through their diversity of languages and founded colonies everywhere, each group occupying the country upon which they lit and to which God led them, so that every continent was peopled by them . . . "[309]

This interpretation of Acts 17:26 in light of the Table of Nations tradition is further substantiated by the allusion to Deut. 32:8: "When the Most High divided the nations (ἔθνη), when he separated the sons of Adam, he set the bounds of the nations (ὅρια ἐθνῶν) according to the number of the angels of God (MT: sons of Israel)." This verse evidently provides the allusion to Adam in Acts 17:26. Furthermore, just as Deut. 32:8 refers to God's having set the "bounds" (ὅρια) of the nations, so also Acts 17:26 refers to God's having set the "boundaries" (ὁροθεσία) of the nations' habitation.[310]

Conclusion

In his two-volume work, Luke emphasizes the nations of the world in a way that reflects a fundamental engagement with the OT account of the postdiluvian origins of the nations. We have seen that there is almost a subtext in Luke-Acts that retells the story of the flood (Genesis 6–9), the Table of Nations (Genesis 10), and the Tower of Babel (Genesis 11).[311] Thus, the genealogy in Lk. 3:23–38 identifies Jesus as a descendant of Noah based in part on the Table of Nations tradition of *Jubilees*. The sending out of the seventy-two in Lk. 10:1–24 probably alludes to the traditional number of nations in the world. In Acts 2:1–13, the outpouring of the Spirit at Pentecost is seen as a reversal of God's confusion of the tongues after the flood, and the *pars pro toto* catalogue of "Jews from every nation under heaven" is related to the more extensive Table of Nations, particularly as mediated through Jewish–Christian tradition based on *Jubilees* 8–9. Peter's speech in the Temple (Acts 3:11–26) cites Gen. 12:3, which, in turn, presupposes the Table of Nations in Genesis 10. Luke's account of the Apostolic Council in Acts 15 emphasizes the "nations" and applies to the Gentile believers the commandments which, according to Genesis 9 and the Jewish tradition based on this passage, were given to Noah after the flood. Finally, Paul's speech on the Areopagus refers to the postdiluvian distribution of the earth among the nations. An important confirmation of our thesis that Luke is dependent on the Table of Nations tradition in *Jubilees* 8–9 comes in the next chapter. There we will show that an early Jewish–Christian text – one of the first commentaries on Acts – displays a similar dependence on *Jubilees* 8–9.

Luke very artfully brings together the *Urzeit* with the *Endzeit* by linking this Table of Nations tradition with the OT and Jewish expectation of the restoration of Israel and the eschatological pilgrimage of the nations.[312] For Luke, the promised inclusion of the nations in Israel's return and restoration had already begun. "Jews from every nation under heaven" (Acts 2:5–11) had been regathered to Jerusalem at Pentecost, inaugurating both Israel's restoration and the subsequent mission to the nations. The promised Spirit of the restoration had come. Although Peter had preached in the Temple that the time of universal restoration that God announced long ago through his holy prophets was still in the future (Acts 3:21), nevertheless the fallen tent of David had already in some sense been rebuilt (Amos 9:11), and this has direct implications for the nations and their participation in Israel of the restoration (Acts 15).

4

PSEUDO-CLEMENTINE *RECOGNITIONS* 1.27–71

Introduction

In the last chapter, we saw that Luke-Acts contains a view of the nations rooted in Genesis 9–11, particularly as mediated through the *Book of Jubilees*. In Pseudo-Clementine *Recognitions* 1.27–71, we find additional evidence for this argument. For the Pseudo-Clementine text is probably the earliest extensive commentary on Luke-Acts,[1] and it contains a similar view of the nations rooted in Genesis 9–11, particularly as mediated through the *Book of Jubilees*. Some of these comparisons have already been noted in Chapter 3. In the following, we shall examine *Rec.* 1.27–71 in its own right. Then, we will attempt to draw further comparisons between the Pseudo-Clementine text and Luke-Acts.

Pseudo-Clementine *Recognitions* 1.27–71

The Pseudo-Clementines have attracted considerable attention as a source for the development of Christianity in general and Jewish Christianity in particular.[2] Ever since the Tübingen School in the nineteenth century, many attempts have been made to unravel the literary complexities of the Ps.-Clementines and to get back to the supposed Jewish–Christian source material.[3] Within the Ps.-Clementine *Recognitions*, 1.27–71 has been isolated as a Jewish–Christian source,[4] which can possibly be dated to ca. 100–15 CE, somewhere in the traditional land of Israel.[5]

> Arnold Stötzel dates the source between 70 and 135 CE, because it expects a future return to the Land.[6] Against this suggestion, Jones argues that *Rec.* 1.27–71 employs Hegesippus' work (written ca. 173–90 CE) and seems to presuppose the edict of Hadrian (*Rec.* 1.39.3).[7] Hence, Jones himself dates the composition to about 200 CE.[8] It is not clear, however, that *Rec.* 1.39.3 actually presupposes the edict of Hadrian: "Thus, everyone who has pleased God in his unspeakable wisdom will be delivered

from the war that, on account of those who have not believed, is ready to come to destroy them. As they did not want to do what was in their free will, this very thing, when they have left their country and when this place [i.e. Jerusalem] that has been up-rooted from them is no longer there for them, even though against their will, they will endure, as is pleasing to God, so that they might be sober." Given the substantial dependence of *Rec.* 1.27–71 on Luke-Acts (see further below), this text may well allude instead to Lk. 21:24: ". . . and they will fall by the edge of the sword and be taken away as captives among all nations (καὶ αἰχμαλωτισθήσονται εἰς τὰ ἔθνη πάντα); and Jerusalem will be trampled on by the nations, until the times of the nations are fulfilled." As Jones himself admits, the reference to "the war" that, according to *Rec.* 1.39.3, would come upon the unbelievers must refer to the first Jewish war, although he considers that it has "coalesced in the mind of the author" with the second Jewish war.[9] As soon as the necessity of an allusion to the edict of Hadrian is eliminated, and it is appreciated that the text refers to the first Jewish war and not the second (cf. also 1.64.2), then the only remaining evidence for a later date for the composition is supposed dependence of *Rec.* 1.27–71 on Hegesippus, which is open to other interpretations.[10] In that case, *Rec.* 1.27–71 may have been written between ca. 100 and 115 CE, allowing some time to elapse after the writing of Luke-Acts (ca. 80–90 CE?).[11] This was the period just before the disastrous Diaspora Revolt (115–17 CE),[12] when eschatological expectations of the return to the Land and the restoration of Israel were apparently at a new high since the first Jewish war.[13] To suggest this dating, we need not assume that this Jewish–Christian group identified with Diaspora Jews in any particular way, only that it shared the same traditional hope of return to the Land which smol-dered and occasionally flared up in the period between 70 and 135 CE.[14] While this Jewish–Christian group certainly would have had no sympathy with hopes of reestablishing the sacrifi-cial cult in the Temple, it may well have expected the Temple (or at least the Temple mount itself) to be restored to its original and only legitimate function as a place of prayer (see further below).

The source presently occurs within a section of the *Recognitions* that recounts Peter's instruction of Clement in Caesarea (1.22–74). Peter's identification with the Hebrews/Jews (cf. 1.32.1), and his view about the inclusion of the nations in the privileges of Israel as contributing to "confusion" (1.42.1 Syriac) are considered indications that the true author of the source is a "Jewish Christian."[15] We may also note that like *Jub.* 12:26 ("Hebrew . . . the language of the creation"), *Rec.* 1.30.5 considers Hebrew to be the original language of humanity.[16]

In the following, we shall examine the important theme of the nations which runs throughout *Rec.* 1.27–71 and contributes significantly to its unity.[17] Our text divides into two unequal parts: (1) the plight of humanity, and (2) the solution to this plight. The first part (*Rec.* 1.27–38) briefly sketches the history of sinful humanity from creation down to the time of the Israelite monarchy, showing that idolatry is the root of all evil and that every nation, even the elect one, is idolatrous. Then, skipping over the exilic period and most of the Second-Temple period, the second part (*Rec.* 1.39–71) presents the main concern of the text: the salvation of the world through the coming of the long-promised Prophet like Moses and the proclamation of the early church. While the Jewish nation is the primary focus of the two parts, the text never loses sight of the other nations of the world. Seen as a whole, the text presents a salvation– historical continuum into which Jesus and the mission of the early church are integrated.[18]

The plight of sinful humanity (Rec. 1.27–38)

The first part of *Rec.* 1.27–71 is largely a retelling of the biblical narrative from Genesis 1 to 2 Kings 25. As such, it can be compared to other examples of the "Rewritten Bible," such as the *Book of Jubilees* and Ps.-Philo's *Biblical Antiquities.*[19] As we shall see, our text clearly uses the *Book of Jubilees* as a source.[20] The first part of our text begins by presenting the plight of humanity in terms of the number of generations from the creation of Adam to the advent of Abraham (*Rec.* 1.27.1–33.2).[21] Thereafter, the text ceases to count the generations and focuses instead on the plight of Abraham and his descendants down to the time of the monarchy (1.33.3–38.5). This numbering of the generations agrees with *Jubilees* (and the Septuagint) against the Masoretic text, for according to *Rec.* 1.32.1, Abraham arises in the twenty-first generation, which assumes the inclusion of the second Kainam as the thirteenth generation.[22]

Even before the creation of Adam, the whole world was designed for the purpose of human habitation (1.28.4), and natural boundaries were formed that there might be a suitable dwelling-place for humans who were about to come (1.27.8–9).[23] In the second part, the text reintroduces the creation of the world and explains the hierarchy in it (cf. 1.45.1–4; 51.1). Nothing is said in the first part about the fall in the Garden of Eden. Indeed, the first seven generations apparently lived in righteousness (cf. 1.28.4–29.1). For our text, the problem of humanity first began in the eighth generation, when righteous men who had been living in the likeness of angels rejected their previous manner of life owing to the beauty of women and indiscriminately had intercourse (1.29.1; cf. Gen. 6:2).[24] From this point on, sin steadily increased in the world and subverted the whole creative order (1.29.2–3). Hence, the narrative moves rapidly to the radical divine solution to the problem. In the tenth generation, God brought the flood on the wicked and thereby purified the world (1.29.4).

After the flood, Noah, his sons, and their wives make a new beginning, although this one fails just as the first did (1.29.5–31.3). In the twelfth generation, they began to increase by the blessing with which God had blessed them (1.30.1). However, already in the thirteenth generation, evil began to gain the upper hand, with sexual sin again the cause of the decline.[25] Noah's middle son (Ham) abused his father; hence, his offspring was accursed to slavery (1.30.2; cf. Gen. 9:20–27). From here on, the Hamites become a constant source of grief for humanity.

It was also in the thirteenth generation that the earth was divided among the sons of Noah: "While his elder brother [Shem] received as a lot the middle portion of the earth, which contains the region Judaea, and the third [Japheth] received the eastern portion, the western part fell to him [sc. Ham]" (1.30.3).[26] This terse summary is not directly based on the Table of Nations in Genesis 10 or 1 Chronicles 1, but rather on the more geographically oriented account in *Jubilees* 8, which likewise refers to the division of the earth by lot among the sons of Noah, with Shem receiving the middle portion of the earth (cf. *Jub.* 8:12, 19)[27] and Ham receiving a portion in the West (cf. *Jub.* 8:22; 10:29). The idea that Shem is the oldest of the three brothers is found in *Jub.* 4:33.[28] There is, however, no corresponding text in *Jubilees* which indicates that Japheth received only the eastern portion (cf. *Jub.* 8:25–8). It appears, therefore, that *Rec.* 1.30.3 either misunderstands or corrects the geographical location of the lots apportioned to Noah's sons (assuming that our Jewish–Christian source is using the version of *Jubilees* that is familiar to us).[29] Furthermore, unlike *Jubilees*, our text does not mention that the division of the earth among the sons of Noah concluded with an oath incumbent upon each of the sons not to violate each others' territories (cf. *Jub.* 9:14). As we shall see presently, however, violation of the allotted portions is seen as a great evil. Here it is important to emphasize that *Jubilees* 8 forms the backdrop for the rest of *Rec.* 1.27–71. Whenever the text refers to the world or the nations, it presupposes the Table of Nations as refracted through the lens of *Jubilees*.

The account goes on to explain that the accursed Hamites were the chief cause of the spread of sacrifice, idolatry, and sin in the postdiluvian world. Already in the fourteenth generation, "one of the cursed seed was the first to build an altar for the purpose of magic and in order to give the honor of blood to demons" (1.30.4). As time goes on, the depravity of humanity becomes steadily worse. In the fifteenth generation, men first worshiped fire and constructed idols (1.30.5). "Now until that time," the text states, "one language had prevailed, the language pleasing to God: Hebrew." This idea, which clearly alludes to the situation before the confusion of languages at the Tower of Babel, may well be derived from *Jub.* 12:25–6. According to that text, Abraham had to be taught Hebrew, since it had ceased to be the universal language after Babel: "Then the Lord God said to me: 'Open his mouth and his ears to hear and speak with his tongue in the revealed language.' For from the day of the collapse [sc. the Tower of Babel] it had disappeared from the mouth(s) of all mankind. I opened his mouth, ears, and lips and began to speak Hebrew with him – in the language of the creation."[30]

To this point the situation was evidently relatively localized because the descendants of Noah had not yet moved to their respective inheritances which Noah had apportioned to them throughout the world (cf. 1.30.3). It was not until the sixteenth generation – three generations after the earth was divided by lot – that "people arose from the east and came to the places of the portions of their fathers" (1.30.6).[31] As we shall see, this migration leads to further problems for humanity, for which the Hamites are again to blame (see below on 1.31.2).

The trouble resumes in the seventeenth generation, when Nimrod, a descendant of Ham (cf. Gen. 10:8), accedes to the throne in Babylon and builds a city.[32] From there he migrates to Persia and teaches the inhabitants to worship fire (1.30.7). Again, the role of the Hamites in spreading the practice of sacrifice is emphasized. In the eighteenth generation, the influence of Nimrod continues, as more cities are built, this time with walls around them.[33] In addition, people arranged for armies, weapons, judges, and law, just as they wished; they built temples, and they bowed down to their rulers as if to gods (1.31.1).[34]

In the nineteenth generation, the descendants of Ham perpetrate further crimes. According to *Rec.* 1.31.2, "the grandsons of the one who was cursed after the flood left the boundary of their land (for they had received as an allotted portion the western part) and drove those to whom the middle portion had fallen to the east, into Persia. They then dwelt in the place of

those who had been expelled."[35] Here we have another idea that is drawn
from the *Book of Jubilees*. As we have seen, the notion that Noah divided
the earth by lot among his three sons is found in *Jubilees* 8. Likewise, the
idea that the descendants of Ham illegally took territory that rightfully
belonged to Shem and his descendants is found in *Jub.* 10:27–34:

> In the fourth week, during the first year – at its beginning – of the
> thirty-fourth jubilee [1639], they were dispersed from the land
> of Shinar. (28) Ham and his sons went into the land which he was
> to occupy, which he had acquired as his share, in the southern
> country. (29) When Canaan saw that the land of Lebanon as far
> as the stream of Egypt was very beautiful, he did not go to his
> hereditary land to the west of the sea. He settled in the land of
> Lebanon, on the east and west, from the border of Lebanon and
> on the seacoast. (30) His father Ham and his brothers Cush and
> Mitzraim said to him: 'You have settled in a land which was
> not yours and did not emerge for us by lot. Do not act this way,
> for if you do act this way both you and your children will fall
> in the land and be cursed with rebellion and in rebellion your
> children will fall and be uprooted forever. (31) Do not settle
> in Shem's residence because it emerged by their lot for Shem
> and his sons. (32) You are cursed and will be cursed more than
> all Noah's children through the curse by which we obligated
> ourselves with an oath before the holy judge and before our
> father Noah.' (33) But he did not listen to them. He settled in the
> land of Lebanon – from Hamath to the entrance of Egypt – he
> and his sons until the present. (34) For this reason that land was
> named the land of Canaan.

This passage clinches a very important point for *Jubilees*: how it is that
even in the Bible one reads the misleading phrase "the land of Canaan"
(Gen. 11:31; 12:5; 13:12; 16:3; 17:8). It was not because the land belonged
to Canaan, but rather because he stole it from Shem and his descendants.
When *Rec.* 1.27–71 appropriates this idea, it adopts the main point of
Jubilees 8–10: Israel's ancestral right to the promised land.[36] However,
Rec. 1.27–71 does not include from *Jubilees* the idea that by taking Shem's
territory, Canaan fell under a second curse (cf. *Jub.* 9:14–15; 10:30–2).
Shem's patrimony was the center, it was holy; there God dwells and is
worshiped, and there no outsider such as Canaan, so horribly condemned
by two curses, should venture. It was only right that Israel, Shem's descendants, later drove the children of Canaan from the land they had
stolen from its legitimate owners.[37] As our Jewish–Christian source puts

it, "They took possession of it in their tribal portions as the land of their fathers" (*Rec.* 1.38.3).

From the foregoing it can be seen that the text paints a very bleak picture of the human condition since the flood. In the twentieth generation, therefore, signs of judgment begin to emerge: a son first died the death of his soul before his father, due to impious intercourse (Latin: "the sin of incest") (1.31.3). By the twenty-first generation, the whole world was in error and was on the verge of being destroyed by fire because of its ungodliness. The scourge had already begun in Sodom in order to pass through all the world (1.32.1). It is at this crucial moment that Abraham, from the line of the Shemites whom the Hamites had expelled from their land and the ancestor of the Hebrews/Jews, was able to please God and therefore saved the world (1.32.1–3).[38] This was not the ultimate solution to the plight of sinful humanity, but a temporary reprieve. Nevertheless, Abraham's favor with God foreshadowed the ultimate solution, which would come in Jesus (see below). The idea in our text that Abraham saved the whole world apparently stems from the Abrahamic blessing in Gen. 12:3 (cf. 18:18; 22:18; 26:4; 28:14), which states that all the nations of the world would be blessed in Abraham and his seed (cf. Gal. 3:8, 16; Acts 3:25).[39] In the original context of Genesis, these nations are the very ones that had already been introduced in the Table of Nations of Genesis 10. Likewise in our text, the nations of the world are introduced in order to set the stage for the crucial advent of Abraham and his descendants.

Moreover, as a result of Abraham's recognition of the Creator-God, "the angel approached him and testified to him concerning his election and the land which was incumbent upon his race. It was not that he would give, but he promised him that he would requite and return" (1.32.4).[40] Thus, Abraham becomes here a crucial figure in both the salvation of the world and in the restoration of his descendants to their land. From here on, these two elements – the world/nations and the Land/Israel, the universal and the particular – become a constant refrain in the text, thus demonstrating the substantial unity of *Rec.* 1.27–71.

With the advent of Abraham, the text now ceases the enumeration of generations and focuses on Abraham's descendants (1.33.3–38.5).[41] Abraham's first two sons, Ishmael and Eliezar, are explained as products of the patriarch's pre-enlightenment days (1.33.3–5),[42] whereas his third son Isaac was born to his lawful wife after Abraham came into knowledge of the truth from God (1.34.1–2; cf. Gal. 4:21–31). From Isaac, in turn, came Jacob, the "twelve" sons of Jacob, and the "seventy-two" patriarchs of the tribes of Israel (1.34.2). Given the aforementioned emphasis in our text on the world/nations and the Land/Israel, we may wonder whether the text intends the reader to draw a connection between the 72 descendants of the twelve and the traditional 70 or 72 nations of the world listed in the Table of Nations in Genesis 10.[43] The very fact that the text repeats the numbers "twelve" and "seventy-two" in the subsequent context (cf. 1.40.4, alluding to Lk. 10:1, 17) suggests that special emphasis is put on them. As we have seen in Chapter 3, a numerical relationship exists between Israel and the 70 nations already in the Hebrew Bible. According Gen. 46:27 MT, "all the persons of the house of Jacob who came into Egypt were seventy"[44] (cf. Exod. 1:5). Hence, when Deut. 32:8 MT states that "When the Most High gave the nations their inheritance, when he separated the sons of man, he set the boundaries of the peoples according to the number of the sons of Israel (לְמִסְפַּר בְּנֵי יִשְׂרָאֵל; LXX κατὰ ἀριθμὸν ἀγγέλων θεοῦ)," this number would be traditionally set at 70. Given that the Hebrew and Greek Bibles do not account for the number 72 as applied to the patriarchs of the tribes of Israel,[45] we conclude that *Rec.* 1.34.2 alters the number of Hebrews who entered Egypt to 72, in order to create a parallel between the two groups chosen by Moses to assist him and the two groups of Jesus' disciples (1.40.4). The number 72, in turn, has implications for the nations of the world, for the text is alert to the issue of numerology, particularly with respect to Israel and the nations (cf. 1.42.1, where people from the Gentiles are called to complete the number that was shown to Abraham in Gen. 15:5).[46]

The rest of the first part of *Rec.* 1.27–71 concentrates on the history of the Israelites, including the sojourn and exodus from Egypt (1.34.3–7), the wilderness wanderings (1.35.1–37.5), the conquest of the Land (1.38.1–3), the period of stability under the Judges (1.38.4), and the period of the monarchy (1.38.5). Several salient points can be derived from this history for our purposes. First, Moses was sent to deliver the people of the Hebrews from Egypt "so that it might go forth and journey to the land of its fathers" (1.34.4), that is, to Judea (1.35.1, 6). This mention of the fatherland relates back to the aforementioned idea that the land originally belonged to the Shemites and that Abraham and his descendants would receive their land back (1.31.2; 32.4; see also below on 1.38.3).

Second, the golden calf incident (1.35.5–36.2) reveals the people's love of idolatry, which they had acquired from their long sojourn in Egypt and their "evil upbringing with the Egyptians" (1.36.1). Here again, the Hamites are seen to have a pernicious influence. Therefore, Moses struck a compromise solution: the people could continue to sacrifice as long as they did so in the name of God (Latin: "to God alone") (1.36.1).[47] This would at least eliminate the idolatrous aspect of their sacrificing.

Third, the text goes on to make clear that sacrifice is not the ideal for the people. It is merely a temporary expedient to help curb half of the desire for idolatry, i.e., the worship of other gods (1.36.1). The other half of the remedy (i.e., the elimination of sacrifice altogether) would come when God raises up the Prophet like Moses, to whom the people must listen in all matters or face annihilation (Latin: "his soul will be banished from his people") (1.36.1–2).[48] In order to teach the people by experience that he does not desire sacrifice, God will give the people a "place" (the Tabernacle?) to sacrifice (1.37.1),[49] but he will also subject them to repeated exiles and restorations, "in order that they might understand that they were ransomed whenever they observed the law without sacrifices and that, when they returned to their place and offered sacrifices, they were thrust out and were cast forth from it, so that they might cease sacrificing forever" (1.37.4).[50] On this view, Deuteronomic theology is reshaped, so that during the period of divine judgment in exile the people are encouraged not merely to repent of past sins (especially idolatry),[51] but more specifically to abandon the Temple cultus, according to the motto "to obey is better than sacrifice" (1 Sam. 15:22; cf. *Rec.* 1.37.2, citing Hos. 6:6 LXX: "God desires kindness, not sacrifices").[52] A somewhat similar adaptation of the Deuteronomic theology is found in Stephen's Speech in Acts 7, where the Temple and sacrifice are likewise disparaged (vv. 42, 47–50; see further below).

This interesting adaptation of the Deuteronomic view of Israel's history stands in some tension with the aforementioned promise to Abraham that the land would be returned to his descendants (1.32.4). Ironically, the tension is rooted in the problem of idolatry and sacrifice. Abraham and his descendants were promised that the stolen land would be returned to them as a reward for Abraham's correct perception of the one true God in a world committed to idolatry and illicit sacrifice (1.32.1–4). Now, however, the nation would repeatedly lose the Land precisely because it persists in a sacrificial system which has partially idolatrous roots and which God allowed only so that they would redirect their idolatry and sacrifice to him.

Fourth, the text goes on to state that the people "went up to the land of their fathers and, by the providence of God, in the very moment when they were simply seen, put the evil nations to flight. They took possession of it in their tribal portions as the land of their fathers" (1.38.3). This mention of the patriarchal land again recalls that the Hamites had illegitimately taken the land from the Shemites and that the angel had promised its return to its proper owners, the Shemites, especially Abraham and his descendants (cf. 1.31.2; 32.4). Furthermore, the division of the Land among the tribes may allude to the division of the earth among the sons of Noah.[53]

Finally, after a brief comment on the period of the Judges (1.38.4), the first part of *Rec.* 1.27–71 concludes with a disparaging comment about the period of decline during the monarchy: "When they made for themselves [rulers who were] tyrants rather than kings, they abolished the place that had been predestined for them as a house of prayer, in preference for a temple. [. . .] So it was that by the occasional bad kings who ruled over them they were led into greater impiety" (1.38.5).[54] This seems to assert that during the monarchic period the purpose of the Solomonic Temple was changed from a house of prayer into a cultic sacrificial center.[55] As we have seen, our text holds that the sacrificial cult was never God's perfect will, but that Moses allowed it in order to keep the people from practicing idolatry (1.36.1). In order to maintain this position, the text apparently adduces evidence from the dedication of the Solomonic Temple that the original purpose of the building was as a house of prayer rather than as a place of sacrifice (1 Kgs. 8:27–53).[56] Indeed, Solomon's prayer mentions nothing at all about sacrifices,[57] whereas it does emphasize praying both in and towards the Temple.[58] Obviously, Jesus' Cleansing of the Temple (Mk. 11:15–17 parr.) and his citation of Isa. 56:7 ("My house will be called a house of prayer for all nations") play a major role in this Jewish–Christian interpretation of the original purpose of the Solomonic Temple.[59] From this perspective, Jesus' mission was to restore the original function of the Temple as a house of prayer (see below on 1.39.1–2).[60] The fallen tent of David would be rebuilt (cf. Acts 15:16).

From Solomon's dedicatory prayer in the Temple, our text was also able to develop the aforementioned modified Deuteronomic theology, according to which the people could expect repeated exiles and restorations if they persisted in sacrificing (1.37.3–4). Thus, we read in 1 Kgs. 8:33–4: "When your people Israel, having sinned against you, are defeated before an enemy but turn again to you, confess your name, pray and plead with you in this house, (34) then hear in heaven, forgive the sin of your people Israel, and bring them again to the land that you gave to their ancestors." Similarly in vv. 46–51 we read:

> If they sin against you – for there is no one who does not sin – and you are angry with them and give them to an enemy, so that they are carried away captive to the land of the enemy, far off or near; (47) yet if they come to their senses in the land to which they have been taken captive, and repent, and plead with you in the land of their captors, saying, 'We have sinned, and have done

wrong; we have acted wickedly'; (48) if they repent with all their heart and soul in the land of their enemies, who took them captive, and pray to you towards their land, which you gave to their ancestors, the city that you have chosen, and the house that I have built for your name; (49) then hear in heaven your dwelling place their prayer and their plea, maintain their cause (50) and forgive your people who have sinned against you, and all their transgressions that they have committed against you; and grant them compassion in the sight of their captors, so that they may have compassion on them (51) (for they are your people and heritage, which you brought out of Egypt, from the midst of the iron-smelter).

The Jewish–Christian author of *Rec.* 1.27–71 interprets Solomon's prayer as describing the necessary precondition for restoration to the Land – observance of the Law without sacrifices (1.37.4).[61] Solomon's prayer also contains universalistic strains, which suit the theme of Israel and the nations in our text.[62] Thus, we read in 1 Kgs. 8:41–3: "Likewise when a foreigner, who is not of your people Israel, comes from a distant land because of your name (42) – for they shall hear of your great name, your mighty hand, and your outstretched arm – when a foreigner comes and prays towards this house, (43) then hear in heaven your dwelling place, and do according to all that the foreigner calls to you, so that all the peoples of the earth may know your name and fear you, as do your people Israel, and so that they may know that your name has been invoked on this house that I have built." In light of this passage and Isa. 56:7, we may wonder whether the reference to a "house of prayer" in *Rec.* 1.38.5 implicitly includes the nations.

Solomon's prayer bases the plea for deliverance from exile on the fact that God ransomed his people from Egypt (cf. 1 Kgs. 8:51, 53). If Solomon's prayer of dedication in the Temple is as important to the Jewish–Christian interpretation of the history of Israel as we have argued, then this mention of the exodus from Egypt reinforces the exodus typology that accompanies the Prophet-like-Moses motif in our text (e.g., *Rec.* 1.36.2–1.37.3; 1.39.1).

The coming of the Prophet like Moses (Rec. 1.39–71)

The second part of our text skips over the exile and practically the whole Second-Temple period[63] and proceeds directly to the coming of the Prophet like Moses as the solution to the plight of sinful humanity, for

whom idolatry and sacrifice have become a way of life. Thus, we read in
Rec. 1.39.1–2: "Then, as there was this need for the required reformation,
the time came when it was fitting for the prophet to appear who was proclaimed earlier by Moses. At his coming, by the mercy of God, he would
admonish [or: instruct] them first to stop and cease with their sacrificing.
(2) In order that they should not think that they were being deprived of
the forgiveness of sins that accrued through sacrifices and in order that
this might not be a hindrance with the result that they would not believe, baptism through water for the forgiveness of sins was instituted."[64]
Although this Prophet performed signs as Moses did, the people did not
believe (1.40.1–2; 1.41.1–2).[65] The Prophet like Moses even appointed
twelve apostles and seventy-two disciples, "so that the multitudes might
understand even thus through a type that this one was the prophet to
come who had been previously announced by Moses" (1.40.4). We have
already considered this numeric symbolism in *Rec.* 1.34.2, where the
numbers "twelve" and "seventy-two" may indicate particular and universalistic aspects of Israel's existence, respectively. Here the universalistic
aspect recedes in favor of the typological connection with ancient Israel,
at least for the moment (see below). Despite all the signs he performed,
the people crucified the Prophet, although he transformed even this into
something good (1.41.2). Nevertheless, because of their unbelief (and
their persistence in sacrificing), the people will be exiled from the land,[66]
so that in exile they can come to their senses (1.39.3).

Up to this point, the second part of our text is concerned mainly with
the Jewish nation, although just as in Lk. 10:1, 17, the number seventy-
two may be a proleptic indication that the universal aspect is about to be
introduced.[67] However, with the crucifixion of the Prophet like Moses,
the scope of the text immediately expands to include the universal. The
"whole world suffered with him in his passion," the text states (1.41.3;
cf. 1.41.4; 53.2), referring to the many physical disturbances which accompanied the crucifixion, including the darkening of the sun, the uproar
of the stars, the shaking of the sea, the shattering of mountains, the opening
of graves, and the tearing of the veil of the Temple. The latter represents
one last sign that the Temple cult is now defunct. Nevertheless, when
even these portents do not convince the people, the text explicitly transfers attention to the nations: "Therefore, since it was meet, because they
[sc. the Jewish majority] were not persuaded, for people from the gentiles
to be called for the completion of the number that was shown to Abraham,
this confusion arose" (1.42.1).[68] Just as Abraham was able to save the
world in his own day from destruction by fire (1.32.2), so now the promise
which God spoke to Abraham in Gen. 15:5 – that his descendants would

be as many as the stars in heaven – allows the inclusion of the nations among those who would be saved.[69] Here, the nations are counted as part of the descendants of Abraham,[70] just as they are in Paul (cf. the citation of Gen. 15:5 in Rom. 4:18). As with the twice repeated numbers twelve and seventy-two (cf. 1.34.2; 40.4), there is evidently here a numerical relationship between Israel and the nations. Likewise, Paul has the idea of the completion of a number, albeit the completion of the full number of the nations rather than of Israel (cf. Rom. 11:25).

The rest of the second part of our text describes events during the week of years after Jesus' passion (*Rec.* 1.43.1–71.6). The reference to "one week of years" which passed from the time of the passion of Jesus (1.43.3) evidently ties the narrative into the chronology of the seventy weeks of Dan. 9:24–7, according to which an "anointed one" is cut off after the sixty-two weeks and the Temple is desolated (v. 26).[71] For not only does our text stress that Jesus is an anointed one (1.45.4–48.6), but it also "predicts" the destruction of the Temple and the erection of "the abomination of desolation in the holy place" (1.64.2; cf. Dan. 9:27; 11:31; 12:11; Lk. 21:24: ἄρχι οὗ πληρωθῶσιν καιροὶ ἐθνῶν).

During this nascent period, the church in Jerusalem grows under the leadership of James, whom Jesus appointed as bishop (1.43.1, 3).[72] The priests become afraid lest the whole nation should come to faith, and they frequently inquire about whether Jesus was the promised Prophet like Moses. However, the church refuses to answer these questions, while they look for a "convenient time" (1.43.1–3; 44.2–3).[73] Meanwhile, the church itself begins to ask James and Peter for answers to its own questions. Whereas James seems reluctant to teach (1.44.1), Peter is more forthcoming, explaining what the Christ is and why he is so called (1.44.4–53.6).[74] In the process, Peter makes some comments that continue the universalistic motif of our text (1.45.1–2, 4):

> God, who made the world and who is Lord of everything, appointed chiefs over everything, even over plants and rocks, springs and rivers, and every creature. For there are many that I might enumerate like them. (2) Thus, he appointed as chiefs an angel over the angels, a spirit over spirits, a star over the stars, a bird over the birds, a beast over the beasts, an insect over the insects, a fish over the fish, and over humans, a human, who is the Christ. [. . .] (4) The reason that he might be called Christ is that he was the Son of God and became human. And because he was the first chief, his Father anointed him in the beginning with the oil that comes from the tree of life.

This passage recalls the creation story that was recounted at the beginning of our text (1.27.1–28.4), thus tying together the two parts. Christ is seen as the chief over all humanity from creation. Perhaps we can detect here the influence of the genealogy of Jesus in Lk. 3:23–38, which culminates in "son of Adam, son of God."

Peter proceeds to make another universalistic statement (1.50.1–4):

> What I am saying is that when Christ came, it was fitting and right for the Jews to believe him, for it was delivered to them to await him for redemption, just as the fathers, who knew everything well, delivered to them. It was not fitting for those who were from the peoples in error, who had heard neither of his name nor of his coming. (2) But the prophet [i.e., Isaiah] revealed beforehand incredible things, and he proclaimed what came to pass and said, 'He will be a hope for the nations' [Isa. 11:10]. That is, the nations will hope in him and not the Jews who received and heard, (3) which thing thus happened. For when he came, those who were awaiting him on the basis of tradition did not recognize him, but those who had not previously heard a single thing recognized him when he came, and because he has gone, they are expecting him. (4) Thus all these things of the prophecy that was not believed we exactly fulfilled, and he became the hope of the nations.

The fact that the majority of the Jewish nation failed to believe in their own long-awaited Prophet was a potentially embarrassing situation for the early church, a situation that had to be explained if aspersion was not to be cast on Jesus himself. Both the present passage[75] and Paul explain the majority Jewish response to Jesus as the foreordained will of God, and both cite Isa. 11:10 in order to explain why Jesus became "the hope of the nations" (Rom. 15:12).[76] Only through Jesus, as Peter goes on to say, is it possible for the evils of humans to be purified and expiated and for this creation to live (1.51.1).

The daylong exchange between the church and various hostile religious parties on the steps of the Temple (1.55.1–65.5) brings out more particularistic and universalistic aspects. On the one hand, Caiaphas objects to Jesus' teaching about the poor: "... he called the poor blessed and promised earthly rewards so that they, the virtuous, would inherit the earth and would be filled with foods and drink and things similar to these" (1.61.2).[77] Evidently, this understands Jesus to have taught a this-worldly messianic kingdom in which the saints will literally inherit the earth (cf. Matt. 5:5).[78] In answering this objection, Thomas did not seek to correct Caiaphas' understanding of Jesus' teaching, but rather defended it as biblical (1.61.3). At first sight, it may seem difficult to reconcile this idea of world domination with the aforementioned belief that the earth was divided by lot among the sons of Noah into territories. But as we saw in Chapter 3, this is precisely what the *Book of Jubilees* espouses. There, Shem receives the temperate middle of the earth as the position from which he and his descendants are expected to exercise universal sovereignty. Thus, *Jubilees* itself interprets the Abrahamic promise of land (Gen. 12:7; 13.14–17; 15:7, 18–21; 17:8) as an eschatological hope that Israel will inherit and rule the world (cf. *Jub.* 19:21–2; 22:11–14). At Bethel (cf. Gen. 28:13–14), God transfers this Abrahamic promise of universal sovereignty to Jacob (*Jub.* 32:18–19): "I am the Lord who created heaven and earth. I will increase your numbers and multiply you very much. Kings will come from you, and they will rule wherever mankind has set foot. (19) I will give your descendants all of the land that is beneath the sky. They will rule over all nations just as they wish. Afterwards, they will gain the entire earth, and they will possess it forever."[79] From the perspective of *Jubilees*, therefore, the two ideas – inviolable territories distributed to the sons of Noah and the notion of Israel's universal sovereignty – are not strictly incompatible, especially if the eschatological judgment of the wicked nations takes place before Israel assumes universal sovereignty.[80] Since, as we have seen, the *Book of Jubilees* is well known to be a source of *Rec.* 1.27–71, our text (1.61.2) may have appropriated the idea of Israel's universal sovereignty directly from *Jubilees*, although the same idea is found in other Jewish writings of the Second-Temple period which contain the Table of Nations tradition.[81]

On the other hand, we also find an expression of universalism in the debate on the steps of the Temple. In Peter's parting shot to the priests (1.63.2 – 64.4), we read: "Finally I counseled them that before we should go to the nations to preach the knowledge of the God who is above all, they should reconcile their people to God by receiving Jesus" (1.63.2).[82] Peter considers the repentance of the Jewish nation a precondition of the mission to the nations.[83] Particularism still has priority over universalism, much as it does in Paul's missionary work (cf. Rom. 1:16; 2:10; 3:1–2; 9:3–4; Acts 13:46). Peter goes on to state not only that sacrifice is useless for redemption and eternal life, but that God is even more angered about the priests' sacrificing "after the end of the time of sacrifices" (1.64.1), that is, after the coming of Jesus (cf. 1.39.1) and the rending of the veil in the Temple (1.41.3). Therefore, Peter predicts the destruction of the Temple and the beginning of the mission to the nations (1.64.2–3):

"Precisely because of this the temple will be destroyed, and they will erect the abomination of desolation in the holy place. Then, the gospel will be made known to the nations as a witness for the healing of the schisms that have arisen so that also your separation will occur. (3) For throughout the ages the whole world was infested by an evil will either openly or obscurely."[84] This last sentence summarizes everything that was said in the first part of our text, on the plight of sinful humanity (*Rec.* 1.27–38). Thus, the whole world – both Israel and the nations – stands in need of God's salvation. The mission to Israel and the mission to the nations are integrally intertwined. Whereas at first, the mission to the Jewish nation was a precondition for the mission to the nations (cf. 1.63.2), now the mission to the nations is expected actually to effect the needed change in Israel. The exact mechanism by which this is supposed to happen is not elaborated here. Perhaps we are to think of the jealousy motif based on Deut. 32:21, which Paul also used to explain in part how the Jews would come to faith in the time before the parousia (Rom. 10:19; 11:11, 14).[85] For if the growth of the Jerusalem church caused jealousy among unbelieving Jews,[86] how much more would the success of the mission to the nations cause jealousy among the same?

The text mentions Paul, but not by name and certainly not as the "apostle to the nations" (Rom. 11:13) who was recognized as such at the Apostolic Council by James, Peter, and John (Gal. 2:8–9). It does not even recognize a mission to the nations before the destruction of the Temple in 70 CE (cf. *Rec.* 1.64.2),[87] which is well after the time of Paul's death. To the contrary, our text regards Paul as chiefly responsible for preventing the repentance of the Jewish nation and for persecuting the church. During his seven-day discourse in the Temple (1.68.3–69.8), James "persuaded all the people together with the high priest so that they should immediately make haste to proceed to baptism" (1.69.8). In other words, the whole nation was on the verge of coming to faith. At that very moment, however, an "enemy" (Latin: "a certain hostile person"), whose description fits that of the Apostle Paul, turns the priests against James and the other members of the church, with the result that James is killed and the church, scattered (1.70.1–8). Under the authority of the priests, the "enemy" goes on to Damascus and then to Jericho in order to persecute and kill believers (1.71.3–6). This is perhaps evidence of the conflict within Jewish Christianity, which pitted Paul against the Jerusalem church. The Jewish–Christians whom Paul attacks according to the Pseudo-Clementine source are similar to the Hellenists in Jerusalem who, according to the canonical Book of Acts, aroused Saul's wrath (cf. Acts 9:1–2). In both texts, the Jewish Christians whom Saul/Paul attacks affirm the abrogation of the Temple cult and the ritual law by the death of Jesus (cf. Acts 6:13–14).[88] From here onward, the two texts share several points in common: the preaching of the Hellenists in Jerusalem leads to the martyrdom of Stephen/James, their expulsion from the city, and their flight to Damascus/Jericho.

Despite this vilification of Paul, our text contains several striking parallels to Paul's own theology.[89] In *Rec.* 1.42.1, for example, the citation of Gen. 15:5 is applied to the inclusion of the nations as descendants of Abraham in a way that is similar to Paul's citation of Gen. 15:5 in Rom. 4:18.[90] In *Rec.* 1.50.2 (Syriac only), the citation of Isa. 11:10 is used to show that Jesus is the hope for the nations in a way that is directly comparable to Paul's citation of the same passage in Rom. 15:12. In fact, the wild, anti-Pauline polemic that is used here obscures the real issue that separated Paul and the group of Jewish Christians behind our text.

The Jewish–Christian author of our text sees the exile of unbelieving Jews and the destruction of the Temple as an important confirmation of the truth of the Christian faith. After the war and the destruction of the Temple, those of the Jewish people who have been exiled because they did not believe in Jesus can expect to return from exile and to be restored to the Land when they change their minds about Jesus (1.39.3).[91] As we have seen, God had always ransomed the people from exile in the past (1.37.4), and he would do so in the future as well. With the Temple destroyed, the people would presumably not be led into any further sacrificial activity that would cause another exile. Thus, even after the destruction of the Temple, Judea remains the homeland of all Jews, including both Jewish Christians and those who are yet to become Jewish Christians.

Summary

The theme of Israel and the nations runs throughout *Rec.* 1.27–71 and contributes substantially to the salvation–historical program of the work. Drawing on the *Book of Jubilees*, our text posits that all nations, including the Jewish nation, stem from one antediluvian progenitor and his family, and that after the flood the world was divided among the sons of Noah as a habitation for the nations. From here, the text traces a line from *Urzeit* to *Endzeit* through Abraham and his descendants to the coming of the promised Prophet like Moses and Messiah, who is seen as the first chief of creation. Just as Abraham effected a provisional salvation for the whole world, so also Jesus effects final salvation for it. However, since many Jews persist in their unbelief, the nations are allowed to be included as Abraham's descendants in their stead. Ultimately, however, the text expects the return of unbelieving Jews to the Land, when they repent of their current attitude about Jesus.

Pseudo-Clementine *Recognitions* 1.27–71 and Luke-Acts

We have seen that *Rec.* 1.27–71 covers the history of sinful humanity from creation to the persecution of the church by Paul. If most of this account is devoted to the coming and passion of the Prophet like Moses (1.39.1–42.4) and the growth and dispersion of the earliest church in Jerusalem (1.43.1–71.6), we may ask what relationship, if any, exists between *Rec.* 1.27–71 and Luke-Acts. In the history of research, the question has not been put in this way. Normally, the relationship between our text and the canonical Acts of the Apostles is considered, but not Luke-Acts as a whole.[92] Luke-Acts is not responsible for the aforementioned outline of *Rec.* 1.27–71 (i.e., the plight of sinful humanity [1.27–38] and the coming of the Prophet like Moses [1.39–71]), but Luke's two-volume work is clearly fundamental both to the overall structure of the Pseudo-Clementine source and to individual ideas within the text. A comparison of Luke-Acts and *Rec.* 1.27–71 also reveals that both writings have in common the use of a Jewish source which helps to explain some aspects of their universalism.

Parallels between *Rec.* 1.27–71 and Luke's Gospel

The fact that our source knows Luke's Gospel can be shown by many parallels.[93] In some cases, of course, we may question whether the source knows Luke's Gospel or rather the parallel in Matthew, which the source also uses.[94] In many cases, however, the parallels are to Lukan special material, which has no corresponding Matthean tradition. Furthermore, the parallels are not just from one part of Luke, but run straight across the whole Gospel.

To begin with, we must notice that the idea of the Prophet like Moses (*Rec.* 1.36.2) is found not only in Acts 3:22–3 (see below), but also implicitly in the account of the Transfiguration (Lk. 9:35 parr.), where the "listen to him" (αὐτοῦ ἀκούετε) alludes to Deut. 18:15 (αὐτοῦ ἀκούσεσθε). Furthermore, as soon as we entertain the possibility that the seventy-two in Lk. 10:1–20 foreshadows the mission to the nations in Acts,[95] then we must consider a similar possibility for *Rec.* 1.27–71, where, as in Luke's Gospel, the number "seventy-two" occurs twice in juxtaposition to the "twelve" (1.34.2; 40.4).[96] Lk. 6:13 refers to Jesus' choosing of the Twelve, "whom he named apostles," just as *Rec.* 1.40.4 (Latin) refers to Jesus' choosing the Twelve, "whom he called apostles."

There are still further parallels to Luke's Gospel. According to *Rec.* 1.54.6–7, the scribes and Pharisees received the key to the kingdom of heaven and hid it. This can be compared with the "Western" text of Lk. 11:52, which pronounces woe on lawyers for hiding the key of knowledge (ἐκρύψατε τὴν κλεῖδα τῆς γνώσεως). Moreover, Lk. 17:26–7 compares the days of the Son of Man to the days of Noah: "Just as it was in the days of Noah, so too it will be in the days of the Son of Man. They were eating and drinking, and marrying and being given in marriage, until the day Noah entered the ark, and the flood came and destroyed all of them." This can be compared to *Rec.* 1.29.1–5, which describes the situation leading up to and including the flood.[97]

As for other parallels to Luke, we need look no further than Jesus' Cleansing of the Temple (Lk. 19:45–46 parr.), which, as we have seen, was probably determinative for the Deuteronomic theology in our text (*Rec.* 1.37.3–4), insofar as it recalls for our author Solomon's dedicatory prayer in the Temple (1 Kgs. 8:27–53).[98] The idea in *Rec.* 1.39.3, that unbelieving Jews will be exiled from Jerusalem ("when they have left their country and when this place that has been uprooted from them is no longer there for them"), alludes to Lk. 21:24, where it is predicted that "they will fall by the edge of the sword and be taken away as captives among all nations (καὶ αἰχμαλωτισθήσονται εἰς τὰ ἔθνη πάντα); and Jerusalem will be trampled on by the nations, until the times of the nations are fulfilled." Once again, this represents Lukan special material, with no corresponding Matthean tradition. Finally, the darkening of the sun that transpired during the crucifixion (*Rec.* 1.41.3) shows certain dependency on the "Western" text of Lk. 23:45 (καὶ ἐσκοτίσθη ὁ ἥλιος). There can be no doubt that our Jewish–Christian source uses Luke's Gospel throughout his account.

Parallels between *Rec.* 1.27–71 and Acts

The fact that *Rec.* 1.27–71 knew Acts can also be shown by many parallels.[99] Three clear examples conclusively demonstrate this fact:

(1) The report that Peter fled from persecution in Jerusalem, and that Paul pursued him with murderous intentions to Damascus, bearing letters

from the chief priest (*Rec.* 1.71.3–4),[100] sounds like a parody of Acts 9:1–2; 22:4–5; 26:10–12.[101]

Acts 9:1–2	*Rec.* 1.71.3–4
Meanwhile Saul, still breathing threats and murder against the disciples of the Lord, went to the high priest (2) and asked him for letters to the synagogues at Damascus, so that if he found any who belonged to the Way, men or women, he might bring them bound to Jerusalem.	Then, he told us how the enemy, before the priests, promised Caiaphas the high priest that he would massacre all those who believe in Jesus. (4) He departed for Damascus to go as one carrying letters from them so that when he went there, the nonbelievers might help him and might destroy those who believe.

(2) The same citation of Deut. 18:15 + Lev. 23:29 is found both in *Rec.* 1.36.2 and in Acts 3:22–3:[102]

Acts 3:22–3 (cf. Lk. 9:35)	Deut. 18:15 LXX	*Rec.* 1.36.2
The Lord your (pl.) God	The Lord your (sg.) God	The Lord your (pl.) God
will raise up	will raise up	will raise up
for you (pl.)	for you (sg.)	for you (pl.)
from your (pl.) brothers	from your (sg.) brothers	
a prophet like me.	a prophet like me.	a prophet like me.
Listen (pl.) to him according to	Listen (pl.) to him.	Listen (pl.) to him in all matters.
all that he says to you.		

	Lev. 23:29 LXX	
(23) And it will be that every soul who does not listen to that prophet will be utterly rooted out of the people.	Every soul who will not be humbled in that same day will be utterly rooted out from her people.	Everyone who is not obedient to him will die in death. This shows that he will give up his soul to destruction. [Lat.: For whoever should not hear that prophet, his soul will be banished from his people.]

The citation of Deut. 18:15 in these two passages differs from the Septuagint. Both *Rec.* 1.36.2 and Acts 3:22 rearrange the OT text by putting "the Lord your God will raise up for you" before "like me," rather than after it as in the Septuagint. Moreover, both texts use plural pronouns rather than singular. After the citation of Deut. 18:15, both texts append a word from Lev. 23:29 (cf. Deut. 18:19) to the effect that the disobedient person's soul will be destroyed or banished. As Max Turner has recently argued, the Prophet-like-Moses Christology provides the linchpin of Luke's ecclesiology, which maintains that the Jewish–Christian church is the true Israel of the restoration.[103] The Pseudo-Clementine source has evidently appropriated this idea from Acts.

(3) In *Rec.* 1.65.2–3, the description of Gamaliel and his address to the crowd are directly parallel to Acts 4:34–9:

Acts 5:34–9	*Rec.* 1.65.2–3
But a Pharisee in the council named Gamaliel, a teacher of the law, respected by all the people...	But Gamaliel, who was the head of the nation and who was, because it was advantageous, secretly our brother in the matter regarding faith, perceived that they were intensely gnashing their teeth in the great anger towards us with which they were filled. He said these things: (3) "Cease and keep your peace, O people, the children of Israel [Latin: O Israelite men], for we do not know the nature of this trial that has come upon us. Therefore, leave these men alone, for if this matter is of human origin, it will come to naught, but if it is of God why then are you transgressing in vain, as you are not able to do a thing? For it befits the will of God to be continually victorious over all things."
(35) Then he said to them, "Men, Israelites, consider carefully what you propose to do to these men. [...] (38) So in the present case, I tell you, keep away from these men and let them alone; because if this plan or this undertaking is of human origin, it will fail; (39) but if it is of God, you will not be able to overthrow them – in that case you may even be found fighting against God!"	

Both texts describe Gamaliel as a leading member of the Jewish nation. Both texts have Gamaliel speak to the crowd with the direct address, "Men, Israelites." And both texts make a contrast between an undertaking of human origin that is bound to failure and an undertaking of divine origin that is insurmountable.

The foregoing three examples establish a literary relationship between Acts and *Rec.* 1.27–71. Table 5 shows other possible parallels between these two texts, which vary in degree of probability and significance.

Table 5. *Parallels between Acts and* Rec. *1.27–71*

Acts	Recognitions
1:7: It is not for you to know the times or periods that the Father has set by his own authority.	**1.43.3:** Now, while they were frequently beseeching us and while we were looking for a convenient time, one week of years passed from the time of the passion of Jesus.
1:13–14: When they had entered the city, they [sc. the eleven] went to the room upstairs where they were staying . . . (14) All these were constantly devoting themselves to prayer, together with certain women, including Mary the mother of Jesus, as well as his brothers.	**1.66.1:** We came and related to James what had been said. As we spoke to him, we ate, and we all lodged with him and were praying all night that on the following day, in the coming discussion, our word of truth might prevail and be victorious.
1:23, 26: So they proposed two, Joseph called Barsabbas, who was also known as Justus, and Matthias. (26) And they cast lots for them, and the lot fell on Matthias; and he was added to the eleven apostles.	**1.60.5:** . . . Barabbas, who had become an apostle in the stead of Judas the traitor . . .
2:22: You that are Israelites, listen to what I have to say: Jesus of Nazareth, a man attested to you by God with deeds of power, wonders, and signs that God did through him among you, as you yourselves know . . .	**1.41.1:** Then one of the scribes called out from the middle of the crowd and said, "Your Jesus performed signs and wonders as a magician and not as a prophet."
2:38: Peter said to them, "Repent, and be baptized every one of you in the name of Jesus Christ so that your sins may be forgiven; and you will receive the gift of the Holy Spirit."	**1.69.8:** . . . he [sc. James] persuaded all the people together with the high priest so that they should immediately make haste to proceed to baptism.
3:1: One day Peter and John were going up to the temple at the hour of prayer, at three o'clock in the afternoon.	**1.66.2** (cf. 53.4): On the next day, James the bishop also ascended to the temple with our entire congregation.

Table 5. (*cont.*)

Acts	Recognitions
3:25: You are the descendants of the prophets and of the covenant that God gave to your ancestors, saying to Abraham, "And in your descendants all the families of the earth shall be blessed" (Gen. 12:3; 18:18; 22:18; 26:4; 28:14).	**1.32.2:** Now when the world was in error, and owing to ungodliness, was on the verge of being destroyed not by water but by fire, and when the scourge had begun in Sodom in order to pass through the whole world, he [sc. Abraham], by his knowledge of God and his love for him, by means of which he had especially pleased him, saved the whole world from being destroyed (cf. Gen. 12:3).
4:3: So they arrested them and put them in custody until the next day, for it was already evening.	**1.65.4** (cf. 71.2): Now, since this day is passing away, I wish to speak with them here before you all tomorrow so that I may confute their word of error.
4:4: But many of those who heard the word believed; and the number of men about five thousand.	**1.71.2:** Before the dawn, we went down to Jericho. We numbered about five thousand men.
4:5–7: The next day their rulers, elders, and scribes assembled in Jerusalem, (6) with Annas the high priest, Caiaphas, John, and Alexander, and all who were of the high-priestly family. (7) When they had made the prisoners stand in their midst, they inquired, "By what power or by what name did you do this?"	**1.55.1:** Since then the high priest with the rest of the priests had often bidden us either to teach or to learn the things regarding Jesus, our whole company went to the temple at the counsel of the whole church . . .
4:13: Now when they saw the boldness of Peter and John and realized that they were uneducated and ordinary men, they were amazed and recognized them as companions of Jesus.	**1.62.2** (62.5; 63.1): Again, he [sc. Caiaphas] found fault with me [sc. Peter] as with someone rash, "For while you were untaught and a fisher by trade you became a teacher by chance."
4:18: So they [sc. rulers of the Jews, including Caiaphas (cf. vv. 5–6)] called them [sc. Peter and John (cf. v. 1)] and ordered them not to speak or teach at all in the name of Jesus.	**1.62.1:** After him, Caiaphas gave heed to me [sc. Peter], sometimes as if exhorting me and sometimes as if finding fault with me. He said, "Be silent and do not proclaim about Jesus that he is the Christ."

Table 5. (*cont.*)

Acts	Recognitions
6:7: The word of God continued to spread; the number of the disciples increased greatly in Jerusalem, and a great many of the priests became obedient to the faith.	**1.43.3:** The church in Jerusalem, which was established by our Lord, was growing while it was led uprightly and straightforwardly by James ...
6:7: The word of God continued to spread; the number of the disciples increased greatly in Jerusalem, and a great many of the priests became obedient to the faith.	**1.69.8:** ... all the people together with the high priest so that they should immediately make haste to proceed to baptism.
6:14: ... for we have heard him say that this Jesus of Nazareth will destroy this place and will change the customs that Moses handed on to us.	**1.36.1:** Therefore, he [sc. Moses] allowed them to sacrifice.
7:6–7: And God spoke in these terms, that his descendants would be resident aliens in a country belonging to others, who would enslave them and mistreat them during four hundred years. (7) "But I will judge the nation that they serve," said God, "and after that they shall come out and worship me in this place" (cf. Gen. 15:13–16).	**1.32.4:** ... the angel approached him [sc. Abraham] and testified to him concerning his election and the land which was incumbent upon his race. It was not that he would give, but he promised him that he would requite and return. **1.34.3:** For four hundred years they multiplied in the blessing and promise of God (cf. Gen. 15:13–16).
7:42–3: But God turned away from them and handed them over to worship the host of heaven, as it is written in the book of the prophets: "Did you offer to me slain victims and sacrifices forty years in the wilderness, O house of Israel? (43) No; you took along the tent of Moloch, and the star of your god Rephan, the images that you made to worship; so I will remove you beyond Babylon."	**1.36.1:** Because of this, even Moses, when he came down from Mount Sinai and saw the crime, understood, as a good and faithful steward, that it was not possible for the people easily to cease and stop all of the desire of the love of idolatry ...

Table 5. (*cont.*)

Acts	Recognitions
7:54: When they heard these things, they became enraged and gnashed their teeth at Stephen.	**1.53.1** (cf. 65.2, 5): Hence because there was not a little debate about Christ, those from the Jews who did not believe were excessively gnashing their teeth over us . . .
7:57 (cf. 21:28): . . . with a loud shout all rushed together against him.	**1.70.1:** Then a certain man who was the enemy entered the temple near the altar with a few others. He cried out and said . . .
8:1: That day a severe persecution began against the church in Jerusalem, and all except the apostles were scattered throughout the countryside of Judea and Samaria.	**1.71.2** (after the outbreak of persecution): Before the dawn, we went down to Jericho.
8:2: Devout men buried Stephen and made loud lamentation over him.	**1.71.5:** We buried two brothers in that place [sc. Jericho] at night.
8:5, 14: Philip went down to the city of Samaria and proclaimed the Messiah to them. (14) Now when the apostles at Jerusalem heard that Samaria had accepted the word of God, they sent Peter and John to them.	**1.57.3:** Now because they had received a command that they should not enter into their [sc. the Samaritans'] city (cf. Matt. 10:5), they devised a way by which they would neither speak with these with whom they refused to speak nor be silent . . .
12:3: After he saw that it pleased the Jews, he proceeded to arrest Peter also. (This was during the festival of Unleavened Bread.)	**1.44.1:** Therefore, as we twelve apostles were gathered in the days of the Passover with the greater part of the community at Jerusalem . . . [i.e., the time of the debate and the subsequent persecution]
13:15: After the reading of the law and the prophets, the officials of the synagogue sent them a message, saying, "Brothers, if you have any word of exhortation for the people, give it."	**1.67.3:** So as to excite and entice us, he said, if you know something, do not be reluctant to tell our people also, for they are your brothers in respect to the fear of God.

Table 5. (*cont.*)

Acts	*Recognitions*
13:46–7 (cf. 18:6; 28:28): It was necessary that the word of God should be spoken first to you [Jews]. Since you reject it and judge yourselves to be unworthy of eternal life, we are now turning to the nations. For so the Lord has commanded us, saying, "I have set you to be a light for the nations, so that you may bring salvation to the ends of the earth" (Isa. 49:6).	**1.42.1:** Therefore, since it was meet, because they were not persuaded, for people from the gentiles to be called for the completion of the number that was shown to Abraham, this confusion arose.
14:15 (Paul speaking): Men, why are you doing these things?	**1.63.2:** Finally, I counseled them that before we should go to the nations to preach the knowledge of the God who is above all, they should reconcile their people to God by receiving Jesus. **1.70.2** (Paul speaking): What are you doing, O men, the children of Israel?
15:20: . . . but we should write to them to abstain only from things polluted by idols and from fornication and from whatever has been strangled and from blood.	**1.30.1:** In the twelfth generation, they began to increase by the blessing with which God had blessed them, and they received the first commandment, that they should not eat blood, for the flood had taken place precisely because of this.
21:7: When the seven days [of Paul's purification] were almost completed, the Jews from Asia, who had seen him in the temple, stirred up the whole crowd.	**1.69.8–70.1:** In seven full days he [sc. James] persuaded all the people together with the high priest so that they should immediately make haste to proceed to baptism. (70.1) Then a certain man who was the enemy entered the temple near the altar with a few others. He cried out and said . . .
21:30: Then all the city was aroused, and the people rushed together. They seized Paul and dragged him out of the temple, and immediately the doors were shut.	**1.71.2:** When evening arrived, the priests closed the temple, and we came to James' house and prayed there.
21:40 (cf. 15:12): When he had given him permission, Paul stood on the steps and motioned to the people for silence; and when there was a great hush, he addressed them in the Hebrew language, saying . . .	**1.55.2** (cf. 66.4): . . . and we stood on the stairs with our whole company of believers. When everyone was silent, when there was great stillness, the high priest first began to soothe the people . . .

As might be expected, these parallels with Acts stem mostly from the second part of our text, i.e., from *Rec.* 1.39–71, the section which most overlaps with the subject matter of Acts. Nevertheless, the first part of our work (*Rec.* 1.27–38) also shows some parallels with Acts (cf. 1.32.4; 36.1, 2). The distribution of parallels covers much of the Book of Acts, with some notable concentrations (Acts 4, 6, 7, 8, 21) and gaps (Acts 10–11, 15–20, 22–28).[104] Although not all of these parallels are equally weighty, we may take it as virtually certain that *Rec.* 1.27–71 knew and used Acts, although the latter is not explicitly mentioned as a source.[105] As we have suggested, our text can be characterized as the first extensive commentary on the Book of Acts,[106] although the author obviously takes a critical stance at certain crucial points. For example, the author corrects Luke's positive presentation of Paul and his mission, to which most of Acts is devoted.[107] Even in this regard, however, Acts itself may have provided fuel for the anti-Pauline polemic when it records, for instance, the Jewish case against Paul before Felix: "We have, in fact, found this man a pestilent fellow, an agitator among all the Jews throughout the inhabited world, and a ringleader of the sect of the Nazarenes" (Acts 24:5).

Jubilees as a source for *Rec.* 1.27–71 and Luke-Acts

In considering the influences that contributed to the overall design of *Rec.* 1.27–71, F. Stanley Jones makes an important observation:[108]

> The author [of *Rec.* 1.27–71] . . . seems to have been influenced by the review of biblical history in Acts 7 as an example of how he might proceed. Acts 7 perhaps sparked the idea of composing a "universal history," and not just a book of acts. The *Book of Jubilees* proved particularly helpful as R 1 began his account with the creation story. R 1's version is better than Acts 7 insofar as it not only begins at creation but also pursues some clear goals. For example, material from *Jubilees* is adopted to explain how the land of Israel belonged to the Hebrew race even before the time of Abraham. This theme is pursued by the author throughout his composition and forms a remarkable witness to Christian justification for Christian inheritance of the land. The author has developed a distinctively Christian form of deuteronomistic theology.

Jones emphasizes two influences that contributed to the formation of the overall structure of *Rec.* 1.27–71. First, he credits the review of biblical history in Acts 7 with supplying the decisive impulse for writing a "universal history" from a Deuteronomic perspective. We may remark that while Acts 7 certainly contributed to the author's unique Deuteronomic theology,[109] the latter derives more fundamentally from Jesus' Cleansing of the Temple in Lk. 19:45–6 parr., seen against the background of 1 Kgs. 8:27–53. This OT passage also reinforces the author's rejection of sacrifice and his emphasis on the participation of the nations. Moreover, the idea for a universal history is not limited to Acts 7; it is implicit at many other points in Luke-Acts. As discussed in Chapter 3, for example, there is almost a subtext in Luke-Acts, which retells the story of the Flood (Genesis 6–9), the Table of Nations (Genesis 10), and the Tower of Babel (Genesis 11). As for beginning *Rec.* 1.27–71 with a creation account, we must recall that the genealogy in Lk. 3:23–38 traces Jesus' lineage from Joseph (v. 23), through Noah (v. 36) and his sons, back to Adam, son of God (v. 38; cf. Acts 17:26). This genealogy is evidently where *Rec.* 1.27–71 derives its interest in the origins of Jesus,[110] frequently referring to him as the "Son" in this connection.[111] In fact, one of the main reasons that our text includes the creation account in the first part might be in order to make a Christological point in the second part. Hence, by examining Luke-Acts as a whole, rather than Acts in isolation, we begin to see the total sweep of biblical history, which informed the writing of *Rec.* 1.27–71.

Second, Jones credits the *Book of Jubilees*, especially its creation account and its Land theology, with inspiring the beginning of the Ps.-Clementine text and its emphasis on the Land, respectively. In response to this suggestion, we have just discussed a more probable reason why *Rec.* 1.27–71 begins with creation. Similarly, while *Jubilees* clearly influences the Land theology of *Rec.* 1.27–71 (cf. 1.30.3), Luke-Acts provides the main catalyst for expectations of return and restoration to the Land which permeate the later Jewish–Christian source.[112] In other words, Luke-Acts is the primary impulse for theology and historiography in *Rec.* 1.27–71. This does not diminish the importance of *Jubilees* as a source for *Rec.* 1.27–71, but it does put *Jubilees* into perspective. Based on our observations in Chapter 3, Luke-Acts itself appears to have used *Jubilees* as a source.[113] In that case, Luke-Acts is probably the main catalyst even in the use of *Jubilees* in *Rec.* 1.27–71.

Conclusion

If we are correct that *Rec.* 1.27–71 is oriented primarily on Luke-Acts and secondarily on *Jubilees* through Luke-Acts, then we may be able to learn about Luke-Acts and its use of *Jubilees* by studying *Rec.* 1.27–71.

We have already begun to see in Chapter 3 how studying the later Jewish–Christian source can be of considerable help in the exegesis of Luke-Acts (see esp. on Acts 15:20, 29). More importantly for the purposes of the present chapter, *Rec.* 1.27–71 confirms our interpretation that the emphasis on the nations in Luke-Acts is in part influenced by the Table of Nations tradition in *Jubilees* 8–9. For *Rec.* 1.27–71 clearly refers to Jerusalem as the center of the earth and to the division of the earth among the sons of Noah (1.30.3). Using this method we can penetrate the fundamental theological conceptions which compelled the early Christian movement in Jerusalem to mission both at home and abroad. Both Luke-Acts and *Rec.* 1.27–71 have the conception of a centrifugal movement away from the Holy City to the ends of the earth that is matched by a centripetal movement back to the center as the place of OT and Jewish eschatological expectations. This conception is shaped by the *imago mundi* in *Jubilees* 8–9.

5

THEOPHILUS OF ANTIOCH

Introduction

We continue our survey of the early Christian reception of the Genesis Table of Nations tradition by examining the work of Theophilus of Antioch. This second-century Greek apologist used the authoritative *Book of Jubilees* in order to combat pagan philosophy. In the process, he clearly alludes to *Jubilees* 8–9 and perhaps even to an accompanying map.

Theophilus was a bishop of Antioch in the late second century (169–77 CE).[1] He completed *Ad Autolycum*, his only extant work, sometime after Marcus Aurelius had died (3.28), that is, after 180 CE, during the reign of Commodus (180–92 CE). *Ad Autolycum* provides some biographical information about its author. Theophilus lived near the Tigris and Euphrates rivers (*Autol.* 2.24), converted to Christianity by reading the Greek OT (1.14), and then lived among Christians who were an opposed and denigrated minority (3.4).

Theophilus was very likely a "Jewish Christian," however carefully that vexed term must be defined.[2] Whereas he explicitly states that he is a Christian (1.12),[3] his Jewishness must be inferred from the text. Several lines of evidence can be adduced. First, Theophilus presupposes that the Law and the Prophets are "our writings" (3.29), that Abraham is "our Patriarch" (3.24) and "our forefather" (3.28), as is David (3.25, 28). Likewise, the Hebrews of the exodus story are "our forefathers" (3.20). These first-person plurals indicate Theophilus' identification with the Jewish people, and they are not merely an extension of Pauline usage, in which the reference to Abraham as "our forefather" and "our father" includes believing Gentiles (Rom. 4:1, 11–12).[4] For Theophilus makes it clear that he regards "the Hebrews (also called Jews)" as "the righteous seed of pious and holy men, Abraham, Isaac, and Jacob" (*Autol.* 3.9). Second, Theophilus' theology[5] and exegesis[6] are strongly Jewish. His dependence on Jewish apologetics[7] and his own emphasis on biblical history[8] and monotheism[9] make his writings thoroughly Jewish in character. As

Skarsaune remarks, "Were it not for some NT quotations and allusions, and the inclusion of the Logos Christology in his account of creation, Theophilus could be taken for a Jewish author."[10] Although Judaism was the matrix of early Christianity as a whole, there may be enough evidence to suggest that Theophilus himself was Jewish.

In his three books against Autolycus, Theophilus writes as an apologist who seeks to present the Christian truth and to debunk certain Greek notions. In Book 1, Theophilus assembles various catechetical materials in order to justify his own faith in the invisible Creator God and in the resurrection. In Book 2, he brings out the contradictions of the Greek philosophers and poets on the origin of the world, and contrasts them with the prophets, who were inspired by God. In Book 3, he continues some of the themes developed in Book 2, and writes a world chronicle to demonstrate the antiquity and accuracy of "our religion" (3.29), which includes OT history. Theophilus' tract constitutes an important repository of early interpretive traditions.

Jewish geographical conceptions

Given Theophilus' Jewish background and perspective, we are not surprised to find elements of Jewish geographical tradition in his apology. For purposes of the present study, we will concentrate on several statements in Book 2. In *Autol.* 2.11–32, Theophilus provides an exegetical treatment of the primeval history in Genesis 1–11 that betrays influence from Jewish geographical tradition.[11] Grant suggests that most of the treatise on Genesis 1–11 in *Autol.* 2.11–32 probably existed separately prior to its inclusion in *Ad Autolycum*.[12]

The first evidence of Jewish geographical tradition comes in Theophilus' description of the rivers of paradise from Gen. 2:10–14. Having cited Gen. 2:10–14 in *Autol.* 2.20, Theophilus proceeds to comment on this passage:

> To show that paradise is of earth and was planted on the earth, scripture says: "And God planted paradise in Eden to the east, and he set man there ..." (Gen. 2:8). By the expressions "also from the earth" and "to the east" the divine scripture clearly teaches us that paradise is under this very heaven which are the east and the earth ...
>
> The scripture indicated that a river flows out of Eden to water paradise, and that from there it is divided into four sources. Two called Phison and Geon water the eastern regions

(τὰ ἀνατολικὰ μέρη), especially Geon, which encircles the
whole land of Ethiopia and is a river which they say (φασιν)
appears in Egypt, where it is called the Nile. The other two
rivers are well known to us (they are called the Tigris and the
Euphrates) because they are on the edge of our own regions.

Of the four rivers of paradise, Theophilus discusses only one of them in
any depth. First, he does not identify the Phison, which Josephus equates
with the Ganges (*Ant.* 1.38), but states that the Geon, encircling Ethiopia,
appears in Egypt, "where it is called the Nile." Likewise, Josephus states
that the Geon that flows through Egypt is called the Nile by the Greeks
(*Ant.* 1.39). Theophilus explicitly follows (Jewish) tradition here (φασιν).
Whereas some Greco-Roman writers looked to the West for the source
of the Nile (cf. Herodotus 2.33; Dio Cassius 75.13),[13] others, including
some Jewish authors, put it in the east (cf. Ptolemaios 1.17.5; *Jub.* 8:23:
"The Gihon River goes until it reaches the right side of the Garden of
Eden").[14] Whereas Philo rejects the view that treats the rivers of paradise
as real, opting instead for an allegorical interpretation of the rivers as
symbolizing the four cardinal virtues (*Quaest. Gen.* 1.12), Theophilus
emphasizes the concrete, geographical reality of both paradise and the
rivers of paradise. Second, Theophilus also gives no explanation for the
Tigris and the Euphrates. The reason for this, however, is twofold. On
the one hand, these two rivers are well known to Theophilus because
they border on "our regions" (κλίματα)[15] and hence require no further
description. On the other hand, scripture itself fails to give the location of
the Euphrates, as Philo also recognized and attempted to explain (*Quaest. Gen.* 1.13).

The second evidence of Jewish geographical tradition in *Autol.* 2.11–
32 comes in Theophilus' account of the postdiluvian settlement of the
earth based on Genesis 10–11 (*Autol.* 2.32):

> Those who love learning and antiquities can judge whether what
> has been said by us through the holy prophets is merely recent
> or not by considering this: though there were originally only a
> few men at the time in Arabia and Chaldea, after the division
> of their languages they gradually began to become many and to
> multiply over the whole earth. Some turned to dwell to the east,
> some to the parts of the great continent and the region to the
> north so that they reached the Britons in the arctic zones. Others
> inhabited the land of Canaan, which is also called Judea and
> Phoenicia, and the regions of Ethiopia and Egypt and Libya and

the so-called torrid zone and the areas extending to the west. The rest, beginning with the lands from the sea coast and Pamphylia, inhabited Asia and Greece and Macedonia and finally Italy and the so-called Gauls and Spains and Germanies. Thus the whole world is now filled with inhabitants. Since, then, the settlement of the world by humanity had a triple beginning, in the east and south and west, later the other parts of the earth were also inhabited when people came to be very numerous. Writers who do not know these things want to call the world spherical or to compare it with a cube. How can they speak truthfully in these matters when they do not know how the world was created or how it was inhabited? As men gradually *increased and multiplied* (Gen. 9:1) on the earth, as we have said, the islands of the sea and other regions were thus inhabited (cf. Gen. 10:5).

Although nothing is mentioned here about Noah and his sons, the account is nevertheless clearly based on Genesis 10–11, as the immediately preceding context shows (*Autol.* 2.30–1). Theophilus describes the settlement of the world as radiating out from Arabia and Chaldea (i.e., the land of Shinar; cf. Gen. 10:10; 11:2) and proceeding in a counterclockwise direction in three major population movements, which seem to correspond to the three continents – Asia, Europe, and Libya/Africa.[16] The text states that one population movement turned to dwell to the east, which stands for the continent of Asia. Another group is said to have settled "the great continent," which signifies Europe (cf. Herodotus 4.42, 45). The third movement is described as settling Canaan, Ethiopia, Egypt and Libya, which collectively stand for Libya/Africa. Canaan is correctly included with the African lands because according to Gen. 10:6, Canaan is one of the descendants of Ham, who occupied Africa.

Although the text clearly affirms that "the settlement of the world by humanity had a *triple* beginning" (τριμεροῦς οὖν γεγενημένης τῆς κατοικήσεως τῶν ἀνθρώπων ἐπὶ τῆς γῆς κατ' ἀρχάς), Theophilus anomalously adds a fourth population which overlaps with the Asian and European movements already mentioned: "The rest, beginning with the lands from the seacoast and Pamphylia, inhabited Asia and Greece and Macedonia and finally Italy and the so-called Gauls and Spains and Germanies." Theophilus obviously sees this fourth movement as a subsequent development caused by overpopulation: "... later (μετέπειτα) the other parts of the earth were also inhabited when people came to be very numerous (χυδαίων)."[17] The point is clear: the Greeks, against whom Theophilus polemicizes in *Ad Autolycum*, were established as a people at a later date than much of the rest of human-ity, including, of course, the Jews. Hence, "those who love learning and antiquities can judge whether what has been said by us through the holy prophets is merely recent or not . . ." Theophilus evidently uses the fact that Judea was among the earliest lands to be settled in order to bolster his claim that the Jewish scriptures are more ancient. Moreover, he uses the primeval history of human settlement to polemicize against comparatively recent Greco-Macedonian (and Roman) intrusion in the East. This mes-sage is quite in keeping with the point of *Jubilees* 8–9. As we discussed in Chapter 2, *Jubilees* regards the original boundaries of the nations as fixed and inviolable, with intruding nations being liable to a terrible curse and divine judgment. Theophilus seems to reflect that tradition at this point.

There is further evidence that Theophilus' account of the settlement of the earth is dependent on the *Jubilees* 8–9 tradition. First, the emphasis on the three continents of the inhabited world is reminiscent of *Jubilees* 8–9, which presupposes these same continents when it chooses the Tanais, the Nile and Gadir as the precise boundaries between the territories of the three sons of Noah.[18]

Second, when Theophilus writes that "some turned to dwell to the east," this is directly comparable to *Jub.* 8:21, which states that Shem was given "all the land of the east" as his portion. Moreover, *Jubilees* repeatedly emphasizes the location of Shem's portion as being in the east.

Third, when Theophilus writes that "some [turned] to the parts of the great continent and the regions to the north so that they reached the Britons in the arctic zones," this seems to rely on *Jub.* 8:29: "This is the land that emerged for Japheth and his children as his hereditary share which he would occupy for himself and his children throughout their generations forever: five large islands and a large land in the north." *Jubilees* repeatedly emphasizes that Japheth's portion lies in the north (cf. 8:25). Although *Jubilees* does not explicitly mention Britain, the fifth "great island" in Japheth's portion (*Jub.* 8:29) may well be Britain.[19]

Fourth, when Theophilus writes that "Others inhabited the land of Canaan, which is also called Judea and Phoenicia, and the regions of Ethiopia and Egypt and Libya and the so-called torrid zone and the areas extending to the west," this reflects the description of Ham's territory, which proceeds from east to west (*Jub.* 8:22; 9:1).[20]

Finally, and perhaps most tellingly, Theophilus describes three κλίματα corresponding to the three continents, specifically "the arc-tic zones" (τὰ ἀρκτικὰ κλίματα), "the so-called torrid zone" (ἡ καλουμένη διακεκαυμένη [ζώνη]), and "the regions extending to the West" (τὰ μέχρι δυσμῶν κλίματα παρατείνοντα). Strabo gives an overview of the ways that Greek attempts to divide the world into zones, including, for example, that of Poseidonius (ca. 135–50 BCE), who critiqued the usual division of the earth into five zones – one uninhabited (torrid) zone, two inhabitable (temperate) zones, and two uninhabited (frigid) zones – and replaced it with divisions based on astronomical criteria.[21] Theophilus' three climates can best be compared to *Jubilees* 8, where Shem receives the most favorable portion in the temperate "center of the earth" (8:12–21), Ham receives the hot southern portion (vv. 22–4), and Japheth receives the cold northern portion (vv. 25–30). If Theophilus is dependent on *Jubilees* at this point, he could be the first known Syrian to transmit the Table of Nations tradition of *Jubilees* 8–9, which, as we shall see in the next chapter, resurfaces in the medieval Syriac *Chronicle to the Year 1234*.[22]

Based on this evidence, it appears probable that Theophilus used the *Book of Jubilees* in his description of how the postdiluvian world was settled. Since, as we have seen, Theophilus was very likely Jewish, his exposure to *Jubilees* seems quite plausible, especially since he clearly refers to other non-biblical Jewish writings, including the *Sibylline Oracles*.[23] Moreover, Theophilus may possibly refer to *Jubilees* by name in his writings. In *Autol.* 2.29, after citing the Septuagint text of Gen. 4:1–2, Theophilus continues: "There is a fuller narrative about these sons (τὰ μὲν οὖν κατ᾽ αὐτοὺς πλείω ἔχει τὴν ἱστορίαν), in addition to an exegetical treatment; those who love learning can obtain a most accurate narrative from the book itself which is entitled *Genesis of the World* (Γένεσις κόσμου)." Grant notes that *Genesis of the World* is "possibly, but not certainly, the book of Genesis."[24] A possibility that Grant does not consider, however, is that Theophilus is referring to the *Book of Jubilees*, which is commonly called "the Little Genesis" (ἡ Λεπτὴ Γένεσις or *Parva Genesis*).[25] Indeed, two Greek fragments of the *Book of Jubilees* contain the exact expression "Genesis of the World" in reference to the teaching that Moses received on Sinai.[26] Since *Jubilees* itself claims to record what "the Lord told to Moses on Mount Sinai when he went up to receive the tablets of the law and the commandment by the word of the Lord . . ." (Prologue), *Genesis of the World* may refer to *Jubilees*.[27] Interestingly enough, Syncellus (5.26–8) quotes from a pseudepigraphic work ("the so-called *Life of Adam*") for the sake of those who love learning (φιλομαθίας χάριν), a work that Hermann Rönsch suggests may be an epitome of the *Book of Jubilees*.[28]

Further evidence substantiates the possibility that *Genesis of the World* refers to *Jubilees*. In *Autol.* 2.30, Theophilus refers back to this *Genesis of the World* as follows: "To replace Abel, God allowed Eve to conceive and bear a son, who was called Seth; from him the rest of the human race is derived up to the present day. For those who desire and love learning, it is easy to make a description of all the generations from the holy scriptures. And there already exists for us a partial account elsewhere (καὶ γὰρ ἐκ μέρους ἡμῖν γεγένηται ἤδη λόγος ἐν ἑτέρῳ λόγῳ), as we said above (2.29) – the order of the genealogy in the first book, which is on history." The juxtaposition of "the holy scriptures" to the aforementioned work leads us to believe that *Genesis of the World* is not the biblical book of Genesis and increases the likelihood that it is the *Book of Jubilees*. Somewhat further in the same passage, Theophilus continues: "And the story of Noah, by some called Deucalion, has already been explained to us in the book which we mentioned before; if you will, you too can read it."[29] And likewise in *Autol.* 2.31: "As for the three sons of Noah and their relationships and their genealogies, we have a brief catalogue (ὁ κατάλογος ἐν ἐπιτομῇ) in the book previously mentioned."[30] Hence, if Theophilus clearly used the *Book of Jubilees* (see above on *Autol.* 2.32), and if the work *Genesis of the World* is clearly different from the biblical book of Genesis and has an express connection to the language of *Jubilees*, then we may plausibly propose that the work to which Theophilus refers is none other than the *Book of Jubilees*.

After this discussion of how the postdiluvian world was settled, Theophilus concludes *Autol.* 2.32 with a final geographical point which is of some interest to us:

> Writers who do not know these things want to call the world spherical or to compare it with a cube (βούλονται τὸν κόσμον σφαιροειδῆ λέγειν καὶ ὡσπερεὶ κύβῳ συγκρίνειν αὐτόν). How can they speak truthfully in these matters when they do not know how the world was created or how it was inhabited? As men gradually *increased and multiplied* (Gen. 9:1) on the earth, as we have said, the islands of the sea and other regions were thus inhabited (cf. Gen. 10:5).

There are many unanswered questions in this short passage. It is not immediately apparent, for example, why Theophilus would bring up the issue of the shape of the world in the context of the postdiluvian settlement of the world. From the train of thought in the passage, it seems unmotivated. Clearly, Theophilus is reacting against (Greek) conceptions that the world is spherical or cubic.[31] But why should Theophilus' understanding of the creation of the world and its postdiluvian settlement be so obviously adverse to these two conceptions of the world's shape?[32] Moreover, what shape does Theophilus think the world has – and on what basis? Presumably Theophilus' conception was planar rather than three-dimensional, like a sphere or a cube.[33] Perhaps the dispersion of the peoples from a common center (the Tower of Babel; cf. *Autol.* 2.31) to the rest of the world suggested to Theophilus the general shape of the world: a disk surrounded by Ocean and containing islands, the islands being the last places to be settled after the mainland had already been inhabited. In his discussion of the six days of creation, Theophilus cites Isa. 40:22 ("This is God, who made the heavens like a vaulted ceiling and stretched it out like a tent to live in"), suggesting perhaps that the earth has a rectangular shape. In his *Christian Topography*, Cosmas Indicopleustes (fl. 540 CE) sharply attacks those who believed the world to be spherical, presenting the earth instead as a rectangle surrounded by Ocean – a conception which, he claims, goes back to Ephorus of Cyme (ca. 405–330 BCE).[34] Cosmas ridiculed the idea that people could hang upside down by their toes, and that rain could fall *up* in the southern hemisphere. Such a view was quite common among Christians.[35]

There is yet another possible reason for Theophilus' reaction against the (Greek) conceptions: his source for this section may have contained a world map which was neither spherical nor cubic. As we have seen, the *Book of Jubilees* is arguably one of Theophilus' main sources for the present section, and a source to which he frequently refers in *Ad Autolycum*. Although *Jubilees* 8–9 mentions nothing about the shape of the world that was divided among the sons of Noah, it is often assumed to be a disk.[36] If the manuscript of *Jubilees* which Theophilus consulted contained such a map, that would explain both the basis for Theophilus' critique of other conceptions and the reason for bringing up a subject that was seemingly unmotivated by the previous context. Several modern scholars entertain the possibility that the *Book of Jubilees* originally contained a world map.[37] While manuscript support for this view is wholly lacking, there is, as we have seen in Chapter 1, at least some literary evidence that Jews were involved in producing world maps during the Second-Temple period. Therefore, it is not impossible that Theophilus consulted a map.

Conclusion

We have seen evidence that as early as ca. 180 CE a Christian was using Greek *Jubilees* as an apologetic tool. Theophilus presupposes the validity of the image of the world in *Jubilees* 8–9 and argues on the basis of it. If this is correct, the date of Greek *Jubilees* is pushed back to a period even earlier than at first suspected. As we have seen, the *Book of Jubilees* was originally written in Hebrew and was subsequently translated from Hebrew into Greek, and from Greek into Latin, Ethiopic and perhaps also Syriac. Some textual evidence survives from each of these languages, although the only complete text of *Jubilees* now extant is the Ethiopic version, which appeared relatively late in the book's textual transmission. Unfortunately, no copy of the crucial Greek translation has come down to us from antiquity.[38] According to James C. VanderKam, all that remains of it is a series of paraphrases of or allusions to material in *Jubilees* found in the writings of several Greek authors, especially Epiphanius (ca. 315–403 CE) and the Byzantine chronographers Syncellus and Cedrenus.[39] There is insufficient evidence for precisely dating the Greek translation of *Jubilees*, although it is not impossible that the Greek version was very early, as the recently identified fragments of Greek *1 Enoch* show.[40] William Adler[41] and VanderKam[42] agree with Heinrich Gelzer's thesis that the traditions from *Jubilees* in chronographers such as Syncellus were derived from the works of the fourth-century Alexandrian authors Panodorus and Annianos.[43] With the evidence of Theophilus, it may be possible now to push back the date even further.

Another early reference to Greek *Jubilees* comes from a letter (*P. Oxy.* 4365) dating to the end of the third century or the beginning of the fourth century CE, in which someone urges a woman, who is addressed as "my dearest lady sister" and greeted "in the Lord," to lend him the *(Book of) Ezra/Esdras*, since he had lent her "the Little Genesis" (τὴν Λεπτὴν Γένεσιν).[44] Taken together, the letter and Theophilus' *Ad Autolycum* show that *Jubilees* was popular and circulated in early Christianity. This impression will be strengthened in the next two chapters, as we continue our investigation of the *Jubilees* 8–9 tradition.

6

HIPPOLYTUS OF ROME

Introduction

As we saw in Chaper 5, the second-century Greek Apologist, Theophilus of Antioch, may give us the earliest explicit reference to Greek *Jubilees*. There is also evidence that Greek *Jubilees* remained popular in the following centuries (cf. *P. Oxy.* 4365). This may be due in part to the growth of the Christian world/universal chronicles, which frequently incorporated *Jubilees* 8–9 material at the beginning of larger chronographies. While Eusebius of Caesarea (ca. 260–340 CE) is often acknowledged as the first to establish the format and style of the Christian world chronicle, forerunners of his chronographic approach are found in the work of Sextus Julius Africanus and of Hippolytus, who wrote within fifteen years of one another (ca. 220–35 CE).[1] Since we know relatively little about the lost *Chronographies* of Africanus, except through fragments that have come down to us in other authors,[2] we will do well to concentrate on the *Chronicon* of Hippolytus, which survives basically intact.[3]

Given the paucity of our direct textual evidence for the Greek version of *Jubilees*, it is surprising that Hippolytus' *Chronicon* (234/5 CE) has not been given more consideration as a source for that version, for the *Chronicon* contains a large section called the "Division of the Earth" (Διαμερισμὸς τῆς γῆς, §§ 44–239) which, like *Jubilees* 8–9, covers the parceling of the earth among the sons of Noah based on the Table of Nations in Genesis 10.[4] The title of this section probably derives from Gen. 10:25, which gives the reason that one of Eber's son was called Peleg (Greek: Φαλεκ): "... for in his days the earth was divided" (ὅτι ἐν ταῖς ἡμέραις αὐτοῦ διεμερίσθη ἡ γῆ).[5] While the suggestion has been made that the lost chronography of Julius Africanus was the first of the Christian chronographies to incorporate the *Jubilees* 8–9 tradition,[6] Bauer and Helm suggested that Hippolytus is the first chronographer to have included the *Diamerismos* material, that Julius Africanus contains no hint of it, and that subsequent chronographies are dependent on Hippolytus for this material.[7] Did Hippolytus use *Jubilees* 8–9 for the *Diamerismos*? Unfortunately, Bauer and Helm failed to answer this question in their discussion of the *Diamerismos*' sources.[8] Earlier, in his major study of the *Chronicon*, Bauer had expressed the opinion that there was no connection between the *Diamerismos* and *Jubilees* 8–9, but he did not elaborate on how this conclusion was reached.[9] Equally unsubstantiated is the opposite opinion of A.-M. Denis: "La *Chronique d'Hippolyte* contient une 'division de la terre entre les fils de Noé,' que certains font dériver de *Jub.*, 8 et 9."[10]

The purpose of the present chapter is to explore whether Hippolytus may have used the Greek version of *Jubilees* 8–9 in writing his *Diamerismos*.[11] The strongly geographical content of the two writings provides an excellent means by which to test literary dependence. To this end, the following study proceeds in five steps: (1) a survey of Hippolytus and his understanding of Judaism; (2) an examination of the purpose of Hippolytus' *Diamerismos*; (3) an overview of the *Diamerismos* itself; (4) a detailed comparison of the *Diamerismos* with *Jubilees* 8–9; and (5) a short account of the *Wirkungsgeschichte* of Hippolytus' *Diamerismos*.

Hippolytus and his understanding of Judaism

Hippolytus of Rome (ca. 170–236 CE), the last Roman Christian author to write in Greek, was a presbyter and perhaps bishop in the Roman church. Before considering whether Hippolytus may have appropriated the Greek *Jubilees* tradition, we must consider the possible influence of Jewish tradition on him. While a comprehensive study of this matter remains a desideratum,[12] a few seminal observations can be offered here. First of all, Hippolytus may have used the Greek *Testaments of the Twelve Patriarchs* as a source for his exegesis.[13] If so, this may be an indication of Jewish influence on his thinking. For although the texts, as they have come down to us, contain unmistakable Christian passages,[14] these contributions are minor compared to the abundance of Jewish material.[15] Sources for some of the individual *Testaments* have now been identified among the Qumran scrolls, showing that they originally enjoyed considerable status within the Qumran community.[16] Again, however, there are formidable methodological problems in isolating original Jewish traditions in works of the so-called "OT Pseudepigrapha" which have been transmitted by Christians.[17]

Second, Hippolytus' *Diamerismos* identifies the Romans with the Κίτιοι/Κιτιαῖοι.[18] According to Gen. 10:2, 4, Kittim is the son of Javan son of Japheth. Originally, the name Kittim referred to the inhabitants of Kition on Cyprus (cf. Josephus, *Ant.* 1.128; Hippolytus, *Chron.* 73).[19]

In Hellenistic–Jewish texts, the name is applied to the Macedonians (e.g., 1 Macc. 1:1; 8:5).[20] In Dan. 11:30 LXX, כתים is translated Ῥωμαῖοι, although this is an isolated instance, and the Greek-speaking reader would not necessarily know that Kittim stood in the *Vorlage*. Indeed, as a search of the TLG database and of A.-M. Denis' concordance to the Greek pseudepigrapha[21] reveals, Kittim as a name for the Romans does not seem to have been at all common in Greek-speaking Jewish and Christian circles.[22] In contrast, Qumran scrolls regularly use Kittim as a cryptonym for the Romans, at least in the later texts (after 63 BCE).[23] Very likely, therefore, Hippolytus' identification of the Kittim with the Romans stems from a source with close ties to the Qumran community.[24] Interestingly enough, the only place in Hippolytus' writings where Kittim occurs is in the *Diamerismos*.

Third, Hippolytus seems to be familiar with and sympathetic to the Essenes in his *Refutation of All Heresies* (9.18–31).[25] Although his description of the Essenes may depend on Josephus' very similar account (*JW* 2.119–66; cf. *Ant.* 18.11–22),[26] this is probably not the case, or at least not completely, because, with the publication of the Qumran scrolls, Hippolytus has been shown to be correct in describing the Essenes as believing in the resurrection of the body (*Ref.* 9.27; cf. 4Q521 line 12),[27] whereas Josephus claims that they do not (*JW* 2.154–5).[28] Furthermore, as John J. Collins has observed, it is quite possible that Hippolytus has preserved some authentic details of Essene eschatology that were omitted by Josephus.[29] For Hippolytus mentions the Essenes' belief in "both a judgment and a conflagration of the universe" (*Ref.* 9.27), an eschatological expectation that finds striking confirmation in 1QH 11.29–36. Hence, however "Christianized" his account may be, Hippolytus seems to have independent access to at least some reliable information about the Essenes.

Taken together, this evidence converges on one point: Hippolytus evidently has a special affinity for Essene/Qumran tradition.[30] If this is correct, then it is not unreasonable to expect that he should also have access to the "book" of Noah tradition from *Jubilees* 8–9, which, as we have seen, is also found at Qumran (cf. 1QapGen. 16–17).[31]

Purpose of Hippolytus' *Chronicon*

The *Chronicon*, whose full title is "The Compilation of Times and Years from the Creation of the World Until the Present Day" (Συναγωγὴ χρόνων καὶ ἐτῶν ἀπὸ κτίσεως κόσμου ἕως τῆς ἐνεστώσης ἡμέρας, §1), calculates the age of the world from creation to the "present day," that is, until the thirteenth year of Alexander Severus (= 5738 *anno mundi* or 234/35 CE).[32] Hippolytus' purpose in making these calculations is to counteract an imminent expectation of the parousia, the downfall of the Romans (the Kittim!), and the final judgment of the world – eschatological hopes which Bauer and Helm call an "Erbstück des Judentums."[33] Hippolytus wants to show that the sixth millennium, which, it was hoped, would usher in the new era, was still over two and a half centuries away (6000 – 5738 = 262 years).[34]

If Hippolytus' purpose in writing the *Chronicon*, and hence his purpose in including the *Diamerismos*, was to counter contemporary apocalyptic speculation, then it is interesting to note that *Jubilees* 8–9 is apocalyptically oriented.[35] According to *Jub.* 1:27, Moses is told about everything "from the beginning of creation till my sanctuary has been built among them for all eternity" (*Jub.* 1:27). This includes the expected eschatological judgment by sword and fire (*Jub.* 9:15). Moreover, as we have seen in Chapter 2, the Samaritan *Asatir* (4.19), which comes within the context of a division of the earth very much like *Jubilees* 8–9 (*Asatir* 4.13–18), makes a similar calculation of the end based on the assumption of 6,000 years of human history: "And when Noah had finished the division of the land by the astronomical calculation of the day, he found that there were still four thousand three hundred years less seven years to come after the flood, of the six thousand from the beginning of the creation and three hundred and seven since the flood." It is easy to see how this kind of fixed date could give rise to apocalyptic speculation among those who calculate that the time of the end was at hand. Hence, we may consider how this "Erbstück des Judentums" may have contributed to the apocalyptic expectations in Hippolytus' day, given the aforementioned earlier influence of *Jubilees* 8–9 on the Third Sibyl and the War Scroll. *Jubilees* 8–9 looks forward to the final judgment of the nations (9:15). Perhaps Hippolytus was countering eschatological expectations to which *Jubilees* 8–9 in part gave rise in the Christian church.[36] If Hippolytus incorporates *Jubilees* 8–9 into his *Chronicon*, it will be in order to neutralize its apocalyptic influence.

Overview of the *Diamerismos*

Occurring towards the beginning of the *Chronicon*, the *Diamerismos* is sandwiched between two major sections which mark it off as an independent literary unit: on the one hand, the "Book of the Origin of Humanity" (Βίβλος γενέσεως ἀνθρώπων, §§ 22–42), which lists the patriarchs from Adam to Noah, and, on the other hand, the *Stadiasmos of the Great Sea* (§§ 240–613), which provides a sailing handbook and a coastal description for circumnavigating the Mediterranean.[37] Although, unlike §§ 22–42, the *Diamerismos* is not explicitly entitled a "book," the paragraph which transitions to the "beginning of the chronography" (Ἀρχὴ τοῦ χρονογράφου, § 43), that is, the *Diamerismos*, refers to "other books" in such a way as to suggest that the source of the *Diamerismos* may also be considered a "book": "But you will find the beginning [of the chronography] in fuller detail in other books; however, we have written the *Diamerismos* only in brief" (ἀλλ' ἐν ἄλλοις βίβλοις εὑρήσεις πλατυτέρως τὴν ἀρχήν, ἡμεῖς δὲ τὸν διαμερισμὸν μόνον ἐν συντόμῳ γεγράφαμεν). Although these "other books" might refer exclusively to works that Hippolytus himself has written,[38] they may also include the "book" of Noah recorded in *Jubilees* 8–9, from which he drew as a source. An initial clue for this latter possibility is that, as in *Jubilees*, the foregoing section of the *Chronicon* prefaces the *Diamerismos* with a genealogy of the sons of Shem from Arpachshad to Peleg (§§ 36–41; cf. *Jub.* 8:1–8) and a date for the division of the earth (§ 42; cf. *Jub.* 8:10). Moreover, Syncellus (5.26–8) indicates that, for the sake of those who love learning, he has briefly (ἐν συντόμῳ) summarized information from the so-called *Life of Adam* (ταῦτα ἐκ τοῦ βίου λεγομένου Ἀδαμ φιλομαθίας χάριν ἐν συντόμῳ ἐστοιχείωσα). Rönsch suggests that this pseudepigraphon is an epitome of the *Book of Jubilees*.[39] We shall adduce further evidence below.

Like *Jubilees* 8–9, the *Diamerismos* consists of two interrelated parts. The first part (§§ 44–55) outlines the portions given to the three sons of Noah and the boundaries between them, according to the order: Shem, Ham, and Japheth. The second and larger part (§§ 56–197) introduces the sons of these three brothers (this time in reverse order: Japheth, Ham, and Shem) and the portions given in turn to them. Finally, the *Diamerismos* appends some miscellaneous geographical information (§§ 202–39),[40] which Hippolytus repeatedly claims to have added himself.[41] This corroborates our suggestion that Hippolytus wrote the rest of the *Diamerismos* on the basis of another source(s).

Comparison of Hippolytus' *Diamerismos* with *Jubilees* 8–9

General comparisons

As we have already begun to see, many general comparisons can be made between *Jubilees* 8–9 and Hippolytus' *Diamerismos*: (1) both explicitly refer to the "division of the earth" (*Jub.* 8:11; *Chron.* 44); (2) both have

an apocalyptic orientation; (3) both give the contents of a "book" which
is prefaced by a genealogy of the sons of Shem from Arpachshad to Peleg
and a date for the division of the earth; (4) both have a similar two-part
structure, describing first the division of the earth among the sons of Noah
and then the further subdivision of the earth among Noah's grandsons;
(5) and both use the term "lot, share" in referring to the portions of the earth
assigned to the sons of Noah (*Jub.* 8:11; *Chron.* 89, 197).[42] We may now
proceed to some more specific comparisons between the two writings.[43]

Specific observations

1   *The portions given to Noah's sons*

Both *Jubilees* 8–9 and Hippolytus' *Diamerismos* present the distribution
of the earth among the sons of Noah in the same order: Shem, Ham, and
Japheth (*Jub.* 8:12–30; *Chron.* 44–55). We shall examine each of these in
turn. First, Shem's portion is described in our two writings as follows:

Jub. 8:12–16, 21	*Chron.* 47
(12) In the book there emerged as Shem's lot the center of the earth which he would occupy as an inheritance for him and for his children throughout the history of eternity: from the middle of the mountain range of Rafa, from the source of the water from the Tina River. His share goes toward the west through the middle of this river. One then goes until one reaches the water of the deeps from which this river emerges. This river emerges and pours its waters into the Me'at Sea. This river goes as far as the Great Sea. Everything to the north belongs to Japheth, while everything to the south belongs to Shem. (13) It goes until it reaches Karas. This is in the bosom of the branch [lit., tongue] which faces southward.	(47) . . . and to Shem, the first-born [son], [was given] the length from Persia and Bactra to India, and the breadth from India to Rinocorura . . .

(14) His share goes toward the Great Sea and goes straight until it reaches to the west of the branch that faces southward, for this is the sea whose name is the Branch of the Egyptian Sea.

(15) It turns from there southward toward the mouth of the Great Sea on the shore of the waters. It goes toward the west of Afra and goes until it reaches the water of the Gihon River and to the south of the Gihon's waters along the banks of this river.

(16) It goes eastward until it reaches the Garden of Eden, toward the south side of it – on the south and from the east of the entire land of Eden and of all the east. It turns to the east and comes until it reaches to the east of the mountain range named Rafa. Then it goes down toward the bank of the Tina River's mouth.

(21) . . . all the land of Eden, all the land of the Erythrean Sea, all the land of the east, India, (that which is) in Erythrea and its mountains, all the land of Bashan, all the land of Lebanon, the islands of Caphtor, the entire mountain range of Sanir and Amana, the mountain range of Asshur which is in the north, all the land of Elam, Asshur, Babylon, Susan, and Madai; all the mountains of Ararat, all the area on the other side of the sea which is on the other side of the mountain range of Asshur toward the north . . .

The description in *Jubilees* is obviously much longer than the one in the *Diamerismos*, as would be expected if the latter is an abridgement (see above on §43). Nevertheless, both descriptions define Shem's territory in roughly the same geographical terms.[44] In fact, all of the limits given in the *Diamerismos'* bare description are consistent with the lands and natural boundaries listed in *Jub.* 8:12–16, 21. Even the one apparent exception, "Rinocorura" ('Ρινοκόρουρα),[45] can be explained if *Jubilees* was the *Vorlage*.[46] A maritime town located about thirty miles south of Raphia, Rinocorura (el-'Arish) had long been a border town. Depending on the source one consults, Rinocorura lies on the border of Palestine and Egypt,[47] or near the border of "Phoenicia" and Egypt,[48] or on the border of Syria and Egypt.[49] According to Josephus (*Ant.* 13.396), Rinocorura was the southernmost coastal town held by the Jews under Alexander Jannaeus. Already in Isa. 27:12 LXX, Rinocorura is seen as a geographical boundary: "On that day, the Lord will fence all around from the channel of the River [= the Euphrates] to Rinocorura (ἕως 'Ρινοκορούρων; MT: עד־נחל מצרים), and you will gather the sons of Israel one by one." If Isaiah means by "the River of Egypt" the Gihon/Nile (corresponding to "the River" [Euphrates] in Mesopotamia),[50] then the Septuagint has substituted Rinocorura for the Gihon/Nile as the boundary marker. Likewise, the *Diamerismos* may have substituted Rinocorura for an original reference to the Gihon/Nile as a boundary between Shem and Ham.[51] An Armenian text, which is called *The Peoples of the Sons of Noah* (1660 CE) and strongly resembles Hippolytus' *Diamerismos*, describes the territory of Shem as follows:[52]

> And the border of Shem is around the middle part of the earth [cf. *Jub.* 8:12], to the east and to the west; the land of the Persians, that of the Syrians, Palestine *as far as the river Nile*.

Where Hippolytus' *Diamerismos* has "as far as Rinocorura" (ἕως 'Ρινοκορούρων), the Armenian text has "as far as the river Nile," perhaps preserving a reading that is closer to the Hebrew *Vorlage* of *Jubilees*.[53] Seen in this light, the *Diamerismos* preserves a hint of the original *Jubilees* text when it refers a few lines later to the Gihon/Nile as Ham's river (§51). Especially important is the geographical conception in §156: "Ham has the River Gihon, called the Nile, which circles all Egypt and Ethiopia;[54] the mouth of the Western Sea separates between Ham and Japheth." Here the Gihon/Nile evidently functions as a boundary between Ham and Shem, just as "the mouth of the Western Sea" (τὸ στόμα τῆς ἑσπερινῆς θαλάσσης), i.e., the Straits of Gibraltar,[55] functions as a boundary between Ham and Japheth.[56] It is noteworthy that in describing territorial boundaries, *Jub.* 8:15 also refers to "the mouth of the Great Sea."[57] We are obviously dealing with the same geographical conceptions in our two writings.

The reason for the change from an original Gihon to Rinocorura is perhaps not too difficult to surmise. The *Diamerismos* (or rather its source!) evidently wants to summarize Shem's territory ("... the length from Persia and Bactra to India, and the breadth from India to Rinocorura") in terms of the idealized borders of the Seleucid Empire under Antiochus III (ca. 223–187 BCE), whom Josephus says "ruled over Asia" (*Ant.* 12.129). In 212, Antiochus began his so-called *anabasis* to the "Upper Satrapies," bringing Commagene and Armenia under direct Seleucid rule; he restored Seleucid suzerainty over Parthia and Bactria (210–206 BCE), thereby earning for himself the surname "The Great"; and he renewed links with the Indian frontier (Polybius 11.39.11–12).[58] In several campaigns against the Ptolemaic kingdom (202–198 BCE), Antiochus established Seleucid control over southern Syria, Phoenicia, and Judea[59]; Rinocorura now marked the border between the Seleucid and Ptolemaic realms, as we have seen. By the treaty of Apamea (188 BCE), Antiochus relinquished Seleucid holdings west of the Taurus mountain range;[60] however, he still ruled a huge realm, from southern Turkey, through Syria and Palestine to Babylonia, Iran, and central Asia.[61] By thus expressing Shem's territory in terms of the extent of the Seleucid Empire, the source of Hippolytus' *Diamerismos* (Greek *Jubilees*) tacitly accuses the Seleucids (the Kittim of Japheth![62]) of seizing a domain that rightfully belonged to the Shemites.[63] As discussed in Chapter 2, *Jubilees* 8–10 also implies that the Seleucid occupation of the East is illegitimate. For the sons and grandsons of Noah had taken an oath that they would not trespass each other's territories on penalty of a terrible curse (*Jub.* 9:14–15). Now that the Seleucids, like the Canaanites before them (*Jub.* 10:27–34), had blatantly violated the oath, the implication is that they, too, stood under a curse. We may suspect that Hippolytus' *Diamerismos* epitomizes Greek *Jubilees* at this point, inadvertently leaving in the geographical details that apply to the situation under Hellenistic rule. If this interpretation is correct, then by using Rinocorura instead of Gihon to mark the boundary of the Shemite territory, Greek *Jubilees* was even more effective than the Hebrew *Vorlage* in emphasizing the Seleucids' intrusion.

The description in *Jubilees* also describes Shem's lot as "the center of the earth" (*Jub.* 8:12), for which the *Diamerismos* has no corresponding description. Nevertheless, in the very next lines, the *Diamerismos* seems to assume that Shem's portion lies in the middle of the earth, when it describes the territories of Ham and Japheth relative to Shem: Ham has "the portions to the South" (§ 48)[64] and Japheth has "the portions to the North" (§ 49).[65] Later, we read that Ham has territories "towards the [Mediterranean] Sea" (§ 150)[66] and that the tribes of Shem inhabit "toward the East" (§§ 159).[67] These directional indicators presuppose a point of reference in the geographical middle of all three portions, that is, Terra Sancta itself.[68] Although writing in Rome, Hippolytus adopts the standpoint of Palestine, most likely because he is following a source.

Second, Ham's portion is described in the two writings as follows:

Jub. 8:22–3	*Chron.* 48
(22) For Ham there emerged a second share toward the other side of Gihon – toward the south – on the right side of the garden. It goes southward and goes to all the fiery mountains. It goes westward toward the Atel Sea; it goes westward until it reaches the Mauk Sea, everything that descends into it is destroyed.	(48)... and to Ham, the second [son], from Rinocorura to Gadeira, the [portions] to the South...
(23) It comes to the north to the boundary of Gadir and comes to the shore of the sea waters, to the waters of the Great Sea, until it reaches the Gihon River. The Gihon River goes until it reaches the right side of the Garden of Eden.	

Here again, the description in *Jubilees* is more extensive than the one in the *Diamerismos*.[69] Nevertheless, both descriptions define Ham's territory in roughly the same geographical terms: (1) both contain the ordinal "second"; (2) both list Gadir/Gadeira as the westernmost limit of Ham's lot; and (3) both have the directional indicator "to the South." If, as we have suggested, Rinocorura substitutes for an original Gihon/Nile, then we have a further correspondence between our two texts. We should also observe that, unlike its previous description of Shem's territory, the *Diamerismos* does not use any lands in describing Ham's territory. This may be due to the fact that in *Jub.* 8:22–3, the description of the limits of the Ham's portion contains no inventory of the lands corresponding to the inventory of the lands of Shem in *Jub.* 8:21. Thus, while the *Diamerismos* may radically abridge the *Jubilees* description, it nonetheless retains the essence of the original.

Third, Japheth's portion is described in our two writings as follows:

Jub. 8:25–9	*Chron.* 49
(25) For Japheth there emerged a third share on the other side of the Tina River toward the north of the mouth of its waters. It goes toward the Northeast, (toward) the whole area of Gog and all that is east of them.	(49) and to Japheth, the third [son], from Media to Gadeira, the [portions] to the North.
(26) It goes due north and goes toward the mountains of Qelt, to the north and toward the Mauq Sea. It comes to the east of Gadir as far as the edge of the sea waters.	
(27) It goes until it reaches the west of Fara. Then it goes back toward Aferag and goes eastward toward the water of the Me'at Sea.	
(28) It goes to the edge of the Tina River toward the Northeast until it reaches the bank of its waters toward the mountain range of Rafa. It goes around the north.	
(29) . . . five large islands and a large land in the north.	

Once again, the description in *Jubilees* is longer than that in the *Diamerismos*.[70] Yet both descriptions delineate roughly the same geographical territory and have several important features in common: (1) the ordinal "third"; (2) Gadir/Gadeira as the westernmost limit of Japheth's territory; and (3) the directional indicator "to the North."

In sum, our comparison of the distribution of the earth among the sons of Noah in *Jubilees* 8 and the *Diamerismos* (*Chron.* 47–9) reveals a high degree of correspondence between the two descriptions. This correspondence cannot be explained as a mere result of the influence of common Jewish and Hellenistic traditions. Although this part of the *Diamerismos* is very much shorter than the *Jubilees* description, we must conclude that the former is dependent on the latter, and that Hippolytus himself abbreviated the Greek version of *Jubilees*.

2   *The portions given to the sons of Ham, Shem, and Japheth*

Whereas in *Jubilees* 9:1–13 the three sons of Noah divide their shares among their own sons according to the order from south to north (Ham, Shem, Japheth), the *Diamerismos* has the order Japheth, Ham, and Shem (§§ 56–197), possibly reflecting a chiastic pattern already evident in §§ 50–2. Perhaps Hippolytus of Rome wanted thereby to emphasize the Japhethite nations, for, as we have seen, Hippolytus is concerned with the apocalyptic end of the Roman Empire and shows special interest in the origins of the Roman people. There is another significant difference between the two descriptions. Whereas, as we have seen, Hippolytus greatly abbreviates the geographical detail of *Jubilees* 8, he not only abbreviates the geographical detail of *Jubilees* 9 but also expands the *Vorlage* in order to give greater scope to the origins of contemporary nations. In this regard, the second part of the *Diamerismos* is more like Josephus' update of the biblical Table of Nations (*Ant.* 1.122–47) than the original *Jubilees Vorlage*. Indeed, we may suspect the influence of Josephus on the *Diamerismos* at this point, although the actual overlap with Josephus is minimal.[71] In the following comparison, only the *Jubilees* text will be cited in full, and the *Diamerismos* will be cited as necessary.

Following the order in *Jubilees*, we encounter, first of all, the description of the territory of Ham's sons in *Jub.* 9:1:

> Ham divided (his share) among his sons. There emerged a first share for Cush to the east; to the west of him (one) for Egypt; to the west of him (one) for Put; to the west of him (one) for Canaan; and to the west of him was the sea.

The *Jubilees* text evidently infers the relative geographical location of the sons of Ham from the order of their presentation in Gen. 10:6. The corresponding section in the *Diamerismos* (*Chron.* 92–157) has a similar concept when it lists the sons of Ham in the same order (§§ 93–8) and then states that "their dwelling-place is from Rinocorura to Gadeira towards the South lengthwise" (§ 130; cf. § 136). However, the *Diamerismos* goes well beyond *Jubilees* by listing (1) the contemporary nations that stem from Ham's sons (§§ 92–130, 131–3), (2) the countries of Ham both in Africa and in Asia Minor (§§ 137–49, 150–1), and (3) the islands and the river of Ham (§§ 152–6). The text contains the idea that Ham gave rise to some of the nations of Asia Minor (§§ 111–17, 131–2) and that the Hamites possess countries (§§ 150–1) and islands (§§ 152–3) which would normally be considered part of Japhethite territory. These notions may reflect an Egyptian provenance for this material, or it may be an attempt to deal with the difficult expression "Afreg" (= Africa?) which is included in the description of Japheth's territory in *Jub.* 8:27.[72]

Second, we come to the description of the territory of Shem's sons in *Jub.* 9:2–6:

> (2) Shem, too, divided (his share) among his sons. (2) There emerged a first share for Elam and his children to the east of the Tigris River until it reaches the east of the entire land of India, in Erythrea on its border, the waters of the Dedan, all the mountains of Mebri and Ela, all the land of Susan, and everything on the border of Farnak as far as the Erythrean Sea and the Tina River. (3) For Asshur there emerged as the second share the whole land of Asshur, Nineveh, Shinar, and Sak as far as the vicinity of India, (where) the Wadafa River rises. (4) For Arpachshad there emerged as a third share all the land of the Chaldean region to the east of the Euphrates which is close to the Erythrean Sea; all the waters of the desert as far as the vicinity of the branch of the sea which faces Egypt; the entire land of Lebanon, Sanir, and Amana as far as the vicinity of the Euphrates. (5) There emerged for Aram as the fourth share the entire land of Mesopotamia between the Tigris and Euphrates to the north of the Chaldeans as far as the vicinity of the mountain range of Asshur and the land of Arara. (6) For Lud there emerged as the fifth share the mountain range of Asshur and all that belongs to it until it reaches the Great Sea and reaches to the east of his brother Asshur.

There is greater geographical detail here than in the previous description of the sons of Ham, and the *Diamerismos* follows suit accordingly. The *Diamerismos* begins with a general remark that the Shemites "inhabited to the East" (οὗτοι πρὸς ἀνατολὰς ᾤκησαν, § 159)[73] and concludes with a more specific summary: "The dwelling-place of all the sons of Shem is from Bactra to Rinocorura, which divides Syria and Egypt and the Red Sea from the mouth of the [river] toward the Arsinoe of India" (πάντων δὲ τῶν υἱῶν τοῦ Σήμ ἐστιν ἡ κατοικία ἀπὸ Βάκτρων ἕως Ῥινοκορούρων τῆς ὁριζούσης Συρίαν καὶ Αἴγυπτον καὶ τὴν ἐρυθρὰν θάλασσαν ἀπὸ στόματος τοῦ κατὰ τὸν Ἀρσινοΐτην τῆς Ἰνδικῆς, § 188; cf., similarly, § 195). As usual, the *Diamerismos* abbreviates the geographical detail in Greek *Jubilees*; nevertheless, the *Vorlage* is perceptible in terms such as the vicinity of India/Bactra and the Erythrean/Red Sea. Scholars have debated what

Jubilees means by the description of Asshur's share as extending "as far as the vicinity of India, (where) the Wadafa River rises" (9:3).[74] One wonders whether the difficult expression, στόμα τοῦ κατὰ τὸν ᾽Αρσινοΐτην τῆς ᾽Ινδικῆς,[75] which also seems to refer to a river, preserves something of the Greek *Vorlage* which gave rise to the confusion in the Ethiopic version. This problem well illustrates how a pseudepigraphon can sometimes become garbled in the process of transmission, especially when the text is translated into one or more intermediate languages and then epitomized.[76]

Between these two geographical descriptions of the Shemite territory, the *Diamerismos* goes well beyond the corresponding section in *Jubilees* 8:11 – 9:15 by listing (1) the contemporary nations that stem from Shem's sons (§§ 160–86, 190–2) and (2) the countries of Shem (§ 194). Some of this material derives from the Septuagint.

Finally, we come to the description of the territory of Japheth's sons in *Jub.* 9:7–13:

> (7) Japheth, too, divided the land among his sons as an inheritance. (8) There emerged for Gomer a first share eastward from the north side as far as the Tina River. North of him there emerged (as a share) for Magog all the central parts of the north until it reaches the Me'at Sea. (9) For Madai there emerged a share for him to occupy on the west of his two brothers as far as the islands and the shores of the islands. (10) For Javan there emerged as the fourth share every island and the islands that are in the direction of Lud's border. (11) For Tubal there emerged as the fifth share the middle of the branch which reaches the border of Lud's share as far as the second branch, and the other side of the second branch into the third branch. (12) For Meshech there emerged a sixth share, namely all the (region on the) other side of the third branch until it reaches to the east of Gadir. (13) For Tiras there emerged as the seventh share the four large islands within the sea which reach Ham's share. The islands of Kamaturi emerged by lot for Arpachshad's children as his inheritance.

The geographical detail of *Jubilees* is preserved in abbreviated form in the *Diamerismos*. There the geographic distribution of the Japhethite nations is described as extending "from Media to the Western Ocean, looking to the North" (*Chron.* 79; cf., similarly, §§ 83 ["from Media to Gadeira, the portions to the North"], 86), corresponding to *Jubilees*' emphasis on the North (9:8; cf. 8:25, 26, 28, 29) and the distribution from the portions of Gomer and Magog to the Great Sea (9:6) and to Gadir (9:12).

The *Diamerismos* also stresses the many islands in the Japhethite portion (*Chron.* 73: "the islands of the nations" [Gen. 10:5]), corresponding to *Jubilees'* emphasis on islands (9:9, 10, 13; cf. 8:29).[78] The *Diamerismos* provides the names of these islands (i.e., the British Isles, Sicily, Euboia, Rhodes, Chios, Lesbos, Cythera, Zacythus, Cephallenia, Ithaca, Kerkyra, and the Cyclades, and a certain part of Asia called Ionia [§§ 6–8]), whereas *Jubilees* does not. This second part of the *Diamerismos* also goes well beyond *Jubilees* 9 in listing (1) the contemporary nations that stem from Japheth (§§ 56–73, 80), (2) the countries of Japheth (§ 84), and (3) the river of Japheth (§ 90).

Perhaps the strongest evidence of Hippolytus' dependence on *Jubilees* at this point is seen in his treatment of the Medes. The *Diamerismos* mentions the Μῆδοι several times. They first appear in the list of the sons and grandsons of Japheth and the nations that stem from them, where Madai (Gen. 10:2; 1 Chr. 1:5) is given as the forefather of the Medes (§ 59, Μαδάι, ἀφ' οὗ Μῆδοι).[79] Later, they appear in another list of the nations of Japheth (§ 80.1), including the list of six Japhethite nations that understand writing (§ 82.5). However, their next appearance is in the list of the nations of *Shem* (§ 190.3). Although this could be explained as an error, another possibility suggests itself when we consult the *Book of Jubilees*. According to *Jub.* 10:35, "Japheth and his sons went toward the sea and settled in the land of their share. Madai saw the land near the sea but it did not please him. So he pleaded (for land) from Elam, Asshur, and Arpachshad, his wife's brother. He has settled in the land of Medeqin near his wife's brother until the present." With some plausibility, therefore, the *Diamerismos* can list the Medes who stem from Madai as Shemites based on territory and intermarriage, even though they are actually sons of Japheth.

In sum, the second part of the *Diamerismos* (§§ 56–197) deviates more substantially than the first from the *Jubilees Vorlage* both in order of presentation and in the material included. We may suspect that Hippolytus has heavily edited his source in accordance with his own designs and emphases. Nevertheless, use of the *Vorlage* seems to account for several features in our text.

The *Wirkungsgeschichte* of Hippolytus' *Diamerismos*

The *Wirkungsgeschichte* of the *Diamerismos* seems to confirm that Hippolytus uses *Jubilees* 8–9. This is not the place to consider the highly ramified tradition of Hippolytus' *Diamerismos*, which has already been the subject of several detailed studies.[80] We may simply point out, however, that where the *Diamerismos* is used as a source, material from *Jubilees* 8–9 is often included with it. In some cases, this *Jubilees* material includes the account of Canaan's violation of the oath (*Jub.* 9:14), when he intruded into Shem's territory (10:27–34). This is a very important observation for our study, because it further substantiates that Greek *Jubilees* may have been the basis for the *Diamerismos*. As we have suggested, the latter incorporates from Greek *Jubilees* a description of Shem's borders in terms of the extent of the Seleucid Empire as it was known under Antiochus III ("the Great"). The intent of Greek *Jubilees*, as of its Hebrew *Vorlage*, was to emphasize that the Seleucids (the Kittim of Japheth) had encroached upon Shem's eternal heritage. If writings that are dependent on Hippolytus' *Diamerismos* include additional material from *Jubilees* 8–10, then it is likely that Hippolytus himself had access to the same material. In the following, we shall examine three examples that are particularly relevant for the present study. More could have been added, but they would have added little to the survey intended here.[81]

Epiphanius

First, Epiphanius (ca. 315–403 CE), a native of Palestine and the founder of a monastery near Eleutheropolis in Judea, apparently uses the *Diamerismos* as a source at several points.[82] Although A. Bauer at first denied this possibility,[83] he later revised his opinion: "Auch Epiphanios ist nicht, wie ich früher . . . mit A. v. Gutschmid angenommen habe, von einer selbstständigen Bearbeitung, sondern ebenfalls von Hipp[olytos] abhängig."[84] More recently, Juhani Piilonen has further documented the dependence of Epiphanius, *Ancoratus* 113 on Hippolytus: "As for Epiphanius' relation to Hippolytus, the revised opinion of Adolf Bauer . . . proves correct. Epiphanius cannot claim the honour of having written his Διαμερισμός quite independently of Hippolytus' chronicle. Instead, he can claim the honour of having treated his model in an original manner. He started with the Semite and continued with the Hamitic and Japhetic peoples, whereas Hippolytus had done just the reverse."[85] Here we should notice, however, that this is the same order as that in *Jub.* 8:11–30 and an exact reversal of the order in Genesis 10. Epiphanius also has some distinctive *Jubilees* material that Hippolytus does not include.[86] For example, just as in *Jub.* 9:14, the *Ancoratus* (112.1; 114.1; see also below on *Pan.* 66.83.3–84.4) refers to the oath that Noah required his sons to swear so that they would not intrude into each other's portions. Furthermore, just as in *Jub.* 10:29, Ham is said to have taken part of Shem's portion (*Ancoratus* 113.7; 114.3).

The *Panarion* of Epiphanius also shows extensive influence from both Hippolytus' *Diamerismos* and the *Book of Jubilees*. One passage in particular (*Pan.* 66.83.3–84.4) deserves to be cited in full:[87]

> (83.3) The ignoramus [i.e., Mani] did not know that they [sc. the children of Israel] took their own land back which had been seized from them, and that retribution was exacted for the pact that was made between them, with a true decision and an oath. (4) For when Noah was saved from the flood – and his wife, with his three sons and their three brides – he alone divided the whole world (cf. *Jub.* 8:10–9:15). As is logical and nothing foolish or false, he distributed it among his three sons, Shem, Ham, and Japheth, by casting lots in Rhinocorura. (5) For Rhinocorura means Neel, and its inhabitants actually call it that; but in Hebrew it means "lots," since Noah cast the lots for his three sons there (cf. *Jub.* 8:11). (6) And the land from Rhinocorura to Gadiri fell <to **Ham**>, including Egypt, the Marean Marsh, Ammon, Libya, Marmaris, Pentapolis, Macatas, Macronas, Leptis Magna, Syrtis, and Mauritania, out to the so-called Pillars of Hercules and the interior of Gadiri. (7) These were Ham's possessions to the south. But he also owned the land from Rhinocorura eastwards, Idumaea, Midianitis, Alabastritis, Homeritis, Axiomitis, Bugaea, and Diba, out to Bactria. (8) The same lot sets a boundary between **Shem** and the lands to the east. Roughly, Shem's allotment was Palestine, Phoenicia and Coele-Syria, Commagene, Cilicia, Cappadocia, Galatia, Paphlagonia, Lazia, Iberia, Caspia, and Carduaea, out to Media in the north. (9) From there this lot assigned the northern lands to **Japheth**. But in the west <Japheth was assigned> the land between Europe and Spain, and Britain, <Thrace, Europe, Rhodope> and the peoples who border on it, the Venetians, Daunians, Iapygians, Calabrians, Latins, Oscans [and] Megarians, out to the inhabitants of Spain and Gaul, and the lands of the Scots and Franks in the north. (84.1) After these allotments, Noah called his three sons together and bound them with an oath, so that none of them would encroach on his brother's allotment and be covetous of his brother (cf. *Jub.* 9:14). (2) But Ham's son Canaan was covetous and invaded Palestine and took it; and the land was named Canaan because Canaan settled in it after leaving his own allotment (cf. *Jub.* 10:27–34), which he thought was hot (cf. *Jub.* 8:30).

(3) And he settled in Shem's land, which is now called Judaea, and fathered the following sons: Amorraeus, Girgashaeus, Pherizaeus, Jebusaeus, Hivaeus, Arucaeus, Chittaeus, Asenaeus, Samaraeus, Sidonius and Philistiaeus. (4) And so, to show that the number of their sins against the oath was reaching completion, the Lord says in the Law, "The sins of the Amorites have not yet been completed" (Gen. 15:16). And therefore [Israel] remained in the desert and loitered in the wilderness, until the Amorites condemned themselves by going to war with the wronged sons of Shem.

Here we see the influence of both traditions side-by-side. On the one hand, the *Diamerismos* tradition of Hippolytus is apparent especially in the use of Rhinocorura as a boundary marker. On the other hand, the *Jubilees* 8–9 tradition comes through in many ways, as indicated parenthetically above.[88] Significantly, Epiphanius' text ties in the account of Canaan's intrusion into Shem's territory as an example of how the oath was violated, an account that stems ultimately from *Jub.* 10:27–34.[89] These observations lead to the conclusion that Epiphanius either supplemented Hippolytus' *Diamerismos* with material from *Jubilees* 8–10[90] or used an earlier, unabridged edition of the *Diamerismos* that already contained the additional *Jubilees* material.[91] Perhaps, however, it should not be ruled out that Epiphanius used a recension of the lost Greek version of *Jubilees*, that is, a copy of the work that presumably stood behind Hippolytus' *Diamerismos*.[92]

This possibility is made all the more probable when we realize that a similar tradition is found (independently?) in later rabbinic literature.[93] Without considering Hippolytus' *Diamerismos* and its textual transmission, Himmelfarb suggests that a passage in the medieval work, *Midrash Aggadah*, Lek-Leka 13.7 on Gen. 12:6 ("The Canaanite was then in the land") may be based on a collection of excerpts from *Jubilees* which was used by Byzantine chronographers such George Syncellus (and, we may add, Epiphanius).[94] Like *Jubilees* 8–9, this midrash gives an account of the division of the earth among Noah's sons and the violation of Shem's portion by the Canaanites:[95]

> For the land of Israel had fallen to the portion of Shem, as it says, "Melchizedek, king of Salem" (Gen. 14:18). When the Holy One, blessed be he, divided the world among them, Noah made his three sons swear that none of them would enter the territory of another. But the seven nations passed through the land of Israel

and transgressed the oath. Therefore, the Holy One, blessed be he, commanded, "You shall utterly destroy them." At the time that Abraham passed through, they had not yet entered there except for the Canaanites. Thus the land of the seven nations fell to Israel, for all the lands of the seven nations had fallen to the portion of Shem. Thus it says, "He set up boundaries for the nations according to the number of the sons of Israel" (Deut. 32:8).

George Syncellus

Second, George Syncellus (fl. ca. 800) uses the *Diamerismos* tradition, allegedly as transmitted through Abydenus (second century CE?), who is also a source for Eusebius (ca. 260–339).[96] In his important *Ecloga Chronographica*, Syncellus writes a chronicle from creation to the time of Diocletian (285 CE), which was posthumously extended to 813 CE.[97] The section attributed to Abydenus (Sync. 46.10–48.84) actually seems to be a composite of various sources, including Eusebius, Hippolytus, and *Jubilees* 8–9.[98] For instance, the very first paragraph of the Abydenus quote (Sync. 46.10–16), referring to the division of languages at the Tower of Babel, is taken directly from Eusebius, *Chronica* 17.11–24 (cf. also *Praep. Ev.* 9.14.1–2).[99]

According to Syncellus, Abydenus records that there were "72 nations that were dispersed throughout the whole inhabited world, which Noah the righteous divided thusly among his three sons in year 2572 of the world, when he was 934 years old, according to the divine oracle" (Sync. 46.19–22).[100] What follows is an expanded citation of the *Diamerismos* in Hippolytus' *Chronicon*, which sketches the borders of the territories that Noah gave to each of his three sons (Sync. 46.23–47.11; cf. *Chron.* §§41–9). This may give credence to the aforementioned possibility of an earlier, unabridged edition of Hippolytus' *Diamerismos*.[101] Of course, insofar as Hippolytus himself is using a source at this point, the Abydenus material in Syncellus may go back to the earlier source as well. As we shall see, the influence of *Jubilees* on this section is palpable.

After describing the division of the earth among Noah's sons, the Abydenus quote continues:[102]

> Thus having divided [the world], drawn up a will *in writing* (ἐγγράφως), as they say (ὡς φασιν), and having read his testament (τὴν διαθήκην αὐτοῦ) to them, he sealed it, retaining it for himself until the year 2592 from Adam, in which he also fell asleep. When he was about to die, he enjoined his three sons

that no one should trespass the borders of his brother, and that no one should be lawlessly subject to another, as this one will be the cause of strife with them and of wars with one another. And he gave his testament (τὴν διαθήκην αὐτοῦ) to Shem as his firstborn son and the one most favored of God. Shem also received after Noah the hegemony and inherited from him the special honors of the blessings, as it states in Genesis [9:26]. And he fell asleep on Mt. Lubar.

This passage provides evidence of a written tradition about Noah's division of the world among his sons. Whereas *Jubilees* refers to a "book" of Noah in this regard,[103] the Abydenus quote describes a "will" or "testament" of Noah,[104] for which we find parallels elsewhere.[105] Also in other ways, the Abydenus material is not simply a citation of *Jubilees* 8–9, at least not in the form that it has come down to us in the Ethiopic version. For instance, the date for the death of Noah (2592) is clearly not from *Jubilees*, and neither is the whole idea that Noah sealed his will until the day of his death. Indeed, the closest parallel to the notion that Noah waited until the end of his life to complete the division of the world among his sons is found in the Samaritan *Asatir* (4.36–8), which, as we have seen in Chapter 2, stands in the same tradition as *Jubilees* 8–9.

Nevertheless, the Abydenus material has several salient features that reflect the *Jubilees* tradition. First, Noah's injunction to his sons not to trespass each other's allotted territories clearly originates from *Jub.* 9:14: "In this way Noah's sons divided [the earth] for their sons in front of their father Noah. He made [them] swear by oath to curse each and every one who wanted to occupy the share which did not emerge by his lot." Second, the unbiblical detail that Noah "slept" on "Mt. Lubar" stems originally from *Jub.* 10:15: "Noah slept with his fathers and was buried on Mt. Lubar in the land of Ararat" (cf. Gen. 9:29, which states merely, ". . . and he died"). Hence, although the text explicitly refers to the canonical book of "Genesis" (Γένεσις), some of this material also derives from *Little Genesis*, which is consistent with the fact that the passage qualifies the assertion by attributing it to received tradition (ὥς φασιν). A similar qualification is found earlier in Syncellus in an explicit reference to the *Book of Jubilees* as *Little Genesis*: ὥς ἐν Λεπτῇ φέρεται Γενέσει, ἥν καὶ Μωϋσέως εἶναί φασί τινες ἀποκάλυψιν (Sync. 3.16–17).[106]

The Abydenus quote continues with an account of the aftermath of Noah's death:[107]

In the year 2791 of the world, which is 200 years after the death of Noah, Canaan, the son of Ham, attempting a new thing,

entered the borders of Shem and settled there, thus violating
the command of Noah, along with the 7 nations that came from
him, the Amorites, the Hittites, the Perizzites, the Hivites, the
Girgashites, the Jebusites, and the Canaanites, whom God utterly
destroyed through Moses and Joshua. And at various times, God
restored the Patriarchal Land to the sons of Israel through the
Judges . . .

Again, this section has no counterpart in Genesis, and it must go back
ultimately to the account in *Jub.* 10:27–34, which describes how "the
land of Canaan" received its name illegitimately. Although the Abydenus
quote reports only the most essential features of this story (and adds
several unique elements), the convergence is unmistakable. By intruding into the territory of Shem, Canaan fundamentally violated Noah's
command.

Immediately after the Abydenus quote, Syncellus provides a list of
"The Names of the 72 Nations That Were Given a New Name by the
Originators Who Were Spread Abroad" (Sync. 48.12–55.8). This list,
which includes the descendants of the three sons of Noah and the names
of the peoples who stem from them, closely resembles Hippolytus'
Diamerismos. There are differences in the order of presentation
(Syncellus, like Epiphanius, begins with Shem, whereas Hippolytus starts
with Japheth) and in the specific contents; nevertheless, the two lists over-
lap considerably. A separate study would be necessary to ascertain how
Syncellus received and shaped this list.

In light of this evidence, the following conclusion emerges: George
Syncellus cites a source that contains side-by-side not only fragments
of Hippolytus' *Diamerismos* but also an epitome of *Jubilees* 8–9 and
10:27–34. Whether the Abydenus quote originally contained both of these
elements, or Syncellus supplemented Abydenus with various materials
that he found appropriate is difficult to say with certainty.[108] The situation
is complicated by the possibility that Hippolytus himself may have written
both shorter and longer versions of the *Diamerismos*. Nevertheless, it
is uncanny that Hippolytus' *Diamerismos* appears once again with the
Jubilees tradition.

Syriac tradition

A final example in which Hippolytus' *Diamerismos* appears to be mixed
with *Jubilees* 8–9 material is found in Syriac tradition. Working back-
wards from the *Chronicle* of Michael the Syrian (1166–99 CE), which

stands at the end of a long tradition, Witold Witakowski examines the account of the division of the earth among the descendants of Noah in an extensive number of Syriac sources, including Ephrem the Syrian (306–73), the *Cave of Treasures* (ca. 350), the *Apocalypse of Pseudo-Methodius* (end of the seventh century), the *Edessene Apocalypse of Pseudo-Methodius* (also at the end of the seventh century), the *Chronicle to the Year 724*, *On the Families of Languages* (ninth century), *Commentary on Genesis to Exodus 9* (first half of the eighth century), the *Book of Scholia* of Theodore BarKoni (ca. 791/2), the *Commentary to the Bible* of Isho'dad of Merv (ca. 850), the *Anonymous Commentary* (ninth/tenth century), the *Book of the Bee* (first half of the thirteenth century), the *Storehouse of Mysteries* and the *Chronography* of Bar Hebraeus (fl. 1264–86), and the *Chronicle to the Year 1234*.[109]

As Witakowski shows, much of the material in these sources on the division of the earth among the descendants of Noah can be traced back to Hippolytus' *Diamerismos*.[110] For example, the *Chronicle* of Michael the Syrian states "that after the flood Noah granted his sons regions of the earth and forbade them to transgress each other's territories. Shem obtained the regions of Persia and Bactria as far as India and (in the west) as far as Rhinocoroura. Ham's territory (in the south) stretched from Rhinocoroura to Gadeira, whereas that of Japheth extended over the north from Media to Gadeira."[111] Obviously, this description of the boundaries of the territories allotted to Noah's sons is exactly what we find in the *Diamerismos* of Hippolytus (*Chron.* 44–9).[112] It is important to notice, however, that this *Diamerismos* material is mixed with elements from *Jubilees* 8–9: (1) that *Noah* parceled out the earth to his three sons (cf. *Jub.* 8:11), and (2) that he prohibited them from transgressing one another's territories (cf. *Jub.* 9:14).[113]

This is not an isolated example in Syriac literature. As Witakowski demonstrates, the Syriac *Chronicle to the Year 1234* provides another case in point: "Thus the region given to Shem is described as being in the midst of the earth, 'from the borders of Egypt and the Red Sea to the Sea of Phoenicia and Syria' and it contains countries from Palestine to Northern India 'and other eastern regions.' The region given to Ham extends from the eastern shore of Gihon to the South over all the Fiery Mountains and to the West to the Sea of Atel (= Atlantic) and the Sea Mahuq, 'into which nothing descends but to perish.' Japheth's share extends from beyond the river Tina (= Tanais), contains the regions of Gog and reaches the mountain *Qtl* and the Sea Mahuq. This northern part also includes five large islands."[114] Many of these elements clearly derive ultimately from *Jubilees* 8–9.[115] This is confirmed by the description of the three climates in the Syriac *Chronicle*:[116]

> The territory of Shem is neither hot nor cold, but temperate both in heat and in frost; the territory of Ham is hot; the territory of Japheth is very cold.

The corresponding passage in *Jub.* 8:30 reads as follows:

> However, it [sc. Japheth's territory] is cold while the land of Ham is hot. Now Shem's land is neither hot nor cold but it is a mixture of cold and heat.

Nevertheless, the Syriac *Chronicle to the Year 1234* also contains a list of peoples/languages having knowledge of writing, which comes ultimately from Hippolytus' *Diamerismos* (§§ 81–2 [six Japhethite nations], §§ 134–5 [four Hamite nations], § 192 [six Shemite nations]).[117] Hence, there can be no doubt that, here again, we find Hippolytus' *Diamerismos* being mixed with *Jubilees* 8–9 material.

The origin of the *Diamerismos* material in Syriac literature is not easy to ascertain. Witakowski considers several possibilities (or some combination of them).[118] First, there may have been intermediate stages in the transmission of Hippolytus' *Diamerismos*, whether in the Greek text itself or in a possible Syriac translation that is no longer extant. Indeed, as we have seen, Hippolytus himself may have produced both a longer and a shorter version of the *Diamerismos*, and only the latter has come down to us intact. Second, Hippolytus' *Diamerismos* may not be the direct source for the Syriac texts. If, as Witakowski indicates, the *Diamerismos* material in Syriac is never attributed to Hippolytus, then one or more excerptors may have been responsible for introducing *Diamerismos* material into Syriac literature.

In the case of the *Chronicle to the Year 1234*, Witakowski suggests that two separate traditions were combined into one text, i.e., *Jubilees* 8–9 and Hippolytus' *Diamerismos*. However, after all that we have seen so far in Epiphanius, Syncellus, and other Syriac literature, it seems unlikely that these independent writings just happened to blend the *Jubilees* 8–9 material with the *Diamerismos* tradition.[119] Rather, it seems more probable that the *Jubilees* 8–9 material was an integral part of the *Diamerismos* tradition from its inception. If this is correct, then the *Wirkungsgeschichte* of the *Diamerismos* further substantiates that Greek *Jubilees* was foundational to Hippolytus' original writing. A more definitive answer to this question must await a comprehensive study of the reception of *Jubilees* in Jewish and Christian sources.

Conclusion

Jubilees 8–9 gives the contents of an apocalyptically-oriented "book" of Noah (8:11–12) which describes the origins of the nations and anticipates their eschatological judgment (9:15). It is possible that this "book" circulated during the Second-Temple period, and that it was used in apocalyptic oracles against the nations, particularly against the Kittim of Japheth – at first the Seleucids and later the Romans. From the perspective of *Jubilees* and the tradition dependent on it, these peoples were imperialistic nations that had usurped the territory of others, and that had therefore incurred the terrible curse for violating the oath Noah had made his sons and grandsons swear (*Jub.* 9:14). Eventually, this Book of Noah seems to have found its way into Christian circles and stoked imminent expectations about the end of the Roman Empire and the coming judgment.[120] The foregoing study offers evidence that Hippolytus' *Diamerismos* may have been based on the Book of Noah material in *Jubilees* 8–9. It seems likely that Hippolytus epitomized and reworked the lost Greek version of *Jubilees* 8–9 and incorporated it into his *Chronicon*. By reusing the very writing that had helped to fuel eschatological hopes in the first place, Hippolytus sought to dampen imminent expectations of the end of the Kittim. The extensive *Wirkungsgeschichte* of Hippolytus' *Diamerismos* shows that *Jubilees* 8–9 material is often found together with the *Diamerismos* tradition, further substantiating that Hippolytus himself was originally influenced by the *Jubilees* tradition.

7

MEDIEVAL *MAPPAEMUNDI*

Introduction

Finally, our investigation comes full circle back to its point of departure. In Chapter 1, we used the Kypros *mappamundi* as a means of introducing the whole vast subject of Jewish geographical conceptions. Then, in Chapters 2–6, we examined the Jewish geographical tradition that probably most influenced Jewish and Christian geographical conceptions through the centuries, that is, Genesis 10 and the Table of Nations tradition, in particular *Jubilees* 8–9. In the present chapter, we return to the Kypros map to explore the possible relevance of our investigation for understanding the medieval *mappaemundi*. With the discussion of Chapters 2–6 in view, it is almost inevitable that speculation should lead one to consider a possible link, however tenuous and indirect, between the Kypros map and the *mappaemundi*. For if the Kypros map reflects Jewish geographical traditions, and if Christian sources received and transmitted the same Jewish geographical traditions, then we may plausibly ask whether these traditions influenced the medieval *mappaemundi*. This possibility is strengthened by the fact that the *Book of Jubilees* was preserved in a Latin version, dating to the fifth to sixth century.[1] Moreover, Greek *Jubilees* had long circulated in the form of extracts in many disparate works, especially the Christian chronographic tradition, as we have seen.

Given the many uncertainties and gaps in our knowledge, the purpose of this chapter must be tentative and cautious, exploring the possibilities and opening up new visas for future investigation. Our research is complicated by at least three major factors. First, we must realize that not all *mappaemundi* are the same. Although some bear a strong family resemblance to each other, others evidently represent quite different traditions. It would be a mistake to try to find a Jewish source for all *mappaemundi*. If such a source is plausible at all, it probably accounts for only a portion of the medieval maps.

Second, the situation is complicated by the fact that the Jewish geographical tradition of *Jubilees* 8–9 may have influenced the medieval *mappaemundi* through literary or cartographic sources. As Robert A. Kraft remarks, "In various ways, pseudepigraphic literatures seem to have been able to serve a wide range of interests in the 'middle ages,' including science (especially astronomical and calendric issues), history, popular piety (especially with folkloristic tales), and ordinary worship (e.g., with models of prayer/hymn language). The interrelationship of such motives among Christian transmitters deserves closer study."[2] It is theoretically possible, therefore, that the medieval *mappaemundi* were influenced directly through literary sources that contained the *Jubilees* tradition.

Of course, the two avenues are not necessarily mutually exclusive, especially if the literary source included a map. We know, for example, that several prominent Christian sources were accompanied by world maps, including Beatus' Commentary on the Apocalypse and Isidore of Seville's *Etymologiae* (illustrating Book 14, *de terra et euis partibus*).[3] Yet how should we go about ascertaining whether there originally was a Jewish map? The problem of establishing a Jewish precursor for the medieval *mappaemundi* is similar to the problem of demonstrating a Jewish original for almost any piece of medieval Christian art. Heinz Schreckenberg and Kurt Schubert have recently shown that certain pieces of medieval Christian art probably represent Jewish pictorial traditions, because they depict scenes that are otherwise found only in Jewish literary sources and/or actually contradict Christian sources.[4] In the case of the medieval maps, however, we cannot employ the same principle of dissimilarity, for, as we have said, *Jubilees* 8–9 strongly influenced Christian tradition. If all we had were formal, typological affinities, the question would be whether the similarities are strong enough to establish influence.[5] As we shall see, however, there is at least some direct evidence that the *Jubilees* tradition was indeed appropriated by the medieval maps.[6] Moreover, we do not need to speculate whether Jews produced world maps. The evidence of Chapter 1, however sketchy, is sufficient to demonstrate this point. The only question now is whether Jewish cartographic tradition survived into the medieval period.

Third, the situation is complicated by the fact that we are dealing here not just with Jewish geographical tradition, but in all probability with a combination of various influences. We have already seen that the epigram of Philip of Thessalonica praises an artistic tapestry, which was made by Queen Kypros and offered as a gift to Emperor Gaius. Woven into the fabric of the tapestry was an image of the world, which may have taken the form of a disk-shaped earth encircled by Ocean. It is possible that Kypros' inspiration was drawn from tapestries and textiles that were associated with the Jerusalem Temple and its priesthood. It is not improbable, however, that she also took as the model for her work the famous Agrippa map erected in the Porticus Vipsanius in Rome. Insofar as both the Agrippa map and the Jerusalem Temple were influenced by Greco-Roman conceptions of the world, the two possible influences may stem from a common cartographic tradition. By the same token, Kypros herself may have blended both Greco-Roman and Jewish traditions into her representation of the world, resulting in a novel, hybrid form – an Orientalized version of the Agrippa map. In any case, the Kypros map opens up a fascinating, new way of explaining the origin and development of the medieval *mappaemundi*. In other words, the medieval maps may not represent, as commonly supposed, merely the "Christianization" of an earlier Roman map; rather, they may represent the first-century "Judaization" of a Roman map which was later adapted by Christians. Seen in this light, the main difference between the Agrippa and Kypros maps, on the one hand, and the medieval Christian maps, on the other, would be that the latter replaced Caesar with Christ as the one who dominates the world (see further below).

In the following, we shall survey the various influences on the medieval *mappaemundi* – Greco-Roman, Jewish, and Christian. Then, we shall return to the question of the Kypros map as a possible "missing link."

Greco-Roman influence

It is unnecessary to discuss extensively the Greco-Roman influence on the medieval *mappaemundi*, for historians of cartography are generally agreed that these maps can be traced back to a Roman precursor, particularly the world map of M. Vipsanius Agrippa which was set up in the Porticus Vipsanius in Rome to symbolize the control of the earth by Caesar Augustus.[7] As Anna-Dorothee von den Brincken observes, "Die abendländliche Weltkarte ist bis ins Zeitalter der Entdeckungen ganz von der römischen Antike bestimmt; für viele Forscher gilt sie überhaupt nur als Rudiment der verlorenen Weltkarte, die Vipsanius Agrippa, des Augustus Schwiegersohn, von der römischen Ökumene anfertigte."[8] We may surmise that the Agrippa map not only became the authoritative standard of world cartography in its own day, but also a precious heirloom for subsequent ages. Certainly, the Agrippa map did not survive intact from classical antiquity; however, the thirteenth-century world map in the Hereford Cathedral, among other medieval maps, is often regarded as a replica of the Agrippa map.[9] The Middle Ages, it is argued, honored ancient tradition and therefore would have faithfully preserved the ancient form of the map.[10] P. D. A. Harvey expresses the *opinio communis*:[11]

> Simple or elaborate, large or small, all these [medieval] maps of the inhabited world are related to each other and to the Hereford map. In the broadest terms, features of their outlines are common to all. They all belong to a single, much ramified tradition which must go back to the Roman period. We cannot suppose that people between the fifth century and the twelfth themselves mapped any substantial part of the known world. The techniques of surveying and calculating geographical coordinates had fallen into disuse, the necessary administrative structure no longer existed and, most important of all, the concept of mapping to scale, of mapping from measurements, had been lost. It follows that where any portion of a world map of this period has a recognizably correct outline, this must go back to a Roman original, and this original was probably a measured and reasonably accurate map of the world, showing coastal outlines, mountains, rivers, towns and boundaries of provinces.

The most important evidence for the Roman origin of the medieval *mappaemundi* is written right on the Hereford map itself.[12] Around the map's border on the left side, we read that "the world began to be measured by Julius Caesar" (*a Iulio Caesare orbis terrarum metiri cepit*). In the lower left corner we find a drawing of an enthroned figure of Caesar Augustus[13] handing over to three geographers an edict, with the imperial seal affixed (*S[igillum] Augusti Cesaris Imperatoris*), that commissions them to survey the whole world.[14] However, since the three geographers belong to the tradition of Julius Caesar's survey,[15] the author of the Hereford map seems to have confused the two events and the two Caesars.[16] Yet we need not follow Kai Brodersen in therefore completely dismissing the whole tradition of Caesar's geographical survey of the world.[17] Insofar as the Agrippa map was based on the earlier survey work mandated by Julius Caesar,[18] the confusion is perhaps understandable. In any case, evidence for Roman influence on the medieval *mappaemundi* appears to be quite strong.[19] A possible major influence on the medieval maps, such as Paulus Orosius (fl. 417), seems to corroborate this impression.[20]

In light of this obvious Roman influence, scholars have often assumed that several characteristic features of the *mappaemundi* also derive from Roman influence: for example, the tripartite division of a circular earth,[21] the notion of a geographical center of the earth,[22] and the placement of East at the top of the map.[23] However, none of these features is the exclusive provenance of Roman culture. Africa/Libya was distinguished from Asia as the third continent by at least 500 BCE;[24] the notion of an omphalos of the earth is very widespread and ancient;[25] orientation on the East is characteristic of many other cultures, and whether it is characteristic of Roman culture is much debated.[26] On the latter point in particular, we must bear in mind that, like Jewish synagogues, Christian churches had long been oriented on the East. Therefore, although the Roman influence on the medieval maps must have been substantial, it cannot be shown to be the only source of influence. There must have been several complementary sources.

OT and Jewish influence

The attempt to understand medieval cartography merely as a vestige of Roman cartography fails to take adequate account of other probable influences on these maps.[27] Even those who acknowledge biblical elements in the medieval *mappaemundi* often regard them as a later accretion under Christian influence, rather than a pre-Christian development.[28] For example, David Woodward writes: "As the influence of the classical tradition declined [in medieval cartography], biblical sources became more prominent. Although originally Roman, the basic structure of the tripartite diagrams now owed their form to the tradition of the peopling of the earth by the descendants of Noah."[29] In other words, the medieval monks were responsible for superimposing the Noah tradition on a Roman map. Likewise, making Jerusalem the center of the earth is often seen as a late medieval Christian adaptation of a Roman map,[30] in which the original center is either Delos or Delphi.[31] And the inclusion of earthly paradise in medieval maps is regarded as the intrusion of a Christian element into the Agrippa map.[32]

The thesis that Christians were responsible for altering a Roman map late in the development of the medieval *mappaemundi* ignores two important considerations. First, the adaptation of the Agrippa world map to a biblical worldview may have already taken place, in part, in the first century CE. As we have seen in Chapter 1, the *mappamundi* of Queen Kypros may well have been an imitation of the Agrippa map; however, this would not have prevented the Jewish artist from incorporating biblical elements which would have been familiar to her from cosmological images, and possibly even a "map," associated with the Jerusalem Temple and its priesthood.[33]

Second, the thesis that Christians were responsible for altering a Roman map late in the development of the medieval *mappaemundi* ignores the existence of the whole *Diamerismos* tradition, dependent ultimately on *Jubilees* 8–9, which had long since been describing the world in a way that is similar to *mappaemundi* like the Hereford map.[34] As we have seen in Chapter 2, *Jubilees* 8–9 already contains numerous features which are familiar from the medieval maps – the tripartite division of the world, with the Nile, the Mediterranean, the Pillars of Hercules (Gades), and the Tanais as physical boundaries between them; the identification of the three continents (Asia, Africa/Libya, and Europe) with Noah's sons, Shem, Ham, and Japheth;[35] paradise and the four rivers which flow out of it; Jerusalem as the center of the world;[36] and the orientation on the East.[37] Moreover, several medieval T-O maps actually list the nations that belong to Asia, Europe and Africa, as if they were trying to imitate the Genesis Table of Nations, without citing it verbatim.[38]

In light of this evidence, it is extremely unlikely that the centrality of Jerusalem on medieval maps should be understood as an impulse of Jerome's commentary on Ezek. 5:5,[39] which was appropriated only in the high Middle Ages.[40] In his letter to Fabiola (*Ep.* 78.20), Jerome explicitly refers to *Jubilees* as *Parva Genesis*,[41] the Latin equivalent of the Greek title, ἡ Λεπτὴ Γένεσις.[42] Hermann Rönsch observes that Jerome tacitly uses *Jubilees* at several places in his *Hebrew Questions on Genesis*.[43] Perhaps, then, Jerome's conception of the Jerusalem in the geographical center of the world was influenced by the *Jubilees* tradition, rather than it being his own independent innovation.

Even if it is mediated through standard Christian sources, Jewish influence on medieval maps should not be gainsaid too hastily. For example, Isidore of Seville (ca. 600–36), whose encyclopedic *Etymologiae* was a major source of geographical information for the Middle Ages in general and for the *mappaemundi* in particular,[44] calls Jerusalem the *umbilicus regionis totius* ("navel of the whole area") (*Etym.* 14.3.21), rather than *umbilicus terrae* ("navel of the earth").[45] This would seem at first to eliminate the possibility of Jewish influence based on the Table of Nations tradition.[46] Nevertheless, Isidore is apparently following Josephus,[47] who refers to the fact that Jerusalem is called the ὀμφαλὸς τῆς χώρας ("navel of the country"), that is, the center of Judea (*JW* 3.52).[48] It is highly likely that Isidore is following Josephus at this point, for in discussing the names of the seventy-two nations of the world (*Etym.* 9.2), Isidore explicitly and extensively cites Josephus' exposition of the Table of Nations (*Ant.* 1.122–47; cf. esp. *Etym.* 9.2.35), including the contemporary equivalents that Josephus provides for the biblical names of the nations. Also

elsewhere, Isidore explicitly refers to Josephus (*Etym.* 3.25.1). There
is even some evidence that Isidore knew the *Book of Jubilees*.[49] Since
Jubilees states that Jerusalem is situated "in the midst of the navel of
the earth" (*Jub.* 8:19; cf. v. 12), Josephus (and Isidore) may have understood Jerusalem to be the navel of the earth as well, despite the fact
that only part of Jerusalem's spatial relationship is mentioned.[50] For, as
Midrash Tanḥuma, *Qedoshim* 10 (ed. S. Buber 78) states in explaining
Ezek. 38:12, "The Land of Israel is located in the center of the world,
and Jerusalem in the center of the Land of Israel."[51] Indeed, Shemaryahu
Talmon argues that Josephus has fused both of these concepts in *JW*
3.52.[52] If, as William D. McCready has argued, Isidore presupposes a
disk-shaped world,[53] then he may well have understood Jerusalem to be
its center.

The disproportionately large Jerusalem at the center of many medieval
mappaemundi is found already in the famous Madaba mosaic map, which
dates to the latter half of the sixth century CE. As Herbert Donner comments: "Undoubtedly, the picture of Jerusalem is the most impressive
image on the whole Madaba map. It is much larger than that of any
other city in Palestine or Lower Egypt. The reason is clear: Jerusalem
was considered 'the navel of the earth,' the very centre of God's salvation history, the place of Jesus Christ's death and resurrection."[54] Indeed,
the Madaba map shows a prominent column in Jerusalem that stands in
the oval square near the Damascus gate at the northern end of the *cardo
maximus*.[55] As we saw in Chapter 1, this column was used by Adamnan
(624–704), whose *De locis sanctis* is based on the account of a pilgrimage by the Gallic bishop Arculf (ca. 680), as proof that Jerusalem is
situated at the center of the world (citing Ps. 73[74]:11–12; Ezek. 38:12),
for the column casts no shadow at midday during the summer solstice.[56]
A Samaritan tradition attributes a similar phenomenon to Jacob's well,
located at the base of Mt. Gerizim, which Judg. 9:37 calls the "navel of the
land/earth" (טבור הארץ, ὀμφαλὸς τῆς γῆς).[57] Hence, even if Jerusalem
appears in the center of *mappaemundi* rather late in the Middle Ages, the
cartographic precedent for this placement, as well as the literary tradition
on Jerusalem as omphalos, is certainly much earlier.[58] As Woodward
notes, Jerusalem in the center of a world map is found as early as the
seventh century, although the practice was not generally established until later.[59] Given the paucity of actual maps that have come down to
us from the ancient period, such early evidence must be considered as
highly significant. Pilgrimage to biblical sites and to the magnificent
new churches of the Holy Land was already well established by the
time of the death of Constantine.[60] Jewish and Christian attachment to

the Land of Israel through the centuries should be seen as a continuous development.[61]

Whether a world map ever accompanied *Jubilees* 8–9 is unknown. Philip S. Alexander argues in favor of such a possibility.[62] Moreover, as we have seen in Chapter 5, Theophilus of Antioch may have been looking at such a map when he was writing his apology, *Ad Autolycum*.[63] Although a few historians of cartography have noted *Jubilees* 8–9 and the tradition dependent on it,[64] none has seriously examined it as a major, contributing factor to the development of the medieval *mappaemundi*.

Nevertheless, there is good reason to suspect that the *Diamerismos* tradition influenced medieval cartography. For instance, historians of cartography have frequently noticed that the medieval *mappaemundi* are associated with world chronicles.[65] Indeed, von den Brincken argues that medieval world maps are largely graphic representations of world chronicles.[66] The Hereford map explicitly refers to itself as "Estorie." Likewise, the *Diamerismos* tradition is deeply embedded in chronography, beginning with the *Book of Jubilees* itself and continuing on into the Christian world chronicles. Interestingly enough, Hippolytus' *Chronicon*, which includes the *Diamerismos*, found its way into Latin literature in the form of the *Liber generationis* (354 CE). The *Liber generationis* is one of the "Alexandrian World-Chronicles," which incorporate Hippolytus' *Diamerismos* and add illustrative materials, including in one case a schematic map of Ocean and its islands.[67] Likewise, a miniature in the Byzantine Octateuch of Genesis 10 offers a novel depiction of the earth colonized by Noah's descendants, represented as divided into three sections or islands by large interior rivers or arms of the sea.[68] Here we begin to see the confluence chronographic tradition, the *Diamerismos* tradition, and Christian cartography.

In addition, historians of cartography have often noticed that the medieval *mappaemundi* have an apocalyptic orientation.[69] Thus, as Woodward states, "The central theme [of the *mappaemundi*] is the earth as a stage for a sequence of divinely planned historical events from the creation of the world, through its salvation by Jesus Christ in the Passion, to the Last Judgment."[70] As we have seen the *Jubilees* 8–9 tradition is also apocalyptically oriented.[71] According to *Jub.* 9:15, Noah made his sons and grandsons swear an oath not to trespass the lots assigned to them in the book that Noah gave them (cf. 8:11–12); otherwise, a curse would come upon the violators, "until the day of judgment on which the Lord God will punish them with the sword and fire because of all the evil impurity of their errors by which they have filled the earth with wickedness, impurity, fornication, and sin." Evidently, the "Book of Noah" fueled apocalyptic expectation in the early church. Therefore, as we discussed in Chapter 6, Hippolytus incorporated the *Diamerismos* into his *Chronicon* in order to quell apocalyptic speculation associated with an imminent expectation of the downfall of the Roman Empire, by setting it within an extended chronological scheme which calculated the end still to be several centuries off. The medieval *mappaemundi* may well represent a further development in the apocalyptic use of the *Diamerismos* tradition, as the ongoing delay of the parousia pushes the date of the end ever further into the indeterminate future.

The clearest evidence that *Jubilees* 8–9 influenced the medieval *mappaemundi* is found in the schematic T-O map that accompanies several medieval manuscripts, the earliest of which dates to the ninth century CE.[72] In this map, the world is divided into three parts, with *oriens* at the top and the following descriptions provided for each part:

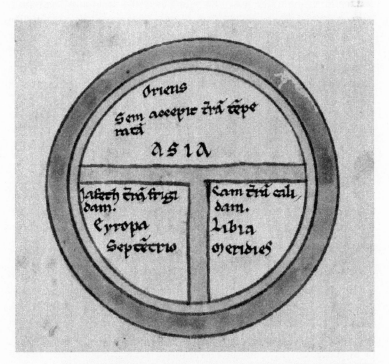

Beatus of Liébana, *Commentary on the Apocalypse, praefatio.* Rylands MS 8, fol. 8ᵛ, twelfth century, Spanish. Diameter, 7 cm. The text reads, "Shem receives the temperate land; Japheth, the cold land; Ham, the hot land." Reproduced by courtesy of the Director and University Librarian, The John Rylands University Library of Manchester.

"Shem receives the temperate land; Japheth, the cold land; Ham, the hot land."

This description obviously stems from *Jub.* 8:30: "However, it [sc. Japheth's hereditary portion of the world] is cold, while the land of Ham is hot. Now Shem's land is neither hot nor cold but is a mixture of cold and heat." We must assume that the similarity between these descriptions and *Jub.* 8:30 is the result of either literary or cartographic dependency; it is hardly likely that they represent independent developments. If this is correct, then we have solid evidence that the *Jubilees* tradition influenced medieval cartography at a relatively early date, and certainly well before the Crusades in the eleventh to thirteenth centuries. Moreover, it is probable that *Jubilees* influenced Christian tradition at an even earlier date. As we have seen in Chapter 5, Theophilus of Antioch (*Autol.* 2.32) also divides the earth into climatic zones based on *Jub.* 8:30,[73] and the inclusion of the list of the climates of the "unknown" nations in Hippolytus' *Diamerismos* (§§ 224–34) may have been prompted by the concept of climates in *Jubilees*. In view of the Syrian tradition represented by Theophilus of Antioch, it is probably no coincidence that, as we have seen in Chapter 6, the Syriac *Chronicle to the Year 1234* appropriates the description of the three climates ultimately from *Jub.* 8:30. Here, within the same geographical region, we see the preservation of a Jewish geographical tradition for over a millennium, right down to the high Middle Ages.

Christian influence

It is unnecessary to establish the Christian influence on the medieval *mappaemundi*, for there can be little doubt that, to some degree at least, the medieval mapmakers shaped any cartographic tradition they may have received, whether it was Greco-Roman or Jewish or both. Catherine Delano Smith refers to Greco-Roman maps that were "Christianized and hijacked into the service of the church."[74] While they did not create *de novo*,[75] the medieval mapmakers also did not simply receive passively. Their additions, omissions, and other modifications to the received tradition are everywhere to be seen on the maps. The clearest example is the habit in many medieval maps of portraying Christ as dominating the world.[76] If, as seems probable, the medieval maps had a Roman and/or Jewish *Vorlage*, it certainly would not have depicted Christ. We have suggested the possibility that the *mappamundi* of Queen Kypros may have copied from the Agrippa map an image of Caesar dominating the world, for Philip's epigram explicitly mentions that the image of the world on the tapestry portrayed the earth as "obedient to great Caesar" (*AP* 9.778). The medieval mapmakers, in turn, may have substituted the image of Christ for that of Caesar. For example, the famous London Psalter map (ca. 1250) portrays the torso of Christ wearing royal garb, looming above the disk-shaped world, and holding a tripartite globus in his left hand.[77] As we saw in Chapter 1, the representation of the globus as a symbol of imperial or royal power was derived from Roman times, where it appears commonly on Roman imperial coinage. The inclusion of Christ at the head of several *mappaemundi* may symbolize the appointment of Christ as sovereign and judge of the earth.[78] Thus, the Hereford map depicts Christ coming down to the earth on the clouds of heaven, in accordance with Mk. 14:62 parr. (citing Dan. 7:14 with Ps. 110:1).

   In light of these considerations, the Christian maker of the Hereford map must have taken no little pleasure in writing in the lower-left corner of the map the Latin text of Lk. 2:1 above the head of the enthroned figure of Caesar Augustus: "A decree went out from Caesar Augustus that the whole world should be described."[79] For this verse not only cleverly links the origins of the Hereford map to salvation history, but it also effectively deconstructs the Roman *Vorlage* upon which the Hereford map may have been based. This becomes clear when we realize the trajectory of Lk. 2:1 within the context of Luke-Acts. As we saw in Chapter 3, the two volumes are unified in part by the decrees of Roman emperors. In Lk. 2:1, the "decree" (δόγμα) of Caesar Augustus controls where Christ is born. By Acts 17:6–7, however, the "decrees" (δόγματα) of the Roman emperor[80] are being subverted by the kingdom of the risen Christ (Acts 17:6–7), who is the new "Lord of all" (Acts 10:36) and the final Judge of the οἰκουμένη (Acts 17:31; cf. Lk. 4:5–8). Hence, by placing Lk. 2:1 above the head of Caesar Augustus on the Hereford map, the medieval mapmaker may be pointing to the fact that the image of the emperor on the *Vorlage* was replaced with Christ.[81]

Conclusion

Medieval *mappaemundi* represent a combination of various interlocking influences – Greco-Roman, Jewish, and Christian. Could it be that the *mappamundi* of Queen Kypros is a kind of "missing link" between the Agrippa map and the *mappaemundi*? On the one hand, of course, certainty on this issue will never be achieved as long as Philip's tantalizingly brief epigram is the only witness to it. On the other hand, to ask the question is almost to answer it. There are strong reasons to suppose that the medieval mapmakers were not tremendously creative individuals, that they were more or less bound to ancient tradition, and that they merely adapted the traditions they received. Therefore, if there is first-century evidence of a map that may have been the product of both Roman and Jewish influences, that map has the strongest possibility of being a distant relative of the medieval maps. We need not suppose that the Kypros map was the only one of its kind in existence. Where there is one, there may have been more. Perhaps similar maps were modeled on the Kypros map or were developed independently in the same milieu – the Jerusalem Temple and its priesthood. Kypros herself may well have been merely imitating or adapting a priestly cartographic tradition. In any case, the Kypros map opens the door to a new way of explaining the origin and development of the medieval *mappaemundi*.

CONCLUSION

The foregoing study has sought to trace the trajectory of an important geographic tradition from its OT and Jewish roots, through its reception in the NT and other early Christian literature, and on into the medieval *mappaemundi*. It remains here merely to summarize our main findings and to suggest their possible significance for the historical investigation of the NT.

In Chapter 1, we opened our discussion with an epigram of Philip of Thessalonia that not only provided an example of the methodological issues involved with a discussion of Jewish geographical lore, but also contributed valuable new insights into the possibility of Jewish cartographic activity in the Second-Temple period. The epigram praises an artistic tapestry, made presumably by Kypros, the last queen of Judea, and offered as a gift to Emperor Gaius. Woven into the fabric of this tapestry was a very impressive image of the world dominated by Caesar. Given the fact that a Hellenistic dynast like Kypros would have traveled with equal facility between Greco-Roman and Jewish worlds, we considered it a promising hypothesis that Kypros may have blended both Roman and Jewish traditions into her representation of the world, resulting in a novel, hybrid form – perhaps an Orientalized rendition of the famous Agrippa map in Rome.

In subsequent chapters, we set out to learn more about Jewish geographical lore in the Second-Temple period and its reception in early Christian tradition. In Chapter 2, therefore, we commenced by examining Genesis 10 – the most logical starting point – and the influential tradition to which it gave rise through the lost "Book of Noah" and *Jubilees* 8–9. We saw that *Jub.* 8:11 refers to *Jubilees* 8–9 as giving the contents of an apocalyptically oriented "book" purportedly written by Noah. Certain Jewish texts from the Second-Temple period provide evidence that this "Book of Noah" was circulated and reused in apocalyptic oracles against the nations, particularly against the imperialistic Kittim (at first the Greco-Macedonians and later the Romans). The "Book of Noah" records the division of the world among the sons and grandsons of Noah after the flood, detailing the inviolable boundaries between the portions, which the children of Noah swore they would never trespass. If a nation should nevertheless violate this oath, the Book of Noah predicts its destruction at the final judgment.

In Chapter 3, we turned to the Christian reception of the Genesis 10 tradition, concentrating our attention on Luke-Acts. Here, the influence of Genesis 10 and the *Jubilees* 8–9 tradition was more subtle than in other Second-Temple texts, but still appreciable. Luke's emphasis on the *Urzeit* and the *Endzeit* of the nations parallels that found in the *Book of Jubilees*. As we have seen, there is almost a subtext in Luke-Acts that retells the story of the Flood (Genesis 6–9), the Table of Nations (Genesis 10), and the Tower of Babel (Genesis 11). Thus, for example, the Lukan genealogy of Jesus in Lk. 3:23–38 uses the seventy-two generations from Adam to Jesus in order to underscore a relationship between Jesus and the original seventy-two nations of the world that descended from Noah according to the Table of Nations. The sending out of the seventy-two in Lk. 10:1–24 probably alludes again to the number of nations in the world. In Acts 2:1–13, the outpouring of the Spirit at Pentecost is seen as a reversal of God's confusion of the tongues after the flood. Furthermore, the *pars pro toto* catalogue of nations in Acts 2:9–11, which represents the "Jews from every nation under heaven," is related to the more extensive Table of Nations, particularly as mediated through Jewish–Christian tradition based on *Jubilees* 8–9. Peter's speech in the Temple (Acts 3:11–26) cites Gen. 12:3, which, in turn, presupposes the Table of Nations in Genesis 10. Luke's account of the Apostolic Council in Acts 15 emphasizes the "nations" and applies to the Gentile believers the commandments which, according to Genesis 9 and *Jub.* 7:20–1, were given to Noah after the flood. Finally, Paul's speech on the Areopagus refers to the postdiluvian distribution of the earth among the nations.

In Chapter 4, we received an important confirmation of our thesis that Luke-Acts is partly dependent on the Table of Nations tradition in *Jubilees* 8–9. For we were able to show that Pseudo-Clementine *Recognitions* 1.27–71 – an early Jewish–Christian text and one of the first commentaries on Acts – displays a similar dependence on *Jubilees* 8–9. We had already begun to see in Chapter 3 how studying this later Jewish–Christian source can be of considerable help in the exegesis of Luke-Acts (see esp. on the so-called "Apostolic Decree" in Acts 15:20, 29). Now we observed that *Rec.* 1.27–71 referred to Jerusalem as the center of the earth and to the division of the earth among the sons of Noah (1.30.3) – ideas that are clearly based on *Jub.* 8:12, 19, 22. Thus, Luke-Acts and the

Jewish–Christian source share the same *imago mundi* through the influence of *Jubilees* 8–9 that is common to both.

In Chapter 5, we continued our survey of the early Christian reception of the Genesis Table of Nations tradition by examining the work of Theophilus of Antioch. This second-century Greek apologist used the authoritative *Book of Jubilees* in order to combat pagan philosophy and perhaps even mentioned the book by name. In the course of his defense, Theophilus clearly alludes to *Jubilees* 8–9 and its *imago mundi* and possibly implies the use of an accompanying map. Thus, Theophilus provides us with our earliest evidence for the existence of the lost Greek version of *Jubilees*. In subsequent centuries, there is evidence that Greek *Jubilees* remained popular in Christian circles.

In Chapter 6, we argued that Hippolytus' *Diamerismos* is based on the Greek version of *Jubilees* 8–9, although Hippolytus had modified the original in several ways. Evidently, the apocalyptically oriented "book" of Noah (*Jub.* 8:11, 12), which describes the origins of the nations and anticipates their eschatological judgment (9:15), found its way into Christian circles and stoked imminent expectations about the end of the Roman Empire and the coming judgment. It seems likely that Hippolytus epitomized and reworked the lost Greek version of *Jubilees* 8–9 and incorporated it into his *Chronicon*, thereby seeking to dampen speculation about the end of the Kittim. Through Hippolytus' *Chronicon*, the Diamerismos tradition based on *Jubilees* 8–9 became a fundamental part of the highly ramified Christian chronographic tradition. Indeed, our study illuminates the development of early Christian chronography and its strong link with Christian cartography.

Finally, in Chapter 7, we returned to our initial question about the possible relationship between the *mappamundi* of Queen Kypros and the medieval *mappaemundi*. Having established in the previous chapters that the *Jubilees* 8–9 tradition was preserved in apocalyptically-oriented Christian circles from the time of the NT and for centuries thereafter, the final chapter argued that this *Jubilees* tradition also influenced the medieval *mappaemundi*. There were too many affinities between the *imago mundi* of *Jubilees* and the cartographic features of the *mappaemundi* for the similarities to be accidental. Most strikingly, several of the medieval maps describe the three climates of earth in the same unique way that *Jub.* 8:30 does, thus demonstrating the influence of the *Jubilees* 8–9 tradition in the *mappaemundi*. Hence, the medieval maps may not represent, as commonly supposed, merely the "Christianization" of an earlier Roman map, but rather the first-century "Judaization" of a Roman map which was later adapted by Christians. At the very least, the Kypros map opens up the possibility that some such scenario took place, even if the Kypros map itself is deemed to have had a less decisive or less direct role in the actual development. In the future, the scholarly discussion of the medieval *mappaemundi* will need to take more account of their Jewish roots, among other sources of influence.

In sum, we may attempt to draw a stemma for the development of the *Jubilees* 8–9 tradition (see Table 6). The picture is far from complete, and there are still many uncertainties. Further work is needed, for instance, on the lost "Book of Noah" in order to ascertain, if possible, both its provenance and the circumstances under which it was originally written. On the other end of the timeline, a comprehensive survey of the medieval *mappaemundi* is needed, in order to determine whether there is additional evidence of Jewish influence on these maps. Ultimately, the work that we have begun here will not be complete until the "OT pseudepigrapha" have been systematically studied in their own right, not only as documents illuminating Second-Temple Judaism, but also as writings preserved in the Christian church. The *Book of Jubilees* will undoubtedly play a key role in this investigation, as we learn more about its transmission through the centuries in various localities and languages groups.

What is the significance of the present study for the historical investigation of the NT? Two suggestions may be offered. First, the foregoing study encourages us to lay aside our modern predilections and to reconsider geographical aspects of the NT on their own terms as integral to historical investigation of the text. Perhaps as a result we shall never again be content with our current Bible atlases for reconstructing NT history, realizing that those very maps – products of modern geographical perspective – detract from genuine investigation of our texts. Such maps will remain useful only for the most superficial orientation, and even then we shall need to bear in mind their distorting tendency. Instead, we shall need to develop an historical imagination that comes from immersing ourselves in the thought world of the NT texts and their environs. In all probability, it will be impossible to replace our present Bible atlases with new ones containing reconstructions of the first-century *imago mundi*.[1] These are now irrevocably lost to us, except insofar as they are preserved, however faintly, in the medieval *mappaemundi*. We must no doubt content ourselves with generating mental maps,[2] which, with some notable exceptions, is all the ancients themselves normally had at their disposal. With this heightened sensitivity to the original geographical framework of the NT, our historical work on the NT will hopefully be established on a firmer historical foundation – all the more so if it is combined with a chronology that likewise approaches the matter from "inside." Our study

Table 6. *Genesis 10, the Lost "Book of Noah," and the* Jubilees 8–9 *Tradition*

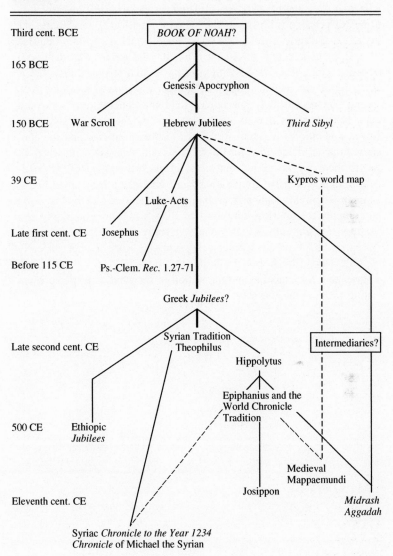

provides a concrete example of what can be accomplished with this kind of contextually sensitive approach.

Second, the present study is significant for the historical investigation of the NT because it illustrates the value of interdisciplinary study. NT Studies is not only a relatively young theological discipline, but also a small segment within the major academic disciplines that deal with antiquity. This means that NT Studies has a dual responsibility. In order to fulfill our responsibility to the other disciplines, we must look beyond our too narrowly specialized field and conduct our work on a much broader basis than is often the case. As the present study has shown, this kind of research stimulates further questions, and the contact with allied fields provides the methods and materials with which to answer them. In the future, our work on the NT will hopefully benefit from more extensive cooperation with scholars in these allied fields. An interdisciplinary team approach may be a useful model for exploring the complex relationship between Christian history/chronography and geography/cartography, which the present study has merely adumbrated. Ultimately, a full-orbed approach to geography, such as that currently being developed by Robert D. Sack, may be helpful in extending our geographical horizons beyond the notion of mere physical place when dealing with our ancient texts.[3]

NOTES

Introduction

1. On the problem of defining the "pseudepigrapha," see most recently Flint 1998–99: 2.24–34.
2. The *Book of Jubilees*, a pseudepigraphon of the mid-second century BCE, presents itself as the divine revelation that Moses received on Mt. Sinai through an "angel of the presence" and wrote down by dictation (cf. *Jub.* 1:26–9). The book is essentially a retelling of Genesis and the first part of Exodus (the story from the time of creation to Israel's arrival at Sinai). It was originally written in Hebrew, fragments of which have been found among the Dead Sea scrolls. From Hebrew, it was translated into Greek and from Greek into Latin and Ethiopic (Ge'ez), the only complete text in existence. See further in Chap. 2.
3. Cf. Scott 1994; 1995a. Indeed, as Bikerman (1952: 71) observes: "... Jewish and Christian scholars until the last century found a niche for each new people in the Biblical Table of Nations (Gen. 10). Even in the time of Voltaire, antiquarians in general had no doubt about the descent of the Chinese from a son of Noah. A learned author rejected the tradition of the Tartars as to their origin ... as inconsistent with Biblical data. In 1731, a well known Orientalist derived the Russians (who are Muscovites) from Mesech, a son of Japhet. He started from this principle: 'It is well known that all peoples descend from Noah.'"
4. Ramsay 1900: 316.
5. P. S. Alexander 1990: 121.
6. Cf. Hengel 1997: 136. On the overlap between geography and history, see now Clarke (1999: 195) who argues that "ancient notions of the terms γεωγραφία (geography) and ἱστορία (history) both incorporated aspects of the modern subjects of geography and history; in other words, that the modern subjects of geography and history, as defined in the narrow, modern sense, do not map exactly into the ancient world." In fact, to complicate matters even further, Strabo introduces his work as one of philosophy! Cf. ibid., 216 with n. 51.
7. Some seminal work has been done, but much more is needed. Cf., e.g., Hengel 1983; L. Alexander 1995a; 1995b; Borgen 1983.
8. This is true both of regional geography and of world geography. Cf., e.g., Goudineau 1996: 465–7, with Fig. 8: "But it is impossible to understand texts or decisions, such as those that created the administrative structure or the road system, if we continue to base our analyses on present-day cartography. It is important to remember that as late as Pliny [d. 79 CE], and perhaps as late as Ptolemy [fl. 146–70 CE], geographical knowledge remained extremely approximate. Book IV of Strabo's *Geography*, devoted to Gaul and completed about A.D. 18, illustrates the point. The information is more or less reliable for southern Gaul ... But for the remainder of Gaul the account is staggering: following Caesar, all the coastlines (including those on the shores of the Atlantic) are described as facing the north and the Pyrenees as running north–south,

parallel to the Rhine and also to the courses of the Garonne, the Loire and the Seine. The coast of Great Britain lies opposite that of Gaul, from the mouth of the Rhine as far as the Pyrenees, and the channel between Britain and Gaul is said to be 320 stades (some 50 km) in width. All the distances are wrong, some of them by a huge margin." According to some modern scholars, world geography was practically unknown to the ancients. Cf., e.g., Talbert 1990.

9. During the past half-century, science and technology have equipped us with a grasp of the earth's appearance far in advance of that available to any previous era. Ironically, this new knowledge, now firmly embedded in our consciousness, imposes an unprecedented, irreversible handicap as we seek to penetrate the perspective of others, such as Greeks, Romans, Jews, and the writers and readers of the NT. The forthcoming, comprehensive *Atlas of the Greek and Roman World* (ed. Richard J. A. Talbert; Princeton: Princeton University Press) also fails to escape this difficulty, even though the overriding rationale for the atlas was to transport users to the ancient world. As Talbert states in an interview (Monaghan 1998: 15), "We really want people to go back in the time machine and look at this physical and cultural landscape on its own terms, its ancient terms." Yet, many of the maps were drawn from military sources, primarily the U.S. National Imagery and Mapping Agency. If, as Talbert (1990: 219) elsewhere suggests, ancients and medievals were incapable of accurate mapping on a large scale, then it would seem necessary for our modern cartographic reconstructions of the ancient world to reflect this more limited perspective.

10. Cf., e.g., Whitfield 1994; Harley and Woodward 1987.

11. Fraser 1972: I.520.

12. Hengel 1994; 1996.

13. See the withering critique and quite despairing assessment of the situation by Bockmuehl (1998).

14. Cf. Charlesworth 1985; Charlesworth and Evans 1993; Evans 1992: 20–47.

15. Kraft 1994: 56, 63. In this connection, Kraft cites as examples the works of Marinus de Jonge on the Christian nature of the *Testaments of the Twelve Patriarchs*. These *Testaments* belong to the so-called "OT Pseudepigrapha" transmitted to us by early and medieval Christianity. In their present form, they constitute a clearly Christian writing addressing Christian concerns. Some scholars consider them basically Jewish, though more or less heavily interpolated and redacted by Christians. They still use them as evidence for ideas current in Judaism around the beginning of the present era. Others, like de Jonge, are of the opinion that such a Jewish *Grundschrift*, if it existed at all, cannot possibly be reconstructed. For him, the *Testaments* must be studied as a Christian composition that makes use of a surprising number of Jewish traditions, probably on the basis of acquaintance with written Jewish sources. With the publication of the Aramaic Levi fragments found at Qumran, the hope of reconstructing the Jewish *Grundschrift* for at least part of the *Testaments of the Twelve Patriarchs* has been given new impetus. Cf., most recently, Kugler 1996. For a response, see de Jonge 1999.

16. Cf. VanderKam 1996a; Bauckham 1983: 7, 51–3, 89ff.

17. Cf. Kugel 1998.

18. Cf. Wright 1998; 1999, which builds on the work of other scholars who have found evidence that some early Christian writers used the Qumran Pseudo-Ezekiel text. Cf. Kister 1990; Bauckham 1992b. See also Brooke 1998–99: I.287.

19. Cf. Milik 1971: 548, 550–1.

20. Cf. Hagedorn and Hagedorn 1987: 60.

21. Cf. Rönsch 1874: 251–382.

22. It can still be debated, however, whether writings such as Pseudo-Philo's *Biblical Antiquities*, the Temple Scroll, and *Jubilees* should be described as "Rewritten Bibles" or as independent accounts drawn from a common tradition. On the "Rewritten Bible," see further Bernstein 1999b: 10–17.

23. VanderKam and Milik 1994.
24. Albani, et al. 1997. None of the essays in that volume is devoted to the NT, and my own essay on "The Division of the Earth in *Jubilees* 8:11–9:15 and Early Christian Chronography" (Scott 1997a) contains the only treatment of early Christian literature.
25. I.e., *Jub.* 1:23 in Rom. 2:29; *Jub.* 2:19 in Rom. 9:24; and *Jub.* 19:21 in Rom. 4:13.
26. Cf. Adler 1994: 144: "In Christian chronography, no other work of Jewish pseude-pigrapha enjoyed a longevity comparable to *Jubilees*."
27. Cf. VanderKam 1998a: 400: "There is no evidence that early Christian writers con-sidered Jubilees canonical, though it was cited fairly often, but it, too [along with *1 Enoch*], became part of the Old Testament canon of the church in Ethiopia."
28. This name for the *Book of Jubilees* may imply a lower authority than the canonical Genesis, although the pseudepigraphon does compress the Genesis account at points.
29. Cf. Kugel 1998: 29 n. 23: "A further complication is presented by such books as *1 Enoch* or *Jubilees*, books that arguably were at one time considered by some readers to be as scriptural as Genesis or Exodus, but that later in the course of their transmission came to be viewed as less authoritative or altogether irrelevant. If so, then – for a time, at least – the interpretations contained within them must not have been viewed as interpretations at all: they were no less scriptural than the interpretations found in Chronicles or Daniel. Did not the books' subsequent change of status mean that these same interpretations reverted back to their original state, that is, turned from Scripture into interpretation (thereby reversing the path traced by the interpretations canonized in Chronicles and Daniel)?" There is a possible difference between the books of *1 Enoch* and *Jubilees*: whereas the former fell into disuse by most of the Christian church during the third century CE, the latter seems to have continued to enjoy some interest well beyond that point.

1   The *mappamundi* of Queen Kypros

1. Cf. Peek 1938: 2339–49. The *Garland* of Philip has long been assigned to the brief reign of Emperor Gaius, more precisely to 40 CE. However, Alan Cameron argues that the anthology was more likely published under Nero (54–68 CE). On the debate, see Cameron 1980: 43–62; 1993: 56–65.
2. If, as we shall argue, the weaver of the tapestry was Jewish, she may have observed the biblical prohibition against mixing wool and linen (cf. Lev. 19:19; Deut. 22:11; Ezek. 44:17–18; see further Yadin 1963: 186–7, 262). On the other hand, gold and other materials could be woven into linen (e.g., Exod. 28:5, 6; *T. Job* 25:7; *Jos. As.* 2:8; 5:5). According to *t. Ketub.* 5.4, R. Yehudah ruled that a husband cannot force his wife to work with flax, since it lacerates the mouth and makes the lips stiffen. This suggests perhaps that Jewish women may have been averse to working with flax.
3. The term *mappamundi*, literally "cloth of the world" (cf. Schuppe 1930: 1413–16), is unknown to classical Latin. It is first recorded in the ninth century, and it was what a world map was normally called in the twelfth and thirteenth centuries, whether drawn on cloth or not (cf. Harvey 1996: 26; Woodward 1987a: 287–8). For some stunning examples of artistic textiles, see Wilckens 1991. See also Tyner 1994: 2–7.
4. Cf. Polybius 3.32.2; 4.28.2–6; 5.31.4–5; Diodorus Siculus 4.60.1; 4.63.1. I am grateful to Katherine Clarke for this point. See also Clarke 1999: 81, 123, 314.
5. In the following, we shall continue to refer to Kypros' production as a "map," although it was probably little more than a generalized image of the world like the Babylonian world map (see further below). Modern cartography should not be used as the stan-dard of what passes for an ancient "map." The definition employed by Harley and Woodward (1987: I.xvi) seems sufficiently inclusive: "Maps are graphic representa-tions that facilitate a spatial understanding of things, concepts, conditions, processes, or events in the human world."

6. Gow and Page (eds.) 1968: 300–1 (no. 6).

7. Cf. *Anth. Pal.* 16.172, a comment by Alexander of Aetolia (b. 315 BCE) on a statue of Aphrodite: "Pallas herself, I think, wrought Aphrodite to perfection, forgetting the judgment of Paris" (Αὐτά που τὰν Κύπριν ἀπηκριβώσατο Παλλὰς τᾶς ἐπ' Ἀλεξάνδρου λαθομένα κρίσιος). See also LSJ, s.v., 175. Therefore, in light of the tapestry described in Philip's epigram, the desire to achieve exactitude and to replicate empire cartographically is much older than the medieval *mappaemundi.* Cf. Tomasch 1998: 5.

8. According to Strabo (*Geog.* 1.1.7; cf. 1.14), Krates of Mallos described the shield of Achilles (Homer, *Il.* 18) as a "replica of the world" (κόσμου μίμημα).

9. Hence, this tapestry should be added to the discussion of cartography and art. For previous discussions of this nexus, see Woodward 1987b.

10. Cichorius 1922: 351–4, followed by Gow and Page 1968: 1.300; Cameron 1993: 65; Peek 1938: 2340, 2344; Stern 1974–84: 1.375–6; Schwartz 1990: 7 n. 10.

11. Another contributing factor to the corruption may have been the influence of φερέκαρπον in line 1. It seems less likely that Philip himself made the mistake when composing the official epigram, although this possibility cannot be completely excluded.

12. Besides Kypros the wife of Agrippa I, Josephus refers to four other members of the Herodian dynasty with the name Kypros: the wife of Antipater (*JW* 1.181; *Ant.* 14.121); the daughter of Herod the Great and Mariamme (*Ant.* 16.196; 18.130); the daughter of Kypros and Antipater, married to Alexas (*Ant.* 18.138); and the daughter of Kypros and Alexas (*Ant.* 18.138). See the stemmata in Kokkinos 1998: 176, 205, 340, and Appendix 1 on Herodian prosopography (363–6).

13. According to the *Suda,* ἄνασσα is synonymous with βασίλισσα ("queen"). The term ἄνασσα is used of various female deities, including Demeter (Homer, *Il.* 14.326), Artemis, the "queen of the gods" (Euripides, *IA* 1523), and the Syrian goddess Derketo, "the queen of the Assyrians" (Ctesias [*FGrH* F3c, 688F, frag. 1εγ]). It is also used of mortals. In the *Odyssey* (6.149, 175), for example, Odysseus addresses Nausicaa, the daughter of the Phaeacians' king, as an ἄνασσα. On ἄνασσα as a Greek form of address, see Dickey 1996: 98, 103. According to the second-century CE lexicographer, Harpocration of Alexandria, who preserves a fragment of Aristotle (frg. 526), the following titles are used of the royal household on Cyprus: "The sons and brothers of the king are called 'lords' (ἄνακτες), whereas sisters and wives [of the king] are called 'ladies' (ἄνασσαι)." This usage may have special relevance to our discussion, if Philip is playing on the connection between Kypros (the name of an island and of a person in Herod's royal household) and the term ἄνασσα (the title of princesses and queens on Cyprus).

14. For reasons that the ἄνασσα is most likely not a member of the imperial household, see Cichorius 1922: 352.

15. Cf. Cameron 1990: 291–4. The identification of Cleopatra depends on whether the epigram was written by Antipater of Thessalonica (client of L. Calpurnius Piso, consul 15 BCE) or Asclepiades of Samos (b. 340–330 BCE). See Gutzwiller 1998: 122, who argues that Cleopatra is the sister of Alexander, murdered about 308 BCE.

16. The text explicitly states that "we have come" (ἤλθομεν), suggesting that the queen's gift comes to the emperor from afar. On Roman "client" kingdoms, see in general Sullivan 1990; Braund 1984.

17. Cf. Schwartz 1990: 59–62. For a fresh discussion of Agrippa I, see now Kokkinos 1998: 271–304, including 279–81 on the territorial extent of Agrippa's kingdom.

18. As a new emperor, Gaius also gave extensive domains to other Hellenistic client kings with whom he had close, personal links. Cf. Wiedemann 1996: 223.

19. Cf. Cameron 1993: 65: "Epigrams that name or address reigning emperors normally and naturally refer only to 'Caesar.'" Hence, it is only by a process of deduction that the identity of a "Caesar" can be ascertained in an epigram.

20. See, however, Cameron 1993: 65: "The 'Caesar' of Philip VI (*AP* ix.778), recipient of a present from the wife of Herod Agrippa, is (despite the commentators) much more likely to be Herod's lifelong friend Claudius than Gaius." No reasons are given for this opinion, but it surely relates to Cameron's view that the *Garland* of Philip was published in the reign of Nero (see above).

21. The precedent for this move is well established. Cf. Mitchell 1997; Braund 1984: 59–67, 184. According to Josephus (*Ant.* 15.26–27; *JW* 1.439), Alexandra sent portraits of her children (Mariamme and Aristobulus/Jonathan) as a gift to Mark Antony in order to ingratiate herself with him.

22. Another example of a woman who engages herself in the political world to help her husband is Turia in the *Laudatio Turiae*, who had saved him and secured his rehabilitation during the proscriptions. Cf. Badian 1996: 822. I am grateful to Katherine Clarke for this example.

23. If, as Schwartz (1990: 48, 50) argues, Josephus' source is merely biased in favor of Kypros, the historical reality behind the positive statements about her in *Ant.* 18.147–9, 159 may be called into question. Unfortunately, however, Schwartz does not interact with Cichorius' thesis at this point, which is based on possibly corroborating evidence in *Anth. Pal.* 9.778 (see merely Schwartz 1990: 7 n. 10). Moreover, Kypros' prominence is well documented in an issue of coins dating from 40/41 CE, which carry the portrait of Agrippa I on the obverse, and his wife Kypros surprisingly *standing* to front on the reverse. Cf. Kokkinos 1998: 289.

24. Cf. Prov. 31:10–31 (esp. vv. 19, 23); see also *m. Ketub.* 5:5: "These are works which the wife must perform for her husband: grinding flour and baking bread and washing clothes and cooking food and nursing her child and making ready his bed and working in wool. If she brought him in one bondwoman, she need not grind or bake or wash; if two, she need not cook or nurse her child; if three, she need not make ready his bed or work in wool; if four, she may sit (all day) in a chair. R. Eliezer says: Even if she brought him in a hundred bondwomen, he should compel her to work in wool, for idleness leads to unchastity." In Greek literature before the Platonic Socrates in *Meno*, the feminine form of σωφροσύνη is associated exclusively with domestic virtue and with weaving in particular (cf. H. F. North 1977: 35–48). Cf. Peskowitz 1997: 197: ". . . referring to literary figures, such as Lucretia, spinners and weavers symbolized the sexual chastity, marital loyality, domesticity, and industriousness expected of elite matrons (Livy, *History [Ad urbe conditia]* 1.57 . . .)."

25. If Kypros sent the tapestry in 39 CE, she would have sent it from Panias (Caesarea Philippi), where coins depicting her were minted. Cf. Kokkinos 1998: 285–6.

26. This event must have taken place before September 39 CE, for at that time Gaius embarked on a trip to Gallia and Germania and did not return to Italy until the summer of 40. In that case, Agrippa's gifts were probably sent in the summer of 39 CE.

27. Cf. Kokkinos 1998: 285 n. 74. I am grateful to the author for a private communication on this point.

28. On Gaius' expedition, see Halfmann 1986: 32, 170–2.

29. Quandt 1962: 22 (no. 26), noting *Anth. Pal.* 9.778 as a parallel.

30. If a mythological background is sought for Philip's description of Kypros' tapestry, we may note that weaving has strong mythological/metaphorical connections in Greco-Roman tradition. Cf. Scheid and Svenbro 1996. Note also that analysis of the weaving imagery in *De rerum natura* shows that the loom helped to shape Lucretius' conception of the world (Snyder 1983: 37–43). Perhaps most importantly for our considerations, Pherecydes of Syros (fl. 544 BCE) describes how "Zas [Zeus] fashions a robe (φᾶρος) both big and beautiful, and on it he embroiders (ποικίλλει) Earth and Ogenos [Ocean] and the abodes of Ogenos . . ." (*P. Grenf.* II.11.i.14–18), how he gives the robe to his bride Chthonie during the wedding, and how she becomes Earth upon donning the robe. Cf. Schibli 1990: 50–77, 165–6; West 1971: 9–11, 15–20, 53–5 (on Oriental parallels); Scheid and Svenbro 1996: 63–6. West (1971: 19) suggests that if Pherecydes specially

mentions earth, sea, and sky, then "it is possibly because he has in view a map on which they were prominently marked. Maps of the world were believed to have first appeared in Greece in the mid sixth century. Anaximander was supposed to have made the first one, and we hear of them next in connection with two more Milesians, Aristagoras and Hecataeus. We gather from Herodotus that they were commonly bordered by the circle of Oceanus." According to West (1971: 49–50, 87), the Babylonian world map, which shows Mesopotamia surrounded by a circular ocean, approximates what Pherecydes' map must have looked like. On the Babylonian world map, see further below.

31. As educated, well-traveled members of the Herodian dynasty, Agrippa and Kypros would have been equally at home in both worlds.

32. Cf. Romm 1992. Note, however, that in her review of this book, Clarke (1995: 266–7) suggests that Romm's treatment of the ancient concept of geographical limits is problematic: "He sees the idea of an encircling Ocean as the answer to the need to make intelligible a world whose actual limits are not known, but it is not made clear how the imagined existence of an indefinite body of water fulfils this need. R[omm]'s point (15) that Homer and Hesiod do not envisage new continents beyond the Ocean, only islands, does not help his argument, and merely draws attention to the fact that the Ocean is *not* seen as delimiting the earth, but has places lying beyond it." Note, however, that the encircling Ocean was not always conceived of as an *indefinite* "edge." For instance, on the Babylonian world map, the encircling Ocean clearly has definite limits, although triangles radiating from its outer edge evidently symbolize the existence of distant islands within the encircling Ocean. See further Horowitz 1998: 29–30.

33. Cf. Bannert 1978: 1561–2; Wolf and Wolf 1983.

34. See further Stanley 1993: 10; Hardie 1985: 11–31; Taplin 1998: 96–115; Harley, Woodward, and Aujac 1987: 131–2. Note that Clement of Alexandria (*Strom.* 6.2.9.4) compares Achilles' shield in Homer to the robe of Chthonie/Ge in Pherecydes (on which see above).

35. In Baebius Italicus, *Ilias Latina* (ca. 65 CE), the Shield of Homer is used for official Neronian propaganda, recalling the earlier use of the Shield in Virgil, *Eclogue* 4. Cf. Schubert 1998: 229–44 (esp. 232ff.).

36. According to the Greek geographer, Agathemerus (after ca. 51 BCE), "(1.1) Anaximander the Milesian, the disciple of Thales, was the first to attempt to draw the inhabited world on a tablet (ἐν πίνακι)...(1.2) The ancients drew the inhabited world as round (στρογγύλην), and Greece lay in the middle (μέσην), and Delphi (lay) in the middle of it for it is the umbilicus of the earth (καὶ ταύτης Δελφούς· τὸν ὀμφαλὸν γὰρ ἔχειν τῆς γῆς)...(1.4)...Ocean was named for quickly encircling (ὠκέως ἀνύειν κύκλῳ) the earth." K. Müller 1965: II.471–2. For text, translation and notes, see Diller 1975: 59–76 (here 60, 67, 72).

37. On attempts to reconstruct Herodotus' conception of the world, see Siebener 1995: 13–19, 320–33.

38. Similarly, the Babylonian world-map clearly presents the world as containing one circular continent in the center, surrounded by Ocean. Cf. Horowitz 1998: 27–9; Clarke 1999: 213: "Early Babylonian maps of Mesopotamia, with Babylon at the centre, form a precise parallel for the centrality of Rome in Strabo's world."

39. As Clarke (1999: 212, 308) demonstrates, Strabo reasserted the Homeric idea of the encircling Ocean in direct opposition to Hellenistic scientists such as Hipparchus. On the limits of the world as equivalent to the inhabited world, see Strabo, *Geog.* 2.5.34; 2.5.5.

40. Cf. F. Romer 1998. See also Städele 1991: 251–5.

41. Cf. Clarke 1999: 308–11.

42. Cf. Horowitz 1998: 20–42, pls. 2, 6; idem 1988: 147–63; VanderKam 1983: 271–8. On the new join to the Babylonian world map, which restores one of the aforementioned triangular regions, see Finkel 1995: 26–7; C. D. Smith 1996: 209–11. In a highly

controversial article, McMenamin (1997: 46–51) argues that a Carthaginian coin of the mid-to-late fourth century BCE contains a schematic map of the world which is oriented on the North. According to the author, the rectangular area in the middle constitutes the Mediterranean Sea, with a central dot representing Sardinia; the British Isles are visible above the Iberian peninsula; the triangular landmass to the right is India; and the irregular shape to the left is the New World (America). It has been argued that the Table of Nations in Genesis 10 (see Chap. 2) had a Phoenician source. Cf. Tsirkin 1991: 117–34.

43. On the worldwide empire of Sargon of Akkad (the "totality of the land under heaven") in the "Sargon Geography," see Horowitz 1998: 67–95. Cf. Tadmor 1999: 55–62.

44. Cf. Metzger 1983–85: I.536. See further Stone 1990: 185; Gandz 1953: 23–53; Brincken 1970: 265.

45. Admittedly, nothing is explicitly stated about the shape of the land, and there are other possible ways of conceiving the spatial distribution of land and sea. For example, the Mediterranean (and other seas/oceans) may have been the fundamental point of orientation, with land surrounding it. But see *4 Ezra* 6:49–52, which comes just a few lines below the passage cited above: "Then you kept in existence two living creatures; the name of one you called Behemoth and the name of the other Leviathan. (50) And you separated one from the other, for the seventh part where the water had been gathered together could not hold them both. (51) And you gave Behemoth one of the parts which had been dried up on the third day [of creation], to live in it, where there are a thousand mountains; (52) but to Leviathan you have the seventh part, the watery part; and you have kept them to be eaten by whom you wish, and when you wish." The allusion to Ps. 74:12–15 in *4 Ezra* 6:52 is drawn from the very same passage that informs the portrayal of Christ and Leviathan on the London Psalter Map of ca. 1250 CE (cf., e.g., Vilnay 1963: 14; see further in Chap. 7). There, Ocean encircles the disk-shaped earth.

46. Cf. J. Collins 1995c: 138–53; idem, 1995b: 43–58. The *imago mundi* of Diaspora Jews in the Hellenistic period is apparently limited to the inhabited world, if their writings are any indication. Cf. Borgen 1997: 19: "As reflected in Philo's writings, his world comprised the area from India in the east to Libya, Rome and the Atlantic ocean in the West, and from Scythia and Germany in the north to Ethiopia in the south." Compare Redpath 1903: 307: "If we may ask . . . what are the extreme limits of the names occurring in the whole LXX, we shall find them, if we omit 'India' as simply part of a title, to be Spain on the west, Persepolis or Parthia on the east, Ethiopia on the south, and Macedonia on the north. Almost all the places in it would be found to have been included within the boundaries of the Greek empire of Alexander the Great and of the kingdoms which took its place." On the dominant tribes that define the world's extremities, see Ephorus' view expressed by Strabo, *Geog.* 1.2.28: Celts (W), Scythians (N), Indians (E), and Ethiopians (S). Cf. Clarke 1999: 199; Goldenberg 1998: 91–3.

47. During his campaigns, Alexander is said to have ascended until he saw the earth like a globe partially submerged in a bowl of water. Cf. *y. 'Abod. Zar.* 3:1, 42c; *Num. Rab.* 13:14.

48. Already in Virgil (*Aen.* 1.278–9), we find the famous promise given by Jupiter to Venus, mother of Aeneas, the legendary founder of Rome: "To these [sc. the Romans] I set neither boundaries nor periods of empire; I have given them dominion without limit" (*his ego nec metas rerum nec tempora pono imperium sine fine dedi*). Cf. Hardie 1986: 364–5 (see also his whole discussion of the Shield of Aeneas, esp. 367–9, 377–86); Cancik 1998: 118–19. Cicero (*Cat.* 3.26; cf. *Somn.* 20; *Ps. Sol.* 2:29) celebrates Pompey as one who "has carried the frontiers of your [the Roman citizens'] empire to the limits not of earth but of heaven (*non terrae sed caeli regionibus terminaret*)." See further Vasaly 1993: 133–5; Syme 1995: 90; Bendlin 1997: 36–8; Brunt 1997: 26–8; Clarke 1999: 116–18.

49. Clarke (1997: 106–7) shows that the idea of Roman rule over the whole inhabited world goes back to the 60s BCE, with Pompey and his victory over all three continents – Libya, Europe, and Asia (cf. Plutarch, *Pomp.* 38.2–3). See further Clarke 1999: 191–2, 309–12; Weinstock 1971: 37–9. Interestingly enough, the notion of encircling one's worldwide empire by means of conquest seems to be quite ancient. According to the *Sargon Legend*, "[The La]nd of the Sea I encircled three times" (Horowitz 1998: 78). See also J. E. Wright 2000: 13, 99, 123, 154, 157, 160–2, 165; Arrian, *Anab.* 4.7.5.

50. The Preamble reads as follows: "A copy is set out below of 'The achievements of Divine Augustus', by which he brought the world under the empire of the Roman people..." (*Rerum gestarum divi Augusti, quibus orbem terrarum imperio populi Romani subiecit...*). On Augustus' announcement of conquest of the whole inhabited world, see esp. Nicolet 1991: 29–56. See further Isaac 1992; Talbert 1990: 215–23. An Augustan milestone describes the Roman achievement in grasping all that is between the Baetis river, which describes Baetica, and the stream of Ocean, which bounds the world: "...from Baetis and the *Ianus Augustus* [at Cordoba, the provincial capital] to the Ocean..." (*ILS* 102). The Gemma Augustea, an exquisite cameo of carved onyx dating from the last years of Augustus, shows Augustus being crowned by *Oecumene*, the personification of global empire since Alexander. Cf. Galinsky 1996: 120–1.

51. Cf. Ehrenberg and Jones 1967: 85–7 (no. 100.24–5).

52. As Fergus Millar points out (1988: 138), "Augustan ideology in general, however, shifted uneasily between the notion of an already achieved universal domination and that of a major eastern enemy [i.e., Parthia] whom it was Rome's destiny to confront; thus an inscription of 2/3 CE from Messene speaks of Gaius, on his eastern campaign as 'fighting against the barbarians for the safety of all men' (*SEG* 23.206)." See also ibid., 140: "...Tiberius' survey [cf. Tacitus, *Ann.* 4.4–5], alluding to the three major rivers, Rhine, Danube and Euphrates, which bounded the empire, is perhaps the best example of the new conceptual framework which saw the empire as a stable geographical entity, with defined boundaries..." See further Millar 1982: 15–20.

53. Cf. Yadin 1963: 169–269; Peskowitz 1993; 1997: 195–7; Adovasio and Andrews 1981: 181–5; Shamir and Baginski 1998: 53–62 (Hebrew).

54. In that case, Kypros may well have had the help of master weavers in producing the tapestry.

55. We may also note that the division of the traditional, bipartite division of the world into earth and sea had a major influence on Roman imperial ideology. Cf. Hardie 1986: 302–10.

56. For a succinct cursus, see Kienast 1996: 294–6.

57. Cf. Schwartz 1990: 47. Kokkinos (1998: 276) suggests that Kypros may have been sent to Rome for her education, and that it was there that she met and married Agrippa I. Her second child, Agrippa II, was born in Rome in 27/28 CE.

58. Josephus lived in Rome after the Jewish War (cf. *Life* 422–3; *Ap.* 1.50). Did he come in contact there with either the Agrippa map or Queen Kypros' tapestry? If so, did either one or both of these influence his *imago mundi* (cf. his exposition of the Table of Nations in *Ant.* 1.120–47)? As a Jerusalemite who was intimately familiar with the Temple cult from personal experience, Josephus would have come under the same cartographic influences that may have informed Kypros' image of the world.

59. Cf. Kokkinos 1998: 271–2.

60. Cf. Roller 1998: 43–53; Schürer 1973–87: I.291, 292, 295, 306, 318; II.104, 310; III.96, 130; Roddaz 1984: 446, 453–63. If M. Agrippa was Pliny's source on the Essenes (*HN* 5.73), then we have additional evidence of his familiarity with the Jewish people. Cf. Goranson 1994: 295–8.

61. Sutherland 1984: 11, 105, 112, 115; Nicols 1974: 65–86; Carter and Metcalf 1988: 145–7; Roddaz 1984: 593–612; A. Barrett 1997.

62. The same text also makes it clear that Herod's grandson, King Agrippa I, reminded M. Agrippa's grandson, Emperor Gaius, of their grandfathers' close personal friendship.

63. Similarly, Agrippa I is known to have used imitation of Roman coins as a means of flattering the emperor. Cf. Kokkinos 1998: 286, referring to coins that Agrippa had minted in Panias in the second year of his reign (37/38 CE): "Obviously this is a series of heavily Romanized coins minted by a grateful client king, which serves to underline not only how flattery towards the emperor for his choice to grant a throne had to be made visible, but also how Agrippa's personal background was tightly bound to Rome. Burnett has recently pointed out that these coins are actually adaptations of Roman *sestertii* and *dupondii* struck in Rome in 37/38 CE, and never circulated east of the Adriatic. Indeed it looks as if Agrippa had brought with him some newly minted specimens, which he copied at the first available moment." Similarly, Agrippa's "Year 5" coins, minted in 40/41, were issued as a further compliment to Gaius (ibid., 289).

64. By modern standards, the Agrippa map may not have been very accurate. If the Peutinger map is any indication, Romans were inept at surveying on a large scale, for this map does not give "correct geographical shapes" by most criteria. More probably, however, the Peutinger map did not intend to be a scale map, but rather a handy itinerarium in pictorial form, showing the most important roads and distances within the Roman Empire. Cf. Fugmann 1998: 25–8.

65. Cf. Roller 1998: 52–3.

66. We may note that in 14 BCE, Herod the Great accompanied M. Agrippa on an expedition to the Kimmerian Bosporus. Roller (1998: 49) suggests that Herod's motivation may have been in part that "he had learned from Strabo [*Geog.* 1.1.1–2] the benefits of geographical knowledge to a ruler." Similarly, ibid., 65: "Strabo may have told Herod about recent architectural developments in Rome and have taught him the value of geography to a ruler [*Geog.* 1.1.16]." Roller (1998: 64–5) argues that although Strabo is not explicitly placed at Herod's court, it is probable that the historian and geographer spent some time with Herod in the 20s BCE.

67. Cf., e.g., Dilke 1985: 41–54; 1987: 207–9.

68. Brodersen 1995: 268–87. For Brodersen's reconstruction of this list based on Pliny, see ibid., 286 (fig. 43).

69. Brodersen 1995: 269–70. Cf. Dilke 1987: 208: "The dimensions of the map are not known, but it must have been rectangular, not circular. It is thought that its height may have been between two and three meters, and its width greater. Like the later Ptolemy and Peutinger maps, it very likely had north at the top. Whether the map was carved in or painted on marble is disputed." Ibid., 209: "It is feasible to reconstruct the possible appearance of Agrippa's world map, and this is being attempted [by John H. Bounds, Sam Houston State University, Texas]. But there must always be serious doubts about the accuracy of such reconstructions, since the data are extremely fragmentary." Cf. Trousset 1993: 137–57, who provides a reconstruction based on Pliny, *HN* 3.3: the Agrippa "map" is viewed as a kind of triptych, with each of the three continents of the world – Europe, Asia, and Africa – painted or carved on one of three walls of the portico, oriented respectively towards the North, the East, and the South, and the vertical hinges between the panels symbolizing the Tanais and Nile rivers. Thus, one enters the portico, standing as it were on the Mediterranean and pointing eastward toward Asia on the far wall (ibid., 156 [fig. 3]).

70. Cf. Dilke 1985: 52: "It is a pity that Pliny, who seems to be chiefly interested in measurements, gives us so little other information about Agrippa's map." Clarke (1999: 236) suggests that the sphere of Billarus, a possible symbol of Mithridatic imperialism over the earth that Lucullus took as booty from Sinope (Strabo, *Geog.* 12.3.11), may have been "a Pontic forerunner to Agrippa's map in Rome."

71. Brodersen 1995: 275–84.

72. Cf. Dilke 1985: 42–3: "Certain phrases in Pliny lead one to suppose that they came from a commentary, not a map. Thus Agrippa is said to have written... that the whole coast of the Caspian from the R. Casus consists of very high cliffs, which prevent landing for 425 miles." For citations of the passages where Pliny explicitly quotes Agrippa, see ibid., 44–52. On written descriptions of land routes with distances between landmarks, see Fugmann 1998: 2–32.
73. Brodersen (1995: 277–8) appeals to Pliny, *HN* 6.208, 211 (cf. 36.101).
74. Brodersen 1995: 279–80.
75. Ibid., 280–4. Brodersen ignores important clues that Strabo continued to add to the *Geography* for a quarter century after 7 BCE. Cf. Clarke 1997: 102–3 and esp. 104–5: "At the other end of Strabo's life-span, the reign of Tiberius is referred to a surprising number of times if the work was only emended after 7/6 B.C. It is of some interest that Strabo appears in the *Suda* as a Tiberian author. Most striking of all is Strabo's description of Rome's evolution as a world power whose empire needs one man at the helm. Tiberius appears at the end as the successor of Augustus, making his predecessor his model, and assisted by his children, Germanicus and Drusus [*Geog.* 6.4.2; cf. 17.3.25]. The passage clearly must have been written between Tiberius' accession in A.D. 14 and the death of Germanicus in 19, as the use of the present tense (παρέχει) confirms." See also Pothecary 1997: 245; Engels 1999: 359–77.
76. Cf. Dilke 1985; Dilke and Dilke 1976: 39–72; Harley and Woodward 1987: 105–6, 177–279; Nicolet 1991; R. French 1994: 114–15.
77. Cf. Brodersen 1995; Podossinov and Chekin 1991: 112–23; Talbert 1987: 210–12; 1990: 215–23; Purcell 1990: 7–29; Bekker-Nielsen 1988: 148–61; Sundwall 1996: 619–43.
78. Isaac 1992: 401–2, citing Millar 1982: 15–20.
79. Talbert 1990: 219; cf. Mattern 1999. For a very different assessment of the Roman army's ability to plan for long-term conquest, see now Roth 1998, who argues that Rome was quite efficient in moving huge amounts of material over vast distances in order to supply its massive reserves of manpower. That would have required an image of the world that was fairly reliable.
80. The few examples which Dilke (1985: 53–4) introduces into the discussion of the Agrippa map seem less significant.
81. Cf. Clarke 1999: 9: "One wonders, if this [i.e., Brodersen's] view were correct, what we should make of explicit references to drawn maps in ancient sources. Herodotus, as so often, provides an example in the bronze plaque (χάλκεον πίνακα) displayed in 499 BC to the Spartans, and on which 'a depiction of the entire world (γῆς ἁπάσης περίοδος) had been engraved, with the whole sea and all the rivers' (5.49). Another famous fifth-century example is the map of the world referred to by Strepsiades in Aristophanes' *Clouds*, and on which Athens, the area of Attica, Euboea, and Sparta could be picked out. Again the word used is ('geographical depiction'), nicely illustrating the fact that these graphic depictions were parallel to verbal descriptions of the earth from Hecataeus onwards."
82. If, as Cichorius suggests, Kypros' gift was sent in the summer of 39 CE, then we should note that Gaius' order to introduce his statue into the Jerusalem Temple was issued sometime during the same period, perhaps as late as his departure from Italy in the autumn of 39 (cf. Kokkinos 1998: 285 n. 74). If Agrippa and his wife had caught wind of Gaius' outrageous plan around this time, then they may have tried to mollify the emperor's demand for exceptional homage by sending tribute to his universal sovereignty in the form of the Kypros map.
83. Nicolet (1991: 113–14) suggests that Augustus ordered Agrippa to produce the world map in order to serve as an illustration of his own *Res Gestae*.
84. Note also that imperial artwork such as the frieze of Minerva on Domitian's Forum Transitorium deploys symbols of textile production as metaphors and exempla of imperial values and morality. Cf. D'Ambra 1993.

85. Cf. Wood 1999: 20.
86. Cf. Polybius 5.105.4: "This moment and this conference for the first time wove together the affairs of Greece, Italy, and Libya." Cited in Clarke 1999: 81 n. 7.
87. Sutherland 1984: 49, 50, 59, 84, 85, 86. See also the Boscoreale Cup, which shows Venus bringing Victoria to crown the globe in Augustus' hand, symbolizing that she grants and recognizes Augustus' rule over the world. Cf. Kuttner 1995: 13–34. On the globus as a symbol of world domination in Roman tradition, see further Weinstock 1971: 39, 41–5, 50–3.
88. Sutherland 1984: 108, 109.
89. K. Miller 1895–98: III.130 (fig. 66.5), 131, referring to Charles duc de Croy 1654: 26 (Tab. XV, Fig. 18 [*sic*]). Unfortunately, Miller's source contains only a drawing and description of the reverse, leaving us to wonder where he might have gained information about the inscription on the obverse.
90. Woodward 1987a: 337; cf. Miller 1895–98: III.131; P. S. Alexander 1982: 197–213 (201 with n. 6); Brincken 1970: 250. Actually, the earliest Roman coins bearing the globus date to about 75 BCE. Cf. Weinstock 1971: 42–3. Both Cicero (*Nat. D.* 2.115–16) and Ovid (*Met.* 1.32–7) describe the earth as a sphere.
91. Brodersen 1995: 77.
92. Sutherland 1984: 31–2.
93. Gnecchi 1912. For this point, I am grateful to Christopher Howgego, Curator of the Heberden Coin Room of the Ashmolean Museum (Oxford).
94. Cf. Weinstock 1971: 38–9, pl. 3.6; Cancik 1997: 131.
95. See further in Chap. 7.
96. It is perhaps no coincidence that the "head/body" (*caput/corpus*) metaphor for Rome and her empire appears precisely in the time of Augustus. Cf. Nicolet 1991: 204 n. 9.
97. Cf. Bendlin 1997: 38, citing Clarke 1996: 138–51; see now Clarke 1999: 169, 187, 210–28 (esp. 216f.). See also Grant 1992: 107–8: ". . . Irenaeus [*Haer.* 3.11.8; 1.10.2] referred to the four cardinal points of the earth, with their four principal winds, as *klimata* and described the existence of Christian churches in Germany (to the North), among the Iberias (the Spanish provinces) and the Celts (West), in the Orient (East), in Egypt and Libya (South), and 'in the middle of the world'. Older Greeks had claimed Delphi for the center of the world, but the rhetorician Aelius Aristides was well aware that 'everything meets here' at Rome. Irenaeus, who preached among the Celts, belonged to the West and presumably viewed Rome as the middle. Christians and others came there from everywhere, as to the center of a circle." Clarke (1999: 223) is careful to qualify the sense in which Strabo conceives of Rome as the "center": not a strictly geographical centrality, but rather "its position at the point where the various lines of movement of goods, people, and idea met." On the other hand, Strabo (*Geog.* 9.3.6) disparaged the notion of Delphi as the omphalos of the earth (cf. Clarke 1999: 225).
98. Kypros resided in Judea at least from about October 41 CE, when Agrippa I returned to Jerusalem and read the Torah at the public ceremony during the Feast of Tabernacles at the end of a Sabbatical year (*m. Sota* 7:8). Cf. Kokkinos 1998: 282. Even before that time, however, both Agrippa and Kypros would have had contact with Jerusalem and would have been well acquainted with Judaism. Although Josephus (*Ant.* 19.331) describes Agrippa as a practicing Jew who was right at home in Jerusalem, his modern biographers tend to minimize his Jewishness, while emphasizing his connection with Rome, his Greco-Roman education, and his Syro-Phoenician ancestry. Cf. Schwartz 1990: 170–1; Kokkinos 1998: 291. We must keep in mind, however, that Agrippa descended from the Hasmoneans through his paternal grandmother's side, and there is evidence that he remained observant (on Herod's Jewishness, see further S. Cohen 1999: 13–24). For instance, the promised wedding of his daughter Drusilla to Epiphanes, son of Antiochus IV of Commagene, did not materialize, because the prince refused to be circumcised (ibid., 295). Agrippa played an important role in the issuing of two

edits of Claudius protecting the rights of Jews in Alexandria and the Diaspora at large (cf. ibid., 290 n. 91), and he supported the Jewish cause at Rome in various other ways as well (e.g., he either averted or postponed Gaius' sacrilegious plan against the Jewish Temple [ibid., 288–9]). As we have seen above, Agrippa had facility in the Hebrew, and this is further documented by Josephus (*Ant.* 18.228–9). The whole Herodian Dynasty would have had a strong affinity for the Jerusalem Temple, not least because Herod the Great, who viewed himself as the king of the Jews, took such pains to restore the Temple to a glory even greater than that of the Solomonic. Indeed, Josephus (*Ant.* 20.189–90) reports that Agrippa's palace afforded him a view of the interior of the Temple of which he was particularly fond.

99. Cf. Hengel 1988; 1990. Hence, for example, Chyutin (1997: 113–27) must consider whether the disposition of the New Jerusalem's main streets are more like the *decumanus* and *cardo* of the Roman *castra* or the Hellenistic Hippodamic city.

100. Depending on when the tapestry was made, we may even need to consider Syrian/Iturean influences in Kypros' production, for the queen was based in Panias (Caesarea Philippi) in the early years of her husband's reign.

101. Cf., e.g., Hengel 1988: 139–40.

102. On the Hellenistic background of *Jubilees* 8–9, see P. S. Alexander 1982: 198–9; F. Schmidt 1990: 126–7, 132–4; Scott 1995a: 16–24.

103. Cf. Ovadiah and Ovadiah 1987: 63–5, pls. LXVI, CLXXX–CLXXXI. See further M. Smith 1982: 199–214.

104. On the chariot theme, see *Lexicon Iconographicum Mythologiae Classicae* 4.2 (1988) 366–85. The synagogue at Beth Alpha also portrays Helios as riding a quadriga at the center of a zodiac circle, although there he carries no globus. On the whole tradition, see further H. Gundel 1992, esp. Tafel 6. On the globus theme, see Gundel 1992: 43, 60–3. See further Brincken 1976: 79ff.

105. Cf. Sanders 1992: 245–7.

106. On priestly and high-priestly vestments, see further Sanders 1992: 92–102.

107. Thus, Josephus (*JW* 5.213) describes the veil of Herod's temple and proposes that the colors are symbols of the cosmos: the scarlet, fine linen, blue, and purple symbolize fire, earth, air, and sea, respectively.

108. In the *Hekhalot Rabbati* (Schäfer, *Synopse*, §201), Rabbi Nehuniah describes to the academy what the "descender to the chariot" can see on the ladder extending from his house to the right foot of the throne of glory: "I will recite the gradations, wonders, and the weaving of the web that is the completion of the world and on which its plaiting stands, the axle of heaven and earth, to which all the wings of the earth and inhabited world and the wings of the firmaments on high are tied, sewn, fastened, hanged, and stand." P. S. Alexander (1997a: 156 = 1999: 115) discusses a rabbinic text (*Tosefta Yom ha-Kippurim* 2:14 [ed. Lieberman, 237–8) that refers to the cosmogonic "stone of weaving" (אבן שתיה) located at the navel of the world (Jerusalem).

109. In Greek culture, such a robe is known as early as the sixth century BCE. See above on the narrative of Pherecydes of Syros (fl. 544 BCE), which relates how Zas (Zeus) wove a robe for his bride Chthonie, embroidered Earth and Ogenos (Ocean) upon it, and by giving it to Chthonie transformed her into Ge (Earth).

110. On the source criticism of Genesis 10, cf. VanderKam 1994b: 50–3; see further in Chap. 2.

111. It is perhaps significant in this regard that the prophet Ezekiel, a hereditary priest who was deeply concerned with details of the cult, seems to have used maps during his public presentations (cf. Ezek. 4:1; 43:11); indeed, his complex architectural and geographic descriptions of a future restoration (chaps. 40–8) seem to require the use of at least a mental map. Cf. Brodsky 1998: 17–29.

112. The artifact was found in Locus 45 (i.e., the southeast side of the Qumran settlement), which Roland de Vaux excavated in 1953 and 1954. Cf. de Vaux 1996: 52–3 (#1229 *Steinscheibe*). I am grateful to F. Rohrhirsch for kindly confirming the inventory

number of the artifact in question. He also offered the view that the "sundial" was actually found south of Locus 45 during the 1954 season.

113. In discussing the cosmological significance of Temple objects, Josephus (*Ant.* 3.182) relates the 70 pieces of which the seven-branched golden lampstand is made (Exod. 25:31–40) to the ten-degree provinces (δεκαμοιρίας) of the seven planets. Later Gnostic speculation includes schemes involving 72 heavens (cf. *1 Apoc. Jas.* 26: 13–18 [*NTApocr.* 1.320]; J. E. Wright 2000: 164).

114. Gleßmer and Albani 1999: 407–42; 1997: 88–115; F. Schmidt 1997: 115–18 (Hebrew); J. E. Wright 2000: 129 (possibly a crude astrolabe).

115. Cf. Gleßmer and Albani 1999: 413: "But if there were such a *gnomon* in the center, what was its shape and height? Depending on different assumptions we will try to explain the structure and special elements of the instrument. Our explanations are necessarily tentative because of the absence of any parallel object. The best we can do is to offer some proposals we have made in the course of examining this object. Our methodology is thus open to criticism, as is the validity of our interpretation." As Gleßmer and Albani indicate (ibid., 417, 418), if this relatively small object was an astronomical instrument, it would have been practically useless. For further critique of the artifact as an astronomical instrument, see Levy 1998: 18–23, who suggests that the artifact was a circular board game called a *mehen* (22). On circular board games in antiquity, see further Swartz 1998: 162.

116. Gleßmer and Albani 1999: 414.

117. Even if, as Gleßmer and Albani suggest, the artifact originally contained a gnomon in the center, its purpose may have been more geographical than astronomical. For there is evidence from a later period that a vertical shaft or column was used as a gnomon in order to demonstrate that Jerusalem is the center of the world. Adamnan (624–704 CE), whose *De locis sanctis* (Migne, *PL* 88.779–814) is based on the account of a pilgrimage by the Gallic bishop Arculf, describes the method (787): "A summary account must be given of a very high column which stands in the center of the city to the north of the holy places facing the passers-by. It is remarkable how this column (which is situated in the place where the dead youth came to life when the cross of the Lord was placed on him) fails to cast a shadow at midday during the summer solstice, when the sun reaches the center of the heavens. When the solstice is passed, however (that is the 8th day before the kalends of July), after an interval of three days, as the day gradually grows shorter it casts a brief shadow at first, then as the days pass a longer one. And so this column, which the sunlight surrounds on all sides blazing directly down on it during the midday hours (when at the summer solstice the sun stands in the center of the heavens), *proves Jerusalem to be situated at the center of the world (Hierusolimam orbis in medio terrae sitam esse protestatur)*. Hence the psalmist, because of the holy places of the passion and resurrection, which are contained within Helia itself, prophesying sings: 'God our King before all ages has worked our salvation in the center of the earth' [Ps. 73[74]:11–12], that is, Jerusalem, which is said to be the center of the earth and its navel (*quae mediterranea et umbilicus terrae dicitur*) [Ezek. 38:12]." Translation adapted from Meehan 1958: 57; cf. Iain Macleod Higgins 1998: 37; see also Woodward 1987: 340. If the Qumran artifact was used for such a demonstration, this might account for its rather small size, and we might expect in that case that the gnomon was disproportionately long. Natural phenomena were sometimes used to demonstrate tenets of Jewish belief (e.g., the so-called "Sabbatical river" in Josephus, *JW* 7.96–9; *b. Sanh.* 65b; *Gen. Rab.* 11:5; 73:6). As we shall see in Chap. 7, the Madaba mosaic map, dating to the latter half of the sixth century CE, contains a picture of a major column in Jerusalem. On the possible use of the Qumran artifact for determining the cardinal points of the year, including summer solstice, see Gleßmer and Albani 1999: 415–18. Taking the latitude of Jerusalem as 31°47′, Gleßmer and Albani (ibid., 416–17) calculate that the sun ascends to only 81° on the summer solstice, and that the gnomon therefore casts a shadow (unless, of course, it

was tilted some nine degrees to the south). Note that Syene (modern Aswan) in Upper Egypt was thought to be situated under the Tropic of Cancer, for at midday on the summer solstice gnomons in this region cast no shadow, the sun being exactly at the zenith (Strabo, *Geog.* 17.1.48; cf. Pliny, *HN* 2.75; Arrian, *Indica* 25.7). No omphalos concept is, however, reportedly connected with this observation; rather, Eratosthenes of Cyrene (ca. 285–194 BCE) used the phenomenon at Syene to calculate the earth's circumference, assuming in his calculations the existence of a center of the sphere. Cf. Harley and Woodward 1987: 153–7; Depuydt 1998: 171–80. On the possible function of the gold-plated tower for sun worship in the idealized Temple of the Temple Scroll (11QT 30.3–31.9), see Sanders 1992: 246. On geographical speculation of the Essenes and its biblical basis in Ezekiel, see Wacholder 1993: 131–8.

118. Note that on the bottom of the artifact near the center, the Hebrew letter ע is inscribed. Cf. Gleßmer and Albani 1999: 412, 415 n. 24. Does this stand for the number 70, corresponding to the approximately 72 lines on the disk? Cf. *I Enoch* 77:9: "I saw big islands in the sea and land – seventy-two in the Erythraean Sea." However, given the correspondence in ancient texts between heaven and earth, not least with regard to the numbers 70 and 72, it is impossible to ascertain whether the number of lines on our artifact pertains to heaven and/or to earth. On the numbers 70 and 72 in OT/Jewish and Greco-Roman tradition, see further the excursus in Chap. 3.

119. On the ancient conception of the encircling Ocean as a boundary ditch or trough, see Horowitz 1998: 62–3.

120. Cf. Scott 1995a: 8–10; Kelly 1996: 177–9.

121. On the conception in the Temple Scroll (11QT) of concentric circles of holiness around Jerusalem, from the borders of the Land of Israel to the Holy of Holies, see Lichtenberger 1994: 94–6. See further Qimron and Strugnell 1994: 142–6 (esp. 145, with n. 72). Compare also the possible continuum from civilization to utter barbarism in Strabo's Romanocentric conception of the world (cf. Clarke 1999: 213–15).

122. Cf. the ten degrees of holiness in *m. Kelim* 1:6–9: all other lands, the land of Israel, the walled cities of Israel, the walled city of Jerusalem, the Temple mount, the rampart, the court of women, the court of the Israelites, the court of the priests, the space between the hall and the altar, the sanctuary, the holy of holies.

123. Cited above.

124. Cited in P. S. Alexander 1997a/99: 155/114: "As the navel is the middle of the person, so is Eretz Israel the navel of the world, as it is written, 'That dwell in the navel of the earth' (Ezekiel 38:12). Eretz Israel is located in the center of the world, Jerusalem in the center of Eretz Israel, the Temple in the center of Jerusalem, the *heikhal* in the center of the Temple, the ark in the center of the *heikhal* and in front of the *heikhal* is the *'even shetiyyah* from which the world was founded."

125. Cf. D. King and Lorch 1992: 194, 196 [fig. 9.9]; see now also D. King 1999: 55. Qiblah is the direction of the sacred shrine Ka'ba in Mecca, towards which Muslims turn five times each day when performing the prescribed ritual prayer. Soon after Muhammad's emigration to Medina in 622, he designated Jerusalem as the qiblah, probably under influence of Jewish tradition. Indeed, praying toward Jerusalem is firmly established both in the OT and in subsequent Jewish tradition. Cf. Amit 1995: 140–5; Scott 1997d: 195–7; "Mizrah," *EncJud* 12 (1972) 180–2. See also Irenaeus, *Adv. Haer.* 1.26.2 ("...they [sc. the Ebionites] worship Jerusalem as the house of God"), which Schoeps (1949: 141) compares to the qiblah. See further Lazarus-Yafeh 1997: 197–205; Shtober 1999: 85–98; Neuwirth 1996: 93–116, 483–95.

126. Cf. D. King 1993: X.19, 22; Podossinov 1993: 42 n. 24, 43 (fig. 21). For a color photograph, see Harley and Woodward 1992: plate 13.

127. D. King 1999: 110–14, 168–70.

128. Cf. ibid., 51–5, 116.

129. The sequence of the names for the gates is very different in these two texts, and although both descriptions proceed in a clockwise direction, they begin at different cardinal

points. Ezek. 48:30–5: Reuben, Judah, Levi; *East*: Joseph, Benjamin, Dan; *South*: Simeon, Issachar, Zebulun; *West*: Gad, Asher, Naphtali. 4Q554 (4QNew Jerusalem[a]) 15.12–16.10: *East*: Simeon, [Levi], Judah; *South*: Joseph, [Benjamin], Reuben; *West*: [Issachar, Zebulon, Gad]; *North*: Dan, Naphtali, Asher. See Chyutin 1997: 23–6, 76–81. Cf. 11QT 39.12–13; 40.11–14.

130. Cf. Chyutin 1997: 83, 85–6, 104–6, 113–30; 1994: 71–97. It is also interesting to note that the orientation of most tombs at Qumran is south–north (i.e., the head is to the south and the feet to the north), although there are a few burials with a west–east orientation, and one tomb, on the periphery of the cemetery, that is east–west. On this phenomenon and possible explanations for it, see J. Collins 1997a: 123–4. See further Fass 1988: 465–73.

131. C. Meyers 1992: 1062.

132. According to *Num. Rab.* 13:14, the molten sea weighed 70 shekels, corresponding to the 70 nations of the world. Cf. Josephus, *Ant.* 8.79. In the Dead Sea scrolls themselves, there may be an indirect reference to the molten sea in the Temple Scroll, which describes the measurements of "the house of the laver" (11QT 31.10–33.7). Cf. Yadin 1983: 1.217–24; Chyutin 1997: 42–3.

133. On the Philonic authorship of Agrippa's letter to Gaius, see D. Schwartz 1990: 179, 200–2; Zeitlin 1965: 22–31; Kokkinos 1998: 383 n. 71.

134. Cf. Scott 1994: 495–9; Borgen 1997: 19–21; Hengel 1995b: 270 n. 6. On Jerusalem as the omphalos of the world, see further in Chap. 2.

135. Cf. Himmelfarb 1991: 63.

2 *Jubilees* 8–9

1. See further Scott 1995a: 5–56.

2. For example, the location of Eden and the four rivers of Paradise (Gen. 2:10–14), Jerusalem as the center (Ezek. 5:5; 38:12), the borders of the Land of Israel (Num. 34:1–29; Joshua 13–19; Ezek. 47:15–20), and orientation on the East.

3. Bikerman 1952: 77–8.

4. As late as the sixteenth century, Montanus' copperplate map of the world, prepared for Plantin's polyglot Bible of 1569–72, attempts to reconcile contemporary knowledge of world geography to Genesis 10. Cf. Delano Smith and Ingram 1991: 123–4.

5. On the controversy over the source-critical analysis of Genesis 10, see VanderKam 1994b: 50–3; Kochanek 1998: 273–99.

6. Genesis 10 also signals the importance of Shem by tracing his descendants to the sixth generation (10:21–31; cf. 11:10–32) and those of Ham (10:6–20) and Japheth (10:2–5) to only the third or fourth generation. See Table 1. Of course, the reason that Shem is considered the most important descendant of Noah is that his descendants give rise to Abraham and the promise-bearers, the chosen people of God (Gen. 12:1–3).

7. On the original, onomastic environment of the names in Genesis 10–11, see Hess 1993: 73–95; Lipinski 1990: 40–53; 1992: 134–61; 1993: 193–215.

8. VanderKam (1994b: 50) evidently omits the Philistines (Gen. 10:14) from the count in order to arrive at the number 70.

9. See further in Chap. 3.

10. Cf. Wevers 1974: 132–40; 1993: 127–61; Rösel 1994: 205–12.

11. MT begins the name with *D*, whereas the Samaritan Pentateuch, the Septuagint, and 1 Chr. 1:7 begin it with *R*.

12. We may visualize this description of Canaan's territory approximately as an equilateral triangle whose apex is Sidon in the north and whose base is determined by Gaza in the west and by Lasha in the east. Cf. P. S. Alexander 1974: 313 (fig. 3); Weinfeld 1993: 52–75.

13. On *Jubilees* as an example of the "Rewritten Bible," see VanderKam 1993: 97–8, 117ff.; 1989b: 211–36; Endres 1987: 15–17 and esp. 196–225, which provides a helpful summary of *Jubilees'* homiletical and exegetical techniques.

14. Proposed dates for the book range from the 5th/4th century BCE to the first century CE. Cf. VanderKam 1977: 207–85. See also VanderKam 1997: 3–24; Stone 1996a: 278–9; Berger 1998: 33, agreeing with H. Stegemann that the date could be as early as the fifth century BCE, because *Jubilees* concludes with the recounting of the conquest of Canaan and therefore reads like a theological preparation for a new land.

15. Cf. VanderKam 1992: 635–48; VanderKam and Milik 1994: 1–185. For a convenient list of the available manuscripts of *Jubilees* at Qumran, see Flint 1998–99: II.45–7.

16. Not only does the Damascus Document cite *Jubilees* as authoritative (CD 16.3–4), but the theology and laws in *Jubilees* are closely parallel to and are often identical with those in writings unique to Qumran. For similarities and differences between *Jubilees* and Qumran, see VanderKam 1977: 258–82.

17. Cf. VanderKam 1989a: I.IX–XVI; II.VI–XIX.

18. Cf. VanderKam 1992: 644: "In general, it is fair to say that the Hebrew fragments confirm once again that the ancient translators of Jubilees performed their task with great care and literalness. Naturally there are exceptions to this statement . . ."

19. Cf. Schiffman 1999: 126–8; Nickelsburg 1999: 102ff.

20. The only *Jubilees* manuscript found at Qumran spanning the portion of the book that could have included chapters 8–9 is 11QJubilees (11Q12), a manuscript dated to about 50 CE which preserves parts of *Jub.* 4:6 to 12:29 (i.e., 4:6–11, 13–14, 16–17 [or 11–12], 17–18 [?], 29–30, 31; 5:1–2; 12:15–17, 28–9). Cf. García Martínez, et al. 1998: 207–20.

21. For later versional evidence of *Jub.* 8:11–9:15, VanderKam (1989a: I.265–6; II.334–5) lists only the Syriac *Chronicle to the Year 1234* 43.17–44.15, which reflects *Jub.* 8:11–30. On this chronicle, see further in Chap. 6.

22. Cf. Maier 1991: 183: "Die bisher bekannten hebräischen Qumranfragmente decken leider keine Passagen in den Kapiteln 8–9 ab, daher ist Vorsicht am Platz." See also P. S. Alexander 1997a: 147, referring to *Jub.* 8:19: "There are problems with this text, and unfortunately neither the Greek nor the Hebrew survives to help us solve them. The phrase 'the center of the navel of the earth' seems a curious tautology and we might suspect that 'navel' has been added secondarily, perhaps in the Greek or the Ethiopic." A slightly revised and expanded version of this article is reprinted under the same title in Levine 1999: 104–19. In the following, a slash separates the respective page numbers of the two articles.

23. For the newly published fragments, see Morgenstern, et al. 1995: 50–3. As Fröhlich (1998: 95) points out, the Genesis Apocryphon adds several important details to the flood narrative of Genesis: ". . . after the Flood, Noah atones for the world (10:13) and an oracle is given concerning his future rule on earth (12:16). The geographical descriptions which follow in the third part of the narrative (Noah walks around the land; the division of the land by Noah, then by his sons, 11:10–14, 16:9?–17:19) are the fulfillment of this oracle." Interestingly enough, the Genesis Apocryphon (6.7) indicates that Noah's wife is called אמזרע ("mother of seed") and that she bore Noah three sons. As Stone (1999: 148) has observed, this "indicates something of the role of new creator and father of humankind which Noah and his wife played. Like Deucalion and Pyrrha they re-seeded the earth." Cf. Qimron 1999: 107: "In this passage, we find the earliest Aramaic attestation of the name of Noah's wife אמזרע 'the mother of all human descendants'. This is a symbolic name for the mother of all surviving human beings." Elsewhere in the Qumran scrolls, the Genesis 10 tradition is apparently used one other time, albeit in a very different way from the geographical emphasis we see in the Genesis Apocryphon and the *Book of Jubilees*. The Qumran Nahum pesher (1QpNah 3.12–4.1) interprets Nah. 3:9 ("Put [Gen. 10:6] and the Lubim [= the Lehabim, Gen.

10:13; 1 Chr. 1:11] are her helpers") to mean: "these are the wicked on[es], the house of Peleg, who have joined Manasseh." The expression "the house of Peleg" (lit., "the house of divisions") stems from Gen. 10:25 ("To Eber were born two sons: the name of the one was Peleg, for in his days the earth was divided") and *Jub.* 8:8 ("In the sixth year [1567] she gave birth to a son for him, and he named him Peleg because at the time when he was born Noah's children began to divide the earth for themselves"), and it may refer to the Pharisees here (cf. CD 20.22–4). In that case, the Qumran text reinterprets the Genesis 10 tradition in light of contemporary events (cf. Tantlevskij 1996: 335).

24. Cf. Fitzmyer 1971: 16–19.
25. García Martínez (1994: 40) regards the Genesis Apocryphon as an independent and more faithful witness to the lost "Book of Noah." On the supposed "Book of Noah," see further below.
26. Cf. VanderKam 1994b: 55–69.
27. Cf. VanderKam 1989a: II.52–8. Section headings have been added to VanderKam's translation in order to show the structure of the passage.
28. Similarly, *Jubilees* goes beyond the biblical flood narrative at various points. Cf. Ruiten 1998: 66–85.
29. Note also the inscription in the mosaic pavement of the En-Gedi synagogue (4th–5th cent. CE), which is a citation of 1 Chr. 1:1–4: "Adam, Seth, Enosh, Kenan, Mahalalel, Jared, Enoch, Methuselah, Lameh, Noah, Shem, Ham and Japheth." Cf. Ovadiah and Ovadiah 1987: 55, pl. CLXXVII. On the problem of the relative ages of Noah's three sons, see further Kugel 1998: 220–1.
30. Cf. Brodersen 1994a: 17–19, 120–2. The ancients were uncertain whether to divide the inhabited world into two or three continents. Cf., e.g., Hardie 1986: 311–13; Cancik 1998: 95–6, 110, referring to "the ancient battle of the continents (Asia/Europe; Orient/Occident)." Polybius named the three continents and, like *Jubilees*, defined them in terms of natural features – the Tanais, the Nile, and the straits at the Pillars of Hercules. Cf. Clarke 1999: 113 with n. 79; on Strabo's conception of the continents, see ibid., 209–10. On the Mesopotamian conception of the continent as a single, relatively small landmass, see Horowitz 1998: 321–4.
31. For example, orientation on the East (cf. P. S. Alexander 1982: 204; Brodersen 1994a: 15); the omphalos-idea (cf. *Jub.* 8:19; cf. Brodersen 1994a: 15; Dionys. Per. 13); differentially blessed portions (*Jub.* 8:18–21; Dionys. Per. 968–9). We may also mention other features that the two writings have in common (e.g., Gadir/Gades, Gihon/Nile, Tina/Tanais, Me'at/Maeotis, Red Sea, Mediterranean).
32. On the Hellenistic background of *Jubilees* 8–9, see P. S. Alexander 1982: 198–9; F. Schmidt 1990: 126–7, 132–4; Scott 1995a: 16–24. On the spatial structure of *Jubilees*, see now Frey 1997: 272–85. David Neiman (1980: 42) argues that the "map of the world as conceived by the authors of Genesis 2 and 10 would have resembled the map of the world as conceived by Homer, with significant differences occasioned by the different centers of their respective worlds." See the comparison of the reconstructed maps (ibid., 41).
33. Contrast the Genesis account, which mentions nothing about Noah's writing a book that parcels out the earth to his sons. Indeed, Noah dies before the Table of Nations is recorded (Gen. 9:29).
34. Cf. Morgenstern, et al. 1995: 40.
35. Cf. VanderKam 1994b: 58: "*Jub.* 8.11 introduces the actual division in language reminiscent of Moses' and Joshua's distribution of the promised land among the tribes: the assigned portions are called lots (!; see Num. 26 and 34; Josh. 14.2; 15.1; 17.4; 18.6, 8–9 [where a book is mentioned as in *Jub.* 8.11], 10; 19.51). Noah is the explicit subject of 'divided'. Other than the names, the entire chapter is without parallel in Genesis." See also F. Schmidt 1990: 126; Cowley 1988: 31–3. In Greek literature, too, lots are cast for land. See, for example, the myth of the return of the

descendants of Heracles to the Peloponnese (cf. Prinz 1979: 309–13). According to Apollodorus (*Bibl.* 1.2.1.4), the universe was divided by lots among the three sons of Kronos, with Zeus obtaining heaven, Poseidon the sea, and Pluto Hades. On the division of the portions among the gods in Greek tradition, see further Schibli 1990: 14, 22 n. 18, 39, 40, 47, 52–3, 57 n. 16, 61 n. 25, 86, 99 n. 54, 100–4, 129; West 1983: 72, 123, 124–6, 138; Bremmer 1998: 42–3; Horowitz, 1998: 126, 145.

36. Cf., e.g., Dimant 1998: 140: "His [sc. Noah's] Moses-like nature is underscored by his allotting the land to his sons sometime before his death, an act which corresponds to Moses' role in allotting Canaan to the Israelite tribes (Numbers 32–6; Deuteronomy 29–34; *Jub.* 8:11)." On Noah's Moses-like role in *Jubilees*, see further ibid., 136–40.

37. Cf. Strasburger 1984: 225–7; Honigmann 1929; Neugebauer 1975: II.725–36, esp. 733, referring to Geminus' division of the earth into three zones: hot, temperate, and cold.

38. Cf. Kidd 1999: 113; Clarke 1999: 150–1, 208, 295. On the threefold division of the world in Hellenistic thinking, see Barton 1994b: 120–2; 1994a: 182–4 (on Claudius Ptolemy, *Tetrabiblos* 2.2); Erotian's reference to τὰ τρία κλίματα τῆς οἰκουμένης (ed. E. Nachmanson *Votum Hippocraticarum collectio cum fragmentis* [1918] 91); Polybius 12.25.7: τρία μέρη διῃρημένης, καὶ τῆς μὲν Ἀσίας, τῆς δὲ Λιβύης, τῆς δ' Εὐρώπης.

39. Cited in Barton 1994b: 119. See also Clarke 1999: 217, 298: "The climatologically privileged temperate zone is a movable feature, shifted by the writers of Stabo's time from Ionia to the centre of power in Italy, providing, in the same way as Strabo's manipulation of the periplus tradition, an interesting example of how yet another strand of the literary tradition could be appropriated and adapted to suit the altered geographical circumstances of a new phase in history."

40. Cited in Clarke 1999: 89; see also 218. As Clarke (ibid., 168–9, 186–7) indicates, Posidonius has a similar vision of Rome's centrality, which is expressed through its tenure of the privileged middle of the climatologically arranged earth. On "environmental determinism" (including climate), which has often been used to advocate the innate superiority of certain races, see ibid., 27–8, 49, 90–1, 218, 295–9.

41. Cf. Syncellus 47.17–20, which, as we shall argue in Chap. 6, is probably dependent ultimately on *Jubilees*: "And he gave his testament to Shem as his firstborn son and the one most favored of God. Shem also received after Noah the hegemony (τὴν ἡγεμονίαν) and inherited from him the special honors of the blessings, as it states in Genesis [9:26]." Cf. also *Asatir* 4.34, 37 (cited below).

42. If the disputed pronoun refers to Japheth (rather than to God), then Gen. 9:26–7 can be read as a blessing of world rule for Shem. As the *Jubilees* passages show, that blessing is then extended to Abraham's descendants, especially Jacob. See further Scott 1992: 134–5.

43. Cf. Frey 1997: 272–9. For further discussion on the location of Eden (whether to the East, in heaven, or somewhere else), see Kugel 1998: 139–42.

44. P. S. Alexander 1997a/1999: 149/105. In light of the east–west median presupposed in the *Book of Jubilees*, it is interesting to note that in the later *Expositio Totius Mundi et Gentium*, the Ὁδοιπορίαι ἀπὸ Ἐδὲμ τοῦ παραδείσου ἄχρι τῶν Ῥωμαίων sketches the overland route from the Garden of Eden in the Far East to Gades in Spain (or Gallia), although not through Jerusalem. Cf. Rougé 1966: 346–57; Fugmann 1998: 24.

45. See further in Chap. 1; cf. also *1 Enoch* 26:1; *Sib. Or.* 5.250; *b. Yoma* 54b; *Pesiq. R.* 10:2; Philo, *Legat.* 294; *Let. Arist.* 83. For the seemingly redundant expression, "in the middle of the navel of the earth" (*Jub.* 8:19), cf. Midrash Tanḥuma, *Qedoshim* 10 (ed. S. Buber 4.78), which explains the citation of Ezek. 38:12 as follows: "The Land of Israel is located in the center of the world, and Jerusalem in the center of the Land of Israel." For *Jubilees*, too, the place where the Temple would eventually be built was "in the middle of the land" (*Jub.* 49:19). Cf. also Agathemerus 1.2 (K. Müller 1965:

II.471): "The ancients drew the inhabited world as round (στρογγύλην), and Greece lay in the middle (μέσην), and Delphi (lay) in the middle of it, for it is the omphalos of the earth (καὶ ταύτης Δελφούς. τὸν ὀμφαλὸν γὰρ ἔχειν τῆς γῆς)..." P. S. Alexander (1997a/1999: 147/104–5) argues that the "curious tautology" was probably in the original text of *Jubilees* and served to rank Sinai and Zion: "Both are 'holy', both are 'centers', but whereas Sinai is only the center of the desert, Zion is the center of the world and its *omphalos*. The resonant epithet *omphalos* establishes Zion's higher status." On the curious notion that Bethlehem was the place "in the middle of the earth" (*in medio mundi*) where Adam was created and Jesus was born, see the Latin addition to the *Life of Adam* in Anderson and Stone 1994: 76 (no. 38 [56]).

46. P. S. Alexander 1997a/1999: 147/104. See further Talmon 1993: 50–75, who argues that in the original context of Ezek. 38:12, the collocation מבור הארץ denotes vulnerability (as unprotected as the human navel), rather than the mythic notion of the omphalos. The concept of the omphalos was widespread in the ancient world. Cf. Tilly 1997: 131–53; Wyatt 1995: 123–32; Brodersen 1995: 49–50, 110, 259.

47. Likewise, *1 Enoch* 26:1, where Enoch comes to the "middle of the earth" (i.e., Jerusalem), is based on Ezek. 38:12. Cf. Himmelfarb 1991: 70.

48. P. S. Alexander 1997a/1999: 149–51/105–7.

49. Cf. F. Schmidt 1990: 127; Gutschmid 1894: 587–8.

50. On Noah as the mediator of divine revelation about the coming judgment, see Elgvin 1996: 148–9. Cf. 4Q418 fr. 201:1; *1 Enoch* 10:1–2; 60:1–6, 25. See further in Chap. 3.

51. Cf. VanderKam 1994b: 46–69; R. H. Charles 1972: 68 n. This point is also crucial to the whole chronological framework of *Jubilees*. Cf. VanderKam 1997: 17. See esp. ibid., 22: "It seems likely that the author's [*Jubilees'*] radical stance on calendrical issues must be related to debates on this subject occasioned by the change of calendar which, according to Dan. 7:25, was imposed on the Jerusalem cult by Antiochus IV. But the larger goals of the system – national freedom and possession of the land – may also be viewed against the backdrop suggested by 1 Macc. 1:11. In a time when Judeans were subject to foreign powers who were at least interested in blending them into the surrounding culture, the writer of *Jubilees* articulated a powerful argument for freedom from foreign domination and Judean possession of their own land. The land was theirs by ancient right, the land of a people who would enjoy political blessings if they lived sincerely according to the covenant. God had accomplished their deliverance and liberty in the past and could do so again for a people true to the extraordinarily ancient covenant."

52. Cf. Talmon 1978: 35–6, who compares Deut. 32:8–9 to Exod. 15:13, 17.

53. The book of *Jubilees* is not only a "midrash" on Genesis and Exodus, but it is also in the form of an apocalypse, insofar as it is a heavenly revelation, mediated to Moses by an angel and set within a narrative framework. The chronological framework extends from creation to the new creation (*Jub.* 1.29), implying the end of the present world typical of apocalyptic literature. In the end-time, Israel will be restored to the Land, and God will again dwell with his people upon Mt. Zion (*Jub.* 1:23–9). Furthermore, *Jubilees* displays the typical apocalyptic belief in a final judgment of cosmic scope. According to *Jubilees*, "the judgment of all" is inscribed in heavenly tablets (5:13; cf. "day of judgment" in 4:19, 23–4; see Garcia Martínez 1997: 247–50; VanderKam 1999: 161–3). The apocalyptic orientation of *Jubilees* 8–9 is continued in 10:22: "Come, let us go down and confuse their tongues so that they do not understand one another and are dispersed into cities and nations and one plan no longer remains with them until the day of judgment." See further J. Collins 1998: 79–84; 1998–99: II.408–9; 1997a: 24–6; Lange 1997: 25–38; Frey 1997: 268–70; Nickelsburg 1999: 103–4.

54. Cf. VanderKam 1994b: 46–69, who considers the underlying purpose of *Jubilees* 8–10 to be an explanation of the presence of non-Shemite peoples in Shemite territory. P. S. Alexander (1997a/1999: 151/107) argues that the intent of *Jubilees* 8–9 is to make

Greek influence in the East illegitimate. See also Mendels 1992: 81–105 (esp. 94–5); Frey 1997: 266. In light of later rabbinic literature, *Jubilees* 8–10 may also defend the Jewish right to the land. See, for instance, the story found in *b. Sanh.* 91a and *Gen. Rab.* 61:7, which describes a dispute carried on before Alexander the Great between the Jews, on the one hand, and the Ishmaelites, Canaanites and Egyptians, on the other. Cf. Kazis 1962: 11–13; Himmelfarb 1994: 121; P. S. Alexander 1997a/1999: 151 with n. 7/107 with n. 10 (citing Procopius, *De bello vandalico* 10.13–22). With rare exceptions, almost all peoples claimed to be autochthonous, which was the noblest origin in the eyes of the Greeks (cf. Bikerman 1952: 76). *Jubilees* provides a story to explain that the Jews, too, could claim priority over their land, despite the fact that they had to conquer it from the Canaanites. On conceptions of the conquest of the Land during the Second-Temple period, see Weinfeld 1993: 209–21.

55. Cf. P. S. Alexander 1997a/1999: 151/107: "Javan (Greece) is a son of Japhet, and so his patrimony, according to the Jubilees schema, belongs to Europe, which ends at the Bosphorus. The Greeks, therefore, have no right of residence in Asia, and in usurping land there they are breaking the solemn agreement entered into by the sons of Noah after the Flood." As in Hellenistic historiography as a whole, conquest is the vital factor that leads *Jubilees* 8–9 (or its source) to look at the world in new ways, or rather, in this case, to oppose the new world order that was set up in the wake of conquest by means of a biblically-based, reactionary synthesis of Herodotean proportions. Cf. Clarke 1999: 69–71.

56. In effect, Jerusalem and Shem's territory has a primeval claim to the status of "asylia." In the Hellenistic period, certain Greek temples and cities came to be declared "sacred and inviolable," meaning immune from war. A famous passage of Tacitus (*Ann.* 3.60–3; 4.14) describes the appeals of many cities for Roman confirmation of the title. Rigsby (1996: 527–31) argues that Jerusalem was granted asylia in the late second century BCE.

57. In 1QapGen. 5.29, the words נוח מלי כתב ("the book of the words of Noah") have now been deciphered. Cf. Steiner 1995: 66–71. But see Dimant 1998: 146 n. 91: "The improved text of 1QapGen. I–XII serves to discard recent arguments in favor of the existence of a *Book of Noah*, a thesis advanced by Steiner..." No citation of this "improved text" is provided.

58. García Martínez 1994: 1–44; also Collins 1997a: 24; but see now García Martínez 1998b: 88–9. Although Dimant (1998: 146) argues that "there is no evidence for the existence of a *Book of Noah*," she nevertheless believes that "a case can be made for the existence of a more comprehensive Hebrew narrative midrash, written perhaps in a style similar to the Aramaic *Genesis Apocryphon*, which would have included at least some of the materials dealing with Noah..." Dimant (ibid., 146 n. 90) notes that the outline of the supposed "Book of Noah" as drawn up by García Martínez would fit as well with such a midrash.

59. Cf. Dimant 1998: 145; Stone 2000: 613–15. I would like to thank Prof. Stone for providing me with a pre-publication copy of this article.

60. Cf. Dimant 1998: 145; Werman 1999: 171–81; Nickelsburg 1998: 157–8.

61. Cf. Bernstein 1999a: 199–231 (esp. 226ff.); Stone 1999: 140; Scott 1997b: 368–81.

62. Included after *T. Levi* 18:2 in MS e (Jonge 1978: 47 [# 57])

63. Alternatively, these references to a "book" of Noah may simply represent a fiction of *Jubilees*, since the text elsewhere refers to "all the books" that Noah had written (*Jub.* 10:14) and even names one of them (10:13; cf. 21:10). *Jubilees* also refers to various other early writings: Enoch records "in a book" the signs of heaven (4:17–19; cf. 21:10); Cainan discovers and transcribes astrological tables inscribed on stone by the Watchers (8:2–4); Abraham copies "his father's books" (12:27); and Jacob sees in a dream seven heavenly tablets with information about the future which he then writes down from memory (32:20–6). In all of these cases, however, the writer transcribes material that has been either revealed or passed down to him, whereas in *Jub.* 8:11–12,

Noah seems to play a more active role in the formulation of his book. We often read of "books" from illustrious figures of the archaic past (e.g., *1 Enoch* 81–2; 92:1; *2 Enoch* 23:6; 33:5, 8–10; 36:1; 47:1–2; 48:6–8; 54:1; 68:1–2). On the production and/or transmission of earthbound, pre-canonical books, see Kraft 1996: 205–9.

64. The *Sefer ha-Razim* presents itself as a book of mysteries revealed to Noah by an angelic mediator and later disclosed to Solomon. Cf. Gruenwald 1980: 227, who also refers to *Jub.* 10:12–14; Stone 1999: 140–1. For a translation of the passage, see Morgan 1983: 17–20. See further Dimant 1998: 134, with n. 54.

65. Cf. Himmelfarb 1994: 127–36. See further Stone, "Noah, Books of" *EncJud* 12 (1971) 1198; 1999: 140. In Stone's translation, the *Book of Asaph* commences: "This is the book of remedies which ancient sages copied from the book of Shem b. Noah, which was transmitted to Noah on Mount Lubar, one of the mountains of Ararat, after the Flood."

66. For comparisons between 1QapGen. 16–17 and *Jubilees* 8–9, see Scott 1995a: 30–3. Bernstein (1999a: 229) regards it as a distinct possibility that the material on the apportionment of the earth among Noah's sons may belong to a separate composition. Unfortunately, he does not refer to *Jub.* 8:11–12 as corroboration for this possibility. Indeed, when discussing the possibility of a "Book of Noah," scholars rarely discuss the evidence of *Jubilees* 8. Garcia Martinez (1994: 1–44) considers *Jubilees* 8–9 as merely one part of his reconstructed "Book of Noah."

67. On the later, radical Gnostic revision of the biblical account of the division of the world among the sons of Noah, see Luttikhuizen 1998: 115–16. See further Quack 1995: 102.

68. For a comparison of *Jubilees* 8–9 and *Ant.* 1.122–47, see Scott 1995a: 40–9. On Josephus' knowledge of *Jubilees*, see also Feldman 1998: 51 with n. 60. On Josephus' antiquarian interests, see Pilhofer 1990: 193–206. Note that the historical significance of Josephus' exposition of the Table of Nations has recently been highlighted in F. Millar 1993b: 5–10. For purposes of the present study, Josephus will not be considered here. On *Ant.* 120–47, see further Feldman 2000: 42–52.

69. This is characteristic of Josephus' treatment of Jewish apocalyptic expectations. Cf., e.g., Jonge 1974: 205–19. Cf. also Ps.-Philo, *Bib. Ant.* 4–5, on which see Jacobson 1996: 331–53.

70. Cf. J. Collins 1983: 354–5; 1972: 21–2; 1997b. Gmirkin (1998: 172–214) argues that the final composition of the War Rule dates to 163 BCE. See, however, Collins 1997a: 99, who suggests a time of origin in the first century BCE.

71. As we have seen above, Apollodorus (*Bibl.* 1.2.1.4) writes that the universe was divided by lots among the three sons of Kronos, with Zeus obtaining heaven, Poseidon the sea, and Pluto Hades.

72. On the identification of Iapetos and Japheth, see Westermann 1983: I.674; Neiman 1973: 123ff.; West 1966: 202–3.

73. According to Ps.-Eupolemos (*apud* Eusebius, *Pr. Ev.* 9.17.9, citing Alexander Polyhistor's "On the Jews"), the Babylonians hold that Kronos was the father of Canaan, the father of the Phoenicians, who was the father of Chus (= Ethiopia) and Mitzraim (= Egypt). Thus, Kronos occupies a genealogical position analogous to that of Ham, who was the father of Cush, Mitzraim, Put, and Canaan (cf. Gen. 10:6). On J. Freudenthal's widely followed emendation of Canaan to Cam, see, however, Doron 1985: 881 n. *u*; Stuckenbruck 1997: 33–6. In the *Antiquities* (1.1–153), Josephus interprets the primeval history in Genesis 1–11, including the Table of Nations, in light of the Hesiodic tradition of the Golden Age and the decline of civilization, in order to make biblical history intelligible to his Greek readers. Cf. Droge 1989: 35–47.

74. Cf. Scott 1995a: 37–40.

75. God had promised that the world would never again be destroyed by a flood (*Jub.* 6:4, 15–16), but this did not preclude the destruction of the world by fire (cf. 1QH 11.29–36; Hippolytus, *Ref.* 9.27 [on Essene eschatology!]), a common apocalyptic

theme which is often associated with the flood, as the two great destructions that punctuate the history of the world (e.g., *Sib. Or.* 2.196–213; 3.60–1, 84–7, 669–92 ["God will judge all men by war and sword and fire and torrential rain. There will also be brimstone from heaven" cf. Ezek. 38:22]; 4.171–8; cf. J. Collins 1983: 323, 388 n. *f2*; Bekkum 1998: 128–9). For other similarities between the Third Sibyl and *Jubilees* 8–9, see Scott 1995a: 36–40.

76. The latter incorporate the *Diamerismos* tradition, which is partly dependent on the tradition reflected in *Jubilees* 8–9. See further in Chap. 6.

77. For a recent survey of the eschatological war in 1QM, see J. Collins 1997a: 91–109. As Collins and many other scholars are careful to point out, the War Rule appears to be a composite document. Our purpose here is to understand 1QM as the final redactor may have intended it.

78. In a forthcoming publication, H. Eshel ("The Kittim in the War Scroll and Pesharim") argues that the identity of the "Kittim" changes over time in the Qumran community: from the Hellenistic kingdoms in general in early Qumran compositions, to the Seleucids in particular in later compositions, and finally to the Romans (ca. 63 BCE onwards). See the pre-publication version of the paper at the following URL: http://orion.mscc.huji.ac.il/orion/symposiums/4th/papers/Eshel99.html. On the identity of the Kittim, see further Brooke 1991: 135–59, who emphasizes the role of biblical stereotypes in the *pesharîm*, and discounts their historical value. The method of the *pesharîm*, however, involves correlation of the biblical passage with historical events. The recognition of these events, where possible, is an essential element in the understanding of the texts. See also Lichtenberger 1996: 224–8; Stemberger 1983: 16–25. On 4Q285, see J. Collins 1995a: 59. Gog does not figure prominently in the War Rule (cf. merely 1QM 11.16) and Magog not at all. 4QpIsa^a 7 iii:11 refers to the battle of the *Kittim*, and there are several other mentions of the *Kittim* in the context of battle; 4QpIsa^a 7–10 iii:25 mentions Magog. *Tg. Onq.* Num. 24:24 understands the Kittim as Romans. Similarly, *Tg. Neof.* Gen. 10:4 and *Gen. Rab.* 37:1 interpret Kittim as Italy.

79. Alternatively, Dan. 12:1 may be referring to the time of trouble "such as below has not occurred since they [sc. the people of Israel] became a nation (גוי) until that time."

80. Cf. Qimron 1986: 99, who lists בָּלָה "confusing" under "Words Mainly Attested in the DSS and in the Tannaitic and Amoraitic [MH²] Literature." Note, however, that the verb בלל "confuse" is used in Gen. 11:7, 9 of the confusion of language at the Tower of Babel, and that it has now been found in another Qumran scroll that refers to the confusion of languages at Babel (cf. 4Q464 frg. 3 i:5). See further in Chap. 3.

81. This expression has no apparent Qumran parallel, but Gen. 10:5, 32 uses the Niph. of פרד of peoples separating or dividing from parent stock: "From these [sc. the sons of Javan] the coastland peoples separated . . . (32) These are the families of Noah's sons, according to their genealogies, in their nations; and from these the nations separated on the earth after the flood."

82. The term משפחה "clan" in the wider sense of people or nation occurs in Gen. 10:5, 18, 20, 31, 32; 12:3; 28:14. Gen. 10:30 refers to the territorial "dwelling-place" (מושב) of the descendants of Joktan, which extended from Mesha in the direction of Sephar, the hill country of the east. CD 3.1 refers to "the sons of Noah and their clans" (בני נח ומשפחותיהם). Note especially 1QM 2.13–14: "During the following ten years, the war shall be divided against all the sons of Ham (14) according to [their clans in] their [set]tlements (למ]שפחותם במ[שבותם). During the remaining ten years, the war shall be divided against all [the sons of Japh]eth in their settlements." See also 4Q287 (4QBlessings^b) 5.13: "the families of the earth" (משפחות הארמה).

83. This phrase does not occur in the OT, but see Deut. 19:14: "You must not move your neighbor's boundary marker, set up by former generations, in your inheritance that you will inherit in the land that the Lord your God is giving you to possess." This seems to correspond to the view of *Jubilees*. Just as Israel was not to move the

inner-tribal boundaries in the Land, so also the nations were not to remove the inter-national boundaries on the earth. As we have seen, *Jubilees* also has the concept of the division of the earth among the sons and grandsons of Noah into territorial "lots" (cf. *Jub*. 8:11) or "(hereditary) shares" (*Jub*. 8:17, 21, 22, 24, 25, 29; 9:2, 3, 4, 6, 8, 9, 10, 11, 12, 13, 14). The whole issue is "inheritance" (cf. *Jub*. 9:13).

84. That is, "the seven nations of vanity" (11.8–9; cf. 4.12; 6.6; 9.9), the "Kittim" (11.11; cf. 15.2; 16.6, 8; 17.12, 14, 15; 18.2, 4; 19.10, 13), "Asshur" (11.11; cf. 18.2; 19.10), "all lands" (11.13), the "peoples" (11.13), "all the sons of man" (11.14), "the nations" (11.15; 12.11, 14), "Gog" (11.16), the "nations" (12.11), the "ki]n[gdoms" (12.15). In much of the rest of the War Rule there is a heavy emphasis on the war against "(all) the (wicked) nations" (cf. 14.5, 7; 15.1, 2, 13; 16.1; 19.6, 10). See the summary in Aune 1998–99: II.643: "In 1QM it is clear that the adversaries of the 'Sons of Light' in the eschatological battle are 'all nations' (15:1; 16:1), also called 'all the nations of wickedness' (15:2), presumably a coalition led by the 'king of the Kittim' (15:2). The enemies of the Sons of Light are identified with the traditional biblical enemies of Israel, though the name Kittim (perhaps a generic term for Israel's ancestral foes) occurs with particular frequency. In 1QM 1:1–7, Edom, Moab, the sons of Ammon, the Kittim of Asshur, the Kittim in Egypt, and the sons of Japhet are mentioned, while in 1QM 2:10–14, the list of enemies includes: Aram-Naharaim, the sons of Lud, the sons of Aram, Uz, Hul, Togal, Mesha, the sons of Arphaxad, the sons of Asshur and Persia, the Kadmonites, Elam, the sons of Ishmael, and Ketura, Ham, Japhet. These may be ciphers for the enemies of Israel during the Greco-Roman period, though their latter-day equivalents are far from obvious."

85. On the background of the forty-year period (i.e., the forty-year schema of Exodus) and its sabbatical structure, see García Martínez 1998a: 184–90.

86. Cf. Gmirkin 1998: 202: "Significantly, the detailed list of nations to be conquered in the first nine years of fighting roughly corresponds to the Seleucid empire at the time of the Maccabees, and included territories not ruled by Rome prior to the second century CE." It is interesting to note that if the War Rule reflects Greco-Roman war tactics, the Greco-Roman tactical treatises appear to have nothing approaching the worldwide scope of the eschatological war envisioned by the Qumran text. Cf. Duhaime 1988: 133–51.

87. On the war against Japheth, see also 1QM 18.2: "and the shout of the holy ones when they pursue Asshur; the sons of Japheth will fall, never to rise again; the Kittim will be crushed without . . ."

88. Himmelfarb 1994: 120–3. See further Reeves 1999: 148–77, which includes an example from *Jubilees* (32:2) in *Pirqe de-Rabbi Eliezar*.

89. For the text, see Buber 1960–61: 32.

90. On the tradition that identifies Melchizedek with Shem as an apologetic to demonstrate that Shem had indeed inhabited Salem (= Jerusalem) in ancient times and hence that all of Canaan had originally been given to Shem as his inheritance after the flood, see Kugel 1998: 290–1. Nevertheless, there is at least some evidence that the apologetic issue was not forgotten by Christians. Cf. Epiphanius, *Pan*. 46.84.6, which follows a passage that is dependent on *Jubilees* 8–9: "In the time of Naason the head of the tribe of Judah and Joshua the son of Nun, the sons of Shem took their own land. There was no wrong involved, but a righteous judgment."

91. The suggested dates of composition vary from 250–200 BCE to the tenth or eleventh century CE. Cf. Crown 1989: 223–4.

92. Cf. *Asatir* 1.2 (Gaster 1927: 184): "And he [sc. Adam] gave to Kain the West: and he gave to Hebel the North and the South." Gaster notes that a similar account is found in *Gen. Rab*. 22:7.

93. However, *Asatir* 4:15 mentions several books that Noah gives to the sons of Shem, including the "Book of Astronomy" to Elam. In *Jub*. 8:2–4, however, it is Cainan who discovers and transcribes astrological tables inscribed on stone by the Watchers.

94. Cf. *Asatir* 4.13–38 (Gaster 1927: 228–36).
95. Another Samaritan chronicle that has affinities with the *Book of Jubilees* is the *Tolidah* ("Genealogy"), which, beginning with a discussion of the meridian of Mt. Gerizim, sets out the Samaritan method of calendar calculation. Cf. J. Bowman 1977: 39–61 (esp. 51 n. 21, 52 n. 31, 55 n. 62).
96. On this tumultuous period, see e.g. Hengel 1989b: 63–78; an expanded version of the same is available in Hengel 1980: 33–48. See also Sherwin-White and Kuhrt 1993: 188–216. Perhaps another stone of offense would have been Antiochus' cultic status as in some way "divine." Cf. ibid., 202–10.
97. Hengel (1980: 38–41) describes pro-Seleucid and pro-Ptolemaic factions among Palestinian Jews in the period before the Seleucids which finally prevailed over the Ptolemies. Other Jews no doubt took a position similar to that of the Egyptian people as "illuminated by apocalyptic-sounding texts such as the Demotic chronicle and the Potter's Oracle, which dreamed of the end of foreign rule in Egypt" (ibid., 37).
98. On Berossus and the fragments attributed to him in ancient literature, see Verbrugghe and Wickersham 1996. It is interesting to note that the distribution of the earth among three sons of a world ruler is known in a Persian tradition dating to the early eleventh century CE. Cf. R. Levy 1967: 28: "When he had realized the intention which he had kept concealed, Faridun divided the world between his sons. To one he granted Rum [Greece] and the West, to the next Tur [Turania] and China, and to the third the plain of the heroes and the land of Iran. First consider Salm. To him he allotted the region of Rum and the West, commanding him to lead an army against the West, whose throne of sovereignty he ascended with the title of 'Lord of the West'. Then he allotted to Tur the Turanian land, making him master of the Turks and of China. When it came to the turn of Iraj, his father selected him to be king of Iran, and moreover master of the plain of the lance-wielders [Arabs] too. Also, beholding that he was worthy, he yielded to him the dais of royalty, the princely diadem, the sword, the seal, the ring and the crown. Those princes who had insight, good sense and judgment entitled him 'Sovereign of Iran'. All three sons reigned in peace and happiness as Lords of the Marches." This evidence seems to call into question Fergus Millar's thesis (1993: 6) that, except for Josephus' exposition of the Table of Nations (*Ant.* 1.122–47), "a noteworthy 'amnesia' marked the historical consciousness of the inhabitants of the Near East of the period."
99. Cf. Kraft 1994: 56–8.

3   Luke-Acts

1. Cf., e.g., Cadbury 1958: 8–9; Maddox 1982: 3–6.
2. For previous work on this subject, see Scott 1994: 483–544. On geographic aspects of Paul's mission, see Scott 1995a. See also now Béchard 1997: 182–247, which elaborates on my earlier study of Genesis 10 in Acts.
3. Steyn 1989: 409–11.
4. Kurz 1984: 175–6. Kurz acknowledges, however, that Gen. 11:12–13 LXX would have had to be consulted for the inclusion of Καινάμ in Lk. 3:36, unless Codex A of 1 Chr. 1:17–24 or a nonextant equivalent were used.
5. 1 Chronicles 1–3 LXX begins with Adam (1:1) and traces his descendants through Noah and his three sons to postdiluvian nations (vv. 4–27); thereafter, 1 Chronicles focuses on the descendants of Abraham (1:28–54) down to Jacob ("Israel") and his twelve sons (2:1–2), and then the descendants of Judah and his son David down to the Chronicler's own time (2:3–3:24). For a comparison between 1 Chronicles and the Lukan genealogy, see the table in Fitzmyer 1981–85: I.492–4.
6. Cf. Fitzmyer 1981–85: I.491: "It is obvious that Luke could have consulted his Greek OT in the passages cited above and constructed the list accordingly, either digging out

the others from literature unknown to us or filling them in himself. Yet many modern commentators ... prefer to think that Luke has made use of a previously existing genealogy. This is, in my opinion, more likely. But, obviously, such a genealogy might well have depended on the same OT passages as have been mentioned above."
7. Cf., similarly, Bauckham 1991: 102–3: "... since the [Lukan] genealogy shows striking independence of the LXX in the generations between Abraham and David, it is most likely not dependent on the LXX for the generations between Adam and Abraham." For a table of divergencies between Lk. 3:31–4 and the relevant biblical passages in the Septuagint, see ibid., 95–6.
8. Cf. Bauckham 1990: 327; 1991: 96.
9. In Gen. 11:13, the figures for Kainam's lifespan (130 years to the birth of Shelah and 330 years after it) are the same as those for his son Shelah. Hence, as Bauckham (1991: 98) has rightly seen, this duplication makes it very probable that Kainam is a secondary addition to the Septuagint genealogy. Note that Josephus also has 130 years to the birth of Shelah, but like the MT does not include Kainam. Cf. Fraenkel 1984: 186–90.
10. Rook 1983: 148–50. See also VanderKam 1988: 71–85; Bauckham 1991: 96–8. A more difficult issue is whether the tradition that includes Kainam son of Arpachshad is earlier than either the Septuagint or *Jubilees*. Rook (1983: 148–56) argues that *Jubilees* used the chronology of the Samaritan Pentateuch for the patriarchal period and adapted it to fit his narrative purpose. The problem is that the Samaritan Pentateuch does not actually include the second Kainam in his genealogy. However, since the chronologies of the Samaritan Pentateuch and *Jubilees* are otherwise virtually identical between Adam and Shelah (see the comparative table in Rook 1983: 154), there would seem to be room in Samaritan Pentateuch for the second Kainam (b. 1375 *anno mundi*) between Arpachshad and Shelah. Bauckham (1991: 98–101) provides an additional argument that a form of the genealogy from Shem to Abraham which included Kainam son of Arpachshad was already known before *Jubilees*. On the assumption that the *Apocalypse of Weeks* is based on a scheme of ten weeks of seven generations that predates *Jubilees*, the second week in the series must presuppose the second Kainam in order to fill out the full complement of seven names (*1 Enoch* 93:4), so that Abraham occurs at the end of the third week, exactly where the *Apocalypse* indicates (93:5). On this interpretation, see further below. Another option is to suppose that the author of *Jubilees* added Kainam in order to make possible the analogy in *Jub.* 2:23 between the twenty-two kinds of works created on the six days of creation and the "twenty-two chief men from Adam to Jacob" (cf., e.g., Wevers 1993: 153–4; VanderKam 1988: 76). On this hypothesis, see, however, Bauckham 1991: 97.
11. See esp. Bauckham 1990: 371–3, followed by Brooke 1998: 49.
12. Bauckham tries to overcome this problem by several arguments: (1) numerical schemes are not always explicit, as 1 Chr. 6:1–15 shows (1990: 318); (2) the seventh place in the Lukan genealogy is occupied by Enoch, just as in Jewish tradition (1990: 319, citing *1 Enoch* 60:8; 93:3; *Jub.* 7:39; *Lev. Rab.* 29:11; Jude 14); (4) David appears at the end of the fifth week (1990: 325; 1991: 102); (3) the names Joseph and Jesus appear at the end of the sixth and seventh (jubilee!) weeks of generations, respectively, and these point to the consummation of human history, where the names Joseph and Jesus again appear, this time at the end of the tenth and eleventh weeks (1990: 319, 324, 328; 1991: 101).
13. Cf. VanderKam 1995: 80–100; 1998b: 101–2; Frey 1997: 262–4.
14. Cf. R. Bauckham, 1990: 315–26; 1991: 98–100. Bauckham's generational interpretation of the *Apocalypse of Weeks* resembles the prior attempt of C. F. A. Dillmann (cf. K. Koch 1983: 414).
15. Bauckham's approach is by no means the only possible one, since the *Apocalypse of Weeks* does not provide an explicit genealogy of seven generations per week. For a chronological analysis of the scheme in the *Apocalypse of Weeks*, see

202 Notes to page 47

Koch 1983: 403–30, who argues that, in analogy to Dan. 9:24–7, the *Apocalypse* divides human history into ten "weeks" of 490 years each (= 7 × 70 years). Bauckham (1990: 321; 1991: 99) rejects this and other non-generational interpretations. Roger T. Beckwith (1996: 242–9) calls the generational interpretation of the *Apocalypse of Weeks* "a complete misunderstanding," opting instead for a chronological scheme in which the "weeks" actually vary in length of time (cf. also VanderKam 1993: 110–11; 1998b: 99). For an attempt at a synchronization of the Apocalypse of Weeks with the chronology of the *Book of Jubilees*, see Dimant 1993: 70–2; Frey 1997: 268–9.

16. Thus, the second week (*1 Enoch* 93:4) would include the following seven generations: Methuselah, Lamech, Noah, Shem, Arpachshad, Kainam, Shelah. The Jewish–Christian source in Ps.-Clementine *Recognitions* 1.27–71 counts the number of generations from the creation of Adam to the advent of Abraham (*Rec.* 1.27.1–33.2), following a scheme which is consistent with the *Book of Jubilees*. See further in Chap. 4. On Enochic material in *Jubilees* (or vice versa), see VanderKam 1978: 229–51 (esp. 231ff.).

17. The royal genealogy for the same period, from Rehoboam to Jeconiah, contains seventeen generations (1 Chr. 3:10–16) – too many for the supposed seven-generation week of the *Apocalypse*. Therefore, Bauckham (1990: 322–3; 1991: 100) arbitrarily selects for the sixth week the following seven names from the genealogy of Ezra, based on Ezra 7:1–3: Amariah, Ahitub, Zadok, Shallum, Hilkiah, Azariah, Seraiah. Hence, he is able to claim that the period of the divided monarchy down to 586 BCE *could* fit the scheme of the *Apocalypse of Weeks*. But where else do we find this kind of mingling of priestly and royal genealogies? To be sure, 4Qpseudo-Daniel ar[c] (4Q245) gives an abbreviated (and fragmentary) list of the names of high priests from the patriarchal period (Qahat) down to the Hasmoneans of the Hellenistic age ([Jona]than, Simeon), followed by a list of kings, including David, Solomon and Ahaziah. However, as J. Collins (1999: 52) suggests, "the separate lists of kings and priests were meant to show that the two offices, the kingship and the high priesthood, had always been distinct (even Jonathan and Simon had not laid claim to kingship). In this case, the lists of priests and kings in 4Q245 may be setting up a critique of the combination of priesthood and kingship under the Hasmoneans. Such a critique would be highly compatible with the expectation of two messiahs, of Aaron and Israel, at Qumran." See further Flint 1996: 137–50; also Adler 1997: 24–47. Nevertheless, it is interesting to note that H. Eshel (1996: 92) has recently argued that 4Q522 6–7 should be translated: "And he [sc. King Solomon] will serve as first priest." Cf. 1 Kgs. 8:62–6.

18. As Bauckham (1990: 324) himself acknowledges, "The Lukan genealogy certainly does not conform to the details of this scheme; but the principle to be seen in the Apocalypse of Weeks . . . is illuminating in relation to the genealogy." See also ibid., 320–1: "The author of the Lukan genealogy could easily have seen this [ten-generation scheme] as an inadequacy of the Apocalypse of Weeks. He has therefore not simply reproduced its scheme, which in any case would not easily coincide with his own understanding of world history in its later periods, but he has used it as a model for constructing his own scheme of eleven weeks of generations." We should not underestimate, however, that Bauckham's proposal presupposes that the author of the Lukan genealogy tacitly used a recondite and obscure principle in order to create a completely novel genealogical scheme. For example, unlike the *Apocalypse of Weeks*, which places the giving of the law at Sinai at the end of the fourth week (*1 Enoch* 93:6), the Lukan genealogy according to Bauckham's reconstruction ends the fourth week with Admin son of Arni (1990: 316). Moreover, unlike the *Apocalypse of Weeks*, which places the building of the Temple at the end of the fifth week (*1 Enoch* 93:7), the Lukan genealogy according to Bauckham's reconstruction ends the fifth week with David.

19. For a chart that applies this scheme to Lk. 3:23–38, see Bauckham, 1990: 316–17. Bauckham (ibid., 319) regards *1 Enoch* 10:12 as "the text on which this genealogy

[i.e., the Lukan genealogy] must have been based." See also ibid., 320: "The author of the Lukan genealogy must have been inspired by I Enoch 10:12. . ."

20. Cf. Bauckham, 1990: 320: "It is not easy to tell from the Enoch literature exactly when the binding of the fallen angels occurred, but it certainly happened after Enoch's translation and during the lifetime of his son Methuselah. So a reader might easily suppose that it should be dated in the generation after Enoch's. Thus from I Enoch 10:12 it appears that the whole of world history from Adam to the Last Judgment comprises seventy-seven generations, seven up to and including Enoch, followed by a further seventy. For anyone familiar with I Enoch 10:12 the Lukan genealogy of Jesus would clearly designate Jesus the last generation before the end."

21. For a convenient overview of variant readings in the Lukan genealogy of Jesus, see Swanson 1995: 54–61.

22. Although Fitzmyer (1981–85: I.491) reports that manuscript U contains 72 names, I count 77 (including God) based on Swanson's edition.

23. Fitzmyer 1981–85: I.491.

24. Bauckham, 1990: 318–19; 1991: 101.

25. It seems gratuitous to suppose that the original author of the genealogy wanted to express an imminent expectation of the parousia within the generation of Jesus' contemporaries (so Bauckham, 1990: 325).

26. Cf. M. Johnson 1988: 232: "Thus the genealogy when incorporated or written by Luke may have had only seventy-two names, and consequently the parallel with the twelvefold periodizations of history in the above-mentioned apocalypses is seriously weakened." The same observations hold for Bauckham's elevenfold periodization of history.

27. Heer 1910: 32–106. Heer's argument need not be accepted in every detail. He seems to overplay, for instance, the possibility that Luke appropriated Paul's typological comparison of Christ to Adam.

28. Cf. Metzger 1992: 209: "In general the shorter reading is to be preferred, except where (a) parablepsis arising from homoeoteleuton may have occurred; or where (b) the scribe may have omitted material which he deemed to be (i) superfluous, (ii) harsh, or (iii) contrary to pious belief, liturgical usage, or ascetical practice." See also Aland and Aland 1989: 281; Royse 1995: 242ff.

29. Fitzmyer, 1981–85: I.492; Bauckham, 1990: 371; 1991: 101 n. 19.

30. Cf. Bauer and Helm 1955: XIX–XX (emphasis mine): "Die verschiedenen Handschriften und Handschriftengruppen der Chroniken unterscheiden sich voneinander nicht wie sonst Codices durch bloße Schreiberversehen, sondern durch weit einschneidendere Änderungen, *Zusätze*, Auslassungen u. dgl. Mit Recht sagt de Boor . . . , daß die starken Verschiedenheiten der Nikephoroshss. daher rühren, daß keiner der Abschreiber zu ungebildet war, um nicht den Namen- und Zahlenreihen seiner Vorlage aus der Bibel, aus den Kirchenschriftstellern oder den Martyrologien eines oder das andere *hinzufügen* zu können. Dieselbe Beobachtung läßt sich auch an den zahlreichen Ableitungen der Chronik des Hippolyt machen, nicht bloß bei den späteren Benutzern und Bearbeitern, bei denen dies eigentlich selbstverständlich ist, sondern auch schon an den Abschriften der Übersetzungen. So stellen z.B. die beiden Hss. GC des l.g.I innerhalb der Überlieferung dieses Textes, obwohl er nichts sein soll als eine Wiedergabe der Chronik Hippolyts in lateinischer Sprache, eine durch gewisse Besonderheiten . . . von den übrigen verschiedene Gruppe dar. Die Handschriften, welche christliche Chroniken enthalten, lehren also die Fortdauer einer Erscheinung kennen, die durch die Textkritik schon für die Tradition der Evangelien festgestellt wurde, und die an der Bildung dieser Beteiligten halten sich ebenfalls für berechtigt, zu dem Überkommenen hinzuzusetzen, was zu ihrer Kenntnis gekommen war und was ihnen als wahr galt, zu ändern und zu streichen, wo sie besser unterrichtet zu sein glaubten. Eine Diorthose dieser so entstandenen und lange unkontrolliert umlaufenden Texte setzt bei den Evangelien erst spät, bei der Chronikenliteratur

204 Notes to pages 48-50

überhaupt niemals ein." For insertions into even the most reliable manuscript of Hippolyus' *Chronicon* (H₁), see, for example, §§51, 52, 109, 128, 176, 238, 241, 267, 271, 274, 288, 290, 294.

31. Witakowski 1993: 650: "Moreover long lists of this kind could easily undergo change, either by the elimination of the items which were unknown to the Syrians . . . or by the addition of other topo- or ethnonyms, which, having entered the intellectual horizon of one or another Syriac author, in due time became introduced into the lists."

32. Irenaeus, *Haer.* 3.22.3 (ed. Doutreleau 1974: 438). The text is also available in Greek: Διὰ τοῦτο ὁ Λουκᾶς τὴν ἀπὸ τῆς γεννήσεως τοῦ κυρίου ἡμῶν μέχρι 'Αδὰμ γενεαλογίαν ἑβδομήκοντα δύο γενεὰς ἔχουσαν ἐπιδείκνυσι, τὸ τέλος συνάπτων τῇ ἀρχῇ καὶ σημαίνων ὅτι αὐτός ἐστιν ὁ πάντα τὰ ἔθνη ἑξῆς τοῦ 'Αδαμ διεσπαρμένα καὶ πάσας τὰς γλώσσας καὶ γενεὰς τῶν ἀνθρώπων σὺν αὐτῷ τῷ 'Αδὰμ εἰς ἑαυτὸν ἀνακεφαλαιωσάμενος. On Irenaeus' doctrine of recapitulation, see further Donovan 1997: 87–90, 136 n. 4, 150, 157; C. R. Smith 1994: 313–31.

33. Bauckham (1990: 372) questions whether Irenaeus knew a text with precisely 72 names from Jesus to Adam. Much depends, of course, on whether Irenaeus includes Adam and/or Jesus in the count. As we have seen in Chap. 2, deriving the traditional number of the nations (70/72) from Genesis 10 requires some creative accounting. See, for example, Augustine's vacillation between 73 and 72 nations (*De civ. D.* 16.6). On the use of patristic evidence for textual criticism, see in general Fee 1995: 191–207.

34. So Bauckham, 1990: 372.

35. Cf. Clement of Alexandria, Strom. 1.21.142.1: "Ephorus and many other historians say that there are seventy-five (πέντε καὶ ἑβδομήκοντα) nations and languages, following the words of Moses: 'All the souls of Jacob's house who went down to Egypt numbered seventy-five (πέντε καὶ ἑβδομήκοντα).'" It seems unlikely that this comment has anything to do with the fourth-century BCE historian from Cyme, for there is no other evidence that Ephorus or any other Greek historian claimed that there are 75 nations. Moreover, the comment contains an enthymematic argument whose logic hinges on Jewish tradition. Whereas the Hebrew text of Gen. 46:27 (cf. Exod. 1:5) records that 70 individuals went down with Jacob into Egypt (cf. also Josephus, *Ant.* 2.176), the Septuagint gives 75. The missing part of the syllogism is the tradition based on Deut. 32:8 MT, which equates the number of the nations with the number of the sons of Israel. See further below on the number 70/72 in Lk. 10:1–24. In the later midrashim, a dispute over the correct number of the nations, whether 72 or 75, becomes explicit (cf. *Gen. Rab.* 44:19; *Lev. Rab.* 23:2; *Song Rab.* 2:5).

36. Thus, in our view, Bauckham was right to look to the *Jubilees* tradition in order to explain the presence of the second Kainam in the Lukan genealogy.

37. 1 Chr. 2:9–24 is a text that presents serious problems of interpretation in its own right. Cf. Braun 1986: 25–35.

38. There is also an impressive range of witnesses (A, D, 33, 565, 1079, many versions) which support the reading τοῦ 'Αμιναδὰβ τοῦ 'Αράμ, instead of a reading that involves three names.

39. Cf. Wilson 1973; Bovon 1983: 403–14; Scott 1994: 524–43. Also relevant here is the discussion of the development of Greek ethnography in Sterling 1992: 20–102.

40. Cf. Lk. 2:1 (the decree of Caesar Augustus went out that "the whole inhabited world should be registered"); 4:5 (the devil showed Jesus "all the kingdoms of the world"); 21:25–6 (before the coming of the Son of Man, signs upon the earth will cause "distress among the nations" and foreboding of that which is coming "upon the world"); Acts 11:28 (there would be a great famine "over the whole inhabited world"); 17:6 (Paul and his companions "have been turning the inhabited world upside down"), 31 (God "will judge the world"); 19:27 ("all Asia and the inhabited world" worship Artemis); 24:5 (Paul was found to be an "agitator among all the Jews throughout the world").

This list could be greatly expanded by the many references in Luke-Acts to γῆ in the sense of the "earth" (cf. Lk. 2:14; 5:24; 10:21; 11:31; 12:49, 51, 56; 16:17; 18:8; 21:23, 25, 33, 35; 23:44; Acts 1:8; 2:19; 3:25; 4:24, 26; 7:49; 8:33; 10:11, 12; 11:6; 13:47; 14:15; 17:24, 26; 22:22).

41. Cf. Salmon 1988: 79, 80.

42. Cf. Ravens 1995: 253–4.

43. Cf. Allison 1998: 143–5; Jarick 1997: 270–87.

44. Cf. Meier 1997: 635–72; Evans 1993: 154–70; Clark 1998: 173–7. The symbolism of the number twelve is so strong in Luke's narrative that after the death of Judas, an election had to take place in order to restore the full complement to the Twelve. Cf. O'Brien 1999: 210.

45. In the parallel passage to Lk. 22:30, Matt. 19:28 uses παλιγγενεσία ("renewal, restoration") to describe the time when Jesus would be seated on the throne of his glory and his followers would also sit on twelve thrones, judging the twelve tribes of Israel. Josephus (Ant. 11.66) uses the same term for the restoration of Israel to the land in the time of Zerubbabel: "Those who heard [the good news of Darius' decision to allow the return] thanked God for giving them back the land of their fathers, and turned to drinking and partying, and spent seven days in feasting and celebrating the regaining and restoration of their native land (τὴν ἀνάκτησιν καὶ παλιγγενεσίαν τῆς πατρίδος)."

46. On the textual problem in Lk. 10:1, 17, see Metzger 1968: 67–76; 1994: 126–7. As we shall see in Chap. 4, it is important for our considerations that Ps.-Clem. Rec. 1.40.4 has "seventy-two selected disciples."

47. Cf., e.g., Schürmann 1994: 51, 54.

48. Horbury 1986: 522.

49. Cf., e.g., Bovon 1989–96: 45, 49; T. Lane 1995; Tannehill 1986: 232–7; O'Brien 1999: 207 n. 16. Cf. also Wenham 1991: 5–7, who suggests that Luke includes the mission of the 70 because he himself was one of them.

50. Cf. Kronholm 1978: 212.

51. As we have seen, it takes some creative counting to arrive at either 70 or 72 as the number of the nations of the world. Because 1 Chronicles 1 limits the Table of Nations to the most essential information and eliminates the extra material found in Gen. 10:1b, 5, 9–12, 18b–21, 23a, 30–2, its version of the Table comes closer than Genesis does to the conception of a total of 70 nations of the world. The number 70 is achieved by ignoring Nimrod (Gen. 10:8–11; 1 Chr. 1:10). Thus, the Table of Nations includes 14 sons of Japheth (Gen. 10:2–5; 1 Chr. 1:5–7), 30 sons of Ham (Gen. 10:6–20; 1 Chr. 1:8–16), and 26 sons of Shem (Gen. 10:21–31; 1 Chr. 1:17–23). The Septuagint has a higher count because, as we have seen, it adds Kainan between Arpaxad and Sala to the list of the sons of Shem (Gen. 10:22, 24). For a commentary on the Greek text of Genesis 10, see Wevers 1993: 127–46. The count of 72 nations from the sons of Noah is also commonly found in later Syriac tradition. Cf. Witakowski 1993: 636, 639, 644, 645, 646. See further Sperber 1971: 882–6.

52. Cf. Dan. 12:1; Sir. 17:17; Jub. 15:31–32; Hebr. T. Naph. 8:3–9:4; 1 Enoch 89:59; 90:22, 25; Philo, Post. 91; Tg. Ps-J Gen. 11:7–8; Deut. 32:8–9; Ps.-Clem. Rec. 2:42; 8:50; Irenaeus, Adv. Haer. 3.12.9; Mekilta, Shirata 2; see further Mach 1992: 22–5, 62, 77–8; Gaston 1982: 65–75 (esp. 68, 71).

53. Cf. Wevers 1995: 512–13.

54. Note that 4QDeutʲ 12.12–14, which preserves parts of Deut. 32:7–8, contains the reading בני אלוהים for v. 8 (line 14). Cf. Ulrich, et al. 1995: 90. Unfortunately, 4QpaleoDeutʳ Frg. 35, which preserves parts of Deut. 32:6–8, is missing this section of v. 8. Cf. Skehan, et al. 1992: 146. There are no other occurrences of Deut. 32:8 in the Qumran scrolls.

55. According to b. Hag. 12b, the sages used Deut. 32:8 to support their contention that the world rests on twelve pillars. Obviously, this understands the number of the children of

Israel as 12 rather than as 70. Likewise in *Midrash Aggadah* Lek-Leka 13.7 on
Gen. 12:6 (cited in Chap. 2), Deut. 32:8 is understood to refer to the twelve tribes
of Israel. Cf. Himmelfarb 1994: 120–3. In Hermas, *Sim.* 9.17.1–4, there is a correspondence between the twelve tribes of Israel and the twelve (sic!) nations of the
world.

56. Gen. 46:27 LXX reads "seventy-five" (cf. also Exod. 1:5 in 4QExod[b] and 4QGen-
Exod[a]). A spurious fragment of Ephorus of Cyme (ca. 405–330 BCE) corrects the
idea that there must be 75 nations and languages based on Gen. 46:27 LXX, arguing
that the number is traditionally 72 (*ap.* Clement of Alexandria, *Strom.* 1.21.142.1;
cf. Felix Jacoby, *FGrH* IIA, frg. 70, no. 237; IIC, frg. 70, no. 237). See further above
on the Lukan genealogy of Jesus (Lk. 3:23–38).

57. On the number of Jacob's descendants who went down to Egypt, see Kugel 1998:
482–4. On the use of the number 70 in scripture, see Otto 1993: 1000–27 passim.

58. Cf., e.g., Flusser, 1971: 1198–9. On the interpretive difficulties in identifying the
seventy shepherds, see, however, VanderKam 1997: 89–109. Cf. also Plato, *Politicus*
271d–277d.

59. Cf. Kugel 1998: 236.

60. For example, the 70 large cattle that were slaughtered and burnt during the Feast of
Tabernacles (Num. 29:12–34) are frequently taken as offerings for the sake of the 70
nations (cf. *b. Sukkah* 55b; *Song Rab.* 1:64; *Lam. Rab.* 1:23).

61. The text reads as follows:... ὅστις κατὰ ἀριθμὸν τῶν υἱῶν Ἰσραήλ, οἳ
εἰσῆλθον εἰς Αἴγυπτον, οἵ εἰσιν ἑβδομήκοντα, καὶ πρὸς τὰ ὅρια τῶν ἐθνῶν
περιγράψας γλώσσαις ἑβδομήκοντα... (Rehm and Strecker 1992: 243).

62. Cf. Williams 1997: 16: "In the fifth generation after the flood, now that men were
multiplying from Noah's three sons, the children and their children, who had been born
successively, became a world-population of seventy-two chief men and patricians.
(9) And as they expanded and moved far away from Mt. Lubar and the Armenian
highlands, or region of Ararat, they reached the plain of Shinar [*Jub.* 10:19] where
they presumably chose [to live]. (Shinar is now in Persia, but anciently it belonged
to the Assyrians.) (10) In Shinar they joined themselves together and consulted about
building a tower and city. From the region near Europe which borders on Asia they
were all called 'Scythians', which corresponds to the name of the era. (11) They began
the erection of their tower and built Babylon. But God was displeased with their foolish
work, for he dispersed their languages, and divided them from one into seventy-two,
to correspond with the number of the men then living. This is why they were called
'Meropes', because of the 'divided' language. A blast of wind blew the tower over
[*Jub.* 10:26]. (12) So they were dispersed right and left over the whole earth, with
some going back where they came from and others further east, while others reached
Libya. (13) Anyone who wants the facts about them can discover how each one who
went further obtained his allotment in each particular country. For example, Egypt fell
to Mistrem, Ethiopia to Cush, Axomitia to Phut, Regman, Sabakatha and Ludan, also
known as Judad, obtained the land near Garamitia." See also Epiphanius, *Pan.* 39.8.2–5
(Williams 1997: 259–60): "But, as I have already explained in connection with the
generations discussed above, in the foregoing Sects, all humanity then consisted of
seventy-two men, who were princes and patricians. Thirty-two were of Ham's stock
and fifteen were of Japheth's but twenty-five were of Shem's. And thus the tower and
Babylon were built. (3) After this tribes and languages were dispersed all over the earth.
And since the seventy-two persons [who] were then building the tower were scattered
by the languages – because they had been confused, and [made strangers to] the single
language they had known – each has been infused with a different one by God's will.
(4) This was the beginning of all the ways of talking there are even to this day, so
that [anyone who] cares to, can discover the person who originated each language.
(5) For example, Iovan acquired Greek – the Ionians, who possess the Greeks' ancient
language, are named for him. Theras acquired Thracian; Mosoch, Mossynoecian;
Thobel, Thessalian; Lud, Lydian; Gephar, Gasphenian; Mistrem, Egyptian; Psous,

Axomitian; and Armot, Arabian. And not to mention them individually, each of the rest was infused with a language of his own. And from then on the people who spoke each language after them have multiplied in the world."
63. Bauer and Helm 1955: 53. See also the fragment of Hippolytus' introduction to the Psalms, which connects the 72 psalms attributed to David in the Psalter with the 72 nations of the world: "Diesen vier Sängern [sc. Asaph, Heman, Ethan, Jeduthun] gestellte er [sc. David] 288 Männer zu, so dass zu jedem einzeln von ihnen 72 Männern gehörten, die mit Begleitung von Musikinstrumenten sangen: indem er diese 72 Sänger mit Beziehung auf jene 72 Völker, deren Sprachen vor Zeiten verwirrt wurden, in der prophetischen Voraussicht bestellte, dass alle Völker einst Gott preisen werden (Ps. 71[72]:17). Jene wollten nämlich damals den Turm bauen, waren 72 verbündeten Völker. Als aber der gerechte Zorn über sie losbrach, trat eine Teilung der 72 Sprachen ein, und da sie nicht mehr gleich sprachen, gerieten sie in Feindschaft, indem sie von 288 Fürsten unterjocht und von ihnen vertrieben wurden. Die damals verstreut wurden, als sie aus dem Osten, wo sie auch zu dem Turmbau sich erfrechten, auswanderten, waren: von Ham 32, von Sem 25, von Japhet 15; das macht im Ganzen 72. Dadurch weissagte er, dass am Ende der Zeiten alle Völker Gott preisen werden (Ps. 71[72]:17)." Achelis 1897: 127–8.
64. Cf. Rehm and Strecker 1994: 76–7: est enim uniuscuiusque gentis angelus, cui credita est gentis ipsius dispensatio a deo, qui tamen cum apparuerit, quamvis putetur et dicatur ab his quibus praeest, deus, tamen interrogatus non sibi dabit ipse tale testimonium. deus enim excelsus, qui solus potestatem omnium tenet, in septuaginta et duas partes divisit totius terrae nationes eisque principes angelos statuit.
65. See, e.g., the associations made by Price 1980: 51.
66. Cf. Dreizehnter 1978: 102; Burrows 1936: 390: "The number 70 is used principally to denote natural groups of individuals in a family, human or divine; of clans in a people; or peoples in the human race."
67. Cf. Sbordone 1940: 37–9.
68. The number 72 may also occur outside astrological tradition. For example, according to Appian (*Syr.* 62), Seleucus I "had seventy-two satraps under him, so much of the earth did he rule" (σατραπεῖαι δὲ ἦσαν ὑπ' αὐτῷ δύο καὶ ἑβδομήκοντα· τοσαύτης ἐβασίλευε γῆς).
69. On the notion of countries coming under the influence of the zodiac, see further below on Acts 2:9–11.
70. Cf. Kroll 1930: 12–13, who argues here for a Babylonian origin of the number 72. See, however, W. Gundel 1949a: 1241: "Die Zahl 72 ergibt sich von selbst aus den 72 Göttern der ägyptischen Fünftagewoche, sowie aus den 36 Dekane, zu denen dann noch 36 Pentaden in den Salmeschiniaka durch 'die mächtigen Führer' und durch besondere Sterne astronomisch bestimmt waren."
71. Cf. Hunger and Pingree 1989: 137; Horowitz 1998: 169. Note that MUL.APIN has a 360-day calendar, divided into 72 pentads (Hunger and Pingree, 1989: 139). See further Neugebauer 1975: II.590–3, 698–9. See also Koch-Westenholz 1995.
72. Cf. W. Gundel 1936: 23–5, 123–34 (esp. 126). See also Gundel 1949a: 1240–6.
73. Cf. Gundel 1969: 39. On these 72 pentad deities, see further ibid., 27, 40, 97, 258, 267–8, 295 n. 1, 347. On the relationship of *P. Oxy.* 465 to the Salmeschiniaka, see Kroll 1931: 843–6. On "subdecans" of the 72 pentads, cf. Tegtmeier 1990: 73–8, which includes a diagram (77) illustrating the relationship between the pentads and the signs of the zodiac; Quack 1995: 97–122.
74. Cf. *Her.* 175; *Praem.* 65; *Fug.* 185; *Mos.* 2.123–4; *Spec. Leg.* 1.87; compare Rev. 12:1; Wisd. 18:24; Josephus, *Ant.* 3.181–2; 4Q186; 4Q561. On the zodiac in early Judaism, see e.g. Charlesworth 1987: 926–52. On astrology, see further *Jub.* 8:3–4; 12:16–17 (on which see Ps.-Clem. *Rec.* 1.32.3 in Chap. 4).
75. Cf. Albani 1993: 3–42; 1994; Gleßmer 1996: 259–82. On astrology in the Qumran scrolls, see further Greenfield and Sokoloff 1995: 507–25; Wise 1994: 13–50; Albani 1998–99: II.278–330; Böttrich 1997: 222–45; F. Schmidt 1998: 189–205.

76. Gleßmer and Albani 1999: 407–42. As discussed in Chap. 1, however, this artifact may actually represent a schematic map of the world, with Jerusalem in the center of the traditional 70/72 nations.
77. Cf. Ovadiah and Ovadiah 1987: 54–6, pl. CLXXVII; Levine 1981: 140–5. Note also that the fifth-century synagogue at Jerash (Gerasa) in Transjordan contains a mosaic floor with another reference to the sons of Noah: the left corner of mosaic features the heads of two people, labeled ΣΗΜ and ΙΑΦΕΘ, with a dove holding a twig in its beak and sitting on a branch above them. Cf. Barrois 1930: 259, pl. IXb; Pringent 1990: 85–96 (esp. 85–8), 159–73 (on the zodiac); Goodenough 1953–68: I.259–60. On the whole question, see further Stemberger 1975: 11–56. A fifth-century synagogue at Misis (ancient Mopsuestia in Cilicia) features a mosaic flood depicting Noah's ark (the lid of which reads ΚΙΒωΤΟΣ ΝωΕ) and the animals surrounding it. Cf. A. Ovadiah 1978: II.864–6, pl. 18. Compare the coins issued by Apamea (nicknamed ἡ Κιβωτός) in Phrygia under a succession of Roman emperors (ca. 192–253 CE): the reverse depicts a man and a woman standing in a big open chest bearing the name ΝΩΕ; on it is a bird, with another bird flying to it holding a branch in its claws. Cf. Hilhorst 1998: 63–5; Harl 1992: 97–125.
78. No zodiacal circle with symbols appears, however, as is commonly found at other synagogues (e.g., Beth-Alpha, Na'aran, Hammath-Tiberias and Susiyah).
79. Cf. Lieberman 1974: 16: "The Holy One, Blessed be he, showed Abraham all of the Zodiac (שהמזלות) surrounding his *Shekhina*; . . . and said: just as the Zodiac surrounds me, with my glory in the center, so shall your descendants multiply and camp under many flags, with my *Shekhina* in the center." Cited in Klein 1980: 43–4.
80. Cf. Ovadiah and Ovadiah 1987: 63–5, pls. LXVI, CLXXX–CLXXXI. See further M. Smith 1982: 199–214. The chariot theme is common in representations of Helios. Cf. *Lexicon Iconographicum Mythologiae Classicae* 4.2 (1988) 366–85. The synagogue at Beth Alpha portrays Helios riding a quadriga at the center of a zodiac circle, although he carries no globus. On the whole tradition, see further H. G. Gundel 1992: esp. Tafel 6.
81. Cf. H. G. Gundel 1992: 43, 60–3. See further Brincken 1976: 79ff.
82. Cf. Gutmann 1984: 1337.
83. Cf. Burrows 1936: 392:

MUL.APIN:	32 (Path of Enlil)	+ 23 (Path of Anu)	+ 15 (Path of Ea) = 71
Table of Nations:	32 (Ham)	+ 23 (Shem)	+ 15 (Japheth) = 70
Sons of Jacob:	33 (Leah)	+ 23 (Zilpah and Bilhah)	+ 14 (Rachel) = 70

Note, however, that in order to arrive at the total for Shem, Burrows (1936: 391–2) subtracts four names from the Table of Nations in 1 Chronicles 1. For a list of the stars in each of the paths of the three gods (Enlil – the god of the earth, Anu – the god of the sky, and Ea – the god of waters), see Hunger and Pingree 1989: 137–9; J. Koch 1989: 16.

84. Metzger 1994: 150–1. Note, however, that the NT textual critic, Gordon Fee, regards the geographical distribution of the textual witnesses to be strongly in favor of 72 (personal communication).
85. As we shall see in Chap. 4, a similar dilemma is met in Ps.-Clem. *Rec.* 1.34.2 and 1.40.4.
86. *Pace* Marshall 1978: 415, followed by Schürmann 1994: 54. In view of the sending out of the 72 in pairs, it is interesting to note that half of 72 is 36. This happens to be the number of decan-gods, each of which is thought to rule over 10° of the 360° zodiac. In the *Testament of Solomon* 18, for example, the 36 decans are demons that cause mental and physical illnesses in humans (cf. W. Gundel 1969: 286–7). It may be significant in this regard that the Lukan account of the sending of the 72 emphasizes healing and overpowering demons (cf. Lk. 10:9, 17, 20).

87. At the very beginning of Acts, the disciples endeavor to replace Judas, thereby reconstituting the Twelve who represent the twelve tribes of Israel (Lk. 22:30) and witness to the restoration of Israel taking place in the nation's midst. Cf. Acts 1:15, where the beginning size of the group which met in Jerusalem is described as 120 persons (12 × 10?).

88. Based on her extensive research on Jewish onomastics in the Second-Temple period, Tal Ilan of the Hebrew University kindly shared with me in a private communication that it is very rare for Jews of this period to mention tribal affiliation, even among Babylonian Jews. Besides Anna, the only other known case is "Tobit . . . of the tribe of Naphtali" (Tob. 1:1). Furthermore, whereas names such as Ephraim or Manasseh occur infrequently, Joseph was the second most common name in the Second-Temple period (almost 200 people). Ilan doubts, however, that the popularity of this name is due to northern influence, any more than the popularity of Ishmael in the same period is due to Arab influence. We may note, however, that hope for the return of the nine/ten northern tribes (collectively called "Joseph") was apparently nurtured in the Second-Temple period. Cf. Schuller 1989–90: 349–76 (esp. 368–70).

89. Cf. Bauckham 1997a: 185; Ravens 1995: 47. Note that in Lk. 2:25, Simeon's hope for the "consolation" (παράκλησις) of Israel may also include the hope of restoration for the northern tribes, for Jer. 38(31):9 uses the same term of God's returning Ephraim (either one of the northern tribes or the whole northern kingdom of Israel) to the land. For the emphasis on Israel and the nations in Luke-Acts, see further pp. 50–5.

90. As we mentioned in Chap. 1, Strabo (*Geog.* 17.3.24) conceptualized the Roman Empire and the entire world as spreading in concentric circles around Rome.

91. See Chap. 2. See further Hengel 1995b: 270, 303; Bauckham 1996b: 417–27; L. Alexander 1995a: 29–31; Scott 1994: 525–7; Borgen 1997: 19–21; Klauck 1986: 129–47; Poorthuis and Safrai 1996; Stegemann 1983: 154–71; Frey 1997: 277–9; Lichtenberger 1994: 94–6; Schultz 1993: 28–37.

92. Cf. Ego 1989: 87–91, 94–7, 105, 107, 109–10, 170–1. The Ezekiel cycle painted on the north wall in the synagogue at Dura-Europos (NC1) seems to portray the Mount of Olives (note two [olive] trees growing out of the top) as an omphalos (cf. the cross-hatching on the Delphic omphalos) which is split down the middle in accordance with the prophetic word of Zech. 14:4: "And in that day his feet shall stand on the Mount of Olives, which lies before Jerusalem on the east; and the Mount of Olives shall be split in two from east to west by a very wide valley, so that half of the Mount will withdraw northward, and the other half southward." If the bodies and limbs in the picture are meant to come out of the valley (cf. the valley of dry bones in Ezek. 37:1–14), then this underscores the omphalos function of the Mount as the point of junction between heaven, earth, and the underworld. See further Goldstein 1995: 148.

93. Bauckham 1996b: 425–6.

94. L. Alexander (1993: 34–41, 120–3) makes the interesting observation that αὐτόπται ("eyewitnesses"), such as those whose accounts Luke claims to pass on (Lk. 1:2), almost always occur in connection with the verification of pieces of information from or about distant places; hence, αὐτόπται are particularly associated with geographical information.

95. This centrifugal and centripetal movement begins already in Luke's Gospel. Cf. Bauckham 1997a: 185: "As has often been observed, Simeon and Anna [Lk. 2:25–38] form one of the pairs of man and woman of which Luke is fond. But Anna's role complements Simeon's in more respects than this. Simeon, presumably a native of Jerusalem, waiting for the consolation of Israel (2:25), hails the Messiah Jesus as the one who will fulfil Israel's destiny to be a light to the nations (2:31–32). He represents the hope of the centrifugal movement of salvation out from Jerusalem to the Gentiles. Anna, a returnee from the diaspora of the northern tribes, waiting for the redemption of Jerusalem (2:38), recognizes the Messiah Jesus as the one who will fulfil Jerusalem's destiny to be the centre to which all the tribes of Israel are regathered. She represents the hope of the centripetal movement of salvation as the diaspora returns to Zion.

Thus together Simeon and Anna represent these two key aspects of the eschatological salvation predicted in Isaiah 40–66."

96. Cf. Brawley 1987: 34–6, esp. 36: "In the geography of Acts emphasis repeatedly falls on Jerusalem from beginning to end." See also Koet 1996: 128–42. Contrast Loveday Alexander, who finds "a decisive shift from the Jerusalem-centred perspective of the earlier part of Acts" to "a narrative of Mediterranean travel" in the pragmatic periplus tradition (1995b: 17–57, with an appendix containing "Toponyms in the Pauline Travel Narratives [of Acts]" and eight maps). Somewhat similarly, Brown (1997: 284) suggests the possibility that the list in Acts 2:9–11 describes the areas evangelized by missionaries from the Jerusalem church (e.g., the East and Rome), as distinct from areas evangelized from other centers like Antioch (e.g., through the journeys of Paul). See further pp. 68–84.

97. For a different view, see Green 1997: 14–15.

98. Cf. Kartveit 1989: 110–17; Scott 1994: 525–7. See also Clarke 1999: 168: "... Posidonius' universal history may have moved in a circle from Rome, then east, south, west, north, east, and back to Rome..."

99. Cf. Scott 1994: 530–41.

100. Cf. Pokorny 1995: 198–210. The literature is divided on whether to interpret the neuter singular ἐσχάτου as referring particularly to one "end" of the earth (e.g., Rome or Spain) or as referring to all the "ends" of the earth. C. K. Barrett (1994–98: I.80) suggests a compromise interpretation: "The truth probably is that the phrase does refer to Rome, but to Rome not as an end in itself but as representative of the whole world." On the notion, see further Becking 1995: 573–6; Maiburg 1983: 38–53.

101. It is interesting to note that the oldest extant Roman itinerarium (*CIL* 11.3281–4), dating to ca. 7 BCE–47 CE, describes the route from Gades in Spain (traditionally the western extreme of the inhabited world) to Rome. Cf. Fugmann 1998: 6.

102. On the Aeneas legend, see Vasaly 1993: 133–4.

103. Similarly, Strabo (*Geog.* 15.3.2) says that after conquering the Medes, Cyrus and the Persians noticed that their native land was situated somewhat on the edges (ἐπ' ἐσχάτοις που) of the empire and so moved their royal seat to Susa. Cited in Clarke 1999: 213.

104. Cf. Clarke 1999: 111 n. 75.

105. Ellis 1991a: 277–86; 1991b: 123–32.

106. Cf. Tajra 1994: 102–7 (Excursus 2: "'Usque ad ultimum terrae,' Did Paul Visit Spain between his two Roman Captivities?").

107. Cf. Pokorny 1995: 207; Unnik 1973: 386–401; Thornton 1977–78: 374–5; Horst 1983: 20.

108. Cf. L. Alexander 1995b: 40–1; 1995a: 30–1. Alexander argues that in the worldview centered on Jerusalem that we find in the Book of Acts, even the Aegean may have been *terra incognita*. In fact, Alexander argues here that Luke's story has two mental maps, one centered on Jerusalem and one on the Mediterranean. In the first fifteen chapters of Acts the world map of Acts 2 is presupposed. With the crossing of the Bosporus in Acts 16:11, the narrative shifts to a Mediterranean-centered map in which Jerusalem is no longer the center of a circle but the eastern edge of a westerly voyage. As we have argued, however, Jerusalem remains central to Acts from first to last. Moreover, although I have also argued that two images of the world influence the narrative in (Luke-)Acts (see Scott 1994: 522ff.), I do not postulate the same shift in "maps" after Acts 16. For another example of Rome as *terra incognita* to peoples in the east, see Strabo, *Geog.* 17.1.54, where ambassadors of Queen Candace of Ethiopia are said to have asserted that "they did not know who Caesar was or where they should have to go to find him." Cited in Clarke 1999: 220.

109. Cf. Romm 1992; Clarke 1999: 199; Goldenberg 1998: 91ff. Goldenberg has shown that a group of rabbinic sources use the same topos as found in the traditional Greco-Roman

sources (i.e., the pair of toponyms/gentilics "Scythia(n)" and "Ethiopia(n)," the peoples at the northern and southern ends of the inhabited world, as a figure of speech to denote geographic extremes), except that the rabbinic texts substitute for "Ethiopia(n)" the other southern toponymn/gentilic in East Africa, which is even further south, that is, "Barbaria(n)." The same figure of speech, Goldenberg argues, appears in Col. 3:11, with the same sense of racial and geographic extremes. Cf. also Goldenberg 1999: 69.

110. Goldenberg 1998: 97 n. 23; cf. Scott 1995a: 169–73 (esp. 171).
111. See further Cancik 1997: 131–2.
112. Cf. Weinstock 1971: 38–9.
113. Pokorny 1995: 205.
114. Ibid., 208.
115. On the Roman imperial ideology of dominion over the whole inhabited world surrounded by Ocean, see further in Chap. 1.
116. In Chap. 1, we examined a particularly interesting example of this imperial ideology in the first-century epigram of Philip of Thessalonica, which describes an artistic tapestry given as a gift by a queen to the reigning Roman emperor, containing "a perfect copy of the harvest-bearing earth, all the land-encircling ocean girdles, obedient to great Caesar, and the gray sea too" (*AP* 9.778).
117. Controlling the center of a world empire is the key to controlling the whole. Cf. Plutarch, *Alex.* 65.6–8: "It was Calanus, as we are told, who laid before Alexander the famous illustration of government. It was this. He threw down upon the ground a dry and shrivelled hide, and set his foot upon the outer edge of it; the hide was pressed down in one place, but rose up in others. He went all round the hide and showed that this was the result wherever he pressed the edge down, and then at last he stood in the middle of it, and lo! it was all held down firm and still. The similitude was designed to show that Alexander ought to put most constraint upon the middle of his empire and not wander far away from it."
118. Irenaeus, *Haer.* 1.10.2 (Rousseau 1979: 154). Cf. Hengel 1997: 137–8. Later, however, Origen's *Commentary on Matthew* (Klostermann 1933: 76) lists several peoples (Seres, Ariacins, Britons, Germans, Dacians, Sarmatians, Scythians and Ethiopians, especially those "on the other side of the river" [Zeph. 3:10]) to indicate the far reaches of the world where the gospel has not yet fully penetrated. Cited in Goldenberg 1998: 99 n. 27.
119. Mendels 1996: 431–52. To Mendels' collection of Hellenistic heroes who make a circuit we may add the Argonauts (cf. Dräger 1996: 1066–70 [with a map of their route from Lemnos and back again in a counterclockwise circle]; Hunter 1996: 154). If we widen the scope somewhat and consider political examples, we may also add Plutarch, *Caesar* 58.6, which is potentially significant in view of Luke's interest in the proclamation of the kingdom of God: "For he [sc. Caesar] planned and prepared to make an expedition against the Parthians; and after subduing these and marching around the Euxine by way of Hyrcania, the Caspian Sea, and the Caucasus, to invade Scythia; and after overrunning the countries bordering on Germany and Germany itself, to come back by way of Gaul to Italy, and so complete this circuit of his empire (καὶ συνάψαι τὸν κύκλον τοῦτον τῆς ἡγεμονίας), which would then be bounded on all sides by Ocean [i.e., include the whole οἰκουμένη]." If we widen the net still further we may include the whole periplus tradition. For example, the *Periplus of Maris Erythraei* describes two round-trip trade routes originating from ports in Egypt – one sailing to Africa and another to India (cf. Casson 1989). Pomponius Mela's *De chorographia* describes the world in the form of a voyage which begins at the Straits of Gibraltar and circumnavigates the coasts of the three continents (cf. Brodersen 1994b).
120. Mendels 1996: 439; cf. also 1992: 256. We may point out, however, two biblical wanderers whom Mendels does not consider. First, the Book of the Watchers (*1 Enoch* 1–36) depicts Enoch as journeying to the ends of the earth (East [chaps. 28–33], North

[34], West [35], and South [36]), which may be an attempt to explain how he walked with God or the angels (אלהים, Gen. 5:24). See further Himmelfarb 1991: 66–72. Second, and more to the point, the *Genesis Apocryphon* (1QapGen. 11.11) reports Noah as saying that after disembarking from the ark, he "went out and walked through the length and breadth of the earth" (נפקת וחלכת בארעא לאורכהא ולפותיהא). Morgenstern et al. 1995: 46–7. The translation of ארעא as "earth" rather than "land" follows the summary of this passage given in Greenfield and Qimron 1992: 70. According to Weinfeld (1993: 209 n. 54), Abraham established a juridical claim to the promised land by "encircling the land" (1QapGen. 21.15–19) and by "walking about the land" (Gen. 13:17).

121. Mendels 1996: 447 n. 29.
122. On Isa. 66:18–21, see further below. This passage is alluded to in *Ps. Sol.* 17:31, which likewise expects "nations (ἔθνη) to come from the ends of the earth to see his [sc. Messiah's] glory, to bring as gifts (δῶρα) her [sc. Jerusalem's] sons who had been driven out..." Cf. Scott 1995a: 82–3. In *JosAs* 15:7; 19:6, Joseph's bride Aseneth is a prototypical proselyte who is described in terms which make her an allegory of the eschatological Zion, in which all the nations will take refuge with God.
123. Riesner 1994: 213–25, 233, 235–8, *et passim*. See Scott 1995a: 145–7.
124. See further VanderKam 1998b: 10–11, 13–14, 30–2, 33, 53, 54–5, 58, 64, 66, 67–9, 71–2, 75, 77–8; Fitzmyer 1984: 430–7.
125. Cf. Falk 1994: 206: "Perhaps the theological significance of Pentecost for the early Christian community (Acts 2) should be considered as evidence for a link between this festival [i.e., Pentecost] and a new/renewed covenant, but until this hypothesis is placed on a more firm foundation, all that can be said is that an annual covenant renewal ceremony was held in connection with the Feast of Pentecost by the group at Qumran and those who followed the calendar of Jubilees." See further Pfann 1999: 337–52 (esp. 342–5).
126. Cf. VanderKam 1998b: 30; Eiss 1997: 172: "Die Aufforderung an ihn [sc. Moses] in Jub 6,11.20ff., die er auf dem Berg Sinai erhält, kommt einer Bestätigung des Noahbundes gleich, die mit einem eidlichen Geschehen verbunden ist (6,11). Nach Jub 1,1 stieg Mose am 16. Tag des 3. Monats auf den Berg Sinai zum Empfang der Gesetzestafeln. Nach Meinung des Autors müßte der Bundesschluß bzw. die Bundeserneuerung selbst dann am. 15. Tag stattgefunden haben. Die in der Geschichte von Noah bis Mose erkennbare Traditionslinie der Bestätigung und Erneuerung des Bundesgeschehens wird fortgesetzt und in jedem Wochenfest aktualisiert." In interpreting Acts 2, most scholars tend to emphasize the connection of Pentecost with the giving of the law at Sinai. Cf. Harris 1996: 143–59; Turner 1996: 280–9; Weinfeld 1978: 7–18. For the probable scriptural peg which allowed the author of *Jubilees* chronologically to align the festival with both the Noachic and the Sinaitic covenants, see VanderKam 1993: 121–2; 1998b: 30; see also Nodet and Taylor 1998: 385–97. Insofar as Acts 2 reflects the giving of the law at Sinai, it is interesting to note the rabbinic conception that God's voice was heard in seventy languages, so that all the nations might understand the revelation (cf. *b. Shabb.* 88b; *Exod. Rab.* 5:9; 28:6).
127. Cf. Bergler 1998: 143–91.
128. Passover was another pilgrimage festival that was seen in light of the eschatological pilgrimage of the nations to Zion. See below on Jer. 38(31):8.
129. On the Joel citation, see Wall 1998: 443–9; O'Brien 1999: 212.
130. Cf. *b. Soṭah* 36b, which interprets "a tongue I did not know I hear" (Ps. 81:5) to mean that Joseph (possibly symbolic of the entire people of Israel) was supernaturally given the ability to speak all 70 languages of the world. See Kugel 1998: 457–8; 1986: 95–100. According to rabbinic tradition, members of the Sanhedrin must be conversant with all the 70 languages of the nations (cf. *b. Sanh.* 17a,b; *Menaḥ.* 65a). This tradition is already found in the Qumran scrolls. Cf. CD 14.8–10: "And the inspector who is

over all the camps will be between thirty and fifty years of age, mastering every secret of men and every language (ולכל לשון)."

131. C. K. Barrett 1994–98: I.108. See further D. Smith 1996: 183–5.
132. A Qumran fragment (4Q464 frg. 3 i) apparently contains the same connection between the confusion (נבלה) of languages at the tower of Babel (*l.* 5) and the eschatological prophecy about the reversal of the curse of Babel in Zeph. 3:9, expecting God to "make the peoples pure of speech" (*l.* 9). Since *l.* 8 refers to the "holy tongue" (לשון הקודש), the editors of the text plausibly suggest that this is an eschatological prophecy, relating to the reversal of the curse of the tower of Babel, when all the nations will forever speak a pure (i.e., single) language, perhaps Hebrew. Cf. Stone and Eshel 1992: 248–53; also, E. Eshel, 1997: 5–7; Weitzman 1999: 35–45. See also *T. Jud.* 25:3.
133. Cf. Wedderburn 1994: 32 n. 14: "Traditionally much has been made of the symbolism of this event as a reversal of the Tower of Babel...; yet Dupont rightly notes that this account does not describe a reversal to a single, universal language as one might expect if this symbolism were intended. All understand the speakers in their many diverse languages..." In order for us to argue that Acts 2 is alluding to the expected reversal of the confusion at Babel, it is not necessary to assume that the text sees the process as completed at Pentecost. More likely, Acts 2 understands the event as proleptic.
134. Cf. *Jub.* 10:26 ("The Lord sent a wind at the tower and tipped it to the ground"); *Sib. Or.* 3.101–3 ("But immediately the immortal one imposed a great compulsion on the winds. Then the winds cast down the great tower from on high, and stirred up strife for mortals among themselves"); Josephus, *Ant.* 1.118 ("But the gods sent winds against it and overturned the tower and gave to every man a peculiar language"); Epiphanius, *Pan.* 2.11 ("A blast of wind blew the tower over").
135. Cf. Theophilus, *Autol.* 2.31, referring to the Tower of Babel episode: "As for the three sons of Noah and their relationships and their genealogies, we have a brief catalogue in the book previously mentioned [sc. *Autol.* 2.30]. Now, however, we shall mention the remaining facts about cities and kings and about the events which occurred when 'there was one lip and one tongue' [Gen. 11:1]. Before the languages were divided (πρὸ τοῦ τὰς διαλέκτους μερισθῆναι), the previously mentioned cities were in existence. But when they were about to be divided (διαμερίζεσθαι), they took counsel with their own judgment... From that time he [sc. God] diversified the tongues of men, 'giving each a different language' (ἐνήλλαξεν τὰς γλώσσας τῶν ἀνθρώπων, δοὺς ἑκάστῳ διάφορον διάλεκτον) [Gen. 11:7]."
136. Cf. Turner 1996: 267–315 (esp. 297ff.); O'Brien 1999: 210.
137. If the reference to "all those who are afar off" (πᾶσιν τοῖς εἰς μακράν) in Peter's speech (Acts 2:39) includes Diaspora Jews, then there may be a further link to the list of Nations in Acts 2:9–11. See, however, C. K. Barrett 1994–98: I.155–6. In light of the focus in Acts 2:5–11 on the restoration of Israel, it is perhaps necessary to reevaluate the conception of the Land in Luke's two-volume work. For a negative evaluation, see e.g. Strecker 1983: 189–90, 195–6; Allison 1997: 643–4.
138. Cf. Wedderburn 1994: 41.
139. On Jewish pilgrimage festivals, see e.g. Tsafrir 1995: I.369–76.
140. Cf. Bauernfeind 1980: 41: "Das Partizipium κατοικοῦντες vor τὴν Μεσοποταμίαν u[nd] den folgenden Namen steht in einer gewissen – von L[u]k[as] wohl übersehenen – Spannung zu εἰς Ἰερουσαλὴμ κατοικοῦντες v 5, es soll plusquam-perfektisch Personen bezeichnen, die früher in Mesopotamien usw. angesiedelt waren; die Wahl des Wortes erklärt man damit, daß für den ersten dieser Namen die Wortbil-dung Μεσοποταμῖται umgangen werden soll."
141. Cf. Wedderburn 1994: 40. For a different solution, see D. Schwartz 1992: 126: "In other words, we would suggest that an earlier version of this story told of Galileans (the apostles) who astounded the residents of Jerusalem, who came from diverse parts of Judaea, by their ability to speak in the various dialects or accents of Palestinian

Aramaic (2:5a[–b? see below], 6–8, 13ff.). Later, however, the addition of 2:5b – or more probably, the transformation of something like 'devout people from all over the land' to 'devout people from all nations under heaven' – and vv. 9–11(12), perhaps due to a desire to foreshadow the Gentile mission, turned the account into one which portrays Gentile presence as well – not without leaving traces of the earlier account."

142. Cf., e.g, Fitzmyer 1993: 29: "If some of the Roman sojourners in Jerusalem were among the three thousand Jews converted to Christianity according to the Lucan account (Acts 2:10–11, 41), they may have formed the nucleus of the Christian community in Rome on their return there. Thus the Roman Christian community would have had its matrix in the Jewish community, possibly as early as the 30s, and thus was made up at first of Jewish Christians and God-fearing Gentiles (or even of *proselytoi*, Acts 2:11, also mentioned in Roman Jewish funerary inscriptions), who had associated themselves with Jews of Rome." See also Bauckham 1996b: 426: ". . . Luke provides us, in his portrayal of the first preaching of the gospel in Jerusalem to the crowd drawn from all nations under heaven (Acts 2:5–11), with a programmatic account of the earliest missionary strategy of the Jerusalem church."

143. Cf. Deut. 2:25; 4:19; 9:14; 29:19; Eccl. 1:3; 3:1; Bar. 5:3; Lk. 17:24; Acts 4:12; Col. 1:23. Note that already in the "Sargon Geography," which probably dates to the Neo-Assyrian period, Sargon is described as "the king of the universe, when he conquered the totality of the land under heaven." The text includes a lengthy list of the places and peoples that Sargon had conquered. Cf. Horowitz 1998: 67–95.

144. The MT reads differently: "the dread and fear of you upon the peoples everywhere under heaven (תחת כל השמים)."

145. Unlike the LXX, the MT has "all" (כל) before "the heaven" (השמים).

146. For another passage that refers to the Jewish Diaspora as scattered under heaven, cf. Zech. 2:10–11: "Flee from the land of the north, says the Lord; therefore, I will gather you from the four winds of heaven. Return safe to Zion, you who dwell [with] daughters of Babylon." See further Rabinowitz 1971: 1373–5; Scott 1997c.

147. See further Merrill 1988: 261–72. According to Isa. 43:5–6, the sons and daughters of God would be regathered "from the ends of the earth" (ἀπ᾽ ἄκρων τῆς γῆς).

148. Whether Luke has a concept of the restoration of Israel is a contentious point in the modern discussion of Acts. For the view that Luke has such a concept, see e.g. Jervell 1972: 41–74; 1996b: 16, 23, 29, 35–6, 39–40, 44, 46–7, 58, 64, 72, 78, 91, 92, 97, 110–11; 1996a: 104–26; Tiede 1986: 278–86; Turner 1996: 306–15, 418–27; Ravens 1995; Seccombe 1998: 349–72 (esp. 351); Turner 1996: 346–7. For the opposite view, see Räisänen 1991: 94–114; P. Walker 1996: 94–102. Bauckham (1997a: 185 n. 77) presents a mediating view: "Perhaps the fact that Luke does not express the content of Anna's praise of God (2:38), as he does Simeon's (2:28–32), is connected with the fact that, although there are allusions later in his work to the hope of the regathering of all the tribes of Israel (Luke 22:30; Acts 26:7) and there are pilgrims from the diaspora of the northern tribes present at Pentecost (Acts 2:9), this theme does not feature in the rest of Luke's work in the way that the subject-matter of Simeon's song [i.e., the nations] does." Note, however, that Bauckham attributes far greater significance to the theme of restoration in his forthcoming essay, "The Restoration of Israel in Luke-Acts," in J. M. Scott (ed.), *Restoration: Old Testament, Jewish, and Christian Conceptions* (JSJSup 113; Leiden: Brill).

149. Cf. Bauckham 1996b: 426, 480.

150. Most scholars date Luke-Acts after the fall of Jerusalem to ca. 80–90 CE (e.g., Fitzmyer 1981–85: I.53–7; Esler 1987: 27–9). However, some scholars argue for a date in the 60s (e.g., Hemer 1989: 365–410; Moessner 1989: 308–15). If Luke ends his book of Acts without describing the outcome of Paul's trial in Rome because the trial has not yet taken place, then Acts must be dated about 63 CE, its preceding companion volume, the Gospel of Luke, somewhat earlier. The centrality that Luke attributes to Jerusalem may well support a pre-70 dating of the two-volume work. Furthermore,

the very fact that Paul's letters appear to be unknown in Acts may be evidence for its relatively early date.

151. Ever since the exile, Israel had expected the eschatological ingathering of the dispersed remnant of the people of God to Jerusalem (cf., e.g., Mic. 2:12–13; 4:6–8; Zeph. 3:14–20). Often this ingathering of the remnant was connected with the concept of a meeting in Jerusalem which would include the whole world, whereby the nations would also confess YHWH as their Lord and would make a pilgrimage to Zion (cf. Isa. 60:1–14; Mic. 4:1–5; Isa. 2:1–5).

152. Tiede 1986: 286.

153. See also Jeremias 1969: 62–71, who gives historical evidence that visitors came to Jerusalem from all over the then-known world.

154. However, the use of the participles κατοικοῦντες and ἐπιδημοῦντες, belonging to the same semantic field, creates asymmetry in the list, since they occur at different positions relative to the ends and in different syntactical relationships to the names.

155. By the time of Claudius Ptolemaeus (fl. 146–70 CE), the Arabian peninsula had been divided into Arabia Felix in the south and Arabia Deserta. Therefore, it is difficult to ascertain exactly what Luke (or his source) meant by this toponym. On Arabia, see further Bowersock 1983; Millar 1993b: 387–436; Hengel and Schwemer 1997: 106–26.

156. Alternatively, the appositives may modify all of the preceding names in vv. 9–11, especially if, as some scholars suggest, the last two names in the list (i.e., Cretes and Arabs) were inserted secondarily. However, given the aforementioned 3–9–3 structure of the list, this suggestion is unlikely. On proselytes in Acts, see now Levinskaya 1996.

157. Unlike the first four members of Luke's list, which were part of the Parthian Empire during the first century CE, the other members of the list lay west of the Euphrates and were therefore part of the Roman Empire. The latter includes, besides Rome itself, both Roman provinces and other constituent territories: (1) Judea became a Roman procuratorial province in 6 CE; (2) Cappadocia was a procuratorial province from 17 to 72 CE; (3) Pontus was not a province in its own right, but parts of the old Pontic kingdom came into the Roman provincial regime in the early empire to form the northeastern districts of Galatia (Pontus Galaticus and Pontus Polemoniacus); (4) Asia became a Roman province in 133 BCE; (5) Phrygia was not a Roman province, but rather a large and ill-defined geographical region which stretched across much of west central Anatolia; (6) Pamphylia was not a Roman province, but was part of the Roman province of Asia from its creation, and in 80 BCE it was attached to Cilicia before reverting to Asia in the 40s, and then being assigned to Galatia from 25 BCE; (7) Egypt became a Roman province in 30 BCE; (8) Libya was not a Roman province, but Cyrene was annexed as a Roman province sometime around 75/4 BCE; (9) Crete became a Roman province, united with Cyrene, in the time of Augustus; (10) Arabia was a territory consisting of several parts (see above), which became a Roman province in 105 CE.

158. It is difficult to think of any reason why Judea and Cappadocia would be linked. In Jewish tradition we hear of the friendship between Abraham and the ancestors of the Pergamenes (Josephus, *Ant.* 14.255) and of the alleged kinship between Jews and Spartans (*Ant.* 12.226–7; 1 Macc. 12:20; cf. Gruen 1996: 254–69), but never, to my knowledge, of a special relationship between Jews and Cappadocians.

159. Cf. Metzger 1994: 253–4. There is sparse patristic evidence for reading "Armenia," "Syria," or "India."

160. Dibelius 1968: 82.

161. So C. K. Barrett 1994–98: I.121, 123.

162. Bauckham 1996b: 419. See ibid., 420, for "the Jewish Diaspora according to Acts 2:9–11 on a map of the world according to Strabo."

163. Bauckham 1996b: 419, followed by L. Alexander 1995a: 30. See also Legrand 1995: 29: "Judea occupies its rightful position as the centre of the entire perspective as it does in the letter of Agrippa and, in general, in the Jewish conception of the world."

164. The same applies to the similar suggestion by Stegner (1979: 206–14), who perceives in the list a convoluted pattern of correspondences based on the opposition of the four points of the compass. If, however, as we shall consider below, the list is influenced in part by Isa. 11:11–12, then it is interesting to note that Isa. 11:12 refers to the ingathering of the dispersed of Israel and Judah "from the four ends of the earth" (ἐκ τῶν τεσσάρων πτερύγων τῆς γῆς). On the four cardinal points, see also Isa. 43:5–6; Ps. 72(71):10; *1 Enoch* 28–36 (East [28–33], North [34], West [35], and South [36]); 4QAstronomical Enoch[b] (4Q209) frag. 23.1–9 (= *1 Enoch* 76:13–77:4; note that 77:1–4 explains the meaning of the cardinal points); 4QAstronomical Enoch[c] (4Q210) frag. 1 ii:1–17 (= *1 Enoch* 76:3–10); Jarick 1997: 270–87; Podossinov 1991: 233–86; 1993: 33–43; N. Lewis 1989: 14, 45; Muchowski 1994: 319–27.

165. Bauckham's geographical analysis ignores this essential grammatical point. If Luke had meant for ᾿Ιουδαίαν to stand alone in the center or to culminate a series running from east to west, he would have constructed the list differently. For the use of τε καί in Luke-Acts, see, e.g., Lk. 22:66; Acts 4:27; 5:14; 8:12; 9:2, 15; 14:1, 5; 15:32; 19:10, 17; 20:21; 22:4; 26:20. See further Elliott 1990: 202–4; Levinsohn 1987: 121–36.

166. In a personal communication, R. Bauckham agrees with my observation, explaining the grammatical structure of Acts 2:9–11 as putting emphasis on Mesopotamia and Rome as the most important centers of the Diaspora in east and west. However, he makes a distinction between the geographical order of the list and its grammatical structure.

167. Cf. Dupont 1979: 56: "This list obviously does not pretend to be exhaustive, for we know that the peoples of the earth, according to the Jewish theory based on Genesis 10, are seventy in number (and that is the reason the rabbis imagined that God's voice divided on Sinai into seventy voices)." Tertullian (*Adv. Jud.* 7.4, 7–9) adduces an expanded and somewhat modified citation of Acts 2:9–11 to show that all nations have believed in Christ.

168. On the worldwide Diaspora, see, e.g., Deut. 30:4–5; Neh. 1:8–9; *Sib. Or.* 3.271; *Ps. Sol* 9:2; Josephus, *JW* 2.398; 7.43. It is unnecessary here to detail the extent of the Jewish Diaspora. For a cartographic survey, see Bloedhorn, et al. 1992. For a geographic survey, see Schürer 1973–87: 3/1.1–86; Trebilco 1997: 287–91.

169. As we have seen, L. Alexander has another explanation for the allegedly restricted scope of the "mental map" presupposed in Acts 2:9–11.

170. So Wedderburn 1994: 44; Dupont 1979: 57.

171. Dupont (1979: 57) suggests that "it was useful to include a few out of the way and unimportant nations, to show that even they were represented in Jerusalem." According to Legrand (1995: 38–41), the list of nations in Acts 2:9[-11?] describes the missionary territory apportioned to Peter during the Apostolic Council (Gal. 2:9). Although Phrygia and Pamphylia (Acts 2:10) are connected with the Pauline ministry in Acts, Legrand argues that these belong to the so-called First Missionary Journey, prior to the Jerusalem accord. We may comment, however, that there is nothing in Luke's *pars pro toto* list of nations to suggest that its scope is restricted particularly to the Petrine mission. The correspondences which Legrand (ibid., 42–4) finds between Luke's list and 1 Pet. 1:1 (i.e., Babylon?/Mesopotamia, Cappadocia, Pontus, Asia) do not strengthen the case. On Gal. 2:9, see further Scott 1995a: 151–7.

172. Cf. Conzelmann 1972: 31; L. Johnson 1992: 43.

173. Cf. Schmitt 1991: 49–50 (§6 = col. I.12–17): "Proclaims Darius, the king: These (are) the countries which fell to my lot; by the favour of Auramazda I was their king: Persia, Elam, Babylonia, Assyria, Arabia, Egypt, (the people) who (dwell) by the Sea, Lydia, Ionia, Media, Armenia, Cappadocia, Parthia, Drangiana, Aria, Chorasmia, Bactria,

Sogdiana, Gandara, Scythia, Sattagydia, Arachosia, (and) Maka, all round twenty-three countries." See further Herzfeld and Walser 1968: 288–97, 357–9; E. Schmidt 1970: III.108–11, 145–63.
174. Cf. Groneberg 1992.
175. Cf. Gropp 1985.
176. Cf. Seibert 1985; 1984.
177. Cf. Orth 1992.
178. Cf. Waldmann 1983.
179. Cf. Waldmann 1985.
180. Cf. J. Wagner 1983.
181. Cf. Pill-Rademaher, et al. 1988.
182. Cf. Hackstein 1991: 217–27. Similarly, Clarke 1999: 205–6.
183. Cf. Cook 1983: 42–3: "...the Greeks generally continued to know the great power in Asia as the Medes... And it is not only the Greeks; Jews, Egyptians (who also used the word Mede as a term of abuse) and even Minaeans from southern Arabia continued almost indefinitely to speak of the Medes and not of the Persians." See, however, Tuplin 1994: 235–56; 1996: 140–1, who argues that for most of the classical period everyone knew that the Achaemenid Empire was a Persian one and spoke of it as such; "Mede" was not used interchangably with "Persian" but was the ossification of what was already strictly a terminological inexactitude, which was largely reserved for contexts in which the focus of thought was on the collective mass of an oriental power threatening the Hellenic world.
184. Cf. Clarke 1999: 109, 226–7.
185. For a full discussion of this matter, see Milikowsky 1997: 265–95.
186. For further parallels to Acts 2:9–11, see Horst 1985: 53–4; Görg 1976: 15–18.
187. Although Paulus writes in the second half of the 4th cent. CE, he evidently draws from ancient traditions. Thus W. Gundel (1949b: 2382) writes: "Der Wert der Eisagogika [= Elementa Apotelesmatica] besteht vornehmlich darin, daß P[aulus] sehr alte Quellen ausschöpft, die uns einen Einblick in die älteste Systematik der hieratischen und der vulgären Astrologie gewähren. So ist der geographische Gesichtskreis seiner zodiakalen Länder ein sehr kleiner. Die Verteilung von etwas mehr als zwölf Ländern an die einzelnen Zodiakalgötter weist auf Ägypten als Zentrum der Oikumene hin und wird mit guten Gründen auf die Zeit von Alexander dem Großen zurückgeführt..." Ernst Weidner (1963: 117) suggests that Paulus' list stems from a time when Persia was at the height of its power.
188. Lüdemann 1987: 46–7, following Weinstock 1948: 43–6. Cf. also Güting 1975: 151; Brinkman 1963: 418–27.
189. Note the astronomical thrust of Deut. 4:19 (cited above).
190. We may also note that Acts 17:28 cites Aratus' Phaenomena, which is a work on constellations.
191. For further critique of the use of Paulus as the background for Acts 2:9–11, see Metzger 1980: 46–56; Barrett 1994–98: I.121–2; Schneider 1980: I.254–5; Wedderburn 1994: 45–7.
192. Table 3 compares Acts 2:9–11 to Paulus Alexandrinus, Elementa Apotelesmatica 1.2 (ed. E. Boer); Manilius, Astronomica 4.741–805 (ed. G. P. Goold); Dorotheus Sidonius, Carmen Astrologicum 427–8 (ed. D. Pingree); Claudius Ptolemaeus, Tetrabiblos 2.3 (ed. F. Boll and E. Boer); and Hermes Trismegistos (W. Gundel 1969: 312). The one exception to the rule is the Latin list of Hermes Trismegistos, which does include several names of peoples at the beginning. Claudius Ptolemy's list comes the closest to Luke's list in terms of content, perhaps because it is also the longest list (see Table 2); even Judea is included. In fact, Ptolemy (Tetrabiblos 2.3) lists Judea among other countries (i.e., Idumea, Coele Syria, Phoenicia, Chaldea, Orchinia, and Arabia Felix) which are "situated about the center of the whole inhabited world" (περὶ τὸ μέσον ἐσχηματισμένα τῆς ὅλης οἰκουμένης). See also Tetrabiblos

2.4, where Judea is listed among "nations" which are "about the center" (περὶ τὸ μέσον). Ptolemy's astrological ethnography depends on the Stoic Posidonius. Cf. Boll 1894: 181–235. On astrological geography, see further Bouché-Leclercq 1963: 327–47; Barton 1994a: 179–85; 1994b: 119–21; H. Gundel 1972: 573–5; Weidner 1963: 117–21; Richer 1994. It is also interesting to note that Dan. 8:2–6 may contain traces of ancient astrological geography insofar as the ram stands for Persia and the male goat for Syria. Cf. Hengel 1988: 168 n. 256.

193. See Table 2; also W. Gundel 1969: 244, 312, 379–83.
194. C. K. Barrett 1994–98: I.122, citing Josephus, *Ap.* 2.282; *JW* 2.398; 7:43; *Ant.* 14.114–18; *Sib. Or.* 3.271; Philo, *Flacc.* 45–6.
195. Cf. Scott 1994: 495–9. See, however, Bauckham 1996b: 418–19.
196. The OT contains many passages about the worldwide Jewish Diaspora and some of them contain a *pars pro toto* list of the nations to which the Jews have been scattered in the world (e.g., Isa. 11:10–12; 66:18–20; see further below).
197. Cf. Bauckham 1997a: 166–70 *et passim*.
198. Cf. Younger 1998: 215, 222–3.
199. For further parallels between Luke 1–2 and Acts 2, see Ravens 1995: 27.
200. Goulder 1964: 158. A similar interpretation is found in Holzmann 1892: 330: "Die 16 Völkerschaften erinnern übrigens an die 16 Enkel Noahs Gen. 10,1.2.6.21.22." See also Güting 1975: 154–5; Kilpatrick 1975: 48–9, who argues that the list is drawn up from the point of view of Rome, thus eliminating the difficulty about Judea.
201. Wedderburn (1994: 47) calls Goulder's suggestion "a *tour de force* of ingenuity." It seems forced, for example, to squeeze the first 13 names of Luke's list into the 16 grandsons of Noah. Furthermore, these 13 names describe a rather convoluted route to Rome, skipping, for example, from Asia Minor to Africa before jumping to the imperial capital. Finally, there is no textual warrant for excluding Crete and Arabia from the original list.
202. Scott 1994: 527–30. For a critique of this view, see Bauckham 1996b: 419 n. 9.
203. See, for example, the aforementioned influence of Isa. 49:6 in Lk. 2:36; Acts 1:8; 13:47.
204. Cf. Bauernfeind 1980: 41: "... L[u]k[as] wird eine Reihe genannt haben, die ihm aus anderen Anlässen (Schule? Verzeichnis von Ländern blühenden synagogalen Lebens? oder christlicher Gemeinden?) geläufig war."
205. See further in Chap. 2.
206. Jones 1995a. See further in Chap. 4.
207. Bauer and Helm 1955: 10–43. See further in Chap. 6.
208. There are obviously tensions and inconsistencies in the *Diamerismos*, some of which can be explained by the fact that the *Diamerismos* is really a compilation and reworking of several different sources. Cf., e.g., Bauer and Helm 1955: 34 n. 2, 40 n. 1, 41 n. 4, 42 n. 14. See further in Chap. 6.
209. Parthians do not appear in Josephus' exposition of the Table of Nations (*Ant.* 1.122–47).
210. Cf., similarly, Josephus, *Ant.* 1.124.
211. Additional evidence for the dependence of the *Diamerismos* on *Jubilees* 8–9 will be discussed in Chap. 6.
212. Note that Josephus regards Elam as the progenitor of the Persians (*Ant.* 1.143).
213. Cf. Piilonen 1974.
214. Note that in Acts 2:11 Ἰουδαῖοι is in apposition to Ῥωμαῖοι.
215. Josephus (*Ant.* 1.125) identifies Meshech son of Japheth (Gen. 10:2; 1 Chr. 1:5) with the Cappadocians. Ps.-Philo, *LAB* 4.7 lists *Cappadoces* among the descendants of Ham. The *Diamerismos* lists a number of Hamite countries in Asia Minor (§§151–2), but Cappadocia is not one of them.
216. The notion that Ham owns territory in Asia Minor may reflect an Egyptian provenance for the material in Hippolytus, or it may be an attempt to deal with the difficult

expression "Afreg" (= Africa?) which is included in the description of Japheth's territory in *Jub.* 8:27. On the interpretative problem, see Wintermute 1983–85: II.74 n. *x*; VanderKam 1989a: II.55 n.

217. Cf. P. S. Alexander 1982: 208, 209.
218. For the translation, see Barrett 1994–98: I.123, who compares Josephus, *Ant.* 16.160 (ἡ πρὸς Κυρήνῃ Λιβύη) and Dio Cassius 53.12.
219. For the identification of the Romans with the Kittim in the *Diamerismos*, see further in Chap. 6.
220. Josephus (*Ant.* 1.128) identifies Kittim with Cyprus. The Romans are not mentioned in his exposition of the Table of Nations (*Ant.* 1.120–47).
221. Josephus (*Ant.* 1.137) does not realize that biblical Caphtor is Crete.
222. The Arabs do not appear in Josephus' exposition of the Table of Nations. See further Millar 1993a: 23–45.
223. Here is a summary of the identifications in the *Diamerismos*:

Acts 2:9–11	Diamerismos
Parthians	Shem
Medes	Japheth *and* Shem
Elamites	Shem
Mesopotamia	Shem
Judea	[Shem]
Cappadocia	Japheth
Pontus	[Japheth?]
Asia	Japheth
Phrygia	Ham
Pamphylia	Ham
Egypt	Ham
Cyrene	Ham
Romans	Japheth
Cretans	Ham
Arabs	Shem

224. Once again, the presence of 'Ιουδαίαν disturbs the list. Perhaps the original list had a Japhethite nation here?
225. The application of the *Diamerismos*' identifications to Luke's list is done here merely for heuristic purposes. We need not assume that Luke had exactly this arrangement in mind as he composed the list. The mixture would be somewhat different if the identifications were changed, but there would still be a mixture of nations from each of the sons of Noah.
226. "(18) I am coming to gather all nations and tongues; and they will come and see my glory. (19) And I will set a sign among them, and from them I will send those who have been saved to the nations – to Tarsis, Phoud, Loud, Mosoch, and Thobel, and to Greece, and to the distant islands – who have neither heard my name nor seen my glory. And they will declare my glory among the nations. (20) And they will bring your brothers from all the nations as a gift to the Lord . . . to my holy city Jerusalem, says the Lord . . ." See Scott 1995a: 12–14.
227. Shem is represented by Lud; Ham, by Put; and Japheth, by Tarshish, Tubal, Meshech, and Javan.
228. Cf., e.g., Maiburg 1983: 47: "Irenaeus [*Haer.* 1.10.2] zählt nicht beliebige Provinzen und Völker auf, sondern beschreibt, beginnend mit seiner näheren, ihm bekannten Umgebung [Kelten], in west-östlicher Richtung fortschreitend, (halb)kreisförmig die äußersten Punkte der Oikumene, bis zu denen Christen schon vorgedrungen sind."

Note also that although Strabo's order of presentation in his *Geography* follows the general principle of movement from west to east, his professed privileging of the civilized Mediterranean may explain why he sometimes deviates from a strictly geographical sequence by discussing one place before another. Cf. Clarke 1999: 214–15.

229. Cf. Bauernfeind 1980: 41: "... es kam ja nur auf die Fülle und Buntheit der Namen an ..." For example, Epiphanius, *De Mensuris et Ponderibus*, embellishes the *Letter of Aristeas* (i.e., the Alexandrian Jewish story of the making of the Greek translation of the Torah for the library of Ptolemy II Philadelphus, at the instigation of his librarian, Demetrius of Phalerum). After a lengthy citation from the *Letter of Aristeas*, which gives a list of the names of the 72 translators of the Septuagint, 6 from each of the 12 tribes of Israel, Epiphanius continues with a statement by Demetrius that is designed to provoke the king to acquire more volumes for the library, which already has "books from all over the world" (τὰς πανταχοῦ γῆς βίβλους): "We hear that there are still many more [books] in the world (ἐν τῷ κόσμῳ) among the Ethiopians and the Indians, the Persians and Elamites and Babylonians, the Assyrians and Chaldeans, and among Romans and Phoenicians, the Syrians and the Romans in Greece ... But also among those in Jerusalem and in Judea (παρά τε Αἰθίόψι καὶ Ἰνδοῖς, Πέρσαις τε καὶ Ἐλαμίταις καὶ Βαβυλωνίοις, Ἀσσυρίοις τε καὶ Χαλδαίοις, παρὰ Ῥωμαίοις τε καὶ Φοίνιξι, Σύροις τε καὶ τοῖς ἐν τῇ Ἑλλάδι Ῥωμαίοις ... Ἀλλὰ καὶ παρά τοῖς ἐν Ἱεροσολύμοις τε καὶ ἐν τῇ Ἰουδαίᾳ) ..." (Moutsoula 1973: 168–9, lines 270–5; for the Syriac version, see Dean 1935: 25 [§52c]). A reason for the choice and arrangement of these nations is difficult to perceive. Sidney Jellicoe (1978: 45) argues that the novel idea that the 72 translators worked in pairs derives from Lk. 10:1ff., which in turn was influenced by the Aristean account of the origin of the Septuagint itself. If that is correct, then perhaps Epiphanius' list of nations is dependent on Acts 2:9–11. Note that the two lists have two names in common (the Elamites and the Romans). There is also a structural and grammatical similarity between the two lists.

230. Kilpatrick (1975: 49) suggests that the combination of Cretans and Arabs in Luke's list is due to Ezek. 30:5 in the Lucianic manuscripts of the Septuagint ("Persians and Cretans and Lydians and Libyans and all Arabia").

231. Cf. Ziegler 1975: 86–7. See further Hollerich 1999.

232. P. S. Alexander 1992: 983. Cf. Uehlinger 1990: 264–6; Schnabel 1997: 754; Davids 1997: 1178; O'Brien 1999: 212.

233. Cf. Kronholm 1978: 212–14.

234. As we have seen, Tertullian (*Adv. Jud.* 7.4, 7–9) adduces an expanded and somewhat modified citation of Acts 2:9–11 to show that all nations have believed in Christ. On Acts 2:5 as an anticipation of the worldwide mission to follow, see also O'Brien 1999: 211.

235. Cf. Jervell 1972: 58–60; Turner 1996: 308–12.

236. Cf. Gen. 18:18 (καὶ ἐνευλογηθήσονται ἐν αὐτῷ πάντα τὰ ἔθνη τῆς γῆς); 22:18 (καὶ ἐνευλογηθήσονται ἐν τῷ σπέρματί σου πάντα τὰ ἔθνη τῆς γῆς); 26:4 (καὶ ἐνευλογηθήσονται ἐν τῷ σπέρματί σου πάντα τὰ ἔθνη τῆς γῆς); 28:14 (καὶ ἐνευλογηθήσονται ἐν σοὶ πᾶσαι αἱ φυλαὶ τῆς γῆς καὶ ἐν τῷ σπέρματί σου).

237. Luke substitutes the broader term αἱ πατριαί to signal that πᾶσαι αἱ πατριαὶ τῆς γῆς denotes both the Jewish nation and the other nations of the world.

238. Assuming, of course, that Acts 15 and Gal. 2:1–10 describe the same meeting.

239. Bockmuehl 1995: 93.

240. Daniel R. Schwartz (1996: 278) suggests that "Luke took over the *Fragestellung* of the Izates story [Josephus, *Ant.* 20.34–48], although it was somewhat inappropriate for his own context." We must question, however, whether Luke already knew the works of Josephus (cf. Hengel and Schwemer 1997: 9).

241. Cf. Horn 1996: 479–505.

242. James restates Peter's position in other words: "Simeon has related how God first looked favorably on the Gentiles, to take from among them a people for his name." Does this mean that in addition to Israel God has established a people in his name? If so, how are the new people to be regarded in relation to Israel? James goes on to give an answer.

243. On the complex textual problem presented by Acts 15:20, 29; 21:25, see Strange 1992: 87–105; Head 1993: 438–42. Most likely, the original text contained merely the four prohibitions, without the Golden Rule.

244. For further intepretive options, see C. K. Barrett 1994–98: II.725–6.

245. Cf. Chilton and Neusner 1995: 104–8. Similarly, Robert Wall (1998: 450) sees the tent of David as referring to the restoration of the Davidic/messianic kingdom (cf. Acts 1:6).

246. Jervell 1972: 52–3. Cf., with modifications, Turner 1996: 312–15. Note that according to Amos 9:7 (just a few verses prior to the citation of Amos 9:11–12!), nations such as the Philistines and the Arameans receive the same kind of redemption that Israel received at the time of the exodus from Egypt.

247. Cf. Bauckham 1996b: 453–4; 1996a: 158–64. On the other OT texts that are part of the combined citation (Hos. 3:5; Jer. 12:15–16; Isa. 45:21), see ibid., 454–8. See further Nägele 1995: 71–107; Ådna 1997: 1–23. Note, however, that although Acts 15:15 introduces the citation as "the words of the prophets" (οἱ λόγοι τῶν προφητῶν), C. K. Barrett (1994–98: II.725) argues that only Amos 9:11–12 is quoted: "the slight verbal echoes of Jer. 12.15; Isa. 45.21 can hardly count as prophetic sayings that agree or disagree with anything."

248. Similar options confront us in the interpretation of "tent of Zion" (אהל ציון) in 4Q372 1:13, which seems to refer to the Jerusalem Temple. Cf. Schuller 1989–90: 361.

249. Scholars sometimes consider this possibility before opting for a metaphorical interpretation. Cf. Nägele 1995: 90–5; Ådna 1997: 21–2; Bauckham 1996a: 164.

250. Cf., e.g., *T. Ben.* 9:2: "But the Temple of God will be in your portion, and the last will be more glorious than the first; and there the twelve tribes and all the nations will be gathered together (καὶ δώδεκα φυλαὶ ἐκεῖ συναχθήσονται καὶ πάντα τὰ ἔθνη), until the Most High will send forth his salvation in the visitation of an only-begotten prophet." Note that συνάγειν is used of Israel's return from exile in connection with the gathering of the nations in Jerusalem (cf., e.g., Isa. 66:18; Jer. 3:17–18; Tob. 13:15; 14:6). See further Wilken 1993: 1–19.

251. Cf. Ps. 96:7–8; Isa. 2:2–3; 25:6; 66:23; Jer. 3:17; Mic. 4:1–2; Zech. 14:16.

252. Cf. Isa. 56:8: "Thus says the Lord God, who gathers the outcasts of Israel, 'I will gather others to them besides those already gathered.'" Note the Targum's reading of the same verse (with departures from MT given in italics): "Thus says the Lord God who *is about to* gather the outcasts of Israel, 'Yet will I *bring near their exiles, to gather them.*'" Cf. Sperber 1959–73: III.112–13; Chilton 1987: 109. See further Evans 1997: 299–328.

253. Cf. Koenen 1990: 28–9.

254. Westermann 1986: 338. However, this would be an extraordinary idea, unparalleled anywhere else in Jewish literature. The very word Levites specifies tribal descent. Perhaps, then, the text envisions the priests and Levites as being taken from among "your brothers" (v. 20) whom the nations bring to Jerusalem.

255. Cf., e.g., Chilton 1997: 1164–5.

256. After the destruction of the Temple in 70 CE, it is improbable that the early church would have invented a saying about the Temple as the place of prayer for all nations. Indeed, despite the embarrassment that the saying went unfulfilled, the church evidently preserved an authentic logion at this point. Cf. Evans 1995a: 362 n. 49.

257. Ådna 1993. This is not the place to review other major proposals for the interpretation of Jesus' Temple action. See merely Sanders 1985: 61–76; Evans 1995b: 319–44;

1995a: 345–65. Ådna's dissertation also includes a complete and competent survey of the secondary literature (1993: 3–18 *et passim*).

258. Cf. also Neusner 1989: 81–4.

259. Cf. Lk. 24:53: "... and they were continually in the temple blessing God"; Acts 3:1: "Peter and John were going up to the temple at the hour of prayer, at three o'clock in the afternoon"; 22:17: "After I [sc. Paul] had returned to Jerusalem and while I was praying in the Temple..." See further Acts 5:12, 42; 21:26. According to the summary in Acts 2:41–7, the disciples spent much time together in the Temple day by day (v. 46), and their devotion to "the prayers" (v. 42) may refer above all to Temple prayer. See further Falk 1995: 267–301 (esp. 269–76); Bachmann 1980: 332–69. If, as Acts 9:32–5 reports, "all the residents of Lydda" were brought to faith, and if, as Josephus (*JW* 2.515) states, the whole population of Lydda went to Jerusalem for the Feast of Tabernacles before the outbreak of the war in 66 CE, then we have additional evidence that worship at the Temple remained important to early Christians, even those outside the land.

260. Cf. Hengel 1981: 240: "... the Temple on Mount Zion had not yet lost all its functions; instead of being a place of sacrifice it was a 'house of prayer for all nations'; as one might say, it had become the universal centre of all synagogues." See also Hengel 1995a: 42: "... for the primitive community in Jerusalem the Temple had changed from being a place of sacrifice to a place of prayer." On the Temple as a place of prayer, see now Betz 1997: 467ff. If Paul is said to have gone to the Temple to fulfill a Nazarite vow (Acts 21:23–6), that could be an exception that proves the rule.

261. On the Temple as a place of James' activity, see also Ps.-Clem. *Rec.* 1.66.2ff. The Temple was also the place where James is said to have been martyred. For an overview of the Christian sources on this, see Lüdemann 1983: 231–3; Hengel 1985: 75–9; Evans 1999: 233–49. According to Acts 21:17–26, however, it was James who also asked Paul to demonstrate his continuing devotion to the Temple by an act of sacrificial piety, in order to counter the rumor that Paul was disloyal to the Law. Matt. 5:23–4 also possibly shows that Jewish Christians continued to offer sacrifices in the Temple.

262. Cf. Falk 1995: 285–92.

263. See also Schiffman 1999: 564, referring to the liturgical texts from the Qumran corpus which present morning and late afternoon prayers on the analogy of the daily sacrifices in the Temple: "Yet someone collected these texts, and it seems most likely that they were recited daily at Qumran. If so, we can see prayer already replacing Temple worship, even before the destruction of the Temple in 70 CE. To put it another way, sectarian groups may have experienced the destruction of the Temple before the rest of Israel. To them an illegitimate shrine was the same as a non-existent shrine. Their solution, the replacement of sacrifice with prayer, would become that of all Israel in the aftermath of the Great Revolt (66–73 CE), when Rabbinic Judaism made synagogue liturgy and individual prayer the norm..."

264. Cf. Wehnert 1997: 213–38; Bauckham 1996b: 460–1; 1996a: 172–8; Jervell 1995: 227–43. For a critique of the common understanding, see Wedderburn 1993: 362–89; C. K. Barrett 1994–98: II.734. The Holiness Code includes legislation pertaining to the resident alien (LXX: προσήλυτος!) on sacrificing to idols (Lev. 17:8–9; 20:2–5), eating animal blood (17:10–16), and illicit sexual relations (Leviticus 18). See further Joosten 1996: 54–79.

265. But see C. K. Barrett 1994–98: II.737.

266. Thus, εἰδωλόθυτα (cf. Lev. 17:8–9); αἷμα (cf. Lev. 17:10–12); πνικτά (cf. Lev. 17:13); πορνεία (cf. Lev. 18:26, referring back to vv. 6–23).

267. As James Lindenberger kindly reminded me in a private communication, OT scholars commonly interpret the Apostolic Decree in light of Genesis 9.

268. Millard 1995: 71–90. Cf., similarly, Böcher 1989: 327–8; Segal 1990: 195, 197; 1995: 7–27. Nanos (1996: 53) represents a mediating position: "We thus have in the apostolic decree a snapshot of a stage in the historical development from laws that had been

originally addressed to gentile sojourners in the land of Israel (Mosaic model) to laws that were later developed to address the situations of the Diaspora where Jews were the ones sojourning among gentiles and living under their laws (Noahide Commandment model)." See further ibid., 166–238.

269. Stone 1999: 133–49.

270. Bockmuehl 1995: 94–5; also Segal 1990: 195–201; Nodet and Taylor 1998: 222–9; Tomson 1990: 177–86; Dunn 1998: 661–2; Sanders 1992: 269; Kugel 1998: 224–6. For the largely negative assessment of the relationship of the Apostolic Decree to the Noachic Commandments, see C. K. Barrett 1994–98: II.734; Wehnert 1997: 236–7; Klaus Müller 1994; Flusser and Safrai 1986: 173–92; Goodman 1994: 53–4; Flusser 1994: 582–5; Heiligenthal 1994: 585–7; Klinghardt 1988: 176–80; Blomberg 1998: 408–9. See further Uchelen 1986: 253ff.; N. Cohen 1992: 46–57; Porton 1994: 5–6, 17, 102, 222, 223, 228.

271. See also *Sib. Or.* 3.756–81, which contains the expectation that after the great judgment, there will be "a common law for men throughout the whole earth" (κοινόν τε νόμον κατὰ γαῖαν ἅπασαν ἀνθρώποις): nations are to worship the living God, to avoid adultery and homosexuality, and to refrain from killing their children.

272. Cf., similarly, Nanos 1996: 55 n. 55: "The Qumran book of *Jubilees* dates from the first century or earlier as an independent witness to the concept of the Noahide Commandments operative in Judaism in a format similar to the apostolic decree prior to the later, formalized development in rabbinic Judaism (*Jub.* 7:20–21) . . . " Several scholars make an unnecessarily sharp distinction between the Noachic covenant of Gen. 8:21–9:17 and the tradition, found in *Jub.* 7:20–39, of Noah's instruction of his sons after the flood to avoid fornication, blood pollution, and injustice. Cf. Bauckham 1990: 322; Dexinger 1977: 123–4; Black 1985: 289–90. There can be no doubt that, according to *Jubilees*, the prohibition against eating blood was associated with the Noachic covenant (*Jub.* 6:10: "Noah and his sons swore an oath not to consume any blood that was in any animate being. During this month he made a covenant before the Lord God forever throughout all the history of the earth"). See on this esp. Kugel 1994: 328–9; 1998: 667–8. Moreover, when Noah exhorts his grandchildren to avoid the shedding of human blood and the eating of animal blood (*Jub.* 7:27–33), the juxtaposition of murder and the consumption of blood shares the priestly outlook of its source, God's covenant with Noah in Gen. 9:4–5. This is particularly apparent in Noah's warning that the earth will become polluted by improper use of blood (*Jub.* 7:33).

273. For a comparison of Luke-Acts to Ps.-Clem. *Rec.* 1.27–71, see Chap. 4.

274. Translation of the Syriac from Jones 1995a: 56. The Latin version of *Rec.* 1.30.1 is similar: "In the twelfth generation, after God had blessed the human beings and they began to be multiplied, they received the precept that they should not taste blood. For precisely because of this the flood was brought about." Without mentioning this text, however, A. F. J. Klijn (1968: 305–12) argues that the Apostolic Decree influenced the rule about blood only during the revision of the "Grundschrift" of the Ps.-Clementines.

275. Cf. Ps.-Clem. *Hom.* 8.15.4 (Rehm and Strecker 1992: 128), where the giants are said not to have been satisfied with the manna with which God supplied them for food and to have desired the eating of blood (γεῦσις τῶν αἱμάτων), thereby eventually precipitating the flood. See also Ps.-Philo, *LAB* 3:11: "The Lord spoke again to Noah and to his sons, saying, 'Lo, I will establish my covenant with you and with your seed after you, and I will not again destroy the earth by the water of a flood. Everything that moves and is alive will be food for you. But meat with the blood of the soul you shall not eat. Indeed, whoever will shed the blood of a man, his own blood will be shed, because man was made in the image of God. But you, increase and multiply and fill the earth like a multitude of fish that multiplies in the waves.' "

276. Cf. Dimant 1998: 129: "With all their differences, the various legends reflect the same basic transgressions committed by the antediluvians, later epitomized in the sins prohibited, according to the rabbis, to all mankind: murder, idolatry or blasphemy,

and fornication." Note that R. H. Charles (1972: 61) called *Jub.* 7:20–39 "a fragment of the lost book of Noah." As we shall see below, Martha Himmelfarb makes a similar assertion with regard to this passage.

277. The antediluvian giants were guilty of drinking blood (cf. *1 Enoch* 7:5). The giants, in turn, corrupted humanity with their evil way, thus setting the stage for divine judgment (cf. *Jub.* 5:1–2). See further Stuckenbruck 1997.

278. If the Apostolic Decree goes back to the Jerusalem church, and if the framer of the Decree was the same as the author of the NT letter of James, then it is interesting to note that that Catholic epistle is evidently familiar with the *Book of Jubilees*. Cf. Davids 1993: 228–30.

279. Assuming that πνικτόν/πνικτά refers to meat containing blood.

280. *Jubilees* itself is very concerned about the eating of blood. Cf. *Jub.* 6:7: "But you are not to eat animate beings with their spirit – with the blood – (because the vital force of all animate beings is in the blood) so that your blood and your vital forces may not be required from the hand of any man." A few lines later the text continues (6:10–14): "Noah and his sons swore an oath not to consume any blood that was in any animate being. During this month he made a covenant before the Lord God forever throughout all the history of the earth. (11) For this reason he told you, too, to make a covenant – accompanied by an oath – with the Israelites during this month on the mountain and to sprinkle blood on them because of all the words of the covenant which the Lord was making with them for all times. (12) This testimony has been written regarding you to keep it for all times so that you may not at any time eat any blood of animals or birds throughout all the days of the earth. (As for) the person who has eaten the blood of an animal , or cattle, or of birds all the days of the earth – he and his descendants will be uprooted from the earth." See also *Jub.* 11:2: "During this jubilee [sc. the 35th jubilee] Noah's children began to fight one another, to take captives, and to kill one another; to shed human blood on the earth, to consume blood . . . " This text shows that eating blood is part of a general malaise that characterized the postdiluvian period.

281. Cf. Bauckham 1996b: 465–6.

282. Cf. VanderKam 1999: 165–9, who argues that Lev. 18:26–8 explains why Noah needed to make atonement for the earth after the flood (*Jub.* 6:2): the biblical passage, which is directly preceded by laws about illicit sexual relations (Lev. 18:6–23), could have reminded the author of *Jubilees* about the connection between such offenses (which the angels of Genesis 6 had committed) and defilement of the land on which they were committed. VanderKam (ibid., 169) concludes his discussion of *Jub.* 6:2 with the following observation: "In using the angel story [i.e., Asael/Azazel] to establish halakhic points . . . , the author [of *Jubilees*] follows the same procedure he will use in ch. 7 where the sins that led to the flood will become the subject of laws about shedding and covering blood." This dovetails with Stone's aforementioned suggestion that several OT pseudepigrapha attempt to trace priestly traditions back to Noah.

283. Dimant 1998: 137. She continues (ibid.): "The analogy is made explicit between Noah's prohibition of shedding and eating blood, and similar Torah injunctions, as well as with the prescription to sprinkle blood on the altar (Exod. 24:8; Lev. 17:10; *Jub.* 6:6–14). By placing Noah's covenant in the third month (*Jub.* 6:1), *Jubilees* takes the analogy further and identifies the celebration of Noah's covenant with the festival of *shavuot*, implying the well-known view that *shavuot* celebrates the giving of the Torah. In this way not only is Noah's covenant turned into a prototype of the Sinai covenant, but Noah himself becomes a figure analogous to Moses. Characteristically, *Jubilees* attaches to the celebration a future forecast prophesying that the sons of Noah and the Israelites will forget this injunction and eat blood (*Jubilees* 18–19)."

284. A separate study would be needed to examine ancient practices of blood consumption. To mention just one interesting example, Posidonius (*apud* Athenaeus 2.45F), born in Apamea on the Orontes in Syria around 135 BCE, proscribes the friendship toasts among the Carmanians in southeastern Iran: "One should not drink toasts as the

Carmanians do, says Posidonius: as marks of friendship in their cups, they open facial veins, mix the dripping blood in their cup and quaff it off in the belief that to taste each other's blood is the ultimate in friendship (τέλος φιλίας νομίζοντας τὸ γεύεσθαι τοῦ ἀλλήλων αἵματος). After swallowing, he says, they anoint their heads with rose perfume preferably, otherwise with quince or iris perfume [orris] or nard to repel the effects from the potion and avoid harm from the fumes of the wine." Cf. Kidd 1999: 359 (frg. 283).

285. Cf. *Jub.* 7:28–32 (emphasis mine): "For I myself see that the demons have begun to lead you and your children astray; and now I fear regarding you that after I have died you will shed human blood on the earth and (that) you yourselves will be obliterated from the surface of the earth. (28) For everyone who sheds human blood and *everyone who consumes the blood of any animate being* will all be obliterated from the earth. (29) *No one who consumes blood* or who sheds blood on the earth will be left. He will be left with neither descendants nor posterity living beneath the heaven because they will go into Sheol and will descend into the place of judgment. All of them will depart into deep darkness through a violent death. (30) No blood of all the blood which there may be at any time when you sacrifice any animal, cattle, or (creature) that flies above the earth is to be seen on you. Do a good deed for yourselves by covering what is poured out on the surface of the earth. (31) *Do not be one who eats (meat) with the blood; exert yourselves so that blood is not consumed in your presence.* Cover the blood because so was I ordered to testify to you and your children together with all humanity. (32) *Do not eat the life with the meat* so that your blood, your life, may not be required from every person who sheds (blood) on the earth."

286. On this translation of the text, see Steiner 1995: 67 n. 13.

287. After *T. Levi* 18:2 in MS e (de Jonge 1978: 47 [# 57]). This archaic-sounding title may reflect an original Hebrew or Aramaic *Vorlage*. Cf. 1QapGen. 5.29: כתב מלי נוח "the book of the words of Noah" (Morgenstern, et al. 1995: 40–1; Steiner 1995: 66–71). Martha Himmelfarb (1994: 133–4) suggests that the *Book of Asaph* incorporated material from a Second-Temple source, possibly called "the book of Noah about blood," which stands behind *Jub.* 10:1–14 and 7:27–33. Cf., similarly, Charles 1972: 61, 78. Note also that according to 1QapGen. 11.16–17, God gave to Noah and his sons "everything to eat of the vegetables and herbs of the earth, but you shall eat no blood of any kind." See further Stone (1999: 137–41), who argues that three sequential pseudepigrapha found in the Qumran caves and attributed to the ancestors of the Levites (viz., Aramaic Levi, Testament of Qahat, and Visions of Amram) found it important to trace the priestly tradition they enfolded back specifically to Noah.

288. Cf. Stone 2000: 614, referring to the aforementioned Greek addition to the Greek *Testament of Levi* as a fragment of Aramaic Levi: "The phrase 'concerning the blood' and attribution to Noah may be explained by Gen. 9:1–7 combined with Gen. 8:20–1. A similar stress on the transmission of teaching from antiquity is to be found in 4QTQahat ar and 4QVisions of Amram ar which are associated with Aramaic Levi. The question remains, of course, whether a 'Book of Noah (concerning the blood)' actually existed, or whether Aramaic Levi invented this title to enhance the authority of the priestly tradition it promoted." I am grateful to Prof. Stone for a prepublication copy of this article.

289. Cf. Strange 1992: 93–6.

290. On Noah as a "just man," see Rose 1994: 191–202.

291. Καὶ γὰρ βρωμάτων τινῶν ἀπέχεσθαι προσέταξεν ὑμῖν, ἵνα καὶ ἐν τῷ ἐσθίειν καὶ πίνειν πρὸ ὀφθαλμῶν ἔχητε τὸν θεόν, εὐκατάφοροι ὄντες καὶ εὐχερεῖς πρὸς τὸ ἀφίστασθαι τῆς γνώσεως αὐτοῦ, ὡς καὶ Μωυσῆς φησιν· Ἔφαγε καὶ ἔπιεν ὁ λαὸς καὶ ἀνέστη τοῦ παίζειν. καὶ πάλιν· Ἔφαγεν Ἰακὼβ καὶ ἐνεπλήσθη, καὶ ἐλιπάνθη, καὶ ἀπελάκτισεν ὁ ἠγαπημένος· ἐλιπάνθη, ἐπαχύνθη, ἐπλατύνθη, καὶ ἐγκατέλιπε θεὸν τὸν ποιήσαντα αὐτόν. τῷ γὰρ Νῶε ὅτι συγκεχώρητο ὑπὸ τοῦ θεοῦ, δικαίῳ ὄντι,

226   Notes to pages 92–94

πᾶν ἔμψυχον ἐσθίειν πλὴν κρέας ἐν αἵματι, ὅπερ ἐστὶ νεκριμαῖον, διὰ Μωυσέως ἀνιστορήθη ὑμῖν ἐν τῇ βίβλῳ τῆς Γενέσεως (Goodspeed 1914: 112).

292. *Erubescat error uester Christianis, qui ne animalium quidem sanguinem in epulis esculentis habemus, qui propterea suffocatis quoque et morticinis abstinemus, ne quo modo sanguine contaminemur uel intra uiscera sepulto* (Dekkers 1954: 104). Cf. also Tertullian, *De Mon.* 5.

293. To my knowledge, Ps.-Clem. *Rec.* 1.30.1 has never before been used to interpret the Apostolic Decree. Resch (1905: 28–30) and Strange (1992: 99, 100–1, 104–5) also suggested that πνικτόν/πνικτά be understood simply as an extension of the prohibition of blood, but they did not explain why, in so succinct a set of rules, it was felt necessary to reinforce particularly the avoidance of the consumption of blood. For a "demonological" rationale for the prohibition of blood and strangulated things, see Wedderburn 1993: 384–9. On the other hand, the double prohibition against blood in Acts may reflect the close tie in *Jub.* 7:27–32 between consuming blood and shedding blood.

294. The other occurrence is in Lk. 3:23–38, where in conformity with his universalistic emphasis, Luke traces the lineage of Jesus from Joseph (v. 23), through Noah (v. 36), to Adam (v. 38), in a way that mirrors the Table of Nations in 1 Chr. 1:1–2:2 beginning with Adam (1:1). See further pp. 44–9.

295. Cf. Fitzmyer 1981–85: II.1170.

296. Cf. Sato 1988: 285, who classifies Lk. 17:26–7, 30 par. as a "'heilsgeschichtlicher' Vergleich," an example of which is Isa. 54:9 (ibid., 280–1).

297. Cf. Fishbane 1985: 374–5. A similar typological use of the flood with respect to the exile occurs in Sifré Deuteronomy *Eqev* 43 (ed. Finkelstein 101), where the phrase "and you shall soon perish" (Deut. 11:17) is rephrased as follows: "I will exile you immediately, and I will not grant you any extension." While God granted an extension of 120 years to the generation of the flood, YHWH will not be so generous to the Israelites, because unlike the generation of the flood, they had previous generations to learn from.

298. Cf. Ezek. 14:12–20, which also makes a comparison of Noah with the Judean exile. See Wahl 1992: 542–53.

299. Cf. P. Miller 1995: 161–3.

300. Cf. Dimant 1998: 135–6, 41 (also adducing the comparison to Matt. 24:37–9; Lk. 17:26–7); P. S. Alexander 1997b: 323: "The Qumran literature shows a marked interest in the biblical story of the Flood, possibly because the Community believed that the evil conditions which provoked the Flood were being replicated in their days. They too were living at the end of history, just prior to a cataclysmic divine judgment of God on the wickedness of their generation. Like righteous Enoch and Noah they had to stand out against the prevailing evil and warn their contemporaries of the impending doom." For a survey of Noah materials at Qumran, see García Martínez 1998b: 86–108; Dimant 1998: 123–50; Bernstein 1998–99: I.128–59 (esp. 138ff.); 1999a: 199–231; Stone 1999: 133–49. Note that 4Q176 8–11, 10–11 quotes Isa. 54:9–10 MT.

301. As Barrett (1994–98: II.745) points out, the prohibitions of the Apostolic Decree are characterized as "these necessary (requirements)" (τούτων τῶν ἐπάναγκες [Acts 15:28]) because they are deemed a condition of salvation (cf. 15:1, 5).

302. Indeed, according to the *Damascus Document*, Jacob's male descendants were cut off in the wilderness precisely because they walked in the stubbornness of their hearts, they disobeyed God's commandments, each one doing what was right in his own eyes, "and they ate blood" (CD 3:5–7). Fröhlich (1998: 86) suggests that this phrase, "and they ate blood," "may be a later addition referring to the violation of the Noachic laws (Gen. 9:3–6, the prohibition of consuming blood)." Note also that in the Epistle of Enoch (*1 Enoch* 82–105), the author pronounces woe (eschatological damnation) upon his opponents for consuming blood, among other heinous sins (89:11).

303. Cf. Dimant 1998: 126, who suggests that in the Qumran literature "Noah as righteous remnant was seen as a prototype of the righteous at the End of Days, a concept central to the thinking of the Qumran community and apocryphal works related to it." See also ibid., 141: "The emblematic analogy between the flood and the eschaton was not confined to theoretical speculations. It had immediate practical implications for the Qumranites. For the analogical relationships were perceived as expressions of a divine, premeditated law which governs history, and thus as providing indications for the nature of the eschaton, and the correct behavior to be practiced at its eve. Such an interest may well account for the presence of the Noachic and Enochic literature at Qumran."
304. Cf. Benjamins 1998: 139, 141.
305. A somewhat similar procedure is detected in *1 Enoch* by Nickelsburg (1999: 101).
306. Cf. *'Arukh* 3:324 s.v. נח: "From Noah God derived all the seventy nations and gave them lands. He gave Gothia to the Goths, and Egypt to the Egyptians, and thus he apportioned to all." As Goldenberg (1998: 100) points out, the purpose of the pairing (Gothia/Goths, Egypt/Egyptians) in this passage, as in many other rabbinic texts, is to indicate geographic extremes as a merism representing the extent of the whole world.
307. In Jewish tradition, Noah is frequently seen as a second Adam.
308. On the other hand, it is possible that the passage presupposes the existence of antediluvian nations, as in Philo, *Abr.* 40 and *4 Ezra* 3:7–10.
309. Gärtner 1955: 151. Josephus (*Ant.* 2.94) also relates that Joseph affirmed the unity of all humanity: "Nor did he open the market to the natives only, for Joseph held that all men, in virtue of their kinship (κατὰ συγγένειαν), should receive succour from those in prosperity." This is not just an apologetic ploy on Josephus' part to rehabilitate the image of contemporary Jews, who were charged with misanthropy (cf. Feldman 1992: 407, 527). Nor is it a merely a rare example of Josephus' appreciation of Hellenistic culture (cf. Barclay 1996: 360 n. 54). Rather, this is evidence of how deeply rooted Josephus' thinking is in the Table of Nations tradition, which he expounds at the beginning of his *Antiquities* (1.122–47). We may also ask whether Josephus' interpretation of Joseph also reflects the Hellenistic concept of the unity of humanity that Tarn (1948) attributed to Alexander the Great (cf. Plutarch, *Alex.* 329B–D). On Tarn's view, see, however, Sterling 1992: 56 n. 8.
310. Cf. 1QM 10:12ff.: "He who created the earth and the limits of her divisions . . . the confusion of language and the separation of peoples, the abode of clans."
311. Joseph Fitzmyer (1979: 98) adduces some interesting parallels between the infancy narratives of Luke and Matthew and the story of Noah as preserved in the Genesis Apocryphon (1QapGen.; cf. also *1 Enoch* 106–7). For instance, in parallel to Mary's conception through the overshadowing of the Holy Spirit (Lk. 1:35; Matt. 1:18), Noah's father Lamech suspects that Noah was conceived through the visit of an angel to Noah's mother Batenosh.
312. As we noted in Chap. 2, the juxtaposition of *Urzeit* and *Endzeit* – the beginning of the nations and their cataclysmic end – occurs not only in *Jubilees* 8–9 itself, but also in Dan. 12:1 and the War Rule. On *Urzeit/Endzeit* typology of Noah and the flood in *1 Enoch*, see Nickelsburg 1998: 142–3; Dimant 1998: 135–6, 141: "In the context of a sequence of periods which compose the historical process, the flood is situated at the beginning of the present historical sequence, while the eschaton concludes this sequence. Thus, the flood and the eschatological end are opposing counterparts of the same symmetry between the primordial and final judgments (see *1 Enoch* 93:4, 9–10; 91:12–13)."

4 Pseudo-Clementine *Recognitions* 1.27–71

1. Cf. Jones 1995b: 617–35; 1995a: 141.
2. Cf. Jones 1982a: 1–33; 1982b: 63–96.

3. Even distinctively Jewish materials have been found in the Pseudo-Clementines. For instance, Adler (1993: 15–49) suggests that the encomium in *Homilies* 4–6 was part of a longer Jewish missionary tract composed in Alexandria in the second century CE.

4. For purposes of the present chapter, the results of Jones' preliminary source-critical investigation are followed (1995a: 111–55).

5. Cf. *Rec*. 1.37.2 (Syriac): "At that time, the prophet who is to say these things to them will be sent out. Those who believe in him will be led, through the wisdom of God, to a fortified place of the land, as if to life, and preserved because of the battle that will afterwards come to destroy those who have not been persuaded because of their doubt." Where exactly this place of refuge might have been cannot be determined with certainty. The source ends its account with the congregation fleeing to Jericho (1.71.2), and so Jones plausibly suggests that this represents the first stopping point on the way to the unspecified place of refuge within the Land (1995a: 158). However, Jones rejects Strecker's opinion (1981: 230) that the place of refuge was Pella, for "Pella does not lie 'in the land' at all but is rather a city of the Decapolis" (Jones 1995a: 158). This argument overlooks, however, that if *Rec*. 1.27–71 is otherwise dependent on the *Book of Jubilees* (see below and Jones 1995a: 138–9, 158, 161 n. 13, 162), then the source may well presuppose the ideal boundaries of the Promised Land in Gen. 15:18–20 (cf. *Jub*. 14:18), which obviously include Pella in the Transjordan (Ammorite territory). There is even evidence that *Jubilees* understood the whole territory allotted to Shem as part of the pre-Sinaitic "holy land" (cf. Dimant 1998: 138 n. 73; Weinfeld 1993: 208 with n. 51). On the Pella tradition, see Eusebius, *HE* 3.5.3. This testimony is questioned by many (e.g., Lüdemann 1983: 243, 265–86; Murphy-O'Connor 1995: 15–17); it is defended by Hengel 1976; Blanchetière and Pritz 1993: 93–110; Reid 1997: 900–2. See further Wehnert 1991: 231–55; Stemberger 1998: 230–2. Even Syria cannot be excluded as a possibility for the provenance of the text, for Syria was considered to lie within the Land (or within the future messianic kingdom). For example, a recently published ossuary inscription from Jerusalem mentions a certain "Ariston of Apamea," who may be identical with the Ariston mentioned in the Mishnah. According to *m. Ḥallah* 4:11, "Ariston brought his firstfruits from Apamea, and they [sc. the priests] accepted them from him, for they said, 'He who owns [land] in Syria is as one who owns [land] in the outskirts of Jerusalem.' " Cf. Ilan 1991–92: 150–4; Hengel 1995b: 298. According to Jewish tradition, including 1QapGen. 21.16–17, the "Taurus Amanus" mountain range forms the northern border of Israel. Cf. *m. Sheb*. 6:1; *y. Ḥal*. 4.4; *Exod. Rab*. 23:5; *b. Git*. 8a. See further P. S. Alexander 1992: 986.

6. Stötzel 1982: 32.

7. Jones 1995a: 159.

8. Jones 1995a: 163. In reviewing Jones' book, Richard Bauckham (1997b: 420–1) seeks to provide additional evidence for dating *Rec*. 1.27–71 to about 200 CE. Drawing upon Jones' comment (1995a: 128) that this Pseudo-Clementine source differs from other parts of the Pseudo-Clementines in interpreting the "sons of God" in Gen. 6:2 as righteous men (*Rec*. 1.29) rather than as angels (cf., e.g., *Jub*. 5:1), Bauckham observes that the only other Christian writer before 300 CE who adopts this interpretation is Julius Africanus, thus making it possible to argue that both Africanus and the author of the source in *Rec*. 1.27–71 may have derived this interpretation from Palestinian rabbinic tradition, in which it had already come to prevail by about 200 CE. For a chronological survey of the early Christian uses of the Enochic angel story based on Gen. 6:1–4, see VanderKam 1996: 60–88; cf. also W. Wagner 1996: 137–55. On euhemeristic interpretations of Genesis 6, see Adler 1989: 125ff. VanderKam (1996: 80) makes a similar observation to that of Bauckham: "As the last pages of the present survey will show, the sort of interpretation found in the Recognitions will come to dominate Christian exegesis of Gen. 6:1–4. The first extant evidence for it appears only in the third century; by the fourth century it will, for all practical purposes, have forced

the angelic reading from the field." In response to Bauckham, however, we must recognize that the Pseudo-Clementine source most probably originated in a Palestinian, "Jewish–Christian" circle, and that therefore the most relevant comparative material is Palestinian–Jewish, rather than Christian *per se*. In Jewish sources, the earliest datable interpretation of Gen. 6:1–4 as referring to humans ("sons of judges") is, as most scholars acknowledge, expressed by R. Simeon b. Yohai (ca. 150 CE) in *Gen. Rab.* 26:5 (cf. Ruiten 1997: 66 n. 21; P. S. Alexander 1972: 61; Bauckham 1983: 51; Kooij 1997: 43–51). Note, however, that Kugel (1998: 209–10) has now adduced even earlier evidence for this interpretation. Therefore, the interpretation of Gen. 6:1–4 as referring to humans was current well before 200 CE, and nothing stands in the way of dating the Pseudo-Clementine source to the period just before the Diaspora Revolt.

9. Jones 1995a: 163 with n. 20, following Strecker 1981: 231 (referring to *Rec.* 1.39.3): "...wo offenbar die erste und zweite Belagerung Jerusalems nicht mehr unterschieden wird: denn erst Hadrian erließ das Edikt zur Vertreibung der Juden aus Jerusalem, das hier anscheinend vordatiert ist..." Cf., similarly, Lüdemann 1983: 243.
10. Jones 1995a: 142–5.
11. As we noted in Chap. 3, most scholars date Luke-Acts after the fall of Jerusalem to ca. 80–90 CE, although some scholars argue for a date in the 60s. The latter option seems plausible, since, as we have seen, Luke-Acts maintains the salvation–historical centrality of Jerusalem. Moreover, the Book of Acts ends without describing the outcome of Paul's trial in Rome, perhaps because by the time of writing the event has not yet taken place.
12. On the dating of the revolt, see esp. Horbury 1996a: 284–95.
13. Cf. Horbury 1996a: 295–303; Hengel 1989a: 655–86; Scott 1997d: 173–218.
14. On early Christian expectations of Israel's return to the Land, see Heid 1993; Horbury 1996b: 207–24.
15. On the vexed problem of definition, see Taylor 1990: 313–34; Hagner 1997: 579–80; Stemberger 1998: 228–9.
16. Cf. Jones 1995a: 160.
17. Since the original Greek of our text is lost, the following discussion will necessarily be dependent on the surviving Syriac and Latin versions. The English translations of these versions are from Jones 1995a: 51–109. For purposes of the present study, the Syriac version is followed throughout, with reference to the Latin as necessary. For critical editions of the Syriac version, see Lagarde 1861; Frankenberg 1937: 35–77. For the Latin version, see Rehm and Strecker 1994: 23–49.
18. Seen as a whole, *Rec.* 1.27–71 is somewhat similar to Josephus' *Antiquities*, which likewise begins with creation, reworks biblical history, and extends the narrative to the author's own time.
19. Cf., e.g., Nickelsburg 1984: 89–156; Evans 1992: 46–7, with further bibliography.
20. Cf. Jones 1995a: 138–9; Rönsch 1874: 322–5.
21. On the primal history according to the Ps.-Clementines, see Schoeps 1950: 1–37, who adduces a parallel to *Rec.* 1.27–71 in *Rec.* 4.9–13 par. *Hom.* 8.10–20; 9.3–7.
22. On Kainam son of Arpachshad, see further in Chap. 3 on the genealogy of Jesus in Lk. 3:23–38.
23. The natural boundaries between human territories are also a feature of the *Book of Jubilees*. Cf. P. S. Alexander 1982: 205–8. See also the allusion to Deut. 32:8 in Acts 17:26.
24. On the use of Gen. 6:1–4 in Ps.-Clem. *Rec.* 1.29.1, see VanderKam 1996: 76–80; Jones 1995a: 128. Insofar as *Rec.* 1.29.1 traces the origin of evil to the influence of the angels of Genesis 6 (rather than to the fall in Gen. 3:16–19), the text partakes of a tradition that Stone (1999: 133–49) has called "the Enoch–Noah axis." See also VanderKam 1999: 153–4. Note, however, that the text seems to combine both human and angelic interpretations of Gen. 6:1–4. See further n. 8 above.

25. The condemnation of Ham and his descendants with regard to their sexual practices is a recurring theme in rabbinic literature. According to *b. Sanh.* 108b, for example, Ham inappropriately copulated while still in the ark. See further Aaron 1994: 740–1.

26. The Latin version reads as follows: "In the meanwhile, his older brother [Shem] received the lot for habitation that is in the middle of the earth (*in medio terrae*), in which is located the land of Judea; the younger [Japheth] received the region of the east, while he [Ham] took the region of the west."

27. On Judea/Jerusalem as the middle of the earth, see also *1 Enoch* 26:1; Justin, *Dial.* 115.1; 119.3; Ephr. Syr. *Serm. de fide* 5.61 (CSCO 212; SSyr. 89.54.18). On Shem's lot in the middle of the earth, see further in Chap. 2; Frey 1997: 277–9.

28. The LXX, Philo (*Quaest. in Gen.* 2.79), and most rabbinic sources regard Japheth as the oldest son.

29. Cf. Jones 1995a: 139: "While the use of Jubilees cannot be doubted, it should also be remarked that the dependency is by no means one of blind adoption. [. . .] When in the partitioning of the world the eastern and western lots are perhaps the inverse of the lots in Jubilees (contrast R 1.30.3 with Jubilees 8:8–30), this is not because as Charles assumed, there is a mistake in the Latin R, but as not only the Syriac but also R 1.31.2 confirm, because the author of our source is possibly consciously altering the version in Jubilees." Jones refers here to R. H. Charles (1972: 84 n. 29), who remarks (1) that the view in *Jub.* 10:29 (". . . he [sc. Canaan son of Ham] did not go to his hereditary land to the west of the sea") is otherwise found only in works dependent on *Jubilees*, and (2) that in Ps.-Clem. *Rec.* 1.30.3 (Latin), *orientis* as the lot of the younger son (Japheth) should read *occidentis* and *occidentis* as the lot of the middle son (Ham) should read *orientis*.

30. On Hebrew as the original language of humankind, see Kugel 1998: 235–7; Weitzman 1999: 35–45. On Hebrew as the "holy tongue," see p. 214 n. 132.

31. The Latin version reads as follows: "In the sixteenth generation, the sons of man moved from the east and came to the lands of their fathers. Each one called the place of his lot his own name." Both Syriac and Latin versions include the interesting detail that these people named the places either after themselves or after their fathers' names. Josephus has a similar detail in *Ant.* 1.122: "Noah's children had sons, who were honored by having their names conferred upon the nations by the first occupants of the several countries. Japheth, son of Noah, had seven sons. These, beginning by inhabiting the mountains of Taurus and Amanus, advanced in Asia up to the river Tanais and in Europe as far as Gadeira, occupying the territory upon which they lit, and, as no inhabitant had preceded them, giving their own names to the nations." This is not the only place in *Rec.* 1.27–71 that has affinities with Josephus. See below on Josephus' identification of Ishmael with the Arabs.

32. Cf. Horst 1990: 220–32. Nimrod is frequently regarded as the builder of the Tower of Babel (cf. Kugel 1998: 229–32). According to *b. Ḥag.* 13a, it was a descendant of Nimrod who attempted to ascend into heaven and become like the Most High (Isa. 14:14).

33. On the beginnings of city-building by the descendants of Noah, see *Jub.* 11:2; Ps.-Philo, *LAB* 4.8.

34. Cf. *Jub.* 11:2: "During this jubilee [sc. the 35th jubilee] Noah's children began to fight one another, to take captives, and to kill one another; to shed human blood on the earth, to consume blood; to build fortified cities, walls, and towers; men to elevate themselves over peoples, to set up the first kingdoms; to go to war – people against people, nations against nations, city against city; and everyone to do evil, to acquire weapons, and to teach warfare to their sons. City began to capture city and to sell male and female slaves."

35. The Latin version reads as follows: "In the nineteenth generation, the descendants of the one who was cursed after the flood left their proper boundaries, which they had received by lot in the western regions, expelled those who had received the middle part of the earth into the lands of the east, and drove them to Persia, while they themselves took the places of the expelled in an unjust way."

36. Cf. VanderKam 1994b: 46–69. As we saw in Chap. 2, *the Book of Jubilees* probably took its perspective about the original owners of the Land from the Song of Moses (Deut. 32:8–9), which strongly implies that during the original division of the world among the nations, God established Israel's right to the Land, i.e., God's own land.

37. On the concept of the Land in *Rec.* 1.27–71, see further Heid 1992–93: 1–5; 1993; Strecker 1983: 197–8.

38. The idea that Abraham turned from astrology to the worship of God as Creator (*Rec.* 1.32.3) is reflected in *Jubilees* 11–12, which depicts Abraham as one who seeks the true God and then rejects idolatry and astrological prognostication (see esp. 12:16–17). On Abraham as astrologer in Jewish tradition, see Stemberger 1975: 37–9; Scott 1992: 93–5.

39. On Gal. 3:8, 16, see Scott 1992: 180–2.

40. The Latin version reads: "Hence, an angel also came to him in a vision and instructed him more fully concerning the things he had begun to perceive. And he also showed him what was due to his race and posterity, and he promised that these places not so much are to be given to them as they are to be returned." The text may be a paraphrase of *Jub.* 14:13–15, which is based on Gen. 15:13–16 (cf. Acts 7:6–7).

41. For Strecker (1981: 221), *Rec.* 1.33 marks the beginning of the source.

42. If our text regards Ishmael as the progenitor of "the tribes of the Arabs" (1.33.3; Latin: "the barbarian nations"), then it is interesting to note that Josephus (*Ant.* 1.214) is the only other source prior to this which supports this identification. Cf. Millar 1993a. This is the second time that *Rec.* 1.27–71 has material that is otherwise distinctive to Josephus (see above, n. 31).

43. See the discussion in Chap. 3.

44. Gen. 46:27 LXX reads "seventy-five," as do Philo (*Mig.* 36) and Acts 7:14.

45. Num. 11:16 refers to Moses' choosing of the seventy elders. Cf. Horbury 1986: 503–27.

46. A direct relationship between the 70 who went down to Egypt and the 70 nations of the world is explicitly mentioned in Ps.-Clem. *Hom.* 18.4.3. See further in Chap. 3.

47. Compare the distinction in both Judaism and Christianity between the Decalogue, given by God directly to the people, and other laws given indirectly through Moses; see, e.g., Horbury 1988: 759–60.

48. Cf. Teeple 1993.

49. As we shall see below, this "place" is evidently not the Jerusalem Temple. Although the Latin version can be understood in this way (1.37.2: "This place, however, which seemed for a while to be chosen, though it was often ravaged by attacks of enemies and military destructions, they would also finally hear to be destined to thorough destruction"), the Syriac text has nothing about the Temple at this point.

50. The Latin version reads: "When it fled to the mercy of God it was called back from there so that by these things it might be taught that when it offers sacrifices it is expelled and given over into the hands of enemies, but when it effects mercy and justice without sacrifices it is freed from captivity and restored to the fatherland." On the idea of exile, see further Scott 1997c. Cf. Carroll 1997: 67: "In conformity with the discourse of education, so prominent in the book of Hosea (cf. 10:11), the motif of the return to Egypt or deportation to Assyria represents a *sentimental education* on the part of Israel, whereby the nation finally learns what it has failed to learn when living in its own land. Exile as *education* is a major trope in the scroll of Hosea."

51. Cf. Steck 1967.

52. Note that Hos. 6:6 is cited in Matt. 9:13; 12:7. See further Mic. 6:6–8; Amos 5:23; Jer. 7:21–3. On the prophetic critique of the sacrificial system, see G. Anderson 1992: 881–2.

53. Cf. VanderKam 1994b: 58: "*Jub.* 8.11 introduces the actual division in language reminiscent of Moses' and Joshua's distribution of the promised land among the

tribes: the assigned portions are called lots (!; see Num. 26 and 34; Josh. 14.2; 15.1; 17.4; 18.6, 8–9 [where a book is mentioned as in *Jub.* 8.11], 10; 19.51)." Compare the Latin version of *Rec.* 1.38.3: "... and they received their paternal inheritance by appointed lot." On Noah's Moses-like role in the *Book of Jubilees*, see further in Chap. 2.

54. Likewise, for example, in *1 Enoch* 89:54, the period after the founding of the Davidic dynasty and the building of the Temple is characterized as a time of apostasy.

55. The Latin version gives a different impression: "... they built for the royal ambition a temple precisely in the place that had been predestined for them for prayer ..." On this reading, building the Solomonic Temple constitutes the violation of God's will.

56. On the Jerusalem Temple as a place of prayer, see Lk. 2:37 ("She never left the Temple but worshiped there with fasting and prayer night and day"); 18:10 ("Two men went up to the Temple to pray, one a Pharisee and the other a tax collector"); 2 Macc. 10:26 ("Falling upon the steps before the altar, they implored him to be gracious to them and to be an enemy to their enemies and an adversary to their adversaries, as the law declares"); 3 Macc. 2:10 ("And because you love the house of Israel, you promised that if we should have reverses and tribulation should overtake us, you would listen to our petition when we come to this place and pray"). The latter alludes to Deut. 4:30; 30:1–6; 1 Kgs. 8:33–4, 48–50.

57. Contrast 2 Chr. 7:12, where the Lord appeared to Solomon and said to him with reference to his prayer of dedication: "I have heard your prayer, and have chosen this place for myself as a house of sacrifice."

58. Note that 1 Kgs. 8:48 is important for the later rabbinic discussion of the direction of prayer in the Diaspora (Sifré Deut. 29 [ed. Finkelstein, 47]). Cf. Amit 1995: 140–5; Isa. 60:7 LXX; Dan. 6:11; 1 Esdr. 4:58; *m. Ber.* 4:5. See further in Chap. 1.

59. As a means of countering the charge of misanthropy which had been leveled against Jews, Josephus modifies Solomon's prayer to emphasize that the Temple is for all people (*Ant.* 8:116–17), perhaps reflecting on Isa. 56:7. It is unlikely that *Rec.* 1.38.5 "strongly implies that the tabernacle had no sacrifices ..." (Voorst 1989: 98), for that would apparently contradict 1.37.1.

60. This is evidently an interpretation of the eschatological expectation, based on 2 Sam. 7: 13 (1 Chr. 17: 12), that the Messiah would build the Temple (cf. Isa. 44:28; Zech. 6:12–13; *Tg. Zech.* 6:12–13; *Tg. Isa.* 53: 5).

61. Cf. *Rec.* 1.69.2: "Then he [sc. James] spoke also concerning the Books of Kingdoms with respect to how, when and by whom they were written, and with respect to how it is proper for us to employ them." No doubt some of his remarks included Solomon's prayer of dedication (1 Kings 8), including Jesus' role in returning the Temple to its original function (although it must be admitted that James does not polemicize here against the Temple or sacrificing; but he does urge baptism, which is the substitute for sacrificing [cf. 1.39.2]).

62. On the nations, see 1.32.2; 34.2; 38.3; 42.1; 50.1–4; 61.2; 63.2; 64.2–3. Cf. also Schwemer 1991: 356.

63. Skipping over the exile and the Second-Temple period is characteristic of Jewish apocalyptic literature. Cf. VanderKam 1997.

64. On the emphasis on baptism in *Rec.* 1.27–71, see further Jones 1995a: 161–2.

65. The collocation "signs and wonders" occurs frequently in the OT in reference to divine displays which attest to the sending of a human messenger, especially Moses (cf. Exod. 7:3; Deut. 4:34; 6:22; 7:19; 13:1, 2; 26:8; 28:46; 29:3; 34:11; Isa. 8:18; 20:3; Jer. 32:20, 21; Ps. 78:43; 105:27; 135:9; Neh. 9:10). The same collocation of terms is used in the NT of Jesus (cf. Acts 2:22) and the apostles (cf. Acts 2:19, 43; 5:12), including Paul himself (cf. Rom. 15:19; Acts 15:12). Just as Jesus of Nazareth was accredited by God through miracles, wonders and signs, which God did among the people through Jesus (cf. Acts 2:22), so also Paul was accredited as an apostle

through similar displays which attested to his divine sending and message (cf. 2 Cor. 12:12; Acts 14:3). On Moses as a model of the sign prophets, even down to the first century, see Gray 1993: 112–44 (esp. 115, 125–8, 137, 141–2).

66. On the question of whether this refers to the decree of Hadrian in 135 CE, which expelled the Jewish nation from the Land (cf. Eusebius, *HE* 4.6.3), see pp. 97–8.

67. See further in Chap. 3.

68. The Latin version reads: "But since it was necessary for the nations to be called in place of those who remained unbelievers so that the number that was shown to Abraham might be filled, the saving proclamation of the kingdom of God was sent out into the whole world."

69. Does this mean that like the other descendants of Abraham, these nations would need to be circumcised (cf. 1.33.5), especially in light of prophecies predicting that the Gentile nations would become, like Israel, God's own people (Zech. 2:11 [MT 2:15]; cf. Isa. 19:25)? If so, this may be one of the points that separates Paul and the Jewish Christians behind our text (see below on 1.70.1ff.). Cf., however, Jones 1995a:164 (author's emphasis): "It is highly unlikely that he [sc. the author of *Rec.* 1.27–71] would have demanded circumcision of the gentile believers, for the very notion of calling the *nations* to complete the number shown to Abraham . . . contradicts the view that these gentiles should first have to convert to Judaism (e.g., submission to circumcision) before entering Christianity." See also Bauckham 1996b: 474. Donaldson (1990: 3–27) argues that the predominant Jewish eschatological expectation was that in the end-times the Gentiles would be converted to the God of Israel as Gentiles, rather than by having to become proselytes. But it is not at all clear that the evidence he examines really supports this conclusion.

70. Cf. Stroumsa 1996, who argues that ethnic terms were deeply irrelevant for Christians, citing, among other texts, Gal. 3:28 and the *Epistle to Diogenes* 5.1–5. While we might add Acts 15:14 as possible additional support for this thesis, a text like Ps.-Clem. *Rec.* 1.42.1 tells a different story. Compare also Ephrem's concept of the "church from the Nations" (cf. Darling 1987) rather than a "third race" (so Stroumsa).

71. Traditional Christian exegesis saw in Dan. 9:26 a reference to the death of Christ. On the use of Daniel 9 in Jewish and Christian sources, see, e.g., Beckwith 1996: 217–75; Adler 1996: 201–38; A. Collins 1996: 69–76.

72. See Hengel 1985: 71–104; Bauckham 1996b: 415–80.

73. Does this "convenient time" relate to the aforementioned chronological speculation based on Dan. 9:24–7?

74. Note, however, that *Rec.* 1.44.4–52.6 (with differences regarding the exact extent of the material) is often considered a secondary insertion of the redactor who established the entire framework and fundamental content of the novel. Cf. Jones 1995a: 135–6.

75. Unlike the Syriac version, the Latin version of *Rec.* 1.50.2 does not have the citation of Isa. 11:10 and it speaks of "the prophets" rather than "the prophet."

76. Note that Isa. 11:11 goes on to give a *pars pro toto* list of the nations from which the people, who are scattered to the four corners of the earth, will be gathered. See the discussion on Acts 2:9–11 in Chap. 3.

77. The Latin version reads: "He [sc. Jesus] said the poor were blessed; he promised that there would be earthly rewards; he placed the highest reward in earthly inheritance; and he promised that those who observed righteousness would be filled with food and drink."

78. Cf. Jones 1995a: 129. On this earthly kingdom, see also *Rec.* 1.55.4, which distinguishes between the kingdom of heaven and the resurrection of the dead. A messianic kingdom will be established with the second coming of Christ (1.69.4).

79. See further Scott 1992: 134–5.

80. Already in *Jubilees* 8–9, the eschatological judgment of the nations is expected (*Jub.* 9:15).

81. See further in Chap. 2.

82. The Latin version reads: "At the end I warned them that before we should go to the nations to preach to them the knowledge of God the Father, they should be reconciled to God by accepting his Son." In both the Syriac and the Latin versions of *Rec.* 1.63.2, the mission to the nations is future, whereas in 1.42.1 (Latin) "the saving proclamation of the kingdom of God was sent out into the whole world."

83. When this universalistic statement appears on Peter's lips, it probably recalls Peter's reputation as an apostle to the nations. Cf. Bauckham 1992a: 575–7. Paul knows Peter as a traveling missionary (cf. 1 Cor. 9:5).

84. In the Latin version, the latter half of 1.64.2 reads somewhat differently: "Then the gospel will be proclaimed to the nations as a testimony of you, so that your unbelief might be judged on the basis of their belief."

85. Cf. Bell 1994.

86. Cf. *Rec.* 1.43.1: "For again increasingly, as if by the jealousy of God at all times, we [sc. Jewish Christians] grew even more numerous than they [sc. unbelieving Jews], so that their priests were afraid lest by the providence of God and to their shame, the whole nations should come to faith. They were frequently sending and asking us to speak to them about Jesus, whether he is the prophet who was foretold by Moses, that is the eternal Christ."

87. Cf., similarly, *Rec.* 3.61.2; *Hom.* 2.17.4, cited in Jones 1995a: 130.

88. See, however, Hill 1992: 41–101, who argues that Acts 6:11–14 does not support the interpretation that Stephen was a radical critic of the Temple. For the purpose of the present study, it will suffice to note that the Pseudo-Clementine source seems to hold the negative view of the Temple of which Stephen was reportedly accused. On Hill's position, see further Hagner 1997: 580–1.

89. Jones (1995a: 142) denies that *Rec.* 1.27–71 knows the Pauline letters: "Contrary to other sections in the *Pseudo-Clementines* that draw on Paul's own letters in order to attack this missionary [cf., e.g., *Epistula Petri* 2.4, 6 with Gal. 2:11–21], the author of the source of R 1.27–71 never displays evidence of knowing the content of Paul's letters. It should not be doubted, however, that the author of the source knew of Paul's letters, though he might never have read them or taken their content seriously."

90. Other parallels to Paul's theology are admittedly weaker. In *Rec.* 1.32.1–3, for example, the allusion to Gen. 12:3 may be compared to Gal. 3:8, 16 (cf. also Acts 3:25). In 1.34.1–2; 40.4, the connection between the 12 tribes of Israel and the 70 nations (based on Deut. 32:8) can be compared perhaps to Rom. 11:25–6.

91. The Latin version is even more explicit: "But the nonbelievers will be exiled from the place and the kingdom so that perhaps against their will they might understand and be obedient to the will of God." Paul speaks similarly of the "obedience of faith" (Rom. 1:5; 16:26).

92. Cf. Jones 1995b: 617–35; 1995a: 141–2; 1997: 223–45.

93. Cf. Jones 1995a: 3, 140 nn. 99–100, comparing *Rec.* 1.41.3 with Lk. 23:45 and *Rec.* 1.54.5–6 with the "Western" text of Lk. 11:52.

94. On the use of Matthew in *Rec.* 1.27–71, see Jones 1995a: 3, 140 with n. 99, 142, 155, 157. In addition, we may point out that the periodization of history in *Rec.* 1.27–71 may be similar to that in Matthew's Gospel, depending on the outcome of the scholarly debate on that controversial point. According to R. Walker (1967), for example, Matthew's scheme of salvation history is oriented around the Gentile mission, which begins in 70 CE (see further the debate between Gundry 1994: 436–7 and Davies and Allison 1997: 202). In a similar way, *Rec.* 1.27–71 regards the mission to the nations as beginning only after the destruction of the Temple (1.64.2–3). Moreover, just as Matthew springs from the exile to Christ (Matt. 1:17), so also *Rec.* 1.27–71 skips over the exile and practically the whole Second-Temple period and proceeds directly to the coming of the Prophet like Moses (1.39.1–2). Also, Matthew's Gospel presents Jesus as the new Moses. Cf. Allison 1993.

95. See Chap. 3.

96. Cf. Jones 1995b: 617–35; 1995a: 141–2. Jones (1995b: 626) explains the "seventy-two" in *Rec.* 1.34.2 as dependent on "seventy-five" in Acts 7:17: "Seventy-two is a most unusual number to have going to Egypt and is most readily explained as an awkward attempt by R 1 to speak of seventy-two followers of Moses, which the author needed as a prefiguration of Jesus' followers (R 1.40.4 [Lk. 10:1, 17])."

97. Also, the disciple of John uses the words of Jesus in Lk. 7:24–8 (or Matt. 11:7–11) to argue that John is the Messiah (*Rec.* 1.60.1). Just as in Lk. 4:23; 5:31 Jesus is likened to a "physician," so also in *Rec.* 1.64.3 he is called a "physician." The Temple will be destroyed because the Jews did not recognize the time of their visitation from God (Lk. 19:45), just as in *Rec.* 1.64.2–3.

98. Luke-Acts has a strongly Deuteronomic character. Cf. Moessner 1989; Römer and Macchi 1995: 178–87; Baasland 1995: 191–226.

99. The following parallels are drawn largely from Jones 1995b: 622–9, who describes each one according to their order in *Rec.* 1.27–71 and in terms of the probability of their dependence on Acts (most secure instances, probable instances, possible instances). Other attempts have been made to establish a relationship between the Pseudo-Clementines and Acts. Cf., e.g., Martyn 1977: 267, 269, 273, 279ff. As Martyn (ibid., 273) points out, "It is clear that he [sc. the author of the source] intends radically to correct Acts, perhaps even to replace it."

100. Such letters from the highest Jewish communities in the mother country to the Diaspora communities are attested by Luke in Acts 28:21 and also by early rabbinic tradition (cf. Taatz 1991).

101. Cf. Jones 1995b: 624–5. Hengel and Schwemer (1997: 50–1) point out that Luke tends to depict Paul the persecutor in rather too glaring colors. In that case, *Rec.* 1.71.3–4 further magnifies and distorts Paul as the persecutor of the early church.

102. Cf. Jones 1995b: 625–6, 631.

103. Cf. Turner 1996: 311–12.

104. Cf. Jones 1995b: 629: "The author of R 1 was accordingly influenced by the entire book of Acts throughout all sections of his writing." *Pace* Wehnert 1997: 185: "Der zweite Teil der Apg war für den antipln. Autor dieses Werkes [i.e., *Rec.* 1.27–71] offensichtlich unbrauchbar..." Wehnert's study of the Ps.-Clementines (ibid., 145–86) almost completely ignores *Rec.* 1.27–71 for the discussion of Acts.

105. By the same token, our text does not explicitly mention the *Book of Jubilees* as a source, although there can be little question that *Jubilees* was also used in our text.

106. Cf. Jones 1995b: 629: "If, as was concluded above, the author of R 1 truly knew and used Acts, R 1.27–71 presents one of the first 'commentaries' on Acts." Jones hesitates to call our text "the first commentary" because he regards the textual variants to the Greek NT to be the oldest commentary (ibid., 629 n. 47). Cf. Strange 1992: 37, who understands by "the Western text" "a broad stream of textual tradition, and a way of handling the text," with a "commentary-like character" (40).

107. Epiphanius (*Pan.* 30.16.6–9) has an interesting remark about Jewish–Christian acts of the apostles, which may relate to *Rec.* 1.27–71 and its evaluation of Paul: "They say that there are other Acts of apostles; and these contain much utterly impious material, with which they deliberately arm themselves against the truth. (7) They prescribe certain decrees and directions in the 'Degrees of James,' if you please, as though he discoursed against the temple and sacrifices, and the fire on the altar – and much else that is full of nonsense. (8) Nor are they ashamed to accuse Paul here with certain false inventions of their false apostles' villainy and imposture. They say that he was a Tarsean – which he admits himself and does not deny. But they suppose that he was of Greek parentage, taking the occasion for this from the (same) passage he frankly said, 'I am a man of Tarsus, a citizen of no mean city' (Acts 21:39). (9) They then claim that he was Greek and the son of a Greek mother and father, but that he had gone up to Jerusalem, stayed a while, and desired to marry a daughter of the high priest. He therefore became proselyte and was circumcised. But since he still could not get that

sort of girl he became angry, and wrote against circumcision, and the Sabbath and Legislation." Cf. F. Williams 1997: 132–3; see further Voorst 1989: 44–5.

108. Jones 1995b: 631–2. Cf., similarly, Martyn 1977: 269: "[*Rec.* 1.33ff.] begins precisely where the redemptive–historical sketch in Stephen's speech takes its beginning (Acts 7:2ff.), but also that it runs somewhat parallel to it: Abraham, Isaac, Jacob, the twelve Patriarchs, the seventy-five (Acts) or seventy-two (R) who entered Egypt, and Moses, together with Moses' promise that God would raise up another prophet like him."

109. For instance, Stephen's radical temple criticism in Acts 7:41–3 may have inspired the link in our Pseudo-Clementine source between the wilderness story and the eventual building of the Temple because of the idolatrous bent of the people (cf. *Rec.* 1.35.5–36.1; 37.1–2; 38.5). For according to Acts 7:41, the idolatrous Israelites are said to have rejoiced "in the work of their hands," and Acts 7:48, which refers at least in part to the Temple, makes the point that God does not dwell in houses "made with [human] hands." Hence, the author of the Pseudo-Clementine source could have concluded, as modern scholars often do, that the building of the Temple was an act continuous with the fashioning of the golden calf at Sinai.

110. Cf. *Rec.* 1.43.1 ("They were frequently sending and asking us to speak with them about Jesus, whether he is the prophet who was foretold by Moses, that is, the eternal Christ"); 44.2 ("Caiaphas the high priest sent priests to us to come to him so that either we might persuade him that Jesus is the eternal Christ or that he might persuade us that he is not . . . "), 4; 1.45.1–2 ("God, who made the world and who is lord of everything, appointed chiefs over everything, even over plants and rocks, springs and rivers, and every creature. For there are many that I might enumerate like them. [2] Thus, he appointed as chiefs an angel over the angels, a spirit over spirits, a star over the stars, a bird over the birds, a beast over the beasts, an insect over the insects, a fish over the fish, and over humans, a human, who is the Christ"), 4 ("The reason that he might be called Christ is that he was the Son of God and became human. And because he was the first chief, his Father anointed him in the beginning with the oil that comes from the tree of life"); 63.1 ("Against all we said that Jesus is the eternal Christ").

111. Cf. *Rec.* 1.45.4 (cited above); 48.4; 63.2 Latin; 69.7 ("But he spoke also concerning the Son the matter of how, and from whom, and that it is not that he is without beginning, and that therefore the matter of when [he was begotten] is not said concerning him").

112. For example, the allusion to Isa. 49:6 in Acts 1:8; the allusion to Deut. 30:4–5 (cf. Neh. 1:8–9; 2 Macc. 2:18) in Acts 2:5; the citation of Amos 9:11–12 in Acts 15:16–18.

113. Cf. Acts 1:8 (*Jub.* 8:12); Acts 2:2 (*Jub.* 10:26); Acts 2:9–11 (*Jub.* 8–9); Acts 15:20, 29 (*Jub.* 7:20).

5   Theophilus of Antioch

1. Cf. Grant 1988: 143.

2. Cf. Grant 1970: xvii–xix; 1988: 165–6. Ultimately, there may be no distinction in Theophilus' mind between being a Jew and being a Christian. Cf. Grant 1988: 166: "Because of his ambiguous theology one cannot be sure that he reflects Christianity rather than Judaism or if, indeed, there was a clear line between the two in his mind." For example, when he claims that "only the Christians have held the truth" (*Autol.* 2.33), he is dealing specifically with the inferiority of all Greek writers vis-à-vis the OT prophets. In no way is his comment designed to disparage Jews, for as he goes on to state in the same text, "only the Christians have held the truth – we who are instructed by the Holy Spirit and who spoke in the holy prophet and foretold everything."

3. Cf. Grant 1988: 165: "There [sc. Book 1 of *Ad Autolycum*] Theophilus clearly states that he is a Christian but explains the name as based on being 'anointed with the oil

of God,' without any reference to Christ (1.12)." However, this passage may allude to 2 Cor. 1:21 (ὁ δὲ βεβαιῶν ἡμᾶς σὺν ὑμῖν εἰς Χριστὸν καὶ χρίσας ἡμᾶς θεός), in which case Theophilus' reference to being "anointed with the oil of God" strongly implies Christ.

4. However, Theophilus does clearly make use of the Pauline letters elsewhere in his three-volume work. Cf. Grant 1988: 163–4.

5. Grant 1988: 165: "... his [sc. Theophilus'] teaching is essentially Jewish in tone and is based on the Old Testament as understood by Hellenistic Jews – not allegorizers like Philo but the more literal-minded exegetes in view in his *Questions on Genesis ...*"

6. Theophilus' exegesis of the OT is essentially Jewish in nature. Cf. Grant 1970: xiv–xv; 1988: 157–9; Skarsaune 1996: 415–17.

7. The *Contra Apionem* of Josephus provided a model for Theophilus' apologetic; indeed, Josephus was one of his main sources outside the OT (cf. *Autol.* 3.20, 21, 22, 23, 26, 29).

8. See especially *Autol.* 2.11–32 and 3.16–26. On Theophilus' biblical chronology, see Grant 1988: 155–6.

9. Cf. Grant 1970: xv: "The theology of Theophilus ... is the most radically monotheistic to be found among the Greek Christian apologists. ... in part, and most important, it is due to his proximity to Hellenistic Judaism, with which most of his doctrine has close affinities."

10. Skarsaune 1996: 414.

11. Cf. Grant 1992: 109.

12. Grant 1970: x.

13. The Peutinger map (ca. 335–66 CE), known from a twelfth-century copy, represents the Nile as a river which arises in the mountains of Cyrenaica and flows eastward to a point just above the delta (cf. K. Miller 1888). This may, of course, have been influenced by the elongated deformation of the map.

14. The famous Madaba mosaic map portrays the Nile as originating in the East (cf. Donner 1984: 255–6). On the various conceptions of the source and course of the Nile, see further Werner 1993: 14 n. 30, 15 n. 32, 32–6; Honigmann 1936.

15. On the ancient notion of κλίματα, see further pp. 130–1.

16. In subsequently summarizing the three population movements, Theophilus proceeds in a clockwise direction: "in the east and the south and the west ..."

17. Grant (1992: 109) suggests that Theophilus' "discussion of colonization looks like a garbled version of Josephus [*Ant.* 1.120–47]." However, Josephus mentions nothing of world colonization due to overpopulation, a theme that is familiar, for example, from Philo (*Legat.* 45–6) and Diodorus Siculus (1.28.2–3); cf. Scott 1995b: 556–62. For discussion of the traditions on which Theophilus relies in *Autol.* 2.32, see further pp. 132–3.

18. Cf. P. S. Alexander 1982: 204. The Nile was traditionally regarded as the boundary between Libya/Africa and Asia; Gadir/Cadiz, also known as the Pillars of Heracles, was regarded as the boundary between Libya/Africa and Europe; and Tanais/Don was regarded as the boundary between Europe and Asia. Cf. Strabo, *Geog.* 1.2.25, 28; 1.4.7; 2.4.6–7; 2.5.26, 31; 7.4.5; 11.1.1, 5; 11.7.4; 12.3.27; 17.3.1.

19. Cf. P. S. Alexander 1982: 207.

20. According to *Jub.* 10:27–34, Canaan illegitimately occupied the so-called "land of Canaan."

21. Cf. Strabo, *Geog.* 2.2.1–3. His discussion of zones continues in *Geog.* 2.3 (also 2.5.16). See the discussion on the climates in Chap. 2. On the use of κλίματα in the antediluvian cosmography of Annianus, see Adler 1989: 122–5.

22. As Drijvers (1996: 173) points out, the cultural tradition of Syriac Christianity "was not fundamentally different from what was thought and written in Greek-speaking Syria, where Syriac however was also well known and well understood." Note, however, that the question of Jewish influence on early Syriac Christianity and its

supposed Jewish–Christian character has been hotly debated and has not to date reached generally accepted conclusions. Cf. Drijvers 1992. On the *Book of Jubilees* in Syriac tradition, see also Bundy 1991: 752–3; Brock 1978.

23. Cf. *Autol.* 2.3, 31, 36, 38.
24. Grant 1970: 73 n. 29.1. Aristobulus (*ap.* Eusebius, *Praep. Ev.* 13.12.3) contains a possible parallel: "So also by the giving of the Law Moses has spoken to us the whole genesis of the world, words of God (καθὼς καὶ διὰ τῆς νομοθεσίας ἡμῖν ὅλην τὴν γένεσιν τοῦ κόσμου θεοῦ λόγους εἴρηκεν ὁ Μωσῆς)."
25. Cf., e.g., Hagedorn 1997; Jerome, *Ep.* 78.20 (Hilberg 1996: 68). The Hebrew title of the *Book of Jubilees* is apparently given in CD 16.3–4, where it is cited and called "The Book of the Divisions of the Times according to Their Jubilees and Their Weeks." Elsewhere, *Jubilees* is also called, for example, Βίβλος τῆς Διαθήκης (cf. Hagedorn and Hagedorn 1987: 60), τὰ Ἰωβηλαία (Epiphanius, *Pan.* 39.6.1), Μωυσέως Ἀποκάλυψις (Syncellus 3.16–17; 27.34), and Βίου Ἀδαμ (Sync. 4.21–2). See further Rönsch 1874: 461–82.
26. Denis 1970a: 70–102. Frg. 2.1: διδασκόμενος παρὰ τοῦ ἀρχαγγέλου Γαβριὴλ τὰ περὶ τῆς γενέσεως τοῦ κόσμου. Frg. 48.1: καταλιπὼν δὲ Μωϋσῆς τὰς κατ᾽ Αἴγυπτον διατριβὰς εἰς τὴν ἔρημον ἐπιλοσόφει διδασκόμενος παρὰ τοῦ ἀρχαγγέλου Γαβριὴλ τὰ περὶ τῆς γενέσεως τοῦ κόσμου.
27. Note, however, that Epiphanius (*Pan.* 39.6.6) uses ἡ Γένεσις τοῦ κόσμου of the canonical Book of Genesis in distinction to the *Book of Jubilees*, called here τὰ Ἰωβηλαία and ἡ λεπτὴ Γένεσις (Epiphanius, *Pan.* 39.6.1, 5). On the other hand, Syncellus (47.11–20) refers to Γένεσις in a passage that clearly incorporates material from *Jubilees* (see further in Chap. 6).
28. Rönsch 1874: 280.
29. On the identification of Noah with Deucalion, see, for example, Philo, *Praem.* 23. See further Stern 1974–84: II.301; Hilhorst 1998: 56–65.
30. Cf. also *Autol.* 3.19: "This Noah had three sons, as we have explained in the second volume (2.30–1); their names are Sem and Cham and Iapheth. They had three wives, one for each, and there were Noah himself and his wife. (Some persons call this man a eunuch.) Eight human lives, then, were saved in all – those who were in the ark."
31. Cf. Grant 1970: 83 n. 32.4. For a diachronic survey of the images of the world in Greco-Roman sources, see Bannert 1978; see also Brincken 1976; Lindgren 1992.
32. David Woodward's comment (1987a: 326) does not seem to apply here: "In reaction to the classical geographers, the early fathers of the church were also anxious to stress that knowledge of the earth was of strictly secondary importance to the Christian, whose eyes should be on a higher spiritual plane."
33. The Hebrew Bible offered various possibilities for understanding the shape of the earth, which in any case was considered bounded (cf. Ps. 48:11; 65:6; Isa. 40:28; Job 28:24). Some texts suggest a circular shape for the earth (cf. Job 22:7; 26:10; Prov. 8:27; Isa. 40:22), whereas others seem to support a rectangular shape (cf. Job 37:3; Isa. 11:12; Rev. 7:1; 20:8). See further in Chap. 2.
34. Cf. Wolska-Conus 1968–73. Like Theophilus, Cosmas describes his vision of the world in the context of the postdiluvian settlement of the world. The four rivers of paradise correspond to the Nile, the Tigris, the Euphrates and the Ganges. And Noah's sons divide the earth according to the three continents. According to Revel-Neher (1990–91: 78), the iconographical motives in Cosmas' *Topography* "prove the existence of a Jewish model from which the artist copied extant schemes and specific formulae."
35. Cf. McCready 1996: 108–27.
36. Cf. P. S. Alexander 1982: 203: "Though it is not actually stated, it may be readily assumed that the world was represented as a disc, as on the Ionian and early Christian maps. This is a view which could be given Biblical support (cf. Job 26:10; Prov. 8:27), and it fits in most easily with the author of *Jubilees*' notion that the earth has a centre point (VIII 19)." Cartographic reconstructions of the *imago mundi* of

Jubilees normally have a disk shape. This is a common assumption for ancient maps in general. Cf. Harley, Woodward, and Aujac 1987: 135: "We have almost no details of Anaximander's map, but it is traditionally accepted that 'ancient maps' (which are probably those from Ionia) were circular, with Greece in the middle and Delphi in the center. Herodotus [4.36.] confirms the regularity of the form of these maps: 'For my part, I cannot but laugh when I see numbers of persons drawing maps of the world without having any reason to guide them; making, as they do, the ocean-stream to run all round the earth, and the earth itself to be an exact circle, as if described by a pair of compasses, with Europe and Asia just of the same size.' "

37. Cf., e.g., P. S. Alexander 1997a/1999: 149/105. See further in Chap. 7.
38. Cf. Kraft 1994: 68: "Very few Greek manuscripts of allegedly Jewish pseudepigrapha have survived from the period prior to the ninth century. To what extent this is a reflection of official orthodox hostility, or even of censorship, or is simply due to the general paucity of materials that have survived from that period is difficult to determine."
39. Cf. VanderKam 1989a: I.XI–XII; II.XI–XIV; Denis 1970a: 70–102; Milik 1971: 545–57.
40. Cf. Puech 1996. As is well known, the Greek NT cites *1 Enoch* 1:9 in Jude 14–15, which is perhaps additional evidence that a Greek version of *1 Enoch* circulated in the first century CE.
41. Adler 1990: 483, 491–2.
42. VanderKam 1989a: II.XIV.
43. Gelzer 1885: 249–97.
44. Cf. *P. Oxy.* 4365 (Rea 1996: 44–5): "To my dearest lady sister, greetings in the Lord. Lend the *(Book of) Ezra/Esdras*, since I lent you the *Little Genesis*. Farewell in God" (τῇ κυρίᾳ μου φιλτάτῃ ἀδελφῇ ἐν κ[υρί]ῳ χαίρειν. χρῆσον τὸν Ἔσδραν, ἐπεὶ ἔχρησά σοι τὴν Λεπτὴν Γένεσιν. ἔρρωσο ἐν θ[ε]ῷ). See further Hagedorn 1997. The interest shown here in *Ezra/Esdras* (= *4 Ezra*?) and *Jubilees* may have been motivated by apocalyptic speculation.

6 Hippolytus of Rome

1. Cf. Croke 1992: 116–31. The present chapter revises and expands my earlier article (Scott 1997a: 295–323).
2. Cf. Routh 1814: 124–95, which does not contain the *Diamerismos* tradition. Note that William Adler is currently preparing a translation and commentary on the fragments of Africanus' *Chronographies*.
3. This is not to say that the complex textual situation of Hippolytus' *Chronicon* has been completely clarified, but rather that this writing has at least come down to us in several recensions and versions, with one thought to be particularly close to the supposed original. See further Bauer and Helm 1955: IX–XXXI.
4. According to Gelzer (1885: 294), Africanus knew from the *Book of Jubilees* (8:11) the story of how Noah divided by lot the territories of the earth that his three sons would receive.
5. The paronomasia occurs only in the Hebrew text: the name "Peleg" (פלג) is derived from "divided" (נפלגה).
6. Cf. Adler 1990: 491–2, who regards Leo Grammaticus 13.17–18 to be "an authentic extract from the third-century chronicle of Africanus." Cf. already Gelzer 1885: 294.
7. Cf. Bauer and Helm 1955: XXX: "Für diesen Abschnitt der christlichen Weltchronik [i.e., the *Diamerismos*] war Hippolyt der ursprüngliche Gewahrsmann; weder Afrikanus vor ihm noch später Eusebius haben in ihren Werken etwas ähnliches geboten." On the *Wirkungsgeschichte* of the *Diamerismos*, see further pp. 149–58.
8. Bauer and Helm (1955: 13 n. 2) regard certain "additions" in Hippolytus' *Diamerismos* (§§73–8, 202–23) to have taken place before Hippolytus "in den

jüdisch-hellenistischen Bearbeitung des Diamerismos." Bauer and Helm (ibid., 26 n. 2) reckon that Hippolytus used an earlier *Diamerismos* that already contained many contradictions. On 27 n. 15, Bauer and Helm refer to "the original Diamerismos" (so also 33 n.). Ibid., XXIX–XXX: "Es muß versucht werden, die vor Hippolyt liegende Entstehungsgeschichte des Diamerismos zu ermitteln und die Entstehungszeit der einzelnen Bestandteile festzustellen, aus denen die verhältnismäßig junge, von Widersprüchen strotzende Fassung in der Chronik entstanden ist, der Anteil muß geschieden werden, der in diesem geographisch-ethnographischen Sammelsurium einerseits den hellenistisch-jüdischen Erweiterungen der Völkertafel der Genesis und andererseits Anleihen bei der antiken geographischen und ethnographischen Literatur zufällt." Note also that in his comprehensive study of the use of *Jubilees* in Christian sources, Rönsch (1874: 252–382) does not consider Hippolytus at all, arguing that an explicit citation of the pseudepigraphon occurs for the first time in Christian sources towards the end of the fourth century (ibid., 321–2).

9. Cf., e.g., Bauer 1905: 151 n. 2 [emphasis mine]: "Erhalten ist uns davon [i.e., Hellenistic-Jewish precursors of Hippolytus' *Diamerismos*] nur das sogenannte Buch der Jubiläen oder die kleine Genesis aus dem ersten nachchristlichen Jahrhundert, die jedoch mit dem Diamerismos des Hippolytos *keine Berührung* zeigt . . ." See also Bauer and Strzygowski 1906: 24.

10. Denis 1970b: 155 (emphasis mine). See also R. H. Charles 1972: lxxx: "The Διαμερισμὸς τῆς γῆς which is assigned to this writer [sc. Hippolytus] is based on *Jub.* viii–ix"; Berger 1998: 36; P. S. Alexander 1982: 212: "The text of Jubilees in its Greek and Latin versions was certainly known to the Church fathers, and some patristic accounts of the Table of the Nations, such as the *Diamerismos* of Hippolytus, appear to have drawn on it." Such opinions go back ultimately to Gutschmid 1894: 239, 585–717, who holds that *Jubilees* 8–9 is "the model for all later versions of the Table of Nations" (587).

11. Other possibilities are (1) that Hippolytus used a source that had already incorporated Jubilees 8–9 or (2) that both Hippolytus and *Jubilees* go back to a common source.

12. For the interim, see Scholten 1991: 504–7; Simonetti 1997: 27–31; Phillips 1989.

13. Jean Daniélou (1973: 260) believes that Hippolytus' notion of the Antichrist arising from the tribe of Dan, his idea that Benjamin is a type of the Apostle Paul, and his particular interest in Joseph as a type of Christ, all derive from the *Testaments of the Twelve Patriarchs*. Moreover, L. Mariès (1951–52: 381–96) argues that Hippolytus' notion of the Levitical descent of Jesus Christ derives from the *Testaments*. See, however, de Jonge 1991a: 204–19 (esp. 216–19); Hollander and de Jonge 1985: 77–8, 81.

14. On the Christian character of the *Testaments*, see Hollander and de Jonge 1985: 83–5 *et passim*; de Jonge 1991b: 147–63; 1993: 1–28.

15. Cf. VanderKam 1994a: 40; Kee 1983: 777.

16. Cf., e.g., VanderKam 1994a: 40–1; Stone and Greenfield 1996; Stone 1996b; Kugler 1996.

17. Cf. Kraft 1994. See further in the Introduction to the present volume.

18. Cf. *Chron.* 72 (καὶ Κίτιοι, ἀφ' οὗ Ῥωμαῖοι <οἱ> καὶ Λατῖνοι), 200 (Ῥωμαῖοι οἱ καὶ Λατῖνοι καὶ Κιτιαῖοι), 215 (Ῥωμαίων δὲ τῶν καὶ Κιτιέων [τῶν καὶ Λατίνων κεκλημένων] ἔθνη). The *Diamerismos* appears to have a special interest in the Kittim (cf. §§72–5). In early Jewish and Christian literature, Χεττιείμ and Χεττιίμ also occur as orthographic variations.

19. See also Eusebius, *Onomasticon*, s.v. Χεττιείμ (Judg. 1:26): γῆ Χεττιείμ ἡ Κύπρος; Tsirkin 1991: 122.

20. See already the Hebrew inscriptions from the sixth century BCE which apply Kittim to the Greeks in general. Cf. Renz 1995: 353–4 *et passim*.

21. Denis 1987.

22. The name does not occur at all, for example, in Aland and Aland 1988.

23. As was mentioned in Chap. 2, H. Eshel ("The Kittim in the War Scroll and Pesharim" [forthcoming]) argues that the identity of the "Kittim" changes over time in the Qumran community: from the Hellenistic kingdoms in general in early Qumran compositions, to the Seleucids in particular, and finally to the Romans (after 63 BCE). Insofar as Hippolytus' *Diamerismos* contains material that refers to the geopolitical situation under Antiochus III (see below on the description of Shem's territory in *Chron.* 47), the identification of Kittim with the Romans in the same text appears to stem from a different period. There was never any question that the *Diamerismos* is a composite text.

24. In this particular case, the source is not likely to be *Jubilees* 8–9, since the latter does not explicitly mention Kittim (nor indeed any of Noah's greatgrandsons). Moreover, Javan's portion, which would presumably include Kittim's, does not seem to extend to Italy (cf. *Jub.* 9:10: "For Javan there emerged as the fourth share every island and the islands that are in the direction of Lud's border"). From the perspective of *Jubilees*, Italy seems to be part of Tubal's portion (cf. *Jub.* 9:12; P. S. Alexander 1982: 209). Yet, if *Jubilees* is closely connected with the Qumran community, which identified the Kittim with Rome, then there must have been different perspectives on this matter within the community.

25. For the text, see Vermes and Goodman 1989: 62–73. See also Cansdale 1997.

26. On the debate over this point, see, e.g., Black 1956: 172–5; Burchard 1977: 1–41 (with a synopsis of the two Greek texts on pp. 8–20); Hardwick 1989: 51–7, who argues that Hippolytus did not read Josephus' description of the Essenes in the *Jewish War*, but rather probably used a Christian source (Hegesippus?) who relied on Josephus and Christianized the material. On Josephus and Hippolytus, see further Baumgarten 1984; Marcovitch 1988; Nodet and Taylor 1998: 398 n. 143; Rajak 1994: 152–3.

27. See further Puech 1993: 703–69; Elgvin 1996: 142–3.

28. Cf. VanderKam 1994a: 78–81; Beall 1988: 162 n. 270. Puech (1999: 553 n. 21) is critical of scholars who emphasize Josephus' views about the Essenes, without doing justice to the ancient account of Hippolytus.

29. Cf. Collins 1997a: 114–15.

30. Cf. Hinson 1989; 1992. Hinson does not discuss the first two lines of evidence to which we referred above. Nodet and Taylor (1998) have recently reasserted the thesis that Christianity emerged from the Essenes. On Essene parallels to Christian rituals described by Hippolytus, see ibid., 423–4. If, as often argued, Hebrews was written to Rome (cf., e.g., W. Lane 1991: lviii–lx; Attridge 1989: 9–10) and was also influenced by the Essenes (cf., e.g., Hughes 1977: 10–15; but see Lane 1991: cv, cviii; Hurst 1997: 998–9; Attridge 1989: 29), then we may have additional (and possibly early) evidence of Essene influence in Rome. On echoes of Essene influence in Jewish Christianity, see Goranson 1998–99: II.549–50.

31. Burchard (1977: 39) argues that Hippolytus has more than a merely encyclopedic interest in the Essenes and the other Jews whom he describes in *Ref.* 9.18–30: they implicitly provide evidence of how the "true teaching" revealed to Noah came to the Christians. Interestingly enough, Eusebius (*HE* 2.16ff.) and many later Church Fathers claim that Essenes were precursors of Christianity. Burchard proposes that Hippolytus was, in fact, the first Father to suggest this idea.

32. On the authorship of the *Chronicon*, see, however, Brent 1995: 271: "Indeed the anonymity of the work [sc. the *Chronicon*] needs to be emphasised in view of the too quick assumption, which we have seen to be all too common for the health of the discussion, that it must have been by Hippolytus since the Statue must both have been his, and he himself the author of every work on the list."

33. Cf. Bauer and Helm 1955: XXVIII. See also Schwarte 1966: 153–4.

34. Cf. Bauer and Helm 1955: IX. On Hippolytus' apocalyptic perspective, see, e.g., VanderKam 1996: 93–5; Adler 1996: 220, 226–7; Landes 1988: 144–9; Potter 1994: 106–8. On the chronological discrepancies between the *Chronicon* and Hippolytus' commentary on Daniel, see Brent 1995: 273–84.

35. Cf. Adler 1989: 81–2: "There is, broadly speaking, a congruity of interests between Christian chronography and the Jewish literature of the Second Temple Period, especially the Jewish apocalypses. Christian chronography was originally conceived as a highly specialized form of Jewish/Christian apocalypticism. Both the Christian universal chronicle and the Jewish apocalypse characteristically encompassed the whole course of human history, and both were known to periodize human history according to some artificial scheme. For both, matters of precise reckoning of time figured importantly, especially insofar as this involved the dating of feasts and commemorations, and eschatological expectation." Note that both *Jubilees* and Hippolytus have systems of chronology that date events from the creation of the world, although each system gives very different dates for the individual events. On the chronological system in *Jubilees*, see VanderKam 1995; Rook 1983: 126–69. Compare the chart of the chronological system of *Jubilees* (VanderKam 1995: 86–9) with the chart of the chronological system of Hippolytus' *Chronicon* (Bauer and Helm 1955:193–6). For example, *Jubilees* (8:10) dates the division of the world to the 33rd jubilee (= 1569 anno mundi), whereas Hippolytus (*Chron.* 42) calculates 2,767 years from the time of Adam to Peleg ("in his days the earth was divided" [Gen. 10:25]).

36. As we suggested in Chap. 5, *P. Oxy.* 4365 shows an interest in *Jubilees* and *Ezra* (= *4 Ezra*?) which may have been motivated by apocalyptic speculation.

37. Cf., e.g., Casson 1989. The purpose of this first-century CE periplus is to provide a sailing manual for merchants trading between Roman Egypt and eastern Africa, southern Arabia, and India. See further Purcell 1996: 1141–2.

38. In an earlier work, the *Refutation of All Heresies* (ca. 218–22 CE), Hippolytus already refers to a *Diamerismos*-like work as a "book." Thus in *Ref.* 10.30.4–5 we read: "In the time of Phalek, the descendants of Noah were scattered. These were the 72, from whom also [stem] the 72 nations, whose names we have also set forth in other books (ὧν καὶ τὰ ὀνόματα ἐτεθείμεθα ἐν ἑτέραις βίβλοις)..." This statement is directly comparable to the beginning of the *Diamerismos* (*Chron.* 45–6, 53): "(45) The division of the earth happened after the flood among the three sons of Noah – Shem, Ham and Japheth. (46) The tribes of the three brothers were dispersed...(53) The languages were confused upon the earth after the flood. Therefore, the confused languages were 72..." Bauer (1905: 158–62) believes that Hippolytus refers here to the *Chronicon*; however, the *Chronicon* was written after the *Refutation of All Heresies*. Perhaps, therefore, the *Refutatio* refers to an earlier version of the *Chronicon* which was later updated (cf. Brent 1995: 270–99).

39. Rönsch 1874: 280. Syncellus' citations from *Jubilees* and the allied *Life of Adam* (cf. Sync. 4.21–2: ἐκ τῆς Λεπτῆς Γενέσεως καὶ τοῦ λεγομένου βίου ᾿Αδάμ) are, as he himself recognizes, epitomized forms of these works (Sync. 5.26–7). Cf. Adler 1989: 183.

40. The appendix to the *Diamerismos* includes material on (1) the colonies of the "unknown" nations (§§ 202–23); (2) the climates of the "unknown" nations (§§ 224–34); (3) the twelve most famous mountains (§235); (4) the most famous rivers (§§ 236–7); and (5) the sources of the rivers of Paradise (§§ 238–9). It is difficult to ascertain the origin of these diverse materials. For example, the twelve most famous mountains may have a connection with the twelve mountains from which, according to Hermas, the stones for building of the Tower of Babel were quarried (*Sim.* 9.1.1–10), and which represent the nations that inhabit the whole world (*Sim.* 9.17.1–4).

41. Cf. §§ 202 ("I thought it necessary also to disclose to you the colonies of the unknown nations and their names and their climates, how they dwell and which nation is near which, in order that that you might not be unacquainted with these things"), 224 ("And this appeared necessary for me to disclose to you: the climates of the unknown nations and most famous mountains and the best-known rivers which pour out into the Sea, in order that you might not be unaware of these things"), 225 ("I will begin, therefore, to speak about the unknown nations from East to West, how they dwell"),

236 ("The names of the twelve mountains of the earth having been therefore shown, it is necessary also to disclose to you the most famous rivers").

42. The term used in §§ 89 and 197 is μέρος, denoting "portion, share" (cf. LSJ, s.v., 1104). The same term is implied in §§ 48, 49, 83, 188. For the analogous term (חלק "portion, possession, lot") in the Genesis Apocryphon, see 1QapGen. 16.14; 17.7, 11, 15, 19. Cf. Beyer 1984–92: I.580–1; II.348.

43. One wonders whether *Jubilees* may have also inspired the inclusion of some of the "extra" lists in the *Diamerismos*: e.g., the climates of the unknown nations (§§ 224–34; cf. *Jub.* 8:30; Theophilus, *Autol.* 2.32); the descendants of Noah who understood writing (§§ 81–2, 134–5, 192; cf. *Jub.* 8:2, 11); the most famous mountains and rivers (§§ 235, 236–7; cf. P. S. Alexander 1982: 207–8).

44. On the limits of Shem's territory, see also *Chron.* 188, 191, 195. For the description of the boundaries of Shem's territory in the Genesis Apocryphon, see 1QapGen. 16.15–20: "(15)...go out the waters of the Tina River...(16) up to the Tina River...(17) [to] the Great Salt Sea, and this boundary runs as a spring from this bay...(18)...that runs to the west and passes...(19)...till it reaches...(20)...to the East..."

45. For other occurrences of Rinocorura in the *Diamerismos*, see §§ 48, 130, 136, 188, 191, 195, 196.

46. Adler (1990: 495–6) considers the presence of "Rinocorura" in Epiphanius' elaboration of the Table of Nations as an indication that Epiphanius abandoned the geography of *Jubilees*. Charles (1972: 70 n. 13) tries to see in "Karas" (*Jub.* 8:13) the remains of an original Ῥινοκορούρα.

47. Cf. *PW* II.1 (1920) 841–2. The Madaba mosaic map places Rinocorura on the Mediterranean coast between Ostrakine and Betylion, with the following caption coming just below the name Rinocorura and its cartographic symbol: ὅροι Αἰγύπτον κ[αὶ] Παλαιστίνης. Cf. Donner and Cüppers 1977: 156, 158; Donner 1992: 77–8. A map of the Holy Land drawn in the margin of an eighth-century copy of Paul Orosius' *Histories* (Orosius Codex 621, St. Gall) indicates Rinocorura as the boundary town between Egypt and Palestine, albeit separately from the *Fluvius Egypti* (cf. Delano Smith 1991: 150). The Peutinger map shows Rinocorura on the Mediterranean coast between "Pelusio" and "Ascalone" (cf. K. Miller 1888: segmentum IX 5; see further idem 1896: 813).

48. Cf. Strabo, *Geog.* 16.4.24: Ῥινοκόλουρα τῆς πρὸς Αἰγύπτῳ Φοινίκης. According to Strabo (16.2.33), Phoenicia extended all the way to Pelusium, which was a generally recognized border town between Egypt and Asia – the town at the easternmost mouth of the Nile that formed the natural entry to Egypt to the northeast, on the route upriver to Memphis. Cf. Thompson 1996: 1134–5; Kees 1937: 407–15.

49. Cf. Diod. Sic. 1.60.6 ("This city [sc. Rinocoloura], which lies on the border between Egypt and Syria not far from the sea-coast..."); Polybius 5.80 (Ῥαφίας ἣ κεῖται μετὰ Ῥινοκόλουρα πρώτη τῶν κατὰ Κοίλην Συρίαν πόλεων ὡς πρὸς τὴν Αἴγυπτον).

50. So Bar-Deroma 1960: 50; cf. Koehler and Baumgartner 1995: II.687; Redpath 1903: 302. Cf. *Jub.* 10:29: "When Canaan saw that the land of Lebanon as far as the stream of Egypt was very beautiful, he did not go to his hereditary land to the west of the sea." This reference to "the stream of Egypt" seems to mean the Nile, for the point is that Canaanites settled in Shemite rather than in Hamite territory, the Nile (Gihon) being the boundary between the two (*Jub.* 8:22). Cf. VanderKam 1989a: II.63 n. on *Jub.* 10:29. In the map of the Holy Land accompanying a medieval manuscript of Rashi's Bible on Num. 34:3 (Munich #5, p. 139v, dated 1233 CE), the "Nile" (נילוס) forms the southern boundary of the "Land of Canaan" (ארץ כנען). Cf. Delano Smith and Gruber 1992: 31. Rabbinic literature does not seem to include Rinocorura as a border. Cf. Reeg 1991: 171–86. However, *t. Sheb.* 4:10 mentions the name Raphiah deHagra ("Raphia of the wall") as a name of a province located on the border between Egypt and Palestine. Cf. Abel 1967: I.308–10. Furthermore, the boundaries of the Land according

to Judah ben Ilai (*y. Hall.* 60a) include Naḥal Mizraim, which P. S. Alexander (1992: 987) takes to mean Wadi el-'Arish; see also his interpretation of the boundaries of the Land described in Ezek. 47:15–20 (ibid., 985). Note the comment of Esarhaddon (680–699 BCE) about passing through Raphia on his way to Egypt (*ANET*, 292): "(Then) I removed my camp from Musru and marched directly towards Meluhha [i.e., Egypt] – a distance of 30 double-hours from the town of Apku which is in the region of Samaria (*Sa-me-[ri-na]*) as far as the town of Rapihu (in) the region adjacent to the 'Brook of Egypt' – and there is no river (all the way)!" Here, the "Brook of Egypt" would seem to be referring to Wadi el-'Arish. On the suggestion of identifying the Wadi of Egypt with the brook of Besor south of Gaza, see Weinfeld 1993: 53 n. 2.

51. In a passage that has much in common with both *Jubilees* 8–9 and Hippolytus' *Diamerismos*, Epiphanius, *Pan.* 66.83.4–5 describes Rinocoroura as the place where Noah divided the world among his three sons by casting lots and then adds the following reason: "For Rinocoroura is translated 'Neel,' and so the natives naturally call it; but in Hebrew it is translated 'lots,' since Noah cast the lots for his three sons there (Ῥινοκόρουρα γὰρ ἑρμηνεύεται Νέελ, καὶ οὕτω φύσει οἱ ἐπιχώριοι αὐτὴν καλοῦσιν· ἀπὸ δὲ τῆς Ἑβραΐδος ἑρμηνεύεται κλῆροι, ἐπειδήπερ ὁ Νῶε ἐκεῖ ἔβαλε τοὺς κλήρους τοῖς τρισὶν υἱοῖς αὐτοῦ)." Cf. F. Williams 1997: 302. As Holl (1915–33: III.125 n. 1) points out, Epiphanius evidently associates the word נחל ("river") in the name נחל מצרים ("River of Egypt" [Isa 27:12]) with the Hebrew word נחלה (Greek κλῆρος, "lot"). As far as I am able to ascertain, the name Νέελ occurs nowhere else in Greek literature. Perhaps it is a corruption of Νεῖλος ("Nile"). See, however, Epiphanius, *Ancoratus* 112.3, which describes Rinocoroura as lying between Egypt and Palestine, opposite the Red Sea: καὶ τῷ μὲν Σὴμ τῷ πρωτοτόκῳ ὑπέπεσεν ὁ κλῆρος ἀπὸ Περσίδος καὶ Βάκτρων ἕως 'Ινδικῆς ·τὸ μῆκος, πλάτος δὲ ἀπὸ 'Ινδικῆς ἕως τῆς χώρας Ῥινοκουρούρων· κεῖται δὲ αὕτη ἡ Ῥινοκουρούρων ἀνὰ μέσον Αἰγύπτου καὶ Παλαιστίνης, ἀντικρὺ τῆς ἐρυθρᾶς θαλάσσης. Abel (1967: I.301) argues that Νέελ transcribes נחל ("wadi") and compares Νεελκεράβα in Cyril of Scythopolis (*Sabas* 16), referring to Wadi Qarawa.

52. Cf. Stone 1981: 225 (emphasis mine).

53. On the relationship between the Armenian text and Hippolytus, see Stone 1981: 221: "A much expanded form of the same body of material, in the section dealing with the descendants of Japheth, may be observed in the second chapter of *The History of the Caucasian Albanians* by Moses Dasxuranc'i. In a note to this passage, Dowsett points out that in it Dasxuranc'i is dependent on the Chronicle by Hippolytus which was published, in its Armenian version, by Sarghissian. Chabot does not reckon Hippolytus' Chronicle among the sources used by Michael the Syrian, and a particularly close relationship exists between Michael's work and the text published here, as is indicated at a number of points in the Commentary below. It thus seems that there may be some intermediate link in the transmission." Unfortunately, Stone does not consider the *Jubilees* 8–9 tradition, which might have helped to clarify several aspects of the Armenian text.

54. Cf. *Jub.* 8:23: "The Gihon River goes until it reaches the right side of the Garden of Eden."

55. In discussing the countries of Ham, the *Diamerismos* mentions "Mauretania which stretches to the Pillars of Heracles before Gadeira" (Μαυριτανία ἡ παρεκτείνουσα μέχρι Ἡρακλείων στηλῶν κατέναντι Γαδείρων [§149]). On the relationship between Mauretania in Libya and the Strait of Gibraltar, see Strabo, *Geog.* 3.5.5; 17.3.2.

56. Cf. Strabo, *Geog.* 2.5.26: "Now as you sail into the strait at the Pillars, Libya lies on your right as far as the stream of the Nile, and on your left hand across the strait lies Europe as far as the Tanais. And both Europe and Libya end at Asia."

57. Cf. P. S. Alexander 1982: 205: "According to Jubilees VIII 15 the Mediterranean is joined to the outside Ocean by a narrow channel which is compared to a mouth. The reference is, of course, to the Straits of Gibraltar, and precisely the same metaphor is used by Ps.-Aristotle [*De Mundo* III (393a.17)]." However, a TLG search failed

to surface a single example of the expression στόμα θαλάσσης/θαλάττης with reference to the Strait of Gibraltar, although "the mouth of the Caspian/Hyrcanian Sea" was found (cf. Posidonius, frg. 47a [ed. W. Theiler]; Strabo, *Geog.* 2.1.17; 2.5.14; 7.2.4; 11.1.5; 11.11.7). Moreover, in elaborating the doctrine of the four gulfs of the οἰκουμένη (i.e., Mediterranean, Persian, Caspian, Arabian), Agathemerus refers to the "mouth" of Lake Maeotis (3.10), of the Persian Sea (3.12), and of the Caspian Sea (3.13). Cf. Diller 1975: 63.

58. Cf. Hengel 1989b: 70: "[Antiochus III's] prestige in the west was increased by his successful campaign in the eastern provinces as far as Bactria and 'India,' which was seen as an *imitatio Alexandri*. To distinguish himself from the kings of Armenia, Parthia and Bactria, who had become vassals, he took the title 'The Great King.'" See also the somewhat expanded version in Hengel 1980: 39.

59. Cf. Waldmann 1987.

60. In contrast, *Jubilees* 8–9 assigns all of Asia, including Asia Minor, to Shem. Cf. Scott 1995a: 23 with n. 68. Genesis 10 itself seems to have made Asia Minor "the centre of the habitation of Japheth's descendants" (so Tsirkin 1991: 123).

61. Cf. Sherwin-White and Kuhrt 1993: 215: "From Cilicia, to the borders of ancient Iran, from the river Oxus to the Arab-Persian gulf, from Seistan to Palestine, the Seleucids ruled, directly or through local rulers subject to them." For historical maps covering this period, see Waldmann 1983; 1985.

62. Cf. 1 Macc. 1:1 ("Alexander son of Philip, the Macedonian, who came from the land of Kittim"); 8:5 ("King Perseus of the Kittim").

63. An additional factor may be that the Shemites had been given rule over the world by virtue of Shem's primogeniture and their privileged position in the temperate middle of the world (see Chap. 2). This is certainly how Syncellus' source understands the geopolitical situation: "And he gave his testament to Shem as his firstborn son and the one most favored of God. Shem also received after Noah the hegemony (τὴν ἡγεμονίαν) and inherited from him the special honors of the blessings, as it states in Genesis [9:26]" (Sync. 47.17–20). See further pp. 153–5.

64. Cf. § 130: "And also their dwelling-place is from Rinocorura to Gadeira, the [portions] towards the South lengthwise." Cf. *Jub.* 8:22: "For Ham there emerged a second share toward the other side of the Gihon – *toward the south* – on the right side of the garden."

65. Cf. also §§ 79 ("These nations of Japheth were spread from Media to the Western Ocean, looking toward the North [βλέποντα πρὸς βορρᾶν]"), 83 ("Their boundaries are from Media to Gadeira, the [portions] toward the North..."), 86 ("Here the borders of Japheth leave off until the islands of the Britains, all [countries] looking towards the North [πᾶσαί τε πρὸς βορρᾶν βλέπουσαι]"), 197.

66. Cf., similarly, Josephus, *Ant.* 1.130. In the Septuagint πρὸς θάλασσαν denotes "to the West," i.e., the direction of the Mediterranean Sea from the perspective of the Land (cf., e.g., Exod. 26:22, 27; 37:10; Num. 35:5; Josh. 18:14; Ezra 3:7; Zech. 14:4; Ezek. 41:12; 45:7).

67. Cf. also § 170: "And Arphaxad begat Cainan, whence comes the Samites towards the East."

68. For a map showing the intersection of the three portions at the Land, see Aharoni and Avi-Yonah 1993: 21.

69. For other descriptions of Ham's territory in the *Diamerismos*, see §§ 130, 136. The extant fragments of the Genesis Apocryphon do not include a description of Ham's territory.

70. For other descriptions of Japheth's territory in the *Diamerismos*, see §§ 79, 83. Cf. 1QapGen. 16.9–12: "(9) the bay that is between them ... up to the Tina River ... (10) and all the land of the north till it reaches ... (11) And this boundary passes (through) the waters of the Great Sea till it reaches ..."

71. See, for example, on the Japhethites in Scott 1995a: 48–9 (Table 3). As this table shows, the attempt to identify the scriptural names with contemporary peoples and places is found also in the targumim and the later midrashim.

72. On the interpretative problem, see Wintermute 1985: 74 n. *x*; VanderKam 1989a: II.55 n. Note that Cleodemus Malchus recounts a legend that the sons of Abraham joined with Heracles in his war on the Libyan giant Antaeus and that Heracles married the daughter of one of these sons (i.e., Aphranes), who became the eponymous progenitor of Africa (cf. Josephus, *Ant.* 1.239–41; Eusebius, *Praep. Evang.* 9.20.2–4; Holladay 1983: 245–59). Note also that Ps.-Philo, *LAB* 4.7 lists *Cappadoces* among the descendants of Ham.

73. Cf. *Jub.* 9:2, 4, where the phrase "to the east" also appears, although not in an absolute sense but relative to the Tigris and Euphrates rivers, respectively.

74. See the discussion of interpretative options in VanderKam 1989a: II.56 n. on *Jub.* 9:3. For another solution, see Gutschmid 1894: 594.

75. I could find no parallel to this expression in TLG. Cf. Josephus, *Ant.* 1.147: "These, proceeding from the river Cophen, inhabited parts of India and of the adjacent country of Seria" (οὗτοι ἀπὸ Κωφῆνος ποταμοῦ τῆς Ἰνδικῆς καὶ τῆς πρὸς αὐτῇ Σηρίας τινὰ κατοικοῦσι). On the latter country, see Reinink 1975.

76. Cf. Kraft 1994: 56–8. However, the work of VanderKam on the Qumran fragments of the *Book of Jubilees* shows the accuracy of the later ancient translators who translated *Jubilees* into Greek before 200 CE and then into Ethiopic and Latin as early as 500 CE. The later versions generally agree with the Hebrew fragments from the Dead Sea caves. Cf. VanderKam 1988: 72: "Though one is compelled now to use granddaughter versions of Jub[ilees] for most of the book, there is every reason to believe that the text, despite its distance in time from the original, has been transmitted with remarkable accuracy. This verdict follows from a comparison of the published Hebrew fragments of the book with the critical text of the Ethiopic version (and the Latin where extant). The Ethiopic rarely deviates from the Hebrew texts, and in some cases it may even preserve readings that are superior to those of the Hebrew fragments." The extraordinary degree to which Jubilees was faithfully preserved even in the later versions may be an indication of the authority with which this writing was thought to have been endowed.

77. For example, even though Kainam son of Arpachshad is found in *Jub.* 8:1, the occurrence of this name in *Chron.* 170 (καὶ Ἀρφαξὰδ ἐγέννησε τὸν Καϊνάν) clearly stems from Gen. 10:24 LXX (cf. 11:12). As we discussed in Chap. 3 on the genealogy of Jesus (Lk. 3:23–38), the inclusion of the second Kainam is a point of convergence between *Jubilees* and the LXX against the MT.

78. Cf. 1QapGen. 17.17.

79. Cf., similarly, Josephus, *Ant.* 1.124.

80. On the *Wirkungsgeschichte* of the *Diamerismos*, see the stemma in Bauer and Helm 1955: XIV and in Bauer 1905: Tafel V. See further von Gutschmid 1894: 585–717. In light of the Egyptian provenance of the Third Sibyl, it is significant that the *Diamerismos* tradition of Hippolytus was carried on by "the Alexandrian World-Chronicles," which is represented by three works: the "Golenischev World-Chronicle" (preserved by a fifth-century papyrus), *Excerpta Latina Barbari*, and the *Chronicon Paschale*. Cf. Bauer and Strzygowski 1906; Dindorf 1832: I.43–64 (text); II.234–49 (annotations). We may note here that the anonymous tenth-century Jewish author of Josippon, who wrote a history of Judaism to the destruction of Jerusalem in 70 CE, starts his work with a Table of Nations which may go back in part to Hippolytus' *Diamerismos*, as the identification of the Romans with the Kittim shows (1.25–6; cf. Flusser and Safrai 1978–80: 1.7). On Josippon's idea of Esau's grandson, Zepho, as the king of the Kittim and the forebear of Romulus, who founded the city of Rome, see Feldman 1993: 494 n. 59. On the *Wirkungsgeschichte* of Hippolytus' *Diamerismos*, see also Arentzen 1984: 114.

81. See, for example, the *Chronicle* of John Malalas (ca. 480–ca. 570 CE) 1.6 (Jeffreys et al. 1986: 5): "Then the tribes of the sons of Noah, I mean of Shem, Ham and Japheth, the three brothers, were divided. The tribe of Shem took as the length of its

territory the land from Persia and Bactria as far as India and, as for the breadth, as far as Rhinokourouroi, that is, from the East as far as the region of the South, including Syria and Media and the river called the Euphrates. The tribe of Ham, Noah's second son, took for its territory the land from Rhinokourouroi in Egypt and in a southward direction as far as the region of the West, and all Libya and the river Nile known as gold-flowing and Africa and as far as Mauritania and the Pillars of Herakles and the great Adriatic Sea. The tribe of Japheth, Noah's third son, took the territory from Media to the North as far as the British Isles, including all the area of the Pontic Sea as far as the region of the West, and the rivers Danube and Tanais and the area by the Caucasus mountains and the Abasgoi, all those nations, beginning from the river Tigris which divides Media and Babylonia and up to the Pontic Sea, the area near Rhodes, Cyprus and Attalesis. The three tribes were divided throughout the earth in 72 nations, as Eusebios Pamphilou, the most learned chronicler, has stated." The interesting thing about this particular version of the *Diamerismos* tradition is that the subsequent context refers to the Kronos myth (1.8): "From this tribe of Shem, Noah's first son, which held Syria, Persia and the remaining areas of the East, there was born and appeared a man who was of the race of giants, named Kronos, given that name by Damnos his father after the planet. He was a strong man who was the first to practice ruling, that is, the governing and controlling of other men." As we discussed in Chap. 3, the Kronos myth was incorporated with the Book of Noah tradition in the Third Sibyl.

82. Cf., e.g., Holl 1915–33: I.136 n. 18 (on *Ancoratus* 112–14). See also II.66.81–3.
83. Bauer 1905: 163–7; cf., similarly, Adler 1990: 496–7.
84. Bauer and Helm 1955: IX n. 1.
85. Piilonen 1974: 35–6. Piilonen estimates that 156 of the 188 names in Epiphanius' list (i.e., 83 percent) stem from Hippolytus' *Diamerismos* (ibid., 35).
86. Epiphanius refers explicitly to the *Book of Jubilees* in his writings. On Epiphanius' indebtedness to *Jubilees*, see in general Adler 1990: 476ff.
87. Cf. F. Williams 1994: 302–3.
88. The notion that Canaan left his allotted portion because he considered it too hot can also be compared to Strabo's statement (*Geog.* 15.3.10) that Alexander moved his capital from Susa to Babylon in order to avoid the extreme heat of Susa. Cf. Clarke 1999: 213.
89. See further VanderKam 1994b: 46–69.
90. On Epiphanius' tendency to blend material from *Jubilees* with the Christian chronographic tradition, see Adler 1990: 481–2, 490.
91. On the possible existence of an earlier edition of Hippolytus' *Diamerismos*, see above on *Ref.* 10.30.4–5 and *Chron.* 43.
92. It is interesting to note that Epiphanius (*Pan.* 26.1.3) explicitly mentions a book of Noriah, wife of Noah.
93. Cf. Himmelfarb 1994: 120–2, who argues that "there is no evidence that the Greek version of *Jubilees* was still in circulation in R. Moses' time [i.e., the eleventh century]" (ibid., 117).
94. Ibid., 117, 122.
95. Translation adapted from Himmelfarb 1994: 121. Cf. Buber 1960–61: 32.
96. According to Eusebius (*Praep. Ev.* 9.41.1), Abydenus wrote a Chaldean history called Ἀσσυριακὰ καὶ Βαβυλωνιακά, for which he used excerpts from Alexander Polyhistor, among others.
97. Mosshammer 1984.
98. On the use of *Jubilees* in Syncellus, who often attributes *Jubilees* material to Josephus, see Adler 1989: 10 (explicit citations), 182–8 (Syncellus' text of *Jubilees*), 188–93; also Rönsch 1874: 299–302; but see Sync. 8:1–2, where Syncellus juxtaposes ὁ Ἰώσηππος and ἡ λεπτὴ Γένεσις. According to Gelzer (1885: 286), the traditions from *Jubilees* in the writings of Byzantine chronographers such as Syncellus were derived from the works of fourth-century Alexandrian authors Panodorus and

Annianus through the *Chronographies* of Sextus Julius Africanus. It is interesting to note, however, that Syncellus' chronological scheme, while clearly echoing *Jubilees*, was formulated in declared opposition to Africanus. Cf. Andrei 1996: 62–5.

99. See further Adler 1989: 36–7.

100. It should be noted that the date for the division of the earth is not that of *Jubilees*, which apparently sets it at 1569 *anno mundi*. Cf. *Jub*. 8:10, on which see VanderKam 1995: 87.

101. See above on *Chron*. 43; cf. *Ref*. 10.30.4–5.

102. Sync. 47.11–20. García Martínez (1994: 25) translates the first line somewhat differently: "Upon making these partitions and his will once engraved, as they say, he handed his sealed testament to them."

103. *Jub*. 8:11–12: "When he [sc. Noah] summoned his children, they came to him – they and their children. He divided the earth into the lots which his three sons would occupy. They reached out their hands and took the book from the bosom of their father Noah. (12) In the book there emerged as Shem's lot . . . "

104. For García Martínez (1994: 39, 44), Abydenus' account of the division of the world among Noah's sons is decisive for including *Jub*. 8:10–9:15 (along with 1QapGen. 16–17) in a hypothetically reconstructed "Book of Noah."

105. Cf. Rönsch 1874: 275. For example, combining both terms, a commentary on Job by Didymus the Blind (ca. 310–98 CE) refers to *Jubilees* as "the Book of the Covenant" (τὴν βίβλον τῆς διαθήκης). Cf. Hagedorn and Hagedorn 1987: 60. Just as Syncellus (47.12) distances himself from "the Covenant" with the words, ὥς φασιν, Didymus distances himself from "the Book of the Covenant" with the words, εἰ τῷ φίλον παραδέξασθαι τὴν βίβλον τῆς διαθήκης.

106. Cf. Adler 1994: 145: "Although Byzantine historians quote freely from *Jubilees* and *Enoch*, they often hedge their citations with warnings about their dangers and corruptions 'by Jews and heretics' [Sync. 4.21–3; 27.11]. In later Byzantine chronicles, these warnings have hardened into positive hostility. A 'joke . . . and a diversion (γέλως . . . καὶ παιγνία)' is the way Michael Glycas characterizes *Jubilees*, certainly clear testimony to the declining status of this literature in later Greek chronicles."

107. Sync. 47.21–7. Already during Noah's lifetime, the borders of Shem had been disputed. Cf. Sync. 101.10–12: "In the year 2838 of the world, when Phalek was 67 years old, Kainan died, and the sons of Shem fought with the sons of Ham over the borders of Palestine (καὶ οἱ υἱοὶ τοῦ Σὴμ ἐπολέμησαν πρὸς τοὺς υἱοὺς Χὰμ περὶ τῶν ὁρίων τῆς Παλαιστίνης)." See above on Rhinocorura.

108. To complicate matters even further, Syncellus (4.19–20) acknowledges dependence on intermediaries ("some historians") when he first appeals to *Jubilees*. Cf. Adler 1989: 7, 182.

109. Cf. Witakowski 1993.

110. We may note, however, that the interest of Syriac tradition in Genesis 10 was not restricted to the *Diamerismos*. Cf. D. J. Lane 1999: 241, referring to Arhrahat, *Demonstration* 5, which dates to 337 CE: "The identification of the beasts is based on a juxtaposition of Daniel with Gen. 6:10 (the sons of Noah) and Gen. 10 (the table of the nations), so that the three sons of Noah, Shem, Ham and Japheth, are types of the later kingdoms. The sons of Ham are the seed of Nimrod, and so stand for Babylon; Japheth, understood as the younger, is the originator of both Persians and Medes as the Greeks are brothers of the Medes; the sons of Shem are taken as the sons of Esau. Japheth the younger gives way to Shem the elder, signalling the displacement of the Greeks by the Romans."

111. Witakowski 1993: 635, summarizing Chabot 1899–1924: I.15.

112. Cf. Adler 1994: 171 n. 69: "When Michael [the Syrian] (2.2), followed by Bar Hebraeus (p. 7), describes the division of the earth among Noah's sons, he departs from the geographical boundaries of *Jubilees* 8 and substitutes it with a scheme attested as early as the chronicle of Hipppolytus."

113. Witakowski does not mention these two points.
114. Cf. Witakowski, 1993: 647, referring to J.-B. Chabot 1937: 31.16–33.27. For an English translation of this passage of the Syriac *Chronicle*, see VanderKam 1989a: II.334–5.
115. Witakowski 1993: 652: "All the toponyms of the Syriac match those of the Ethiopic [four examples], although of course spelling differences and distortions have been unavoidable." In addition, we may point out (1) that the idea that Shem's region is located in the middle of the earth recalls *Jub.* 8:12, 19; (2) that the phrase about the Sea Mahuq "into which nothing descends but to perish" recalls *Jub.* 8:22 ("... it [sc. the boundary of Ham's territory] goes westward until it reaches the Mauk Sea, everything that descends into which *is* destroyed"; see the note on the textual problem in VanderKam 1989a: II.54); (3) that the reference to the five large islands in Japheth's territory agrees with *Jub.* 8:29; (4) the description of Ham's territory as beginning "from the right side of the Garden of Eden" corresponds to *Jub.* 8:22 ("on the right side of the garden"); (5) the summary statement that Japheth's territory belongs to him and his posterity "throughout their generations forever" alludes to *Jub.* 8:29; (6) and the reference to "Afgara" resembles *Jub.* 8:27 ("Aferag").
116. Cf. Witakowski 1993: 647, citing Syriac *Chronicle* 32.8–10. See also Chap. 5 on the description of the climates in Theophilus, *Autol.* 2.34, another Syrian source.
117. Witakowski 1993: 652, referring to Syriac *Chronicle* 32.11–15: "Quindecim linguae sunt in mundo, quae sciunt scripturam et litteras. E Semo, quinque: Hebraei, Syri, Babylonii, Persae, Elamitae, Arabes. E Iaphetho, sex: Graeci, Iberi, Franci, Armeni, Medi, Alani. E Chamo, quattuor: Aegyptii, Cushitae, Phoenices, Indi."
118. Witakowski 1993: 650–2.
119. Witakowski (1993: 651) quite rightly refrains from making firm conclusions at this point in time: "It would be premature to discuss more extensively the ways, apparently more than one, by which *Diamerismos* material penetrated Syriac literature. Perhaps we should wait for a clarification of the transformation of this material in Greek, since otherwise we would risk explaining the variations in Syriac by internal reasons whereas they may be caused by translation of various Greek *Vorlagen*."
120. We may also note incidentally that the Book of Noah tradition may have entered gnostic circles, for like *Jub.* 8:11–12, the *Apocalypse of Adam* (4:1–9) regards Noah as the one who divided the earth among his three sons; the immediately following context speaks of a judgment by fire (5:1–14; cf. *Jub.* 9:15). Cf. MacRae 1983: 714–15.

7 Medieval *mappaemundi*

1. Cf. VanderKam 1989a: I.XIV, 270ff. (citation of the Latin text); II.XVII–XVIII, 337ff. (English translation of the Latin text).
2. Cf. Kraft 1994: 82 n. 38.
3. Cf. Edson 1993; Delano Smith 1991: 145–6.
4. Schreckenberg and Schubert 1992; K. Schubert 1990–91. Cf. also Stichel 1979.
5. Cf. P. S. Alexander 1982: 212–13: "We observed earlier that the cartographic affinities of the Jubilees world map are with Patristic and mediaeval Christian world maps which show a similar blend of Ionian and Biblical elements. We were careful to speak of 'affinities' and not of 'influence', but the question of influence may be legitimately raised: Jubilees may, in fact, have had a profound influence on Christian cartography. The text of Jubilees in its Greek and Latin versions was certainly known to the Church fathers, and some patristic accounts of the Table of the Nations, such as the *Diamerismos* of Hippolytus, appear to have drawn on it. Whether or not this bolder hypothesis of direct influence can be proved remains to be seen. Enough has been said, however, to put beyond any doubt the typological affinity of the Jubilees and the early Christian world maps. The conclusion appears unassailable:

the Jubilees world map has the distinction of being the earliest attested example of the *imago mundi* which predominated in Christian circles right through the patristic and mediaeval periods down almost to the time of Christopher Columbus."

6. Often the key to interpreting the medieval maps lies not in the text which accompanies the maps (*pace* Edson 1997), but rather in the traditions that inform the maps. A classic example of this is the London Psalter map (ca. 1250 CE), whose placement in the text is practically impossible to comprehend without independently knowing the extensive, Christian tradition based on Ps. 74:12–17 (cf. Edson 1997: 137: "The existence of a world map in a psalter is rare, and its presence here may indicate that a world map was an increasingly common image, now finding its way into books which would not ordinarily have one. However, the patient reader, who has followed us so far, will remember the connection between maps and calendars in medieval computus manuscripts"; see Higgins 1998: 34–9). Similarly, the thirteenth-century *mappamundi* known as the Ebstorf map, which represents the world quite literally as the body of Christ, with his head at the top (east), his two hands spanning right (north) and left (south), his feet at the bottom (west), and his navel in the middle (Jerusalem), must be understood in light of Eph. 1:22–3; Col. 1:15–20 and/or an ancient Orphic tradition (cf. West 1983: 72–3, 88–90, 239–41). What was common knowledge to the medieval mapmakers needs to be rediscovered today through painstaking, diachronic study of the embedded traditions.

7. Cf., e.g., Kliege 1991: 22, 48–9. The idea of tracing the medieval maps back to the Agrippa map is attributed to Konrad Miller. Gradually, Miller's approach has become entrenched in modern cartographic scholarship. For a discussion of the Agrippa map, see Chap. 1.

8. Brincken 1970: 250.

9. Cf. Harvey 1996: 22–6. For other medieval maps that are considered direct descendants of the Agrippa map, see Harvey 1991: 21.

10. Brincken 1968: 168: "Und weil das Mittelalter das Alte besonders hoch in Ehren hielt, bewahrte es treulich die antike Form. Daher ist es methodisch nicht unberechtigt, aus den mittelalterlichen *mappaemundi* die Agrippa-Karte rekonstruieren zu wollen, wenn man dabei auch vorsichtig zu Werke gehen muß." Edson (1997: 11) argues that since the Roman Empire did not disappear all at once, but dwindled and declined unevenly from place to place, even continuing its existence for another millennium in Constantinople, it is likely that whatever world maps the Romans made, some must have survived to influence the mapmakers of the Middle Ages.

11. Harvey 1996: 22. On this view, see P. S. Alexander 1997a/1999: 153/111–12: "Parts of Harvey's tradition-history are plausible, but parts are not. That the ancestor of the Hereford family of maps goes back at least to the fifth century is a conclusion demanded by the basic stemmatics of the manuscripts. But that the ancestor-map was some sort of official Roman world map, based on information derived from the efficient Roman methods of surveying, seems to me to be totally off-target. In fact I would suggest that Harvey and other historians of cartography are guilty of naively misreading the Hereford map. The Hereford map, and others like it, were never meant to be 'real' geography. Their significance was symbolic and theological right from the start. The Hereford map was so seriously out of joint with the geographical knowledge of its day that it cannot have been intended to be taken literally."

12. For a reproduction of the Hereford map, see, e.g., Whitfield 1994: 21.

13. The Latin text of Lk. 2:1 (*Lucas in euuangelio: Exiit edictum ab Augusto Cesare, ut describeretur huniuersus orbis*) is written above the head of the enthroned figure. See further p. 169.

14. The edict reads as follows: "Go into the whole world and report back to the Senate on every continent; and to confirm this I have attached my seal to this document" (*ite in orbem universum: et de omni eius continentia referte ad senatum: et ad istam confirmandam huic scripto sigillum meum apposui*). We may perhaps compare the bematists on Alexander the Great's expedition to the East.

15. Cf. *Cosmographia Iulii Caesaris* 1 (Riese 1964: 21–3). Even around the map's border on the upper left side, where we read that "the world began to be measured by Julius Caesar," the text continues with a description of territories surveyed by the three geographers: the whole East by Nicodoxus, the North and the West by Theodocus, and the South by Policlitus. Cf. Harvey 1996: 54.
16. Cf. Wiseman 1992: 22–42, 227–30 (Appendix 1: The world survey: Latin texts).
17. Brodersen 1995: 262–7.
18. Cf., e.g., Dilke 1987: 207.
19. Note also the miniature of Caesar Augustus that accompanies the richly illustrated *Liber floridus* of Lambert of St. Omer (ca. 1112–15 CE): the emperor is depicted as sitting on his royal throne, with a sword in his right hand and a globus in his left hand. The globus is drawn in the schematic form of a typical T-O map, with the upper half of the circle labeled "Asia," the left quarter labeled "Europa," and the right quarter, "Africa." Cf. Brincken 1992: pl. 26. But see P. S. Alexander 1997a/1999: 153 n. 12/111 n. 18: "Curiously Julius Caesar's survey of the empire is alluded to in the bottom left corner of the Hereford map, but this, in my view, cannot be used to link the Hereford map to the Agrippan map. It is simply a learned piece of *doctrina* on the part of Richard of Holdingham or some other medieval scholar."
20. Cf. Janvier 1982. On Orosius as a possible major source for *mappaemundi*, see Woodward 1987a: 300–1; J. Williams 1997.
21. Ruberg (1980: 555) assumes that simple T-O maps are Roman in origin but have been Christianized by labeling the three continents with the sons of Noah.
22. Ovid (43 BCE–17 CE) regards Delphi as the center of the earth (*Met.* 10.167–8); he also holds the Homeric concept of the earth as a disk surrounded by Ocean (*Met.* 2.5–7). Suetonius (*Jul.* 79.3) refers to the rumors that Julius Caesar intended to move the seat of the Roman Empire to Alexandria or Ilium, perhaps in order to rule closer to the center of the perceived geographical center of the inhabited world (cf. Nicolet 1991: 192). On the importance of governing from the center of the world, see the advice allegedly given to Alexander (Plut. *Alex.* 65.6–8). On Rome as the political, rather than the geographical, center of the world, see Vasaly 1993: 133–4; Clarke 1999: 210–28. See further in Chap. 1.
23. K. Miller (1895–98: VI.143–5) argued for the eastern orientation of all Roman maps. Cf. also Woodward 1987a: 337: "An eastern orientation is usually, but by no means exclusively, found on the tripartite *mappaemundi*, and it follows the late Roman Sallustian tradition adopted by the Christian world."
24. Cf. Herodotus 2.16; 3.96, 115; 4.42, 198; Xenophon, *Mem.* 2.1.10: "In Asia the rulers are the Persians; the Syrians, Lydians and Phrygians are the ruled. In Europe the Scythians rule, and the Maeotians are ruled. In Libya, the Carthaginians rule, and the Libyans are ruled." On the three continents and their boundaries, see Strabo, *Geog.* 1.4.7–8; 2.5.26; Arrian, *Anab.* 3.30.7–9. As we mentioned in Chap. 2, Dionysius Periegetes outlines the world by continents (Africa/Libya, Europe, and Asia). See further Polybius 12.25.7; Werner 1993: 27ff.
25. Cf. Pindar, *Pyth.* 4.74; Bacchylides 4.4; Aeschylus, *Eum.* 40, 166. Indeed, it was Ptolemy (*Tetrabiblos* 2.3; cf. 2.4) who listed Judea, along with several adjacent lands (i.e., Idumea, Coele Syria, Phoenicia, Chaldea, Orchinia, and Arabia Felix), as "situated about the center of the whole inhabited world" (περὶ τὸ μέσον ἐσχηματισμένα τῆς ὅλης οἰκουμένης). See further Herrmann (1959) and the discussion of Acts 1:8 in Chap. 3.
26. Cf. Brincken 1968: 176: "Eine Ostung der Agrippa-Karte ist zwar angenommen worden, einwandfrei erwiesen ist sie nicht"; ibid., 180: "Die verschiedene Entwicklung der christlichen Kartographie in Ost und West zeigt, daß die Ostung eben nicht genuin christlich ist. Wurzeln finden sich allerdings sowohl im Alten Testament als vielleicht auch bei den Römern." See also Drinkard 1992: 204; Podossinov 1991; 1993: 38, who argues that the orientation on the East in the medieval *mappaemundi* is the result of a

long development which can be traced from Homer, through Herodotus, to the Middle Ages, when it received an additional justification through the Roman tradition.

27. Cf. Brincken 1968: 122: "... zweifellos ist die lateinische Kartographie des Mittelalters ganz von der römischen bestimmt ... Wenn man freilich die mittelalterliche Kartenkunst nur als Rudiment der römischen auffaßt, gerät die Wertung zu negativ. Es darf nicht außer acht gelassen werden, daß man damals ganz andere Anforderungen an die Karte stellte als der moderne Mensch oder auch der Araber jener Tage. Vielmehr fertigte man eine Tafel der Hauptplätze des Heilsgeschehens und der in die Heilsgeschichte hineingenommenen Geschichte der weltlichen Mächte der Erde an. Man wollte nicht die exakte Abbildung der Welt, sondern ihr Bild, die Gesamtvorstellung von ihr, skizzieren. Die Weltkarte in diesem Sinne is *imago mundi*, sie ist Zeugnis von Weltanschauung, Mythos und Religion."

28. French (1995: II.795) seems to suggest that Eusebius of Caesarea's map of Palestine, which was supposedly appended to his *Onomasticon*, was largely responsible for the subsequent development of the medieval *mappaemundi*: "Eusebius reoriented Ptolemy's large scale map of Asia to the East. This corresponds to the convention of the schematic maps, but it also reflects the belief that the Garden of Eden was a historical place literally located in the East. Thus the entire map is oriented in the direction of creation. The scale is extremely variable, and topographical detail is limited to select stylized lakes, rivers, mountains and cities. The symbol for Jerusalem occupies a proportionally larger space than its size warranted, and dominates the centre of the map. Eusebius created a totally idealized biblical Palestine by deliberately omitting contemporary place-names and locating only biblical place-names. It is perhaps hard to appreciate how revolutionary Eusebius' map was in his time. It promoted a radical world view that struck an immediate response in the hearts of Christians who were sympathetic to the idea of the importance of Palestine as the scene of God's revelation to mankind throughout history as disclosed in the Bible. The appeal of Eusebius' topographical map to Christians completely transformed map making for approximately one thousand years as Christian cartography with its biblical orientation displaced classical map making." There are several difficulties with this suggestion. (1) It is not clear how a *regional* map of Palestine developed into a *mappamundi*. (2) The map in question is actually from a copy of Jerome's *Holy Places* dating to about 1150 CE. (3) The extent to which this was Jerome's work, in or about 380–91, or his reworking of a map made by Eusebius for the *Onomasticon*, remains largely unresolved. Cf. Delano Smith 1991: 144, 147–8.

29. Woodward 1987a: 328. Cf. also Brincken 1968: 137; Lecoq 1989b.

30. Cf. Woodward 1987a: 340–2, who argues that the concept of placing Jerusalem at the center of the world seems to have been introduced in the seventh century but was not generally established until the twelfth or even the thirteenth, when the Crusades caused a shift in the structure of the *mappaemundi* toward centering the maps on Jerusalem. See further Higgins 1998; Hengevoss-Dürkop 1991.

31. Cf. Brincken 1992: 70, who argues that the earliest medieval maps (e.g., the Henry of Mainz map) do not have Jerusalem as the center, but rather Delos. See also Brincken 1991: 401: "Erst die Kreuzzugsbewegung belebt das Interesse für Asien als den eigentlichen Orient und sucht das Zentrum der Welt mit dem Propheten Ezechiel [5, 5] in Jerusalem, wie dies der Kirchenvater Hieronymus [Comm. in Hiezechielem 5, 5] längst in seinem exegetischen Werk gefordert hatte: Auch die Kartographie zieht die entsprechenden Konsequenzen, jedoch erst im Hochmittelalter." See further Woodward 1987a: 340–1. Note, however, that already during the Republic, at least one Roman author is skeptical that the earth even has an *umbilicus*, let alone that Delphi could properly be so called (cf. Varro, *Ling.* 7.17; see also Strabo, *Geog.* 9.3.6). On the concept of the navel of the earth, see further Brodersen 1995: 49–50, 110, 259; Clarke 1999: 225.

32. Kliege 1991: 109–10, 119.

33. P. S. Alexander (1997a: 154) argues that the ancient ancestor of the Hereford map was a symbolic Christian world map originating in the East, and that this early Christian map was in turn more or less identical to the *Jubilees* map and may have descended from it. As P. S. Alexander (ibid., 154–5) states, "Jubilees represents the *fons et origo* of an *imago mundi* which prevailed in Christian Europe down to the time of Columbus." In his later reworking of the same article, Alexander (1999: 113) adds at this point: "Also relevant is the type of early Christian text known as a 'Division (*Diamerismos*) of the World.' A classic example of this genre, worked and reworked in Latin and Greek throughout late antiquity, is found in the Chronicle of Hippolytus (§§44ff.). These *Diamerismoi* contain a detailed ethnography based on the Table of Nations in Gen. 10. They are, in many respects, verbal analogues to the medieval *mappaemundi*, and some of them may show the influence, whether direct or indirect, of Jubilees."

34. Kliege (1991: 113–14) gives a list of sources for medieval maps, but *Jubilees* is not mentioned. Edson (1997: 15) argues that since the details of the division of the continents among the three sons of Noah are far from clear in Genesis 10, "the medieval mapmakers clearly superimposed *their own* tripartite formula on the existing three-continent schema." This assessment not only ignores intervening Jewish and Christian tradition, but it also attributes more creativity to medieval mapmakers than seems likely.

35. Cf. Braude 1997: 103–42, who argues not only that the notion of dividing the world into three or more continents did not exist before the seventeenth century (109), but also that Alcuin (732–804 CE) was the first authority to identify the three sons of Noah with the three continents (112). See also Lewis and Wigen 1997. On the antiquity of the notion of the three continents, see above. As for the antiquity of the identification of the continents with the sons of Noah, see merely *Jubilees* 8–9 and Hippolytus, *Chron.* 44–51.

36. It is interesting to note that a Jewish grave inscription from Rome (3rd–4th century CE?) contains a dome-shaped, crosshatched outline of an omphalos like that preserved at Delphi. Cf. Noy 1995: 221–3. Although a single such object is always dangerous as a basis for generalization, we may wonder whether the omphalos symbolizes an eschatological expectation about Jerusalem.

37. The *Jubilees* map, whether it was physical or mental, was probably oriented on the East. We may deduce this from *Jub.* 8:22–3: "For Ham there emerged a second share toward the other side of the Gihon – toward the south – on *the right side* of the garden. [...] The Gihon River goes until it reaches the right side of the Garden of Eden." Ham's territory in the South lay "on the right side" of the Garden of Eden, because East was at the top of the map. Likewise, the Hebrew word ימין denotes both "right hand" and "south," because when facing east, the right hand is toward the south. Orientation on the East is a standard feature in Jewish sources. Cf. N. Lewis (1989: 14, 45), where when stating abutters or boundaries of a property, the scribes consistently adhere to the Semitic practice of giving the east first; the west is usually given second, followed by north and south in either order. The inside, north wall of the synagogue at Dura-Europos (NC1) depicts the Mount of Olives as split in two down the middle in accordance with Zech. 14:4: "And in that day his feet will stand on the Mount of Olives, which is in front of Jerusalem on the east; and the Mount of Olives will be split in its middle from east to west by a very large valley, so that half of the mountain will move toward the north and the other half toward the south." Hence, the viewer of the painting sees through the valley created by the split and looks towards the East. Cf. Goldstein 1995: 146–53. See also, e.g., *1 Enoch* 76:2–3, where the description of the twelve winds begins with the East. As discussed in Chap. 1, the expected New Jerusalem contains two main streets, the broader of which runs east–west and is 126 cubits wide (5Q15 1 i:3–7).

38. See, e.g., the Table of Nations (*Gentes Asie, Europe, Affrice diverse*) in the *Liber floridus* of Lambert of St. Omer (Kliege 1991: 135, pl. 4) and the verso of the London Psalter map (ibid., pl. 12).

39. Cf. Jerome, *Commentary on Ezekiel* 5:5 (Migne, *PL* 25, 52b): "Jerusalem is situated in the middle of the world (*Jerusalem in medio mundi sitam*). This is affirmed by the prophet [Ezek. 5:5], showing it to be the navel of the earth (*umbilicum terrae*), and by the psalmist [Ps. 73(74):11–12] expressing the birth of the Lord: 'Truth,' he says, 'rose from the earth'; and next the passion: '[God] worked,' he says, 'salvation in the middle of the earth (*salutem in medio terrae*).' For the eastern parts, of course, it is surrounded by the area that is called Asia; for the western parts, by that which is called Europe; from the South, Libya and Africa; from the North, Scythia, Armenia and also Persides and by all the nations of the Black Sea. It is, therefore, situated in the midst of the peoples (*in medio igitur gentium posita est*)." Translation adapted from Higgins 1998: 34. On the Ps. 73(74):11–12 tradition, see also Cyril, *Catech.* 13.28 (Reischl and Rupp 1967: 86–7). See further Wilken 1992: 64, 254, 344–6; Jeremias 1926: 40–88. On Jerome's views on Jerusalem, see further Perrone 1999.
40. *Pace* Brincken 1968: 139; 1993: 453–77, who credits Jerome as the possible incidental originator of the Western *mappaemundi*. The concept of Jerusalem as the geographical center of the world is more widespread and ancient than this view allows. Cf. Wilken 1992: 11, 30, 94–5, 230; Higgins 1998: 34–9. It is interesting to note that through the centuries, some Christian groups held to a literal fulfillment of biblical prophecies regarding a coming restoration of Jewish rule in Jerusalem, which underscores the centrality of the Jerusalem. Cf. Wilken 1985; 1993.
41. Cf. Hilberg 1996: 68. See Rönsch 1874: 266–7.
42. On the *Little Genesis*, see further in Chap. 5.
43. Rönsch 1874: 267–70. More obvious, of course, is Jerome's use of Josephus, *Ant.* 1.122–47 in his treatment of Genesis 10. Cf. Hayward 1995: 138–46.
44. Isidore's fame is reflected in inscriptions such as those found on the great medieval *mappaemundi*: the Ebstorf map (ca. 1270 CE) admonishes the reader: "If you wish to know more, read Isidore!" Cited in Kish 1978: 163.
45. I am grateful to Evelyn Edson for drawing this passage to my attention. Cf. Lindsay 1911 (no page numbers in this edition). See also J. K. Wright 1965: 259–60.
46. Higgins (1998: 34) considers Isidore to be dependent on Jerome's *Commentary on Ezekiel* at this point. For a comprehensive table of the sources of Isidore's *Etymologiae*, see Philipp 1912–13: Teil II: Textausgabe und Quellenangabe.
47. So also Philipp 1912–13: 13–14: "Kretschmer ist sogar der Ansicht, Isidors Karte sei auf Jerusalem gezentret gewesen. Diese Annahme ist a priori falsch. Die mittelalterlichen Karten zeigen deutlich, daß diese erst mit den Kreuzzügen Jerusalem diese Bedeutung für die Kartographie erhielt. Es ist gerade das Charakteristikum der sämtlichen Beatuskarten, daß sie noch nicht Jerusalem als Zentrum haben. Erst im 15. s. verschwindet dann wieder dies Zentrum von den Karten. Sehen wir uns nun auch einmal die Isidorstelle an, auf der Kretschmer und andere fußen, so erkennen wir, daß in ihr auch gar nicht das erhaltenen ist, was man herausgelesen hat, zumal wenn wir uns von unseren jämmerlichen Textausgaben frei machen: XIV 3, 21: in medio autem Judaeae civitas Hierosolyma est, quasi umbilicus regionis totius. So geben den Text die meisten codices; unsere Ausgaben haben freilich das mir unverständliche 'terrae' für 'totius'. Wir sind aber in der Lage, die Textfrage einwandfrei zu lösen, da wir die unmittelbare Quelle Isidors kennen. Hegesipp b. iud. III 6: in medio autem Judaeae civitas Hierosolyma quasi umbilicus regionis totius . . . nuncupatur; endlich ergibt es sich aus Hegesipps Quelle Joseph b. iud. III 52 ganz einwandfrei, daß Jerusalem als der Nabel Judäas oder Palästinas, nicht aber der gesamten Erde gilt. Kretschmer hat freilich Recht, wenn er behauptet, daß den Juden Jerusalem auch als ὄμφαλος τῆς γῆς galt, aber diese Absicht war längst antiquiert, als die Juden, wie ja auch die Griechen, die bis Hekataeus in Delphi den Nabel der Erde sahen, einen weiteren Gesichtskreis bekamen und ihrer Abgeschlossenheit entrückt wurden. Josephus, der Zeitgenosse des Judenbesiegers Titus, hat diese Anschauung von der zentralen Lage Jerusalems in dem

Erdkreis nicht mehr haben können, ja, er zweifelt sogar leise an der zentralen Lage der heiligen Stadt für ihre Landschaft." It is clearly incorrect to say that from Josephus' time on, the notion of Jerusalem's position as the navel of the earth became antiquated. Scripture itself, especially in the Septuagint and Vulgate versions of Ezek. 38:12, guaranteed that Jerusalem would long continue to be regarded as the ὀμφαλὸς τῆς γῆς.

48. Cf. Scott 1995a: 41. See also *Ep. Arist.* 83.
49. On the possible use of *Jub.* 2:23 in Isid. *Etym.* 16.26.10, see Rönsch 1874: 344–6. Philipp (1912–13: 19) does not include the *Book of Jubilees* as a direct source for the geography of Isidore's *Etymologiae.*
50. In addition, Josephus (*Ap.* 1.197, citing Hecataeus of Abdera) refers to the Temple and its stone walls as "approximately in the center of the city" (κατὰ μέσον μάλιστα τῆς πόλεως).
51. Cf. P. S. Alexander 1997a/1999: 155/114.
52. Talmon 1993: 56: "It is impossible to determine with precision whether the word 'country' (χώρα) here signifies Judea or the world as a whole. It appears that Josephus fused two ancient concepts. One of these is apparent in the book of *Jubilees* (8:19) . . . "
53. Cf. McCready 1996.
54. Cf. Donner 1992: 87; also 30–1.
55. Donner 1992: 88.
56. Higgins 1998: 37 (with other examples of the same tradition on pp. 38ff.); cf. also French 1992: 45–81 (esp. 55); J. K. Wright 1965: 260. Although, as Woodward (1987a: 340) rightly indicates, "Such an observation of the sun is impossible astronomically (unless the column was leaning ten degrees toward the south), Jerusalem being some ten degrees north of the Tropic of Cancer," it is possible that a (pre-70 CE) artifact found at Qumran may have been used for just such a purpose. The extent to which this artifact has any genetic relationship to medieval qiblah maps, which portray the Ka'ba in Mecca at the center of the world and surrounded by the nations, may have a bearing on our question about the possible Jewish background of the medieval *mappaemundi.* For soon after Muhammad's emigration to Medina in 622, he designated Jerusalem as the qiblah, probably under influence of Jewish tradition. Therefore, the Christian *mappaemundi* and qiblah maps could go back ultimately to a common Jewish tradition.
57. The tradition is preserved by Peter Comestor (d. ca. 1179), a biblical scholar in Paris who relates in his tremendously popular *Historia scholastica* (Migne, *PL* 198, 1567–8 [§58: "*De puteo Samaritanae*"]), that at the summer solstice the sun casts no shadow on the Jacob's well, and furthermore that "sunt qui dicunt locum illum esse umbilicum terrae nostrae habitabilis." Cited in Eliade 1971: 13; cf. also J. K. Wright 1965: 260–1; W. Müller 1961: 189. Wells were often used in the ancient world for such a solar observation (cf., e.g., Cockle 1996: 1459), and the 100-feet-deep Jacob's well would have suited this purpose superbly. We may observe incidentally that if a medieval monastic like Peter Comestor preserved a relatively obscure Samaritan tradition about Jacob's well (cf., however, John 4:4–26), how much more would medieval monks have been likely to preserve the well-attested Jewish tradition about the centrality of Jerusalem.
58. As we have seen, there is a sizeable body of Christian literature through the centuries that views the earthly Jerusalem as the center of the world. It is an oversimplification to state that before the Crusades Christians commonly thought of the heavenly Jerusalem as the spiritual center.
59. Woodward 1987a: 342 n. 262.
60. The first known Christian pilgrim, a Cappadocian bishop named Alexander, went to Jerusalem soon after 200 CE "to pray and visit the sites there" (Eusebius, *HE* 6.11.2). One hundred years later, Eusebius (*Dem. Ev.* 6.18.23) declared that "all who believe in Christ come here [sc. to Jerusalem] from every part of the world . . . " The earliest surviving Christian account of a pilgrimage is that of the pilgrim who came from Bordeaux in 333 CE. See further Wilken 1996; Vogt 1992: II.688; Pullan 1993.

61. Cf. Meyers and Strange 1981; Wilkinson 1990: 51–2: "The element of pilgrimage...seems to have been part of the church from its start, even if it remained unofficial. The origins of Christian pilgrimage therefore grow out of the practice of Jewish pilgrimage, and this seems to be a good reason why Christian pilgrims should have visited so great a quantity of holy places connected with the Old Testament. Readers of Eusebius would therefore be well advised to understand literally his references to pilgrimage, since all the documents studied so far seem to support it. And in any case an early origin for pilgrimage is far easier to defend than any idea that it was invented later on."

62. P. S. Alexander 1997a/1999: 149/105: "The geographical centrality of Jerusalem is presented by the author of Jubilees in a very concrete way. His treatment of the Table of Nations in Genesis 10 projects a remarkably vivid *imago mundi*, one so coherent and cartographic that it probably once existed as a drawn map... The world is visualized as a more or less circular land mass surrounded by the waters of ocean, its disc disected east–west by a median running through the Garden of Eden and the Straits of Gibraltar, and and north–south by a median running through Mount Zion and Mount Sinai. The medians intersect at Zion, which stands, consequently, at the center of the earth." See also P. S. Alexander 1982: 197: "In its exposition of the Table of the Nations (Gen. X), Jubilees VIII–IX offers a remarkably complete and coherent picture of the inhabited world. The account is so full of precise, visual detail that it is hard to avoid the suspicion that the author was describing not merely an image which he saw in his mind's eye, but one which lay physically before him in the shape of a world map. Indeed, it is possible that such a map was an integral part of his original manuscript. Cosmographies in the form of text with accompanying map are well enough attested in antiquity: two examples which spring readily to mind are the *Periodos* of Hecataeus of Miletus, and the famous Babylonian world map, BM 92687. The loss of the map and the survival of the written text would not be hard to explain. There is a well-known tendency for copyists to omit text-figures of all kinds, especially if, as would have been the case with the putative Jubilees world map, those figures were complicated and liable to tax a scribe's powers of artistic reproduction. It is, perhaps, just conceivable that the author of Jubilees managed to carry all the details of his world picture in his head." See further F. Schmidt 1990: 122, 127–8; Delano Smith and Gruber 1992: 32: "The presence of maps in Rashi's writings raises a number of wider questions concerning medieval cartography. They demonstrate a cartographically sophisticated context. Was there already a tradition in Hebrew biblical commentary of, literally, mapping out the text?" Historians of cartography frequently ponder whether literary texts presuppose maps. Cf., e.g., Armin 1992; Siebener 1995: 13–19, 320–33.

63. See Chap. 5 on Theophilus, *Autol.* 2.32.

64. Cf. Brincken 1968: 137–8, 176, who gives very short shrift to *Jubilees* 8–9 and the *Diamerismos* of Hippolytus, without realizing that the latter is very probably based on *Jubilees* 8–9, and that the *Jubilees* tradition had a long and influential history. Brincken (ibid., 138) observes that Hippolytus neither includes a map in his *Chronicon* nor mentions the existence of such a map, although the production of such a map would be conceivable ("denkbar jedoch wäre die Anfertigung schon"). See also the important statement by Arentzen 1984: 114: "Bereits das 'Buch der Jubiläen' aus der Zeit um 100 v.Chr. bezeugt die geographische Deutung der biblischen Beschreibung der Teilung, die mit den alttestamentlichen Völkertafeln (Gen 10 und 11,10–32; 1. Chr 1,5–23) und der Sprachverwirrung nach dem Turmbau zu Babel (Gen 11,1–9) in Verbindung gebracht werden konnte. Hippolyt von Rom reicht in seiner Chronik diesen Ansatz an das christliche Abendland weiter, wo die Verbindung Asiens mit Sem, Europas mit Japhet und Afrikas mit Ham zu einem Topos der Kartographie wird, der sich bis in die Inkunabelzeit [i.e., the fifteenth century] behaupten kann."

65. Cf., e.g., Brincken 1968; Edson 1997: 97–131.

66. Cf. Brincken 1968: 123–4, followed by Woodward 1987a: 288–90, 334.
67. Cf. Bauer and Strzygowski 1906: Table II; also Baldwin and Cutler 1991: 62. One wonders whether the tradition about Alexander the Great that found its way into medieval *mappaemundi* (cf. Lecoq 1993) may have been influenced, in part, by the Alexandrian World-Chronicles, which preserved this tradition (cf. Fraser 1996: 11–13).
68. Cf. Weitzmann and Bernabò 1999: I.58.
69. The apocalyptic orientation of the *mappaemundi* is shown, for example, by the fact that they sometimes depict the kingdom of Gog and Magog (cf. Gen. 10:2; Ezek. 38:1–39:29) as enclosed behind a great wall in northern or north-eastern Asia, waiting to overrun the world in the end-time. Cf. Lecoq 1993: 92–103; Woodward 1987a: 332–3. See further Andersen 1932; P. J. Alexander 1985; Westrem 1998. Once again, we are dealing here with traditional expectations of the restoration of Israel that both Jews and Christians alike had nurtured for centuries. Cf. Wilken 1985: 453, 459–60. Furthermore, the Samaritan book of *Asatir* (4.29) mentions that Gog and Magog are located from "from Bab el Abwab ['Gate of Gates'] and onwards," evidently referring to the Caspian Gates. Cf. Gaster 1927: 232 n. 29.
70. Woodward 1987a: 334. Of course, one reason that eschatology is built into these medieval maps is that the places of reward and punishment are geographically determined from creation.
71. Also otherwise, geographical material in Jewish sources is often presented with an apocalyptic orientation. See, for example, Nickelsburg 1999: 97, who states concerning the cosmological/geographical material in the apocalyptic book of *1 Enoch*: "This preponderance of cosmological material is not presented for its own sake, however... In the Book of the Watchers and the Book of Parables, cosmology undergirds eschatology. Enoch's first journey, to the West, climaxes in his visions of the places of punishment... In his second journey, from the far West to the East, several new places of eschatological import for human beings are added and, again, chapters 32–34 document his journey to paradise."
72. Destomes 1964: 22.2, pl. VIIIb; Arentzen 1984: 123; Edson 1997: 15 (fig. 1.6), 156; Woodward 1987a: 331 (fig. 18.33), 346 (fig. 18.52); J. Williams 1994–98: I.57 (fig. 30a); II (figs. 238, 270); III (fig. 238). In a private communication, Williams suggests that the T-O map accompanying the genealogical table in Beatus' *Commentary on the Apocalypse* was not in the original but inserted by someone conscious of the distribution of the world among the sons of Noah in the T-O map tradition. Cf. also Williams 1994–98: I.55–8. In the same communication, Williams also agreed that the *Book of Jubilees* would be a logical place to begin tracing the tradition of the three climates that is found in the T-O map of the Beatus manuscripts.
73. As we saw in our discussion of Theophilus of Antioch (169–77 CE), the fusion of Greek thinking about the *klimata* of the earth and the Jewish Table of Nations tradition occurred much earlier than historians of cartography have generally assumed.
74. Delano Smith 1991: 145.
75. See, however, Edson 1993: 184: "I would like to entertain the idea that these maps were not copies of some hypothetical classical model, but genuine medieval creations, drawn from the available geographic texts: Isidore's *Etymologies*, Orosius' *Seven Books of History*, and for Biblical places, St. Jerome's dictionary of sites in the Holy Land. However much medieval scholars denied originality, we do not need to always believe them. While they struggled to copy the giants who went before them, the classical heritage was inevitably transformed to fit the needs of a very different world." Similarly, historians of medieval art now tend to depreciate the ancient heritage of medieval works of art in favor of seeing them as products elucidating their own time and place. Cf. Nees 1997: 962. I am grateful to Evelyn Edson for this reference.
76. Cf. Woodward 1987a: 290, 335.
77. On the London Psalter map, see Brincken 1992: 85–9; Kliege 1991: 82–3, 167–71; Whitfield 1994: 19.

78. Cf. also Lecoq 1989a.
79. Cf. Brincken 1970; Harvey 1996: 54.
80. The fact that a different Roman emperor was reigning by the time of the events in Acts 17:6–7 is irrelevant to Luke's point.
81. Alternatively, the mapmaker, like Dante, may have thought of God and Caesar as two forces that rule the world – one earthly and the other heavenly. I am grateful to Evelyn Edson for this suggestion.

Conclusion

1. For a partial attempt at sensitivity to this issue, see Monson (1978), who orients maps on the East mostly for practical considerations of the "Wide-Screen Project."
2. Cf., e.g., Stein and Niederland 1989; Downs 1977; Gould and White 1986; G. King 1996; Jarvis 1998; Portugali 1996; R. King 1990.
3. Cf. Sack 1986; 1997.

BIBLIOGRAPHY

Aaron, David H. 1994, "Early Rabbinic Exegesis on Noah's Son Ham and the So-called 'Hamitic Myth.'" *JAAR 63*, 721–59.

Abel, F.-M. 1967, *Géographie de la Palestine*. 2 vols. 3rd edn. Etudes Bibliques 28. Paris: Librairie Lecoffre.

Achelis, Hans. 1897, *Hippolytus Werke, Bd. 1: Exegetische und homiletische Schriften, 2.Hälfte: Kleinere exegetische und homiletische Schriften*. GCS. Leipzig: Hinrichs.

Adler, William. 1989, *Time Immemorial: Archaic History and Its Sources in Christian Chronography from Julius Africanus to George Syncellus*. Dumbarton Oaks Studies 26. Washington, DC: Dumbarton Oaks Research Library and Collection.

1990, "The Origins of the Proto-Heresies: Fragments from a Chronicle in the First Book of Epiphanius' *Panarion*." *JTS 41*, 472–501.

1993, "Apion's 'Encomium of Adultery': A Jewish Satire of Greek Paideia in the Pseudo-Clementine *Homilies*." *HUCA 64*, 15–49.

1994, "Jacob of Edessa and the Jewish Pseudepigrapha in Syriac Chronography." In John C. Reeves (ed.), *Tracing the Threads: Studies in the Vitality of Jewish Pseudepigrapha*, 143–71. SBLEJL 6. Atlanta, GA: Scholars Press.

1996, "The Apocalyptic Survey of History Adapted by Christians: Daniel's Prophecy of 70 Weeks." In J. C. VanderKam and W. Adler, *The Jewish Apocalyptic Heritage in Early Christianity*, 201–38. CRINT 3.4. Assen: Van Gorcum; Minneapolis: Fortress.

1997, "Exodus 6:23 and the High Priest from the Tribe of Judah." *JTS N.S. 48*, 24–47.

Ådna, Jostein. 1993, "Jesu Kritik am Tempel. Eine Untersuchung zum Verlauf und Sinn der sogenannten Tempelreinigung Jesu, Markus 11,15–17 und Parallelen." Ph.D. dissertation, University of Oslo.

1997 "Die Heilige Schrift als Zeuge der Heidenmission. Die Rezeption vom Amos 9,11–12 in Apg 15,16–18." In J. Ådna, et al. (eds.), *Evangelium, Schriftauslegung, Kirche. Festschrift für Peter Stuhlmacher zum 65. Geburtstag*, 1–23. Göttingen: Vandenhoeck & Ruprecht.

Adovasio, James M., and Rhonda L. Andrews. 1981, "Textile Remains and Basketry Impressions from Bad edh-Dhra and a Weaving Implement from Numeria." In Walter E. Rast and R. Thomas Schaub (eds.), *The Southeastern Dead Sea Plain Expedition: An Interim Report of the 1977 Season*, 181–5. AASOR 46. Cambridge, MA: American Society of Oriental Research.

Aharoni, Yohanan, and Michael Avi-Yonah. 1993, *The Macmillan Bible Atlas*. 3rd edn. New York: Macmillan.

Aland, Kurt, and Barbara Aland. 1988, *Griechisch-deutsches Wörterbuch zu den Schriften des Neuen Testaments und der frühchristlichen Literatur.* 6th edn. Berlin/New York: de Gruyter.

1989, *The Text of the New Testament: An Introduction to the Critical Editions and to the Theory and Practice of Modern Textual Criticism.* 2nd edn. Trans. Erroll F. Rhodes. Grand Rapids: Eerdmans; Leiden: Brill.

Albani, Matthias. 1993, "Der Zodiakos in 4Q318 und die Henoch-Astronomie." *Forschungsstelle Judentum, Theologische Fakultät Leipzig, Mitteilungen und Beiträge 7* 3–42.

1994, *Astronomie und Schöpfungsglaube. Untersuchungen zum Astronomischen Henochbuch.* WMANT 68. Neukirchen-Vluyn: Neukirchener Verlag.

1998–99, "Horoscopes in the Qumran Scrolls." In Peter W. Flint and James C. VanderKam (eds.), *The Dead Sea Scrolls: A Comprehensive Assessment,* II.278–330. 2 vols. Leiden: Brill.

et al. (eds.). 1997, *Studies in the Book of Jubilees.* TSAJ 65. Tübingen: Mohr-Siebeck.

and U. Gleßmer. 1997, "Un instrument de mesures astronomiques à Qumrân." *RB 104,* 88–115.

Alexander, Loveday. 1993, *The Preface to Luke's Gospel: Literary Conventions and Social Context in Luke 1.1–4 and Acts 1.1.* SNTSMS 78. Cambridge: Cambridge University Press.

1995a, " 'In Journeyings Often': Voyaging in the Acts of the Apostles and in Greek Romance." In C. M. Tuckett (ed.), *Luke's Literary Achievement: Collected Essays,* 17–49. JSNTSup 116. Sheffield: Sheffield Academic Press.

1995b, "Narrative Maps: Reflections on the Toponomy of Acts." In M. Daniel, et al. (eds.), *The Bible in Human Society: Essays in Honour of John Rogerson,* 17–57. JSOTSup 200. Sheffield: Sheffield Academic Press.

Alexander, Paul J. 1985, "Gog and Magog." In *The Byzantine Apocalyptic Tradition,* 185–92. Berkeley: University of California Press.

Alexander, Philip S. 1972, "The Targumim and Early Exegesis of 'Sons of God' in Genesis 6." *JJS 23,* 60–71.

1974, "The Toponymy of the Targumim, with Special Reference to the Table of Nations and the Boundaries of the Land of Israel." D. Phil. thesis, Oxford University.

1982, "Notes on the 'Imago Mundi' of the Book of Jubilees." *JJS 33,* 197–213.

1990, "Review of Alain Desremaux and Francis Schmidt, *Moïse Géographe: Recherches sur les représentations juives et chrétiennes de l'espace.*" *JJS 41,* 120–2.

1992, "Geography of the Bible (Early Jewish)." *ABD 2,* 977–88.

1997a, "Jerusalem as the Omphalos of the World: On the History of a Geographical Concept." *Judaism 46,* 147–58.

1997b, " 'Wrestling against Wickedness in High Places': Magic in the Worldview of the Qumran Community." In Stanley E. Porter and Craig A. Evans (eds.), *The Scrolls and the Scriptures: Qumran Fifty Years After,* 318–37. JSPSup 26. Roehampton Institute London Papers 3. Sheffield: Sheffield Academic Press.

1999, "Jerusalem as the Omphalos of the World: On the History of a Geographical Concept." In Lee I. Levine (ed.), *Jerusalem: Its Sanctity and Centrality to Judaism, Christianity, and Islam*, 104–19. New York: Continuum.

Allison, Dale C., Jr. 1993, *The New Moses: A Matthean Typology*. Minneapolis: Fortress.

1997, "Land in Early Christianity." In Ralph P. Martin and Peter H. Davids (eds.), *Dictionary of the Later New Testament and Its Developments*, 642–4. Downers Grove, IL: InterVarsity Press.

1998, *Jesus of Nazareth: Millenarian Prophet*. Minneapolis: Fortress.

Amit, David. 1995, "Architectural Plans of Synagogues in the Southern Judean Hills and the 'Halakah.'" In Dan Urman and Paul V. M. Flesher (eds.), *Ancient Synagogues: Historical Analysis and Archaeological Discovery*, 129–56. SPB 47.1. Leiden: Brill.

Andersen, Andrew R. 1932, *Alexander's Gate, Gog and Magog, and the Inclosed Nations*. Cambridge, MA: Medieval Academy of America.

Anderson, Gary A. 1992, "Sacrifice and Sacrificial Offerings (OT)." *ABD 5*, 870–86.

and Michael E. Stone (eds.). 1994, *A Synopsis of the Books of Adam and Eve*. SBLEJL 5. Atlanta, GA: Scholars Press.

Andrei, Osvalda. 1996, "The 430 Years of Ex. 12:40, from Demetrius to Julius Africanus: A Study in Jewish and Christian Chronography." *Henoch 18*, 9–67.

Arentzen, Jörg-Geerd. 1984, *Imago Mundi Cartographica. Studien zur Bildlichkeit mittelalterlicher West- und Ökumenekarten unter besonderer Berücksichtigung des Zusammenwirkens von Text und Bild*. Münstersche Mittelalter-Schriften 53. Munich: Wilhelm Fink.

Armin, Wolf. 1992, "Hatte Homer eine Karte? Zu einer poetischen Weise, Küstenlinien und Länderformen darzustellen." In Klaus Döring and Georg Wöhrle (eds.), *Antike Naturwissenschaft und ihre Rezeption*, I.3–36. 2 vols. Bamberg: Collibri-Verlag.

Attridge, Harold W. 1989, *The Epistle to the Hebrews*. Hermeneia. Philadelphia: Fortress.

Aune, David E. 1998–99. "Qumran and the Book of Revelation." In Peter W. Flint and James C. VanderKam (eds.), *The Dead Sea Scrolls After Fifty Years: A Comprehensive Assessment*, II.622–48. 2 vols. Leiden: Brill.

Baasland, Ernst. 1995, "Rhetorischer Kontext in Apg 15,13–21. Statuslehre und die Actareden." In Tord Fornberg and David Hellholm (eds.), *Texts and Contexts: Biblical Texts in their Textual and Situational Contexts. Essays in Honor of Lars Hartman*, 191–226. Oslo: Scandinavian University Press.

Bachmann, M. 1980, *Jerusalem und der Tempel. Die geographisch-theologischen Elemente in der lukanischen Sicht des jüdischen Kultzentrums*. BWANT 6.9 (109). Stuttgart: Kohlhammer.

Badian, Ernst. 1996, "*Laudatio Turiae*." In Simon Hornblower and Antony Spawforth (eds.), *OCD*, 822. 3rd edn. Oxford: Oxford University Press.

Baldwin, Barry, and Anthony Cutler. 1991, "Alexandrian World Chronicle." *The Oxford Dictionary of Byzantium* I. 62. Oxford: Oxford University Press.

Bannert, Herbert. 1978, "Weltbild." *PW Suppl. 15*, 1557–83.

Barclay, John M. G. 1996, *Jews in the Mediterranean Diaspora: From Alexander to Trajan (323 BCE-117 CE)*. Edinburgh: Clark.

Bar-Deroma, H. 1960, "The River of Egypt (Naḥal Mizraim)." *PEQ 92*, 37–56.

Barrett, Anthony A. 1997, "Review of Kevin Herbert, *Roman Imperial Coins. Augustus to Hadrian and Antonine Selections, 31 BC-AD 180.*" *Bryn Mawr Classical Review* 97.5.3 (online).

Barrett, C. K. 1994–98, *The Acts of the Apostles.* 2 vols. ICC. Edinburgh: Clark.

Barrois, A. 1930, "Chronique." *RB 39*, 257–65.

Barton, Tamsyn S. 1994a, *Ancient Astrology.* Sciences of Antiquity. London: Routledge.

1994b, *Power and Knowledge: Astrology, Physiognomics, and Medicine under the Roman Empire.* Ann Arbor: University of Michigan Press.

Bauckham, Richard. 1983, *Jude, 2 Peter.* WBC 50. Waco, TX: Word.

1990, *Jude and the Relatives of Jesus in the Early Church.* Edinburgh: Clark.

1991, "More on Kainam the Son of Arpachshad in Luke's Genealogy." *ETL 67*, 95–103.

1992a, "The Martyrdom of Peter in Early Christian Literature." In Wolfgang Haase (ed.), *ANRW* II.26.1, 539–95. Berlin: de Gruyter.

1992b, "A Quotation from 4QSecond Ezekiel in the Apocalypse of Peter." *RevQ 15*, 437–45.

1996a, "James and the Gentiles (Acts 15.13–21)." In Ben Witherington, III (ed.), *History, Literature, and Society in the Book of Acts*, 154–84. Cambridge: Cambridge University Press.

1996b, "James and the Jerusalem Church." In R. Bauckham (ed.), *The Book of Acts in Its First Century Setting, Vol. IV: The Book of Acts in Its Palestinian Setting*, 415–80. Grand Rapids, MI: Eerdmans; Carlisle: Paternoster.

1997a, "Anna of the Tribe of Asher (Luke 2:36–38)." *RB 104*, 161–91.

1997b, "Review of F. Stanley Jones, *An Ancient Jewish Christian Source on the History of Christianity: Pseudo-Clementine Recognitions 1.27–71.*" *JJS 42*, 420–1.

Bauer, Adolf. 1905, *Die Chronik des Hippolytus im Matritensis graecus 121.* TU 29.1. Leipzig: Hinrichs.

and Rudolf Helm (eds.). 1955, *Hippolytus Werke, Bd. 4: Die Chronik.* GSC 46. Berlin: Akademie-Verlag.

and Josef Strzygowski. 1906, *Eine alexandrinische Weltchronik. Text und Miniaturen eines griechischen Papyrus der Sammlung W. Goleniscev.* Denkschriften der Kaiserlichen Akademie der Wissenschaften, Phil.-hist. Klasse 51.2. Vienna: Hölder.

Bauer, Walter. 1988, *Griechisch-deutsches Wörterbuch zu den Schriften des Neuen Testaments und der frühchristlichen Literatur.* 6th edn. Berlin/New York: de Gruyter.

Bauernfeind, Otto. 1980, *Kommentar und Studien zur Apostelgeschichte.* WUNT 22. Tübingen: Mohr-Siebeck.

Baumgarten, Albert I. 1984, "Josephus and Hippolytus on the Pharisees." *HUCA 55*, 1–25.

Beall, Todd S. 1988, *Josephus' Description of the Essenes Illustrated by the Dead Sea Scrolls.* SNTSMS 58. Cambridge: Cambridge University Press.

Béchard, Dean Philip. 1997, "Paul among the Rustics: A Study of Luke's Socio-Geographical Universalism in Acts 14:8–20." Ph.D. dissertation, Yale University.

Becking, B. 1995, "Ends of the Earth אפסי ארץ." In Karel van der Toorn, et al. (eds.), *Dictionary of Deities and Demons in the Bible*, 573–6. Leiden: Brill.

Beckwith, Roger T. 1996, "The Year of the Messiah: Jewish and Early Christian Chronologies, and Their Eschatological Consequences." In *Calendar and Chronology, Jewish and Christian: Biblical, Intertestamental and Patristic Studies*, 217–75. AGJU 33. Leiden: Brill.

Beitzel, Barry J. 1994, "Exegesis, Dogmatics, and Cartography: A Strange Alchemy in Earlier Church Traditions." *Archaeology in the Biblical World* 2, 8–21.

Bekker-Nielsen, Tønnes. 1988, "*Terra Incognita*: The Subjective Geography of the Roman Empire." In Askel Damsgaard-Madsen, et al. (eds.), *Studies in Ancient History and Numismatics Presented to Rudi Thomsen*, 148–61. Århus: Århus University Press.

Bekkum, Wout J. van. 1998, "The Lesson of the Flood: מבול in Rabbinic Tradition." In Florentino García Martínez and Gerard P. Luttikhuizen (eds.), *Interpretations of the Flood*, 124–33. Themes in Biblical Narrative: Jewish and Christian Traditions 1. Leiden: Brill.

Bell, Richard H. 1994, *Provoked to Jealousy: The Origin and Purpose of the Jealousy Motif in Romans 9–11*. WUNT 2.63. Tübingen: Mohr-Siebeck.

Bendlin, Andreas. 1997, "Peripheral Centres – Central Peripheries: Religious Communication in the Roman Empire." In Hubert Cancik and Jörg Rüpke (eds.), *Römische Reichsreligion und Provinzialreligion*, 35–68. Tübingen: Mohr-Siebeck.

Benjamins, H. S. 1998, "Noah, the Ark, and the Flood in Early Christian Theology: The Ship of the Church in the Making." In Florentino García Martínez and Gerard P. Luttikhuizen (eds.), *Interpretations of the Flood*, 134–49. Themes in Biblical Narrative: Jewish and Christian Traditions 1. Leiden: Brill.

Berger, Klaus. 1998, "Jubiläenbuch." *RAC 19/Lfg. 146*, 31–8.

Bergler, Siegfried. 1998, "Jesus, Bar Kochba und das messianische Laubhüttenfest." *JSJ 29*, 143–91.

Bernstein, Moshe J. 1998–99, "Pentateuchal Interpretation at Qumran." In Peter W. Flint and James C. VanderKam (eds.), *The Dead Sea Scrolls After Fifty Years: A Comprehensive Assessment*, I.128–59. 2 vols. Leiden: Brill.

1999a, "Noah and the Flood at Qumran." In Donald W. Parry and Eugene Ulrich (eds.), *The Provo International Conference on the Dead Sea Scrolls: Technological Innovations, New Texts, and Reformulated Issues*, 199–231. STDJ 30. Leiden: Brill.

1999b, "Pseudepigraphy in the Qumran Scrolls: Categories and Functions." In Esther G. Chazon and Michael Stone (eds.), *Pseudepigraphic Perspectives: The Apocrypha and Pseudepigrapha in Light of the Dead Sea Scrolls*, 1–26. STDJ 31. Leiden: Brill.

Betz, Hans Dieter. 1997, "Jesus and the Purity of the Temple (Mark 11:15–18): A Comparative Religion Approach." *JBL 116*, 455–72.

Beyer, Klaus. 1984–92, *Die aramäischen Texte von Toten Meer*. 2 vols. Göttingen: Vandenhoeck & Ruprecht.

1994, *Die aramäischen Texte vom Toten Meer. Ergänzungsband*. Göttingen: Vandenhoeck & Ruprecht.

Bikerman, Elias J. 1952, "Origines Gentium." *CP 47*, 65–81.

Black, Matthew. 1956, "The Essenes in Hippolytus and Josephus." In W. D. Davies and David Daube (eds.), *The Background of the New Testament and Its Eschatology*, 172–5. Cambridge: Cambridge University Press.

1985, *The Book of Enoch or I Enoch: A New English Edition*. SVTP 7. Leiden: Brill.

Blanchetière, François, and Ray Pritz. 1993, "La migration des 'Nazaréens' à Pella." In F. Blanchetière and Moshe D. Herr (eds.), *Aux Origines Juives du Christianisme*, 93–110. Cahiers du Centre de recherche française de Jérusalem, Série Hommes et sociétés 2. Jerusalem: Peeters.

Bloedhorn, Hanswulf, et al. 1992, "Die jüdische Diaspora bis zum 7. Jahrhundert n. Chr." *TAVO* B VI 18. Wiesbaden: Reichert.

Blomberg, Craig L. 1998, "The Christian and the Law of Moses." In I. Howard Marshall and David Peterson (eds.), *Witness to the Gospel: The Theology of Acts*, 397–416. Grand Rapids, MI: Eerdmans.

Böcher, Otto. 1989, "Das sogenannte Aposteldekret." In Hubert Frankemölle and Karl Kertelege (eds.), *Vom Urchristentum zu Jesus. Für Joachim Gnilka*, 325–36. Freiburg: Herder.

Bockmuehl, Markus. 1995, "The Noachide Commandments and New Testament Ethics, with Special Reference to Acts 15 and Pauline Halakhah." *RevB 102*, 72–101.

1998, " 'To Be or Not to Be': The Possible Futures of New Testament Scholarship." *SJT 51*, 271–306.

Boll, Franz. 1894, "Studien über Claudius Ptolemäus. Ein Beitrag zur Geschichte der griechischen Philosophie und Astrologie." *Jahrbuch für classische Philologie Suppl. Bd. 21*, 51–244.

Borgen, Peder. 1983, "Philo, Luke and Geography." In *Paul Preaches Circumcision and Pleases Men and Other Essays on Christian Origins*, 59–71. Relieff 8. Dragvoll-Trondheim: TAPIR.

1997, "Philo and His World." In *Philo of Alexandria: An Exegete for His Time*, 14–29. NovTSup 86. Leiden: Brill.

Böttrich, Christfried. 1997, "Astrologie in der Henochtradition." *ZAW 109*, 222–45.

Bouché-Leclercq, A. 1963, *L'Astrologie grecque*. Paris, 1899. Reprint edn., Paris: Culture et Civilisation.

Bovon, François. 1983, "Israel, die Kirche und die Völker im lukanischen Doppelwerk." *TLZ 108*, 403–14.

1989–96, *Das Evangelium nach Lukas*. 2 vols. EKK 3. Zurich: Benziger Verlag; Neukirchen-Vluyn: Neukirchener Verlag.

Bowersock, G. W. 1983, *Roman Arabia*. Cambridge, MA: Harvard University Press.

Bowman, Alan K., et al. (eds.). 1996, *The Cambridge Ancient History, Vol. X: The Augustan Empire, 43 B.C.–A.D. 69*. 2nd edn. Cambridge: Cambridge University Press.

Bowman, John (ed. and trans.). 1977, *Samaritan Documents Relating to Their History, Religion and Life*. Pittsburgh Original Texts and Translations 2. Pittsburgh: Pickwick.

Braude, Benjamin. 1997, "The Sons of Noah and the Construction of Ethnic and Geographical Identities in the Medieval and Early Modern Period." *The William and Mary Quarterly 54*, 103–42.

Braun, Roddy. 1986, *1 Chronicles*. WBC 14. Waco, TX: Word.

Braund, David. 1984, *Rome and the Friendly King: The Character of the Client Kingship*. London: Croom Helm; New York: St. Martin's Press.

Brawley, Robert L. 1987, *Luke-Acts and the Jews: Conflict, Apology, and Conciliation*. SBLMS 33. Atlanta, GA: Scholars Press.

Bremmer, Jan N. 1998, "Near Eastern and Native Traditions in Apollodorus' Account of the Flood." In Florentino García Martínez and Gerard P. Luttikhuizen (eds.), *Interpretations of the Flood*, 39–55. Themes in Biblical Narrative: Jewish and Christian Traditions 1. Leiden: Brill.

Brent, Allen. 1995, *Hippolytus and the Roman Church in the Third Century: Communities in Tension Before the Emergence of a Monarch-Bishop*. VCSup 31. Leiden: Brill.

Brincken, Anna-Dorothee von den. 1968, "Mappamundi and Chronographia. Studien zur *imago mundi* des abendländischen Mittelalters." *Deutsches Archiv für Erforschung des Mittelalters 24*, 118–86.

1970, " ' ... ut describeretur universus orbis.' Zur Universalkartographie des Mittelalters." In Albert Zimmermann (ed.), *Methoden in Wissenschaft und Kunst des Mittelalters*, 249–78. Miscellanea Mediaevalia 7. Berlin: de Gruyter.

1976, "Die Kugelgestalt der Erde in der Kartographie des Mittelalters." *Archiv für Kulturgeschichte 58*, 77–95.

1991, "Romazentrische Weltdarstellung um die erste Jahrtausendwende." In Anton von Euw and Peter Schreiner (eds.), *Kaiserin Theophanu. Begegnung des Ostens und Westens um die Wende des ersten Jahrtausends: Gedenkschrift des Kölner Schnütgen-Museums zum 1000. Todesjahr der Kaiserin, Bd. 1*, 401–11. Köln: Schnütgen-Museum.

1992, *Fines Terrae. Die Enden der Erde und der vierte Kontinent auf mittelalterlichen Weltkarten*. Monumenta Germaniae Historica 36. Hanover: Hahnsche Buchhandlung.

1993, "Hieronymus als Exeget 'secundum historiam'. Von der Chronik zum Ezechiel-Kommentar." *Deutsches Archiv für Erforschung des Mittelalters 49*, 453–77.

Brinkman, J. A. 1963, "The Literary Background of the 'Catalogue of the Nations' (Acts 2,9–11)." *CBQ 25*, 418–27.

Brock, S. 1978, "Abraham and the Ravens: A Syriac Counterpart to Jubilees 11–12 and its Implications." *JSJ 9*, 135–52.

Brodersen, Kai. 1994a, *Dionysios von Alexandria, Das Lied von der Welt*. Hildesheim: Olms.

1994b, *Pomponius Mela, Kreuzfahrt durch die alte Welt*. Darmstadt: Wissenschaftliche Buchgesellschaft.

1995, *Terra Cognita. Studien zur römischen Raumerfassung*. Spudasmata 59. Hildesheim: Olms.

Brodsky, Harold. 1998, "Ezekiel's Map of Restoration." In H. Brodsky (ed.), *Land and Community: Geography in Jewish Studies*, 17–29. Studies and Texts in Jewish History and Culture 3. Bethesda, MD: University Press of Maryland.

Brooke, George J. 1991, "The Kittim in the Qumran Pesharim." In Loveday Alexander (ed.), *Images of Empire*, 135–59. Sheffield: JSOT Press.

1998, "Shared Intertextual Interpretations in the Dead Sea Scrolls and the New Textament." In Michael E. Stone and Esther G. Chazon (eds.), *Biblical*

Interpretations: Early Use and Interpretation of the Bible in Light of the Dead Sea Scrolls, 35–57. STDJ 28. Leiden: Brill.

1998–99, "Parabiblical Prophetic Narratives." In Peter W. Flint and James C. VanderKam (eds.), *The Dead Sea Scrolls After Fifty Years: A Comprehensive Assessment*, I.271–301. 2 vols. Leiden: Brill.

Brown, Raymond E. 1997, *An Introduction to the New Testament*. ABRL. New York: Doubleday.

Brunt, P. A. 1997, "Laus Imperii." In Richard A. Horsley (ed.), *Paul and Empire: Religion and Power in Roman Imperial Society*, 25–35. Harrisburg, PA: Trinity Press International.

Buber, Solomon (ed.). 1960–61, *Midrash Aggadah*. 2 vols. in 1. Vienna, 1893–94. Reprint edn., Jerusalem.

Bundy, David. 1991, "Pseudepigrapha in Syriac Literature." *SBL 1991 Seminar Papers*, 745–65. Atlanta, GA: Scholars Press.

Burchard, Christoph. 1974, "Zur Nebenüberlieferung von Josephus' Bericht über die Essener Bell 2,119–161 bei Hippolyt, Porphryrius, Jossipus, Niketas Choniates und anderen." In Otto Betz, et al. (eds.), *Josephus-Studien. Untersuchungen zu Josephus, dem antiken Judentum und dem Neuen Testament. Otto Michel um 70.Geburtstag gewidmet*, 77–96. Göttingen: Vandenhoeck & Ruprecht.

1977, "Die Essener bei Hippolyt. Hippolyt, Ref. IX 18, 2–28, 2 und Josephus, Bell. 2, 119–161." *JSJ 8*, 1–41.

Burrows, Eric. 1936, "The Number Seventy in Semitic." *Or N.S. 5*, 389–92.

Cadbury, H. J. 1958, *The Making of Luke-Acts*. London: SPCK.

Cameron, Alan. 1980, "The Garland of Philip." *GRBS 21*, 43–62.

1990, "Two Mistresses of Ptolemy Philadelphus." *GRBS 31*, 287–311.

1993, *The Greek Anthology from Meleager to Planudes*. Oxford: Clarendon Press.

Cancik, Hubert. 1997, "Die 'Repraesentation' von 'Provinz' (nationes, gentes) in Rom. Ein Beitrag zur Besinnung von 'Reichsreligion' vom 1. Jahrhundert v. Chr. bis zum 2. Jahrhundert n. Chr." In H. Cancik and Jörg Rüpke (eds.), *Römische Reichsreligion und Provinzialreligion*, 129–43. Tübingen: Mohr-Siebeck.

1998, "The End of the World, of History, and of the Individual in Greek and Roman Antiquity." In John J. Collins (ed.), *The Encyclopedia of Apocalypticism, Vol. I: The Origins of Apocalypticism in Judaism and Christianity*, 84–125. New York: Continuum.

Cansdale, Lena. 1997, *Qumran and the Essenes: A Re-Evaluation of the Evidence*. TSAJ 60. Tübingen: Mohr-Siebeck.

Caquot, André. 1980, "Deux notes sur la géographie des Jubilés." In Gérard Nahon and Charles Touati (eds.), *Hommage à Georges Vajda. Etudes d'histoire et de pensée juives*, 37–42. Leuven: Peeters.

Carroll, Robert P. 1997, "Deportation and Diasporic Discourses in Prophetic Literature." In J. M. Scott (ed.), *Exile: Old Testament, Jewish and Christian Conceptions*, 63–85. JSJSup 56. Leiden: Brill.

Carter, Giles F., and William E. Metcalf. 1988, "The Dating of the M. Agrippa Asses." *The Numismatic Chronicle* 145–7.

Casson, Lionel. 1989, *The Periplus Maris Erythraei: Text with Introduction, Translation, and Commentary*. Princeton: Princeton University Press.

Chabot, J.-B. (ed.). 1899–1924, *Chronique de Michael le Syrien, patriarche jacobite d'Antioche (1166–1199)*. 4 vols. Paris: Leroux.

— 1937, *Chronicon Anonymum ad annum Christi 1234 pertinens*. CSCO; Scriptores Syri 3.14. Leuven: Ex Officina Orientali et Scientifica.

Charles duc de Croy. 1654, *Regum et imperatorum Romanorum numismata aurea, argentea, aerea, a Romulo et c. Iul. Caesare usque ad Iustinianum Aug. Curâ & impensis Caroli, Ducis Croyiaci et Arschotani. Olim congesta, aerique incisa: nunc insigni auctario locupletata, & breui commentario illustrata, cum indice rerum, in numismatib. disignatarum, copiosissimo. Accessere Antonii Augustini, Antiquitatum Romanar. Hispanarumq. in nummis veterum, dialogi*. Antwerp: Aertssens.

Charles, R. H. 1972, *The Book of Jubilees or the Little Genesis*. Oxford: Clarendon, 1902. Reprint edn., Jerusalem: Makor.

Charlesworth, James H. (ed.). 1983–85, *The Old Testament Pseudepigrapha*. 2 vols. Garden City, NY: Doubleday.

— 1985, *The Old Testament Pseudepigrapha and the New Testament*. SNTSMS 54. Cambridge: Cambridge University Press.

— 1987, "Jewish Interest in Astrology during the Hellenistic and Roman Period." In Wolfgang Haase (ed.), *ANRW* II.20.2, 926–52. Berlin/New York: de Gruyter.

— and Craig A. Evans (eds.). 1993, *The Pseudepigrapha and Early Biblical Interpretation*. JSPSup 14. Sheffield: JSOT.

Chilton, Bruce. 1987, *The Isaiah Targum*. ArBib 11. Wilmington: Glazier.

— 1997, "Temple." In Ralph P. Martin and Peter H. Davids (eds.), *Dictionary of the Later New Testament and Its Developments*, 1159–66. Downers Grove, IL: InterVarsity.

— and Jacob Neusner. 1995, *Judaism in the New Testament: Practices and Beliefs*. London/New York: Routledge.

Chyutin, Michael. 1994, "The New Jerusalem: Ideal City." *DSD 1*, 71–97.

— 1997, *The New Jerusalem Scroll from Qumran: A Comprehensive Reconstruction*. JSPSup 25. Sheffield: Sheffield Academic Press.

Cichorius, Conrad. 1922, *Römische Studien. Historisches, Epigraphisches, Literargeschichtliches aus vier Jahrhunderten Roms*. Leipzig/Berlin: Teubner.

Clark, Andrew C. 1998, "The Role of the Apostles." In I. Howard Marshall and David Peterson (eds.), *Witness to the Gospel: The Theology of Acts*, 169–90. Grand Rapids, MI: Eerdmans.

Clarke, Katherine. 1995, "Review of James S. Romm, *The Edges of the Earth in Ancient Thought* (1992)." *JRS 85*, 266–7.

— 1996, "Between Geography and History: Strabo's Roman World." D. Phil. thesis, Oxford University.

— 1997, "In Search of the Author of Strabo's *Geography*." *JRS 87*, 92–110.

— 1999, *Between Geography and History: Hellenistic Constructions of the Roman World*. Oxford Classical Monographs. Oxford: Clarendon.

Cockle, W. E. H. 1996, "Syene." In Simon Hornblower and Antony Spawforth (eds.), *OCD*, 1459. 3rd edn. Oxford: Oxford University Press.

Cohen, Naomi G. 1992, "Taryag and the Noahide Commandments." *JJS 43*, 46–57.

Cohen, Shaye J. D. 1999, *The Beginnings of Jewishness: Boundaries, Varieties, Uncertainties*. Berkeley: University of California Press.

Collins, Adela Yarbro. 1996, "Numerical Symbolism in Jewish and Early Christian Apocalyptic Literature." In *Cosmology and Eschatology in Jewish and Christian Apocalypticism*, 55–138. JSJSup 50. Leiden: Brill.

Collins, John J. 1972, *The Sibylline Oracles of Egyptian Judaism*. SBLDS 13. Missoula, MT: Society of Biblical Literature.

1983, "Sibylline Oracles." *OTP* I: 317–472.

1995a, *The Scepter and the Star: The Messiahs of the Dead Sea Scrolls and Other Ancient Literature*. ABRL. New York: Doubleday.

1995b, "A Throne in the Heavens: Apotheosis in Pre-Christian Judaism." In J. J. Collins and M. Fishbane (eds.), *Death, Ecstasy, and Other Worldly Journeys*, 43–58. Albany, NY: State University of New York Press.

1995c, "A Throne in the Heavens." In *The Scepter and the Star: The Messiahs of the Dead Sea Scrolls and Other Ancient Literature*, 138–53. ABRL. New York: Doubleday.

1997a, *Apocalypticism in the Dead Sea Scrolls*. The Literature of the Dead Sea Scrolls. London: Routledge.

1997b, *Seers, Sibyls and Sages in Hellenistic-Roman Judaism*. Leiden: Brill.

1998, *The Apocalyptic Imagination*. Rev. edn. Grand Rapids, MI: Eerdmans.

1998–99, "Apocalypticism and Literary Genre in the Dead Sea Scrolls." In Peter W. Flint and James C. VanderKam (eds.), *The Dead Sea Scrolls After Fifty Years: A Comprehensive Assessment*, II.403–30. 2 vols. Leiden: Brill.

1999, "Pseudepigraphy and Group Formation in Second Temple Judaism." In Esther G. Chazon and Michael Stone (eds.), *Pseudepigraphic Perspectives: The Apocrypha and Pseudepigrapha in Light of the Dead Sea Scrolls*, 43–58. STDJ 31. Leiden: Brill.

Conzelmann, Hans. 1972, *Die Apostelgeschichte*. 2nd edn. HNT 7. Tübingen: Mohr-Siebeck.

Cook, J. M. 1983, *The Persian Empire*. London: Dent.

Cowley, Roger W. 1988, *Ethiopian Biblical Interpretation: A Study in Exegetical Tradition and Hermeneutics*. University of Cambridge Oriental Publications. Cambridge: Cambridge University Press.

Croke, Brian. 1992, "The Origins of the Christian World Chronicle." In *Christian Chronicles and Byzantine History, 5th–6th Centuries*, 116–31. Aldershot, Hampshire: Variorum.

Crown, Alan D. (ed.). 1989, *The Samaritans*. Tübingen: Mohr-Siebeck.

D'Ambra, Eve. 1993, *Private Lives, Imperial Virtues: The Frieze of the Forum Transitorium in Rome*. Princeton: Princeton University Press.

Daniélou, Jean. 1973, *A History of Early Christian Doctrine Before the Council of Nicea, Vol. II: The Gospel Message and Hellenistic Culture*. London: Darton, Longman and Todd.

Darling, R. A. 1987, "The 'Church from the Nations' in the Exegesis of Ephrem." In Hans J. W. Drijvers, et al. (eds.), *IV Symposium Syriacum 1984*, 111–21. Orientalia Christiana Analecta. Rome: Pont. Inst. Stud. Orient.

Davids, Peter H. 1993, "The Pseudepigrapha in the Catholic Epistles." In James H. Charlesworth and Craig A. Evans (eds.), *The Pseudepigrapha and Early Biblical Interpretation*, 228–45. JSPSup 14. Sheffield: JSOT.

1997, "Tongues." In Ralph P. Martin and Peter H. Davids (eds.), *Dictionary of the Later New Testament and Its Developments*, 1177–9. Downers Grove, IL: InterVarsity Press.

Davies, W. D., and Dale C. Allison, Jr. 1997, *The Gospel According to Saint Matthew*. ICC. Edinburgh: Clark.

Dean, James Elmer (ed.). 1935, *Epiphanius' Treatise on Weights and Measures*. Studies in Ancient Oriental Civilization 11. Chicago: University of Chicago Press.

Dekkers, E. 1954, *Quinti Septimi Florentis Tertulliani Opera, Pars I: Opera Catholica, Adversus Marcionem*. Corpus Christianorum, Series Latina. Turnhout: Brepols.

Delano Smith, Catherine. 1991, "Geography or Christianity? Maps of the Holy Land Before AD 1000." *JTS 42*, 143–52.

1996, "Imago Mundi's Logo: The Babylonian Map of the World." *Imago Mundi 48*, 209–11.

and Mayer I. Gruber. 1992, "Rashi's Legacy: Maps of the Holy Land." *The Map Collector 59*, 30–5.

and Elizabeth Morley Ingram. 1991, *Maps in Bibles 1500–1600: An Illustrated Catalogue*. Travaux d'Humanisme et Renaissance 256. Genève: Librairie Droz.

Denis, Albert-Marie. 1970a, "Liber Jubilaeorum." In *Fragmenta Pseudepigraphorum Quae Supersunt Graeca*. PVTG 3. Leiden: Brill.

1970b, *Introduction aux pseudépigraphes grecs d'Ancien Testament*. SVTP 1. Leiden: Brill.

1987, *Concordance grecque pseudépigraphes d'Ancien Testament*. Louvain-la-Neuve: Université Catholique de Louvain.

Depuydt, Leo. 1998, "Gnomons at Meroë and Early Trigonometry." *The Journal of Egyptian Archaeology 84*, 171–80.

Destomes, Marcel (ed.). 1964, *Mappemondes, A.D. 1200–1500. Catalog préparé par la Commission des Cartes Anciennes de l'Union Géographique Internationale*. Monumenta Cartographica Vetustioris Aevi 1; Imago Mundi Suppl. 4. Amsterdam: Israel.

Dexinger, Ferdinand. 1977, *Henochs Zehnwochenapokalypse und offene Probleme der Apokalyptikforschung*. SPB 29. Leiden: Brill.

Dibelius, M. 1968, "Der Text der Apostelgeschichte." In *Aufsätze zur Apostelgeschichte*, 76–83. 5th edn. Ed. Heinrich Greeven. FRLANT 60. Göttingen: Vandenhoeck & Ruprecht.

Dickey, Eleanor. 1996, *Greek Forms of Address From Herodotus to Lucian*. Oxford: Clarendon.

Dilke, A. O. W. 1985, *Greek and Roman Maps*. Ithaca, NY: Cornell University Press.

1987, "Maps in the Service of the State: Roman Cartography to the End of the Augustan Era." In J. B. Harley and David Woodward (eds.), *The History of Cartography, Vol. I: Cartography in Prehistoric, Ancient, and Medieval Europe and the Mediterranean*, 201–11. Chicago/London: University of Chicago Press.

and Margaret Dilke. 1976, "Perception of the Roman World." *Progress in Geography 9*, 39–72.

Diller, Aubrey. 1975, "Agathemerus, *Sketch of Geography*." *GRBS 16*, 59–76.

Dimant, Devorah. 1993, "The Seventy Weeks Chronology (Dan 9:24–27) in the Light of New Qumranic Texts." In A. S. van der Woude (ed.), *The Book of Daniel in the Light of New Findings*, 57–76. BETL 106. Leuven: Peeters.

1998, "Noah in Early Jewish Literature." In Michael E. Stone and Theodore A. Bergren (eds.), *Biblical Figures Outside the Bible*, 123–50. Harrisburg, PA: Trinity Press International.

Dindorf, L. 1832, *Chronicon Paschale*. 2 vols. Corpus Scriptorum Historiae Byzantinae. Bonn: Weber.

Donaldson, T. L. 1990, "Proselytes or 'Righteous Gentiles'? The Status of Gentiles in Eschatological Pilgrimage Patterns of Thought." *JSP 7*, 3–27.

Donner, Herbert. 1984, "Transjordan and Egypt on the Mosaic Map of Madaba." *Annual of the Department of Antiquities, Jordan 18*, 249–57.

1992, *The Mosaic Map of Madaba: An Introductory Guide*. Palestina Antiqua 7. Kampen: Kok Pharos.

and Heinz Cüppers. 1977, *Die Mosaikkarte von Madeba, Teil I: Tafelband*. Abhandlungen des Deutschen Palästinavereins. Wiesbaden: Harrassowitz.

Donovan, Mary Ann. 1997, *One Right Reading? A Guide to Irenaeus*. Collegeville, MN: The Liturgical Press.

Doron, R. 1985, "Pseudo-Eupolemus." *OTP* II: 872–82.

Doutreleau, Louis. 1974, *Irénée de Lyon, Contre les hérésies Livre III*. SC 210. Paris: Cerf.

Downs, Roger M. 1977, *Maps in Minds: Reflections on Cognitive Mapping*. New York: Harper & Row.

Dräger, Paul. 1996, "Argonautai." *Der neue Pauly* I: 1066–70.

Dreizehnter, Alois. 1978, *Die rhetorische Zahl. Quellenkritische Untersuchungen anhand der Zahlen 70 und 700*. Zetemata 73. Munich: Beck.

Drijvers, Hans J. W. 1992, "Syrian Christianity and Judaism." In J. Lieu, et al. (eds.), *The Jews among Pagans and Christians*, 147–73. London: Routledge.

1996, "Early Syriac Christianity: Some Recent Publications." *VC 50*, 159–77.

Drinkard, Joel F., Jr. 1992, "Direction and Orientation." *ABD 2*, 204.

Droge, Arthur J. 1989, *Homer or Moses? Early Christian Interpretation of the History of Culture*. HUT 26. Tübingen: Mohr-Siebeck.

Duhaime, Jean. 1988, "The War Scroll from Qumran and the Greco-Roman Tactical Treatises (1QM)." *RevQ 13*, 133–51.

Dunn, James D. G. 1998, *The Theology of Paul the Apostle*. Grand Rapids, MI: Eerdmans.

Dupont, Jacques. 1979, *The Salvation of the Gentiles: Essays on the Acts of the Apostles*. New York: Paulist Press.

Edson, Evelyn. 1993, "The Oldest World Maps: Classical Sources of Three VIIIth Century Mappaemundi." *The Ancient World 24*, 169–84.

1997, *Mapping Time and Space: How Medieval Mapmakers Viewed Their World*. The British Library Studies in Map History 1. London: The British Library.

Ego, Beate. 1989, *Im Himmel wie auf Erden. Studien zum Verhältnis von himmlischer und irdischer Welt im rabbinischen Judentum*. WUNT 2.34. Tübingen: Mohr-Siebeck.

Ehrenberg, Victor, and A. H. M. Jones. 1967, *Documents Illustrating the Reigns of Augustus & Tiberius*. 2nd edn. Oxford: Clarendon.

Ehrman, Bart, and Michael W. Holmes (eds.). 1995, *The Text of the New Testament in Contemporary Research: Essays on the* Status Quaestionis. Grand Rapids: Eerdmans.

Eiss, Werner. 1997, "Das Wochenfest im Jubiläenbuch und im antiken Judentum." In Matthias Albani, et al. (eds.), *Studies in the Book of Jubilees*, 165–78. TSAJ 65. Tübingen: Mohr-Siebeck.

Elgvin, Torleif. 1996, "Early Essene Eschatology: Judgment and Salvation According to *Sapiential Work* A." In Donald W. Parry and Stephen D. Ricks (eds.), *Current Research and Technological Developments on the Dead Sea Scrolls*, 126–65. STDJ 20. Leiden: Brill.

Eliade, Mircea. 1971, *The Myth of the Eternal Return or, Cosmos and History*. Trans. Willard R. Trask. Bollingen Series 46. Princeton: Princeton University Press.

Elliott, J. K. 1990, " τε in the New Testament." *TZ 46*, 202–4.

Ellis, E. Earle. 1991a, "'Das Ende der Erde' (Apg 1,8)." In Claus Bussmann and Walter Radl (eds.), *Der Treue Gottes trauen. Beiträge zum Werk des Lukas für Gerhard Schneider*, 277–86. Freiburg: Herder.

1991b, "'The End of the Earth' (Acts 1:8)." *BBR* I: 123–32.

Endres, John C. 1987, *Biblical Interpretation in the Book of Jubilees*. CBQMS 18. Washington, DC: Catholic Biblical Association of America.

Engels, Johannes. 1999, *Augusteische Oikumenegeographie und Universalhistorie im Werk Strabons von Amaseia*. Geographica Historica 12. Stuttgart: Franz Steiner.

Eshel, Esther. 1997, "Hermeneutical Approaches to Genesis in the Dead Sea Scrolls." In Judith Frishman and Lucas Van Rompay (eds.), *The Book of Genesis in Jewish and Oriental Christian Interpretation*, 1–12. Traditio Exegetica Graeca 5. Leuven: Peeters.

Eshel, Hanan. 1996, "A Note on a Recently Published Text: The 'Joshua Apocryphon.'" In M. Poorthuis and Ch. Safrai (eds.), *The Centrality of Jerusalem: Historical Perspectives*, 89–93. Kampen: Pharos.

Esler, P. F. 1987, *Community and Gospel in Luke-Acts: The Social and Political Motivation of Lucan Theology*. SNTSMS 57. Cambridge: Cambridge University Press.

Evans, Craig A. 1992, *Non-Canonical Writings and New Testament Interpretation*. Peabody, MA: Hendrickson.

1993, "The Twelve Thrones of Israel: Scripture and Politics in Luke 22:24–30." In C. A. Evans and James A. Sanders, *Luke and Scripture: The Function of Sacred Tradition in Luke-Acts*, 154–70. Minneapolis: Fortress.

1995a, "Jesus' Action in the Temple and Evidence of Corruption in the First-Century Temple." In *Jesus and His Contemporaries: Comparative Studies*, 319–44. AGJU 25. Leiden: Brill.

1995b, "Jesus and the 'Cave of Robbers': Towards a Jewish Context for the Temple Action." In *Jesus and His Contemporaries: Comparative Studies*, 345–65. AGJU 25. Leiden: Brill.

1997, "Aspects of Exile and Restoration in the Proclamation of Jesus and the Gospels." In J. M. Scott (ed.), *Exile: Old Testament, Jewish, and Christian Conceptions*, 299–328. JSJSup 56. Leiden: Brill.

1999, "Jesus and James: Martyrs of the Temple." In Bruce Chilton and C. A. Evans (eds.), *James the Just and Christian Origins*, 233–49. Leiden: Brill.

272   *Bibliography*

Falk, Daniel K. 1994, "4Q393: A Communal Confession." *JJS 45*, 184–207.

1995, "Jewish Prayer Literature and the Jerusalem Church in Acts." In Richard Bauckham (ed.), *The Book of Acts in Its First Century Setting, Vol. IV: The Book of Acts in Its Palestinian Setting*, 267–301. Grand Rapids, MI; Carlisle: Paternoster.

Fass, David E. 1988, "The Symbolic Uses of the North." *Judaism 37*, 465–73.

Fee, Gordon D. 1995, "The Use of the Greek Fathers for New Testament Textual Criticism." In Bart Ehrman and Michael W. Holmes (eds.), *The Text of the New Testament in Contemporary Research: Essays on the Status Quaestionis*, 191–207. Grand Rapids, MI: Eerdmans.

Feldman, Louis H. 1992, "Josephus' Portrait of Joseph." *RB 99*, 379–417.

1993, *Jew and Gentile in the Ancient World: Attitudes and Interactions from Alexander to Justinian*. Princeton: Princeton University Press.

1998, *Josephus's Interpretation of the Bible*. Hellenistic Culture and Society 27. Berkeley: University of California Press.

2000, *Flavius Josephus: Translation and Commentary, Vol. III: Judean Antiquities 1–4*. Brill: Leiden.

Finkel, Irving. 1995, "A Join to the Map of the World: A Notable Discovery." *British Museum Magazine 23*, 26–7.

Fishbane, Michael. 1985, *Biblical Interpretation in Ancient Israel*. Oxford: Clarendon.

Fitzmyer, Joseph A. 1971, *The Genesis Apocryphon*. 2nd edn. BiOr 18. Rome: Pontifical Biblical Institute.

1979, "The Contribution of Qumran Aramaic to the Study of the New Testament." In *A Wandering Aramean: Collected Aramaic Studies*, 85–113. SBLMS 25. Missoula, MT: Scholars Press.

1981–85, *The Gospel according to Luke*. 2 vols. AB 28–28A. Garden City, NY: Doubleday.

1984, "The Ascension of Christ and Pentecost." *Theological Studies 45*, 409–40.

1993, *Romans*. AB 33. New York: Doubleday.

Flint, Peter W. 1996, "4Qpseudo-Daniel arᶜ (4Q245) and the Restoration of the Priesthood." *RevQ 17/65–68*, 137–50.

1998–99, "'Apocrypha,' 'Other Previously-Known Writings,' and 'Pseudepigrapha' in the Dead Sea Scrolls." In P. W. Flint and James C. VanderKam (eds.), *The Dead Sea Scrolls After Fifty Years: A Comprehensive Assessment*, II.24–66. 2 vols. Leiden: Brill.

Flusser, David. 1971, "Seventy Shepherds, Vision of." *EncJud 12*, 1198–9.

1994, "Noachitische Gebote I. Judentum." *TRE 24*, 582–5.

and Shmuel Safrai. 1978–80, *The Josippon (Josephus Gorionides) Edited with an Introduction, Commentary and Notes*. 2 vols. Jerusalem: Bialik Institute.

and Shmuel Safrai. 1986, "Das Aposteldekret und die Noachitischen Gebote." In Edna Brocke and Hans-Joachim Barkenings (eds.),"*Wer Tora vermehrt, mehrt Leben." Festgabe für Heinz Kremers zum 60.Geburtstag*, 173–92. Neukirchen-Vluyn: Neukirchener Verlag.

Fraenkel, Detlef. 1984, "Die Überlieferung der Genealogien Gen 5:3–28 und Gen 11:10–26 in den 'Antiquitates Iudaicae' des Flavius Josephus." In Albert Pietersma and Claude Cox (eds.), *De Septuaginta: Studies in*

Honour of John William Wevers on his Sixty-fifth Birthday, 175–200. Mississauga, ONT: Benben.

Frankenberg, Wilhelm. 1937, *Die syrischen Clementinen mit griechischen Paralleltext. Eine Vorarbeit zu dem literargeschichtlichen Problem der Sammlung*. TU 48.3. Leipzig: Hinrichs.

Fraser, P. M. 1972, *Ptolemaic Alexandria*. 3 vols. Oxford: Clarendon.

1996, *Cities of Alexander the Great*. Oxford: Clarendon.

French, Dorothea R. 1992, "Journeys to the Center of the Earth: Medieval and Renaissance Pilgrimages to Mount Calvary." In Barbara N. Sargent-Baur (ed.), *Journeys Toward God: Pilgrimage and Crusade*, 45–81. Occasional Studies Series 5. Kalamazoo, MI: SMC XXX Medieval Institute Publications, Western Michigan University.

1995, "Mapping Sacred Centers: Pilgrimage and the Creation of Christian Topographies in Roman Palestine." In *Akten des XII. Internationalen Kongresses für christliche Archäologie*, II.792–7. 2 vols. Jahrbuch für Antike und Christentum Ergänzungsband 20. Münster: Aschendorffsche Verlagsbuchhandlung.

French, Roger. 1994, *Ancient Natural History*. London: Routledge.

Frey, Jörg. 1997, "Zum Weltbild im Jubiläenbuch." In Matthias Albani, et al. (eds.), *Studies in the Book of Jubilees*, 261–92. TSAJ 65. Tübingen: Mohr-Siebeck.

Fröhlich, Ida. 1998, "'Narrative Exegesis' in the Dead Sea Scrolls." In Michael E. Stone and Esther G. Chazon (eds.), *Biblical Perspectives: Early Use and Interpretation of the Bible in Light of the Dead Sea Scrolls*, 81–99. STDJ 28. Leiden: Brill.

Fugmann, Joachim. 1998, "Itinerarium." *RAC 19/Lfg. 146*, 2–31.

Galinsky, Karl. 1996, *Augustan Culture: An Interpretative Introduction*. Princeton: Princeton University Press.

Gandz, Solomon. 1953, "The Distribution of Land and Sea on the Earth's Surface According to Hebrew Sources." *PAAJR 22*, 23–53.

García Martínez, Florentino. 1994, "4QMess Ar and the Book of Noah." In *Qumran and Apocalyptic: Studies on the Aramaic Texts from Qumran*, 1–44. 2nd edn. STDJ 9. Leiden: Brill.

1997, "The Heavenly Tablets in the Book of Jubilees." In Matthias Albani, et al. (eds.), *Studies in the Book of Jubilees*, 243–60. TSAJ 65. Tübingen: Mohr-Siebeck.

1998a, "Apocalypticism in the Dead Sea Scrolls." In John J. Collins (ed.), *The Encyclopedia of Apocalypticism, Vol. I: The Origins of Apocalypticism in Judaism and Christianity*, 162–92. New York: Continuum.

1998b, "Interpretations of the Flood in the Dead Sea Scrolls." In Florentino García Martínez and Gerard P. Luttikhuizen (eds.), *Interpretations of the Flood*, 86–108. Themes in Biblical Narrative: Jewish and Christian Traditions 1. Leiden: Brill.

and Eibert J. C. Tigchelaar (eds.). 1997, *The Dead Sea Scrolls Study Edition, Vol. 1: 1Q1–4Q273*. Leiden: Brill.

et al. (eds.). 1998, *Qumran Cave 11, II: 11Q2–18, 11Q20–31*. DJD 23. Oxford: Clarendon.

Gärtner, B. 1955, *The Areopagus Speech and Natural Revelation*. ASNU 21. Lund: Gleerup.

Gaster, Moses. 1927, *The Asatir: The Samaritan Book of the "Secrets of Moses."* London: Royal Asiatic Society.

Gaston, Lloyd. 1982, "Angels and Gentiles in Early Judaism and in Paul." *SR 11*, 65–75.

Geffcken, Joh. 1902, *Die Oracula Sibyllina*. GCS 8. Leipzig: Hinrich.

Gelzer, Heinrich. 1885, *Sextus Julius Africanus und die byzantinische Chronographie, 2.1: Die Nachfolger des Julius Africanus.* Leipzig: Teubner.

Gleßmer, Uwe. 1996, "Horizontal Measuring in the Babylonian Astronomical Compendium *MUL.APIN* and in the Astronomical Book of *1 Enoch.*" *Henoch 3*, 259–82.

——— 1997, "Un instrument de mesures astronomiques à Qumrân." *RB 104*, 88–115.

——— and Matthias Albani. 1999, "An Astronomical Measuring Instrument from Qumran." In Donald W. Parry and Eugene Ulrich (eds.), *The Provo International Conference on the Dead Sea Scrolls: Technological Innovations, New Texts, and Reformulated Issues*, 407–42. STDJ 30. Leiden: Brill.

Gmirkin, Russell. 1998, "Historical Allusions in the War Scroll." *DSD 5*, 172–214.

Gnecchi, Francesco. 1912, *I Medaglioni Romani*. 3 vols. Milan: Hoepli.

Goldenberg, David. 1998, "Scythian-Barbarian: The Permutations of a Classical Topos in Jewish and Christian Texts of Late Antiquity." *JJS 49*, 87–102.

——— 1999, "Geographia Rabbinica: The Toponym Barbaria." *JJS 50*, 53–73.

Goldstein, Jonathan A. 1995, "The Judaism of the Synagogues (Focusing on the Synagogue of Dura-Europos)." In Jacob Neusner (ed.), *Judaism in Late Antiquity*, 109–57. Handbuch der Orientalistik 1.17.2. Leiden: Brill.

Goodenough, Erwin R. 1953–68, *Jewish Symbols in the Greco-Roman Period.* 13 vols. Bollingen Series 37. New York: Pantheon Books.

Goodman, Martin. 1994, *Mission and Conversion: Proselytizing in the Religious History of the Roman Empire*. Oxford: Oxford University Press.

Goodspeed, Edgar J. 1914, *Die ältesten Apologeten. Texte mit kurzen Einleitungen.* Göttingen: Vandenhoeck & Ruprecht.

Goranson, Stephen. 1994, "Posidonius, Strabo, and Marcus Vipsanius Agrippa as Sources on Essenes." *JJS 45*, 295–8.

——— 1998–99, "Others and Intra-Jewish Polemic in Qumran Texts." In Peter W. Flint and James C. VanderKam (eds.), *The Dead Sea Scrolls: A Comprehensive Assessment*, II.534–51. 2 vols. Leiden: Brill.

Gordon, Robert P. 1982, "*Terra Sancta* and the Territorial Doctrine of the Targum to the Prophets." In J. A. Emerton and Stefan C. Reif (eds.), *Interpreting the Hebrew Bible: Essays in Honour of E. I. J. Rosenthal*, 119–32. University of Cambridge Oriental Publications 32. Cambridge: Cambridge University Press.

Görg, M. 1976, "Apg 2,9–11 in außerbiblischen Sicht." *BN* I: 15–18.

Goudineau, C. 1996, "Gaul." In Alan K. Bowman, et al. (eds.), *The Cambridge Ancient History, Vol. X: The Augustan Empire, 43 B.C. – A.D. 69*, 464–502. 2nd edn. Cambridge: Cambridge University Press.

Gould, Peter, and Rodney White. 1986, *Mental Maps*. 2nd edn. Boston: Allen & Unwin.

Goulder, M. D. 1964, *Type and History in Acts*. London: SPCK.

Gow, A. S. F. and D. L. Page. 1968, *The Greek Anthology: The Garland of Philip and Some Contemporary Epigrams, Vol.* I. Cambridge: Cambridge University Press.

Grant, Robert M. 1970, *Theophilus of Antioch*, Ad Autolycum. Oxford: Clarendon.

1988, *Greek Apologists of the Second Century.* Philadelphia: Westminster.

1992, "Early Christian Geography." *VigChr 46*, 105–11.

Gray, Rebecca. 1993, *Prophetic Figures in Late Second Temple Jewish Palestine: The Evidence from Josephus.* New York/Oxford: Oxford University Press.

Green, J. B. 1997, "Acts of the Apostles." In Ralph P. Martin and Peter H. Davids (eds.), *Dictionary of the Later New Testament and Its Developments*, 7–24. Downers Grove, IL: InterVarsity Press.

Greenfield, Jonas C., and Elisha Qimron. 1992, "The Genesis Apocryphon Col. XII." *Abr-Nahrain Supplement 3*, 70–7.

Greenfield, J. C., and M. Sokoloff. 1995, "An Astronomical Text from Qumran (*4Q318*) and Reflections on Some Zodiacal Names." *RevQ 16*, 507–25.

Groneberg, Brigitte. 1992, "Die Elamitischen Reiche." *TAVO* B IV 11. Wiesbaden: Reichert.

Gropp, Gerd. 1985, "Iran unter den Achämeniden (6.-4.Jahrhundert v.Chr.)." *TAVO* B IV 22. Wiesbaden: Reichert.

Gruen, Erich S. 1996, "The Purported Jewish-Spartan Affiliation." In Robert W. Wallace and Edward M. Harris (eds.), *Transitions to Empire: Essays in Greco-Roman History, 360–146 B.C., in Honor of E. Badian*, 254–69. Oklahoma Series in Classical Culture 21. Norman/London: University of Oklahoma Press.

Gruenwald, Ithamar. 1980, *Apocalyptic and Merkavah Mysticism.* AGJU 14. Leiden: Brill.

Gundel, Hans Georg. 1992, *Zodiakos. Tierkreisbilder im Altertum: Kosmische Bezüge und Jenseitsvorstellungen im antiken Alltagsleben.* Kulturgeschichte der antiken Welt 54. Mainz am Rhein: Philipp von Zabern.

Gundel, Wilhelm. 1936, *Neue astrologische Texte des Hermes Trismegistos. Funde und Forschungen auf dem Gebiet der antiken Astronomie und Astrologie.* Abhandlungen der Bayerischen Akademie der Wissenschaften, Phil.-hist. Abteilung N.F. 12. Munich: Verlag der Bayerischen Akademie der Wissenschaften.

1949a, "Paranatellonta." *PW 18.3*, 1214–75.

1949b, "Paulus von Alexandreia." *PW 18.3*, 2376–86.

1969, *Dekane und Dekansternbilder. Ein Beitrag zur Geschichte der Sternbilder der Kulturvölker.* 2nd edn. Warburg, 1936. Reprint edn., Darmstadt: Wissenschaftliche Buchgesellschaft.

1972, "Zodiakos." *PW 2.19*, 462–709.

Gundry, Robert H. 1994, *Matthew: A Commentary on His Handbook for a Mixed Church under Persecution.* 2nd edn. Grand Rapids, MI: Eerdmans.

Güting, Eberhard. 1975, "Der geographische Horizont der sogenannten Völkerliste des Lukas (Acta 2,9–11)." *ZNW 66*, 149–69.

Gutmann, Joseph. 1984, "Early Synagogue and Jewish Catacomb Art and Its Relation to Christian Art." In Wolfgang Haase (ed.), *ANRW* II.21.2, 1313–42. Berlin: de Gruyter.

Gutschmid, Alfred von. 1894, *Kleine Schriften, Bd. 5: Schriften zur römischen und mittelalterlichen Geschichte und Literatur.* Ed. Franz Rühl. Leipzig: Teubner.

Gutzwiller, Kathryn J. 1998, *Poetic Garlands: Hellenistic Epigrams in Context.* Hellenistic Culture and Society 28. Berkeley: University of California Press.

Hackstein, Katharina. 1991, "Situative Ethnizität und das Kartieren ethnischer Gruppen im Vorderen Orient." In Wolfgang Röllig (ed.), *Von der Quelle zur Karte. Abschlußbuch des Sonderforschungsbereichs "Tübinger Atlas des Vorderen Orients,"* 217–27. Weinheim: VCH Verlagsgesellschaft.

Hadas-Lebel, Mireille. 1990, *Jérusalem contre Rome.* Paris: Cerf.

Hagedorn, Dieter. 1997, "Die 'Kleine Genesis' in P. Oxy. LXIII 4365." *ZPE 116,* 147–8.

Hagedorn, U. and D. Hagedorn, 1987, "Kritisches zum Hiobkommentar Didymos' des Blinden." *ZPE 67,* 59–78.

Hagner, D. A. 1997, "Jewish Christianity." In Ralph P. Martin and Peter H. Davids (eds.), *Dictionary of the Later New Testament and Its Developments,* 579–87. Downers Grove, IL: InterVarsity Press.

Halfmann, Helmut. 1986, *Itinera principum. Geschichte und Typologie der Kaiserreisen im Römischen Reich.* Heidelberger Althistorische Beiträge und Epigraphische Studien 2. Stuttgart: Steiner.

Hardie, Philip R. 1985, "*Imago mundi*: Cosmological and Ideological Aspects of the Shield of Achilles." *JHS 105,* 11–31.

1986, *Virgil's Aeneid: Cosmos and Imperium.* Oxford: Clarendon.

Hardwick, Michael E. 1989, *Josephus as an Historical Source in Patristic Literature Through Eusebius.* BJS 128. Atlanta, GA: Scholars Press.

Harl, Marguerite. 1992, "Le nom de l''arche' de Noé dans la Septante. Les choix lexicaux des traducteurs alexandrins, indices d'interprétations théologiques?" In *La langue de Japhet. Quinze études sur la Septante et le grec des chrétiens,* 97–125. Paris: Cerf.

Harley, J. B., and David Woodward (eds.). 1987, *The History of Cartography, Vol. I: Cartography in Prehistoric, Ancient, and Medieval Europe and the Mediterranean.* Chicago: University of Chicago Press.

(eds.). 1992, *The History of Cartography, Vol. II.1: Cartography in the Traditional Islamic and South Asian Societies.* Chicago: University of Chicago Press.

Harley, J. B., David Woodward, and Germaine Aujac. 1987, "The Foundations of Theoretical Cartography in Archaic and Classical Greece." In J. B. Harley and D. Woodward (eds.), *The History of Cartography, Vol. I: Cartography in Prehistoric, Ancient, and Medieval Europe and the Mediterranean,* 130–47. Chicago/London: University of Chicago Press.

Harris, W. Hall III. 1996, *The Descent of Christ: Ephesians 4:7–11 and Traditional Hebrew Imagery.* AGJU 32. Leiden: Brill.

Harvey, P. D. A. 1991, *Medieval Maps.* London: The British Library.

1996, *Mappa Mundi: The Hereford World Map.* London: The British Library.

Hayward, C. T. R. 1995, *Saint Jerome's Hebrew Questions on Genesis.* Oxford Early Christian Studies. Oxford: Clarendon.

Head, P. 1993, "Acts and the Problem of Its Texts." In B. W. Winter and A. D. Clark (eds.), *The Book of Acts in Its First Century Setting, Vol. I: The Book of Acts in Its Ancient Literary Setting,* 438–42. Grand Rapids, MI: Eerdmans; Carlisle: Paternoster.

Heer, Joseph M. 1910, *Die Stammbäume Jesu nach Matthäus und Lukas. Ihre ursprüngliche Bedeutung und Text-Gestalt und ihre Quellen*. BibS (F) 15. Freiburg: Herder.

Heid, Stefan. 1992–93, "Das Heilige Land: Herkunft und Zukunft der Judenchristen." *Kairos 34/35*, 1–26.

1993, *Chiliasmus und Antichrist-Mythos. Eine frühchristliche Kontroverse um das Heilige Land*. Bonn: Borengässer.

Heiligenthal, Roman. 1994, "Noachitische Gebote II. Neues Testament." *TRE 24*, 585–7.

Hemer, Colin J. 1989, *The Book of Acts in the Setting of Hellenistic History*. Ed. Conrad H. Gempf. WUNT 49. Tübingen: Mohr-Siebeck.

Hengel, Martin. 1976, *Die Zeloten. Untersuchungen zur jüdischen Freiheitsbewegung in der Zeit von Herodes I. bis 70 n.Chr.* 2nd edn. AGJU 1. Leiden: Brill.

1980, *Jews, Greeks and Barbarians: Aspects of the Hellenization of Judaism in the pre-Christian Period*. London: SCM.

1981, *The Atonement: The Origins of the Doctrine in the New Testament*. Philadelphia: Fortress.

1983, "Luke the Historian and Geographer in the Acts of the Apostles." In *Between Jesus and Paul: Studies in the Earliest History of Christianity*, 97–128. Trans. John Bowden. London: SCM Press.

1985, "Jakobus der Herrenbruder – der erste 'Papst'?" In Erich Gräßer and Otto Merk (eds.), *Glaube und Eschatologie. Festschrift für Werner Georg Kümmel zum 80.Geburtstag*, 71–104. Tübingen: Mohr-Siebeck.

1988, *Judentum und Hellenismus. Studien zu ihrer Begegnung unter besonderer Berücksichtigung Palästinas bis zur Mitte des 2.Jh.s v.Chr.* 3rd edn. WUNT 10. Tübingen: Mohr-Siebeck.

1989a, "Messianische Hoffnung und politischer 'Radikalismus' in der 'jüdisch-hellenistischen Diaspora'. Zur Frage der Voraussetzungen des jüdischen Aufstandes unter Trajan 115–117." In David Helholm (ed.), *Apocalypticism in the Mediterranean World and the Near East: Proceedings of the International Colloquium on Apocalypticism*, 655–86. 2nd edn. Tübingen: Mohr-Siebeck.

1989b, "The Political and Social History of Palestine from Alexander to Antiochus III (333–187 B.C.E.)." In W. D. Davies and Louis Finkelstein (eds.), *The Cambridge History of Judaism, Vol. II: The Hellenistic Age*, 63–78. Cambridge: Cambridge University Press.

1990, *The "Hellenization" of Judaea in the First Century After Christ*. Philadelphia: Trinity Press International.

1994, "Aufgaben der neutestamentlichen Wissenschaft." *NTS 40*, 321–57.

1995a, "The Geography of Palestine in Acts." In Richard J. Bauckham (ed.), *The Book of Acts in Its First Century Setting, Vol. IV: The Book of Acts in Its Palestinian Setting*, 27–78. Grand Rapids, MI: Eerdmans; Carlisle: Paternoster.

1995b, "Jerusalem als jüdische *und* hellenistische Stadt." In Bernd Funck (ed.), *Hellenismus. Beiträge zur Erforschung von Akkulturation und politischer Ordnung in den Staaten des hellenistischen Zeitalters: Akten des Internationalen Hellenismus-Kolloquiums 9.–14. März 1994 in Berlin*, 269–306. Tübingen: Mohr-Siebeck.

1996, "Tasks of New Testament Scholarship." *BBR 6*, 67–86.

1997, *"Nuntii Personarum et Rerum*: Problems of a History of Earliest Christianity." *Biblica 78*, 131–41.

and Anna Maria Schwemer. 1997, *Paul Between Damascus and Antioch: The Unknown Years*. London: SCM.

Hengevoss-Dürkop, Kerstin. 1991, "Jerusalem – Das Zentrum der Erbstorf-Karte." In Hartmut Kugler (ed.), *Ein Weltbild vor Columbus. Die Erbstorfer Weltkarte: Interdisziplinäres Colloquium 1988*, 205–22. Weinheim: VCH Acta humaniora.

Herrmann, Hans-Volkmar. 1959, *Omphalos*. Münster: Ascherdorff.

Hertog, Cornelis G. den. 1995, "Erwägungen zur Territorialgeschichte Koilesyriens in frühhellenistischer Zeit." *ZDPV 111*, 168–84.

Herzfeld, Ernst, and Gerold Walser, 1968, *The Persian Empire: Studies in Geography and Ethnography of the Ancient Near East*. Wiesbaden: Steiner.

Hess, Richard S. 1993, *Studies in the Personal Names of Genesis 1–11*. AOAT 234. Neukirchen-Vluyn: Neukirchener Verlag.

Higgins, Iain Macleod. 1998, "Defining the Earth's Center in a Medieval 'Multi-Text': Jerusalem in *The Book of John Mandeville*." In Sylvia Tomasch and Sealy Gilles (eds.), *Text and Territory: Geographical Imagination in the European Middle Ages*, 29–53. The Middle Ages Series. Philadelphia: University of Pennsylvania Press.

Hilberg, Isidorus (ed.). 1996, *Sancti Eusebii Hieronymi Epistulae, Pars II: Epistulae LXXI–CXX*. CSEL 55. Vienna: Verlag der Österreichischen Akademie der Wissenschaften.

Hilhorst, A. 1998, "The Noah Story: Was It Known to the Greeks?" In Florentino García Martínez and Gerard P. Luttikhuizen (eds.), *Interpretations of the Flood*, 56–65. Themes in Biblical Narrative: Jewish and Christian Traditions 1. Leiden: Brill.

Hill, Craig C. 1992, *Hellenists and Hebrews: Reappraising Division Within the Earliest Church*. Minneapolis: Fortress.

Himmelfarb, Martha. 1991, "The Temple and the Garden of Eden in Ezekiel, the Book of the Watchers, and the Wisdom of ben Sira." In Jamie Scott and Paul Simpson-Housley (eds.), *Sacred Places and Profane Spaces: Essays in the Geographies of Judaism, Christianity, and Islam*, 63–78. Contributions to the Study of Religion 30. New York: Greenwood.

1994, "Some Echoes of *Jubilees* in Medieval Hebrew Literature." In John C. Reeves (ed.), *Tracing the Threads: Studies in the Vitality of Jewish Pseudepigrapha*, 115–41. SBLEJL 6. Atlanta, GA: Scholars Press.

Hinson, E. Glenn. 1989, "Did Hippolytus Know Essenes Firsthand?" *Studia Patristica 18*, 283–9.

1992, "Essene Influence in Roman Christianity: A Look at the Second-Century Evidence." *Perspectives in Religious Studies 19*, 399–407.

Holl, Karl (ed.). 1915–33, *Epiphanius, Ancoratus und Panarion*. 3 vols. GCS 25, 31, 37. Leipzig: Hinrichs.

Holladay, Carl R. 1983, *Fragments from Hellenistic Jewish Authors, Vol. I: Historians*. SBLTT 20; Pseudepigrapha 10. Chico, CA: Scholars Press.

Hollander, H. W., and M. de Jonge. 1985, *The Testaments of the Twelve Patriarchs: A Commentary*. SVTP 8. Leiden: Brill.

Hollerich, Michael J. 1999, *Eusebius of Caesarea's* Commentary on Isaiah: *Christian Exegesis in the Age of Constantine*. The Oxford Early Christian Series. Oxford: Clarendon.

Holzmann, H. J. 1892, *Die Synoptiker – Die Apostelgeschichte*. 2nd edn. HKNT. Freiburg: Akademische Verlagsbuchhandlung.

Honigmann, Ernst. 1929, *Die sieben Klimata und die* πόλεις ἐπίσημοι. *Eine Untersuchung zur Geschichte der Geographie und Astrologie im Altertum und Mittelalter*. Heidelberg: Winter.

1936, "Nil." *PW 17.1*, 555–66.

Horbury, William. 1986, "The Twelve and the Phylarchs." *NTS 32*, 503–27.

1988, "Old Testament Interpretation in the Writings of the Church Fathers." In Martin Jan Mulder (ed.), *Mikra: Text, Translation, Reading and Interpretation of the Hebrew Bible in Ancient Judaism and Early Christianity*, 727–87. CRINT 2.1. Assen: van Gorcum; Philadelphia: Fortress.

1996a, "The Beginnings of the Jewish Revolt under Trajan." In Peter Schäfer (ed.), *Geschichte – Tradition – Reflexion. Festschrift für Martin Hengel zum 70. Geburtstag, Bd. I: Judentum*, 282–304. Tübingen: Mohr-Siebeck.

1996b, "Land, Sanctuary and Worship." In John Barclay and John Sweet (eds.), *Early Christian Thought in Its Jewish Context*, 207–24. Cambridge: Cambridge University Press.

Horn, Friedrich Wilhelm. 1996, "Der Verzicht auf die Beschneidung im frühen Christentum." *NTS 42*, 479–505.

Horowitz, Wayne. 1988, "The Babylonian Map of the World." *Iraq 50*, 147–63.

1998, *Mesopotamian Cosmic Geography*. Mesopotamian Civilizations 8. Winona Lake, IN: Eisenbrauns.

Horst, P. W. van der. 1983, "Hellenistic Parallels to the Acts of the Apostles (1.1–26)." *ZNW 74*, 17–26.

1985, "Hellenistic Parallels to the Acts of the Apostles (2.1–47)," *JSNT 25*, 49–60.

1990, "Nimrod after the Bible." In *Essays on the Jewish World of Early Christianity*, 220–32. NTOA 14. Freiburg: Universitätsverlag; Göttingen: Vandenhoeck & Ruprecht.

Hughes, Phillip E. 1977, *A Commentary on the Epistle to the Hebrews*. Grand Rapids, MI: Eerdmans.

Hunger, Hermann, and David Pingree. 1989, *MUL.APIN: An Astronomical Compendium in Cuneiform*. AfO Beiheft 24. Horn, Austria: Ferdinand Berger.

Hunter, Richard. 1995, "The Divine and Human Map of the *Argonautica*." *Syllecta Classica 6*, 13–27.

1996, "Argonauts." In Simon Hornblower and Antony Spawforth (eds.), *OCD*, 154. 3rd edn. Oxford: Oxford University Press.

Hurst, L. D. 1997, "Qumran." In Ralph P. Martin and Peter H. Davids (eds.), *Dictionary of the Later New Testament and Its Developments*, 997–1000. Downers Grove, IL: InterVarsity.

Ilan, Tal. 1991–92, "New Ossuary Inscriptions from Jerusalem." *Scripta Classica Israelica 11*, 149–59.

Isaac, Benjamin. 1992, *The Limits of Empire: The Roman Army in the East*. Rev. edn. Oxford: Clarendon.

Jacobson, Howard. 1996, *A Commentary on Pseudo-Philo's* Liber Antiquitatum Biblicarum *with Latin Text and English Translation, Vol. I.* AGJU 31. Leiden: Brill.

Janvier, Yves. 1982, *La géographie d'Orose.* Paris: Société d'Edition "Les Belles Lettres."

Jarick, John. 1997, "The Four Corners of Psalm 107." *CBQ 59*, 270–87.

Jarvis, Brian. 1998, *Postmodern Cartographies: The Geographical Imagination in Contemporary American Culture.* Chicago: Pluto Press.

Jeffreys, Elizabeth, et al. (trans.). 1986, *The Chronicle of John Malalas.* Byzantina Australiensia 4. Melbourne: University of Melbourne.

Jellicoe, Sidney. 1978, *The Septuagint and Modern Study.* Winona Lake, IN: Eisenbrauns.

Jeremias, Joachim. 1926, *Golgotha.* Angelos 1. Leipzig: Pfeiffer.

1969, *Jerusalem in the Time of Jesus: An Investigation into Economic and Social Conditions during the New Testament Period.* London: SCM.

Jervell, Jacob. 1972, "The Divided People of God: The Restoration of Israel and Salvation for the Gentiles." In *Luke and the People of God: A New Look at Luke-Acts,* 41–74. Minneapolis: Augsburg.

1995, "Das Aposteldekret in der lukanischen Theologie." In Tord Fornberg and David Hellholm (eds.), *Texts and Contexts: Biblical Texts in Their Textual and Situational Context. Essays in Honor of Lars Hartman,* 227–43. Oslo: Scandinavian University Press.

1996a, "The Future of the Past: Luke's Vision of Salvation History and Its Bearing on His Writing of History." In Ben Witherington III (ed.), *History, Literature, and Society in the Book of Acts,* 104–26. Cambridge: Cambridge University Press.

1996b, *The Theology of the Acts of the Apostles.* New Testament Theology. Cambridge: Cambridge University Press.

Johnson, Luke Timothy. 1992, *The Acts of the Apostles.* Sacra Pagina Series 5. Collegeville, MN: Glazier.

Johnson, Marshall D. 1988, *The Purpose of the Biblical Genealogies, with Special Reference to the Setting of the Genealogies of Jesus.* 2nd edn. SNTSMS 8. Cambridge: Cambridge University Press.

Johnstone, William. 1997, *1 and 2 Chronicles, Vol. I: 1 Chronicles 1–2 Chronicles 9. Israel's Place among the Nations.* JSOTSup 253. Sheffield: Sheffield Academic Press.

Jones, F. Stanley. 1982a, "The Pseudo-Clementines: A History of Research, Part I." *The Second Century 2,* 1–33.

1982b, "The Pseudo-Clementines: A History of Research, Part II." *The Second Century 2,* 63–96.

1995a, *An Ancient Jewish Christian Source on the History of Christianity: Pseudo-Clementine Recognitions 1.27–71.* SBLTT 37. Christian Apocrypha Series 2. Atlanta, GA: Scholars Press.

1995b, "A Jewish Christian Reads Luke's Acts of the Apostles: The Use of the Canonical Acts in the Ancient Jewish Christian Source behind Pseudo-Clementine *Recognitions* 1.27–71." In Eugene H. Lovering, Jr. (ed.), *SBL 1995 Seminar Papers,* 617–35. Atlanta, GA: Scholars Press.

1997, "An Ancient Jewish Christian Rejoinder to Luke's Acts of the Apostles: Pseudo-Clementine *Recognitions* 1.27–71." *Semeia 80,* 223–45.

Jonge, Marinus de. 1974, "Josephus und die Zukunftserwartung seines Volkes." In Otto Betz, et al. (eds.), *Josephus-Studien. Untersuchungen zu Josephus, dem antiken Judentum und dem Neuen Testament*, 205–19. Göttingen: Vandenhoeck & Ruprecht.

1978, *The Testaments of the Twelve Patriarchs: A Critical Edition of the Greek Text.* PVTG 1.2. Leiden: Brill.

1991a, "Hippolytus' 'Benedictions of Isaac, Jacob and Moses' and the Testaments of the Twelve Patriarchs." In *Jewish Eschatology, Early Christian Christology and the Testaments of the Twelve Patriarchs: Collected Essays*, 204–19. NovT 63. Leiden: Brill.

1991b, "The Main Issues in the Study of the Testaments of the Twelve Patriarchs." In *Jewish Eschatology, Early Christian Christology and the Testaments of the Twelve Patriarchs*, 147–63. NovTSup 63. Leiden: Brill.

1993, "The Transmission of the Testaments of the Twelve Patriarchs by Christians." *VigChr 47*, 1–28.

1999, "Levi in Aramaic Levi and in the Testament of Levi." In Esther G. Chazon and Michael Stone (eds.), *Pseudepigraphic Perspectives: The Apocrypha and Pseudepigrapha in Light of the Dead Sea Scrolls*, 71–89. STDJ 31. Leiden: Brill.

Joosten, J. 1996, *People and Land in the Holiness Code: An Exegetical Study of the Ideational Framework of the Law in Leviticus 17–26.* VTSup 67. Leiden: Brill.

Karttunen, Klaus. 1988, "Expedition to the End of the World: An Ethnographic τόπος in Herodotus." *StudOr 64*, 177–81.

Kartveit, Magnar. 1989, *Motive und Schichten der Landtheologie in 1 Chronik 1–9.* CBOT 20; Stockholm: Almquist & Wicksell.

Kazis, Israel J. (ed.). 1962, *The Book of the Gests of Alexander of Macedon: Sefer Toledot Alexandros ha-Makdoni. A Mediaeval Hebrew Version of the Alexander Romance by Immanuel ben Jacob Bonfils.* The Mediaeval Academy of America 75. Cambridge, MA: The Mediaeval Academy of America.

Kee, H. C. 1983, "Testaments of the Twelve Patriarchs." *OTP* I: 775–828.

Kees, H. 1937, "Pelusion." *PW 19.1*, 407–15.

Kelly, Brian E. 1996, *Retribution and Eschatology in Chronicles.* JSOTSup 211. Sheffield: Sheffield Academic Press.

Kidd, I. G. 1999, *Posidonius, III: The Translation of the Fragments.* Cambridge Classical Texts and Commentaries 36. Cambridge: Cambridge University Press.

Kienast, D. 1996 "M. Vipsanius Agrippa," *Der Neue Pauly. Enzyklopädie der Antike*, 1A. 294–6.

Kilpatrick, G. D. 1975, "A Jewish Background to Acts 2:9–11?" *JJS 26*, 48–9.

King, David A. 1993, "Makka as the Centre of the World." In *Astronomy in the Service of Islam*, 1–26. Aldershot, Hampshire (UK): Variorum.

1999, *World-Maps for Finding the Direction and Distance to Mecca: Innovation and Tradition in Islamic Science.* Islamic Philosophy, Theology and Science Texts and Studies 36. Leiden: Brill.

and Richard P. Lorch. 1992, "Qibla Charts, Qibla Maps, and Related Instruments." In J. B. Harley and David Woodward (eds.), *The History of*

282   *Bibliography*

Cartography, 2.1: Cartography in the Traditional Islamic and South Asian Societies, 189–205. Chicago: University of Chicago Press.

King, Geoff. 1996, *Mapping Reality: An Exploration of Cultural Cartographies*. New York: St. Martin's Press.

King, Russell. 1990, *Visions of the World and the Language of Maps*. Trinity Papers in Geography 1; Dublin: Department of Geography, Trinity College.

Kish, George. 1978, *A Source Book in Geography*. Cambridge, MA: Harvard University Press.

Kister, Menahem. 1990, "Barnabas 12:1; 4:3 and 4QSecond Ezekiel." *RB 97*, 63–7.

Klauck, Hans-Josef. 1986, "Die heilige Stadt. Jerusalem bei Philo und Lukas." *Kairos 28*, 129–47.

Klein, Michael L. 1980, "Palestinian Targum and Synagogue Mosaics." *Immanuel 11*, 33–45.

Kliege, Herma. 1991, *Weltbild und Darstellungspraxis hochmittelalterlicher Weltkarten*. Münster: Nodus.

Klijn, A. F. J. 1968, "The Pseudo-Clementines and the Apostolic Decree." *NovT 10*, 305–12.

Klinghardt, Matthias. 1988, *Gesetz und Volk Gottes. Das lukanische Verständnis des Gesetzes nach Herkunft, Funktion und seinem Ort in der Geschichte des Urchristentums*. WUNT 2.32. Tübingen: Mohr-Siebeck.

Klostermann, E. (ed.). 1933, *Origenes Werke, Bd. 11*. GCS 38.2. Leipzig: Teubner.

Koch, Johannes. 1989, *Neue Untersuchungen zur Topographie des babylonischen Fixsternhimmels*. Wiesbaden: Harrassowitz.

Koch, Klaus. 1983, "Sabbatstruktur der Geschichte. Die sogenannte Zehn-Wochen-Apokalypse (1 Hen 93,1–10; 91, 11–17) und das Ringen um die alttestamentlichen Chronologien im späten Israelitentum." *ZAW 95*, 403–30.

Kochanek, Piotr. 1998, "Les strates rédactionelles de la table des nations et l'inversion de la loi de primogéniture." *ETL 74*, 273–99.

Koch-Westenholz, Ulla. 1995, *Mesopotamian Astrology: An Introduction to Babylonian and Assyrian Celestial Divination*. Carsten Niebuhr Institute Publications 19. Copenhagen: The Carsten Niebuhr Institute of Near Eastern Studies, Museum of Tuscalanum Press; University of Copenhagen.

Koehler, Ludwig, and Walter Baumgartner. 1995, *The Hebrew and Aramaic Lexicon of the Old Testament*. 3 vols. Ed. M. E. J. Richardson. Leiden: Brill.

Koenen, K. 1990, *Ethik und Eschatologie im Tritojesajabuch. Eine literarkritische und redaktionsgeschichtliche Studie*. WMANT 62. Neukirchen-Vluyn: Neukirchener Verlag.

Koet, Bart J. 1996, "Why did Paul Shave his Hair (Acts 18:18)?" In M. Poorthuis and Ch. Safrai (eds.), *The Centrality of Jerusalem: Historical Perspectives*, 128–42. Kampen, The Netherlands: Kok Pharos.

Kokkinos, Nikos. 1998, *The Herodian Dynasty: Origins, Role in Society and Eclipse*. JSPSup 30. Sheffield: Sheffield Academic Press.

Kooij, Arie van der. 1997, "Peshitta Genesis 6: 'Sons of God' – Angels or Judges?" *JNSL 23*, 43–51.

Kraft, Robert A. 1994, "The Pseudepigrapha in Christianity." In John C. Reeves (ed.), *Tracing the Threads: Studies in the Vitality of Jewish Pseudepigrapha*, 55–86. SBLEJL 6. Atlanta, GA: Scholars Press.

1996, "Scripture and Canon in Jewish Apocrypha and Pseudepigrapha." In Magne Sæbø (ed.), *Hebrew Bible/Old Testament: The History of Its Interpretation, Vol. I: From the Beginnings to the Middle Ages (Until 1300)*, 199–216. Göttingen: Vandenhoeck & Ruprecht.

Kroll, W. 1930, "Plinius und die Chaldäer." *Hermes 65*, 1–13.

1931, "Salmeschiniaka." *PW Suppl. 5*, 843–6.

Kronholm, Tryggve. 1978, *Motifs from Genesis 1–11 in the Genuine Hymns of Ephrem the Syrian, with Particular Reference to the Influence of Jewish Exegetical Tradition*. ConBOT 11. Lund: Gleerup.

Kugel, James L. 1986, "Two Introductions to Midrash." In Geoffrey H. Hartman and Sanford Budick (eds.), *Midrash and Literature*, 77–103. New Haven: Yale University Press.

1994, "The Jubilees Apocalypse." *DSD 1*, 322–37.

1998, *Traditions of the Bible: A Guide to the Bible As It Was at the Start of the Common Era*. Cambridge, MA: Harvard University Press.

Kugler, Robert A. 1996, *From Patriarch to Priest: The Levi-Priestly Tradition from Aramaic Levi to Testament of Levi*. SBLEJL 9. Atlanta, GA: Scholars Press.

Kurz, William S. 1984, "Luke 3:23–38 and Greco-Roman and Biblical Genealogies." In Charles H. Talbert (ed.), *Luke-Acts: New Perspectives from the Society of Biblical Literature Seminar*, 169–87. New York: Crossroad.

Kuttner, Ann L. 1995, "Augustus' World Rule." In *Dynasty and Empire in the Age of Augustus: The Case of the Boscoreale Cups*, 13–34. Berkeley: University of California Press.

Lagarde, Paul Anton de. 1861, *Clementis Romani Recognitiones Syriace*. Leipzig: Brockhaus; London: Williams & Norgate.

Landes, Richard. 1988, "Lest the Millenium Be Fulfilled: Apocalyptic Expectations and the Pattern of Western Chronography 100–800 CE." In Werner Verbeke, et al. (eds.), *The Use and Abuse of Eschatology in the Middle Ages*, 137–211. Mediaevalia Lovaniensia 1.15; Leuven: Leuven University Press.

Lane, D. J. 1999, "Of Wars and Rumours of Peace: Apocalyptic Material in Aphrahat and Subhalmarhan." In P. J. Harland and C. T. R. Hayward (eds.), *New Heaven and New Earth: Prophecy and the Millennium. Essays in Honour of Anthony Gelston*, 229–45. VTSup 77. Leiden: Brill.

Lane, Thomas. 1995, *The Anticipation of the Gentile Mission of the Acts of the Apostles in the Gospel of Luke: The Mission of the Seventy(-Two) (Luke 10,1–20) Foreshadows the Gentile Mission of Acts*. Rome: Pontificia Universitas Gregoriana.

Lane, William L. 1991, *Hebrews*. 2 vols. WBC 47. Dallas, TX: Word.

Lange, Armin. 1997, "Divinatorische Träume und Apokalyptik im Jubiläenbuch." In Matthias Albani, et al. (eds.), *Studies in the Book of Jubilees*, 25–38. TSAJ 65. Tübingen: Mohr-Siebeck.

Lazarus-Yafeh, Hava. 1997, "Jerusalem and Mecca." *Judaism 46*, 197–205.

Lecoq, Danielle. 1989a, "La 'mappemonde' du *De arca Noe mystica* de Hugues de Saint-Victor (1128–1129)." In Monique Pelletier (ed.), *Géographie du monde au moyen age et à la renaissance*, 9–31. Mémoires de la section de géographie 15. Paris: Editions du C.T.H.S.

1989b, "Rome ou Jérusalem: La cartographie médiévale entre l'influence antique et l'influence chrétienne." *Bulletin du Comité français de Cartographie 121*, 22–39.

1993, "L'image d'Alexandre à travers les mappemondes médievales (XIIᵉ–XIIIᵉ)." *Geographica Antiqua 2*, 63–103.

Legrand, Lucien. 1995, "Gal 2:9 and the Missionary Strategy of the Early Church." In Tord Fornberg (ed.), *Bible, Hermeneutics, Mission: A Contribution to the Contextual Study of Holy Scripture*, 21–83. Missio 10. Swedish Institute for Missionary Research.

Lehman, Manfred R. 1975, "New Light on Astrology in Qumran and the Talmud." *RevQ 32*, 599–602.

Lemaire, A. 1991, "Asher et le royaume de Tyr." In E. Lipinski (ed.), *Phoenicia and the Bible: Proceedings of the Conference held at the University of Leuven on the 15th of March 1990*, 134–52. OLA 44. Studia Phoenicia 11. Leuven: Department Oriëntalistiek; Peeters.

Levine, Lee I. 1981, "The Inscription in the 'En Gedi Synagogue." In L. I. Levine (ed.), *Ancient Synagogues Revealed*, 140–5. Jerusalem: Israel Exploration Society.

1999, *Jerusalem: Its Sanctity and Centrality to Judaism, Christianity, and Islam*. New York: Continuum.

Levinskaya, Irina. 1996, *The Book of Acts in Its First Century Setting, Vol. V: The Book of Acts in Its Diaspora Setting*. Grand Rapids, MI: Eerdmans; Carlisle: Paternoster.

Levinsohn, S. H. 1987, *Textual Connections in Acts*. Atlanta, GA: Scholars Press.

Levy, Abraham. 1998, "Bad Timing: Time to Get a New Theory." *BAR 24/4*, 18–23.

Levy, Reuben (trans.). 1967, *The Epic of the Kings: Shah-Nama, the National Epic of Persia by Ferdowsi*. Persian Heritage Series. Chicago: University of Chicago.

Lewis, Martin W., and Kären E. Wigen. 1997, *The Myth of the Continents: A Critique of Metageography*. Berkeley: University of California Press.

Lewis, Naphtali (ed.). 1989, *The Documents from the Bar Kokhba Period in the Cave of Letters: Greek Papyri*. Judean Desert Studies. Jerusalem: Israel Exploration Society; The Hebrew University of Jerusalem; The Shrine of the Book.

Lichtenberger, Hermann. 1994, "'Im Lande Israel zu wohnen, wiegt alle Gebote der Tora auf.' Die Heiligkeit des Landes und die Heiligung des Lebens." In Reinhard Feldmeier and Ulrich Heckel (eds.), *Die Heiden. Juden, Christen und das Problem des Fremden*, 92–107. WUNT 70. Tübingen: Mohr-Siebeck.

1996, "Das Rombild in den Texten von Qumran." In Heinz-Josef Fabry, et al. (eds.), *Qumranstudien. Vorträge und Beiträge der Teilnehmer des Qumranseminars auf dem internationalen Treffen der Society of Biblical Literature, Münster, 25.–26.Juli 1993*, 221–31. Schriften des Institutum Judaicum Delitzschianum 4. Göttingen: Vandenhoeck & Ruprecht.

Lieberman, S. (ed.). 1974, *Midrash Debarim Rabbah*. 3rd edn. Jerusalem: Wahrmann.

Lindgren, Uta. 1992, "Die Tradierung der Lehre von der Kugelgestalt der Erde von der Antike zur frühen Neuzeit." In Gerhard Bott (ed.), *Focus Behaim Globus, Teil 1: Aufsätze*, 127–30. Nürnberg: Germanisches Nationalmuseum.

Lindsay, W. M. 1911, *Isidori Hispalensis episcopi Etymologiarum sive Originum libri XX*. 2 vols. Oxford: Oxford University Press.

Lipinski, Edouard. 1990, "Les Japhétites selon Gen 10,2–4 et 1 Chr 1,5–7." *ZAH 3*, 40–53.

——— 1991, "The Territory of Tyre and the Tribe of Asher." In E. Lipinski (ed.), *Phoenicia and the Bible: Proceedings of the Conference held at the University of Leuven on the 15th of March 1990*, 153–66. OLA 44; Studia Phoenicia 11; Leuven: Department Oriëntalistiek; Peeters.

——— 1992, "Les Chamites selon Gen 10,6–20 et 1 Chr 1,8–16." *ZAH 5*, 134–61.

——— 1993, "Les Sémites selon Gen 10,21–30 et 1 Chr 1,17–23." *ZAH 6*, 193–215.

Lüdemann, Gerd. 1983, *Paulus, der Heidenapostel, Bd. II: Antipaulinismus im frühen Christentum*. FRLANT 130. Göttingen: Vandenhoeck & Ruprecht.

——— 1987, *Das frühe Christentum nach den Traditionen der Apostelgeschichte. Ein Kommentar*. Göttingen: Vandenhoeck & Ruprecht.

Luttikhuizen, Gerard P. 1998, "Biblical Narrative in Gnostic Revision: The Story of Noah and the Flood in Classic Gnostic Mythology." In Florentino García Martínez and Gerard P. Luttikhuizen (eds.), *Interpretations of the Flood*, 109–23. Themes in Biblical Narrative: Jewish and Christian Traditions 1. Leiden: Brill.

Mach, Michael. 1992, *Entwicklungsstadien des jüdischen Engelglaubens in vorrabbinischer Zeit*. TSAJ 34. Tübingen: Mohr-Siebeck.

Mackay, A. L. 1975, "Kim Su-Hong and the Korean Cartographic Tradition." *Imago Mundi 27*, 27–38.

MacRae, G. 1983, "Apocalypse of Adam." *OTP* I: 707–19.

Maddox, R. J. 1982, *The Purpose of Luke-Acts*. Göttingen: Vandenhoeck & Ruprecht; Edinburgh: Clark.

Maiburg, Ursula. 1983, "'Und bis an die Grenzen der Erde...' Die Ausbreitung des Christentums in den Länderlisten und deren Verwendung in Antike und Christentum." *JAC 26*, 38–53.

Maier, Johann. 1991, "Zu ethnographisch-geographischen Überlieferungen über Japhetiten (Gen 10,2–4) im frühen Judentum." *Henoch 13*, 157–94.

Marcovitch, Miroslav. 1988, "The Essenes as Christians." In *Studies in Graeco-Roman Religions and Gnosticism*, 144–55. Studies in Greek and Roman Religion, 4. Leiden: Brill.

Mariès, L. 1951–52, "Le messie issu de Lévi chez Hippolyte de Rome." *RSR 39*, 381–96.

Marshall, I. Howard. 1978, *The Gospel of Luke: A Commentary on the Greek Text*. NIGTC. Exeter: Paternoster Press.

——— 1999, "'Israel' and the Story of Salvation: One Theme in Two Parts." In David P. Moessner (ed.), *Jesus and the Heritage of Israel: Luke's Narrative Claim upon Israel's Legacy*, 30–57. Luke the Interpreter of Israel 1. Harrisburg, PA: Trinity Press International.

Martyn, J. Louis. 1977, "Clementine Recognitions 1,33–71, Jewish Christianity, and the Fourth Gospel." In Jacob Jervell and Wayne A. Meeks (eds.), *God's Christ and His People: Studies in Honour of Nils Alstrup Dahl*, 265–95. Oslo: Universitetsforlaget.

Mattern, Susan P. 1999, *Rome and the Enemy: Imperial Strategy in the Principate*. Berkeley: University of California Press.

McCready, William D. 1996, "Isidore, the Antipodeans, and the Shape of the Earth." *Isis 87*, 108–27.

McMenamin, Mark A. 1997, "The Phoenician World Map." *Mercator's World 2*, 46–51.

Meehan, Denis (ed.). 1958, *Adamnan's De Locis Sanctis*. Scriptores Latini Hiberniae 3. Dublin: The Dublin Institute for Advanced Studies.

Meier, John P. 1997, "The Circle of the Twelve: Did It Exist During Jesus' Public Ministry?" *JBL 116*, 635–72.

Mendels, Doron. 1987, *The Land of Israel as a Political Concept in Hasmonean Literature: Recourse to History in Second Century B.C. Claims to the Holy Land*. TSAJ 15. Tübingen: Mohr-Siebeck.

1992, "The Concept of Territory: Borders and Boundaries (200–63 B.C.E.)." In *The Rise and Fall of Jewish Nationalism*, 81–105. ABRL. New York: Doubleday.

1996, "Pagan or Jewish? The Presentation of Paul's Mission in the Book of Acts." In Peter Schäfer (ed.), *Geschichte – Tradition – Reflexion. Festschrift für Martin Hengel zum 70.Geburtstag, Bd. I: Judentum*, 431–52. Tübingen: Mohr-Siebeck.

Merrill, Eugene H. 1988, "Pilgrimage and Procession: Motifs of Israel's Return." In Avraham Gileadi (ed.), *Israel's Apostasy and Restoration: Essays in Honor of Roland K. Harrison*, 261–72. Grand Rapids, MI: Baker.

Metzger, Bruce M. 1968, "Seventy or Seventy-two Disciples?" In *Historical and Literary Studies*, 67–76. NTTS 8. Grand Rapids, MI: Eerdmans.

1980, "Ancient Astrological Geography and Acts 2:9–11." In *New Testament Studies: Philological, Versional and Patristic*, 46–56. NTTS 10. Leiden: Brill.

1983, "The Fourth Book of Ezra." *OTP* I: 517–59.

1992, *The Text of the New Testament: Its Transmission, Corruption, and Restoration*. 3rd edn. Oxford: Oxford University Press.

1994, *A Textual Commentary on the Greek Text of the New Testament*. 2nd edn. Stuttgart: German Bible Society.

Meyers, Carol. 1992, "Sea, Molten." *ABD 5*, 1061–2.

Meyers, Eric M., and James F. Strange. 1981, "Jewish and Christian Attachment to Palestine." In *Archaeology, the Rabbis, and Early Christianity*, 155–65. Nashville: Abingdon.

Milik, J. T. 1971, "Recherches sur la version grecque du Livre des Jubilés." *RB 78*, 545–57.

1976, *The Books of Enoch: Aramaic Fragments of Qumran Cave 4*. Oxford: Clarendon.

Milikowsky, Chaim. 1997, "Notions of Exile, Subjugation and Return in Rabbinic Literature." In J. M. Scott (ed.), *Exile: Old Testament, Jewish, and Christian Conceptions*, 265–95. JSJSup 56. Leiden: Brill.

Millar, Fergus. 1982, "Emperors, Frontiers and Foreign Relations, 31 B.C. to A.D. 378." *Britannia 13*, 1–23.

1988, "Nicolet's *L'inventaire du monde*." *Journal of Roman Archaeology 1*, 137–41.

1993a, "Hagar, Ishmael, Josephus and the Origins of Islam." *JJS 44*, 23–45.

1993b, *The Roman East 31 BC–AD 337*. Cambridge, MA: Harvard University Press.

Millard, Matthias. 1995, "Die rabbinischen noachidischen Gebote und das biblische Gebot Gottes an Noah. Ein Beitrag zur Methodendiskussion." *Wort und Dienst 23*, 71–90.

Miller, Konrad. 1888, *Weltkarte des Castorius, genannt die Peutinger'sche Tafel, in den Farben des Originals herausgegeben und eingeleitet*. Ravensburg: Maier.

1895–98, *Mappaemundi. Die ältesten Weltkarten*. 6 vols. Stuttgart: Roth.

1896, *Itineraria Romana. Römische Reisewege an der Hand der Tabula Peutingeriana*. Stuttgart: Strecker und Schröder.

Miller, Patrick D. 1995, "Creation and Covenant." In Steven J. Kraftchick, et al. (eds.), *Biblical Theology: Problems and Perspectives, In Honor of J. Christiaan Beker*, 155–68. Nashville: Abingdon.

Mitchell, Lynette G. 1997, *Greeks Bearing Gifts: The Public Use of Private Relationships in the Greek World, 435–323 BC*. Cambridge: Cambridge University Press.

Moessner, David P. 1989, *Lord of the Banquet: The Literary and Theological Significance of the Lukan Travel Narrative*. Minneapolis: Fortress.

Monaghan, Peter. 1998, "A New Perspective on the Ancient World: Atlas Aims to Bring Classical History to Life." *The Chronicle of Higher Education 44/34*, A14–15.

Monson, J. 1978, *Student Map Manual: Historical Geography of the Bible Lands*. Jerusalem: Pictorial Archive (Near Eastern History).

Morgan, Michael A. (trans.). 1983, *Sepher ha-Razim: The Book of Mysteries*. SBLTT 25. Chico, CA: Scholars Press.

Morgenstern, Matthew, et al. 1995, "The Hitherto Unpublished Columns of the Genesis Apocryphon." *Abr-Nahrain 33*, 30–54.

Mosshammer, Alden A. (ed.). 1984, *Georgii Syncelli Ecloga Chronographica*. Akademie der Wissenschaften der DDR, Zentralinstitut für Alte Geschichte und Archäologie. Leipzig: Teubner.

Moutsoula, Elia D. 1973, "Τὸ ῾Περὶ μέτρων καὶ σταθμῶν᾿ ἔργον ᾿Επιφανίου τοῦ Σαλαμῖνος." *Theologia* [Athens] *44*, 157–98.

Muchowski, Piotr. 1994, "Language of the Copper Scroll in the Light of the Phrases Denoting the Directions of the World." In Michael O. Wise, et al. (eds.), *Methods of Investigation of the Dead Sea Scrolls and the Khirbet Qumran Site: Present Realities and Future Prospects*, 319–27. Annals of the New York Academy of Sciences 722. New York: New York Academy of Sciences.

Müller, Karl. 1965, *Geographi Graeci Minores*. 3 vols. Paris, 1855–61. Reprint edn., Hildesheim: Olms.

Müller, Klaus. 1994, *Tora für die Völker. Die noachidischen Gebote und Ansätze zu ihrer Rezeption im Christentum*. Studien zu Kirche und Israel 15. Berlin: Institut Kirche und Judentum.

Müller, Werner. 1961, *Die heilige Stadt. Roma quadrata, himmlisches Jerusalem und die Mythe vom Weltnabel*. Stuttgart: Kohlhammer.

Murphy-O'Connor, Jerome. 1995, "Pre-Constantinian Christian Jerusalem." In Anthony O'Mahony, et al. (eds.) *The Christian Heritage in the Holy Land*, 13–21. London: Scorpion Cavendish.

Musti, D. 1984, "Syria and the East." In F. W. Walbank, et al. (eds.), *The Cambridge Ancient History, Vol. VII: The Hellenistic World*, 175–218. 2nd edn. Cambridge: Cambridge University Press.

Nägele, Sabine. 1995, *Laubhüte Davids und Wolkensohn. Eine auslegungsgeschichtliche Studie zu Amos 9,11 in der jüdischen und christlichen Exegese*. AGAJ 24. Leiden: Brill.

Nanos, Mark D. 1996, *The Mystery of Romans: The Jewish Context of Paul's Letter*. Minneapolis: Fortress.

Nees, Lawrence. 1997, "Introduction." *Speculum 72*, 959–69.

Neiman, David. 1973, "The Two Genealogies of Japheth." In Harry A. Hoffner (ed.), *Orient and Occident: Essays Presented to Cyrus H. Gordon on the Occasion of his Sixty-fifth Birthday*, 119–26. AOAT 22. Kevelaer: Butzon & Becker; Neukirchen-Vluyn: Neukirchener Verlag.

        1980, "Ethiopia and Kush: Biblical and Ancient Greek Geography." *AncW 3*, 35–42.

Neugebauer, O. 1975, *A History of Ancient Mathematical Astronomy*. 3 vols. Berlin: Springer-Verlag.

Neusner, Jacob. 1989, "Geldwechsler im Tempel von der Mishna her erklärt." *TZ 45*, 81–4.

Neuwirth, Angelika. 1996, "The Spiritual Meaning of Jerusalem in Islam." In Nitza Rosovsky (ed.), *City of the Great King: Jerusalem from David to the Present*, 93–116. Cambridge, MA: Harvard University Press.

Nickelsburg, George W. E. 1984, "The Bible Rewritten and Expanded." In Michael E. Stone (ed.), *Jewish Writings of the Second Temple Period: Apocrypha, Pseudepigrapha, Qumran Sectarian Writings, Philo, Josephus*, 89–156. CRINT 2.2. Assen: Van Gorcum; Philadelphia: Fortress.

        1998, "Patriarchs Who Worry About Their Wives: A Haggadic Tendency in the Genesis Apocryphon." In Michael E. Stone and Esther G. Chazon (eds.), *Biblical Perspectives: Early Use and Interpretation of the Bible in Light of the Dead Sea Scrolls*, 137–58. STDJ 28. Leiden: Brill.

        1999, "The Nature and Function of Revelation in 1 Enoch, Jubilees, and Some Qumranic Documents." In Esther G. Chazon and Michael Stone (eds.), *Pseudepigraphic Perspectives: The Apocrypha and Pseudepigrapha in Light of the Dead Sea Scrolls*, 91–119. STDJ 31. Leiden: Brill.

Nicolet, Claude. 1991, *Space, Geography, and Politics in the Early Roman Empire*. Jerome Lectures 19. Ann Arbor: University of Michigan Press.

Nicols, John. 1974, "The Chronology and Significance of the M. Agrippa Asses." *The American Numismatic Society Museum Notes 19*, 65–86.

Nodet, Etienne, and Justin Taylor. 1998, *The Origins of Christianity: An Exploration*. Collegeville, MN: The Liturgical Press.

North, H. F. 1977, "The Mare, the Vixen, and the Bee: *Sophrosyne* as the Virtue of Women in Antiquity." *Illinois Classical Studies 2*, 35–48.

North, Robert. 1979, *A History of Biblical Map Making*. BTAVO 32. Wiesbaden: Ludwig Reichert Verlag.

Noy, David (ed.). 1995, *Jewish Inscriptions of Western Europe, Vol. II: The City of Rome*. Cambridge: Cambridge University Press.

O'Brien, Peter T. 1999, "Mission, Witness, and the Coming of the Spirit." *BBR 9*, 203–14.

Orth, Wolfgang. 1992, "Die Diadochenreiche (um 303 v.Chr.)." *TAVO* B V 2. Wiesbaden: Reichert.

Otto, E. 1993, "שבע." *TWAT 7*, 1000–27.

Ovadiah, Asher. 1978, "Ancient Synagogues in Asia Minor." In Ekrem Akurgal (ed.), *The Proceedings of the Xth International Congress of Classical Archaeology*, 2.857–66. Ankara: Izmir.

Ovadiah, Ruth, and Asher Ovadiah. 1987, *Hellenistic, Roman and Early Byzantine Mosaic Pavements in Israel*. Bibliotheca Archaeologica 6. Rome: "L'Erma" di Bretschneider.

Peek, W. 1938, "Philippos (36)." *PW 19.2*, 2339–49.

Perrone, Lorenzo. 1999, "'The Mystery of Judaea' (Jerome, *Ep*. 46): The Holy City of Jerusalem between History and Symbol in Early Christian Thought." In Lee I. Levine (ed.), *Jerusalem: Its Sanctity and Centrality to Judaism, Christianity, and Islam*, 221–39. New York: Continuum.

Peskowitz, Miriam B. 1993, "'The Work of Her Hands': Gendering Everyday Life in Roman-Period Judaism in Palestine (70–250 CE), Using Textile Production as a Case Study." Ph.D. dissertation, Duke University.

1997, "Textiles in the Classical Period." In Eric M. Meyers (ed.), *The Oxford Encyclopedia of Archaeology in the Near East*, V.195–7. 5 vols. New York/Oxford: Oxford University Press.

Pfann, Stephen J. 1999, "The Essene Yearly Renewal Ceremony and the Baptism of Repentance." In Donald W. Parry and Eugene Ulrich (eds.), *The Provo International Conference on the Dead Sea Scrolls: Technological Innovations, New Texts, and Reformulated Issues*, 337–52. STDJ 30. Leiden: Brill.

Philipp, Hans. 1912–13, *Die historisch-geographischen Quellen in den Etymologiae des Isidorus von Sevilla*. 2 vols. Quellen und Forschungen zur alten Geschichte und Geographie 25–26. Berlin: Weidmann.

Phillips, L. Edward. 1989, "Daily Prayer in the Apostolic Tradition of Hippolytus." *JTS NS 40*, 398–400.

Piilonen, Juhani. 1974, *Hippolytus Romanus, Epiphanius Cypriensis, and Anastasius Sinaita: A Study of the Διαμερισμὸς τῆς γῆς*. Suomalaisen Tiedaekatemian Toimituksia B 181. Helsinki: Suomalainen Tiedeakatemia.

Pilhofer, Peter. 1990, *Presbyteron Kreitton. Der Altertumsbeweis der jüdischen und christlichen Apologeten und seine Vorgeschichte*. WUNT 2.39. Tübingen: Mohr-Siebeck.

Pill-Rademaher, Irene, et al. 1988, "Römer und Parther (14–138 n. Chr.)." *TAVO* B V 8. Wiesbaden: Reichert.

Podossinov, Alexander V. 1991, "Himmelsrichtung." *RAC 15*, 233–86.

1993, "Die Orientierung der alten Karten von den ältesten Zeiten bis zum frühen Mittelalter." *Cartographica Helvetica 7*, 33–43.

and Leonid S. Chekin. 1991, "Review of J. B. Harley and D. Woodward (eds.), *The History of Cartography, Vol. I: Cartography in Prehistoric, Ancient and Medieval Europe and the Mediterranean* (Chicago, 1987)." *Imago Mundi 43*, 112–23.

Pokorny, Petr. 1995, "'... bis an das Ende der Erde.' Ein Beitrag zum Thema Sammlung Israels und christliche Mission bei Lukas." In *Landgabe. Festschrift für Jan Heller zum 70. Geburtstag*, 198–210. Kampen: Kok Pharos.

Poorthuis, M., and Ch. Safrai (eds.). 1996, *The Centrality of Jerusalem: Historical Perspectives*. Kampen: Kok Pharos.

Porton, Gary G. 1994, *The Stranger Within Your Gates: Converts and Conversion in Rabbinic Literature*. Chicago Studies in the History of Judaism. Chicago/London: University of Chicago Press.

Portugali, Juval. 1996, *The Construction of Cognitive Maps*. The GeoJournal Library 32. Boston: Kluwer Academic Publishers.

Pothecary, Sarah. 1997, "The Expression of 'Our Times' in Strabo's *Geography*." *CP 92*, 235–46.

Potter, David. 1994, *Prophets and Emperors: Human and Divine Authority from Augustus to Theodosius*. Revealing Antiquity 7. Cambridge, MA: Harvard University Press.

Price, Roberto Salinas. 1980, *Homer's Blind Audience: An Essay on the Iliad's Geographical Prerequisites for the Site of Ilios*. San Jerónimo Lídice, Mexico: Casa Huicalco.

Prichard, James B. (ed.). 1969, *Ancient Near Eastern Texts Relating to the Old Testament*. 3rd edn. Princeton: Princeton University Press.

Pringent, Pierre. 1990, *Le Judaïsme et l'image*. TSAJ 24. Tübingen: Mohr-Siebeck.

Prinz, Friedrich. 1979, *Gründungsmythen und Sagenchronologie*. Zetemata 72. Munich: Beck.

Puech, Émil. 1993, *La croyance des Esséniens en la vie future. Immortalité, réssurection, vie éternelle*. Paris: Gabalda.

1996, "Notes sur les fragments grecs du manuscrit 7Q4 = 1 Hénoch 103 et 105." *RB 103–104*, 592–600.

1999, "Some Remarks on 4Q246 and 4Q521 and Qumran Messianism." In Donald W. Parry and Eugene Ulrich (eds.), *The Provo International Conference on the Dead Sea Scrolls: Technological Innovations, New Texts, and Reformulated Issues*, 545–65. STDJ 30. Leiden: Brill.

Pullan, Wendy. 1993, "Mapping Time and Salvation: Early Christian Pilgrimage to Jerusalem." In Gavin D. Flood (ed.), *Mapping Invisible Worlds*, 23–40. Cosmos 9. Edinburgh: Edinburgh University Press.

Purcell, Nicholas. 1990, "The Creation of Provincial Landscape: the Roman Impact on Cisalpine Gaul." In Thomas Blagg and Martin Millett (eds.), *The Early Roman Empire in the West*, 7–29. Oxford: Oxbow Books.

1996, "*Periploi*." In Simon Hornblower and Antony Spawforth (eds.), *OCD*, 1141–2. 3rd edn. Oxford: Oxford University Press.

Qimron, Elisha. 1986, *The Hebrew of the Dead Sea Scrolls*. HSS 29. Atlanta: Scholars Press.

1999, "Toward a New Edition of 1QGenesis Apocryphon." In Donald W. Parry and Eugene Ulrich (eds.), *The Provo International Conference on the Dead Sea Scrolls: Technological Innovations, New Texts, and Reformulated Issues*, 106–9. STDJ 30. Leiden: Brill.

and John Strugnell. 1994, *Qumran Cave 4, V: Miqsat Ma'ase Ha-Torah*. DJD 10. Oxford: Clarendon.

Quack, Joachim Friedrich. 1995, "Dekane und Gliedervergottung. Altägyptische Traditionen im Apokryphon Johannis." *JAC 38*, 97–122.

Quandt, W. (ed.). 1962, *Orphei Hymni*. 3rd edn. Berlin: Weidmann.

Rabinowitz, Jacob J. 1971, "Ingathering of the Exiles." *EncJud 8*, 1373–5.

Räisänen, Heikki. 1991, "The Redemption of Israel: A Salvation-Historical Problem in Luke-Acts." In Petri Luomanen (ed.), *Luke-Acts: Scandinavian Perspectives*, 94–114. Publications of the Finnish Exegetical Society 54. Helsinki: The Finnish Exegetical Society. Göttingen: Vandenhoeck & Ruprecht.

Rajak, Tessa. 1994, "Ciò che Flavio Giuseppe vide: Josephus and the Essenes." In Fausto Parente and Joseph Sievers (eds.), *Josephus and the History of the Greco-Roman Period: Essays in Memory of Morton Smith*, 141–60. SPB 41. Leiden: Brill.

Ramsay, William W. 1900, *A Historical Commentary on St. Paul's Epistle to the Galatians*. 2nd edn. London: Hodder & Stoughton.

Ravens, David. 1995, *Luke and the Restoration of Israel*. JSNTSup 119. Sheffield: Sheffield Academic Press.

Rea, J. R. 1996, *The Oxyrhynchus Papyri, Vol. LXIII*. Graeco-Roman Memoirs 83. London: British Academy.

Redpath, Henry A. 1903, "The Geography of the Septuagint." *AJT 7*, 289–307.

Reeg, Gottfried. 1991, "Grenzen und Gebiete in der rabbinischen Literatur und ihre kartographische Darstellung." In Wolfgang Röllig (ed.), *Von der Quelle zur Karte. Abschlußbuch des Sonderforschungsbereichs "Tübinger Atlas des Vorderen Orients,"* 171–86. Deutsche Forschungsgemeinschaft. Weinheim: VCH.

Reeves, John C. 1999, "Exploring the Afterlife of Jewish Pseudepigrapha in Medieval Near Eastern Religious Traditions: Some Initial Soundings." *JSJ 30*, 148–77.

Rehm, Bernhard, and Georg Strecker (eds.). 1992, *Die Pseudoklementinen, Bd. I: Homilien*. 3rd edn. GCS. Berlin: Akademie Verlag.

1994, *Die Pseudoklementinen, Bd. II: Rekognitionen in Rufins Übersetzung*. 2nd edn. GCS. Berlin: Akademie Verlag.

Reid, D. G. 1997, "Pella, Flight to." In Ralph P. Martin and Peter H. Davids (eds.), *Dictionary of the Later New Testament and Its Developments*, 900–2. Downers Grove, IL: IVP.

Reinink, G. J. 1975, "Das Land 'Seiris' (Shir) und das Volk der Serer in jüdischen und christlichen Traditionen." *JSJ 6*, 27–85.

Reischl, W. C., and J. Rupp (eds.). 1967, *Cyrilli Hierosolymarum archiepiscopi opera quae supersunt omnia*. Munich, 1860. Reprint edn., Hildesheim: Olms.

Renz, Johannes. 1995, *Die althebräischen Inschriften, Teil 1: Text und Kommentar*. Handbuch der althebräischen Epigraphie 1. Darmstadt: Wissenschaftliche Buchgesellschaft.

Resch, G. 1905, *Das Aposteldecret nach seiner außerkanonischen Textgestalt*. TU N.S. 13.3. Leipzig: Hinrichs.

Revel-Neher, Elisabeth. 1990–91, "Some Remarks on the Iconographical Sources of the Christian Topography of Cosmas Indiopleustes." *Kairos 32–3*, 78–97.

Richer, Jean. 1994, *Sacred Geography of the Ancient Greeks: Astrological Symbolism in Art, Architecture, and Landscape*. Albany, NY: State University of New York Press.

Riese, Alexander (ed.). 1964, *Geographi Latini minores*. Heilbronn, 1878. Reprint edn., Hildesheim: Olms.

Riesner, Rainer. 1994, *Die Frühzeit des Paulus. Studien zur Chronologie, Missionsstrategie und Theologie*. WUNT 71. Tübingen: Mohr-Siebeck.

Rigsby, Kent J. 1996, *Asylia: Territorial Inviolability in the Hellenistic World*. Berkeley: University of California Press.

Roddaz, Jean-Michel. 1984, *Marcus Agrippa*. Bibliothèque des Ecoles françaises d'Athènes et de Rom 253. Rome: Ecole française de Rome.

Roller, Duane W. 1998, "Herod and Marcus Agrippa." In *The Building Program of Herod the Great*, 43–53 Berkeley: University of California Press.

Römer, Thomas, and Jean-Daniel Macchi. 1995, "Luke, Disciple of the Deuteronomistic School." In C. M. Tuckett (ed.), *Luke's Literary Achievement: Collected Essays*, 178–87. JSNTSup 116. Sheffield: Sheffield Academic Press.

Romer, F. E. 1998, *Pomponius Mela's Description of the World*. Ann Arbor, MI: University of Michigan Press.

Romm, James S. 1992, *The Edges of the Earth in Ancient Thought: Geography, Exploration, and Fiction*. Princeton, NJ: Princeton University Press.

Rönsch, Hermann. 1874, *Das Buch der Jubiläen oder die Kleine Genesis*. Leipzig: Fues.

Rook, John T. 1983, "Studies in the Book of Jubilees: The Themes of Calendar, Genealogy and Chronology." D. Phil. thesis, Oxford University.

Rose, Christian. 1994, *Die Wolke der Zeugen. Eine exegetisch-traditionsgeschichtliche Untersuchung zu Hebräer 10,32–12,3*. WUNT 2.60. Tübingen: Mohr-Siebeck.

Rösel, Martin. 1994, *Übersetzung als Vollendug der Auslegung. Studien zur Genesis-Septuaginta*. BZAW 223. Berlin/New York: de Gruyter.

Roth, Jonathan P. 1998, *The Logistics of the Roman Army at War (264 BC–AD 235)*. Leiden: Brill.

Rougé, Jean (ed.). 1966, *Expositio Totius Mundi et Gentium*. SC 124. Paris: Cerf.

Rousseau, Adelin (ed.). 1979, *Irénée de Lyon, Contre les Hérésies, Liber I, Tome II: Texte et Traduction*. SC 264. Paris: Cerf.

Routh, Martin Joseph. 1814, *Religuiae Sacrae, Vol. II*. Oxford: Cooke.

Royse, James R. 1995, "Scribal Tendencies in the Transmission of the Text of the New Testament." In Bart Ehrman and Michael W. Holmes (eds.), *The Text of the New Testament in Contemporary Research: Essays on the Status Quaestionis*, 239–52. Grand Rapids, MI: Eerdmans.

Ruberg, Uwe. 1980, "Mappae Mundi des Mittelalters im Zusammenwirken von Text und Bild." In Christel Meier and U. Ruberg (eds.), *Text und Bild. Aspekte des Zusammenwirkens zweier Künste im Mittelalter und frühen Neuzeit*, 550–92. Wiesbaden: Reichert.

Ruiten, J. T. A. G. M. van. 1997, "The Interpretation of Genesis 6:1–12 in *Jubilees* 5:1–19." In Matthias Albani, et al. (eds.), *Studies in the Book of Jubilees*, 59–75. TSAJ 65. Tübingen: Mohr-Siebeck.

1998, "The Interpretation of the Flood Story in the Book of Jubilees." In Florentino García Martínez and Gerard P. Luttikhuizen (eds.), *Interpretations of the Flood*, 66–85. Themes in Biblical Narrative: Jewish and Christian Traditions 1. Leiden: Brill.

Sack, Robert David. 1986, *Human Territoriality: Its Theory and History*. Cambridge: Cambridge University Press.

1997, *Homo Geographicus: A Framework for Action, Awareness, and Moral Concern*. Baltimore/London: Johns Hopkins University Press.

Salmon, Marilyn. 1988, "Insider or Outsider? Luke's Relationship with Judaism." In Joseph B. Tyson (ed.), *Luke-Acts and the Jewish People: Eight Critical Perspectives*, 76–82. Minneapolis: Augsburg.

Sanders, E. P. 1985, *Jesus and Judaism*. Philadelphia: Fortress.

1992, *Judaism: Practice and Belief 63 BCE–66 CE*. London: SCM; Philadelphia: Trinity Press International.

1999, "Jerusalem and Its Temple in Early Christian Thought and Practice." In Lee I. Levine (ed.), *Jerusalem: Its Sanctity and Centrality to Judaism, Christianity, and Islam*, 90–103. New York: Continuum.

Sato, Migaku. 1988, *Q und Prophetie. Studien zur Gattungs- und Traditionsgeschichte der Quelle Q*. WUNT 2.29. Tübingen: Mohr-Siebeck.

Sbordone, Francesco (ed.). 1940, *Hori Apollinis Hieroglyphica*. Naples: Loffredo.

Scheid, John, and Jesper Svenbro. 1996, *The Craft of Zeus: Myths of Weaving and Fabric*. Revealing Antiquity 9. Cambridge, MA/London: Harvard University Press.

Schibli, Hermann S. 1990, *Pherekydes of Syros*. Oxford: Clarendon.

Schiffman, Lawrence H. 1998–99, "The Qumran Scrolls and Rabbinic Judaism." In Peter W. Flint and James C. VanderKam (eds.), *The Dead Sea Scrolls: A Comprehensive Assessment*, II.552–71. 2 vols. Leiden: Brill.

1999, "The Temple Scroll and the Halakhic Pseudepigrapha of the Second Temple Period." In Esther G. Chazon and Michael Stone (eds.), *Pseudepigraphic Perspectives: The Apocrypha and Pseudepigrapha in Light of the Dead Sea Scrolls*, 121–31. STDJ 31. Leiden: Brill.

Schimmel, Annemarie. 1991, "Sacred Geography in Islam." In Jamie Scott and Paul Simpson-Housley (eds.), *Sacred Places and Profane Spaces: Essays in the Geographies of Judaism, Christianity, and Islam*, 163–75. Contributions to the Study of Religion 30. New York: Greenwood.

Schmidt, Erich F. 1970, *Persepolis*. 3 vols. University of Chicago Oriental Institute Publications 70. Chicago: University of Chicago Press.

Schmidt, Francis. 1988, "Naissance d'une geographe juive." In A. Desrumeaux and F. Schmidt (eds.), *Möise géographe. Recherches sur les représentations juives et chrétiennes de l'éspace*, 13–30. Paris: Vrin.

1990, "Jewish Representations of the Inhabited Earth during the Hellenistic and Roman Periods." In A. Kasher, et al. (eds.), *Greece and Rome in Eretz Israel: Collected Essays*, 119–34. Jerusalem: Yad Izhak Ben-Zvi/The Israel Exploration Society.

1997, "Astrologie et prédestination à Qoumrân." *Qadmoniot 30*, 115–18.

1998, "Ancient Jewish Astrology: An Attempt to Interpret 4QCryptic (4Q186)." In Michael E. Stone and Esther G. Chazon (eds.), *Biblical Perspectives: Early Use and Interpretation of the Bible in Light of the Dead Sea Scrolls*, 189–205. STDJ 28. Leiden: Brill.

Schmitt, Rüdiger. 1991, *The Bisitun Inscriptions of Darius the Great: Old Persian Text*. Corpus Inscriptionum Iranicarum, Part I: Inscriptions of Ancient Iran; vol. I: The Old Persian Inscriptions; Texts I. London: School of Oriental and African Studies.

Schnabel, E. J. 1997, "Mission, Early Non-Pauline." In Ralph P. Martin and Peter H. Davids (eds.), *Dictionary of the Later New Testament and Its Developments*, 752–75. Downers Grove, IL: InterVarsity Press.

Schneider, G. 1980, *Die Apostelgeschichte.* 2 vols. HTKNT 5. Freiburg: Herder.

Schoeps, Hans Joachim. 1949, *Theologie und Geschichte des Judenchristentums.* Tübingen: Mohr-Siebeck.

1950, *Aus frühchristlicher Zeit. Religionsgeschichtliche Untersuchungen.* Tübingen: Mohr-Siebeck.

Scholten, Clemens. 1991, "Hippolytos II (von Rom)." *RAC 15*, 492–551.

Schreckenberg, Heinz, and Kurt Schubert. 1992, *Jewish Historiography and Iconography in Early and Medieval Christianity.* CRINT 3.2. Assen: Van Gorcum; Minneapolis: Fortress.

Schubert, Christoph. 1998, *Studien zum Nerobild in der lateinischen Dichtung der Antike.* Beiträge zur Altertumskunde 116. Stuttgart/Leipzig: Teubner.

Schubert, Kurt. 1990–91, "Die jüdische Wurzel der frühchristlichen Kunst." *Kairos 32–33*, 1–8.

Schuller, Eileen. 1989–90, "4Q372 1: A Text about Joseph." *RevQ 14*, 349–76.

Schultz, Joseph P. 1993, "From Sacred Space to Sacred Object to Sacred Person in Jewish Antiquity." *Shofar 12*, 28–37.

Schuppe, A. 1930, "Mappa." *PW 14.2*, 1413–16.

Schürer, Emil. 1973–87, *The History of the Jewish People in the Age of Jesus Christ (175 B.C.–A.D. 135).* 3 vols. in 4. Rev. edn. Ed. Geza Vermes, et al. Edinburgh: Clark.

Schürmann, Heinz. 1994, *Das Lukasevangelium, 2.1: Kommentar zu Kapitel 9,51–11,54.* HTKNT; Freiburg: Herder.

Schwarte, Karl-Heinz. 1966, *Die Vorgeschichte der augustinischen Weltalter-lehre.* Antiquitas 1.12. Bonn: Habelt.

Schwartz, Daniel R. 1990, *Agrippa I: The Last King of Judaea.* TSAJ 23. Tübingen: Mohr-Siebeck.

1992, "Residents and Exiles, Jerusalemites and Judaeans (Acts 7:4; 2:5, 14): On Stephen, Pentecost and the Structure of Acts." In *Studies in the Jewish Background of Christianity*, 117–27. WUNT 60. Tübingen: Mohr-Siebeck.

1996, "God, Gentiles, and Jewish Law: On Acts 15 and Josephus' Adiabene Narrative." In Peter Schäfer (ed.), *Geschichte – Tradition – Reflexion. Festschrift für Martin Hengel zum 70.Geburtstag, Bd. I: Judentum*, 263–82. Tübingen: Mohr-Siebeck.

Schwemer, Anna Maria. 1991, "Irdischer und himmlischer König. Beobachtungen zur sogenannten David-Apokalypse in Hekhalot Rabbati §§ 122–126." In Martin Hengel and A. M. Schwemer (eds.), *Königherrschaft Gottes und himmlischer Kult im Judentum, Urchristentum und in der hellenistischen Welt*, 309–59. WUNT 55. Tübingen: Mohr-Siebeck.

Scott, James M. 1992, *Adoption as Sons of God: An Exegetical Investigation into the Background of ΥΙΟΘΕΣΙΑ in the Pauline Corpus.* WUNT 2.48. Tübingen: Mohr-Siebeck.

1994, "Luke's Geographical Horizon." In David W. J. Gill and Conrad Gempf (eds.), *The Book of Acts in Its First Century Setting, Vol. II: The Book of Acts in Its Graeco-Roman Setting*, 483–544. Grand Rapids, MI: Eerdmans; Carlisle: Paternoster.

1995a, *Paul and the Nations: The Old Testament and Jewish Background of Paul's Mission to the Nations with Special Reference to the Destination of Galatians.* WUNT 84. Tübingen: Mohr-Siebeck.

1995b, "Philo and the Restoration of Israel." In Eugene H. Lovering, Jr. (ed.), *Society of Biblical Literature 1995 Seminar Papers*, 553–75. Atlanta, GA: Scholars Press.

1997a, "The Division of the Earth in *Jubilees* 8:11–9:15 and Early Christian Chronography." In Matthias Albani, et al. (eds.), *Studies in the Book of Jubilees*, 295–323. TSAJ 65. Tübingen: Mohr-Siebeck.

1997b, "Geographic Aspects of Noachic Materials in the Scrolls at Qumran." In Stanley E. Porter and Craig A. Evans (eds.), *The Scrolls and the Scriptures: Qumran Fifty Years After*, 368–81. JSPSup 26; Roehampton Institute London Papers 3. Sheffield: Sheffield Academic Press.

(ed.). 1997c, *Exile: Old Testament, Jewish, and Christian Conceptions.* JSJSup 56. Leiden: Brill.

1997d, "The Self-Understanding of the Jewish Diaspora in the Greco-Roman Period." In J. M. Scott (ed.), *Exile: Old Testament, Jewish, and Christian Conceptions*, 173–218. JSJSup 56. Leiden: Brill.

Seccombe, David. 1998, "The New People of God." In I. Howard Marshall and David Peterson (eds.), *Witness to the Gospel: The Theology of Acts*, 349–72. Grand Rapids, MI: Eerdmans.

Segal, Alan F. 1990, *Paul the Convert: The Apostolate and Apostasy of Saul the Pharisee.* New Haven: Yale University Press.

1995, "Universalism in Judaism and Christianity." In Troels Engberg-Pedersen (ed.), *Paul in his Hellenistic Context*, 1–29. Minneapolis: Fortress.

Seibert, Jakob. 1984, *Die Eroberung des Perserreiches durch Alexander den Großen auf kartographischer Grundlage.* 2 vols. BTAVO 68. Wiesbaden: Reichert.

1985, "Das Alexanderreich (336–323 v.Chr.)." *TAVO* B V 1. Wiesbaden: Reichert.

Shamir, O., and A. Baginski. 1998, "Research of Ancient Textiles Discovered in Israel." *Qadmoniot 31*, 53–62.

Sherwin-White, Susan, and Amélie Kuhrt. 1993, *From Samarkhand to Sardis: A New Approach to the Seleucid Empire.* London: Duckworth.

Shtober, Shimon. 1999, "Judaeo-Islamic Polemics Concerning the Qibla (625–1010)." *Medieval Encounters 5*, 85–98.

Siebener, Wido. 1995, *Das Bild Europas in den Historien. Studien zu Herodots Geographie und Ethnographie Europas und seiner Schilderung der persischen Feldzüge.* Innsbrucker Beiträge zur Kulturwissenschaft 96. Innsbruck: Verlag des Instituts für Sprachwissenschaft der Universität Innsbruck.

Simonetti, Manlio. 1997, *Biblical Interpretation in the Early Church: An Historical Introduction to Patristic Exegesis.* Edinburgh: Clark.

Skarsaune, Oskar. 1996, "Scriptural Interpretation in the Second and Third Centuries." In Magne Sæbø (ed.), *Hebrew Bible/Old Testament: The History of Its Interpretation, Vol. I: From the Beginnings to the Middle Ages (Until 1300)*, 373–442. Göttingen: Vandenhoeck & Ruprecht.

Skehan, Patrick W., et al. (eds.). 1992, *Qumran Cave 4, IV: Paleo-Hebrew and Greek Biblical Manuscripts.* DJD 10. Oxford: Clarendon.

Smith, Christopher R. 1994, "Chiliasm and Recapitulation in the Theology of Ireneus." *VigChr 48*, 313–31.

296   Bibliography

Smith, David. 1996, "What Hope After Babel? Diversity and Community in Gen 11:1–9; Exod 1:1–14; Zeph 3:1–13 and Acts 2:1–3." *HBT 18*, 169–91.

Smith, Morton. 1982, "Helios in Palestine." *Eretz Israel 16*, 199–214.

Smith, Richard J. 1996, *Chinese Maps: Images of "All Under Heaven."* Images of Asia. Oxford: Oxford University Press.

Smith, R. R. R. 1988, "*Simulacra Gentium*: The *Ethne* from the Sebasteion at Aphrodisias." *JRS 78*, 50–77.

Snyder, J. M. 1983, "The Warp and Woof of the Universe in Lucretius' *De Rerum Natura.*" *Illinois Classical Studies 8*, 37–43.

Sperber, A. 1959–73, *The Bible in Aramaic.* 5 vols. Leiden: Brill.

———. 1971, "Nations, the Seventy." *EncJud 12*, 882–6.

Städele, Alfons. 1991, "Die Gestalt der Erde bei Tacitus." *Würzburger Jahrbücher für die Altertumswissenschaft N.F. 17*, 251–5.

Stadelmann, Luis I. J. 1970, *The Hebrew Conception of the World: A Philological and Literary Study.* AnBib 39. Rome: Pontifical Biblical Institute.

Stanley, Keith. 1993, *The Shield of Homer: Narrative Structure in the Iliad.* Princeton: Princeton University Press.

Steck, Odil Hannes. 1967, *Israel und das gewaltsame Geschick der Propheten. Untersuchungen zur Überlieferung des deuteronomistischen Geschichtsbildes im Alten Testament, Spätjudentum und Urchristentum.* WMANT 23. Neukirchen-Vluyn: Neukirchener Verlag.

Stegemann, H. 1983, "'Das Land' in der Tempelrolle und in anderen Texten aus den Qumranfunden." In G. Strecker (ed.), *Das Land Israel in biblischer Zeit. Jerusalem-Symposion 1981*, 154–71. Göttingen: Vandenhoeck & Ruprecht.

Stegner, Werner. 1979, "Beobachtungen zur sogenannten Völkerliste des Pfingstwunders (Apg 2,7–11)." *Kairos 21*, 206–14.

Stein, Howard F., and William G. Niederland (eds.). 1989, *Maps from the Mind: Readings in Psychogeography.* Norman: University of Oklahoma Press.

Steiner, Richard C. 1991, "The Mountains of Ararat, Mount Lubar and הר הקדם." *JJS 42*, 247–9.

———. 1995, "The Heading of the *Book of the Words of Noah* on a Fragment of the Genesis Apocryphon: New Light on a 'Lost' Work." *DSD 2*, 66–71.

Stemberger, Günter. 1975, "Die Bedeutung des Tierkreises auf Mosaikfussböden spätantiker Synagogen." *Kairos 17*, 11–56.

———. 1983, *Die römische Herrschaft im Urteil der Juden.* ErFor 195. Darmstadt: Wissenschaftliche Buchgesellschaft.

———. 1998, "Judenchristen." *RAC 19/Lfg. 147*, 228–45.

Sterling, Gregory E. 1992, *Historiography and Self-Definition: Josephus, Luke-Acts and Apologetic Historiography.* NovTSup 64. Leiden: Brill.

Stern, Menahem (ed.). 1974–84, *Greek and Latin Authors on Jews and Judaism.* 3 vols. Jerusalem: The Israel Academy of Sciences and Humanities.

Steyn, Gert J. 1989, "The Occurrence of 'Kainam' in Luke's Genealogy: Evidence of Septuagint Influence?" *ETL 65*, 409–11.

Stichel, Rainer. 1979, *Die Namen Noes, seines Bruders und seiner Frau. Ein Beitrag zu Nachleben jüdischer Überlieferungen in der außerkanonischen und gnostischen Literatur und in Denkmälern der Kunst.* Abhandlungen der Akademie der Wissenschaften in Göttingen, Phil.-hist. Klasse 3.112. Göttingen: Vandenhoeck & Ruprecht.

Stötzel, Arnold. 1982, "Die Darstellung der ältesten Kirchengeschichte nach den Pseudo-Clementinen." *VigChr 36*, 24–37.

Stone, Michael E. 1981, *Signs of the Judgement: Onomastica Sacra and the Generations from Adam.* University of Pennsylvania Armenian Texts and Studies 3. Chico, CA: Scholars Press.

1990, *Fourth Ezra: A Commentary on the Book of Fourth Ezra.* Hermeneia. Minneapolis: Fortress.

1996a, "The Dead Sea Scrolls and the Pseudepigrapha." *DSD 3*, 270–95.

1996b, "Testament of Naphtali (4Q215)." In James C. VanderKam (ed.), *Qumran Cave 4, Vol. XVII: Parabiblical Texts, Part 3*, 73–82. DJD 22. Oxford: Clarendon.

1999, "The Axis of History at Qumran." In Esther G. Chazon and M. Stone (eds.), *Pseudepigraphic Perspectives: The Apocrypha and Pseudepigrapha in Light of the Dead Sea Scrolls*, 133–49. STDJ 31. Leiden: Brill.

2000, "Noah, Texts of." In Lawrence H. Schiffman and James C. VanderKam (eds.), *Encyclopedia of the Dead Sea Scrolls*, II.613–15. 2 vols. Oxford: Oxford University Press.

and Esther Eshel. 1992, "An Exposition on the Patriarchs (4Q464) and Two Other Documents (4Q464a and 4Q464b)." *Le Muséon 105*, 243–64.

and J. C. Greenfield. 1996, "Aramaic Levi Document (4Q213–214)." In James C. VanderKam (ed.), *Qumran Cave 4, Vol. XVII: Parabiblical Texts, Part 3*, 1–72. DJD 22. Oxford: Clarendon.

Strange, W. A. 1992, *The Problem of the Text of Acts.* SNTSMS 71. Cambridge: Cambridge University Press.

Strasburger, Giesela. 1984, *Lexikon zur frühgriechischen Geschichte.* Zurich/Munich: Artemis.

Strecker, Georg. 1981, *Das Judenchristentum in den Pseudoklementinen.* 2nd edn. TU 70.2. Berlin: Akademie-Verlag.

1983, "Das Land Israel in frühchristlicher Zeit." In G. Strecker (ed.), *Das Land Israel in biblischer Zeit. Jerusalem-Symposium 1981 der Hebräischen Universität und der Georg-August-Universität*, 188–200. Göttingen: Vandenhoeck & Ruprecht.

Stroumsa, Guy S. 1996, "Philosophy of the Barbarians: On Early Christian Ethnological Representations." In Hubert Cancik (ed.), *Geschichte – Tradition – Reflexion. Festschrift für Martin Hengel zum 70. Geburtstag, Bd. II: Griechische und römische Religion*, 339–68. Tübingen: Mohr-Siebeck.

Stuckenbruck, Loren T. 1997, *The Book of the Giants from Qumran: Texts, Translation, and Commentary.* TSAJ 63. Tübingen: Mohr-Siebeck.

Sullivan, Richard D. 1990, *Near Eastern Royalty and Rome, 100–30 BC.* Phoenix Suppl. 24. Toronto: University of Toronto Press.

Sundwall, Gavin A. 1996, "Ammianus Geographicus." *AJP 117*, 619–43.

Sutherland, C. H. V. 1984, *The Roman Imperial Coinage, Vol. I: From 31 BC to AD 69.* Rev. edn. London: Spink and Son.

Swanson, Reuben J. (ed.). 1995, *Luke: New Testament Greek Manuscripts. Variant Readings Arranged in Horizontal Lines against Codex Vaticanus.* Sheffield: Sheffield Academic Press; Pasadena: William Carey International University Press.

Swartz, Joshua. 1998, "Gambling in Ancient Jewish Society and in the Graeco-Roman World." In Martin Goodman (ed.), *Jews in the Graeco-Roman World*, 145–65. Oxford: Oxford University Press.

Syme, Ronald. 1995, "Pompeius and the Parthians." In *Anatolica: Studies in Strabo*, 87–94. Ed. Anthony Birley. Oxford: Clarendon.

298   Bibliography

Taatz, Irene. 1991, *Frühjüdische Briefe. Die paulinischen Briefe im Rahmen der offiziellen religiösen Briefe des Frühjudentums.* NTOA 16. Freiburg: Universitätsverlag; Göttingen: Vandenhoeck & Ruprecht.

Tadmor, Chaim. 1999, "World Dominion: The Expanding World of the Assyrian Empire." In L. Milano, et al. (eds.), *Landscapes: Territories, Frontiers and Horizons in the Ancient Near East,* 55–62. History of the Ancient Near East Monographs 3.1. Padova: Sargon.

Tajra, H. W. 1994, *The Martyrdom of St. Paul: Historical and Judicial Context, Traditions, and Legends.* WUNT 2.67. Tübingen: Mohr-Siebeck.

Talbert, Richard J. A. 1987, "Review of O. A. W. Dilke, *Greek and Roman Maps* (London, 1985)." *JRS 77,* 210–12.

1990, "Rome's Empire and Beyond: The Spacial Aspect." *Cahiers des Etudes Anciennes 26,* 215–23.

Talmon, Shemaryahu. 1978, "'Exil' und 'Rückkehr' in der Ideenwelt des Alten Testaments." In Rudolf Mosis (ed.), *Exil – Diaspora – Rückkehr. Zum theologischen Gespräch zwischen Juden und Christen,* 30–54. Düsseldorf: Patmos.

1993, "The 'Navel of the Earth' and the Comparative Method." In *Literary Studies in the Hebrew Bible: Form and Content. Collected Studies,* 50–75. Jerusalem: Magnes Press, The Hebrew University; Leiden: Brill.

Tannehill, Robert C. 1986, *The Narrative Unity of Luke-Acts: A Literary Interpretation, Vol. 1: The Gospel according to Luke.* Foundations and Facets. Philadelphia: Fortress.

Tantlevskij, Igor R. 1996, "The Historical Background of the Qumran Commentary on Nahum (4QpNah)." In Bernd Funck (ed.), *Hellenismus. Beiträge zur Erforschung von Akkulturation und politischer Ordnung in den Staaten des hellenistischen Zeitalters,* 329–38. Tübingen: Mohr-Siebeck.

Taplin, Oliver. 1998, "The Shield of Achilles Within the *Iliad.*" In Ian McAuslan and Peter Walcot (eds.), *Homer,* 96–115. Oxford: Oxford University Press, on behalf of The Classical Association.

Tarn, W. W. 1948, *Alexander the Great.* 2 vols. Cambridge: Cambridge University Press.

Taylor, Joan E. 1990, "The Phenomenon of Early Jewish-Christianity: Reality or Scholarly Invention?" *VigChr 44,* 313–34.

Teeple, Howard M. 1993, *The Prophet in the Clementines.* Religion and Ethics Institute Occasional Papers 2. Evanston, IL: Religion and Ethics Institute.

Tegtmeier, Ralph. 1990, *Sternenzauber. Das Weltbild der Astrologie.* Cologne: DuMont.

Thompson, Dorothy J. 1996, "Pelusium." In Simon Hornblower and Antony Spawforth (eds.), *OCD,* 1134–5. 3rd edn. Oxford: Oxford University Press.

Thornton, T. C. G. 1977–78, "To the End of the Earth (Acts 1.8)." *ExpTim 89,* 374–5.

Tiede, David L. 1986, "The Exaltation of Jesus and the Restoration of Israel in Acts 1." *HTR 79,* 278–86.

Tilly, Michael. 1997, "Geographie und Weltordnung im Aristeasbrief." *JSJ 28,* 131–53.

Tomasch, Sylvia. 1998, "Medieval Geographical Desire." In S. Tomasch and Sealy Gilles (eds.), *Text and Territory: Geographical Imagination in the European Middle Ages,* 1–12. The Middle Ages Series. Philadelphia: University of Pennsylvania Press.

Tomson, Peter J. 1990, *Paul and the Jewish Law: Halakha in the Letters of the Apostle to the Gentiles.* CRINT 3.1. Assen: Van Gorcum; Minneapolis: Fortress.

Trebilco, P. R. 1997, "Diaspora Judaism." In Ralph P. Martin and Peter H. Davids (eds.), *Dictionary of the Later New Testament and Its Developments,* 287–300. Downers Grove, IL: InterVarsity Press.

Trousset, Pol. 1993, "La 'carte d'Agrippa': Nouvelle proposition de lecture." *Dialogues d'histoire ancienne 19,* 137–57.

Tsafrir, Yoram. 1995, "Jewish Pilgrimage in the Roman and Byzantine Periods." *Akten des XII. Internationalen Kongresses für christliche Archäologie,* I.369–76. 2 vols. Jahrbuch für Antike und Christentum Ergänzungsband 20. Münster: Aschendorffsche Verlagsbuchhandlung.

Tsirkin, Yu. B. 1991, "Japheth's Progeny and the Phoenicians." In E. Lipinski (ed.), *Phoenicia and the Bible: Proceedings of the Conference held at the University of Leuven on the 15th of March 1990,* 117–34. Orientalia Lovaniensia Analecta 44; Studia Phoenicia 11. Leuven: Department Oriëntalistiek; Peeters.

Tuplin, C. J. 1994, "Persians as Medes." *Achaemenid History 8,* 235–56.

1996, "The Place of Persia in Athenian Literature." In *Achaemenid Studies,* 132–77. Historia 99. Stuttgart: Steiner.

Turner, Max. 1996, *Power from on High: The Spirit in Israel's Restoration and Witness in Luke-Acts.* Journal of Pentecostal Theology Supplement 9. Sheffield: Sheffield Academic Press.

Tyner, Judith. 1994, "Geography Through the Needle's Eye: Embroidered Maps and Globes in the Eighteenth and Nineteenth Centuries." *The Map Collector 66,* 2–7.

Uchelen, N. A. van. 1986, "Ethical Terminology in Heykhalot-Texts." In J. W. van Henten, et al. (eds.), *Tradition and Re-interpretation in Jewish and Early Christian Literature: Essays in Honour of Jürgen C. H. Lebram,* 250–8. Leiden: Brill.

Uehlinger, C. 1990, *Weltreich und 'eine Rede'. Eine neue Deutung der sogenannten Turmbauerzählung (Gen 11,1–9).* OBO 101. Freiburg: Universitätsverlag; Göttingen: Vandenhoeck & Ruprecht.

Ulrich, Eugene, et al. (eds.). 1995, *Qumran Cave 4, IX: Deuteronomy, Joshua, Judges, Kings.* DJD 14. Oxford: Clarendon.

Unnik, W. C. van. 1973, "Der Ausdruck ἕως ἐσχάτου τῆς γῆς (Apostel-geschichte I 8) und sein alttestamentlicher Hintergrund." In *Sparsa Collecta, Part 1: Evangelia, Paulina, Acta,* 386–401. NovTSup 29. Leiden: Brill.

VanderKam, James C. 1977, *Textual and Historical Studies in the Book of Jubilees.* HSM 14. Missoula, MT: Scholars Press.

1978, "Enoch Traditions in Jubilees and Other Second-Century Sources." In Paul J. Achtemeier (ed.), *SBL 1978 Seminar Papers, Vol. I,* 229–51. Missoula, MT: Scholars Press.

1983, "1 Enoch 77,3 and a Babylonian Map of the World." *RevQ 11,* 271–8.

1988, "Jubilees and Hebrew Texts of Genesis-Exodus." *Textus 14,* 71–85.

1989a, *The Book of Jubilees.* 2 vols. CSCO 510–11; Scriptores Aethiopici 87–8. Leuven: Peeters.

1989b, "The Temple Scroll and the Book of Jubilees." In George J. Brooke (ed.), *Temple Scroll Studies: Papers Presented at the International Symposium on the Temple Scroll, Manchester, December 1987,* 211–36. JSPSup 7. Sheffield: JSOT Press.

1992, "The Jubilees Fragments from Qumran Cave 4." In Julio Trebolle Barrera and Luis Vegas Montaner (eds.), *The Madrid Congress: Proceedings of the International Congress on the Dead Sea Scrolls, Madrid 18–21 March 1991,* II.635–48. 2 vols. Leiden: Brill; Madrid: Complutense.

1993, "Biblical Interpretation in 1 Enoch and Jubilees." In James H. Charlesworth and Craig A. Evans (eds.), *The Pseudepigrapha and Early Biblical Interpretation,* 96–125. JSPSup 14. Sheffield: JSOT.

1994a, *The Dead Sea Scrolls Today.* Grand Rapids, MI: Eerdmans; London: SPCK.

1994b, "Putting Them in Their Place: Geography as an Evaluative Tool." In John C. Reeves and John Kampen (eds.), *Pursuing the Text: Studies in Honor of Ben Zion Wacholder on the Occasion of his Seventieth Birthday,* 46–69. JSOTSup 184. Sheffield: Sheffield Academic Press.

1995, "Das chronologische Konzept des Jubiläenbuches." *ZAW 107,* 80–100.

1996, "1 Enoch, Enochic Motifs, and Enoch in Early Christian Literature." In J. C. VanderKam and William Adler (eds.), *The Jewish Apocalyptic Heritage in Early Christianity,* 33–101. CRINT 3.4. Assen: Van Gorcum; Minneapolis: Fortress.

1997, "Exile in Jewish Apocalyptic Literature." In J. M. Scott (ed.), *Exile: Old Testament, Jewish, and Christian Conceptions,* 89–109. JSJSup 56. Leiden: Brill.

1998a, "Authoritative Literature in the Dead Sea Scrolls." *DSD 5,* 382–402.

1998b, *Calendars in the Dead Sea Scrolls: Measuring Time.* London: Routledge.

1999, "The Angel Story in the Book of Jubilees." In Esther G. Chazon and Michael Stone (eds.), *Pseudepigraphic Perspectives: The Apocrypha and Pseudepigrapha in Light of the Dead Sea Scrolls,* 151–70. STDJ 31. Leiden: Brill.

and William Adler. 1996, *The Jewish Apocalyptic Heritage in Early Christianity.* CRINT 3.4. Assen: Van Gorcum; Minneapolis: Fortress.

and J. T. Milik. 1994, "Jubilees." In *Qumran Cave 4, Vol. VIII: Parabiblical Texts, Part 1,* 1–185. DJD 13. Oxford: Clarendon.

Vasaly, Ann. 1993, *Representations: Images of the World in Ciceronian Oratory.* Berkeley: University of California Press.

Vaux, Roland de. 1996, *Die Ausgrabungen von Qumran und En Feschcha, IA: Die Grabungstagebücher.* Ed. and trans. Ferdinand Rohrhirsch and Bettina Hofmeir. NTOA Series Archeologica 1A. Freiburg: Universitätsverlag; Göttingen: Vandenhoeck & Ruprecht.

Verbrugghe, Gerald P. and John M. Wickersham. 1996, *Berossos and Manetho, Introduced and Translated: Native Traditions in Ancient Mesopotamia and Egypt.* Ann Arbor: University of Michigan Press.

Vermes, Geza and Martin D. Goodman. 1989, *The Essenes According to Classical Sources.* Oxford Centre Textbooks 1. Sheffield: JSOT.

Vilnay, Zev. 1963, *The Holy Land in Old Prints and Maps.* Jerusalem: Mass.

Vogt, H. J. 1992, "Pilgrim–Pilgrimage." In Angelo Di Berardino (ed.), *Encyclopedia of the Early Church,* II.688. 2 vols. New York: Oxford University Press.

Voorst, Robert E. Van. 1989, *The Ascents of James: History and Theology of a Jewish–Christian Community.* SBLDS 112. Atlanta, GA: Scholars Press.

Wacholder, Ben Zion. 1993, "Geomessianism: Why Did the Essenes Settle at Qumran?" In Stanley F. Chyet and David H. Ellenson (eds.), *Bits of Honey: Essays for Samson H. Levey,* 131–8. South Florida Studies in the History of Judaism 74. Atlanta, GA: Scholars Press.

Wagner, Jörg. 1983, "Die Neuordnung des Orients von Pompeius bis Augustus (67 v.Chr. – 14 n.Chr.)." *TAVO* B V 7. Wiesbaden: Reichert.

Wagner, Walter H. 1996, "Interpretations of Genesis 6.1–4 in Second-Century Christianity." *JRH 20,* 137–55.

Wahl, Harald-Martin. 1992, "Noah, Daniel und Hiob in Ezechiel XIV 12–20 (21–3): Anmerkungen zum traditionsgeschichtlichen Hintergrund." *VT 42,* 542–53.

Waldmann, Helmut. 1983, "Die hellenistische Staatenwelt im 3. Jahrhundert v. Chr." *TAVO* B V 3. Wiesbaden: Reichert.

1985, "Die hellenistische Staatenwelt im 2. Jahrhundert v. Chr." *TAVO* B V 4. Wiesbaden: Reichert.

1987, "Syrien und Palästina in hellenistischer Zeit, 16.1: Die Syrischen Kriege (280–145 v. Chr.); 16.2: Die Makkabaer und die Hasmonäer (167–37 v. Chr.)." *TAVO* B V 16. Wiesbaden: Reichert.

Walker, Peter W. L. 1990, *Holy City, Holy Places? Christian Attitudes to Jerusalem and the Holy Land in the Fourth Century.* The Oxford Early Christian Studies. Oxford: Clarendon.

1996, *Jesus and the Holy City: New Testament Perspectives on Jerusalem.* Grand Rapids, MI: Eerdmans.

Walker, R. 1967, *Die Heilsgeschichte im ersten Evangelium.* FRLANT 91. Göttingen: Vandenhoeck & Ruprecht.

Wall, Robert. 1998, "Israel and the Gentile Mission in Acts and Paul: A Canonical Approach." In I. Howard Marshall and David Peterson (eds.), *Witness to the Gospel: The Theology of Acts,* 437–57. Grand Rapids, MI: Eerdmans.

Wallace, Richard, and Wynne Williams. 1998, *The Three Worlds of Paul of Tarsus.* London/New York: Routledge.

Wedderburn, A. J. M. 1993, "The 'Apostolic Decree': Tradition and Redaction." *NovT 35,* 362–89.

1994, "Traditions and Redaction in Acts 2.1–13." *JSNT 55,* 27–54.

Wehnert, Jürgen. 1991, "Die Auswanderung der Jerusalemer Christen nach Pella. Historisches Faktum oder theologische Konstruktion?" *ZKG 102,* 231–55.

1997, *Die Reinheit des "christlichen Gottesvolkes" aus Juden und Heiden. Studien zum historischen und theologischen Hintergrund des sogenannten Aposteldekrets.* FRLANT 173. Göttingen: Vandenhoeck & Ruprecht.

Weidner, Ernst. 1963, "Astrologische Geographie im Alten Orient." *Archiv für Orientforschung 20,* 117–21.

Weinfeld, Moshe. 1978, "Pentecost as Festival of the Giving of the Law." *Immanuel 8,* 7–18.

1993, *The Promise of the Land: The Inheritance of the Land of Canaan by the Israelites.* The Taubman Lectures in Jewish Studies 3. Berkeley: University of California Press.

Weinstock, Stefan. 1948, "The Geographical Catalogue in Acts 2:9–11." *JRS 38*, 43–6.

1971, *Divus Julius*. Oxford: Clarendon.

Weitzman, Steve. 1999, "Why did the Qumran Community Write in Hebrew?" *JAOS 119*, 35–45.

Weitzmann, Kurt, and Massimo Bernabò. 1999, *The Byzantine Octateuchs*. 2 vols. Princeton: Department of Art and Archaeology in association with Princeton University Press.

Wenham, John. 1991, "The Identification of Luke." *EvQ 63*, 3–44.

Werman, Cana. 1999, "Qumran and the Book of Noah." In Esther G. Chazon and Michael Stone (eds.), *Pseudepigraphic Perspectives: The Apocrypha and Pseudepigrapha in Light of the Dead Sea Scrolls. Proceedings of the International Symposium of the Orion Center for the Study of the Dead Sea Scrolls and Associated Literature, 12–14 January, 1997*, 171–81. STDJ 31. Leiden: Brill.

Werner, Robert. 1993, "Zum Afrikabild der Antike." In Karlheinz Dietz, et al. (eds.), *Klassisches Altertum, Spätantike und frühes Christentum. Adolf Lippold zum 65. Geburtstag gewidmet*, 1–36. Würzburg: Selbstverlag des Seminars für Alte Geschichte der Universität Würzburg.

West, M. L. 1966, *Hesiod: Theogony, Edited with Prolegomena and Commentary*. Oxford: Oxford University Press.

1971, *Early Greek Philosophy and the Orient*. Oxford: Clarendon.

1983, *The Orphic Poems*. Oxford: Clarendon.

Westermann, Claus. 1983, *Genesis*. 3 vols. 3rd edn. BKAT 1. Neukirchen-Vluyn: Neukirchener Verlag.

1986, *Das Buch Jesaia, Kapitel 40–66*. ATD 19. Göttingen/Zurich: Vandenhoeck & Ruprecht.

Westrem, Scott D. 1998, "Against Gog and Magog." In Sylvia Tomasch and Sealy Gilles (eds.), *Text and Territory: Geographical Imagination in the European Middle Ages*, 54–75. The Middle Ages Series. Philadelphia: University of Pennsylvania Press.

Wevers, John William. 1974, *Genesis*. Septuaginta Vetus Testamentum Graecum. Göttingen: Vandenhoeck & Ruprecht.

1993, *Notes on the Greek Text of Genesis*. SBLSCS 35. Atlanta, GA: Scholars Press.

Whitfield, Peter. 1994, *The Image of the World: 20 Centuries of World Maps*. London: The British Library.

Wiedemann, T. E. J. 1996, "Tiberius to Nero." In Alan K. Bowman, et al. (eds.), *The Cambridge Ancient History, Vol. X: The Augustan Empire, 43 B.C. – A.D. 69*, 198–225. 2nd edn. Cambridge: Cambridge University Press.

Wilckens, Leonie von. 1991, *Die textilen Künste. Von der Spätantike bis um 1500*. Munich: Beck.

Wilken, Robert L. 1985, "The Restoration of Israel in Biblical Prophecy: Christian and Jewish Responses in the Early Byzantine Period." In Jacob Neusner and Ernest S. Frerichs (eds.), *"To See Ourselves as Others See Us": Christians, Jews, "Others" in Late Antiquity*, 443–71. Scholars Press Studies in the Humanities. Chico, CA: Scholars Press.

1992, *The Land Called Holy: Palestine in Christian History and Thought*. New Haven: Yale University Press.

1993, *"In novissimis diebus*: Biblical Promises, Jewish Hopes and Early Christian Exegesis." *Journal of Early Christian Studies 1*, 1–19.

1996, "Christian Pilgrimage to the Holy Land." In Nitza Rosovsky (ed.), *City of the Great King: Jerusalem from David to the Present*, 117–34. Cambridge, MA: Harvard University Press.

Wilkinson, John. 1990, "Jewish Holy Places and the Origins of Christian Pilgrimage." In Robert Ousterhout (ed.), *The Blessings of Pilgrimage*, 41–53. Illinois Byzantine Studies 1. Urbana/Chicago: University of Illinois Press.

Williams, Frank (trans.). 1994, *The Panarion of Epiphanius of Salami, Books II and III (Sects 47–80, De Fide)* NHS 36. Leiden: Brill.

1997, *The Panarion of Epiphanius of Salamis, Book I (Sects 1–46)*. NHS 35. Leiden: Brill.

Williams, John. 1994–98, *The Illustrated Beatus: A Corpus of the Illustrations of the Commentary on the Apocalypse. Introduction*. 3 vols. London: Miller.

1997, "Isidore, Orosius and the Beatus Map." *Imago Mundi 49*, 7–32.

Wilson, Stephen G. 1973, *The Gentiles and the Gentile Mission in Luke-Acts*. SNTSMS 23. Cambridge: Cambridge University Press.

Wintermute, O. S. 1985, "Jubilees." *OTP* II: 35–142.

Wise, Michael O. 1994, "Thunder in Gemini: An Aramaic Brontologion (4Q318) from Qumran." In *Thunder in Gemini and Other Essays on the History, Language and Literature of Second Temple Palestine*, 13–50. JSPSup 15. Sheffield: Sheffield Academic Press.

Wiseman, T. P. 1992, "Julius Caesar and the *Mappa Mundi.*" In *Talking to Virgil: A Miscellany*, 22–42, 227–30. Exeter: University of Exeter Press.

Witakowski, Witold. 1993, "The Division of the Earth Between the Descendants of Noah in Syriac Tradition." *Aram 5*, 635–56.

Wolf, Armin, and Hans-Helmut Wolf. 1983, *Die wirkliche Reise des Odysseus. Zur Rekonstruktion des homerischen Weltbildes*. Munich/Vienna: Müller.

Wolska-Conus, Wanda (ed.). 1968–73, *Cosmas Indicopleustès. Topographie chrétienne*. 3 vols. SC 141, 159, 197. Paris: Cerf.

Wood, Susan E. 1999, *Imperial Women: A Study in Public Images, 40 B.C. – A.D. 68*. Mnemosyne 194. Leiden: Brill.

Woodward, David. 1987a, "Medieval *Mappaemundi.*" In J. B. Harley and D. Woodward (eds.), *The History of Cartography, Vol. I: Cartography in Prehistoric, Ancient, and Medieval Europe and the Mediterranean*, 286–370. Chicago/London: University of Chicago Press.

(ed.). 1987b, *Art and Cartography*. Chicago: University of Chicago Press.

Wright, Benjamin G. 1998, "Talking with God and Losing His Head: Extrabiblical Traditions about the Prophet Ezekiel." In Michael E. Stone and Theodore A. Bergren (eds.), *Biblical Figures Outside the Bible*, 290–315. Harrisburg, PA: Trinity Press International.

1999, "Qumran Pseudepigrapha in Early Christianity: Is 1 Clem. 50:4 a Citation of 4QPseudo-Ezekiel (4Q385)?" In Esther G. Chazon and Michael Stone (eds.), *Pseudepigraphic Perspectives: The Apocrypha and Pseudepigrapha in Light of the Dead Sea Scrolls. Proceedings of the International Symposium of the Orion Center for the Study of the Dead Sea Scrolls and Associated Literature, 12–14 January, 1997*, 183–93. STDJ 31. Leiden: Brill.

Wright, J. Edward. 2000, *The Early History of Heaven*. Oxford: Oxford University Press.

Wright, John K. 1965, *The Geographical Lore of the Time of the Crusades: A Study in the History of Medieval Science and Tradition in Western Europe.* New York: American Geographical Society of New York, 1925. Reprint edn., New York: Dover.

Wyatt, Nicolas. 1995, "Le centre du monde dans les littératures d'Ougarit et d'Israël." *JNSL 21*, 123–42.

Yadin, Yigael. 1963, *The Finds from the Bar Kokhba Period in the Cave of Letters.* JDS. Jerusalem: Israel Exploration Society.

1983, *The Temple Scroll.* 3 vols. Jerusalem: The Israel Exploration Society; The Institute of Archaeology of the Hebrew University of Jerusalem; The Shrine of the Book.

Younger, K. Lawson, Jr. 1998, "The Deportation of the Israelites." *JBL 117*, 201–27.

Zeitlin, Solomon. 1965, "Did Agrippa write a letter to Gaius Caligula?" *JQR N.S. 56*, 22–31.

Ziegler, Joseph (ed.). 1975, *Eusebius Werke, Bd. 9: Der Jesaiakommentar.* GCS 9. Berlin: Akademie-Verlag.

INDEX OF ANCIENT LITERATURE

8:19	19, 34, 56, 57, 100, 165, 172, 192 n. 22, 193 n. 31, 194 n. 45, 249 n. 115, 255 n. 52
8:21	130, 140, 142, 144, 199 n. 83
8:22	100, 130, 172, 199 n. 83, 243 n. 50, 245 n. 64, 249 n. 115
8:22–23	144, 253 n. 37
8:22–24	57, 131
8:23	57, 128, 244 n. 54
8:24	199 n. 83
8:25	130, 148, 199 n. 83
8:25–28	100
8:25–29	145
8:25–30	57, 131
8:26	57, 148
8:27	147, 219 n. 216, 249 n. 115
8:28	148
8:29	130, 148, 149, 199 n. 83, 249 n. 115
8:30	151, 157, 168, 173, 243 n. 43
9:1	130, 146
9:1–13	41, 146
9:1–15	32
9:2	199 n. 83, 246 n. 73
9:2–6	39, 147
9:3	148, 246 n. 74
9:4	199 n. 83, 246 n. 73
9:6	80, 148, 199 n. 83
9:7–13	148
9:8	148, 199 n. 83
9:9	149, 199 n. 83
9:10	149, 199 n. 83, 241 n. 24
9:11	199 n. 83
9:12	57, 148, 199 n. 83, 241 n. 24
9:13	149, 199 n. 83
9:14	39, 100, 150, 151, 154, 156, 158, 199 n. 83
9:14–15	37, 102, 143
9:15	34, 138, 158, 166, 173, 233 n. 80, 249 n. 120
10:1–14	36, 225 n. 287
10:12–14	197 n. 64
10:13	196 n. 63
10:14	196 n. 63
10:15	154
10:19	206 n. 62
10:22	195 n. 53
10:26	206 n. 62, 213 n. 134, 236 n. 113
10:27–34	102, 143, 150, 151, 152, 155, 237 n. 20
10:29	100, 150, 230 n. 29, 243 n. 50
10:30–32	102

10:32	39
10:35	78
11:2	92, 224 n. 280, 230 n. 33, 34
12:16–17	207 n. 74, 231 n. 38
12:25–26	101
12:26	99
12:27	196 n. 63
14:13–15	231 n. 40
14:18	228 n. 5
15:31–32	205 n. 52
17:16	4
17:16–18	3
18–19	224 n. 283
19:21	179 n. 25
19:21–22	34, 111
21:1–11	92
21:10	196 n. 63
21:18	92
22:1	63
22:11–14	33, 111
23:30	35
32:2	199 n. 88
32:18–19	34, 111
32:20–26	196 n. 63
44:11–34	49
44:33–34	52
49:19	194 n. 45

Letter of Aristeas

83	255 n. 48

Psalms of Solomon

2:29	183 n. 48
8:15	58
9:2	216 n. 168
17:31	212 n. 122

Pseudo-Philo

Liber Antiquitatum Biblicarum

3:11	223 n. 275
4–5	24, 197 n. 69
4:7	218 n. 215, 246 n. 72
4:8	230 n. 33
8:11	49

Sibylline Oracles

Prologue	33 36
1.11	12
1.288–90	36

IV Dead Sea Scrolls

CD (Damascus Document)

1QH (Thanksgiving Hymns)

1QM (War Rule)

1QapGen (Genesis Apocryphon)

1QpNah

4Q176

VIII Early Christian Writers

160–86	148
170	245 n. 67
176	204 n. 30
188	80, 147, 243 n. 42, 243 n. 44, 243 n. 45
190.1	79, 81
190.3	78, 79, 81, 149
190.10	78, 79, 81
190.12	79, 81
190.14	81
190.15	81
190–92	148
191	243 n. 44, 243 n. 45
192	157, 243 n. 43
192.1	79
192.3	79
193–94	79
194	148
194.7	79
194.8	81
194.11	81
195	147, 243 n. 44, 243 n. 45
196	80, 243 n. 45
197	140, 243 n. 42
200.1	79
200.4	79
200.6	82
200.39	80
200.45	80
200.58	81
202	242 n. 41
202–23	242 n. 40
202–39	139
204	78
205	82
209.4	80
212.2	81
214.15	79
215	81
224	242 n. 41
224–34	168, 242 n. 40, 243 n. 43
225	242 n. 41
233	79
235	242 n. 40, 243 n. 43
235.3	79
235.4	81
235.9	82
236	242 n. 41
236–37	242 n. 40, 243 n. 43
238	204 n. 30
238–9	242 n. 40
240–613	138
241	204 n. 30

267	204 n. 30
271	204 n. 30
274	204 n. 30
288	204 n. 30
290	204 n. 30
294	204 n. 30

Irenaeus

Adversus Haereses
1.10.2	187 n. 97, 211 n. 118, 219 n. 228
1.26.2	190 n. 125
3.11.8	187 n. 97
3.12.9	205 n. 52
3.22.3	204 n. 32

Isidore of Seville

Etymologiae
3.25.1	165
9.2	164
9.2.35	164
14.3.21	164
16.26.10.	255 n. 49

Jerome

Epistulae
78.20	164, 238 n. 25

Justin Martyr

Dialogue with Trypho
20.1	92
115.1	230 n. 27
119.3	230 n. 27

Pseudo-Clementine

Epistula Petri
2.4	234 n. 89
2.6	234 n. 89

Homilies
2.17.4	234 n. 87
4–6	228 n. 3
8.10–20	229 n. 21
8.15.4	223 n. 275
9.3–7	229 n. 21
18.4.3	52, 231 n. 46

5.73	184 n. 60
6.31.136–7	73
6.139	14
6.208	186 n. 73
6.211	186 n. 73
36.101	186 n. 73

Plutarch

Alexander

65.6–8	211 n. 117, 251 n. 22
329 b–d	227 n. 309

Caesar

58.6	211 n. 119
58.6–7	11

Pompey

36.2	73
38.2–3	184 n. 49

Polybius

3.32.2	179 n. 4
3.58.2	59
4.28.2–6	179 n. 4
5.31.4–5	179 n. 4
5.44.9	73
5.80	243 n. 49
5.105.4	187 n. 86
11.39.11–12	143
12.25.7	194 n. 38

Pomponius Mela

De chorographia

1.3–8	10

Procopius

De bello vandalico

10.13–22	196 n. 54

Ptolemaios

1.17.5	128

Sallust

Bellum Catilinae

16.5	58

Strabo

Geographia

1.1.1–2	185 n. 66
1.1.3–10	9
1.1.7	9, 180 n. 8
1.1.14	180 n. 8
1.1.16	185 n. 66
1.2.25	237 n. 18
1.2.28	183 n. 46, 237 n. 18
1.4.7	237 n. 18
1.4.7–8	251 n. 24
2.1.17	245 n. 57
2.2.1–3	237 n. 21
2.3	237 n. 21
2.3.1	33
2.4.6–7	237 n. 18
2.5.5	182 n. 39
2.5.16	237 n. 21
2.5.17	9
2.5.26	237 n. 18, 244 n. 56, 251 n. 24
2.5.31	237 n. 18
2.5.34	182 n. 39
3.5.5	244 n. 55
6.4.1	33
6.4.2	186 n. 75
7.2.4	245 n. 57
7.4.5	237 n. 18
9.3.6	187 n. 97, 252 n. 31
11.1.1	237 n. 18
11.1.5	237 n. 18, 245 n. 57
11.7.4	237 n. 18
11.11.7	245 n. 57
11.13.6	73
12.3.11	185 n. 70
12.3.27	237 n. 18
15.1.73	19
15.3.2	210 n. 103
15.3.10	247 n. 88
16.1.8	73
16.2.33	243 n. 48
16.4.24	243 n. 48
17.1.48	190 n. 117
17.1.54	210 n. 108
17.3.1	237 n. 18

INDEX OF MODERN AUTHORS

336 *Index of Modern Authors*

Sokoloff, M., 207 n. 75
Sperber, A., 205 n. 51, 221 n. 252
Städele, A., 182 n. 40
Stanley, K., 182 n. 34
Steck, O. H., 231 n. 51
Stegemann, H., 192 n. 14, 209 n. 91
Stegner, W., 216 n. 164
Stein, H. F., 258 n. 2
Steiner, R. C., 196 n. 57, 225 n. 286,
225 n. 287
Stemberger, G., 198 n. 78, 208 n. 77,
228 n. 5, 229 n. 15, 231 n. 38
Sterling, G. E., 204 n. 39, 227 n. 309
Stern, M., 180 n. 10, 238 n. 29
Steyn, G. J., 200 n. 3
Stichel, R., 249 n. 4
Stone, M. E., 183 n. 44, 192 n. 14,
195 n. 45, 196 n. 59, 196 n. 61,
197 n. 65, 213 n. 132, 223 n. 269,
225 n. 287, 225 n. 288, 226 n. 300,
229 n. 24, 240 n. 16, 244 n. 52, 244 n. 53
Stötzel, A., 228 n. 6
Strange, J. F., 256 n. 61
Strange, W. A., 221 n. 243, 225 n. 289,
226 n. 293, 235 n. 106
Strasburger, G., 194 n. 37
Strecker, G., 206 n. 61, 207 n. 64,
213 n. 137, 223 n. 275, 228 n. 5,
229 n. 9, 229 n. 17, 231 n. 37, 231 n. 41
Stroumsa, G. S., 233 n. 70
Strzygowski, J., 239 n. 9, 246 n. 80,
257 n. 67
Stuckenbruck, L. T., 197 n. 73, 224 n. 277
Sullivan, R. D., 180 n. 16
Sundwall, G. A., 186 n. 77
Sutherland, C. H. V., 184 n. 61, 187 n. 87,
187 n. 88, 187 n. 92
Svenbro, J., 181 n. 30
Swanson, R. J., 203 n. 21
Swartz, J., 189 n. 115
Syme, R., 183 n. 48

Taatz, I., 235 n. 100
Tadmor, C., 183 n. 43
Tajra, H. W., 210 n. 106
Talbert, R. J. A., 178 n. 8, 178 n. 9,
184 n. 50, 186 n. 77, 186 n. 79
Talmon, S., 195 n. 46, 195 n. 52, 255 n. 52
Tannehill, R. C., 205 n. 49
Tantlevskij, I. R., 193 n. 23
Taplin, O., 182 n. 34
Tarn, W. W., 227 n. 309
Taylor, J. E., 212 n. 126, 223 n. 270,
229 n. 15, 241 n. 26, 241 n. 30

Teeple, H. M., 231 n. 48
Tegtmeier, R., 207 n. 73
Thompson, D. J., 243 n. 48
Thornton, T. C. G., 210 n. 107
Tiede, D. L., 214 n. 148, 215 n. 152
Tilly, M., 195 n. 46
Tomasch, S., 180 n. 7
Tomson, P. J., 223 n. 270
Trebilco, P. R., 216 n. 168
Tsafrir, Y., 213 n. 139
Tsirkin, Y. B., 182 n. 42, 240 n. 19,
245 n. 60
Tuplin, C. J., 217 n. 183
Turner, M., 212 n. 126, 213 n. 136,
214 n. 148, 220 n. 235, 221 n. 246,
235 n. 103
Tyner, J., 179 n. 3

Uchelen, N. A. van, 223 n. 270
Uehlinger, C., 220 n. 232
Unnik, W. C., van 210 n. 107

VanderKam, J. C., 178 n. 16, 179 n. 23,
179 n. 27, 182 n. 42, 188 n. 110,
191 n. 5, 191 n. 8, 192 n. 13, 192 n. 14,
192 n. 15, 192 n. 16, 192 n. 17,
192 n. 18, 192 n. 21, 193 n. 26,
193 n. 27, 193 n. 35, 195 n. 51,
195 n. 53, 195 n. 54, 201 n. 10,
201 n. 13, 202 n. 15, 202 n. 16,
206 n. 58, 212 n. 124, 212 n. 126,
219 n. 216, 224 n. 282, 228 n. 8,
229 n. 24, 231 n. 36, 231 n. 53,
232 n. 63, 239 n. 39, 239 n. 42,
240 n. 15, 240 n. 16, 241 n. 28,
241 n. 34, 242 n. 35, 243 n. 50,
246 n. 72, 246 n. 74, 246 n. 76,
247 n. 89, 248 n. 100, 249 n. 114,
249 n. 115, 249 n. 1
Vasaly, A., 183 n. 48, 210 n. 102
Vaux, R. de, 188 n. 112
Verbrugghe, G. P., 200 n. 98
Vermes, G., 241 n. 25
Vilnay, Z., 183 n. 45
Vogt, H. J., 255 n. 60
Voorst, R. E. van, 232 n. 59, 236 n. 107

Wacholder, B. Z., 189 n. 117
Wagner, J., 217 n. 180
Wagner, W. H., 228 n. 8
Wahl, H. M., 226 n. 298
Waldmann, H., 217 n. 178, 217 n. 179,
245 n. 59, 245 n. 61
Walker, P. W. L., 214 n. 148